T0189781

Lecture Notes in Computer Science

580

Edited by G. Goos and J. Hartmanis

Advisory Board: W. Brauer   D. Gries   J. Stoer

A. Pirotte · C. Delobel · G. Gottlob (Eds)

Advances in Database Technology - EDBT '92

3rd International Conference
on Extending Database Technology
Vienna, Austria, March 23-27, 1992
Proceedings

Springer-Verlag

A. Pirotte   C. Delobel   G. Gottlob (Eds.)

Advances in
Database Technology –
EDBT '92

3rd International Conference
on Extending Database Technology
Vienna, Austria, March 23-27, 1992
Proceedings

Springer-Verlag
Berlin Heidelberg New York
London Paris Tokyo
Hong Kong Barcelona
Budapest

Series Editors

Gerhard Goos
Universität Karlsruhe
Postfach 69 80
Vincenz-Priessnitz-Straße 1
W-7500 Karlsruhe, FRG

Juris Hartmanis
Department of Computer Science
Cornell University
5148 Upson Hall
Ithaca, NY 14853, USA

Volume Editors

Alain Pirotte
University of Louvain, I. A. G. School of Management
1 Place des Doyens, B-1348 Louvain-la-Neuve, Belgium

Claude Delobel
GIP Altair
and
Université de Paris-Sud, LRI, Bât. 490
F-91405 Orsay, France

Georg Gottlob
Technical University of Vienna, Institute for Information Systems
Paniglgasse 16, 1040 Vienna, Austria

CR Subject Classification (1991): D.3.3, E.2, F.4.1, H.2, H.5.1, I.2.1, I.2.4

ISBN 3-540-55270-7 Springer-Verlag Berlin Heidelberg New York
ISBN 0-387-55270-7 Springer-Verlag New York Berlin Heidelberg

This work is subject to copyright. All rights are reserved, whether the whole or part of
the material is concerned, specifically the rights of translation, reprinting, re-use of
illustrations, recitation, broadcasting, reproduction on microfilms or in any other way,
and storage in data banks. Duplication of this publication or parts thereof is permitted
only under the provisions of the German Copyright Law of September 9, 1965, in its
current version, and permission for use must always be obtained from Springer-Verlag.
Violations are liable for prosecution under the German Copyright Law.

© Springer-Verlag Berlin Heidelberg 1992
Printed in Germany

Typesetting: Camera ready by author
Printing and binding: Druckhaus Beltz, Hemsbach/Bergstr.
45/3140-543210 - Printed on acid-free paper

Foreword

These are the proceedings of the third EDBT conference, held in Vienna after the 1988 and 1990 conferences which both took place in Venice. The success of the 1988 and 1990 conferences suggested that there is room for a bi-annual major international database conference in Europe that aims to provide an international forum for presentation of new results in research, development and applications extending the state of the art in database technology.

Judging only from the number of papers submitted (220 from more than 30 countries), the 1992 EDBT conference has attracted a lot of interest. The program committee had the difficult task of selecting the 33 papers included in these proceedings. In addition, in accordance with the policy of the EDBT Foundation to encourage students and young researchers, we are issuing, with our congratulations, best paper awards to Martin Frank, co-author of the paper "Adaptive and automated index selection in RDBMS", and to Philippe Pucheral and Jean-Marie Thévenin, authors of the paper "Pipelined query processing in the DBGraph storage model". This year's conference also features two distinguished scientists as invited speakers: François Bancilhon shares his experience on understanding object databases and Ray Reiter introduces some of his recent ideas on the specification of database updates.

We are grateful to all the people who have helped organize the 1992 EDBT conference: the organizing committee and the conference secretariat run by Brigitte Haberstroh, the program committee members, Esteban Zimanyi for his invaluable help in running the program committee, and also all the reviewers whose names appear in these proceedings.

Vienna, March 1992   Alain Pirotte, Claude Delobel, Georg Gottlob

Sponsorship

Promoted by
  the EDBT Foundation
Sponsored by
  Austrian Industries, Digital Equipment Corporation, Siemens Österreich -
  Programm- und Systementwicklung, Bundesministerium für Wissenschaft
  und Forschung, Vienna Tourist Board, Computer Associates, Software AG,
  IBM Österreich
In cooperation with
  ACM, IEEE, Austrian Computer Society, Christian Doppler Laboratory for
  Expert Systems, ERCIM, GI, SI, BCS, AICA
Under the patronage of
  the European Communities

Organization

Conference Chairman: Claude Delobel (University of Paris-Sud and GIP ALTAIR, France)
Program Committee Chairman: Alain Pirotte (University of Louvain, Belgium)
Organization Chairman: Georg Gottlob (Technical University Vienna, Austria)
Organization Assistant: Brigitte Haberstroh (Technical University Vienna, Austria)
Organization Consultant: Michele Missikoff (IASI-CNR, Italy)
Technical Exhibition Organizer: Austrian Computer Society
Scientific Tutorials Coordinator: Stefano Ceri (Milan Politechnic, Italy)
U.S. Coordinator: H.V. Jagadish (AT&T Bell Laboratories, USA)
Far East Coordinator: H. Sakai (Chu University, Japan)
Local Arrangements: Austrian Computer Society

Program Committee

A. Pirotte (Belgium – chairperson) S. Abiteboul (France)
M. Adiba (France) H. Ait-Kaci (France)
S. Alagic (Yugoslavia) P. Apers (The Netherlands)
E. Bertino (Italy) J. Bubenko (Sweden)
S. Christodoulakis (Greece) H. Demetrovics (Hungary)
D. DeWitt (USA) K. Dittrich (Switzerland)
M. Freeston (Germany) G. Gardarin (France)
S. Gibbs (Switzerland) G. Gonnet (Switzerland)
P. Hitchcock (United Kingdom) M. Jarke (Germany)
L. Kalinichenko (Russia) Y. Kambayashi (Japan)
H. Kangassalo (Finland) E. Komissartschik (Russia)
R. Ladin (USA) Ch. Lecluse (France)
W. Litwin (France) P. Lockemann (Germany)
R. Manthey (Germany) C. Medeiros (Brazil)
A. Mendelzon (Canada) R. Morrison (United Kingdom)
A. Olivé (Spain) D. Roelants (Belgium)
N. Roussopoulos (USA) M. Schrefl (Austria)
A. Sernadas (Portugal) A. Shoshani (USA)
A. Solvberg (Norway) W. Staniszkis (Poland)
P. Stocker (United Kingdom) M. Stonebraker (USA)
L. Tanca (Italy) B. Thalheim (Germany)
P. Valduriez (France) Y. Vassiliou (Greece)
J. Vidart (Argentina) R. Zicari (Italy)
J. Zlatuska (Czechoslovakia)

Additional Referees

F. Andon	C. Bal	H. Balsters
M. Bellosta	B. Ben-Zvi	C. Berrut
A. Berztiss	H. Blanken	P. Bohnlein
D. Boulanger	M. Bouzeghoub	G. Brataas
C. Breiteneder	F. Cacace	J. Chomicki
C. Collet	R. Connor	M. Consens
I. Cruz	Q. Cutts	H. Dahlgren
V. de Antonellis	B. Defude	C. de Maindreville
T. Eiter	S. Gatzin	F. Giannotti
V. Goebel	G. Grahne	P. Grefen
A. Geppert	O. Gruber	S. Grumbach
J. Gulla	O. Gunko	A. Haitsma
M. Hartig	G. Hulin	R. Hull
Y. Ioannidis	D. Jonscher	T. Kakeshita
G. Kappel	G. Kiernan	G. Kirby
E. Knuth	C. Kolovson	A. Kotz
O. Kovalchuk	R. Lanzelotte	A. Lefebvre
O. Lindland	J. Lynngberg	D. Montesi
T. Mueck	D. Munro	J. Naughton
M. Negri	M. Neimat	W. Nejdl
B. Novikov	A. Oelmann	A. Opdahl
B. Polyachenko	R. Ramakrishnan	G. Reichwein
M. Rhiner	B. Riecke	T. Risch
K. Saisho	P. Savino	L. Sbattella
S. Scherrer	C. Sernadas	A. Sikeler
W. Song	S. Spaccapietra	L. Spampinato
H. Takakura	Z. Tari	W. Teeuw
J.-M. Thévenin	V. Vetland	V. Vianu
D. Vista	B. Wangler	G. Willumsen
H. Xu	M. Yang	M. Yoshikawa
P. Zezula	P. Ziane	E. Zimanyi

Contents

Invited Papers

Visual Interfaces and Multimedia Techniques

Deductive Databases

Schema Updatability

Object-Oriented Databases

Updating in Deductive Databases and Knowledge Bases

Indexing Techniques

Parallel Processing

Distributed Databases

Knowledge Bases

Transaction Processing

Query Processing

Panel

Understanding
Object-Oriented Database Systems

François Bancilhon
O_2 Technology
7 Rue du Parc de Clagny
78000 Versailles
France

Abstract

This paper addresses the problem of understanding the current set of commercially available object-oriented database systems. It proposes a classification of these systems based on their external behavior and on the target customers they are aimed at. The classification distinguishes four categories: language oriented database systems, persistent programming languages, engineering database systems and full object-oriented database systems. For each of these categories, a definition is provided, and the characteristics and benefits of the systems are given.

Research on object-oriented data bases (OODBS) started at the beginning of the 1980's with initial efforts such as [6]. It became very active in the mid 1980's with projects such as Orion [4], Observer [11], O_2 [7], Damokles [8], Iris [9] and Exodus [5], to name a few. At the end of the 1980's, a number of start-up companies were created (Versant, Itasca, Objectivity, Object Design and O_2) and joined the already existing object database companies (Servio and Ontos). As a result, seven products are now commercially available.

Of the seven systems, only three originated from research labs, while the four others were the product of industrial start-ups. This means that more than half of the products have had little or no input from the research community.[1]

The market is not growing as fast as some had first expected, but it exists and is developing at a steady rate. For 1991, it is evaluated between $10 and 20 million, depending on whether you count the actual sales of the seven companies or their revenues. This is still very small but enough to guarantee a first base of users of these systems.

The products have been on the market for one or two years or more, and the first users have been using them for some time now. There is a strong user interest coming from various areas: CAD, software engineering, geographic information systems, financial applications, medical applications, telecommunications (network administration), multimedia, etc. Users

---

[1] I leave to the reader to decide whether this is a good or a bad thing.

are moving from the first stage of evaluation (looking at the system and playing with it) to a second stage of evaluation (trying the system on a real application) before they actually move to production development.

At the end of the 1980's, the debate was hot between the proponents of the so-called extended relational systems and the object-oriented database community. At that time, the definition of object-oriented database systems was not so clear and there was some discussion among the proponents of this approach about the definition of an OODBS. The paper [1] was a first proposal. It actually played a role in clarifying the definition and providing a pedagogical tool. It was also endorsed immediately by all the vendors who claimed their systems satisfied every requirement.

It is now time to go back and analyze those systems and to understand what they actually are and how they can be distinguished ¿from one another. The "Manifesto" is not a good tool to perform this analysis because since then:

1. the technology has evolved

2. new features have been added to existing systems

3. new systems have been introduced

4. user needs are better understood through a number of experiments and actual use of the systems.

1 Market

The OODBS field is market driven: vendors analyze the market, listen to user requests and react quickly by adapting their products to these requests. Each vendor has chosen a very specific strategy to react to the market. As forecast in [2], a Darwinian process is taking place: no vendor has disappeared, but all the products are rapidly adapting to the environment. The factors of evolution of the market are the following:

- C++ is pulling the market: a sizable portion of the users come with a C++ requirement (whether they actually use C++ or not).

- Smalltalk is also pulling the market but to a much lesser extent.

- There is a strong concern for standards and open systems.

- The CAD tool builders represent another market niche.

Given these facts, one can identify several types of OODBS users. They can be classified by their motivations:

- *C++ users:*

  These users want to develop in C++; thus they want a database well suited for their needs. This translates into two requirements: they want an object-oriented database system because they believe in object-oriented technology, and they want a solution to the impedance mismatch between C++ and a traditional database system.

- *Engineering application developers:*

  They want a database system well suited for their needs. This translates into data modeling requirements and specific functionality requirements.

- *New application developers:*

  They want support for non-standard data types and extensibility.

- *Database users seeking better database technology:*

  They believe object orientation will improve the development process and the resulting applications.

Of course, these four categories are not necessarily mutually exclusive. The technical answer to the requests of these classes of users would of course be an object-oriented system which offers engineering features and solves the impedance mismatch with C++. Actually life is more difficult than this, and each vendor has reacted differently by addressing a specific market segment.

2 Products

The goal of this paper is to analyze and classify the existing systems. One should analyze them one by one and compare them. This task belongs to the research and scientific community. As a vendor, I cannot do that because my judgement is subject to partiality and I cannot compare O_2 to other systems.

Instead, I provide here a general view of these systems and some clues on how to analyze them. To get to the complete analysis, one should look at the actual systems and apply the classification to them.

As mentioned above, products are rapidly being adapted to the market. Of course, when adapting a product to new requirements, the easiest thing to adapt is the marketing literature. Thus, seen from their marketing brochures, all systems actually look very much alike. Looking at them in detail and reading the user manuals, instead of the marketing brochures, gives quite a different picture: the systems can be classified into distinct categories. This does not necessarily mean that one is better or worse than another, but rather that they are the results of a number of choices and tradeoffs and that some are better adapted for some tasks and others for other tasks. It is thus important for users to understand what each system actually addresses.

The classification I propose is based solely on the user's view of the system: I do not address the issues of their implementation or architecture. I distinguish between four types of systems:

1. language oriented database systems

2. persistent programming languages

3. engineering database systems

4. full object-oriented database systems

Language oriented database systems

Language oriented database systems are database systems specialized for a given programming language.

Thus, if you are using C++ with a traditional database and suffer from the impedance mismatch between these two components, you can replace the traditional system by a different system that will communicate more naturally with C++.

The system is a true database system. It is dependent on a given programming language (C++ in general). The goal of the system is to solve the impedance mismatch between the programming language and the database system; to do so the database data model matches that of the programming language. Thus, the data types manipulated in the database and those manipulated in the programming language are exactly the same.

This concept has nothing to do with object orientation: If the language is object-oriented, the resulting system has an object-oriented flavor, but in general the methods of the objects are managed by a different and more traditional system.

Objects can be declared in the database or in the programming language. Data is moved from one space to another through a *read* and a *write* command. The only thing one can do to database data is read it and write it.

There is a clear and simple notion of persistence: persistent data is in the database and transient data is in the programming language. Data is made persistent by copying it in the database and it is made available to the programming language by copying it into the programming space. Thus the separation between the database and the programming language is clear and simple. The main difference is that there is no (or little) translation in this copying process.

The DDL is in general the same as the declarative part of the language. Thus schema declaration is performed by writing program statements. The system can be high level or low level: in a high level language oriented system, no conversion or operations are needed on the data to be read in or written out. In a low level system, some operations might have to be performed:

- pointer swizling

- type checking

- locking

- index manipulation, etc.

In a high level system, all of these are administered directly by the system; in a low level system, they are taken care of by the programmer. The advantage of high level systems is that programming is simpler. The advantage of low level systems is that they give better control and more flexibility to the programmer and allow him/her, sometimes, to write more efficient code.

The advantage of these systems is that they simplify programming of database applications in the language in question and produce more efficient applications.

Persistent programming languages

Persistent programming language systems are programming languages that offer persistent data management.

Thus, if you are programming in C++ and think you need to manage not only transient data but also persistent, large, shared and secure data, you can switch from a standard C++ compiler to a persistent C++ compiler.

The system is clearly language dependent, since it appears as a compiler or a programming language environment.

As opposed to language oriented database systems, the system does more than suppressing the impedance mismatch: it suppresses the boundary between the database system and the programming language, making them a single and unique system.

Even though some or all of database functionality can be supported, there is no database system *per se* as database users expect to find it. The system is rather a way of fulfilling all database functions in a programming language. Thus, one can, in the programming language, declare persistent data, create, commit and abort transactions, etc.

Here again, the notion of persistent programming language is orthogonal to the issue of object orientation. If the chosen language is object-oriented, the system has an object-oriented flavor, but the methods are not in general managed by the system.

One can perform the same operations on transient and on persistent data. Persistence can be by reachability or by declaration.

- If it is by declaration, the programmer declares that such and such a type is persistent or not, and data are created once and for all as persistent or not. Thus persistence is static. This means that copying is necessary to move from the persistent to the transient space.

- If it is by reachability, certain roots define persistent data, and all data reachable from these roots is persistent. This implies that data can be made persistent or transient at run time by attaching or detaching them from a persistent root. Thus persistence is dynamic.

The advantages of these systems for the user are easier programming (no need to worry about the database) and better performance (if the data format is adapted to the language types).

Engineering database systems

Engineering database systems are databases specialized for engineering and design work.

Thus, if you have an *ad hoc* home-made database system integrated in your CAX development environment, you can replace it by an engineering database system that will deliver a data model well suited for your needs and a number of useful features. Instead of having to develop and maintain such a complex system, you will rely on specialists in this technology to keep the system competitive and up to date.

While traditional database systems were mainly targeted at business-type applications, these systems are true database systems targeted at engineering-type applications. They are normally language independent, because their data model is not chosen to match any specific language.

Such systems have their own data model, which is in general not object-oriented but rather resembles the entity-relationship model, and supports complex object data types with attributes, hierarchical records and relationships. They also offer a number of nice features such as version management, support for long transactions, client/server architecture and distribution. But they are not necessarily object-oriented.

As opposed to the previous systems, an engineering database system is indeed a database system with all the features you are supposed to expect from such a system, and it does not propose to solve the impedance mismatch but rather to bring a database system better suited for CAX applications.

The advantage of such systems is that they well adapted for one specific type of application, that of engineering design. Thus they are good candidates for the repository component of a computer aided design environment.

Full object-oriented databases systems

Full object-oriented databases are database systems that integrate object-oriented technology.

Thus, if you are using a traditional database system and find it difficult or impossible to use for new types of applications, or if you are developing a data-intensive application and want to improve both the development process and the quality of the resulting application, you can switch to a full object-oriented database system.

These systems are true database systems supporting an object-oriented data model. Users accustomed to database systems will find the architecture and the modules they find in a traditional system. They are language independent because their data model is not derived from any specific programming language. These systems offer:

- a complete database data model, with features such as set manipulation and associative access

- an object-oriented data model that supports complex objects, object identity, encapsulation, classes, inheritance, late binding, computational completeness and extensibility

- a true DDL with schema manipulation features

- the ability to store and manipulate both the data (the objects) and the metadata (the classes and the methods) in the system itself

- a query language which is complete, declarative, contains set manipulation operations and supports optimization

- logical to physical data independence (thus a physical and a logical DDL and the ability to modify the physical schema without changing the application)

- the ability to manipulate very large amounts of data

- the ability to develop complete applications in a single environment

The benefits of these systems are:

1. for conventional applications, an improvement of the development process (design, coding, maintenance and evolution are made easier and cheaper) and of the resulting application (applications are better structured, more reliable and easier to customize and modify)

2. for new applications, the ability to deal with new types of data (text, images, figures, sounds, etc.)

3 Meanwhile, in the research community...

While vendors are producing products, the research community is generating prototypes. Some of these prototypes belong in one of the four categories described above, but fortunately the research community is not bound by market considerations and other types of systems are being prototyped: database programming languages and database-style programming languages.

Database programming languages are programming languages running on top of a database system and providing database oriented features.

Thus, if you need to write a database application and want to benefit ¿from the latest technology in terms of programming languages, you should switch to such a system.

There is little chance of seeing any of these systems coming into commercial use because they suffer from the "new programming language syndrome": very few organizations are ready to adopt a new programming language to solve their development problems. This is not to say that this research is not useful: it is indeed extremely important, because it generates technology that can and will be incorporated into existing systems.

Database-style programming languages are programming languages that were targeted to run on top of a database system and which, due to the lack of resources or time (developing a complete database system and language is a huge task, very often out of reach of a research team) end up just being main memory systems, i.e., regular programming languages. These systems are also of interest in the way they address integration problems and in the new features they propose.

Conclusion

I have tried in this paper to reflect on the recent developments in database systems. Many existing systems are presently competing for the market and label themselves object-oriented database systems. Actually, this generic term covers a wide variety of different systems that address different needs through different approaches. I have proposed a classification of these systems, based on their functionality and market objectives.

All of the existing systems will continue to evolve. At this stage, each one belongs rather exclusively to one of the categories I have presented. Most vendors will want to remain generalist and will clearly try to offer the best of all worlds. Therefore we should see the systems evolving toward a common model and the distinctions might become blurred in the future.

The following table summarizes some of the characteristics of each category of systems:

System	Type	Objective	Language independence	Object orientation
LODBS	Database	solve the impedance mismatch	no	-
PPL	Programming language	solve the impedance mismatch	no	-
EDBS	Database	support engineering applications	yes	-
FOODBS	Database	bring OO technology to databases	yes	yes

Acknowledgements

A preliminary version of this paper appeared at the Nafplion Workshop on Database Programming Languages. I wish to thank Fernando Velez for his comments on an earlier draft of this paper. Je le remercie aussi de m'aider à rester lucide sur la qualité de ma production capillaire et scientifique.

References

[1]   M. Atkinson, F. Bancilhon, D. DeWitt, K. Dittrich, D. Maier and S. Zdonick, "The Object-Oriented Database System Manifesto", *Proceedings DOOD 89, Kyoto*, December 1989.

[2]   F. Bancilhon, "Object-oriented database systems", *Proceedings of the 1988 PODS Conference*, Austin, Texas, September 1989.

[3]   F. Bancilhon, G. Barbedette, V. Benzaken, C. Delobel, S. Gamerman, C. Lecluse, P. Pfeffer, P. Richard et F. Velez, "The design and implementation of O_2, an object-oriented database system", *Proceedings of the OODBS II Workshop*, Bad Munster, FRG, September 1988.

[4]   J. Banerjee, H. T. Chou, J. Garza, W. Kim, D. Woelk, N. Ballou and H. J. Kim, "Data model issues for object-oriented applications", *ACM TOIS*, January 1987.

[5]   M. Carey, D. DeWitt and S. Vandenberg, "A Data Model and Query Language for EXODUS", *Proceedings of the 1988 ACM SIGMOD Conference*, Chicago, June 1988.

[6]   G. Copeland and D. Maier, "Making Smalltalk a Database System", *Proc. SIGMOD*, June 1984 .

[7]   O. Deux *et al.*, "The O_2 System", *Communications of the ACM*, Vol. 34, No. 10, October 1991.

[8]   K.R. Dittrich, "Object-Oriented Database Systems: The Notions and the Issues", *in:* K. R. Dittrich U. and Dayal (eds): *Proceedings of the 1986 International Workshop on Object-Oriented Database Systems*, IEEE Computer Science Press.

[9]   D. Fishman *et al.*, "Iris: an object-oriented database management system", *ACM TOIS* 5:1, pp 48-69, January 1986.

[10]   D. Maier, J. Stein, A. Otis, A. Purdy, "Development of an object-oriented DBMS", *Report CS/E-86-005*, Oregon Graduate Center, April 1986.

[11]   A. Skarra, S. Zdonik and S. Reiss, "An object server for an object-oriented database system", *Proceedings of the 1986 International Workshop on Object-Oriented Database Systems*, pp. 196-204, Computer Society Press, IEEE, 1986

On Formalizing Database Updates: Preliminary Report

Raymond Reiter

Department of Computer Science and the Canadian Institute for Advanced Research, University of Toronto, Toronto, Ont. M5S 1A4, Canada

Abstract

We address the problem of formalizing the evolution of a database under the effect of an arbitrary sequence of update transactions. We do so by appealing to a first order representation language called the situation calculus, which is a standard approach in artificial intelligence to the formalization of planning problems. We formalize database transactions in exactly the same way as actions in the artificial intelligence planning domain. This leads to a database version of the frame problem in artificial intelligence. We provide a solution to the frame problem for a special, but substantial, class of update transactions.

We next briefly describe some of the results obtained within this axiomatization. Specifically, we provide procedures for determining whether a given sequence of update transactions is legal, and for query evaluation in an updated database. These procedures have the nice property that they appeal to theorem-proving only with respect to the initial database state. We also address the problem of proving properties true in all states of the database. It turns out that mathematical induction is required for this task, and we formulate a number of suitable induction axioms. Among those properties of database states that we wish to prove are the standard database notions of static and dynamic integrity constraints. In our setting, these emerge as inductive entailments of the database.

1 Introduction

Our concern in this paper is with formalizing the evolution of a database under arbitrary sequences of update transactions. A wide variety of proposals for this exist in the literature (e.g. Grahne [4], Katsuno and Mendelzon [8], Winslett [17], Fagin, Ullman and Vardi [2], Ginsberg and Smith [3], Guessoum and Lloyd [5, 6], Manchanda and Warren [9]). In this paper, we advance a substantially different proposal.

To begin, we take seriously the fact that, during the course of its evolution, a database will pass through different states; accordingly, we endow updatable database relations with an explicit state argument which records the sequence of update transactions which the database has undergone thus far. Secondly, in our approach, the transactions themselves are first class objects, so for example, if the database admits a transaction for changing the grade g of a student st to a new grade g' for the course c, then the first order term $change(st, c, g, g')$ will be an object in the database language. These two features – an explicit state argument for updatable relations, and first order terms for transactions – are the basic ingredients of the *situation calculus*, one of the standard approaches in artificial intelligence to the formalization of planning problems. The essence of our proposal is to specify databases and their update transactions within the situation calculus.

One difficulty with this proposal, which arises immediately, is the so-called *frame problem*, well known in the planning domain. Briefly, this is the problem of how to succinctly represent the invariants of the domain, namely, those relations whose truth values are unaffected by a transaction. Thus, in the example of a grade-changing transaction, it would be necessary to state that the transaction does not affect a teacher's salary. Section 2 describes the problem in more detail, while Sections 3 and 4 describe our axiomatization of databases and transactions, and how these address the frame problem. Finally, in Section 5, we briefly describe our principal results in this approach to a theory of updates.

2 Preliminaries: The Situation Calculus and the Frame Problem

The *situation calculus* (McCarthy [10]) is a first order language designed to represent dynamically changing worlds in which all such changes are the result of named *actions*. The world is conceived as being in some state s, and this state can change only in consequence of some agent (human, robot, nature) performing an action. If α is some such action, then the successor state to s resulting from the performance of action α is denoted by $do(\alpha, s)$. In general, actions may be parameterized. For example, $put(x, y)$ might stand for the action of putting object x on object y, in which case $do(put(A, B), s)$ denotes that state resulting from placing A on B when the world is in state s. Notice that in this language, actions are denoted by function symbols. Those relations whose truth values may vary from state to state are called *fluents*, and are denoted by predicate symbols taking a state term as one of their arguments. For example, in a world in which it is possible to paint objects, we would expect a fluent $colour(x, c, s)$, meaning that the colour of object x is c when the world is in state s.

Normally, actions will have *preconditions*, namely, sufficient conditions which the current world state must satisfy before the action can be performed in this state. For example, it is possible for a robot r to pick up an object x in the world state s provided the robot is not holding any object, it is next to x, and x is not heavy:

$$[(\forall z)\neg holding(r, z, s)] \land \neg heavy(x) \land nexto(r, x, s) \supset Poss(pickup(r, x), s).^1$$

It is possible for a robot to repair an object provided the object is broken, and there is glue available:

$$hasglue(r, s) \land broken(x, s) \supset Poss(repair(r, x), s).$$

---

[1] In the sequel, lower case roman letters will denote variables. All formulas are understood to be implicitly universally quantified with respect to their free variables whenever explicit quantifiers are not indicated.

The dynamics of a world are specified by *effect axioms* which specify the effect of a given action on the truth value of a given fluent. For example, the effect of a robot dropping an object on the fluent *broken* can be specified by:

$$Poss(drop(r, x), s) \land fragile(x) \supset broken(x, do(drop(r, x), s)).$$

A robot repairing an object causes it not to be broken:

$$Poss(repair(r, x), s) \supset \neg broken(x, do(repair(r, x), s)).$$

As has been long recognized (McCarthy and Hayes [11]), axioms other than effect axioms are required for formalizing dynamic worlds. These are called *frame axioms*, and they specify the action *invariants* of the domain, i.e., those fluents unaffected by the performance of an action. For example, dropping things does not affect an object's colour:

$$Poss(drop(r, x), s) \land colour(y, c, s) \supset colour(y, c, do(drop(r, x), s)).$$

Not breaking things:

$$Poss(drop(r, x), s) \land \neg broken(y, s) \land [y \neq x \lor \neg fragile(y)] \supset \neg broken(y, do(drop(r, x), s)).$$

The problem associated with the need for frame axioms is that normally there will be a vast number of them. For example, an object's colour remains unchanged as a result of picking things up, opening a door, turning on a light, electing a new prime minister of Canada, etc. etc. Normally, only relatively few actions in any repertoir of actions about a world will affect the truth value of a given fluent; all other actions leave the fluent invariant, and will give rise to frame axioms, one for each such action. This is the *frame problem*.

In this paper, we shall propose specifying databases and update transactions within the situation calculus. Transactions will be treated exactly as actions are in dynamic worlds, i.e. they will be functions. Thus, for example, the transaction of changing a student's grade in an education database will be treated no differently than the action of dropping an object in the physical world. This means that we immediately confront the frame problem; we must find some convenient way of stating, for example, that a student's grade is unaffected by registering another student in a course, or by changing someone's address or telephone number or student number, etc. etc.

While the frame problem has been recognized in the setting of database transaction processing, notably by Borgida, Mylopoulos and Schmidt [1], it has not received any systematic treatment in the database literature. Neither is its importance widely recognized. The fact is, no adequate theory of database evolution will be possible without confronting the frame problem head-on. The next section provides an example of our approach to specifying database update transactions, and how it deals with the frame problem.

3 The Basic Approach: An Example

We consider a toy education database to illustrate our approach to specifying update transactions.

Relations The database involves the following three relations:

1. *enrolled*($st, course, s$): Student st is enrolled in course *course* when the database is in state s.
2. *grade*($st, course, grade, s$): The grade of student st in course *course* is *grade* when the database is in state s.
3. *prerequ*($pre, course$): *pre* is a prerequisite course for course *course*. Notice that this relation is state independent, so is not expected to change during the evolution of the database.

Initial Database State We assume given some first order specification of what is true of the initial state S_0 of the database. These will be arbitrary first order sentences, the only restriction being that those predicates which mention a state, mention only the initial state S_0. Examples of information which might be true in the initial state are:

$$enrolled(Sue, C100, S_0) \lor enrolled(Sue, C200, S_0),$$

$$(\exists c)enrolled(Bill, c, S_0),$$

$$(\forall p).prerequ(p, P300) \equiv p = P100 \lor p = M100,$$

$$(\forall p)\neg prerequ(p, C100),$$

$$(\forall c).enrolled(Bill, c, S_0) \equiv c = M100 \lor c = C100 \lor c = P200,$$

$$enrolled(Mary, C100, S_0), \quad \neg enrolled(John, M200, S_0), \ldots$$

$$grade(Sue, P300, 75, S_0), \quad grade(Bill, M200, 70, S_0), \ldots$$

$$prerequ(M200, M100), \quad \neg prerequ(M100, C100), \ldots$$

Database Transactions Update transactions will be denoted by function symbols, and will be treated in exactly the same way as actions are in the situation calculus. For our example, there will be three transactions:

1. *register*($st, course$): Register student st in course *course*.
2. *change*($st, course, grade$): Change the current grade of student st in course *course* to *grade*.
3. *drop*($st, course$): Student st drops course *course*.

Transaction Preconditions Normally, transactions have preconditions which must be satisfied by the current database state before the transaction can be "executed". In our example, we shall require that a student can register in a course iff she has obtained a grade of at least 50 in all prerequisites for the course:

$$Poss(register(st, c), s) \equiv \{(\forall p).prerequ(p, c) \supset (\exists g).grade(st, p, g, s) \land g \geq 50\}.$$

It is possible to change a student's grade iff he has a grade which is different than the new grade:

$$Poss(change(st, c, g), s) \equiv (\exists g').grade(st, c, g', s) \land g' \neq g.$$

A student may drop a course iff the student is currently enrolled in that course:

$$Poss(drop(st, c), s) \equiv enrolled(st, c, s).$$

Update Specifications These are the central axioms in our formalization of update transactions. They specify the effects of all transactions on all updatable database relations. As usual, all lower case roman letters are variables which are implicitly universally quantified. In particular, notice that these axioms quantify over transactions.

$$Poss(a, s) \supset$$
$$[enrolled(st, c, do(a, s)) \equiv \qquad\qquad (1)$$
$$a = register(st, c) \vee enrolled(st, c, s) \wedge a \neq drop(st, c)],$$

$$Poss(a, s) \supset$$
$$[grade(st, c, g, do(a, s)) \equiv$$
$$a = change(st, c, g) \vee grade(st, c, g, s) \wedge (\forall g')a \neq change(st, c, g')].$$

It is the update specification axioms which "solve" the frame problem. To see why, let α be *any* transaction distinct from $register(st, c)$ and $drop(st, c)$. We obtain the following instance of the axiom (1):

$$Poss(\alpha, s) \supset \{enrolled(st, c, do(\alpha, s)) \equiv enrolled(st, c, s)\}, {}^2$$

i.e., $register(st, c)$ and $drop(st, c)$ are the only transactions which can possibly affect the truth value of *enrolled*; *all other transactions leave its truth value unchanged* (provided $Poss(\alpha, s)$ is true, of course).[3] But this ability to succinctly represent all of the transactions which leave a given fluent invariant is precisely the kind of solution to the frame problem that we seek. A little reflection reveals those properties of the axiom (1) which solve the problem for us:

1. Quantification over transactions, and
2. The assumption that relatively few transactions (in this case $register(st, c)$ and $drop(st, c)$) affect the truth value of the fluent, so that the sentence (1) is reasonably short. In other words, most transactions leave a fluent's truth value unchanged, which of course is what originally lead to too many frame axioms.

4 An Axiomatization of Updates

The example education domain illustrates the general principles behind our approach to the specification of database update transactions. In this section we precisely characterize a class of databases and updates of which the above example will be an instance.

---

[2] Notice that to obtain this instance we require unique names axioms for transactions, i.e.,

$$change(st, c, g) \neq drop(st, c),$$
$$drop(st, c) \neq register(st, c),$$
$$etc.$$

[3] Since for our example there are just three transactions, this might not seem much of an achievement. To see that it is, simply imagine augmenting the set of transactions with arbitrarily many new transactions, each of which is irrelevant to the truth of *enrolled*, say transactions for changing students' registration numbers, addresses, telephone numbers, fees, etc. etc.

Unique Names Axioms for Transactions For distinct transaction names T and T',

$$T(\mathbf{x}) \neq T'(\mathbf{y})$$

Identical transactions have identical arguments:

$$T(x_1, ..., x_n) = T(y_1, ..., y_n) \supset x_1 = y_1 \wedge ... \wedge x_n = y_n$$

for each function symbol T of $\mathcal{L}$ of sort *transaction*.

Unique Names Axioms for States

$$(\forall a, s) S_0 \neq do(a, s),$$

$$(\forall a, s, a', s').do(a, s) = do(a', s') \supset a = a' \wedge s = s'.$$

Definition: The Simple Formulas The *simple* formulas are defined to be the smallest set such that:

1. $F(\mathbf{t}, s)$ and $F(\mathbf{t}, S_0)$ are simple whenever F is a fluent, the $\mathbf{t}$ are terms, and s is a variable of sort *state* .[4]
2. Any equality atom is simple. Notice that equality atoms, unlike fluents, are permitted to mention the function symbol *do*.
3. Any other atom with predicate symbol other than *Poss* is simple.
4. If S_1 and S_2 are simple, so are $\neg S_1$, $S_1 \wedge S_2$, $S_1 \vee S_2$, $S_1 \supset S_2$, $S_1 \equiv S_2$.
5. If S is simple, so are $(\exists x)S$ and $(\forall x)S$ whenever x is an individual variable not of sort *state*.

In short, the simple formulas are those first order formulas which mention only domain predicate symbols, whose fluents do not mention the function symbol *do*, and which do not quantify over variables of sort *state*.

Definition: Transaction Precondition Axiom A transaction precondition axiom is a formula of the form

$$(\forall \mathbf{x}, s).Poss(T(x_1, \cdots, x_n), s) \equiv \Pi_T,$$

where T is an n-ary transaction function, and Π_T is a simple formula whose free variables are among $x_1, \cdots, x_n, s$.

Definition: Successor State Axiom A successor state axiom for an $(n+1)$-ary fluent F is a sentence of the form

$$(\forall a, s).Poss(a, s) \supset (\forall x_1, \ldots, x_n).F(x_1, \ldots, x_n, do(a, s)) \equiv \Phi_F$$

where, for notational convenience, we assume that F's last argument is of sort *state*, and where Φ_F is a simple formula, all of whose free variables are among $a, s, x_1, \ldots, x_n$.

---

[4] For notational convenience, we assume that the last argument of a fluent is always the (only) argument of sort *state*.

5 Results

We here briefly indicate some of the results we have obtained for first order databases axiomatized as in the previous section. The full details may be found in (Reiter [15]).

5.1 Legal Transaction Sequences

Not all transaction sequences need be legal. For example, the sequence

$$drop(Sue, C100), change(Bill, C100, 60)$$

would be illegal if the *drop* transaction was impossible in the initial database state, i.e. if $Poss(drop(Sue, C100), S_0)$ was false. Even if the *drop* transaction were possible, the sequence would be illegal if the *change* transaction was impossible in that state resulting from doing the *drop* transaction, i.e. if

$$Poss(change(Bill, C100, 60), do(drop(Sue, C100), S_0))$$

was false.

Intuitively, a transaction sequence is legal iff, beginning in state S_0, each transaction in the sequence is possible in that state resulting from performing all the transactions preceeding it in the sequence. Our concern is to characterize the legal transaction sequences. To that end, we require the following:

Definition: A Regression Operator $\mathcal{R}$ Let W be first order formula. Then $\mathcal{R}[W]$ is that formula obtained from W by replacing each fluent atom $F(t, do(\alpha, \sigma))$ mentioned by W by $\Phi_F(t, \alpha, \sigma)$ where F's successor state axiom is

$$(\forall a, s).Poss(a, s) \supset (\forall \mathbf{x}).F(\mathbf{x}, do(a, s)) \equiv \Phi_F(\mathbf{x}, a, s).$$

All other atoms of W not of this form remain the same.

Regression corresponds to the operation of *unfolding* in logic programming.

In what follows, $\mathcal{D}_{uns}$ and $\mathcal{D}_{unt}$ denote the unique names axioms for states and unique names axioms for transactions, respectively (Section 4). $\mathcal{D}_{S_0}$ denotes the initial database, i.e. any set of sentences which mention only the initial state term S_0. (See Section 3 for an example $\mathcal{D}_{S_0}$.)

Theorem 1. *Let $\tau_1, \ldots, \tau_n$ be a sequence of update transactions. There is a formula $R_{\tau_1, \ldots, \tau_n}$ (which is easily obtained using the regression operator and the transaction precondition axioms of Section 3) such that $\tau_1, \ldots, \tau_n$ is legal wrt $\mathcal{D}$ iff*

$$\mathcal{D}_{uns} \cup \mathcal{D}_{unt} \cup \mathcal{D}_{S_0} \models R_{\tau_1, \ldots, \tau_n}.[5]$$

Theorem 1 informs us that *legality testing reduces to first order theorem proving in the initial database $\mathcal{D}_{S_0}$ together with unique names axioms.*

---

[5] See (Reiter [15]) for a description of how to compute $R_{\tau_1, \ldots, \tau_n}$.

5.2 Query Evaluation

Notice that in our formalization of update transactions in the situation calculus, all updates are *virtual*; the database is never physically changed. In order to query a database resulting from a sequence of update transactions we must explicitly refer to this sequence in the query. For example, to ask whether John is enrolled in any courses after the transaction sequence $drop(John, C100), register(Mary, C100)$ has been 'executed', we must determine whether

$$Database \models (\exists c).enrolled(John, c, do(register(Mary, C100), do(drop(John, C100), S_0))).$$

In general, the specific problem we address is this: Given a sequence $\tau_1, \ldots, \tau_n$ of transactions, and a query $Q(s)$ whose only free variable is the state variable s, what is the answer to Q in that state resulting from performing this transaction sequence, beginning with the initial database state S_0? This can be formally defined as the problem of determining whether

$$\mathcal{D} \models Q(do([\tau_1, \ldots, \tau_n], S_0)),$$

where $\mathcal{D}$ denotes some database theory. Here, $do([\tau_1, \ldots, \tau_n], S_0)$ abbreviates the state term

$$do(\tau_n, do(\tau_{n-1}, \cdots, do(\tau_1, S_0) \cdots)),$$

and denotes that state resulting from performing the transaction τ_1, followed by τ_2, ..., followed by τ_n, beginning with the initial database state S_0.

Our principal result is the following:

Theorem 2. (Soundness and Completeness of Query Evaluation) *Suppose that $\tau_1, \ldots, \tau_n$ is a legal transaction sequence. Then whenever $\mathcal{D}$ is a database whose axioms are those of Section 4,*

$$\mathcal{D} \models Q(do([\tau_1, \ldots, \tau_n], S_0))$$

iff

$$\mathcal{D}_{uns} \cup \mathcal{D}_{unt} \cup \mathcal{D}_{S_0} \models \mathcal{R}^n[Q(do([\tau_1, \ldots, \tau_n], S_0))].[6]$$

As was the case for legality testing, *query evaluation reduces to first order theorem proving in the initial database $\mathcal{D}_{S_0}$ together with unique names axioms.*

5.3 Integrity Constraints

In database theory, an *integrity constraint* specifies what counts as a legal database state; it is a property that every database state must satisfy. In our setting, it is natural to represent these as first order sentences, universally quantified over states. In the following examples, $\leq$ is a binary relation between states; $s \leq s'$ means that s' is a possible future of s, i.e. there is some sequence of zero or more transactions which can lead a database from state s to state s'. As it happens, defining $\leq$ requires a second order axiom, the details of which we omit here. A definition is given in (Reiter [15]).

---

[6] Recall that $\mathcal{D}_{uns}$ and $\mathcal{D}_{unt}$ denote the unique names axioms for states and unique names axioms for transactionss, respectively (Section 4), and $\mathcal{D}_{S_0}$ denotes the axioms true of the initial database state.

Examples of integrity constraints

1. No one may have two different grades for the same course in any database state. This is a standard functional dependency.

$$(\forall s)(\forall st, c, g, g').S_0 \leq s \wedge grade(st, c, g, s) \wedge grade(st, c, g', s) \supset g = g'.$$

2. Salaries must never decrease. This is the classic example of a *dynamic* integrity constraint.

$$(\forall s, s')(\forall p, \$, \$').S_0 \leq s \wedge s \leq s' \wedge sal(p, \$, s) \wedge sal(p, \$', s') \supset \$ \leq \$'.$$

Constraint satisfaction defined: A database *satisfies* an integrity constraint IC iff

$$Database \models IC.[7]$$

Not surprisingly, some form of mathematical induction is necessary to establish that a database satisfies an integrity constraint. In [15], we justify the following second order axiom of induction suitable for proving properties of states s in the situation calculus, whenever $S_0 \leq s$.

$$(\forall W).W(S_0) \wedge [(\forall a, s).Poss(a, s) \wedge S_0 \leq s \wedge W(s) \supset W(do(a, s))]$$
$$\supset (\forall s).S_0 \leq s \supset W(s).$$

This is our analogue of the standard second order induction axiom for Peano arithmetic. Frequently, we want to prove sentences of the form

$$(\forall s, s').S_0 \leq s \wedge s \leq s' \supset R(s, s').$$

For example, the following classic dynamic integrity constraint has this form:

$$(\forall s, s', p, \$, \$').S_0 \leq s \wedge s \leq s' \supset sal(p, \$, s) \wedge sal(p, \$', s') \supset \$ \leq \$'.$$

Using the above simple induction axiom we can derive an induction axiom suitable for proving properties of pairs of states s and s' when $S_0 \leq s \wedge s \leq s'$:

$$(\forall R).R(S_0, S_0) \wedge$$
$$[(\forall a, s).Poss(a, s) \wedge S_0 \leq s \supset R(s, do(a, s))] \wedge$$
$$[(\forall a, s, s').Poss(a, s) \wedge S_0 \leq s \wedge R(s, s) \supset R(do(a, s), do(a, s))] \wedge$$
$$[(\forall a, s, s').Poss(a, s') \wedge S_0 \leq s \wedge s \leq s' \wedge R(s, s') \supset R(s, do(a, s'))]$$
$$\supset (\forall s, s').S_0 \leq s \wedge s \leq s' \supset R(s, s').$$

(Reiter [15]) provides a number of examples of integrity constraints and their verification using these induction axioms.

---

[7] This definition should be contrasted with those in Reiter [14, 13]. It seems that there is not a unitary concept of integrity constraint in database theory, and that there are many subtleties involved.

19

6 Conclusions and Extensions

Database transactions have long been treated procedurally. We have outlined a declarative treatment of this notion by appealing to suitable axiomatizations in the situation calculus. A number of issues have not been addressed in this paper; these include the following:[8]

- **Historical Queries:** On our account of database evolution, databases are never physically modified and therefore never forget. It is therefore possible to pose and answer *historical queries*, for example "Did Mary ever get a raise?"
- **Logic Programming Implementation:** It seems that our approach to database updates can be implemented in a fairly straightforward way as a logic program, thereby directly complementing the logic programming perspective on databases (Minker [12]).
- **Indeterminate Transactions:** A limitation of our formalism is that it requires all transactions to be *determinate*, by which we mean that in the presence of complete information about the initial database state a transaction completely determines the resulting state. An example of an indeterminate transaction is registering a student in a multi-section course, without specifying in the parameters of the transaction, in which of the possible sections the student is registered. It is possible to extend the theory of this paper to include indeterminate transactions by appealing to a simple idea for dealing with the frame problem due to Haas [7], as elaborated by Schubert [16].

Acknowledgments Many of my colleagues provided important conceptual and technical advice. My thanks to Leo Bertossi, Alex Borgida, Craig Boutilier, Michael Gelfond, Gösta Grahne, Russ Greiner, Joe Halpern, Hector Levesque, Vladimir Lifschitz, Fangzhen Lin, Wiktor Marek, John McCarthy, Alberto Mendelzon, John Mylopoulos, Javier Pinto, Len Schubert, Yoav Shoham and Marianne Winslett. Funding for this work was provided by the National Science and Engineering Research Council of Canada, and by the Institute for Robotics and Intelligent Systems.

References

1. A. Borgida, J. Mylopoulos, and J. Schmidt. The TaxisDL software description language. Technical report, Department of Computer Science, University of Toronto, 1991.
2. R. Fagin, J.D. Ullman, and M.Y. Vardi. Updating logical databases. In *Proceedings of the ACM Symposium on Principles of Database Systems*, April 1983.
3. M.L. Ginsberg and D.E. Smith. Reasoning about actions I: A possible worlds approach. *Artificial Intelligence*, 35:165–195, 1988.
4. G. Grahne. Updates and counterfactuals. In J. Allen, R. Fikes, and E. Sandewall, editors, *Proceedings of the Second International Conference on Principles of Knowledge Representation and Reasoning (KR'91)*, pages 269–276, Los Altos, CA, 1991. Morgan Kaufmann Publishers, Inc.
5. A. Guessoum and J.W. Lloyd. Updating knowledge bases. *New Generation Computing*, 8(1):71–89, 1990.

[8] See (Reiter [15]) for more details.

6. A. Guessoum and J.W. Lloyd. Updating knowledge bases II. Technical report, University of Bristol, 1991. To appear.

7. A. R. Haas. The case for domain-specific frame axioms. In F. M. Brown, editor, *The frame problem in artificial intelligence. Proceedings of the 1987 workshop*, pages 343–348, Los Altos, California, 1987. Morgan Kaufmann Publishers, Inc.

8. H. Katsuno and A.O. Mendelzon. On the difference between updating a knowledge base and revising it. In J. Allen, R. Fikes, and E. Sandewall, editors, *Proceedings of the Second International Conference on Principles of Knowledge Representation and Reasoning (KR'91)*, pages 387–394, Los Altos, CA, 1991. Morgan Kaufmann Publishers, Inc.

9. S. Manchanda and D.S. Warren. A logic-based language for database updates. In J. Minker, editor, *Foundations of Deductive Databases and Logic Programming*, pages 363–394. Morgan Kaufmann Publishers, Inc., Los Altos, CA, 1988.

10. J. McCarthy. Programs with common sense. In M. Minsky, editor, *Semantic Information Processing*, pages 403–418. The MIT Press, Cambridge, MA, 1968.

11. J. McCarthy and P. Hayes. Some philosophical problems from the standpoint of artificial intelligence. In B. Meltzer and D. Michie, editors, *Machine Intelligence 4*, pages 463–502. Edinburgh University Press, Edinburgh, Scotland, 1969.

12. J. Minker, editor. *Foundations of Deductive Databases and Logic Programming*. Morgan Kaufmann Publishers, Inc., Los Altos, CA, 1988.

13. R. Reiter. What should a database know? *Journal of Logic Programming*. to appear.

14. R. Reiter. Towards a logical reconstruction of relational database theory. In M.L. Brodie, J. Mylopoulos, and J.W. Schmidt, editors, *On Conceptual Modelling: Perspectives from Artificial Intelligence, Databases and Programming Languages*, pages 191–233. Springer, New York, 1984.

15. R. Reiter. On specifying database updates. Technical report, Department of Computer Science, University of Toronto, in preparation.

16. L.K. Schubert. Monotonic solution of the frame problem in the situation calculus: an efficient method for worlds with fully specified actions. In H.E. Kyberg, R.P. Loui, and G.N. Carlson, editors, *Knowledge Representation and Defeasible Reasoning*, pages 23–67. Kluwer Academic Press, 1990.

17. M. Winslett. Reasoning about action using a possible models approach. In *Proceedings of the National Conference on Artificial Intelligence*, pages 89–93. American Association for Artificial Intelligence, 1988.

This article was processed using the LaTeX macro package with LMAMULT style

Concepts for graph-oriented object manipulation

Marc Andries, Marc Gemis, Jan Paredaens, Inge Thyssens, Jan Van den Bussche
University of Antwerp (UIA), Dept. Math. & Comp. Science
Universiteitsplein 1, B-2610 Antwerp, Belgium
E-mail: vdbuss@ccu.uia.ac.be

Abstract: We propose a number of fundamental concepts for graph-oriented database user interfaces. For both schemes and instances we use abstract directed graphs. We represent different kinds of database interactions, such as querying, constraint specification, updating, restructuring, and schema transformation, by means of a uniform graph-transformation framework based on pattern matching. Staying within the same framework, we incorporate viewing and give a formal definition of browsing.

1 Introduction

For as long as database systems are being developed, there has been interest in *visual* or *graphical* user interfaces to them. A good example is QBE [Zlo77], an attractive user interface to relational databases, introduced in the mid-70's.

We can distinguish at least two major types of proposals in the field. One type concerns special-purpose graphical information systems, such as geographical, pictorial or multimedia systems. There, the focus is mainly on highly tuned navigation and interactive manipulation of data of unconventional type and structure.

A second type of database user interfaces is situated in the broader perspective of general-purpose databases (see [SIG90] for some comprehensive reference lists). There, the main objectives are *(i)* the user-friendly specification of a certain set of *associative, set-oriented queries*; and *(ii)* the convenient representation of the result of these queries on the computer screen. Sometimes also some *browsing facilities* are provided. Rather than special-purpose graphics processing, these general-purpose systems emphasize things like efficient menu structures or tractable dialogue-windows. It is this type of interfaces that forms the scope of this paper.

The graphical database user interfaces that were proposed thus far form a rather diverse collection. Some introduce a query language with a graphical syntax, while some others present a way of visually browsing through the database. Furthermore, the proposals are often specifically tuned to their own particular data models. However, a fundamental point in common to most of them is that the database scheme has a *graph-based representation*. To give just two examples, SNAP [BH86] is based on the graphical representation of IFO schemes, and PICASSO [KKS88] employs the representation of a relational database scheme as a hypergraph.

Typically, in such graph-based systems, queries are visually expressed by means of certain graphs which are built from the same components as the schema graph. The actual structure of this query graph specifies which portions of the database are to be retrieved by the query. To draw an analogy, the components of the query graph would correspond to the form-clause of an SQL statement (which also specifies the relevant relations that will participate in the query), while the actual structure of the graph would correspond to the where-clause.

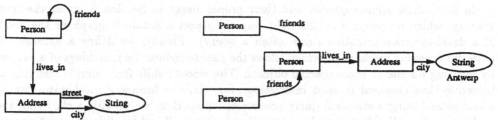

Figure 1: A schema graph (left) and a query graph (right). The schema graph shows the types of objects that can occur in the database. The query graph specifies all persons that have a common friend living in Antwerp.

An example is given in Figure 1. Note here that we do not use the notation of one particular graphical interface, but a simple, uniform formalism that will be used throughout this paper.

In this work, we elaborate and extend the idea of query graph further, by proposing and discussing some general concepts which we think are fundamental to any graph-oriented database user interface. In particular, we do not restrict our attention to simple ad-hoc query facilities, but consider the full spectrum of database manipulations. Our ideas are based on the fact that not only the database schema, but also the actual database instance can be seen as a graph. This was recently observed [AK89, Bee90, GPVG90a, LRV88] in the area of *object oriented database models*.

We will see that the notion of instance graph leads naturally to the use of *graph-pattern-matching* as a uniform object manipulation primitive. Patterns are a simple, elegant formalization of the various query graph representations employed in graphical user interfaces. Actually, the query graph shown in Figure 1 is such a pattern; all matches of the pattern form the answer of the query. Moreover, in a recent paper, Bancilhon and Kim [BK90] argued that the concrete problem of flexible representation and manipulation of objects on a computer screen has certain aspects which make it more than a mere user interface problem. They suggested that solutions to the problem might be more promising if taken from a database point of view. We claim that patterns may be a right step in this direction. In particular, we will see that they offer the user a methodology to specify the information he wants in a quite direct manner (as may be illustrated by the example of Figure 1), while at the same time the "set-oriented" nature so typical to databases can be preserved.

In Section 2 we introduce our object model. The model is general: it does not rely on particular data modeling features. Hence, it lends itself as a uniform framework that can apply to a large class of graphical database user interfaces.

In Section 3 we introduce and motivate patterns. Furthermore, we launch the idea that a user interface should support language constructs for expressing *graph-transformations* based on the pattern-matching paradigm.

In Section 4, we explain how these graph-transformations can be interpreted as database transformations in a variety of ways, from database restructurings, queries and updates to schema manipulations. In particular, the class of queries that can be expressed in this way is far more powerful than the simple query graphs (like the one of Figure 1) typically provided by the average graphical database user interface.

In fact, these simple queries find their proper usage in Section 5 under the term *viewing*, which we propose as the right way to inspect a database graph or the result of a database transformation (most often a query). Finally, we define a natural, yet powerful *browsing* mechanism, which allows the user to reduce the matchings of a pattern by focusing on one or more specific objects. The smooth shift from simple querying to browsing thus obtained is most interesting: for one, our browsing mechanism can be implemented using a standard query processor; for another, we provide a clarifying and unifying look on the diverse scale of browsing facilities offered by different existing user interfaces [AGS90, Gol84, GGKZ85, Hal88, Mot84].

There is already a sparse collection of material in the database literature in which the notion of patterns appears [GSL91, GPVG90a, MZO89]. These papers mainly focus on language details, and are mutually incomparable on many points. This paper's presentation is inspired by the *Graph-Oriented Object Database Model* [GPVG90a]; actually, it may be seen as a follow-up of the companion paper [GPVG90b].

The concepts introduced in this paper are incorporated in the user interface of the Graph-Oriented Object Database Environment, which is currently being developed in a joint effort of Indiana University and the University of Antwerp [PVdBVG+91].

2 Object Model

In this section, we introduce a general model for object databases, based on the *Graph-Oriented Object Database Model* [GPVG90a].[1] This model will turn out useful as a uniform framework for investigating graph based representations of database manipulations.

Database schemes are represented in our model as directed, labeled graphs. As an example, Figure 2 shows the scheme for a hyper-media system [Con87], storing documents which may contain text, graphics and sound information. A rectangular node in the scheme graph represents a *class* of abstract objects. For example, the node Text stands for the class of texts. An oval node represents a *type* of primitive objects. For example, the node Long-String stands for the type of character strings. The edges express properties of abstract objects, e.g., the #chars edge indicates that the number of chars in a text can be kept as information in the system.

Let us have a more detailed look at the example scheme of Figure 2. An info-node represents a node of information in the system. Associated with this node are a creation date, a last modification-date, a name, a comment (either a string or a number), and possibly other info-nodes. Since it is typical in hyper-media systems to have various versions, we need a way to keep track of them. This is facilitated with version nodes. A version node indicates that an info-node has obtained a new version. The node pointed at by the edge labeled old indicates the old version, whereas the edge with the new edge label points to the node corresponding to the new version. We distinguish four subclasses of info-nodes: the classes of text, graphics and sound data, and on the other hand the class of reference nodes specifying references in info-nodes. Associated with a graphics node are its height and width, and the actual data stored as a bitmap. Associated with a text node are its number of words and characters and the actual data stored as a long

---

[1] This model should be viewed as a common denominator of almost all data models, instead as yet another database model. Indeed, in this context, graph-based models were proposed numerous times, dating back to Bachman diagrams.

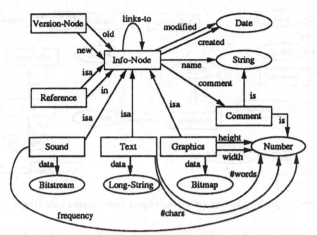

Figure 2: The hyper-media object base scheme.

string. Associated with a sound node are its frequency and the actual data stored as a bit-stream.

We are now ready to formally define a database scheme and its graph-based representation. Throughout this paper, we assume there are infinitely enumerable sets of *abstract object labels* (serving as class names), *primitive object labels* (serving as basic types) and *edge labels* (serving as property names). These three sets of labels are assumed to be pairwise disjoint. Furthermore, we assume there is a function π which associates to each primitive object label a set of constants (e.g., strings, numbers, booleans, ... but also bitmaps, bitstreams,...)

Definition 1 (Database scheme) *A database scheme is a four-tuple* $S = (AOL, POL, EL, P)$ *with*

- *AOL a finite set of abstract object labels;*

- *POL a finite set of primitive object labels;*

- *EL a finite set of edge labels;*

- $P \subseteq AOL \times EL \times (AOL \cup POL)$.

If $(a, e, b) \in P$, then objects of class a have properties of type e being objects of class or type b, as illustrated in the example. [2] Properties are only defined on *abstract object labels*; this corresponds to the intuition that primitive objects have no properties, as their meaning is application-independent [Bee90]. Note also that we do not make any assumptions on the nature of these properties. In particular, at this point, we do not distinguish between composition links, relationship links, or class hierarchy links.

As pointed out in the introduction, almost any graphical database user interface is founded on a graphical representation of the database scheme. Definition 1 naturally

---

[2] One often makes a distinction between single-valued and multi-valued properties. Such a distinction is irrelevant to the scope of this paper.

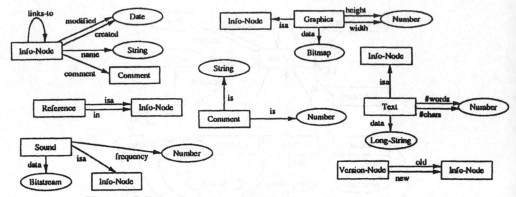

Figure 3: Splitting the hyper-media object base scheme into fragments.

suggests such a graphical representation (as already illustrated in Figure 2), which we refer to as the *normal representation*:

Definition 2 (Normal Scheme representation) *The* normal representation *of a database scheme S is a directed, labeled graph $\mathcal{G}(S)$, with :*

- *For each $a \in AOL$ a unique, rectangular-shaped node labeled a;*
- *For each $b \in POL$ a unique, oval shaped node labeled b;*
- *For every triple $(x, e, y) \in P$ an e-labeled edge from x to y in the graph.*

Note that the graph $\mathcal{G}(S)$ carries all the relevant information necessary to determine S. In other words, the mapping $\mathcal{G} : S \to \mathcal{G}(S)$ is one-to-one.

Figure 2 shows a database scheme in its normal representation, which offers a good overview. Every object-label appears exactly once. However, since schemes may become quite complex in many applications, the normal scheme graph may become too complicated, as too many edges cross each other. This can be dealt with by splitting the normal graph into its *fragments*.[3] Informally, for each class in the scheme we have one fragment, reflecting all properties of the class.

Definition 3 (Fragment) *Let S be a scheme and let $a \in AOL$. The* fragment *of a in S is the subscheme S_a of S whose normal graph $\mathcal{G}(S_a)$ is the subgraph of $\mathcal{G}(S)$ consisting only of a and its outgoing edges.*

We can now split the normal graph $\mathcal{G}(S)$ into its fragment-graphs by considering the (disjoint) union :

$$\mathcal{G}(S_a) \sqcup \mathcal{G}(S_b) \sqcup \ldots \sqcup \mathcal{G}(S_c) \qquad \text{with } AOL = \{a, b, \ldots, c\}$$

---

[3]The notion of fragment was originally introduced in the context of the IFO model [AH87].

It may be useful to discard fragments of *trivial* classes, i.e., classes on which no properties are defined. Indeed, fragments of trivial classes consist solely of one node (without edges), and are thus rather uninteresting.[4]

The result of splitting the hyper-media scheme into its fragments is shown in Figure 3. Although this result now consists of simple components without any crossing edges, it is apparent that thus splitting the graph *completely* is an overkill. In particular, the overview is largely lost here. So we need a more subtle solution, which allows to preserve a balance between simplicity and overview.

Our solution proposes step-wise decomposition/composition of the graph representation of a scheme. It allows the user to "customize" the normal scheme graph by:

- "Focusing in" on one or more classes and their associated properties, by *decomposing* w.r.t. a chosen class name a. Roughly, the fragment of a is split off, forming a new component.

- "Zooming out", by *composing* two subgraphs. Roughly, the two subgraphs are merged into one component.

Algorithm 4 (Decomposition) Input : *A graph G representing a scheme S, and $a \in AOL$.*

Output : *G', the decomposition of G w.r.t. a, also representing S.*

Method : *G' is obtained from G as follows. If a trivial, then the decomposition would not make sense, and we put $G' := G$. Otherwise, all edges leaving a in G are removed, and all nodes that have become isolated by this removal are also removed. Finally, a (disjoint) copy of $\mathcal{G}(S_a)$ is added as an extra component. The resulting graph is G'.*

Algorithm 5 (Composition) Input : *A graph G representing a scheme S, and two designated components G_1, G_2 of G, representing subschemes S_1, S_2 of S, respectively.*

Output : *G', the composition of G on G_1, G_2, also representing S.*

Method : *G' is obtained from G by replacing $G_1 \cup G_2$ by $\mathcal{G}(S_1 \cup S_2)$, where union of schemes is defined in the natural way, component-wise.*

An example of composition and decomposition is given in Figure 4. We thus obtain an "evolutionary" methodology for scheme customization. Typically, in a concrete user interface, the initial scheme representation is the normal graph. This representation can then gradually be customized. Since users may want to change their perspective on the database scheme frequently, the system should provide means to do so, in the spirit of decomposition and composition. The following property essentially states that such a way of scheme customization is "information- and structure-preserving", i.e., at each moment the user has a complete and non-redundant look on the scheme :

---

[4]Discarding the fragment of a trivial class a is without loss of any information relevant to the scheme, if and only if an edge ends in a (or equivalently, if a serves as the domain of some property).

27

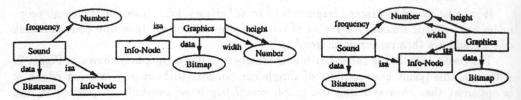

Figure 4: Composing the two leftmost graphs produces the rightmost graph; decomposing the rightmost graph on Graphics produces the two leftmost graphs.

Proposition 6 *Let S be a scheme, and let G' be the result of consecutively applying some decompositions and compositions to $\mathcal{G}(S)$. Then*

1. *$\mathcal{G}(S)$ can be re-obtained from G' by exhaustive application of composition; and*

2. *For each $a \in AOL$, there is exactly one node n in G' labeled a, such that the subgraph of G' consisting of n and its outgoing edges is isomorphic to $\mathcal{G}(S_a)$ (i.e., all properties defined on a in S are shown in G' at n). All other nodes in G' labeled a have no outgoing edges.*

We now discuss database instances. As an example, Figure 5 shows a hyper-media database over the scheme of Figure 2. An instance over a given scheme is again a graph, "generated" by the normal scheme graph.

The nodes of the instance graph are the objects of the database. Abstract objects are rectangular-shaped, and are labeled by their class name; primitive objects are oval-shaped, and are labeled by their type. Primitive objects have an additional label, indicating their actual value (e.g., If there is one group ... for an object of type Long-String in Figure 5).

The edges of the instance graph stand for the various properties that exist between objects of classes and types conforming to the scheme. E.g., in Figure 5, the info-node with name Rock has creation date 04/06/90. Observe that there is no modified edge leaving the object; either this info-node is unmodified or the modification day is unknown.

Formally, we define:

Definition 7 (Database instance) *Let $S = (AOL, POL, EL, P)$ be a database scheme. A database instance over S is a directed, labeled graph $\mathcal{I} = (N, E)$ where:*

- *N is a finite set of labeled nodes; if n is a node in N, then the label $\lambda(n)$ of n must be in $AOL \cup POL$; if $\lambda(n)$ is in AOL (respectively in POL), then n is called an abstract object and is depicted as a rectangular shaped node (respectively a primitive object and is depicted as an oval shaped node);*

- *each primitive node n has an additional label $print(n) \in \pi(\lambda(n))$;*

- *E is a set of labeled edges. Each $e \in E$ has the form (m, α, n) with $m, n \in N$ and label $\alpha \in EL$, such that $(\lambda(m), \alpha, \lambda(n)) \in P$.*

The major rationale for thinking of the database as a graph is to allow for an elegant and uniform expression of a variety of object manipulations in a graphical user interface. This will become clear in the remainder of this paper.

28

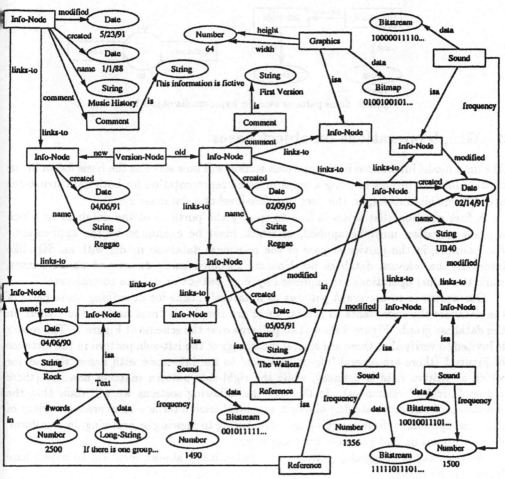

Figure 5: An example of a hyper-media object base instance.

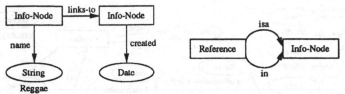

Figure 6: Some patterns over the hyper-media object base.

3 Graph operations on object bases

The data model introduced in the previous section will now serve as the basis for an investigation into the impact of using a *graph oriented* representation for both data structures and data manipulations, on the *user interface*-level of a database system.

A first question that arises is how to specify the portions of the database to which a given operation must be applied, or which must be examined by the application.[5] For example, in the particular case of the relational database model with an SQL-like interface, the relevant database portions are specified using **from**- and **where**-clauses, while the actual operations are expressed by, e.g., **select** or **delete** commands.

Our answer is to use *graph patterns* as a natural means for describing those parts of the database the user wants to access: these are simple all "matches" of the pattern in the database graph. Figure 6 shows two patterns over the scheme of Figure 2. The reader is invited to verify that there are several matchings of the left-side pattern in the instance of Figure 5 (there are several Info-nodes linked to the Info-node with name 'Reggae' for which a creation date is defined), while the right-side pattern matches nowhere (there are no "circular" references). In this and the following sections we will show that the formalism of pattern-matching allows a graphical user interface to express a variety of database operations, from querying or restructuring to viewing or browsing, in a uniform, visually appealing and generally tractable way.

As the example suggests, patterns are syntactically almost identical to object-base instances. Formally:

Definition 8 (Pattern) *A pattern over an object base scheme S is an object base instance over S, with the exception that a pattern may contain primitive nodes without print-labels.*

So, patterns, as instances, conform to the structure of the database scheme. The user can construct patterns in a simple way by copying, duplicating and identifying nodes and edges from the scheme graph (cfr. Section 2). An important advantage is that thus, (syntactically) incorrect queries cannot be formulated. Hence, graph-oriented object manipulation formalisms that are pattern-based allow for a *syntax-directed* way of working, in a much more natural way than text-based interfaces.

The fact that patterns look like database instances also allows us to treat (e.g., store) them in the same way as "real" instances. Since we advocate operations that are based on patterns, it is thus possible to view operations and data on equal grounds. The objects

---

[5]Here, *operation* is interpreted in the most general sense, i.e., we want to treat queries, updates, restructurings, view definitions,...on equal grounds.

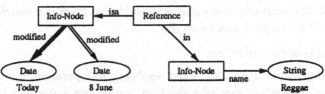

Figure 7: An example of a graph operation. The deletion part (here, an edge is to be deleted) is indicated in outline; the addition part (again an edge in this example) is indicated in bold lines.

of a pattern can be thought of as "computational" or "virtual" objects.[6] For example, it is now possible to specify queries on queries !

The semantic of a pattern is now formally defined as follows:

Definition 9 (Matching) *Let S be a scheme, let $\mathcal{I}$ be an instance over S and let $\mathcal{J}$ be a pattern over S. A matching of $\mathcal{J}$ in $\mathcal{I}$ is a mapping from the nodes in $\mathcal{J}$ to the nodes in $\mathcal{I}$ preserving labels and edges.*

In view of this semantics of patterns, and the way of constructing patterns described after Definition 8, we obtain a way of working reminiscent of the *direct manipulation* paradigm for object manipulation. Indeed, as the user builds a pattern from the scheme graph, he can actually think of this pattern as a "sample" of the images of the matchings in the database. At the same time however, we respect the set-oriented philosophy of databases, since *all* matchings are considered.[7]

We now come to the actual expression of graph operations.

In our framework, an operation is syntactically specified by a pattern together with an action. The action consists of a deletion and an insertion on the pattern. When applying an operation to a database graph, the action is performed on each matching of the pattern in the instance, in parallel. Within each action, the deletion is executed before the insertion, as this seems to be the most natural thing to do.[8] As an example, Figure 7 shows an operation where each Info-node referring to 'Reggae' and dated '8 June' is made up-to-date. More involved examples are presented at the end of the section.

Definition 10 (Graph operation) *Let S be a scheme. A graph operation over S consists of a pattern $\mathcal{J}$ over S, a subpattern $\mathcal{D}$ of $\mathcal{J}$, and another pattern $\mathcal{A}$, which can intersect with $\mathcal{J}$ outside $\mathcal{D}$. $\mathcal{D}$ is called the deletion part, and $\mathcal{A}$ the addition part. Let $F = (\mathcal{J}, \mathcal{D}, \mathcal{A})$. The result of applying F to an instance $\mathcal{I}$ over S is an instance $\mathcal{I}'$ over scheme S', where:*

- *S' is the scheme obtained from S by making the necessary augmentations such that $\mathcal{J} \cup \mathcal{A}$ is a pattern over S';*

- *$\mathcal{I}'$ is obtained from $\mathcal{I}$ by performing for each matching m of $\mathcal{J}$ in $\mathcal{I}$ (in parallel) the following steps:*

  1. Delete the subgraph $m(\mathcal{D})$;

---

[6]This idea also appears in the work of Maier et al. [Mai87, MZO89, ZM89].

[7]Object-centered manipulation will be discussed in Section 5 in the context of browsing.

[8]We point out that the same is done in graph grammars [ENRR86].

> 2. *Add the necessary nodes and edges such that there is a matching of* $(\mathcal{J} - \mathcal{D}) \cup \mathcal{A}$
> *in* $\mathcal{I}'$ *that agrees with* m *on* $\mathcal{J}$.

Two remarks are in order here.

1. According to the definition, when applying an operation, the scheme can never decrease. Indeed, in case of a deletion, we do not know in advance whether the operation will result in the deletion of *all* nodes or edges of a certain type.

2. In fact, as for the present section, the effect of an operation is simply a graph-transformation, i.e., a database-restructuring. However, in Section 4, we will see how the result of an operation can be interpreted in a variety of ways, e.g., as a query, an update, or a schema transformation.

We now launch the proposal that any graphical database user interface should support language constructs providing manipulation facilities along the lines of Definition 10. As the framework proposed here is very general, it may apply to most language paradigms, e.g.:

- applicative (algebraic), by extending an existing algebra with graph operations;

- rule-based (logic), since the pattern-action metaphor agrees well with the rule body-rule head metaphor;

- functional, by viewing a graph operation as an apply-to-all functional (*apply* action *to all* pattern-matchings).

Anyhow, a language supporting the concept of graph operation will provide a set of (graphical) syntactical formats that are special cases (i.e., *restrictions*) of Definition 10. In fact it will be really necessary to impose such restrictions, since Definition 10, in its full generality, may yield operations with ambiguous semantics. One way to go is to devise restricted operations in which either only additions or only deletions may occur [GPVG90b].

On the other hand, graph-oriented languages may well *extend* our framework on some other points. For one, it can be expected that programming constructs like sequencing or recursion are added in an orthogonal way. More interestingly, the pattern matching paradigm may be extended to allow the specification of matchings in a more expressive manner. Analogously, the action-part of an operation may be more than just addition or deletion, e.g., an arbitrary function may be called with parameters bound through the pattern matching. As the scope of the present paper is not on detailed language mechanisms but rather on some relevant concepts in the more general context of graph-oriented user interfaces, we will only briefly touch upon some possible extensions in the following. The discussion of these serves at the same time as illustration of the graph-oriented way of working we propose. See also [GPVdBVG91].

- One possible extension of pattern matching is to allow for *regular expressions* as edge labels [MW89], which provides a succinct representation of complicated matchings whose expression would otherwise require programming constructs. For example, the operation of Figure 8 adds a `related`-edge between the comment about 'Music History' and any other Info-node that is linked to it (directly or indirectly) and which is not a version of it.

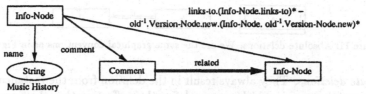

Figure 8: A graph operation using a regular expression as an edge label.

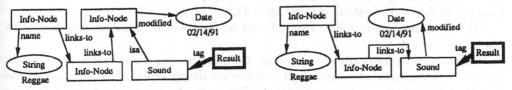

Figure 9: Using inheritance.

- Another useful extension is to support *inheritance* [ABD+89]. In the scheme of Figure 2, one could consider the isa-labeled edges as class-hierarchy links. For example, the operation shown in Figure 9, left, tags each Sound-node in the context of 'Reggae' which was last modified on 02/14/91 with a node labeled Result. This can then be abbreviated as in Figure 9, right, since properties of Info-nodes are inherited by Sound-nodes.

- A possible extension of the notion of action is to allow method calls. Typically, these methods are provided by the underlying object-oriented programming system. For example, the operation in Figure 10 compresses the bitmap of each Graphics-node of 64 by 64 pixels.

4   Interpreting graph-transformations as database tasks

In the previous section we saw how the user can express database-transformations in a graph oriented way. We will now see how these graph-transformations allow the user interface to offer a variety of database tasks in a uniform manner. Our key observation is that each such task can be characterized by its specific effect on scheme and instance of the actual database.

However, recall that in the current form of Definition 10, a graph operation can increase the scheme. A convenient adaptation[9] of the definition can be made to allow also *restrictions* of the scheme in two well defined cases of operations. These operations are

---

[9]For the sake of simplicity, we omitted this adaptation in Section 3.

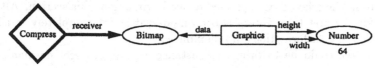

Figure 10: Calling the methods compress of Bitmap-objects

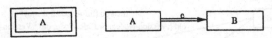

Figure 11: Absolute deletions. We use the same graphical conventions as in Figure 7

called *absolute deletions*. They always result in the deletion from the instance of *all* nodes or edges of a certain type, in which case we define their effect on the scheme as the removal of the corresponding object or edge label. It is readily seen that absolute deletions must have one of the two formats shown in Figure 11.

We are now ready to introduce four different *modes* in which a database transformation can be interpreted.

The most straightforward way to interpret a transformation is in *restructuring mode*. In this mode, the database scheme and instance are simply replaced by the result of the transformation. As its name suggests, this mode is particularly appropriate for performing global database restructurings.

In *query mode*, the result of a transformation is considered only as a query result. I.e., the user adds and deletes derived objects and properties, without affecting the actual database. This situation can be compared to the situation in deductive databases, where rules (in query mode) derive only intentional facts. Note also that, being able to express queries, we automatically obtain a graph-oriented *constraint specification* mechanism. Indeed, it is usual to express a constraint as a query that has some predetermined effect depending on whether or not the database satisfies the constraint [Ull88].

Next we consider *update mode*. Here, the resulting schema of the transformation is disregarded. Thus, the original database scheme remains unchanged. However, the actual contents of the database are updated: the database instance is replaced by the resulting instance of the transformation, except for nodes and edges with labels not present in the original scheme. In this way, it is possible to have "intermediate" derived information during the computation of the update, which is left out in the final result.

Finally, we show how a graph-transformation can be interpreted as a *schema manipulation*. In this mode, the focus is on the transformation of the schema. E.g., the database manager may want to add new classes and properties, or delete no longer needed parts of the scheme. So, the original database scheme is replaced by the resulting scheme of the transformation; the effect of the transformation on the instance is disregarded. The only thing that changes in the actual contents of the database is that objects or properties whose type was deleted from the scheme are removed.

Actually, although our framework allows for a uniform graph-oriented look on restructurings, queries and updates, the last interpretation mode, schema manipulation, may seem a little awkward as it stands now. In fact, the pattern-matching paradigm is not used at all in this case, as the effect of the transformation on the instance (in which patterns are to be matched) is disregarded. In particular, any addition will result in the addition of the corresponding types in the scheme, but only absolute deletions will result in removals from the scheme, as explained in the beginning of this section. Although this is sufficient for the first three interpretation modes, it is not completely satisfactory for expressing scheme transformations in a flexible way.

An alternative could be to bring the instance aspect into schema-manipulation by

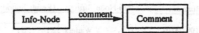

Figure 12: A deletion operation interpreted as a schema transformation

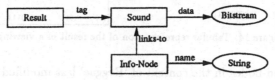

Figure 13: A viewing pattern

looking at the scheme as an instance over itself.[10] In this way, patterns can be matched in the schema, such that the addition or deletion depends on schema information. This is useful in advanced applications, where the schema is typically very large.

For example, consider the deletion operation of Figure 12. Interpreted as a schema-transformation in our new approach, the class Comment is deleted only if there is another class Info-node connected to it. Remark that in the first approach, the class is never deleted, since the operation is not an absolute deletion.

We point out that the interpretation modes presented here can also form the basis for security and authorization, where each user or user group is only authorized to run his programs in the mode he is allowed to.

5 Viewing and browsing

In this section we will propose and discuss techniques for inspecting an instance graph, most often the result of a graph-transformation such as an update or a query. First, we introduce *viewing* as a tool to examine a large instance in a feasible way. Then, we consider *browsing*. It turns out that browsing can be defined in a very elegant manner as a specialization of viewing. Once again, both viewing and browsing will be based on the concept of pattern matching.

In the former sections we defined the result of a database transformation applied to an instance to be another instance. Conceptually, instances are graphs. It is clear that the user will not see these instance graphs on his screen. In general, they will be too large and too complex. Thus, we need a technique to visualize *parts* of the instance. This technique will be called *viewing*.

Informally, viewing can be considered as a special form of querying. More formally, a viewing is specified by a pattern. Each matching of this pattern then defines a part of the instance we are interested in, namely, the image of this matching. For convenience, we will refer to such a matching as a view. Hence, each viewing of an instance results in a set of views, each of which defines a subgraph of the instance.

Example 11 To illustrate the notion of viewing, consider the pattern of Figure 13. This pattern defines a viewing for inspecting the result of the query of Figure 9 on page 12,

---

[10]Note that this is related to the well-known way of looking to the scheme as an instance over a *meta-schema*, as is done, e.g., in data dictionaries. Due to the close relationship between schema graphs and instance graphs in our model, we can actually use the schema itself as meta-scheme.

Info-Node	String	Result	Sound	Bitstream
I1	Wailers	R1	S1	010010010...
I2	UB40	R3	S3	100100111...
I2	UB40	R4	S4	100000111...

Info-Node	String	[Result Sound Bitstream]		
I1	Wailers	R1	S1	010010010...
I2	UB40	R3	S3	100100111...
		R4	S4	100000111...

String	[Bitstream]
Wailers	010010010...
UB40	100100111...
	100000111...

Figure 14: Tabular representation of the result of a viewing

determining all Sound-nodes in the context of 'Reggae' last modified on 02/14/91. Each view then corresponds to one particular Sound-node, with its bitstream data and the Info-node containing it. The reader is invited to verify on Figure 5 that there are three views in this example.

Although not the main focus of this paper, we will now digress on how in the user interface we can actually show the various views resulting from a viewing. What we need for this purpose is an ergonomic way to represent a set of graph matchings by so-called *representation items*, such as diagrams, tables and nested tables, possibly involving the creation of several windows.

Thereto, recall that in the relational model, a tuple is a mapping from a set of attributes to a set of values. On the other hand, a matching is a mapping from a set of pattern nodes to a set of instance nodes. Hence, a viewing can be represented in tabular form as a relation, the attributes of which are the nodes of its pattern, and the values are the nodes of the instance. In this relation, each tuple corresponds to one particular view.

For example, in the user interface, the viewing of Example 11 can be shown as the table of Figure 14, left. Note that we used object identifiers as surrogates for the actual nodes of the instance.[11] In addition, by taking into account the structure of the viewing-pattern as determined by its edges, one could consider representing a viewing as a *nested* rather than a flat relation. E.g., the table of Figure 14, left, could be restructed into the nested table of Figure 14, middle. It might be interesting to investigate ways in which this restructuring could be achieved automatically by the system. One possible direction to go is again to use graph transformations, by representing the set of matchings as one graph.

Often, we are only interested in a restriction of each of the views. For instance, in each of the views generated by the viewing of Example 11, it might be that only modification-dates and frequencies are relevant. For this case, we could easily devise a projection mechanism to filter out the other nodes. In our example, the table of Figure 14, middle would be transformed into the table of Figure 14, right. The projection mechanism could even be incorporated in the pattern specification of the viewing, e.g., by indicating the relevant nodes in another color.

We now turn to *browsing*. Browsing is a well-known technique in user interfaces that enables the user to run through a huge amount of information. Conceptually, browsing starts from one or more specific objects. Then, objects are searched that are related with the given objects in a specified way. Typically, the searched objects are properties of the given objects. In general, the browsing process is then iterated on some of the newly found objects.

---

[11] Alternatively, more visually appealing surrogates, e.g., icons, could be employed.

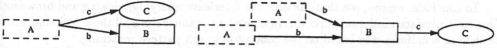

Figure 15: Left: a simple browsing pattern. Right: a more powerful way of browsing. In the former case, the A-node is the only coupled node. In the latter case, both A-nodes are assumed to be coupled.

Here, we consider browsing as an answer-driven query process. Each step in the browsing process is seen as a special case of viewing. Hence, a browsing process is a dynamical sequence of viewings, each of which depends on its predecessor and choices made by the user.

Definition 12 • A browsing step *is a triple* $(\mathcal{J}, N, c)$*, where* $\mathcal{J}$ *is a pattern over the database scheme under consideration,* N *is a set of nodes of the corresponding database instance , and* c *is a partial* coupling function *from the nodes of* $\mathcal{J}$ *to* N*. For each node* n *of* $\mathcal{J}$ *on which* c *is defined,* n *and* $c(n)$ *must have the same label.*

• *Consider the set of views resulting from the viewing specified by* $\mathcal{J}$ *on the instance under consideration. The* result of applying the browsing step $(\mathcal{J}, N, c)$ to that instance *is the set of those views the restrictions of which to the domain of* c *equal* c.

• *A* browsing process *is a sequence of browsing steps* $(\mathcal{J}_1, N_1, c_1), \ldots, (\mathcal{J}_r, N_r, c_r)$ *such that for each* $i = 1, \ldots, r - 1$*, each node in* N_{i+1} *occurs in a view resulting from the browsing step* $(\mathcal{J}_i, N_i, c_i)$.

• *Finally, the* result of a browsing sequence *is obtained by subsequent application of its steps.*

Observe that on the one hand, browsing can be seen as a specialization of viewing. On the other hand, however, a viewing can alternatively be seen as a browsing step whose coupling function is nowhere defined.

In the literature, browsing is usually defined in a much more restricted way [AGS90, Gol84, GGKZ85, Hal88, Mot84]. In a browsing step $(\mathcal{J}, N, c)$, the set N typically consists of a single object. Even more, the user can merely inspect the direct properties of this object. Thus, $\mathcal{J}$ has always the simple shape shown in Figure 15, left. In contrast, our formalism allows a parallel inspection of several objects, while examining much more complex properties, such as indirect properties, closure properties and object sharing. For example, Figure 15, right, shows a browsing step where for two specific A-objects, the c-property of a shared B-object is examined.

In the user interface, the coupling function of a browsing step can be specified in different ways. One could, e.g., think of "dragging" objects from the result of the previous step to the browsing pattern; we will not elaborate on this further. The objects in N_1 will typically arise from an initial viewing. While browsing, the user will build up the sequence of browsing steps dynamically. As such, a browsing process is a dynamical selection.

In general, it is to be expected that while browsing the user will want to backtrack if he comes to a "dead end". Although not developed here, this feature could easily be incorporated by extending the notion of a browsing sequence to that of a *browsing tree*.

To conclude, we propose that the user can interleave querying, viewing and browsing. Our user interface model supports this in an elegant manner since all three techniques are defined in a uniform way based on the concept of graph pattern matching.

6   Conclusion

We proposed some fundamental concepts for graph-oriented object manipulations in graphical database user interfaces, based on pattern matchings. We discussed decomposition and composition algorithms for schema graphs; graph transformations that expressed querying, constraint specification, updating, and schema manipulation; and viewing and browsing.

We feel that an interface design should make elegant and simple tools available to manage these concepts. Of course, on top of this interface design, much more colorful and ergonomic features have to be added to make the system tractable and pleasant to use. The latter topic, however, lies out of the scope of database research.

Let us conclude by comparing with some other, related work. As stressed from the outset, we propose the use of graphs as the basis of a uniform framework for database manipulations. In contrast, models for spatial databases [Güt88], offer graphs as a *separate* concept besides other facilities for data modeling. Hence, such approaches are only seemingly related to ours, as they are geared to another kind of results. Finally, we mention [Zic91], where the issue of consistency of schema transformations in object-oriented database systems is studied. This is done within a minimal framework of schema update primitives, expressed as additions/deletions of nodes/edges in the schema graph. We anticipate that these results also apply to the more expressive framework of graph operations of Section 3, in which we can also express schema transformations, as shown in Section 4.

Acknowledgement   Thanks go to Marc Gyssens for his most helpful comments on Section 5, which greatly improved the presentation. Some anonymous referees helped us in citing the work reported in [Güt88, PVdBVG+91, Zic91].

References

[ABD+89] M. Atkinson, F. Bancilhon, D. DeWitt, K. Dittrich, D. Maier, and S. Zdonik. The object-oriented database system manifesto. *Proc. 1st DOOD*, pp. 40–57.

[AGS90] R. Agrawal, N.H. Gehani, and J. Srinivasan. OdeView: The graphical interface to Ode. *Proc. 1990 SIGMOD*, pp. 34–43.

[AH87] S. Abiteboul and Richard Hull. IFO: A formal semantic database model. *TODS*, 12(4):525–565.

[AK89] S. Abiteboul and P. Kanellakis. Object identity as a query language primitive. *Proc. 1989 SIGMOD*, pp. 159–173.

[Bee90] C. Beeri. A formal approach to object-oriented databases. *DKE*, 5(4):353–382.

[BH86] D. Bryce and R. Hull. SNAP: A graphics-based schema manager. *Proc. Data Eng. Conf.*, pp. 151–164.

[BK90] F. Bancilhon and W. Kim. Object-oriented database systems: In transition. *SIGMOD Record*, 19(4):49–53.

[Con87] J. Conklin. Hypertext: An introduction and survey. *Computer*, 20(9):17–41.

[ENRR86] H. Ehrig, M. Nagl, G. Rozenberg, and A. Rosenfeld, editors. *Graph-Grammars and Their Application to Computer Science.* LNCS 291.

[Güt88] R.H. Gütting. Geo-relational algebra: A model and query language for geometric database systems. *Proc. EDBT'88*, pp. 506–527.

[GGKZ85] K.J. Goldman, S.A. Goldman, P.C. Kanellakis, and S.B. Zdonik. ISIS: Interface for a semantic information system. *Proc. 1985 SIGMOD*, pp. 328–342.

[Gol84] A. Goldberg. *Smalltalk-80—The Interactive Programming Environment.* Addison-Wesley.

[GPVdBVG91] M. Gyssens, J. Paredaens, Jan Van den Bussche, and Dirk Van Gucht. A graph-oriented object database model. Technical Report 91-27, University of Antwerp (UIA). Full, expanded version of [GPVG90a, GPVG90b].

[GPVG90a] M. Gyssens, J. Paredaens, and D. Van Gucht. A graph-oriented object database model. *Proc. 9th PODS*, pp. 417–424.

[GPVG90b] M. Gyssens, J. Paredaens, and D. Van Gucht. A graph-oriented object database model for database end-user interfaces. *Proc. 1990 SIGMOD*, pp. 24–33.

[GSL91] M. Guo, S. Su, and H. Lam. An association algebra for processing object-oriented databases. *Proc. Data Eng. Conf.*, pp. 23–32.

[Hal88] F. Halasz. Reflections on Notecards: Seven issues for the next generation of hypermedia systems. *CACM*, 31(7):836–852.

[KKS88] H.J. Kim, H.F. Korth, and A. Silberschatz. PICASSO: A graphical query language. *Softw. Pract. Exp.*, 18(3):169–203.

[LRV88] C. Lécluse, P. Richard, and F. Velez. O₂, an object-oriented data model. *Proc. 1988 SIGMOD*, pp. 424–433.

[Mai87] D. Maier. Why database languages are a bad idea. *Proc. Workshop on Database Programming Languages.*

[Mot84] A. Motro. Browsing in a loosely structured database. *Proc. 1984 SIGMOD*, pp. 197–207.

[MW89] A. Mendelzon and P. Wood. Finding regular simple paths in graph databases. *Proc. 15th VLDB*, pp. 185–193.

[MZO89] D. Maier, J. Zhu, and H. Ohkawa. Features of the TEDM object model. *Proc. 1st DOOD*, pp. 476–495.

[PVdBVG+91] J. Paredaens, J. Van den Bussche, D. Van Gucht, et al. An overview of GOOD. To appear in *IEEE Data Eng. Bull.*, December 1991.

[SIG90] SIGMOD. Session on user interfaces. *Proc. 1990 SIGMOD*

[Ull88] J. Ullman. *Principles of Database and Knowledge-Base Systems*, volume I. Computer Science Press.

[Zic91] R. Zicari. A framework for schema updates in an object-oriented database system. In *Proc. Data Eng. Conf.*, pp. 2–13.

[Zlo77] M. Zloof. Query-by-example: a data base language. *IBM Syst. J.*, 16(4):324–343.

[ZM89] J. Zhu and D. Maier. Computational objects in object-oriented data models. *Proc. 2nd DBPL*, pp. 139–160.

The Manchester Multimedia Information System

Carole Goble, Michael O'Docherty, Peter Crowther, Mark Ireton, John Oakley and Costas Xydeas

Multimedia Information Systems Laboratory, Department of Electrical Engineering and Department of Computer Science, Victoria University of Manchester, Oxford Road, Manchester, M13 9PL; email: mmis@ee.man.ac.uk

1 Introduction

A Multimedia Information System (MMIS) is a repository for all types of electronically representable data[4]. Conventional databases provide a large set of operations for retrieval of simple data types. The simplest way of extending this to multimedia objects is to store and retrieve on the basis of a few manually entered associated attributes or links.

We believe that the full potential of multimedia databases is realised by a rich set of operations to transparently manipulate data objects of all media, and this is best achieved through content retrieval based on the interpretation of medium objects. Ideally interpretation would be automatic, avoiding the problems of inconsistency, subjectivity and the labour-intensiveness of manual entry. MMISs with content retrieval will have wide application in industry, medicine, education and the military.

The Multimedia Group at Manchester University have experimented with a prototype MMIS for the content retrieval of images and have developed a prototype which is targeted to a in a specific application domain. The project has four goals:

1. to prototype a general MMIS architecture and to demonstrate its applicability to images;
2. to provide an object store for instances[1] to support the above prototype;
3. to develop a representation of instances to support content retrieval ;
4. to investigate the content retrieval of raster images.

Raster images are a rich source of content at levels other than the representation; higher-level constructs range from related groups of picture elements (pixels) to much more abstract concepts such as 'road'. The abstract information in a raster image is hard to extract, but even simple extraction gives enormous help to queries. This potential, coupled with the group's signal processing expertise, has led us to focus on 2-D still raster images.

Such work cannot be done in isolation from an application. An experimental prototype requires an application that has well defined images that are easy to obtain yet sufficiently

---

[1] Hereafter, the term *instance* is used to refer to medium objects that are intended for interpretation in our system.

complex and variable to pose an interesting problem. For demonstration purposes we have chosen as our application a database of images of deciduous tree leaves as this application satisfies the above criteria. Domain knowledge is essential to the tailoring of the system, in particular the image interpretation, and we have access to local expertise.

The paper is divided into five further sections. Section 2 outlines the requirements of the ideal MMIS and of the Manchester MMIS in particular. Section 3 describes the proposed data model and the facilities required to use that model. In Sect. 4 the architecture for the Manchester prototype is described. Finally in Sect. 5 we present our results and proposals for future work.

2 The Manchester MMIS

The Manchester MMIS prototypes an extensible architecture for the creation and storage of automatically derived information about instances. We have specifically addressed raster images and experimented with text and documents. We are particularly interested in composite media—a medium instance composed of a number of other medium instances. Documents are a class of composite media which have document specific information as well as a structure linking other media instances such as text and images.

Our requirements for MMIS-2 are that the user must be able to retrieve items[2] in (at least) three ways:-

by presentation Retrieval based on data type or data structure without sophisticated understanding. This is commonly applied to composite media. Examples of presentation queries[3] are "Retrieve all documents that have voice comments in them" or "Retrieve all images".

by content Retrieval of documents according to their semantic content[3]. The simplest form is based on user entered *labels* (straightforward to implement), the most sophisticated is automatic semantic analysis where descriptions are inferred by the system (difficult but beneficial to the user). Although automatic semantic analysis will never be better than human analysis, human analysis followed by manual labelling is time-consuming and too inflexible.

by association Retrieval of items by associated links to other items. This can be used as a browsing mechanism and subsumes hypermedia[5].

There are a number of mechanisms by which the above queries can be presented:-

data model The user is familiar with the data model and can formulate queries such as "What text attributes are stored?" or, when classification is provided, "What characterises this class?".

directly The user knows exactly what the system stores in relation to each item, e.g. the labels it uses, the primitives it extracts during semantic analysis, or the way it structures composite media. Direct queries are then expressed as logical expressions or set operators, as in conventional databases[6].

---

[2] the term 'item' denotes an object that can be stored in and retrieved from the MMIS

[3] For convenience, the term 'query' in this article refers to anything that specifies a subset of the items stored in the MMIS. Examples are natural language commands, relational algebra/calculus and first order logic.

similarity Queries take the form of a prototype presented to the database, where the prototype may be either of the following:-

- A 'shorthand' version of an item is given on-line by the user and the system must try to match this *sketch* to stored items. The form that a sketch takes varies from one medium to another, and may be meaningless in some. An image sketch might comprise a rough outline of a particular style of house with salient features included such as rectangular Georgian windows with multiple panes[1, 2].
- The user presents an item as prototype. The system interprets the prototype to produce its semantic representation. The semantic representation is then matched against items in the database to retrieve those that are similar[3].

For a realistically substantial system it is undesirable to present users with a large set of items as the result of a query. A measure of the degree to which each item satisfies the query is required so that the candidate instances can be ranked and the best matches examined first. For prototype retrieval, a ranking score can be obtained by measuring the distance of the retrieved item from the prototype. A further source of scores is to assign an importance to each clause of the query; items that satisfy the most important clauses receive the highest score and so on. Scores can be discrete (very good, good, reasonable) or continuous (normalised to the range [0, 1] for item).

A further essential retrieval technique is *browsing*. The user has a set of items (the entire contents of the system or a subset obtained by query) and is allowed to roam over them [9, 10]. The user may wish to generate commented connections between items in a hypermedia fashion. The system should manage the connections for him as sets of 'webs'. Queries can then take the form "Retrieve web X".

3 Semantic Data and its Representation

This section describes briefly the semantic data extracted from instances during interpretation as attributes and structural relationships and how that data is represented. The representation formalism used should ideally be application and medium independent and storage and access efficient; it should be possible to express any information about an instance (*expressive adequacy*); it should be possible to deduce anything from the representation that could have been deduced from the original data (*logical adequacy*); finally, such formalisms should be easy to generate. No formalism will satisfy all these ideals. In particular, complete logical adequacy is infeasible for complex instances such as images—consider the task of asking a person to describe a picture of a room exhaustively, concisely and without repetition. Our model is based on the semantic nets[11] formalism.

Our general aim is to progressively refine low-level data to provide data that is more helpful to users. Low-level data should never be discarded because it is impossible to predict at which levels users will wish to query and because low-level data may be used to infer other data in the light of future knowledge. There is a trade off between the time taken to interpret instances in response to queries and the space required to store representations of the results of interpretation. Our system caters for both approaches—currently, most interpretation is performed pre-query (for better performance) and the results held in an appropriate formalism, but further processing can be performed post-query or by the use of lazy evaluation.

3.1 The Data

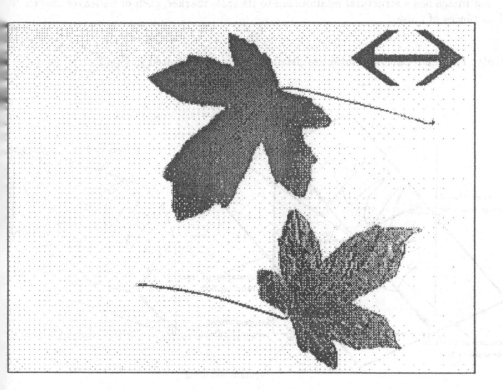

Fig. 1. A typical leaf image with scale marker

Images The basis of interpretation is that images such as the one illustrated in Fig. 1 contain distinct regions of interest that in their processed form are referred to as **Basic Logical ObjecTS** or *blots*.[4] Blots are distinguished from scale markers and noise. Scale markers (designed to be easily distinguishable from other blots of interest) are used to standardise scalar measurements within the image, which are otherwise sensitive to camera sizing.

Image attributes include width, height, time of interpretation, number of leaves contained, number of pieces of noise contained and class. An image's class records whether it is binary, monochrome or colour; the class also indicates the number of bits per pixel for monochrome and colour images and thus indicates what sort of interpretation is required, whether it can be displayed on a particular workstation and so on. Finally, if

---

[4] This term was chosen to avoid confusion between the term 'blob' meaning an 8-connected set of pixels in image analysis terminology, and BLOB meaning a Binary Large OBject in database terminology. Two pixels are 8-connected if they are horizontally, vertically or diagonally adjacent.

a scale marker is identified, then images have a length_scale attribute for converting from pixels to metres.

An image has a structural relationship to its scale marker, each of its leaves and each of its pieces of noise.

Blots The main blot attributes are listed below and illustrated in Fig. 2.

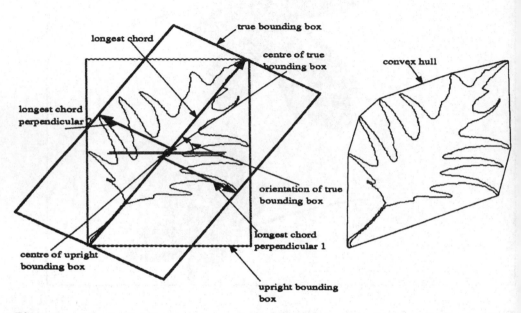

Fig. 2. Aspects of a blot that are expressed as attributes

Area & Perimeter length

Circularity Circularity is the ratio $\frac{Area}{Perimeter^2}$ and is maximum for a circle ($\frac{1}{4\pi}$) and minimum for a line (0). Here it is normalised to give a value in the range 0% (line) to 100% (circle).

Upright bounding box The upright rectangle that exactly fits the outside of the blot.

Longest chord The longest line that can be drawn between any two points on the blot's perimeter.

True bounding box The rectangle that exactly fits the extremities of the longest chord and its two longest perpendiculars.

Length The length of the true bounding box.

Width The width of the true bounding box.

Aspect ratio The ratio $\frac{Length}{Width}$.

Convex hull & Hull area A blot's convex hull is analogous to the shape of an elastic band stretched around its perimeter. Hull area is the area of the convex hull.

Transparency Transparency is the ratio $\frac{\text{Hull area} - \text{Area}}{\text{Hull area}}$. It is low for convex blots and high for incised blots. Here, it is normalised to give a value in the range 0% (completely convex) to 100% (completely transparent).

Irregularity Irregularity is a measure of the unevenness of a blot's perimeter.

Shape class Each blot is given a classification (Sect. 4.1) based on the attributes that are considered to be good shape descriptors—in this case transparency, aspect ratio, irregularity, circularity and numbers of maxima and minima.

If a scale marker is identified, then all attributes that have a length component are expressed using metres as well as pixels.

Blots have structural relationships to other blots in the image to describe relative positions in terms of bearing and bounding box overlap. The bearing of one blot from another is described by one of eight compass directions, (north, north east, east, etc), between the centres of their true bounding boxes; this is augmented by a test of whether or not their true bounding boxes overlap.

Text and documents Text instances within our prototype are simple ASCII data with some structural for each word, number, code and punctuation component. Documents are composite media, represented as components grouped hierarchically in a style similar to ODA[12, 13].

3.2 The Representation

Each instance has an associated semantic description referred to as its *semantic representation*. The semantic representation is a set of facts about the attributes of instances and their structural relationships to other instances. An instance can have structural relationships to its own parts and the parts themselves can also refer to other instances to form hierarchical or graphical structures (useful for representing documents).

The chosen representation is the semantic net. In its simplest form, a semantic net is a graph of unidirectional labelled arcs that can be used to describe structure and attributes. Each arc is a statement of fact; in the case of a structural relationship, both the source and destination of the arc are entities being described with the source having the stated relationship *to* the destination; for an attribute, the source is an entity and the destination is the value of the attribute, with the arc label being the name of the attribute. In practice, the user formulating queries is unaware of the fine distinction between attributes and structural relationships, especially if arc names are meaningful.

Semantic nets are generated by medium interpreters that know what attributes and structural relationships to expect and how to deduce them. Part of the semantic net generated for Fig. 1 is shown in Fig. 3. All node and arc labels take the form *<type>* / *<value>* as explained in Table 1.

For clarity, the type *atom* has been omitted from all arcs in the figures. In the case of images, text, documents and blots, the value is a unique identifier referencing the actual instance in a separate repository (see Sect. 4). Units for floating point values that have dimension are the standard SI units with the addition of the sub-unit radian, a special unit for camera lengths called *pixel*. The pixel unit is abbreviated to p. The enumeration type is analogous to that used in C and is allocated by individual applications. Abstract

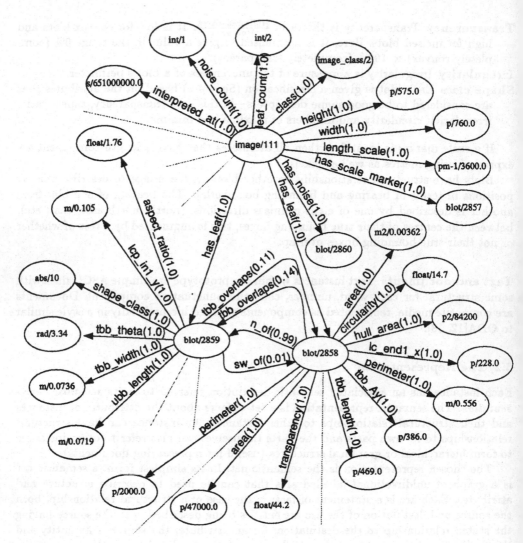

Fig. 3. Part of Fig. 1's semantic net

nodes are used to denote concepts that need more description than a single node allows, as in Fig. 3, where the abstract node *abs/10* represents the concept of a blot's membership of shape class.

All arcs have an extra floating point value called a *score*, used in the ranking of query results (see Sect. 4.3). In the examples in this section, all arcs have been given a score between 0 (false) and 1 (true). Such values can be calculated in any way that is meaningful to the application.

We represent the semantic nets as a set of triples as illustrated in Fig. 4. Each triple represents a fact (arc) as *<source><relationship/score><destination>*.

Table 1. The type and value of node and arc labels

Type	Value
int	integer
float	float
image	instance identifier
text	instance identifier
document	instance identifier
blot	instance identifier
dimension (SI units)	float
enumeration identifier	integer
atom	atom identifier
abstract node	abstract node identifier

```
        :
        :
image/111    class(1.0)              image_class/2
image/111    width(1.0)              p/760.0
image/111    interpreted_at(1.0)     s/651000000.0
image/111    has_leaf(1.0)           blot/2859
image/111    has_scale_marker(1.0)   blot/2857
image/111    leaf_count(1.0)         int/2
blot/2858    tbb_overlaps(0.14)      blot/2859
blot/2858    n_of(0.99)              blot/2859
blot/2858    area(1.0)               m2/0.00362
        :
        :
```

Fig. 4. Part of the triple representation of Fig. 3

This approach leads to simple storage and optimised access. Henceforth, the terms fact, triple, attribute and structural relationship will be used as appropriate—facts are equivalent to triples; attributes and structural relationships are specific uses of triples; triples are expressed as ternary predicates in the query language.

4 Architecture and Capabilities of the Prototype MMIS-2

The general architecture for our (second) prototype, MMIS-2, is shown in Fig. 5. The user interacts with a user interface that gives access to an input part for entering instances, a query part for formulating queries and an output part for presentation of query results and production of hard copy output. Medium instances are stored in the database for access by the interpreters and retrieval by the user interface's output part. An interpreter is provided for each medium and interpretation results are stored in the database. The query engine resolves users' queries according to the interpretation results. The query may be translated into a form more suitable for optimal resolution.

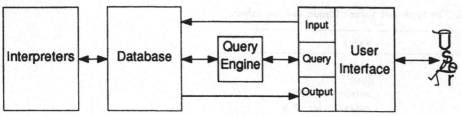

Fig. 5. General architecture for the MMIS prototype

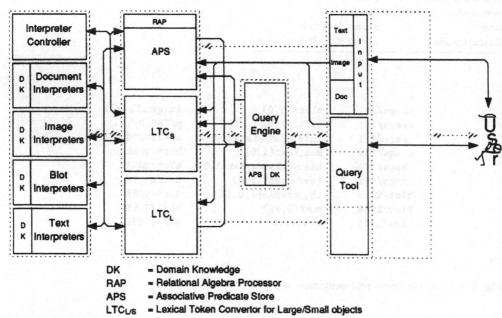

DK = Domain Knowledge
RAP = Relational Algebra Processor
APS = Associative Predicate Store
LTC$_{L/S}$ = Lexical Token Convertor for Large/Small objects

Fig. 6. The architecture of MMIS-2

The specific architecture is shown in Fig. 6. The shaded boxes in the figure correspond to those of the generic architecture. MMIS-2 has a client-server architecture that runs on a network of SUN workstations and includes sharing, multiprocessor implementation and multiuser access (without protection). It has been implemented in C^{++} and Prolog.

4.1 Interpretation

MMIS-2 stores text, documents and 8-bit grey-level images. Interpretation tasks are allocated to individual interpreter processes by the *Interpreter Controller*. The interpretation is hierarchical: document interpreters cause image and text interpreters to be spawned, image interpreters cause blot interpreters to be spawned. Currently only the image and blot interpreters have been implemented. Image interpretation has two levels:-

low-level blots are segmented from the image and their base attributes extracted using hard-coded but modular image analysis algorithms written in C++;

high-level a declarative style of program, written in Prolog, is used to derive more abstract attributes and structural relationships.

Each blot is given a shape classification based on clustering in a multi-dimensional attribute space[14][15]. When a blot is presented to the system it is assigned to the class whose centroid is 'nearest' according to some distance criterion. Class membership is used as a key for prototype retrieval (see Sect. 4.3).

MMIS-2's interpretation is applicable to all images of 2D, non-overlapping objects. Within this application domain any blot that has an area of less than 500 pixels is regarded as noise. Transparency and irregularity are relevant to applications where blots are often incised or where the micro-irregularity of edges is important, respectively.

The database has three components: the *Associative Predicate Store* (APS), the *Lexical Token Converter for Small objects* (LTC$_S$) and the *Lexical Token Converter for Large objects* (LTC$_L$). Interpretation results are stored in the APS as a set of triples where each third of a triple is a token. LTC$_S$ and LTC$_L$ translate tokens to and from small and large objects respectively. Examples of small objects are numbers and atoms; large objects are images and text. The blot's chain code is stored for display. Documents are unusual in that they have a hierarchical semantic net referencing other instances as their raw data representation, as well as a semantic net to represent the results of their interpretation. The system maintains a one-to-one mapping between instances and their identifiers to enable identifier comparison to represent object comparison. In the current prototype the database is a simulation of a hardware tuple store developed at the University of Essex[16], capable of storing and accessing several million tuples and written in C.

4.2 Querying

The query engine is Prolog coupled to a special translator based on Draxler's work[17]. The translator converts Prolog queries to triple store searches and relational operations. The relational operations are provided by the *Relational Algebra Processor* (RAP).

Approximately 10% of each semantic net is derived on demand by the query engine rather than being permanently stored in the semantic representation base. This is done where the cost of storing a particular arc is greater than the cost of slowing the query engine slightly.

The Manchester prototype addresses querying directly and by data model, and partially addresses querying by similiarity (see Sect. 2). Our Query Tool, implemented in Sunview, is purely a development environment for querying. We did not concern ourselves with a user-friendly query language. A typical query session is shown in Fig. 7. Queries return hierarchical sets of instance identifiers called *instance sets*. Instance sets are stored in the the raw database for progressive retrieval by the query tool. For example, the query in Fig. 7 approximates to

> "Retrieve a set where each member contains an image followed by the set of blots within that image that are more than 50% transparent"

This query illustrates the use of direct data known to be held about instances, as previously discussed in Sect. 2. The structure of the returned instance set is shown in Fig. 8.

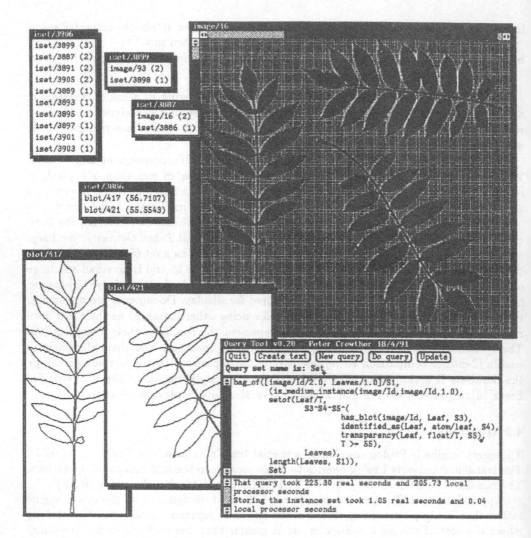

Fig. 7. The query interface of MMIS-2 showing the results of a hierarchical query

The user can navigate through this hierarchy by clicking on the iconic versions of the set members. In Fig. 7, the user has followed the hierarchy down to the level of image 7 and its two highly transparent blots. Hierarchical instance sets are a powerful conceptual grouping mechanism and can be used to retrieve hierarchical instances such as documents. Instance sets contain any type included in the data model, from integers to documents. This gives the user the freedom to formulate queries such as "How many images are in the database?".

There are two ways of refining queries: the first is for the user to modify the initial query according to the system's answer; the second is to restrict the set of items that can

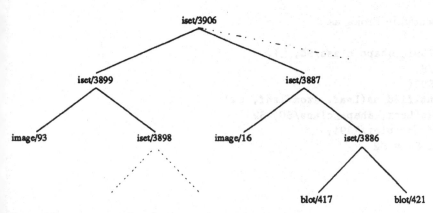

Fig. 8. The structure of an instance set

be in the next query's answer to a proper subset of those that were in the initial query's answer and thus reduce the proportion of the query that is re-evaluated or to reduce the number of objects over which the new query is evaluated.

4.3 Similarity retrieval

Queries of the form "Retrieve images that are similar to image X" are desirable, but too vague. If a user wishes to retrieve an image that is 'similar to' a prototyped image the similarity measures that are most effective are the classification of the item or its sub-objects and the structural relationships of the item's sub-objects. Ie. the objects in the image have a similar shape and/or are positioned with similar spatial relationships.

Instances in a returned instance set are ranked so that the user can first examine those that best match the query—this is especially relevant as interpretation is never exact so query results are always uncertain. MMIS-2 provides scores for arcs so that uncertain statements can be represented. Each arc can be assigned a score from 0 (false) to 1 (true). By using these scores we can go some way to retrieval based on 'similarity' for structural relationships and shape classifications of blots.

We have rejected the use of mathematical probabilities to produce scores because it is difficult to generate a distribution in order to give the probability any theoretical foundation. It is also unclear how to combine probabilities in complex queries when such probabilities may or may not be independent. There are situations, however, when a meaningful score can be generated.

Classification scores The assignment of a score to a blot's classification according to its distance from the centre of the class gives a similarity measure. This distance measure need not be Euclidean[18]. A typical query such as

> "Find all the other leaves that are in the same shape class as the leaf with identifier 7391. Assign each retrieved leaf a score that is its degree of identification multiplied by its distance from the class centroid."

would be presented in Prolog as:

```
class(blot/7391, shape_class/SC, _),
bag_of(Leaf/S,
       S1^S2^(
       identified_as(Leaf, atom/leaf, S1),
       class(Leaf, shape_class/SC, S2),
       Leaf \== blot/7391,
       S is S1 * S2
       ),
       Set
)
```

Classes can be given non-sharp boundaries so that each blot has a degree of membership of several classes, so that queries such as

"Retrieve the blots that fall in class X with a score $\geq$ 0.25 and class Y with a score $\geq$ 0.75."

are possible. This is equated with the general query of

"Retrieve the blots that are somewhat similar to X and very similar to class Y."

Structural relationship scores Compass sectors can be used to describe positional relationships for example on the basis of hard boundaries between compass sectors. Such a scheme means that if the bearing (b) between two blots (S and D) = 22.5° then S is considered to be south west of D, but if b = 22.499999° then S is south of D when there is clearly little difference. A better approach is to use inexact relationships similar to *fuzzy sets*[13]. An alternative way of gaining positional relationships is the degree of overlap of true bounding boxes, so that:-

```
tbb_overlaps(blot/2859, blot/2858, 0.11).
```

means

"Blot 2859's true bounding box overlaps 11% of the true bounding box of blot 2858."

4.4 Browsing

Users may create and destroy arbitrary hypermedia links between image, text and blot instances. The resulting 'web' can be browsed using the keyboard and mouse. Figure 9 shows some browsing in progress. Images are automatically connected to each of their good and bad blots. All links may be navigated in either direction. A link from image 85 to its text description (3875) has been entered manually. Links are stored as triples in the APS, but are kept separate from automatically derived arcs.

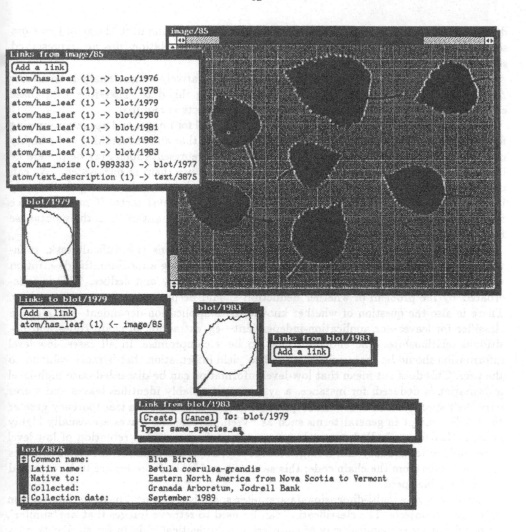

Fig. 9. MMIS-2's hypermedia facility

5 Conclusions

5.1 Results

Although the notion of a MMIS with automatic content retrieval is desirable, it is infeasible unless each MMIS is tailored to the domain of a single application. This implies that the architecture of an MMIS should be easily configurable to new applications.

A database for heterogeneous objects has be implemented by separating storage structures from content querying structures. This database is object-oriented in that host language objects are stored in the large object store (Raw Database/LTC_L). However, a deliberate decision was taken to avoid storing any object schema in the large object store so we do not claim to have built an OODB. Object inter-relationships are represented separately in semantic nets in the APS.

Large amounts of data can be extracted using relatively simple analysis methods. Any system must be capable of storing and processing this data. Therefore a database capable of fast searching of many fixed-size, small objects is required.

Semantic nets have proved to be an expressive model for images and appear promising for other media. They can be stored in a simple fashion that allows searching to be highly optimised and even implemented in hardware. Other representations may be preferable in certain applications, but we have not attempted to use them in our system. We can conclude, however, that knowledge representation formalisms can be managed efficiently in a database if the emphasis is on a small set of high-level facts. If much reliance is made on the topological structure of nets to convey semantics then their database representation is far more difficult to achieve.

Deciding what facts to store in knowledge representations is a difficult task. It involves knowledge of the minimum requirements for describing a medium, the description that is meaningful to users and what it is reasonable to try and deduce. This is exacerbated by the problem of whether deduction should be pre-query, post-query or lazy. There is also the question of whether knowledge is application-dependent—eg. a shape classifier for leaves—or application-independent—eg. extraction of chain codes and positional relationships. The end result has to be a compromise. In all cases, low-level information should be progressively refined to yield information that is more valuable to the user. This does not mean that low-level information can be discarded once high-level information is deduced; for instance, a system that reliably identifies leaves and stores only their species cannot answer the question "Which leaves have a transparency greater than 50%" except in general terms such as "Well, mature oak leaves are usually highly incised, therefore...". Unfortunately, progressive refinement plus retention of low-level data leads to redundancy and a large storage overhead. For example, all blot attributes can be derived from the chain code; this seems unavoidable if queries are to be executed at a reasonable speed.

Clustering in a multi-dimensional parameter space is a powerful basis for comparison of image sub-objects. The classification can be used to retrieve images that are 'similar', by providing an economical way of comparing non-identical objects for similarity on a number of criteria. Similarity retrieval is only feasible if a constrained view of waht is meant by 'similar' is taken. We have found shape classification and structural relationships coupled with certainty scores useful.

5.2 Future Work

We have not researched the types of query asked of a multimedia database. This makes it difficult to demonstrate that the majority of queries can be answered. Future work should include the development of query languages that are safer than Prolog, that are more straightforward for novice users and that use graphical facilities.

One powerful consequence of using Prolog as query language and query engine is that rules can be added easily to perform post-query analysis or to implement user views of the data—eg. the renaming of attributes or the assignment of labels to ranges of values.

Verbalisation, or the mapping of a continuous value to one of a set of perceptual labels is an interesting area of research. For instance, an object's colour could be mapped to [very red, red, not red] to allow users to ask "What red objects are there in the system?". Another example would be the description of a shape class by the verbalisation of the attributes of its blots: "Shape class three is characterised by blots of very high circularity, low transparency, normal irregularity and very high aspect ratio".

The process of ranking query results needs further investigation; this involves the combination of arc scores and the weighting of scores assigned to query sub-clauses. Hypermedia has proved straightforward to implement as a semantic net, but tools that allow browsing of the resultant webs as well as issuing queries have yet to be provided. It may be possible in some circumstances for users to tell the system whether returned items match their query; positive and negative feedback could then be incorporated into the system to improve future analysis.

A simple meta-data description has been used to indicate what attributes and structural relationships each instance should have and whether these were single or multiple, compulsory or optional. Meta-data languages could be developed for use with any application that can be described in terms of base and derived attributes and structural relationships; a description in this new language would then be used to generate an interpreter automatically—only the code to deliver base attributes would have to be written. The meta-data would be employed during interpretation to check that sensible data was being generated and during querying so that queries such as

"Get the images with shape class 2 and score $\geq$ 0.5"

instead of producing no solutions would produce the system message "Instances of type image have no shape class".

6 Acknowledgements

The work of The Multimedia Group is funded by the Systems Integration Division of ICL and the Science and Engineering Research Council.

References

1. Chang S.K. and Kunii T.L: Query-by-pictorial example. IEEE computer **14(11)** (1981) 13–21.
2. Constantopoulos P., Drakopoulos Y. et al: Multimedia document retrieval by pictorial content Multimedia Office filing: The MULTOS approach, North-Holland (1990) 331–349.
3. Conti P., Rabitti F: Image retrieval by semantic content Multimedia Office filing: The MULTOS approach, North-Holland (1990) 299–329.
4. O'Docherty, M.O., Crowther, P.J., Daskalakis C.N., Goble C.A., Ireton M.A., Kay S., and Xydeas C.S.: Advances in the processing and management of multimedia information. ICL Technical Journal, **vol 7 issue 2** (1990) 271–287.
5. Meyrowitz N.: Intermedia: The architecture and construction of an object-oriented hypermedia system and applications framework. OOPSLA '86: Conference on Object-Oriented Programming Systems, Languages and Applications, ACM (1986) 186–201.

6. Date C.J.: An Introduction to Database Systems vol 1. ed. 5th edition, Addison-Wesley, (1986).
7. Gonzalez R.C. et al: A measure of scene content. IEEE CH1318-5/78/0000-0385500.75 (1978) 385–389.
8. Toriwaki J., Hasegawa J., Fukumura T., and Tagaki Y.: Pictorial information retrieval of chest X-ray image database using pattern recognition techniques. Proceedings of MEDINFO '80, (1980) 1154–1158.
9. Christodoulakis S. and Graham S.: Browsing within time-driven multimedia documents. ACM SIGOIS Bulletin 9 (1988) 219–227.
10. Irven JH, Nilson ME, Judd TH, Patterson JF, and Shibata Y.: Multi-media information services: A laboratory study. IEEE Communications Magazine, (1988) 26(6): 27–44.
11. Ringland G.A. and Duce D.A., editors: Approaches to Knowledge Representation—An Introduction. Research Studies Press (1988).
12. ISO. IS 8613: Text and office system—office document architecture (ODA) and interchange formats (1988).
13. Goble C.A., O'Docherty M.H., Crowther P.J., Ireton M.A., Daskalakis C.N., Oakley J.,Kay S., and Xydeas C.S.: The manchester multimedia information system. Proc. of Eurographics Workshop on Multimedia, Stockholm, Spinger-Verlag (1991) (in press).
14. Ireton M.A. and Xydeas C.S.: Classification of shape for content retrieval of images in a multimedia information system. Proc. of 6th IEE International Conference on Digital Processing of Speech in Communications, Loughborough (1991) (to appear).
15. Ireton M.A.: Representing shape data for content retrieval of images in a multimedia database. Internal document (1990).
16. Lavington S.H and Wang J: A formalism for the IFS/2 firmware—part 1. Technical Report CSM-159, University of Essex, Department of Computer Science (1990).
17. Draxler C.: Logic programming and databases. Technical Report 90.09, Institut fur Informatik der Universitat Zurich (1990).
18. Mahalanobis P.C.: On the generalised distance in statistics. Proceedings of the Indian National Institute of Science 2 (1936) 49–55.

This article was processed using the LaTeX macro package with LMAMULT style

Query by Visual Example
— Content based Image Retrieval —

Kyoji HIRATA
NEC Corporation
Kawasaki, Japan

Toshikazu KATO
Electrotechnical Laboratory
Tsukuba Science City, Japan

1. Introduction

"A picture is worth a thousand words." Visual information is a good man-machine communication medium. Users expect a multimedia database system to manage visual data as well as alphanumeric data. Users also expect it to provide a visual interface to accomplish flexible man-machine communication in a user-friendly manner.

In this paper, we will present the idea and the general framework for visual interaction with multimedia database systems. The paper will focus on the visual interface for content based image retrieval.

How can such intelligent retrieval be accomplished? Our basic idea is QVE (query by visual example). A user has only to draw a rough sketch to retrieve the original image and the similar images. The system evaluates the similarity between the rough sketch, i.e. visual example, and each part of the image data in the database automatically. This paper will also give the fundamental algorithms for QVE.

We have been developing an experimental database system, called ART MUSEUM,[1] as an electronic art gallery [1, 2, 3, 4]. The ART MUSEUM database is a collection of artistic full color paintings. The algorithms for QVE are implemented and examined on this system. This paper also includes some experimental results and our current evaluation. The algorithms are quite effective for content based image retrieval.

Section 2 gives a brief survey on visual interfaces and summarizes the idea and the general framework for visual interaction. Section 3 describes the primitive algorithms for QVE. These algorithm enable the system to build a pictorial index, based on the composition of paintings, and to find the original image and similar images automatically. Section 4 shows some experimental results obtained on QVE and our current evaluation.

2. Visual Interface for Content Retrieval

Several experimental image database systems have been proposed to provide visual interfaces. Old style image database systems only accept a combination of key words and

---

[1] ART MUSEUM: multimedia database with sense of color and composition upon the matter of art

index terms in a user's query. Such key words and index terms were prepared by the database manager. Of course, it is quite difficult to describe the image content with such key words. The personnel expense of assigning key words is also an important factor. The QPE system provides a schema of pictorial data in a graphic form as well as in a tabular form [5]. While this system shows the data in a graphic form, its query style is only a substitute for the query languages on alphanumeric data. In the icon-based system, icons and their two dimensional strings are referred to as pictorial keys to image data [6]. A user can specify the target images by placing icons on the graphic display as a visual query. The system evaluates only two dimensional strings of icons in its retrieval process. Therefore, it is difficult to accomplish similarity retrieval, according to the subjective measure presented by the user. The hypermedia system provides an indexing mechanism for multimedia data in a uniformed style [7, 8]. Although this system enables a kind of subjective indexing, its process owes much to the user's effort on defining many links.

We originally want to process visual data and their contents in visual interaction. On this point, although the above systems use graphic devices to show schema, icons and guidelines, their facilities are not sufficient to allow accomplishing such interaction in a user-friendly manner.

Then, what factors are needed in visual interaction? Essential needs are visual queries for content based retrieval of visual data. The requirements for visual interaction can be summarized as follows.

(a)   It is necessary to show visual data to the database in a user-friendly manner. For instance, a user would like to retrieve image data based on database content. Users may provide image data themselves, such as hand-written, rough and partial sketches, as pictorial keys to retrieve some image data.

(b)   Of course, it is necessary to view visual data from the database in a simple manner. For instance, a user would like to browse the database guided by some intelligent navigation facility.

(c)   Users also expect the system to automatically build the pictorial index for content retrieval. Image analysis facilities map individual parts of image data into their abstracted representations, e.g., abstract images on general composition, according to a user's visual perception process.

These needs can be answered by a visual interface, called QVE (query by visual example). The QVE interface proposed in this paper has the following characteristics;

(i)   Simply showing a rough sketch is sufficient to enable retrieving some image data from the system. The powerful pattern recognition algorithms search for the best match candidates on the pictorial index. Currently, the system can accept a hand-drawn rough sketch, a monochrome photo, or a xerographic copy, as well as a full color fair copy as a visual example.

(ii)   A user can also browse through the database, navigated by the similarity measure on the general composition.

(iii) The pictorial index is automatically created by applying on adaptive differential filter, which simulates human's visual perception process. The pictorial index represents the general composition of (full color) images. Thus, users and the database manager don't have to assign any key words or index terms for content retrieval.

The rest of this paper shows the fundamental algorithms and some experimental results of QVE developed for the electronic art gallery ART MUSEUM.

3. Query by Visual Example

3.1 Overview

The general composition of a painting is one of the major parts in a viewer's visual impression. It is assumed that a person may remember an outline of a painting and can draw it as a rough sketch. Our goal is as follows. It would only be necessary for a user to draw an outline sketch of a painting to retrieve the original one. The system automatically evaluates similarity between the sketch and the paintings in the database.

How can a visual interface be organized for content based image retrieval? We have developed an adaptive image abstraction facility and a flexible pattern matching facility. The former is used to describe the outline composition for individual paintings and to refer to it as a pictorial index. The latter is to evaluate any similarity between the sketch and the paintings on the pictorial index. This section describes our approach to QVE (query by visual example).

The QVE in the ART MUSEUM system is composed of the following two stages (see also Fig. 1).

(a)   Adaptive image abstraction: A contour image roughly approximates the composition of the original painting. Therefore, a contour image can be referred to as a pictorial index. We have developed an adaptive differential filter on RGB space to obtain a kind of contour image. The proposed differential filter is based on the Weber-Fechner law [9] of human vision mechanism. The candidates for edge points are adaptively examined in local scope as well as global scope. A map of effective edge points will be called an abstract image. An abstract image has been adopted as a pictorial index for QVE.

(b)   Flexible image matching: A user is liable to draw a sketch uncertainly. Such a sketch may be rough, partial, shifted and sometimes deformed. We have developed a flexible image matching method to evaluate the similarity between the sketch composition and that for individual paintings. Our image matching method calculates the local correlation with shifting them in 2D directions. The matching score is referred to as their similarity value.

In the ART MUSEUM system, the database manager has only to input image data via an image scanner. The system automatically derives their abstract images and appends them to the pictorial index for QVE. A user has only to draw a rough sketch and input it to the system. The system also analyzes the composition of the sketch and evaluates the similarity with the composition of individual paintings on the pictorial index.

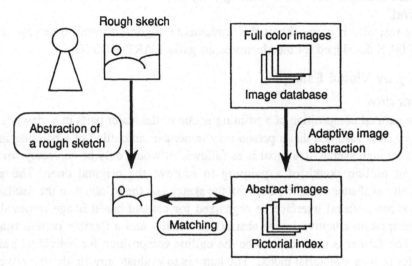

Fig. 1 Overview of QVE (query by visual example)
in the ART MUSEUM system

3.2 Pictorial Index

Abstract images have been adopted for a pictorial index. Based on this concept, what kind of features do they have to have? While the input images are in various sizes, their abstract images should be the same size to make the pattern matching mechanism easier. The abstract images must be small to reduce the memory space cost and the computation cost for pattern matching, while they must be large enough to distinguish one painting from the others. In our current implementation, their size is 64×64 pixels.

Let us introduce the algorithm for deriving abstract images from full color paintings. Its outline is also shown in Fig. 2 and an experimental result is shown in Fig. 3.

[Algorithm 1] A full color image abstraction
(i)   (Input:) Input a full color painting as an RGB intensity value matrix (Fig. 3(a)).
(ii) (Normalization:) Apply the affine transformation and the median filter to the matrix to obtain its regular-sized image (Fig. 3(b)). Here, the regular-sized image is also an RGB intensity value matrix. Its size is currently $M \times N = 64 \times 64$ pixels.

Full color image
↓ Reduction
Regular-sized image
↓ Edge detection in global range
Edge image
↓ Edge detection in local range
Refined edge image
↓ Thinning and shrinking
Abstract image

Fig.2 A Full color image abstraction

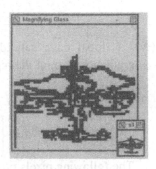

(a) Original full color painting   (b) Regular-sized image   (c) Edge image of global edge candidates

(d) Refined edge image of (local) edge candidates

(e) Abstract image for the pictorial index

Fig. 3 Image abstraction result

(iii) (Gradient in RGB space:) Calculate the gradients for RGB intensity values in four directions, $^1\partial_{ij}, \cdots, {^4}\partial_{ij}$, and the magnitude of the gradient $|\partial_{ij}|$ with each pixel p_{ij} on the regular-sized image.

$$^1\partial_{ij} = \frac{1}{|I_{ij}|}\frac{1}{3}\left\{ (p_{i-1j-1}+p_{ij-1}+p_{i+1j-1}) - (p_{i-1j+1}+p_{ij+1}+p_{i+1j+1}) \right\},$$

$$^2\partial_{ij} = \frac{1}{|I_{ij}|}\frac{1}{3}\left\{ (p_{i-1j-1}+p_{i-1j}+p_{i-1j+1}) - (p_{i+1j-1}+p_{i+1j}+p_{i+1j+1}) \right\},$$

$$^3\partial_{ij} = \frac{1}{|I_{ij}|}\frac{1}{3}\left\{ (p_{i-1j-1}+p_{ij-1}+p_{i-1j}) - (p_{i+1j}+p_{ij+1}+p_{i+1j+1}) \right\},$$

$$^4\partial_{ij} = \frac{1}{|I_{ij}|}\frac{1}{3}\left\{ (p_{ij-1}+p_{i+1j-1}+p_{i+1j}) - (p_{i-1j}+p_{i-1j+1}+p_{ij+1}) \right\},$$

$$|\partial_{ij}| = \max(|^1\partial_{ij}|, \cdots, |^4\partial_{ij}|).$$

Where $|I_{ij}|$ is the intensity power,

$$|I_{ij}| = \left\{ \frac{1}{9} \sum_{r=i-1}^{i+1} \sum_{s=j-1}^{j+1} p_{rs}^2 \right\}^{1/2}.$$

(iv) (Global edge candidates:) Calculate the average and the deviation for the gradients, μ, σ, of the regular-sized image.

$$\mu = \frac{1}{MN}\frac{1}{4} \sum_{i=0}^{M-1} \sum_{j=0}^{N-1} \sum_{k=1}^{4} |^k\partial_{ij}|,$$

$$\sigma = \left\{ \frac{1}{MN}\frac{1}{4} \sum_{i=0}^{M-1} \sum_{j=0}^{N-1} \sum_{k=1}^{4} |^k\partial_{ij}|^2 - \mu^2 \right\}^{1/2}.$$

The following pixels p_{ij} and their map will be regarded as global edge candidates and an edge image, respectively (Fig. 3(c)).

$$|\partial_{ij}| \geq \mu + \sigma.$$

(v) (Local edge candidates:) Calculate the local average and the local deviation for the gradient values, μ_{ij}, σ_{ij}, only with each global edge candidate.

$$\mu_{ij} = \frac{1}{(2m+1)(2n+1)}\frac{1}{4} \sum_{r=i-m}^{i+m} \sum_{s=j-n}^{j+n} \sum_{k=1}^{4} |^k\partial_{rs}|,$$

$$\sigma_{ij} = \left\{ \frac{1}{(2m+1)(2n+1)}\frac{1}{4} \sum_{r=i-m}^{i+m} \sum_{s=j-n}^{j+n} \sum_{k=1}^{4} |^k\partial_{rs}|^2 - \mu_{ij}^2 \right\}^{1/2}.$$

Here, m and n determine the local window size. Currently, the local window size is 7×7 pixels (n = m = 3). The following pixels p_{ij} and their binary map will be regarded as (local) edge candidates and a refined edge image, respectively (Fig. 3(d)).

$$|\partial_{ij}| \geq \mu_{ij} + \sigma_{ij}.$$

(vi)   (Abstract image:) Apply a thinning procedure and a shrinking procedure to the refined edge image. The result is the abstract image of the full color painting (Fig. 3(e)).

The affine transformation, in step (ii), regularizes the input image size into 64 × 64 pixels. This means that the ART MUSEUM system accepts full color images of any size.

The median filter smooths the RGB intensity values to reduce the effect of color noise and small textures. (Just remember the paintings in pointillism!)

The contrast sensitivity of the human eye is proportional to the log-scale of the intensity value. The quantity $|\partial_{ij}| / |I_{ij}|$ is called the Weber ratio [9]. The differential filter, in step (iii), is to simulate the color contrast sensitivity of the human eye with the regular-sized image. This is one of the natural extension of the Weber-Fechner law to the RGB intensity value space. The edge image, created by step (iv), only contains the clearly perceptive boundary points of different colors (Fig. 3(c)).

When a viewer selects some specific objects in a painting, he is involuntarily trying to trace the clearly perceived boundary points. This means that users are paying attention to a specific local area. So, step (v) is to re-examine the boundary points in the local scope considering the Weber-Fechner law. The refined edge image is much more similar to a viewer's visual impression regarding on the paintings composition than the edge image is (Fig. 3(c), (d)).

Gradations of colors may cause a bold boundary line or a noisy pattern on the refined edge image. In order to clarify the abstract image, the thinning procedure and the shrinking procedure are applied in step (vi). The abstract image contains single dot width contour lines without isolated dots (Fig. 3(e)). The abstract image looks like rough sketches which users draw. Thus, the system can accept a rough sketch as a visual example.

The collection of abstract images is referred to as the pictorial index in the ART MUSEUM system.

3.3 Visual Example

A user draws a rough sketch as a visual example in QVE. Such a sketch is composed of line segments which may describe boundaries of objects in a painting.

In order to abstract a rough sketch and to describe its composition, the following algorithm is applied.

[Algorithm 2] A rough sketch abstraction

(i)   (Input:) Input a rough sketch as a monochrome intensity value matrix.

(ii)   (Normalization:) Apply the affine transformation to the matrix to get its regular-sized sketch. Here, the regular-sized sketch is also a 64 × 64 pixel monochrome intensity value matrix.

(iii) (Linear image:) Apply a binarization procedure, a thinning procedure, and a shrinking procedure to the regular-sized sketch. The result is the abstract image of the rough sketch. This is called a linear sketch.

3.4 Content based Image Retrieval

In QVE, content based image retrieval is carried out by flexible image matching between the linear sketch and the abstract images on the pictorial index. A linear sketch has the following properties.

(a) Lines in a linear sketch may be rough and sometimes deformed compared with those for an abstract image of the original painting.

(b) Lines may also be drawn in wrong positions, for instance, shifted positions, compared with those for the abstract image.

(c) White space means "nothing is there" or "I don't remember". In the former case, the abstract image also has a similar white space. In the latter case, it may have objects in that area, just like "don't care". These concepts are quite different from each other.

We have designed an algorithm for content based image retrieval to evaluate the local correlation between a linear sketch and an abstract image. In this process, a local block is also shifted in 2D directions to find the best match position between them. We have also adopted different criteria for each case, to permit the ambiguity of white space; edge-edge, space-space, and edge-space. The algorithm is shown in Fig. 4.

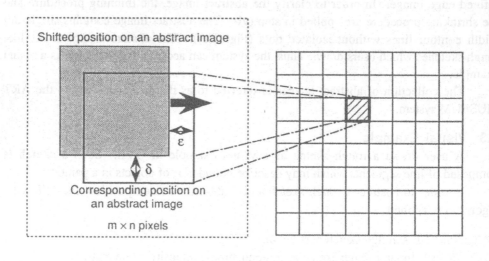

Fig. 4 Content based image retrieval by local/global correlation

[Algorithm 3] Content based image retrieval

(i) (Local block:) Divide an abstract image $P_t = \{p_{ij}\}$ and a linear sketch $Q = \{q_{ij}\}$ into 8×8 local blocks. (Currently, the size for both of the images is $M \times N = 64 \times 64$ pixels. So, each local block size is $m \times n = 8 \times 8$ pixels.)

(ii) (Local correlation:) Calculate the correlation $^{ab}C_{\delta\varepsilon}$ between the local blocks, $^{ab}P_t$ and ^{ab}Q, with shifting ^{ab}Q by δ, ε (Fig. 4).

$$^{ab}C_{\delta\varepsilon} = \sum_{r=ma}^{m(a+1)-1} \sum_{s=nb}^{n(b+1)-1} (\alpha p_{rs} \cdot q_{r+\delta s+\varepsilon} + \beta\, p_{rs} \cdot \overline{q}_{r+\delta s+\varepsilon} + \gamma p_{rs} \oplus q_{r+\delta s+\varepsilon}).$$

Here, coefficients α, β, γ are control parameters used to estimate matching and mismatching patterns. (Currently, $\alpha = 10$, $\beta = 1$, $\gamma = -3$.) The local correlation between these two blocks is defined as follows.

$$^{ab}C = \max(^{ab}C_{\delta\varepsilon}) \quad (\text{for } -m/2 \le \delta \le +m/2,\ -n/2 \le \varepsilon \le +n/2).$$

(iii) (Global correlation:) Calculate the global correlation C_t between the abstract image P_t and a linear sketch Q as a sum of the local correlation values.

$$C_t = \sum_{a=0}^{7} \sum_{b=0}^{7} {}^{ab}C.$$

(iv) (Retrieval:) Apply Steps (i) to (iii) to every abstract image P_t on the pictorial index. Sort $\{C_t\}$ in the descending order. The first one is the best candidate for QVE.

This algorithm examines the correlation, i.e. similarity, between an abstract image and a linear sketch in local scope. Even if a visual example is rough, partial, shifted and deformed, such errors may not affect other local blocks. Therefore, this algorithm accepts a hand-drawn rough sketch as a visual example.

In Steps (ii) and (iv), the correlation $^{ab}C_{\delta\varepsilon}$ between the local blocks, $^{ab}P_t$ and ^{ab}Q, can be calculated with every shifted pattern, with every block, and with every abstract image. Our strategy is also useful for parallel computation.

In Step (ii), terms, $\alpha p_{rs} \cdot q_{r+\delta s+\varepsilon}$ and $\beta\, p_{rs} \cdot \overline{q}_{r+\delta s+\varepsilon}$, are used to count the edge-edge matchings and the space-space matchings, respectively. The term, $\gamma p_{rs} \oplus q_{r+\delta s+\varepsilon}$, is to count the mismatchings. Since the (local) edge candidates are at about 10% of all pixels in an abstract image, we defined $\alpha : \beta = 10 : 1$.

The local blocks for a linear sketch are shifted for $\pm m/2$ and $\pm n/2$ each in Step (ii), as shown in Fig. 4. This means that this algorithm accepts, at most, 12.5% shifted error in a visual example.

4. Experimental Results and Evaluation

The following shows some experimental QVE results and their evaluation for the current stage. We have applied hand-drawn sketch retrieval. Currently, the ART

MUSEUM system contains 205 paintings of full color landscapes and portraits. This section also shows the QVE applications, which are composition based retrieval, xerographic copy (monochrome copy) retrieval and similarity retrieval.

Some general measures are given to evaluate the QVE results. The following values were used.

(a) Recall ratio R_n: This value shows the ratio to retrieve the original full color painting in the best n-candidates. This is the overall image retrieval performance measure.

(b) Deviation D_t: This value shows the relative matching score between individual full color images, P_t, and the visual example, Q, in the normalized scale.

$$D_t = \frac{C_t - \mu}{\sigma} \times 10 + 50,$$

where,

$$\mu = \frac{1}{T} \sum_{i=0}^{T-1} C_t,$$

$$\sigma = \left\{ \frac{1}{T} \sum_{i=0}^{T-1} C_t^2 - \mu^2 \right\}^{1/2}.$$

4.1 Sketch Retrieval

We have applied sketch retrieval, showing each of the 18 visual examples. All of the visual examples in this experiment are hand-drawn sketches. Some of them are rough and only partial, made this way on purpose to examine the image matching facility performance. Some of the results are shown in Fig. 5 with linear sketches, abstract images and deviation values.

The sketch in Fig. 5(a) was drawn while viewing one of Van Gogh's painting. Fig. 5(a) shows the best eight candidates for this visual example. The best candidate for QVE is, of course, the original painting by Van Gogh. In this retrieval, the matching score and deviation value, $D(1) = 88.5$, is much higher than the values for other candidates. Here, $D_1 \geq 80$ means, $C_1 \geq \mu + 3\sigma$.

The sketch in Fig. 5(b) was drawn imaging some paintings. While this sketch is quite rough and deformed, the best three candidates for QVE are quite similar in regard to their composition; trees appear in the right half of each painting. Here, their scores are $D_t \geq 70$, i.e. $C_t \geq \mu + 2\sigma$. In this experiment, the user has especially imagined one of Corot's painting. While it appears as the second best candidate, a reader may feel the best candidate, one of Seurat's painting, is more similar to the sketch.

It can only be expected to retrieve the original painting, if a rough sketch is shown to the system as a visual example. Total recall ratio R_t with 18 visual examples, is summarized in Table 1. In the current state, $R_5 \geq 94.4\%$ from 205 paintings.

The sketch retrieval result suggests that it is possible to retrieve paintings drawn with a similar composition. In sketch retrieval, the candidates for high score, $D_t \geq 70$, i.e. $C_t \geq \mu + 2\sigma$, were quite similar to each other.

Table 1 Sketch Retrieval Evaluation

(a) Matching score for each sketch from 205 paintings

Sketch #	Matching Score		Ranking
	C_t	D_t	
# 1	3992	77.0	1
# 2	4657	100.6	1
# 3	4112	74.4	2
# 4	4544	99.3	1
# 5	4289	88.5	1
# 6	4142	71.7	4
# 7	4309	85.2	1
# 8	4548	92.8	1
# 9	4190	81.8	1
# 10	4109	68.8	1
# 11	4002	66.2	9
# 12	4942	108.4	1
# 13	4227	74.8	3
# 14	4192	80.9	2
# 15	4213	78.1	1
# 16	4146	72.7	2
# 17	4140	80.7	1
# 18	5049	107.5	1

(b) Recall ratio (%) in the best n-candidates from 205 paintings

R_1	R_3	R_5
66.7	88.9	94.4

4.2 Composition based Retrieval

It is known that the general composition for a painting is one of the major factor in the viewer's visual impression. For instance, a horizontal composition gives a stable feeling. Therefore, if it was desired to enjoy some paintings which give a stable impression, it is only necessary to draw a horizontal line and show it to the system in QVE.

Fig. 6 shows the composition based retrieval. While only a horizontal line is drawn in the visual example, many paintings can be found with a similar composition. In composition based retrieval, the score, $D_t \geq 60$, i.e. $C_t \geq \mu + \sigma$, may be sufficient to enable locating similar paintings, since the visual example is only a partial sketch.

4.3 Retrieval by Monochrome Copy

A viewer would often like to find original color photographs from monochrome

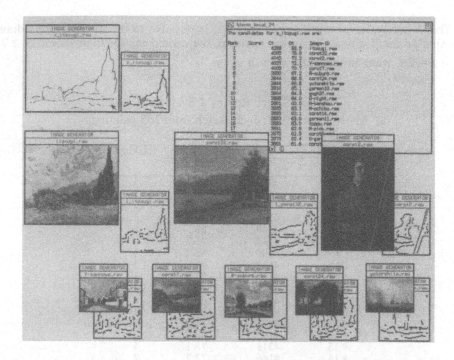

(a) Sketch retrieval by showing a well-drawn sketch

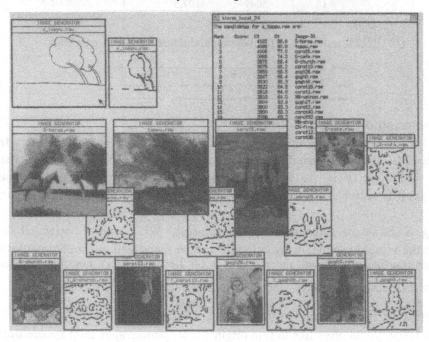

(b) Sketch retrieval by showing a rough sketch

Fig. 5 Some sketch retrieval results

prints or a xerographic copies which appear in some documents. In our system, a user only has to show the monochrome print or the xerographic copy as a visual example, to obtain the original color photograph.

In order to obtain their linear image, a modified version of Algorithm 1 is applied instead of Algorithm 2. Here, the regular-sized image is not an RGB intensity value matrix, but a monochrome one. The abstract image corresponds to the linear sketch.

The visual example in Fig. 7 was a xerographic copy of a painting by Renoir. The best QVE candidate is, of course, the original full color painting by Renoir. In this retrieval, the score, $D_1 = 102.1$, is much higher than the values for other candidates. Here, $D_1 \geq 100$ means, $C_1 \geq \mu + 5\sigma$.

Viewers may expect to be able to retrieve the original full color painting, only if a monochrome print or a xerographic copy is shown to the system as a visual example. The total recall ratio R_t with 10 visual examples is summarized in Table 2. In our current state, $R_1 = 100\%$ from 205 paintings.

Table 2 Sketch Retrieval Evaluation by Monochrome Copy
(from 205 paintings)

| Monochrome | Matching Score | | Ranking |
Copy #	C_t	D_t	
# 21	4634	108.3	1
# 22	5897	136.8	1
# 23	4686	104.8	1
# 24	5122	122.8	1
# 25	4421	95.2	1
# 26	5037	112.8	1
# 27	5054	102.1	1
# 28	4907	106.1	1
# 29	4883	116.4	1
# 30	4589	104.1	1

4.4 Similarity Retrieval

The above results mean that our flexible image matching mechanism gives a good similarity measure for paintings. Therefore, the ART MUSEUM system also provides a similarity retrieval facility from user's full color painting.

Fig. 8 shows a similarity retrieval example. The user specified one of the portraits by Van Gogh. The system retrieved many portraits as the candidates, even though there are many landscapes in the database. In similarity retrieval, the score, $D_t \geq 60$, i.e. $C_t \geq \mu + \sigma$, may be sufficient.

We may expect to use our similarity measure in a clustering procedure. Paintings can be classified from the composition viewpoint. This is useful for dividing a large image data file into several clusters to speed-up the matching procedure.

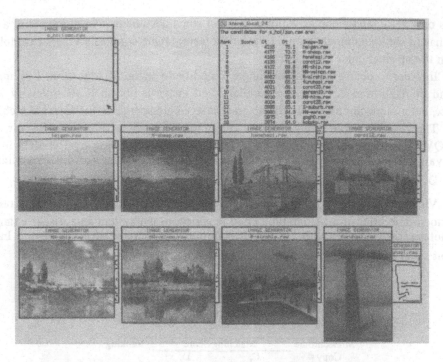

Fig. 6 Composition based content retrieval by a rough sketch

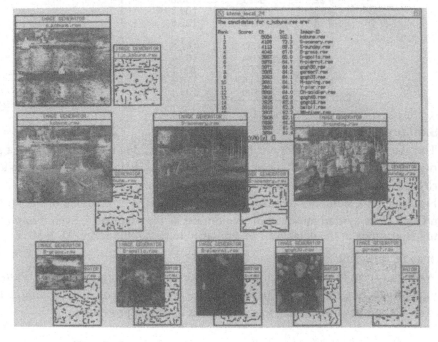

Fig. 7 Image retrieval by a monochrome copy

We may also expect to use our similarity measure in a navigation procedure. Viewers can enjoy paintings with similar compositions without making manual links.

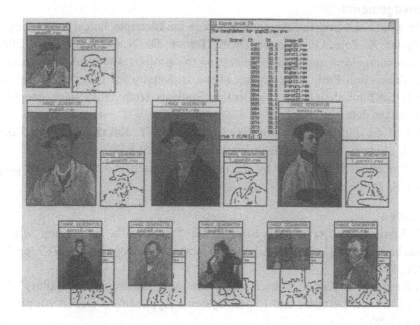

Fig. 8 Similarity retrieval by a full color painting

5. Conclusion

This paper has described the concept of and the general framework for visual interaction with image database systems. The typical interaction style is QVE (query by visual example). We have developed an electronic art gallery, ART MUSEUM system, as a prototype system which provides a visual interaction facility, such as QVE.

Several algorithms were given for QVE, to build a pictorial index, to accept a visual example and to find similar images on the pictorial index. These algorithms are so general that they can be applied to figures, diagrams, photographs, textile patterns and so on, as well as artistic paintings. We have realized a content based image retrieval facility without manual indexing and visual inspection.

This paper also shows some experimental results and current evaluation. Sketch retrieval is quite efficient to find the original painting. A user has only to draw a rough sketch. This facility is easily extended to monochrome photographs and xerographic copies. Composition based retrieval should be investigated from the viewpoint of visual psychology and art. Similarity retrieval is efficient to find paintings with similar compositions. This will also be an effective tool for clustering image data. While these algorithms are quite primitive, they achieved high performance in content based image retrieval.

Acknowledgements

We would like to thank their colleagues in the Electrotechnical Laboratory (ETL), especially Dr. A. Tojo, Dr. T. Yuba, Dr. K. Takase, Dr. N. Otsu, and Mr. K. Fujimura for their encouragement and kind comments on this project. We would also like to thank Prof. K. Tabata and Prof. S. Sugimoto, at the University for Library and Information Science (ULIS) for their kind comments. Students from ULIS have cooperated in obtaining image data.

One of the authors would also like to thank Mr. Y. Kasahara, Mr. Y. Takashima and Mr. H. Shimazu for furnishing an opportunity to visit ETL.

This research is supported by the national research and development project of *Interoperable Database Systems*.

References

[1]   T. Kato, T. Kurita and H. Shimogaki: "Multimedia Interaction with Image Database Systems", Prof. of Advanced Database Symposium ADSS'89, pp.271-278, Dec. 1989.

[2]   T. Kato and T. Kurita: "Visual Interaction with Electronic Art Gallery", Proc. of Int. Conf. on Database and Expert Systems Applications DEXA'90, pp.234-240, Aug. 1990.

[3]   T. Kato, T. Kurita, H. Shimogaki, T. Mizutori and K. Fujimura: "A Cognitive Approach to Visual Interaction", Proc. of Int. Conf. on Multimedia Information Systems MIS'91, pp.109-120, Jan. 1991.

[4]   T. Kato, T. Kurita, H. Shimogaki, T. Mizutori and K. Fujimura: "Cognitive View Mechanism for Multimedia Database System", Proc. of Int. Workshop on Interoperability in Multidatabase Systems IMS'91, pp.179-186, Apr. 1991.

[5]   N. S. Chang and K. S. Fu: "Query-by-Pictorial-Example", IEEE Trans. on Software Engineering, Vol.SE-6, No.6, pp.519-524, June 1980.

[6]   S. K. Chang, C. W. Yan, D. C. Dimitroff and T. Arndt: "An Intelligent Image Database System", IEEE Trans. on Software Engineering, Vol.SE-1, No.5, pp.681-688, May 1988.

[7]   Y. Hara and A. Kaneko: "A New Multimedia Electronic Book and its Functional Capabilities", User-oriented Content-based Text and Image Handling RIAO'88, pp.114-123, 1988.

[8]   N. Yankelovich, N. Meyrowitz and A. van Dam: "Reading and Writing the Electronic Book", IEEE Computer, Vol.21, No.10, pp.15-30, Oct. 1985.

[9]   K. R. Boff, L. Kaufman and J. P. Thomas (ed.): "Handbook of Perception and Human Performance", John Wiley & Sons, 1986.

Optimization of Linear Logic Programs Using Counting Methods

Sergio Greco*

Dip. di Elettr. Informatica Sistem.

Università della Calabria

87030 Rende, Italy

2101gre@icsuniv.bitnet

Carlo Zaniolo

Computer Science Department

University of California

LosAngeles, CA 90024

zaniolo@cs.edu.ucla

Abstract

We present a general solution to the problem of optimized execution of logic programs containing linear recursive rules. Our solution is based on extensions of the classical counting method, which is known to be efficient but of limited applicability. In fact, the range of applicability of the counting method, and its variants proposed by previous researchers, suffer from one or more of the following limitations: the method can be applied only when (1) the adorned program contains one recursive rule, (2) the 'left part' and the 'right part' of the recursive rule do not have any common variable and (3) the relation associated with the left part of the recursive rule is 'acyclic'. In this paper, a simple and unified framework is presented, where those limitations are removed, and the counting method thus become applicable to all programs with linear rules. This framework also allows a simple treatment of programs factorizable into segments, which can be computed separately yielding a much faster execution. A simple factorization technique based on argument reduction is presented that produces optimizations similar to those defined in the literature for RLC-linear programs (i.e., programs with right-linear rules, left-linear rules and a combination of the two).

1 Introduction

In this paper, we address the problem of evaluating queries with bound arguments on programs containing linear recursive rules. Several techniques, based on the propagation of bindings, have been defined in the literature to deal with this problem. These include the *magic-set* method [3,17,4], the *counting* method [3,17], and factorization techniques for special cases, such as those based on the reduction of the program [14] or on the combination of the propagation of bindings with the successive reduction [13].

While the magic-set method can be applied to all programs, the counting method and the factorization techniques can only be applied to restricted classes of linear programs—often yielding an order of magnitude of improvement in efficiency; comparisons between

---

*Work done while visiting MCC, Austin, Texas, and supported by the project "Sistemi Informatici e Calcolo Parallelo" obiettivo "Logidata+" of C.N.R. Italy.

the magic-set method and the counting method can be found in [4,11]. Many recursive programs found in practice are linear, and hence can be optimized by one of the specialized methods. Thus, the problem of identifying and processing these special situations is critical for an efficient implementation of deductive databases [20].

In this paper, we present a unifying framework for the efficient implementation of linear rules, as follows. We first propose extensions to the counting method, to make it applicable to all linear programs — even when the the database contains cycles. Furthermore, we show that, once these programs have been rewritten using the new counting method, the detection of special cases that are treatable by reduction techniques becomes simpler. Thus, we propose extensions to the optimizations defined in the literature [19,14] for programs containing left-linear and right-linear rules.

To illustrate the intuition underlying the different methods, we can use the following well-known example:

Example 1 Consider the following same-generation program SG with query $sg(a, Y)$. The predicates up, down and flat are binary predicates that are non mutually recursive with sg.

$$sg(X, Y) \leftarrow flat(X, Y).$$
$$sg(X, Y) \leftarrow up(X, X1), \ sg(X1, Y1), \ down(Y1, Y).$$

The magic-set method first computes the set of tuples (called *magic set*) that are 'relevant' for the predicate sg and then uses the magic set to restrict the set of answers for the predicate sg. The magic-set method applies the modified goal $sg(a, Y)$ on the following program:

$$m\_sg(a).$$
$$m\_sg(X1) \leftarrow m\_sg(X), \ up(X, X1).$$
$$sg(X, Y) \leftarrow m\_sg(X), \ flat(X, Y).$$
$$sg(X, Y) \leftarrow m\_sg(X), \ up(X, X1), \ sg(X1, Y1), \ down(Y1, Y).$$

The counting method adds information on the distance from the initial node to each tuple belonging to the magic set, thus further constraining the later computation. In our example, the counting method produces the modified query, $sg(a, Y, 0)$, and the following program:

$$c\_sg(a, 0).$$
$$c\_sg(X1, I + 1) \leftarrow c\_sg(X, I), \ up(X, X1).$$
$$sg(X, Y, I) \leftarrow c\_sg(X, I), \ flat(X, Y).$$
$$sg(X, Y, I) \leftarrow c\_sg(X, I), \ up(X, X1), \ sg(X1, Y1, I + 1), \ down(Y1, Y).$$

This program can be further optimized, by dropping the first argument that is redundant for the example at hand, yielding query $sg(Y, 0)$, on the the following program:

$$c\_sg(a, 0).$$
$$c\_sg(X1, I + 1) \leftarrow c\_sg(X, I), \ up(X, X1).$$
$$sg(Y, I) \leftarrow c\_sg(X, I), \ flat(X, Y).$$
$$sg(Y, I) \leftarrow sg(Y1, I + 1), \ down(Y1, Y).$$

The index I in $c\_sg(X, I)$ denotes the distance of the X from the source node a. The computation of the tuple of sg at level I uses only the tuples of sg computed at level $I+1$, i.e., the tuples computed in the previous step. In contrast, the magic-set method joins this set with the result of joining m_sg and up.

However, the basic counting method just described is not as general as the magic-set method, since it can be used only for a restricted class of linear programs and does deal well with cycles in base relations. Thus, in our example, if the relation up, is 'cyclic' the method generates a counting set with infinite tuples. Two different approaches have been defined for dealing with the problem of cycles. The first is based on the combination of the magic-set and the counting method [16], while the second extends the method for cyclic data [11,9,2]. The two methods, in any case, suffer of the other limitations of the classical method.

In this paper, we generalize the counting method to avoid the limitations of the current approaches. Moreover, our approach is conducive to further optimizations that are possible for more restrictive classes of (left-/right-) linear programs [14,13]. The paper is organized as follows. The next section introduces the basic definitions used in the paper. In section 3, an extension of the counting method to handle programs with acyclic databases is presented. Such a method is extended to programs with cyclic databases in section 4. In section 5, we present a technique for reduction of programs rewritten with the extended counting method. Due to space limitations we will omit the formal proofs of our theorems, which can be found in [8].

2   Basic definitions

We now recall some basic concepts [10,20]. Predicates whose definition consists of only ground facts are called *base* predicates while all others predicates are called *derived*. The set of facts whose predicate symbol is a base predicate defines the *database* while the set of clauses whose head predicates symbols is a derived predicate symbol defines the *program*. A *query* is a pair (G, P) where G is a query-goal and P is a program. The *answer* to a query (G, P) is the set of substitutions for the variables in G such that G is true with respect to the minimal model of P [10]. Two queries (Q, P) and (Q', P') are *equivalent* if they have the same answer for all possible databases.

Two variables X and Y in a rule r are connected if they appear in the same predicate or if there exists in r a variable Z such that X is connected to Z and Z is connected to Y. Two predicate P_1 and P_2 appearing in a rule are *connected* if there exists a variable appearing in both P_1 and P_2 or if there exist two connected variables appearing respectively in P_1 and P_2. A predicate p depends on a predicate q if 1) there exists a rule such that p appears in the head and q in the body or 2) if there exists a predicate s such that p depends on s and s depends on q. Two predicates p and q are mutually recursive if p depends on q and q depends on p.

We assume that the program has been partitioned according to a topological order $< P_1, ..., P_n >$. This means that each predicate appearing in P_i depends only on predicates belonging to P_j such that $j \leq i$. We assume also that the computation follows the topological order and that when we compute the component P_i the components $P_1, ..., P_{i-1}$ have been already computed. When we compute the component P_i all the facts obtained from the computation of the components $P_1, ..., P_{i-1}$ are basically treated the same as database facts. A rule in a component P_i is called *exit rule* if each predicate in the body belongs to a component P_j such that $j < i$. All the other rules are *recursive rules*. A recursive rule is said to be *linear* if the body of the rule contains at most one predicate that is mutually recursive with the head predicate. A program is linear if each rule is either an exit rule or a linear recursive rule. A linear recursive rule is of the form $P \leftarrow L, Q, R$ where P and Q are mutually recursive predicates while L and R are conjunctions of predicates not mutually recursive with P. We will denote the conjunctions L and R as *left* part and *right* part respectively.

An *adorned program* is a program whose predicate symbols have associated a string α, defined on the alphabet $\{b, f\}$, of length equal to the arity of the predicate. A character b (resp. f) in the i-th position of the adornment associated with a predicate p means that the i-th argument of p is bound (resp. free).

Let P be program and let P^c be the rewritten program obtained by applying the counting method to P. The program P^c contains a new set of predicates called *counting predicates*. The set of rules defining the counting predicates are called *counting rules*, while the remaining rules are called *modified rules*.

We assume that exit rules and recursive rules in an adorned program P^α have, respectively, the following form: $p(X, Y) \leftarrow E(B)$, and $p(X, Y) \leftarrow L(A), q(X1, Y1), R(B)$, where 1) the variable appearing inside the predicates denote lists of arguments; 2) p and q are mutually recursive predicates whose first and second arguments denote the lists of bound and free arguments, 3) E, L and R are (possibly null) conjunctions of predicates that are not mutually recursive with p and q, 4) the *safety* conditions $Y \subseteq (A \cup Y1 \cup B)$ and (obviously) $X1 \subseteq (X \cup A)$ hold. We assume also that the variables in the head are distinguished. There is no loss of generality in this assumption because each rule can be put in such a form by simple rewriting.

We now review the concept of query graph for an adorned program P [16,11]. Given a query $Q = (q(a, Y), P)$ and a database D we can associate to (Q, D) a graph called *query graph* defined as follows. An arc is a triplet (a, b, c) where are a and b are the source node and the destination node, while c is the label associated with the arc. Given an arc $e = (a, b, c)$ we say that the node a (resp. b) has in output (resp. input) the arc e. The graph associated with (Q, D) is defined as follows:

1. there is an arc from x to $x1$ labeled (L, r, c) if there exists a ground rule r : $p(x, y) \leftarrow L(a), q(x1, y1), R(b)$ such that $L(a) \in D$ and c is the value for the variables appearing both in L and R;

2. there is an arc from $y1$ to y labeled (R, r, c) if there exists a ground rule r : $p(x, y) \leftarrow L(a), q(x1, y1), R(b)$ such that $r(b) \in D$ and c is the value for the variables appearing both in L and R;

3. there is an arc from x to y marked (E, r) if there exists a ground rule $p(x, y) \leftarrow E(b)$ such that $E(b) \in D$.

The query graph G associated with a program can be partitioned into the three subgraphs G_L, G_R and G_E containing the arcs whose first argument of the label is L, R and E respectively.

Consider a graph representation G of a binary relation g. The set of arcs of g can be partitioned with respect to a node s (called source) into the following four disjoint classes [18,1]:

1. *Tree* arcs (g_t): these are the arcs defining the tree T_G obtained by the depth-first search visit of the graph starting from the node s;

2. *Forward* arcs (g_f): these are the arcs that go from a node v_1 to a node v_2 such that v_1 is an ancestor, but not a parent, of v_2 in T_G.

3. *Cross* arcs (g_c): these join two nodes that are not in the relation ancestor-descendant (in T_G).

4. *Back* arcs (g_b): these go from a node v_2 to a node v_1 such that v_1 is an ancestor of v_2 in T_G.

Tree arcs, forward arcs and cross arcs will be called *ahead* arcs. Notice that more than one different partitions are possible.

A node a is said to be *single* (resp. *multiple, recurring*) with respect to a source node s if there is a unique path (resp. a finite number greater than one, an infinite set of paths) from s to a. A graph is a tree if it contains only tree arcs (or equivalently, if each node is single), and is acyclic if it does not contain back arcs (or equivalently, if each node is non-recurring). A cycle is said to be *elementary* if each node is contained only once.

Example 2 Consider the graph defined by the relation *arc* and the source node a.

$$\begin{array}{llll} \text{arc}(a,b) & \text{arc}(a,c) & \text{arc}(d,b) & \text{arc}(c,b) \\ \text{arc}(b,c) \\ \text{arc}(a,d) \end{array}$$

Here, (a,b), (b,c) and (a,d) are tree arcs, (a,c) is a forward arc, (d,b) is a cross arc and (c,b) is a back arc. The nodes a and d are singles, while the nodes b and c are recurring. The arcs (b,c) and (c,b) define an elementary cycle. □

3 Acyclic Databases

For now, we leave the problem of cyclic databases to subsequent sections, and concentrate on the treatment of multiple recursive rules, and the situation where the left part and right part of a rule share variables. For this purpose, we replace the counting indexes with lists, which, operating as stacks, remember the state of the computation for later use. After proving the correctness of the method, we introduce a simpler implementation, where lists are replaced with pointers, to ensure the desired performance level for the method.

3.1 Multiple Linear Rules

The computation of a program rewritten by using the counting method (as well as each linear program rewritten by using the magic-set method) is executed in two different phases: the computation of the counting set and the computation of the answer. The method can thus be viewed as stack-based because during the first phase it remembers the number of applications of the (left part of the) recursive rule, and during the second phase it executes (the right part of) the rule an equal number of times. The presence of more than one recursive rule implies that the exact sequence of rules used need to be memorized during the computation of the counting set, so that the same sequence of rules, but in reverse order, can be executed during the second phase. A list, having as entries the rule numbers, can be used for this purpose. We illustrate this point by means of an example.

Example 3 Consider the following program containing two recursive rules and the query-goal $sg(a,Y)$, which produces the adornment sg^{bf}.

$$r_0 : \quad sg(X,Y) \leftarrow \quad flat(X,Y).$$
$$r_1 : \quad sg(X,Y) \leftarrow \quad up1(X,X1), \quad sg(X1,Y1), \quad down1(Y1,Y).$$
$$r_2 : \quad sg(X,Y) \leftarrow \quad up2(X,X1), \quad sg(X1,Y1), \quad down2(Y1,Y).$$

The computation of the counting set associates to each element the sequence of rules applied to reach the element.

$$c_0 : \quad c\_sg^{bf}(a,[]).$$
$$c_1 : \quad c\_sg^{bf}(X1,[r_1|L]) \leftarrow \quad c\_sg^{bf}(X,L), \quad up1(X,X1).$$
$$c_2 : \quad c\_sg^{bf}(X1,[r_2|L]) \leftarrow \quad c\_sg^{bf}(X,L), \quad up2(X,X1).$$

If we have only one recursive rule, then all elements in the list are the same and it is sufficient to store the length of the list, as per the classical method. During the computation of the right part we need to use the reverse of the sequence of rules used to reach an element during the left part. For example, if we reached element x, starting from source node a, by the application of the left part of rules $r1, r1, r2, r1$, in the computation of the right part we need to apply the rules $r1, r2, r1, r1$. The rewritten rules, with the query-goal $sg(Y,[])$, are as follows:

$$r_0 : \quad sg^{bf}(Y,L) \leftarrow \quad c\_sg^{bf}(X,L), \quad flat(X,Y).$$
$$r_1 : \quad sg^{bf}(Y,L) \leftarrow \quad sg^{bf}(Y1,[r_1|L]), \quad down1(Y1,Y).$$
$$r_1 : \quad sg^{bf}(Y,L) \leftarrow \quad sg^{bf}(Y1,[r_2|L]), \quad down2(Y1,Y).$$

□

The use of lists could result in a performance overhead. In [15], a log of previously used rules was encoded into an integer. We will later propose a more efficient technique using pointers.

The transformation presented above is applicable to programs with more than one mutually recursive predicate and, consequently, to programs whose adornment in the recursive predicate in the body is different from the adornment in the head.

3.2   Shared Variables

The transformation presented in Section 3.1 applies only when the variables appearing in the right part of the recursive rules do not appear in the left part or among the bound variables in the head. This restriction permits us to partition the set of arguments of the recursive predicates into two distinct sets. If a variable in the right part of a recursive rule also appears in the left part, or it is bound in the head, then we need to know its value when computing the answer. This implies that we need to store in the list the values of such variables. (Recall that the pair value and rule number is also labeling the arcs of the query graph associated with the program.) We show first the method by an example and in the next subsection we present the algorithm.

Example 4 Consider the the following example with the query-goal $p(a, Y)$. In the second rule, the variable W appears both in the left and in the right part. In the third rule, the variable X is bound in the head and also appears in the right part.

$$r_0: \ p(X, Y) \leftarrow \ \text{flat}(X, Z).$$
$$r_1: \ p(X, Y) \leftarrow \ \text{up1}(X, X1, W), \ p(X1, Y1), \ \text{down1}(Y1, Y, W).$$
$$r_2: \ p(X, Y) \leftarrow \ \text{up2}(X, X1), \ p(X1, Y1), \ \text{down2}(Y1, Y, X).$$

Each entry in the list defining the path contains two arguments: the identifier of the rule and a list containing the variables that are shared between the left and the right part of the rule. The values of the variables bound in the head appearing also in the right part of the rule (X in the third rule of our example) are not stored in the list because they appear also in the counting predicates. The resulting rewritten program (where the adornment bf have been omitted for brevity) is as follows:

$$c\_p(a, [])$$
$$c\_p(X1, [(r_1, [W])|L])) \leftarrow \ c\_p(X, L), \ \text{up1}(X, X1, W).$$
$$c\_p(X1, [(r_2, [])|L])) \leftarrow \ c\_p(X, L), \ \text{up2}(X, X1).$$
$$p(Y, L) \leftarrow \ c\_p(X, L), \ \text{flat}(X, Y).$$
$$p(Y, L) \leftarrow \ p(Y1, [(r1, [W])|L]), \ c\_p(X, L), \ \text{down1}(Y1, Y, W).$$
$$p(Y, L) \leftarrow \ p(Y1, [(r2, [])|L]), \ c\_p(X, L), \ \text{down2}(Y1, Y, X).$$

The goal $c\_p(X, L)$ in the second modified rule is not necessary since it is always true.

Consider the following database $\{\text{up1}(a, b, 1), \text{flat}(b, c), \text{down1}(c, d, 2), \text{down1}(c, e, 1)\}$, depicted as follows:

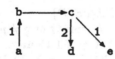

The original program computes the set $S = \{p(b, c), p(a, e)\}$. The set of facts computed by the rewritten program is $\{c\_p(a, []), c\_p(b, [(r_1, [1])]), p(c, [(r_1, [1])]), p(e, [])\}$. Moreover the rewritten program with the query $p(Y, [])$ is equivalent to the original one with respect to the query $p(a, Y)$.

Consider now the database $\{\text{up2}(a, b), \text{flat}(b, c), \text{down1}(c, d, b), \text{down1}(c, e, a)\}$, pictured in the following figure:

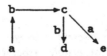

The rewritten program computes now the set $\{c\_p(a, []), c\_p(b, [(r_2, [])]), p(c, [(r_2, [])]), p(e, [])\}$. Also in this case the two program are equivalent with respect to the queries-goal $p(Y, [])$ and $p(a, Y)$. $\square$

3.3 The Extended Counting Algorithm

For a given rule r, $L(r)$ and $R(r)$ denote, respectively, the left part and the right part of r, C_r denotes the list of variables appearing both in $L(r)$ and $R(r)$. D_r denotes the list of variables bound in the head appearing also in $R(r)$. There are three differences with respect to the classical method:

1. the index is substituted with a list whose elements are pairs (r, C) where r is the identifier of a rule and C is a value for C_r;

2. a counting predicate is added in the body of the recursive modified rules (necessary only if bound variable in the head appears also in the right part of the body);

3. the path argument in a counting (resp. modified) rules is incremented (resp. decremented) only if the program defining the predicate in the head of the original rule is not right- (resp. left-) linear.[1]

Algorithm 1 *[Extended Counting Rewriting]*
Input: Query $(q(a, Y), P)$ where the rules in P have form:
$\qquad$ *Exit rules:* $p(X, Y) \leftarrow e(B)$,
$\qquad$ *Recursive rules:* $p(X, Y) \leftarrow a(A), q(X1, Y1), b(B)$
Output: *rewritten query* $(q(Y, []), P^{ec})$
begin
$\quad$ % Generate Counting Rules
$\quad$ $P^{ec} := \{c\_q(a, [])\}$
$\quad$ **for each** rec. rule r s.t. $(L(r)$ is not empty or $q \neq p$ or $X \neq X1)$ **do**
$\quad\quad$ **if** $R(r)$ is empty and $q = p$ and $Y = Y1$ **then**
$\quad\quad\quad$ $P^{ec} := P^{ec} \cup \{c\_q(X1, L) \leftarrow c\_p(X, L), L(A)\}$
$\quad\quad$ **else**
$\quad\quad\quad$ $P^{ec} := P^{ec} \cup \{c\_q(X1, [(r, C_r)|L]) \leftarrow c\_p(X, L), a(A)\}$
$\quad$ % Generate Modified Rules
$\quad$ **for each** exit rule **do**
$\quad\quad$ $P^{ec} := P^{ec} \cup \{p(Y, L) \leftarrow c\_p(X, L), E(B)\}$
$\quad$ **for each** rec. rule r s.t. $R(r)$ is not empty or $q \neq p$ or $Y \neq Y1$ **do**
$\quad\quad$ **if** $L(r)$ is empty and $q = p$ and $X = X1$ **then**
$\quad\quad\quad$ $P^{ec} := P^{ec} \cup \{p(Y, L) \leftarrow q(Y1, L), c\_p(X, L), b(B)\}$
$\quad\quad$ **else**
$\quad\quad\quad$ $P^{ec} := P^{ec} \cup \{p(Y, L) \leftarrow q(Y1, [(r, C_r)|L]), c\_p(X, L), b(B)\}$
end.

Observe that the counting predicate $c\_p(X, L)$ in the body of the modified recursive rules can be omitted if $D_r = \emptyset$, i.e., when no bound variable in the head also appear in the right part of the body.

Theorem 1 *Let $Q = (G, P)$ be an adorned query. Let Q' be the query obtained by application of algorithm 1 to Q. If the graph associated with (P, D) is acyclic, then Q and Q' are equivalent with respect to a database D.* $\qquad\square$

---

[1] The definition of right and left linear programs are given in the next section

3.4 Implementation

The extended counting method adds to each counting predicate an argument denoting the path to reach the element starting from the initial binding. Such an argument, hereafter called *path argument*, is used to select the rule that must be used during the computation of the answer. The technique proposed in [15] (see also [6]) encodes such an information by using a number. Unfortunately this is not practical because the size of the number grows exponentially with the number of steps (the base of the number is equal to the number of rules in the rewritten program).

Our idea is to store for each element in the counting set only the rule used and the address of the tuple used to compute it. In particular, we assume that each tuple is associated with a unique identifier. We use an extended syntax to rewrite our programs. The extended syntax allows to use predicates of the form $O : P$, whose meaning is: "O is the identifier (in our case is the address) for the tuple P".[2] For example, if the element b in the counting set is computed by using the rule r and the tuple a we store the tuple $(b, r, [..], Addr(a))$.

Consider the program of Example 4. The set of counting rules is

$$c\_p(a, r_0, [], nil).$$
$$c\_p(X1, r_1, [W], A) \leftarrow \quad A : c\_p(X, \_, \_, \_), \; up1(X, X1, W).$$
$$c\_p(X1, r_2, [], A) \leftarrow \quad A : c\_p(X, \_, \_, \_), \; up2(X, X1).$$

The list associated with an element can be deduced by 'navigating' the chain defined by the last arguments. The set of rewritten rules is the following with the query-goal $p(Y, \_, nil)$.

$$r_0 : \quad p(Y, R, A) \leftarrow \quad c\_p(X, R, \_, A), \; e(X, Y).$$
$$r_1 : \quad p(Y, R, A) \leftarrow \quad p(Y1, r_1, B), \; B : c\_p(X, R, [W], A), \; down1(Y1, Y, W).$$
$$r_2 : \quad p(Y, R, A) \leftarrow \quad p(Y1, r_2, B), \; B : c\_p(X, R, [], A), \; down2(Y1, Y, X).$$

Notice that in this case when we compute the predicate $B : c\_p(...)$ the variable B is bound and this corresponds to a direct access to the memory. Under this implementation, the method is very similar to the *Bushy-Depth-First* method used in the implementation of $\mathcal{LDL}$ [21].

If the graph associated with the left part of the recursive rules is acyclic and has n nodes, then in the worst case the counting set contains n^2 tuples. In comparison the set of tuples in the magic set is equal, in the worst case, to n. We propose next a modification of the method that reduces the size of the counting set to n. We show this by using the previous example. First we define the predicate up.

$$up(X, X1, [W], r_1) \leftarrow \quad up1(X, X1, W).$$
$$up(X, X1, [], r_2) \leftarrow \quad up2(X, X1).$$

A set of triplets is associated with each node in the counting set. Each element in the set contains the identifier of the rule, the set of common variables between the left and the right part of the rule and the identifier associated with the 'preceding node'. We use here the syntax of $\mathcal{LDL}$ that allows also set terms [5,12].[3] The program computing the counting set is:

---

[2] Many new logic languages support the concept of object ID. Here we use the notation of [22].
[3] $\mathcal{LDL}$ permits, by using grouping rules, to generate set terms.

$c\_p(a, \{(r_0, [], nil)\})$.
$c\_p(X1, < (R, V, A) >) \leftarrow A : c\_p(X, \_), upa(X, X1, V, R),$
$\neg(upa(U, X1, \_, \_)), U \neq X, \neg(c\_p(U, \_))$.

The predicate upa denotes the set of tuples of up that are 'reachables' from the initial binding. Because we are assuming that the database is acyclic, upa coincides with the set of ahead arcs in the query graph. Notice that such a program is not stratified. In the next section we show that it is 'weakly stratified' and that it can be computed efficiently.

4 Cyclic Databases

The counting method is unsafe if the database associated with the left part is cyclic, because it generates paths of infinite length. Two different techniques have been proposed for such a class of programs. The first, called *magic-counting* [16], combines the counting method and the magic-set method, while the second extends the counting method for programs with cyclic data [11,9,2].

We next present an extension of the counting method for cyclic database. Our method differs from those previously defined in the literature because such methods use specialized algorithms while our method is based on the simple rewriting of the original program. The idea is to associate to each vertex in G the acyclic distance from the source node and to nodes that have a back arc in input the length of the elementary cycles containing it.

Example 5 Consider the program of example 1. We, first, divide the set of up arcs that are reachables from the initial binding a (source node) into the two distinct subsets: (1) the ahead arcs upa and (2) the back arcs up_b. Such sets can be computed, in linear time, by using a variant of the depth first search algorithm [18,1]. We assume that the partition of the relation associated with the predicate up into the two subsets upa and up_b has been already done. In this case the database associated with the predicate upa is acyclic and the counting set can be computed as follows:

$c\_sg(a, \{(r_0, [], nil)\})$.
$c\_sg(X1, < (r_1, [], A) >) \leftarrow A : c\_sg(X, \_), upa(X, X1),$
$\neg(upa(U, X1)), U \neq X, \neg(c\_sg(U, \_))$.

After the computation of the predicate c_sg, a unique identifier is associated with each node in the counting set and such nodes are linked. We need now to add the links relative to the back arcs. The following predicate $cycle\_sg$ adds such information.

$cycle\_sg(X1, < (r_1, [], A) >) \leftarrow A : sg\_sg(X, \_), up_b(X, X1)$.

As shown in the previous section, our technique is to associate to each node in the right part of the graph a set of identifiers of the nodes in the left part and then to move in both parts using the same rule. Observe that it is also possible to move in the left part of the graph using back arcs. The predicate f, defined below, computes for a given identifier associated with a node in the counting set the set of identifiers of the nodes preceding it.

$$f(A, S) \leftarrow A : c\_sg(X, S1), \text{ if}(\text{cycle\_sg}(X, S2) \text{ then } S = S1 \cup S2 \text{ else } S = S1).$$

The set of modified rules is then

$$r_0 : \quad sg(Y, S) \leftarrow A : c\_sg(X, \_), f(A, S), flat(X, Y).$$
$$r_1 : \quad sg(Y, S) \leftarrow sg(Y1, T), (r_1, [], A) \in T, f(A, S), down(Y1, Y).$$

The program contains only one recursive rule where no variables are shared between the left part and the right part of the rule. Thus, the arguments denoting the identifier of the rule and the list of the shared variables can be deleted. The resulting program, with the query-goal sg(Y, { nil }), is

$$c\_sg(a, \{nil\}).$$
$$c\_sg(X1, < A >) \leftarrow A : c\_sg(X, \_), up_a(X, X1),$$
$$\neg(up_a(W, X1), W \neq X, \neg c\_sg(W, \_)).$$

$$\text{cycle\_sg}(X1, < A >) \leftarrow A : c\_sg(X, \_), up_b(X, X1).$$

$$f(A, S) \leftarrow A : c\_sg(X, S1), \text{ if}(\text{cycle\_sg}(X, S2) \text{ then } S = S1 \cup S2 \text{ else } S = S1).$$

$$r_0 : \quad sg(Y, S) \leftarrow A : c\_sg(X, \_), f(A, S), flat(X, Y).$$
$$r_1 : \quad sg(Y, S) \leftarrow sg(Y1, T), A \in T, f(A, S), down(Y1, Y).$$

Consider now the following database.

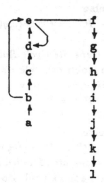

up(a, b)	down(f, g)	flat(e, f)
up(b, c)	down(g, h)	
up(c, d)	down(h, i)	
up(d, e)	down(i, j)	
up(e, f)	down(j, k)	
up(b, e)	down(k, l)	

The counting predicates associate to each value x for the variable X an identifier and the set of identifiers of elements preceding x through an ahead arc. The set of tuples for the predicate counting is then { $o_1 : (a, \{nil\})$, $o_2 : (b, \{o_1\})$, $o_3 : (c, \{o_2\})$, $o_4 : (d, \{o_3\})$, $o_5 : (e, \{o_2, o_4\})$ }. The predicate cycle contains only the tuple $(d, \{o_5\})$.

The predicate f associates to each identifier of tuple in the counting set the identifiers of the tuples in the counting set 'preceding' it. The set of tuples for f is $\{(o_1, \{nil\})$, $(o_2, \{o_1\})$, $(o_3, \{o_2\})$, $(o_4, \{o_3, o_5\})$, $(o_5, \{o_2, o_4\})\}$

Now se consider the computation of the tuples of sg. From the exit rule we obtain the tuple $(f, \{o_2, o_4\})$. Navigating on the relations down and c_sg from f and o_2 we obtain the tuple $(g, \{o_1\})$ while from f and o_4 we obtain $(g, \{o_3, o_5\})$. In the next step from g and o_1 we obtain the tuple $(h, \{nil\})$ that is an answer. From g and o_3, o_5 we obtain the tuples $(h, \{o_2\})$ and $(h, \{o_2, o_4\})$. The following steps compute the tuples $(i, \{o_1\})$, $(i, \{o_3, o_5\})$, $(j, \{nil\})$, $(j, \{o_2\})$, $(j, \{o_2, o_4\})$, $(k, \{o_1\})$, $(k, \{o_3, o_5\})$, $(l, \{nil\})$, $(l, \{o_2\})$, $(l, \{o_3, o_5\})$. □

We next present the algorithm for the extended counting method. We assume that each recursive rule r of the form $p(X,Y) \leftarrow a(A), q(X1,Y1), b(B)$, such that the conjunction denoted by the predicate a is not empty, has been replaced by the following two rules: $a'(X,X1,C_r,r) \leftarrow a(A)$ and $p(X,Y) \leftarrow a'(X,X1,C_r,r), q(X1,Y1), b(B)$. Notice that not all arguments in the predicate a' are necessary. We assume also that the relations associated with the predicate a' has been partitioned, with respect to the binding in the query-goal, into the two subset a'_a and a'_b denoting respectively the sets of ahead and back arcs.

Notation: $L(r)$ and $R(r)$ denote the left and the right part of a recursive rule r while C_r denote the set of common variables between $L(r)$ and $R(r)$.

Algorithm 2 *[Extended Counting Rewriting]*
Input: Query $(q(a,Y),P)$ as in Algorithm 1.
Output: rewritten query $(q(Y, \{(0, [], nil)\}), P^{ec})$
begin
    % *Generate Counting Rules*
    $P^{ec} := \{c\_q(a, \{(r_0, [], nil)\})\}$
    for each rec. rule r s.t. $L(r)$ in not empty or $q \neq p$ or $X \neq X1$ **do**
      if $R(r)$ is empty and $q = p$ and $Y = Y1$ **then**
        $P^{ec} := P^{ec} \cup \{c\_q(X1, < (R, C_r, Id) >) \leftarrow c\_p(X,T), (R,C_r,Id) \in T, a'_a(X,X1,\_,\_),$
$$\neg(a'_a(W,X1,\_,\_), W \neq X, \neg c\_p(W,\_)) \}$$

      else
        $P^{ec} := P^{ec} \cup \{c\_q(X1, < (R, C_r, Id) >) \leftarrow Id : c\_p(X,\_), a'_a(X,X1,C_r,R),$
$$\neg(a'_a(W,X1,\_,\_), W \neq X, \neg c\_p(W,\_)) \}$$

    % *Generate Cycle Rules*
    for each rec. rule r s.t. $L(r)$ in not empty or $q \neq p$ or $X \neq X1$ **do**
      if $R(r)$ is empty and $q = p$ and $Y = Y1$ **then**
        $P^{ec} := P^{ec} \cup \{cycle\_q(X1, < (R, C_r, Id) >) \leftarrow c\_p(X,T),$
$$(R,C_r,Id) \in T, a'_b(X,R,C_r,X1)\}$$

      else
        $P^{ec} := P^{ec} \cup \{cycle\_q(X1, < (R, C_r, Id) >) \leftarrow Id : c\_p(X,\_), a'_b(X,R,C_r,X1)\}$
    % *Generate Modified Rules*
    for each exit rule **do**
      $P^{ec} := P^{ec} \cup \{ p(Y,S) \leftarrow c\_p(X,S), e(B,C_r), \ \ p(Y,S) \leftarrow cycle\_p(X,S), e(B,C_r) \}$
    for each rec. rule r s.t. $R(r)$ is not empty or $q \neq p$ or $Y \neq Y1$ **do**
      if $L(r)$ is empty and $q = p$ and $X = X1$ **then**
        $P^{ec} := P^{ec} \cup \{p(Y,T) \leftarrow q(Y1,T), (r,C_r,Id) \in T, Id : c\_p(X,\_), b(B,C_r)\}$
      else
        $P^{ec} := P^{ec} \cup \{p(Y,S) \leftarrow q(Y1,T), (r,C_r,Id) \in T, f(Id,S), Id : c\_p(X,\_), b(B,C_r)\}$
end.

Here, as in Algorithm 1, the counting predicate $Id : c\_p(X,\_)$ in the body of the modified recursive rules can be omitted if $D_r = \emptyset$, i.e., if no bound head variables appear in the right part of the body.

The following theorem elucidates the correctness of our extended counting method and the effective computability of the transformed program produced by the method.

Theorem 2 *Let $Q = (G, P)$ be an adorned query, and let $Q' = (G', P')$ be the query generated by Algorithm 2 applied to Q. Then, the following properties hold*

1. P' is weakly stratified.

2. Q and Q' are equivalent.

3. If P is a Datalog programs, the computation of the fixpoint of P' terminates. □

The rewritten program consists of a set of modified rules plus a set of *additional rules*. The set of modified rules depends on the set of additional rules. The set of additional rules, in the general case, contains the three distinct sets of rules: (i) counting rules, (ii) 'cycle' rules, and (iii) rules defining the predicate f. In order to compute the set of tuples for the additional rules we need to take the following steps: (1) partition the relation $L(r)$ into ahead-arcs and back-arcs; (2) compute the facts generated by counting rules; (3) compute the facts generated by the 'cycle' rules; (4) compute the predicate 'f'.

The computation of the additional rules, as described above, presents some inefficiencies. The partition of the relation associated with the left parts is done by using an algorithm that is a variation of the depth-first search on a graph. The nodes reached during the search coincides with the nodes in the counting sets. This means that the first two steps can be computed together. The information concerning the back arcs can be 'added' to the path argument of the tuples in the counting set. This means that also the predicate 'f' is not necessary. We assume that we use a *Bushy-Depth-First fixpoint* [7] that computes the set of additional rules that, with such assumption, consists only of counting rules. In practice the algorithm put the information given by the predicate 'f' into the tuples of the counting set. Under these assumptions, the predicate 'f' in the modified rules is no longer necessary, since the navigation is performed using directly the predicate counting that now contains information on back arcs.

Consider the program of Example 5. The set of tuples in the counting set is { $o_1 : (a, \{nil\})$, $o_2 : (b, \{o_1\})$, $o_3 : (c, \{o_2\})$, $o_4 : (d, \{o_3, o_5\})$, $o_5 : (e, \{o_2, o_4\})$ }. The modified rules are:

$$r_0 : \quad sg(Y, S) \leftarrow \quad c\_sg(X, S), \ flat(X, Y).$$
$$r_1 : \quad sg(Y, S) \leftarrow \quad sg(Y1, T), \ A \in T, \ down(Y1, Y).$$

5 Reduction of Linear Programs

One of the advantages of the counting method is the ability to factorize the program, that is, to partition the recursive predicates and the rules defining them into two different recursive cliques. This implies that the new predicates and the rules defining them are simpler. For some classes of programs it is possible to factorize in a better way than the counting method do. This is the case of programs containing only 'left' and 'right linear' rules and only one recursive predicate. We show that the same optimization can be obtained by a simple reduction of the rewritten program. Such a reduction is based on the deletion of the path argument when it is not necessary.

A predicate is of the form $p(X, L)$ where L denotes the path argument and X denotes the list of the remaining arguments of p. Given a recursive rule $r : p(X, L_1) \leftarrow ..., q(Y, L_2), ...$ where q is the predicate mutually recursive with p, we say that r modifies the path argument of p if $L_1 \neq L_2$. Given a predicate p we say that the path argument of p is modified if and only if there exists a recursive rule that modifies it.

Algorithm 3 *[Program Reduction]*
input: A rewritten query Q^{ec}
output: A reduced query Q^{rec}
method: The reduced query Q^{rec} is obtained from the original program Q^{ec} by application of the following rules:
begin

1. *(deletion of argument)* the path argument of a set of mutually recursive predicates S can be deleted if for each predicate $p \in S$ no rules exist that modify the path argument of p;
2. *(deletion of predicates)* a counting predicate appearing in the body of a modified rule can be deleted if it is not connected with any predicate in the rule.

end.

Theorem 3 *Let $Q = (G, P)$ be an adorned query. Let Q' be the query obtained by application of Algorithm 2 to Q, and Q'' be the query obtained by application of Algorithm 3 to Q'. Q'', Q', and Q, are equivalent.* □

Next we show how programs that contain only left-linear and right-linear rules [19,14] can be reduced. Similar results are obtained in [13] by first applying the magic-set transformation and then factoring the rewritten program. Although their technique can be applied also to classes of non-linear programs, our technique, we believe, is simpler and can be extended to classes of non-linear programs.

A rule is said to be *right-linear* (*left-linear*) with respect to an adornment α if (1) the adornment of the recursive predicate in the body is α; (2) each variable in the head that is free (resp. bound) in α occurs in the same position in the recursive predicate in the body; (3) each free (resp. bound) variable in α occurs only once in the recursive predicate. A program is said to be *mixed linear* if it contains only right- and left-linear recursive rules and only one recursive predicate. A mixed linear program is said to be *right-linear* (resp. *left-linear*) if each rule is right- (resp. left-) linear.

When a program consists of left- and right-linear rules, the extended counting method and the reduction that follows can be combined. We show this by the use of an example.

Example 6

$$r_0 : \; p(X, Y) \leftarrow \; flat(X, Y).$$
$$r_1 : \; p(X, Y) \leftarrow \; up(X, X1), \; p(X1, Y),$$
$$r_2 : \; p(X, Y) \leftarrow \; p(X, Y), \; down(Y1, Y).$$

The rewritten program is

$$c\_0 : \; c\_p(a, []).$$
$$c\_1 : \; c\_p(X1, L) \leftarrow \; c\_p(X, L), \; up(X, X1).$$
$$r_0 : \; p(Y, L) \leftarrow \; c\_p(X, L), \; flat(X, Y).$$
$$r_3 : \; p(Y, L) \leftarrow \; p(Y1, L), \; down(Y1, Y).$$

The reduced program is

$$c\_0 : \; c\_p(a).$$
$$c\_1 : \; c\_p(X) \leftarrow \; c\_p(X), \; up(X, X1).$$
$$r_0 : \; p(Y) \leftarrow \; c\_p(X), \; flat(X, Y).$$
$$r_3 : \; p(Y) \leftarrow \; p(Y1), \; down(Y1, Y). \quad □$$

Given a mixed-linear program P, we denote by $exit(P)$, $left(P)$ and $right(P)$ respectively, the sets of exit, left-linear and right-linear rules in P. Let P^{rec} be the reduced rewritten program P_c^{rec} and P_m^{rec} denote the sets of counting rules and the set of modified rules ($P^{rec} = P_c^{rec} \cup P_m^{rec}$). Given a program P, $\bar{P}$ denotes the program obtained from P by projecting out the path argument.

Fact 1 *Let P be a mixed-linear program.* $P^{rec} = exit(\bar{P}^{rec}) \cup left(\bar{P}_c^{rec}) \cup right(\bar{P}_m^{rec})$.

If the program contains only right-linear rules then $P^{rec} = \bar{P}_c^{rec} \cup exit(\bar{P}_m^{rec})$. For right-linear programs the reduction technique give the same optimized program presented in [14]. If the program contains only left-linear rules then $P^{rec} = exit(\bar{P}_c^{rec}) \cup \bar{P}_m^{rec}$. Observe that the rewritten program so obtained is similar to that of [14], except that, in the latter, there is no counting predicate, since the query bindings are pushed directly into the exit rule (in our example the exit rule is $p(Y) \leftarrow flat(a, Y)$).

6 Conclusion

In this paper, we introduced extensions of the counting method that makes it applicable to all programs with linear rules, and to the situations where the database contains cyclic data. The extended method is amenable to reduction techniques that produce further optimizations in the case of left-linear rules, right-linear rules and a combination of the two.

Furthermore, we presented a pointer-based implementation of the method that is computationally efficient. While more extensive measurements and evaluation are planned, our preliminary experience with the Bushy-Depth-First method in the $\mathcal{LDL}$ prototype [7] suggests that this approach yields excellent performance.

Aknowledgements
The authors are grateful to Mimmo Saccà for many useful discussions.

References

[1] A.V. Aho, Hopcroft J.E., and Ullman J.D. *The Design and Analysis of Computer Algorithms*. Addison-Wesley, 1974.

[2] H. Aly and Z.M. Ozsoyoglu. Synchronized counting method. In *Proceedings of the Fifth Intern. Conference on Data Engineering*, pages 366–373, 1989.

[3] F. Bancilhon, D. Maier, Y. Sagiv, and J. Ullman. Magic sets and other strange ways to implement logic programs. In *Proceedings of the Fifth ACM Symposium on Principles of Database Systems*, pages 1–15, 1986.

[4] F. Bancilhon and R. Ramakrishnan. Performance evaluation of data intensive logic programs. In J. Minker, editor, *Foundations of Deductive Databases and Logic Programming*, pages 439–518, Morgan-Kaufman, Los Altos, CA, 1988.

[5] C. Beeri, S. Naqvi, R. Ramakrishnan, O. Shmueli, and S. Tsur. Sets and negation in a logic database language (LDL1). In *Proceedings of the Sixth ACM Symposium on Principles of Database Systems*, pages 21–37, 1987.

[6] C. Beeri and R. Ramakrishnan. On the power of magic. *Journal of Logic Programming*, 10(3 & 4):333–361, 1991.

[7] D. Chimenti, R. Gamboa, R. Krishnamurthy, S. Naqvi, T. Shalom, and C. Zaniolo. The LDL system prototype. In *IEEE Transaction on Knowledge and Data Engineering*, pages 76–90, 1990.

[8] S. Greco and C. Zaniolo. *Optimization of Linear Logic Programs Using Counting Methods*. Research Report, MCC, 1991.

[9] R. Haddad and J. Naughton. A counting algorithm for a cyclic binary query. *Journal of Computer and System Science*, 43(1):145–169, 1991.

[10] J. Lloyd. *Foundations of Logic Programming*. Springer-Verlag, New York, 2nd edition, 1987.

[11] A. Marchetti-Spaccamela, A. Pelaggi, and D. Saccà. Comparison of methods for logic query implementation. *Journal of Logic Programming*, 10(3 & 4):333–361, 1991.

[12] S. Naqvi and S Tsur. *A Logic Language for Data and Knowledge Bases*. Computer Science Press, New York, 1989.

[13] J.F. Naughton, R. Ramakrisnhan, Y. Sagiv, and J.D. Ullman. Argument reduction by factoring. In *Proceedings of the 15th Conference on Very Large Data Bases*, pages 173–182, 1989.

[14] J.F. Naughton, R. Ramakrisnhan, Y. Sagiv, and J.D. Ullman. Efficient evaluation of right-, left-, and multi-linear rules. In *Proceedings of the 1988 ACM SIGMOD Int. Conf. on Management of Data*, pages 235–242, 1989.

[15] D. Saccà and C. Zaniolo. The generalized counting method of recursive logic queries for databases. *Theoretical Computer Science*, 187–220, 1988.

[16] D. Saccà and C. Zaniolo. Magic counting methods. In *Proceedings of the 1987 ACM SIGMOD Int. Conf. on Management of Data*, pages 49–59, 1987.

[17] D. Saccà and C. Zaniolo. On the implementation of a simple class of logic queries for databases. In *Proceedings of the Fifth ACM Symposium on Principles of Database Systems*, pages 16–23, 1986.

[18] R Tarjan. Depth first search of linear graphs algorithms. *SIAM J. Computing*, 1(2):146–160, 1972.

[19] J. Ullman. *Principles of Data and Knowledge-Base Systems*. Volume 2, Computer Science Press, New York, 1989.

[20] J. Ullman. *Principles of Data and Knowledge-Base Systems*. Volume 1, Computer Science Press, New York, 1988.

[21] C. Zaniolo. Design and implementation of a logic based language for data intensive applications. In *Proc. of the Intern. Conf. on Logic Programming*, 1988.

[22] C. Zaniolo. Object identity and inheritance in deductive databases: an evolutionary approach. In *Proc. 1st Int. Conf. on Deductive and Object-Oriented Databases*, 1989.

Generalized Bottom-Up Query Evaluation

Stefan Brass   Udo W. Lipeck

Institut für Informatik, Universität Hannover
Lange Laube 22, D-W 3000 Hannover 1, Fed. Rep. Germany
e-mail: (sb|ul)@informatik.uni-hannover[.dbp].de

Abstract

Our goal is to generalize the well known bottom-up, set-oriented query evaluation for deductive databases in two aspects:

First, we consider arbitrary clauses as rules in the database, not only Horn clauses or clauses with stratified negation. This allows to represent disjunctive information, in the database as well as in answers to queries. We utilize NF^2 relations for modelling sets of disjunctive facts and operations of the corresponding relational algebra for computing consequences and answers. Thus our algorithm should be of practical importance for applying database techniques in generalized deductions.

Second, we parameterize the implicit database completion which underlies query evaluation. The classical rule for Horn clause databases, which only assumes the negation of facts not implied by the database, is not applicable to disjunctive databases. Moreover, the choice of completion often depends on the intended application. Therefore we allow the specification of arbitrary clauses as defaults, and we extend our algorithm to consider such general defaults.

1 Introduction

A deductive database stores formulae which describe facts corresponding to conventional database information, rules for deducing further information, and indefinite information [HPRV89]. Usually, each formula must be an implication with an atom in its head [Llo87], so that disjunctions and purely negative clauses are excluded. But the need for such extensions has been widely accepted, see, e.g., [BH86, RT88, Prz88, RLM89].

An example where disjunctive information arises in practice are rules for diagnosing faults in a computer system, e.g.: "If in some computer X the fan is not running and the power-on light is not burning, then the fuses or the power-supply are faulty."

$$faulty(X, fuses) \vee faulty(X, power\_supply) \leftarrow$$
$$symptom(X, fan\_not\_running) \wedge symptom(X, light\_not\_burning).$$

Of course, one could use a conventional theorem prover to answer queries in such a generalized setting, but probably the performance would not be acceptable in the database context, where large sets of facts have to be handled. Instead, we should try to generalize bottom-up query evaluation, which has the inherent advantage of utilizing powerful database operations and offering many possibilities for further optimization [BR86, Ull89, Bry90].

The first goal of this paper is to demonstrate that *deduction on general clauses can be done in a set-oriented manner applying database techniques.* The style of the computation is very much like the usual bottom-up (semi-naive) evaluation, we only use NF^2-relations to represent sets of disjunctions of facts instead of sets of facts (relations). In principle, everything could be flattened if we had to use a conventional relational database.

Such a generalization with respect to the rules requires a generalization of the underlying database completion. It is well known that it is not sufficient to consider only proper logical consequences of the database state. Usually one assumes the negation of every fact not implied by the database state, but this simple mechanism is not applicable to disjunctive databases, since it leads to inconsistencies [Rei78].

Many completions have been proposed by the deductive database, logic programming, and artificial intelligence communities. No consensus has been reached which is the right one and it seems that this question can only be answered given a particular application. Therefore, in our view, the database completion should be subject of the database design task, and not be given beforehand by the system. This feature will gain particular importance for hierarchical object-oriented systems: there, user-specified properties of object classes act as defaults to be inherited by subclasses, unless overridden by more specific knowledge.

To support such a generalization, we have defined in [BL89] a parameterized CWA, which can be configured by specifying a set of "defaults". It subsumes quite a lot of known database completions, e.g. the CWA versions of [Rei78, Min82, YH85, GP86] and also different versions of circumscription [McC80, MP85, McC86]. So there is a wide range of specifiable database completions, what can also be seen from our results on basic properties of different classes of completions [Bra90]. A further generalization to hierarchical or prioritized completions was already given in [BL91] (in the context of object-oriented specifications), and will briefly be considered in this paper, too.

It is this parameterized CWA that we will use as the "declarative semantics" to measure the correctness of our query evaluation algorithm. So the second goal of this paper is to demonstrate that *even with a quite general database completion, set-oriented computations can still be applied effectively.*

Several other query-evaluation algorithms for non-standard completions have been developed [BS85, YH85, GP86, Prz89, Gin89], but all of them are applicable only to more specific completions, return only single answers at a time, and most have serious efficiency problems (e.g., computing the entire completed database state).

Our paper is structured as follows: In section 2 we will define the basic concepts needed in the sequel and review our parameterized CWA. In section 3, we describe a generalization of bottom-up query evaluation, such that general clauses can be handled. The result of this computation is the input for section 4, where the evaluation of the defaults is explained. An important special case of this will be the implicit assumption of negations, like in stratified databases. Finally, in section 5 we give a short summary of our results and discuss questions of optimization.

2   Fundamental Notions

The application area of a knowledge base determines a signature Σ which consists of a finite set S of sorts (such as *part*), a finite set Ω of sorted constants (e.g., *power_supply: part*), and a finite set Π of sorted predicates (e.g., *faulty(computer, part)*). We will assume the unique names axioms (UNA) and the domain closure axioms (DCA) which require that each element in the carrier set of a sort (e.g., each computer part) can be named injectively by a constant of this sort. Although these assumptions are restrictive, they are quite usual and very useful.

Given such a signature, there are three kinds of inputs to query evaluation: the database state, the defaults, and a query. Let us consider them one after the other.

Definition 2.1 (Database States): *The state of a deductive database is a finite and consistent set Φ of Σ-clauses which are safe, i.e. each variable appearing in a positive literal also appears in a negative one.*

Clauses are disjunctions of positive and negative literals, but we allow rules to be written in various equivalent ways. For example, our knowledge about a faulty computer could be (with abbreviated parts and symptoms):

$$faulty(X, p_1) \vee faulty(X, p_2) \leftarrow symptom(X, s_1) \wedge symptom(X, s_2).$$
$$\neg faulty(X, p_3) \leftarrow symptom(X, s_3).$$
$$symptom(c_1, s_1) \vee error(e_1).$$
$$symptom(c_1, s_2).$$
$$symptom(c_1, s_3).$$
$$faulty(c_1, p_4).$$
$$consists\_of(c_1, p_1).$$
$$\ldots$$
$$consists\_of(c_1, p_5).$$

Our query evaluation algorithm will assume that each rule is given as an implication with a disjunction in the head and a conjunction in the body, both containing positive literals only. So the second rule will have to be rewritten to

$$\leftarrow faulty(X, p_3) \wedge symptom(X, s_3).$$

Obviously, this kind of normalization should be done invisible to the user. In contrast to other completions, our parameterized CWA makes no distinction between logically equivalent formulations. Any such difference would be an extralogical information, which should be specified explicitly and separately from the database state, i.e. typically as a parameter to the completion.

As usual in deductive databases, we also distinguish between a large amount of facts (which can now be also disjunctive facts, i.e. positive ground clauses instead of positive ground literals) and comparatively few deduction rules (any other clause). In the example, only the first two clauses are deduction rules. The facts and disjunctive facts will be represented in the database, while the rules determine the database queries used in deductions. Deduced facts will also be entered into the database, but only temporarily. The safety condition guarantees that we do not have to represent variables in the database.

The task of defaults is now to formalize the implicit assumptions of query evaluation:

Definition 2.2 (Defaults): *A default is a safe Σ-clause δ.*

Typically, negations are assumed by default as long as nothing to the contrary is known. This would be specified in our approach by, e.g.

$$\neg faulty(X, Y).$$

If this particular default seems too optimistic, it can be modified, since in our approach the defaults are subject to specification and not built-in as in most other approaches. We will also use the default $\neg error(X)$, but we will not assume negations of the other predicates (to simplify the example). Of course, our approach is not limited to negations, so a more refined default could be added:

$$faulty(X, p_5) \leftarrow symptom(X, s_5)$$

("symptom s_5 usually indicates that part p_5 is faulty"). The difference to a deduction rule is that we do not run into an inconsistency whenever we observe symptom s_5 without part p_5 being faulty.

If we find such a counterexample, the default rule is not totally abandoned. Instead, the units for assumption or rejection of defaults are their ground instances, or, alternatively, disjunctions of such ground instances. In the example of negations like $\neg p(x)$ as default rules, the usage of ground literals like $\neg p(a)$ as instances would result in the GCWA completion [Min82], while negative ground clauses are taken for the CWA of [YH85], which is equivalent to predicate circumscription [McC80] (with DCA and UNA). Note that there was no difference between these completions for Horn clause databases. One might even consider other such "instantiation mappings" (like "natural consequences" as recently introduced in [Rya91]), but for the sake of simplicity we will only look at these two cases which are sufficient to cover all the special completions mentioned in the introduction.

Definition 2.3 (Default Instances): *Let Δ be a set of defaults. Then we denote the set of ground instances of clauses from Δ by Δ^g, and the set of disjunctions of ground instances by $\Delta^\vee$. We will write Δ^* for one of these two alternatives.*

Now we would like to assume a maximal set of default instances such that the consistency is not destroyed.

Definition 2.4 (Maximal Extension): *Let Δ^* be a set of default instances. A subset $E \subseteq \Delta^*$ is a maximal Δ^*-extension of a state Φ iff*
- *$\Phi \cup E$ is consistent, and*
- *$\Phi \cup E \cup \{\delta\}$ is inconsistent for each $\delta \in \Delta^* - E$.*

In our running example, one maximal extension would be (when using $\Delta^* = \Delta^g$):

$$E_1 := \{ \neg faulty(c_1, p_1), \ \neg faulty(c_1, p_2), \ \neg faulty(c_1, p_3), \ \neg faulty(c_1, p_5),$$
$$faulty(c_1, p_5) \leftarrow symptom(c_1, s_5)\}.$$

There are two other maximal extensions E_2 and E_3 containing $\neg error(e_1)$ instead of $\neg faulty(c_1, p_1)$ resp. $\neg faulty(c_1, p_2)$. If we had used $\Delta^\vee$, we would get supersets of E_1, E_2 and E_3 as maximal extensions, each containing $\neg faulty(c_1, p_1) \vee \neg faulty(c_1, p_2)$.

92

Now the completion, which we call parameterized closed world assumption (CWA), takes the intersection of all maximal extensions:

Definition 2.5 (CWA): *The completed database state determined by Δ^* is*

$$cwa_{\Delta^*}(\Phi) := \Phi \cup \{\delta \in \Delta^* \mid \delta \in E \text{ for each maximal } \Delta^*\text{-extension } E \text{ of } \Phi\}.$$

So, in the example, we can assume neither $\neg faulty(c_1, p_1)$ nor $\neg faulty(c_1, p_2)$ but we might assume their disjunction, depending on the instantiation mechanism. A more complete treatment of the parameterized CWA and its special cases is contained in [BL89].

Our query evaluation algorithm will require that the default rules Δ are represented by special rules within the database state: For each default $\delta \in \Delta$, we introduce a new predicate $notappl_\delta$ ("δ is not applicable") and insert the rule

$$notappl_\delta(x_1, \ldots, x_n) \leftarrow \neg(\delta)$$

(where $x_1, \ldots, x_n$ are the free variables of δ). This is some sort of default normalization: if we consider only defaults of the form $\neg notappl_\delta(x_1, \ldots, x_n)$, we can get the original defaults by contraposition. In the example, three such rules will be introduced:

$$notappl_{\neg faulty}(X, Y) \leftarrow faulty(X, Y),$$
$$notappl_{\neg error}(X) \leftarrow error(X),$$
$$notappl_{p_5 \leftarrow s_5}(X) \vee faulty(X, p_5) \leftarrow symptom(X, s_5).$$

Of course, this should again be invisible to the user.

Now we know the semantics of a database state as defined by the CWA, so that we can proceed to answer queries.

Definition 2.6 (Query): *A query ψ is any Σ-formula of the form*

$$\exists y_1 \ldots \exists y_m \, \psi_1 \vee \cdots \vee \psi_l$$

where the ψ_i are conjunctions of literals (positive or negative) such that $\neg \psi_i$ is a safe clause (i.e. each variable occurring in a negative literal of ψ_i must also occur in a positive literal). The free variables of ψ are called the result variables of ψ.

An answer defines values (constants) for the result variables, such that the resulting formula follows from the completed state. But in the context of incomplete information, we need the slightly more elaborate concept of disjunctive answers (see [Rei78]):

Definition 2.7 (Correct Answer): *Given state Φ, a correct answer to a query ψ is a nonempty set $\Theta = \{\theta_1, \ldots, \theta_n\}$ with substitutions of Σ-constants for the result variables of ψ, such that $cwa_{\Delta^*}(\Phi) \vdash \psi\theta_1 \vee \cdots \vee \psi\theta_n$.*

An answer is minimal if no proper subset is a correct answer, either. It is definite if it consists of a single element.

Again, we apply a normalization invisible to the user. Given a query as in definition 2.6 with result variables $x_1, \ldots, x_n$, we introduce a new predicate *answer* and enter the rules

$$answer(x_1, \ldots, x_n) \leftarrow \psi_i$$

into the database state. So we have to consider only queries of the form $answer(x_1, \ldots, x_n)$ (this transformation does not change the notion of correct answers).

Extension to Priorities and Modeltheoretic Characterization

The parameterized CWA can be generalized further to allow the specification of priorities between conflicting defaults. With this extension, prioritized circumscription and the "perfect model semantics" of [Prz88] become special cases of our approach.

The priorities are specified by defining a level $\lambda(\delta) \in \mathbb{N}$ for each default $\delta \in \Delta$. Then δ_1 will be preferred over δ_2 if $\lambda(\delta_1) < \lambda(\delta_2)$. The level of a default is inherited to its instances (disjunctions get the maximal level of their components). The prioritized CWA differs from the parametrized CWA only in a slight change of the maximal extensions notion:

Definition 2.8 (Prioritized Maximal Extension): *Let Δ^* be a set of default instances and λ be a level mapping for Δ. A subset $E \subseteq \Delta^*$ is a maximal (Δ^*, λ)-extension of a state Φ iff*

- *$\Phi \cup E$ is consistent, and*
- *$\Phi \cup \{\delta' \in E \mid \lambda(\delta') \leq \lambda(\delta)\} \cup \{\delta\}$ is inconsistent for each $\delta \in \Delta^* - E$.*

The assumed defaults can also be characterized by means of minimal Herbrand models, where a model is preferred if it satisfies more default instances, i.e.:

$$\gamma_1 \prec \gamma_2 \ :\Longleftrightarrow \ \{\delta \in \Delta^* \mid \gamma_1 \models \delta\} \supset \{\delta \in \Delta^* \mid \gamma_2 \models \delta\}.$$

For example, in the typical case that Δ^* is the set of negative ground literals, this would result in the usual ordering on the Herbrand models by $\gamma_1 \subset \gamma_2$. The relation of the parameterized CWA to minimal Herbrand models has been studied in much more detail in [BL89]. With priorities, the following ordering corresponds to the CWA:

Definition 2.9 (order on models): *Let Δ^* be a set of default instances and λ be a level mapping for Δ. For each two Herbrand interpretations γ_1 and γ_2 let*

$$\gamma_1 \prec \gamma_2 \iff \text{there is an } i \in \mathbb{N} \text{ such that}$$
$$\{\delta \in \Delta^* \mid \lambda(\delta) < i, \ \gamma_1 \models \delta\} = \{\delta \in \Delta^* \mid \lambda(\delta) < i, \ \gamma_2 \models \delta\} \text{ and}$$
$$\{\delta \in \Delta^* \mid \lambda(\delta) = i, \ \gamma_1 \models \delta\} \supset \{\delta \in \Delta^* \mid \lambda(\delta) = i, \ \gamma_2 \models \delta\}.$$

The CWA assumes exactly those defaults which are true in all $\prec$-minimal Herbrand models of Φ, which therefore are models of the CWA. If we use the disjunctive default instances $\Delta^\vee$, the opposite is true as well:

Theorem 2.10: *For each Δ, λ and Φ, the following holds:*

$$cwa_{(\Delta^*, \lambda)}(\Phi) = \Phi \cup \{\delta \in \Delta^* \mid \text{for each } \prec\text{-minimal Herbrand model } \gamma \text{ of } \Phi \colon \gamma \models \delta\}.$$

For $\Delta^* = \Delta^\vee$, Herbrand models of $cwa_{(\Delta^*, \lambda)}(\Phi)$ are $\prec$-minimal models of Φ.

3 First Generalization: Arbitrary Clauses

Normal bottom-up query evaluation can only be applied to database states consisting of Horn clauses. In this section we will see how it can be generalized to arbitrary sets of clauses. As noted in the introduction, this is necessary for representing disjunctive information and general defaults.

The idea of bottom-up query evaluation is to compute iteratively the set $\hat{\Phi}$ of "consequences", i.e. of facts implied by the database state as the fixpoint of the "direct derivation" operator. This is done by successively entering the heads of those rule instances into $\hat{\Phi}$ whose body literals are already contained in it, until $\hat{\Phi}$ cannot be expanded further.

The generalization which makes this scheme applicable to arbitrary clauses, is to work with disjunctions of facts (positive ground clauses) instead of simple facts. This leads to "positive hyperresolution" which is known in the theorem proving field (e.g: [CL73]). Here $\hat{\Phi}$ is a set of positive ground clauses implied by the database state. This set is initialized with all facts or disjunctions of facts contained in the database state Φ. Now a rule instance

$$p_1 \vee \cdots \vee p_m \leftarrow q_1 \wedge \cdots \wedge q_n$$

can be applied if its body literals are contained in $\hat{\Phi}$ with some disjunctive context:

$$q_i \vee r_{i,1} \vee \cdots \vee r_{i,k_i} \in \hat{\Phi}.$$

Then the application of this rule instance generates the disjunction of the literals in the head of the clause concatenated with all the disjunctive contexts:

$$p_1 \vee \cdots \vee p_m \vee r_{1,1} \vee \cdots \vee r_{1,k_1} \vee \cdots \vee r_{n,1} \vee \cdots \vee r_{n,k_n}.$$

Of course, duplicate literals have to be eliminated. If the rule is a Horn clause ($m = 1$) and we apply it to a set of facts ($k_i = 0$), then it will produce a fact (p_1). Another special case is the application of a negative clause ($m = 0$), which can help to reduce the number of disjuncts in a clause from $\hat{\Phi}$.

Usually, positive hyperresolution contains an optimization to reduce the number of possible rule applications: One defines an ordering on the predicates, and allows to use a disjunction $q_i \vee r_{i,1} \vee \cdots \vee r_{i,k_i}$ from $\hat{\Phi}$ only if the predicate of q_i is minimal in this clause. This distinguishes facts which can be matched to a body literal from the disjunctive context.

Positive hyperresolution is known to be complete with respect to the derivation of the empty clause [CL73] (with an arbitrary partial ordering of the predicates), but we will be interested in the derivation of disjunctions containing facts with the *answer-* and *notappl$_\delta$*-predicates only (see below). It turns out that positive hyperresolution satisfies this modified completeness requirement, too (if we slightly restrict the predicate ordering):

Lemma 3.1: *Let Φ be a database state and $\hat{\varphi}$ be a minimal positive ground clause implied by Φ (i.e. no subdisjunction is implied by Φ). If all the predicates occurring in $\hat{\varphi}$ are maximal with respect to the ordering of the predicates, then $\hat{\varphi}$ is derivable from Φ by positive hyperresolution.*

Implementation with Database Techniques

Of course, we can only utilize positive hyperresolution on large sets of facts if we can implement it with set-oriented database techniques similar to usual bottom-up evaluation.

Since the disjunctions can consist of facts with different predicates and we want to avoid complicated unions we propose to store all the initial disjunctive facts (positive ground clauses) and their consequences in a single database relation *CONSEQ*. The most direct representation is a nested (NF^2) relation, where a tuple in $CONSEQ$ corresponds to a disjunction, and is itself a relation OR consisting of tuples corresponding to the single facts inside the disjunction. These subtuples have the following attributes:

- $pred$, the predicate of this fact.
- $arg1, \ldots, argN$ contain the arguments of this fact. Since we have to accomodate facts with different numbers of arguments, N must be the maximal number of arguments occurring in the database. Unused $argI$ attributes are set to a null value.
- res ("resolvable") is a flag which is T (true) for those facts which can be matched to a body literal in a rule, i.e. which have a minimal predicate in their disjunction.

So we would represent the facts of the computer faults example as follows (we assume the ordering $symptom < faulty < error$):

CONSEQ			
OR			
pred	arg1	arg2	res
symptom	c_1	s_1	T
error	e_1		F
symptom	c_1	s_2	T
symptom	c_1	s_3	T
faulty	c_1	p_4	T
consists_of	c_1	p_1	T
$\ldots$			
consists_of	c_1	p_5	T

Now let us see how the resolution steps can be done on this representation. As in the Horn case, we transform each rule into a database query on $CONSEQ$, producing the new tuples to be entered into the relation.

We will explain the method by means of the first rule of the example from section 2:

$$faulty(X, p_1) \lor faulty(X, p_2) \leftarrow symptom(X, s_1) \land symptom(X, s_2).$$

The query corresponding to this rule will be represented in the NF^2-relational algebra of [SS86]. Although we introduce it in several steps, all subexpressions can be composed into a single query such that no additional temporary relations are needed.

The query is generated in the following way: First we define subexpressions corresponding to the two body literals. The goal is to select those disjunctions which contain a resolvable literal matching the body literal and to restructure the clause into this literal and its disjunctive context. Then we join them over the common variables as usual in bottom-up query evaluation. Finally, we compute the resulting disjunction.

Consider the subquery for the first body literal $symptom(X, s_1)$: The first step is to select those literals from each disjunction which can be used to match it, i.e. which have the predicate symbol '$symptom$', the resolvability flag 'T', and 's_1' as second argument:

$$L1' \equiv \pi \left[\sigma[pred = \text{'}symptom\text{'} \land res = \text{'}T\text{'} \land arg2 = \text{'}s_1\text{'}](OR): MATCH, \ OR \right](CONSEQ).$$

Obviously, we are only interested in disjunctions where the set of matching literals is non-empty:

$$L1'' \equiv \sigma[MATCH \neq \emptyset](L1').$$

Applied to the above example, this results in

L1''							
MATCH				OR			
pred	arg1	arg2	res	pred	arg1	arg2	res
symptom	c_1	s_1	T	symptom	c_1	s_1	T
				error	e_1		F

Next, we unnest the set of matching literals (so we get one tuple for each matching literal) and eliminate the matching literal from the context:

$$L1''' \equiv \mu[MATCH: pred1, arg11, arg12, res1](L1''),$$
$$L1 \equiv \pi\left[pred1, arg11, arg12, \sigma[pred \neq pred1 \vee arg1 \neq arg11 \vee arg2 \neq arg12](OR): C1\right](L1''').$$

This gives us the matching literals together with their disjunctive context:

L1						
pred1	arg11	arg12	C1			
			pred	arg1	arg2	res
symptom	c_1	s_1	error	e_1		F

We do the same for the second body literal, and then join the subqueries of the body literals with respect to the common variables (in this case, only X):

$$BODY \equiv L1 \underset{arg11=arg21}{\bowtie} L2.$$

Obviously, we should apply semi-naive techniques and split this query into two and use only disjunctions computed in the last iteration in $L1$ or in $L2$.

Now we build the derived disjunctions from the two head literals and the contexts of the body literals:

$$DER' \equiv \pi\left[\{('faulty', arg11, 'p_1', '-'), ('faulty', arg11, 'p_2', '-')\} \cup C1 \cup C2: OR\right](BODY).$$

Finally, we have to set the res-flag to the right value:

$$DER \equiv \pi[FLIT \cup TLIT: OR](DER')$$

with

$$FLIT \equiv \pi[pred, arg1, arg2, 'F'](NONMIN),$$
$$TLIT \equiv \pi[pred, arg1, arg2, 'T'](OR - NONMIN),$$
$$NONMIN \equiv \pi[pred, arg1, arg2, res]\left(OR \underset{pred > pred'}{\bowtie} \pi[pred: pred'](OR)\right).$$

Applied to the above example, the query will return

DER			
OR			
pred	arg1	arg2	res
faulty	c_1	p_1	T
faulty	c_1	p_2	T
error	e_1		F

These derived clauses should be inserted into $CONSEQ$ if they are not already contained in it. We should also consider the case that a subdisjunction is already contained in $CONSEQ$, since in this case the new clause is obviously superfluous. So, in fact we insert the following tuples into $CONSEQ$:

$$NEW \quad \equiv \quad DER - \pi[OR](DER \underset{OR \supseteq OR'}{\bowtie} \pi[OR\!: OR'](CONSEQ)),$$

$$CONSEQ := CONSEQ \cup NEW.$$

We could also eliminate disjunctions from $CONSEQ$ which are no longer minimal (because NEW contains a subdisjunction), but probably it is not worth the effort (except at the very end to guarantee the minimality requirement).

The computation continues until NEW is empty.

4 Second Generalization: Arbitrary Defaults

In the last section, we have shown how logical consequences of the database state can be computed by a set-oriented implementation of positive hyperresolution. But this is normally not enough for answering queries, since at least negations should be assumed by default (corresponding to minimal or perfect models etc.), which are a special case of our CWA as introduced in section 2.

Fortunately, the work done in the last section was not superfluous. As an example, let us ask the diagnostic database which parts of our computer c_1 are not faulty:

$$answer(X) \leftarrow consists\_of(c_1, X) \wedge \neg faulty(c_1, X).$$

One of the clauses derived by the method of the last section is $answer(p_3)$. Therefore p_3 is an answer to the query, which can be derived without assuming any default. Another computed clause is

$$answer(p_5) \vee notappl_{\neg faulty}(p_5).$$

If we knew that the default $\neg faulty(p_5)$ is applicable, i.e. $\neg notappl_{\neg faulty}(p_5)$, then the answer p_5 would be correct (with respect to the CWA).

In general, we have to look at the disjunctions of the form

$$answer(\bar{t}_1) \vee \cdots \vee answer(\bar{t}_n) \vee notappl[\delta_1] \vee \cdots \vee notappl[\delta_m]$$

(we write $notappl[\delta_i]$ for the $notappl$ literal corresponding to the default instance δ_i). If Φ implies this disjunction, Φ must also imply

$$answer(\bar{t}_1) \vee \cdots \vee answer(\bar{t}_n) \vee \neg\delta_1 \vee \cdots \vee \neg\delta_m$$

(since $notappl[\delta] \leftarrow \neg\delta$ is the only way to derive $notappl[\delta]$). But this means that

$$\Phi \cup \{\delta_1, \ldots, \delta_m\} \vdash answer(\bar{t}_1) \vee \cdots \vee answer(\bar{t}_n).$$

So the answer $answer(\bar{t}_1) \vee \cdots \vee answer(\bar{t}_n)$ would be correct if $\{\delta_1, \ldots, \delta_m\} \subseteq cwa_{\Delta^*}(\Phi)$, i.e. $\chi := \delta_1 \wedge \cdots \wedge \delta_m$ "justifies" this answer:

Definition 4.1 (Justification): *Let χ be a formula which is equivalent to a conjunction of default instances from Δ^* such that $\Phi \cup \{\chi\} \vdash \psi$ and $\Phi \cup \{\chi\}$ is consistent. Then χ is a justification for ψ.*

Lemma 4.2: *A formula ψ has a justification χ (wrt Φ and Δ^*) iff there is a maximal Δ^*-extension E of Φ such that $\Phi \cup E \vdash \psi$.*

We can easily select the answers which have a justification from the relation $CONSEQ$ computed in the last section (assuming a single predicate $notappl$):

$$JUST\_ANS' \equiv \sigma\big[\sigma[pred \neq \text{'answer'} \land pred \neq \text{'notappl'}](OR) = \emptyset\big](CONSEQ),$$
$$JUST\_ANS'' \equiv \sigma[ANS \neq \emptyset](\pi[\sigma[pred = \text{'answer'}](OR): ANS, \, OR](JUST\_ANS')),$$
$$JUST\_ANS \equiv \pi\big[ANS, \, \sigma[pred = \text{'notappl'}](OR): JUST\big](JUST\_ANS'').$$

JUST_ANS			JUST_ANS	
ANS	**JUST**		**ANS**	**JUST**
$answer(\bar{t}_1)$	$notappl[\delta_1]$		$answer(p_1)$	$notappl_{\neg faulty}(c_1, p_1)$
$\vdots$	$\vdots$		$answer(p_2)$	$notappl_{\neg faulty}(c_1, p_2)$
$answer(\bar{t}_n)$	$notappl[\delta_m]$		$answer(p_3)$	$\emptyset$
$\vdots$	$\vdots$		$answer(p_5)$	$notappl_{\neg faulty}(c_1, p_5)$

The completeness property of Lemma 3.1 guarantees that all justifications consisting of defaults from Δ^g are represented in $JUST\_ANS$ (for $\Delta^* = \Delta^\vee$ see below):

Lemma 4.3: *For $\delta_1, \ldots, \delta_m \in \Delta^g$ and $\bar{t}_1, \ldots, \bar{t}_n$: $\chi := \delta_1 \land \cdots \land \delta_m$ is a justification for $answer(\bar{t}_1) \lor \cdots \lor answer(\bar{t}_n)$ iff there are $1 \leq i_1, \ldots, i_{m'} \leq m$ and $1 \leq j_1, \ldots, j_{n'} \leq n$ with $(\{answer(\bar{t}_{j_1}), \ldots, answer(\bar{t}_{j_{n'}})\}, \{notappl[\delta_{i_1}], \ldots, notappl[\delta_{i_{m'}}]\}) \in JUST\_ANS$.*

Now we have to check for each potential answer (represented by a tuple in $JUST\_ANS$) whether $\{\delta_1, \ldots, \delta_m\} \in cwa_{\Delta^*}(\Phi)$. If it is, $\chi := \delta_1 \land \cdots \land \delta_m$ will be called acceptable:

Definition 4.4 (Acceptable Justification): *Let χ be a justification for ψ. We call χ acceptable (with respect to Δ^* and Φ) iff $cwa_{\Delta^*}(\Phi) \vdash \chi$.*

So a justification χ is acceptable iff it is true in all maximal extensions, i.e. its negation $\neg\chi$ does not hold in any. From lemma 4.2 we conclude that no justification for $\neg\chi$ must exist:

Theorem 4.5: *A justification χ is acceptable iff there is no justification χ' for $\neg\chi$.*

So, we have to look for contradicting justifications. The necessary information is also contained in the relation $CONSEQ$ computed in the last section, namely in the disjunctions of the form $notappl[\delta'_1] \lor \cdots \lor notappl[\delta'_l]$ (which can be read as $\neg\delta'_1 \lor \cdots \lor \neg\delta'_l$):

Corollary 4.6: *A justification $\chi \equiv \delta_1 \land \cdots \land \delta_m$ is acceptable iff there is no minimal disjunction of the form $\neg\delta_{i_1} \lor \cdots \lor \neg\delta_{i_{m'}} \lor \neg\delta'_1 \lor \cdots \lor \neg\delta'_k$ ($m' > 0$, $k \geq 0$) implied by Φ.*

All minimal disjunctions of the latter form can be extracted from $CONSEQ$ by means of the following query:

$$CONFLICT := \sigma\big[\sigma[pred \neq \text{'notappl'}](OR) = \emptyset\big](CONSEQ).$$

CONFLICT
OR
$notappl[\delta_1']$
$\vdots$
$notappl[\delta_l']$

$\vdots$

CONFLICT
OR
$notappl_{\neg faulty}(c_1, p_1)$
$notappl_{\neg faulty}(c_1, p_2)$
$notappl_{\neg error}(e_1)$
$notappl_{\neg faulty}(c_1, p_4)$

Lemma 4.7: For each $\delta_1', \ldots, \delta_l' \in \Delta^g$: $\Phi \vdash \neg \delta_1' \vee \cdots \vee \neg \delta_l'$ iff there are $1 \leq i_1, \ldots, i_{l'} \leq l$ such that $\{notappl[\delta_{i_1}], \ldots, notappl[\delta_{i_{l'}}]\} \in CONFLICT$.

Now by corollary 4.6 we only have to eliminate justifications which overlap with clauses in $CONFLICT$:

$$ANSWERS' \equiv JUST\_ANS \underset{JUST \cap OR \neq \emptyset}{\bowtie} CONFLICT,$$

$$ANSWERS \equiv \pi[ANS](JUST\_ANS - \pi[ANS, JUST](ANSWERS')).$$

So in the example, we get $answer(p_3)$ and $answer(p_5)$ as only correct answers (in correspondence with the GCWA), since the justifications for $answer(p_1)$ and $answer(p_2)$ overlap with $CONFLICT$-clauses.

Extension to Disjunctive Default Instances

If we consider $\Delta^* := \Delta^\vee$ (instead of Δ^g), $answer(p_1) \vee answer(p_2)$ would be an additional answer. But first note that the answers computed in the last subsection remain correct. In fact, the maximal extensions wrt Δ^g and wrt $\Delta^\vee$ are not very different (because of $\Delta^g \subseteq \Delta^\vee$ and the maximality condition):

Lemma 4.8: If E is a $\Delta^\vee$-maximal extension, then $E \cap \Delta^g$ is a Δ^g-maximal extension. If E is a Δ^g maximal extension, then $\{\delta \in \Delta^\vee \mid E \vdash \delta\}$ is a $\Delta^\vee$-maximal extension.

Lemma 4.9: $cwa_{\Delta^g}(\Phi) \subseteq cwa_{\Delta^\vee}(\Phi)$.

It will help to view a justification χ as describing a nonempty set of maximal extensions:

Definition 4.10 (Extensions Covered by a Justification): The set of maximal extensions covered by a justification χ is

$$|\chi| := \{E \mid E \text{ is maximal extension of } \Phi, \Phi \cup E \vdash \chi\}.$$

If χ is a justification for ψ, then ψ is true in all maximal extensions of $|\chi|$. If χ' is a justification for $\neg\chi$, then $|\chi|$ and $|\chi'|$ are disjoint. We are interested in justifications χ for ψ such that there is no contradiction justification, because then $|\chi|$ covers all maximal extensions. So if χ is represented as $\delta_1 \wedge \cdots \wedge \delta_m$ with $\delta_i \in \Delta^*$, then $\{\delta_1, \ldots, \delta_m\}$ is contained in every maximal extension and thus in the completed database state.

So all the potential answers from $JUST\_ANS$ which were rejected had justifications not covering all maximal extensions. Since we are about to give them a second chance, et us compute which answers are blocked by which contradicting justifications:

$$BLOCKED\_BY' \equiv JUST\_ANS \underset{JUST \cap OR \neq \emptyset}{\bowtie} CONFLICT,$$
$$BLOCKED\_BY'' \equiv \pi[ANS, JUST, OR - JUST: AND](BLOCKED\_BY'),$$
$$BLOCKED\_BY := \pi[ANS, OR](\nu[AND: OR](BLOCKED\_BY'')).$$

BLOCKED_BY		
ANS	OR	
	AND	
$answer(\bar{t}_1)$	$notappl[\delta'_{1,1}]$	
$\vdots$	$\vdots$	
$answer(\bar{t}_n)$	$notappl[\delta'_{1,l_1}]$	
	$\vdots$	
	$notappl[\delta'_{k,1}]$	
	$\vdots$	
	$notappl[\delta'_{k,l_k}]$	

BLOCKED_BY		
ANS	OR	
	AND	
$answer(p_1)$	$notappl_{\neg faulty}(c_1, p_2)$	
	$notappl_{\neg error}(e_1)$	
$answer(p_2)$	$notappl_{\neg faulty}(c_1, p_1)$	
	$notappl_{\neg error}(e_1)$	

The set of contradicting justifications is in fact complete, i.e. covering all maximal extensions not covered by the justification for the answer stored in $JUST\_ANS$ (because of Lemma 4.8 we do not have to distinguish between extensions wrt $\Delta^\vee$ and wrt Δ^g):

Lemma 4.11: *For each such tuple in $BLOCKED\_BY$, $answer(\bar{t}_1) \vee answer(\bar{t}_n)$ is true in all maximal extensions not covered by $|\delta'_{1,1} \wedge \cdots \wedge \delta'_{1,l_1}| \cup \cdots \cup |\delta'_{k,1} \wedge \cdots \wedge \delta'_{k,l_k}|$.*

Given this, the disjunction of two such answers is obviously true in all maximal extensions not covered by the conjunction of the contradicting justifications. The important point is that with $\Delta^\vee$, we can construct the disjunction of the justifications for the two answers, while this was not possible with Δ^g.

So the algorithm works as follows: Iteratively take the disjunction of two answers, the conjunction of the contradicting justifications and check, whether this conjunction is inconsistent with the database state (i.e. covers no maximal extensions). If it is, the corresponding answer is correct. This algorithm is complete because the disjuncts of a justification wrt $\Delta^\vee$ are justifications wrt Δ^g and are thus represented in $JUST\_ANS$:

Lemma 4.12: *Let $(\delta_{1,1} \vee \cdots \vee \delta_{1,k_1}) \wedge \cdots \wedge (\delta_{m,1} \vee \cdots \vee \delta_{m,k_m})$ be a justification for ψ. Then each conjunction of the form $\delta_{1,i_1} \wedge \cdots \wedge \delta_{m,i_m}$ is a justification for ψ if it is consistent with Φ. If subconjunctions of these justifications are composed disjunctively, only more maximal extensions may be covered than by the original justification.*

Of course, not every two potential answers should be composed. They should contribute to the ultimate goal of making the set of extensions not covered empty:

Lemma 4.13: *Let $\bigcap_{i=0}^m |\delta'_{i,1,1} \wedge \cdots \wedge \delta'_{i,1,l_{i,1}}| \cup \cdots \cup |\delta'_{i,k_i,1} \wedge \cdots \wedge \delta'_{i,k_i,l_{i,k_i}}| = \emptyset$, $m \geq 1$, and no subintersection be empty. Then there are $\iota \geq 1$ and $\kappa_0, \lambda_0, \kappa_\iota, \lambda_\iota$ such that $\neg\delta_{0,\kappa_0,\lambda_0}$ and $\neg\delta_{\iota,\kappa_\iota,\lambda_\iota}$ occur together in a tuple of $CONFLICT$.*

Note that this lemma can be applied iteratively: When composing the answers 0 and ι, we multiply the contradicting justifications out, and the result can again be entered for answer 0. So we do not loose interesting combinations of potential answers when composing them as follows:

$$DIS' \equiv (\pi[ANS: ANS1, OR: OR1](BLOCKED\_BY)) \underset{\mu[AND](OR1)\cap OR \neq \emptyset}{\bowtie} CONFLICT,$$

$$DIS'' \equiv DIS' \underset{OR \cap \mu[AND](OR2) \neq \emptyset \wedge OR1 \neq OR2}{\bowtie} (\pi[ANS: ANS2, OR: OR2](BLOCKED\_BY)),$$

$$DIS \equiv \pi[ANS1, OR1, ANS2, OR2](DIS''),$$

$$NEW' \equiv \pi\big[ANS1, ANS2, \pi[AND: AND1](OR1) \times \pi[AND: AND2](OR2): OR12\big](DIS),$$

$$NEW'' \equiv \pi\big[ANS1 \cup ANS2: ANS, \pi[AND1 \cup AND2: AND](OR12): OR\big](NEW').$$

NEW''		
ANS	OR	
	AND	
$answer(p_1)$	$notappl_{\neg faulty}(c_1, p_1)$	
$answer(p_2)$	$notappl_{\neg faulty}(c_1, p_2)$	
	$notappl_{\neg error}(e_1)$	

We now have to delete those contradicting "justifications" which are inconsistent with Φ. If none are left, the answer is correct. Finally, we eliminate the tuples of $BLOCKED\_BY$ whose answers are already known to be correct:

$$NEW \equiv \pi\big[ANS, OR - \pi[AND]\big(OR \underset{AND \supseteq OR2}{\bowtie} \pi[OR: OR2](CONFLICT)\big)\big](NEW''),$$

$$BLOCKED\_BY := BLOCKED\_BY \cup NEW,$$

$$ANSWERS := ANSWERS \cup \sigma[OR = \emptyset](BLOCKED\_BY),$$

$$BLOCKED\_BY^- \equiv BLOCKED\_BY \underset{ANS \supseteq ANS'}{\bowtie} \pi[ANS: ANS'](ANSWERS),$$

$$BLOCKED\_BY := BLOCKED\_BY - \pi[ANS, OR](BLOCKED\_BY^-).$$

In the example, the only contradiction justification for the answer $answer(p_1) \vee answer(p_2)$ is deleted, thus this answer is added to $ANSWERS$. $BLOCKED\_BY$ is now empty, so we are finished. Otherwise we had to repeat the disjunctive composition of potential answers, until $BLOCKED\_BY$ is empty or unchanged after some step.

Extension to Priorities

For priorities, we need a generalization of theorem 4.5, which gives a recursive (level-wise) criterion for deciding the acceptability of χ:

Theorem 4.14: *A justification χ which contains defaults auf maximal level l is acceptable wrt $cwa_{(\Delta^*, \lambda)}$ iff for each justification χ' for $\neg\chi$ containing only defaults of level $\leq l$ there is a justification χ'' for $\neg\chi'$ of level $< l$, which is acceptable wrt $cwa_{(\Delta^\vee, \lambda)}$.*

5 Conclusions

This paper has shown that set-oriented query evaluation techniques can still be applied effectively for deductive databases that store arbitrary clauses and that are subject to very eneral (user-specifiable) completions. Such a general setting is of practical importance since incomplete information has to be represented and since more general rules and defaults lead to simpler formulations. We have used nested relations for the representation of disjunctions in the database. A representation with flat relations is possible, but rather complex.

Obviously, we have only presented the basic algorithm, so that many optimizations can still be applied to it. Database systems for NF^2-relations can be expected to use appropriate access paths for evaluating joins and selections. It should be investigated which indexes are helpful for our requirements.

We should also try to make the derivation goal-oriented by applying "magic set" methods to rewrite the rules before they are entered into the algorithm of section 3. This is subject of our future research.

Note that in contrast to the derivation algorithm, our handling of defaults is already goal-oriented. We have successfully avoided to represent all the assumed defaults or to make a complete case analysis of all models (as some other algorithms do). Instead we consider only defaults which are of interest for some potential answer.

The theoretical foundations for evaluating the defaults can also be applied to other derivation algorithms; we are investigating a top-down, OL-resolution based algorithm for computing potential answers and contradicting justifications. Coupling the method suggested by theorem 4.14 with that kind of resolution leads to a query evaluation algorithm which can be specialized to SLDNF-resolution for stratified databases. This top-down version of the algorithm should be especially helpful for applying the "magic set" techniques.

Acknowledgement

We would like to thank Arno Brinkmann and Gerhard Koschorreck for helpful comments.

References

[BH86] N. Bidoit, R. Hull: Positivism vs. minimalism in deductive databases. In *Proc. of the 5th ACM Symp. on Principles of Database Systems (PODS'86)*, 123–132, 1986.

[BL89] S. Brass, U. W. Lipeck: Specifying closed world assumptions for logic databases. In J. Demetrovics, B. Thalheim (eds.), *2nd Symposium on Mathematical Fundamentals of Database Systems (MFDBS'89)*, 68–84, LNCS 364, Springer-Verlag, Berlin, 1989.

[BL91] S. Brass, U. W. Lipeck: Semantics of inheritance in logical object specifications. To appear in: *Proc. of the 2nd International Conference on Deductive and Object-Oriented Databases (DOOD'91)*, LNCS, Springer-Verlag, 1991.

[BR86] F. Bancilhon, R. Ramakrishnan: An amateur's introduction to recursive query processing. In C. Zaniolo (ed.), *Proc. of SIGMOD'86*, 16–52, 1986.

[Bra90] S. Brass: Beginnings of a theory of general database completions. In S. Abiteboul, P. C. Kanellakis (eds.), *Third International Conference on Database Theory (ICDT'90)*, 349–363, LNCS 470, Springer-Verlag, Berlin, 1990.

[Bry90] F. Bry: Query evaluation in recursive databases: bottom-up and top-down reconciled. *Data & Knowledge Engineering 5 (1990)*, 289–312.

[BS85] G. Bossu, P. Siegel: Saturation, non-monotonic reasoning and the closed-world assumption. *Artificial Intelligence 25 (1985)*, 13–63.

[CL73] C.-L. Chang, R. C.-T. Lee: *Symbolic Logic and Mechanical Theorem Proving*. Academic Press, New York, 1973.

[Gin89] M. L. Ginsberg: A circumscriptive theorem prover. *Artificial Intelligence 39 (1989)*, 209–230.

[GP86] M. Gelfond, H. Przymusinska: Negation as failure: Careful closure procedure. *Artificial Intelligence 30 (1986)*, 273–287.

[HPRV89] G. Hulin, A. Pirotte, D. Roelants, M. Vauclair: Logic and databases. In A. Thayse (ed.), *From Modal Logic to Deductive Databases — Introducing a Logic Based Approach to Artificial Intelligence*, volume 2, 279–350. Wiley, 1989.

[Llo87] J. W. Lloyd: *Foundations of Logic Programming*, 2nd edition. Springer-Verlag, Berlin, 1987.

[McC80] J. McCarthy: Circumscription — a form of non-monotonic reasoning. *Artificial Intelligence 13 (1980)*, 27–39.

[McC86] J. McCarthy: Applications of circumscription to formalizing common-sense knowledge. *Artificial Intelligence 28 (1986)*, 86–116.

[Min82] J. Minker: On indefinite databases and the closed world assumption. In D. W. Loveland (ed.), *6th Conference on Automated Deduction*, 292–308, LNCS 138, Springer-Verlag, Berlin, 1982.

[MP85] J. Minker, D. Perlis: Computing protected circumscription. *The Journal of Logic Programming 2 (1985)*, 235–249.

[Prz88] T. C. Przymusinski: On the declarative semantics of deductive databases and logic programs. In J. Minker (ed.), *Foundations of Deductive Databases and Logic Programming*, 193–216, Morgan Kaufmann Publishers, Los-Altos (Calif.), 1988.

[Prz89] T. C. Przymusinski: An algorithm to compute circumscription. *Artificial Intelligence 38 (1989)*, 49–73.

[Rei78] R. Reiter: On closed world data bases. In H. Gallaire, J. Minker (eds.), *Logic and Data Bases*, 55–76, Plenum, New York, 1978.

[RLM89] A. Rajasekar, J. Lobo, J. Minker: Weak generalized closed world assumption. *Journal of Automated Reasoning 5 (1989)*, 293–307.

[RT88] K. A. Ross, R. W. Topor: Inferring negative information from disjunctive databases. *Journal of Automated Reasoning 4 (1988)*, 397–424.

[Rya91] M. Ryan: Defaults and revision in structured theories. In *Proceedings of the IEEE Symposium on Logic in Computer Science (LICS'91)*, 362–373, 1991.

[SS86] H.-J. Schek, M. H. Scholl: The relational model with relation-valued attributes. *Information Systems 11 (1986)*, 137–148.

[Ull89] J. D. Ullman: *Principles of Database and Knowledge-Base Systems, Vol. 2*. Computer Science Press, Rockville, 1989.

[YH85] A. Yahya, L. J. Henschen: Deduction in non-horn databases. *Journal of Automated Reasoning 1 (1985)*, 141–160.

Compilation-Based List Processing in Deductive Databases

Jiawei Han [†]

School of Computing Science
Simon Fraser University
Burnaby, B.C., Canada V5A 1S6
han@cs.sfu.ca

ABSTRACT

List functions occur frequently in deductive database applications. We study efficient evaluation of linear recursions with list functions in deductive databases. Since most linear recursions can be compiled into chain forms, a chain-based query evaluation method is developed, which selects an efficient query evaluation algorithm based on the analysis of compiled forms and finiteness, termination and query constraints. Interesting techniques, such as chain-split, existence checking and constraint-based evaluation, are developed to improve the performance. Moreover, chain-based evaluation can be generalized to the complex recursions compilable to chain forms.

1. Introduction

Efficient evaluation of function-free recursions has been studied extensively in deductive database research [1-3, 6, 11, 24]. However, many deductive database application programs involve list and arithmetic functions [5, 21, 24]. The study of efficient evaluation of such recursions will provide not only new techniques for practical applications but also a deep insight into recursive query processing.

In this paper, we study efficient evaluation of linear recursions with list functions in deductive databases. Since most linear recursions can be compiled into chain forms, a chain-based query evaluation method is developed, which evaluates compiled forms by the analysis of integrity and query constraints and the selection of efficient query evaluation algorithms. Besides the traditional recursive query evaluation algorithms, such as partial transitive closure algorithms [14], Magic Sets and Counting [1], three interesting evaluation techniques are developed: *chain-split, existence checking* and *constraint-based* evaluation. These new techniques are applicable to different kinds of linear recursions and queries under certain circumstances and, when applicable, will improve query evaluation efficiency. Moreover, these techniques can be applied to more complex kinds of recursions compilable to chain forms.

The paper is organized as follows. In Section 2, we introduce functional linear recursion and its compilation. In Section 3, we address finite evaluability and termination in the evaluation of functional linear recursions. In Section 4, we study efficient evaluation of compiled recursions with list functions. In Section 5, we discuss the extension of the technique to more general recursions and the strength and weakness of our method in comparison with

---

[†] The work was supported in part by the Natural Sciences and Engineering Research Council of Canada under Grant A-3723 and a research grant from Centre for Systems Science of Simon Fraser University.

other relevant methods. We summarize our discussion in Section 6.

2. Compilation of Linear Recursions with List Functions

Like many researchers, we assume that a deductive database consists of (i) an *extensional database (EDB)* (a set of database relations), (ii) an *intensional database (IDB)* (a set of predicates defined by Horn-clause rules), and (iii) a set of *integrity constraints (ICs)*.

Definitions. A rule is **linearly recursive** if the head predicate is the sole recursive predicate and appears exactly once in the body. (Notice that we ignore indirect/mutual recursions here). A recursion is **linear** if it consists of one linearly recursive rule and one or more nonrecursive (exit) rules. A recursion is **function-free** if it does not contain function symbols; otherwise, it is **functional**. A **linear recursion with list functions** is a functional linear recursion in which some function symbols are list operators.

Example 1a. A typical linear recursion with list functions, $append(L_1, L_2, L_3)$, is defined by $(1a)$ and $(1b)$, in which L_3 is the concatenation of two lists L_1 and L_2. $[X|L_1]$ denotes a list construction function, $cons(X, L_1)$, which results in a list with X as the head and L_1 as the remaining of the list. The notational conventions used here are similar to Prolog [23]. □

$(1a)$ $append([], L, L)$.

$(1b)$ $append([X|L_1], L_2, [X|L_3]) :- append(L_1, L_2, L_3)$.

To facilitate the analysis of a functional recursion, a **function-predicate transformation** is performed which maps a function together with its *functional variable* to a predicate (called *functional predicate*), where the functional variable is the variable which unifies the returned value(s) of the function. That is, each function of arity n is transformed to a predicate of arity $n + 1$, with the last argument (in our convention) representing the unifying variable. The mapping is performed recursively when there are nested functions. To make explicit the linkage between a function and its functional predicate, we use the name of the function to represent its corresponding functional predicate. For example, $V = f(X_1, ..., X_k)$ is transformed to $f(X_1, ..., X_k, V)$. A similar transformation is also discussed in [16, 20].

Moreover, logical rules in different forms should be *rectified* to facilitate the compilation and analysis [24]. The rules for predicate p is **rectified** if all the functions are mapped to the corresponding functional predicates by the function-predicate transformation, and all the heads of the rules are identical and of the form $p(X_1, ..., X_k)$ for distinct variables $X_1, ..., X_k$.

Example 1b. The recursion *append* can be rectified into $(1a')$ and $(1b')$, where *cons* is a functional predicate corresponding to the same named list construction function. □

$(1a')$ $append(U, V, W) :- U = [], V = W$.

$(1b')$ $append(U, V, W) :- append(U_1, V, W_1), cons(X_1, U_1, U), cons(X_1, W_1, W)$.

Definitions. In the compilation of a linear recursion with the recursive predicate r, we consider that the **first expansion** of r is the recursive rule itself. The **k-th expansion** of r ($k > 1$) is the unification of the recursive rule of r with the $(k - 1)$-th expansion of r. The **0-th expanded exit rule set** is the set of nonrecursive rules of r. The **k-th expanded exit rule set** is generated by the unification of the set of nonrecursive rules of r on the k-th expansion of r. The **compiled form** of r is the union of the set of rule bodies generated by all the expanded exit rules of r.

The study in [7] shows that a function-free linear recursion can be compiled into a highly regular chain form or a bounded recursion (defined below). Obviously, a functional linear ecursion, after being rectified into a function-free one, can be compiled into such forms as well.

Example 1c. The recursion *append* can be compiled into the compiled form $(1c)$ [7]. □

$1c$) $append(U, V, W) =$

$$\bigcup_{i=0}^{\infty} (U = U_0, V = W_i, W = W_0, U_i = [], cons^i(X_i, U_i, U_{i-1}), cons^i(X_i, W_i, W_{i-1})),$$

where

$$cons^i(X_i, U_i, U_{i-1}) = \begin{cases} true & \text{if } i = 0, \\ cons^{i-1}(X_{i-1}, U_{i-1}, U_{i-2}), cons(X_i, U_i, U_{i-1}) & \text{if } i > 0. \end{cases}$$

Definitions. A **chain** of *length* k $(k > 1)$ is a sequence of k predicates with the following properties: (1) all k predicates have the same name, say p, and the l-th p of the chain is denoted as $p_{(l)}$, (2) there is at least one shared variable in every two consecutive predicates, and f i is the variable position in the first predicate, j the variable position in the second, and wo positions contain shared variables, then (i, j) is an *invariant* of the chain in the sense that he i-th variable of $p_{(l)}$ is shared with the j-th variable of $p_{(l+1)}$ for every l where $1 \le l \le k - 1$. Each predicate of the chain is called a **chain element**. A chain element may be formed by a sequence of *connected* (i.e., variable-shared) nonrecursive predicates, which is called a **chain generating path**. A unit-length chain is trivially a chain predicate, and a 0-length chain is defined as a *tautology*.

Definitions. A linear recursion is an **n-chain recursion** if for any positive integer K, there exists a k-th expansion of the recursion consisting of one chain (when $n = 1$) or n synchronous (of the same length) chains (when $n > 1$) each with the length greater than K, and possibly some other predicates which do not form a nontrivial chain. It is a **single-chain recursion** when $n = 1$, or a **multi-chain recursion** otherwise. The recursive rule of an n-chain recursion is called an **n-chain recursive rule**. A recursion is **bounded** if it is equivalent to a set of nonrecursive rules.

The popularly discussed *ancestor* (or *same_generation*) recursion [2] is a typical single- (or double-) chain recursion; and *append* is a single-chain recursion with a chain generating path, "$cons(X_i, U_i, U_{i-1}), cons(X_i, W_i, W_{i-1})$".

3. Finite Evaluability and Termination of Functional Linear Recursions

The compilation of a functional linear recursion greatly facilitates its analysis. Since many functional predicates and *built-in* predicates (e.g., arithmetic, comparison and list operators) are defined on infinite domains, the analysis should ensure that query evaluation can compute all the answers and terminate properly. Two issues should be examined: (1) *finite evaluability*, that is, the evaluation is performed on finite relations and generates finite intermediate relations at each iteration, and (2) *termination*, that is, the evaluation generates all the answers and terminates at finite number of iterations. The study of these issues needs the examination of two kinds of integrity constraints, *finiteness constraints* and *monotonicity constraints* [16].

3.1. Finiteness constraints and finite evaluability

The justification of finite evaluability relies on both query information and finiteness constraints. A **finiteness constraint** $X \to Y$ over a predicate r implies that each value of attribute X corresponds to a finite set of Y values in r [10]. Finiteness constraint is strictly weaker than the functional dependency studied in database theory [24]. It holds trivially for all finite predicates. Since all the EDB relations are finite, all the arguments in EDB relations satisfy the finiteness constraint. In a functional predicate $f(X_1, ..., X_n, V)$, if all the domains for arguments $X_1, ..., X_n$ are finite, V must be finite no matter whether f is a single- or multiple-valued function, that is, $(X_1, ..., X_n) \to V$.

Specific finiteness constraints should be explored for specific functions. In many cases, one argument of a function can be computed from the values of the other arguments and the value of the function. For example, in the functional predicate $sum(X, Y, Z)$, any argument can be finitely computed if the other two arguments are finite. Such a relationship can be represented by a set of finiteness constraints, such as $(X, Z) \to Y$, and $(Y, Z) \to X$. An interesting finiteness constraint, $Z \to (X, Y)$, holds in the functional predicate $cons(X, Y, Z)$, which indicates if the list Z is finite, there is only a finite number of choices of X and Y.

Since query constants may bind some infinite domains of variables to finite ones, the analysis of finite evaluability should incorporate query instantiation information. Similar to the notations used in the Magic Sets transformation [2,24], a superscript b or f is used to adorn a variable to indicate the variable being *bound (finite)* or *free (infinite)*, and a string of b's and f's is used to adorn a predicate to indicate the bindings of its corresponding arguments.

Algorithm 1. *Testing the finite evaluability of a query in an n-chain recursion.*

Input. (1) An n-chain recursion consisting of an n-chain recursive rule and a set of exit rules, (2) a set of finiteness constraints, and (3) query instantiation information.

Output. An assertion of whether the query is finitely evaluable.

Method.

1. Initialization: A variable is finite if it is in an EDB predicate or equivalent to one or a set of constants.

2. Test the finite evaluability of (1) the exit rule set, and (2) the *first expanded exit rule set* (the rule set obtained by unifying the n-chain recursive rule with the exit rule set). This is done by pushing the query binding information into the rules being tested and propagating the finiteness bindings iteratively based on the following two finiteness propagation rules:

   (i) if there is a finiteness constraint $(X_1, ..., X_n) \to Y$ and X_i^b (for $1 \le i \le n$), then Y^b; and

   (ii) if $(X = Y$ or $Y = X)$ and X^b, then Y^b.

3. Return *yes* if every variable in the two sets of rules being tested is finite after the finiteness binding propagation or *no* otherwise. □

Theorem 1. *Algorithm 1 correctly tests the finite evaluability of an n-chain recursion in $O(k)$ time, where k is the number of predicates in the recursion.*

The theorem is proved in [9].

Example 1d. For the predicate $append(U, V, W)$, there are $2^3 = 8$ possible query binding patterns: bbb, bbf, bfb, bff, fbb, fbf, ffb, and fff, among which only three cases, bff, fbf and fff, are not finitely evaluable. One of the above eight cases is verified below.

The query with the binding pattern ffb, such as "$? - append(U, V, [a, b, c])$.", is finitely evaluable because all the variables in the exit rule and the first expanded exit rule are adorned with b after the binding propagation. For example, the adorned first expanded exit rule is $(1a')$.

1a′) $append(U^b, V^b, W^b) :- U^b_1 = [], V^b = W^b_1, cons(X^b_1, U^b_1, U^b), cons(X^b_1, W^b_1, W^b).$

The binding propagation proceeds as follows: (i) U_1 and W are adorned with b from the instantiations in the exit rule and the query; (ii) X_1 and W_1 are adorned with b from the finiteness constraint, $W \rightarrow (X_1, W_1)$, in $cons(X_1, W_1, W)$, (iii) V is adorned with b based on the variable equivalence $V = W_1$, and finally, (iv) U is adorned with b from the finiteness constraint, $(X_1, U_1) \rightarrow U$, in $cons(X_1, U_1, U)$. Therefore, the query is finitely evaluable. □

Notice that the direction of the finiteness binding propagation determines the order of the query evaluation. If there are several choices in the propagation of the finiteness bindings, one can select a preferred order for efficient evaluation.

3.2. Monotonicity constraints and termination of query evaluation

A nonrecursive query, if finitely evaluable, terminates and derives a finite set of answers. However, a finitely evaluable recursive query guarantees only a finite intermediate relation at each iteration but not the termination of iterative processing. Monotonicity constraints are often useful for the termination of iterative processing.

Definition. A **monotonicity constraint** is a relationship $r_i \twoheadrightarrow r_j$, ($\twoheadrightarrow$ represents a partial order), where r_i and r_j are two arguments of a predicate r. The constraint holds in an instance of r if and only if the value in the i-th argument is strictly greater than that in the j-th argument in every tuple, according to some partial order $\twoheadrightarrow$.

Monotonic behavior is typical in arithmetic functions, list functions and term construction functions. Such behavior should be specified as monotonicity constraints and be used in query evaluation. Also, an acyclic EDB relation is a partially ordered finite relation which is useful in the judgement of termination.

Example 2. We examine some monotonic behavior in arithmetic functions, list functions and term construction functions.

1. An arithmetic operation often implies the monotonicity of a function. For example, $F_1 > 0$, $F_2 > 0$, and $F_1 + F_2 = F$ imply that $F > F_1$ and $F > F_2$.

2. The monotonicity of a list manipulation function usually lies at the growing or shrinking of the list. For example, a list construction operation *cons* results in a longer list than the original one, while some other list operations, such as *car* or *cdr*, result in an atom or a list with the length shorter than the original one.

3. The monotonicity of a term constructor/de-constructor is similar to that of a list function. The repetitive application of a term constructor, such as f, results in an increasingly nested sequence of functors, such as $f(f(...f(X)...))$, while the repetitive application of a term de-constructor, such as f^{-1}, results in a less nested sequence of functors.

4. One may like to terminate a recursion after a certain number of iterations when there is no appropriate termination condition. In such cases, the number of iterations is treated as a monotonically increasing function. □

The processing of a single-chain recursion is essentially the iterative processing of a growing sequence of chain elements. An argument in the head predicate is *monotonic* if the argument has certain monotonic behavior as the number of iteration increases. A query terminates if there exists a **termination restraint** which blocks the growth of the monotonic argument. A termination restraint can be provided or implied in a query, a rule, or an EDB relation. The termination of a query evaluation should be justified before the evaluation starts.

Similar tests can be performed for multi-chain recursions.

Example 1e. A query on *append*, if finitely evaluable, always terminates. This is because the lengths of U and W shrink at each iteration based on the monotonicity constraints, $length(U) > length(U_1)$ and $length(W) > length(W_1)$, in $(1b')$. When a query is finitely evaluable, U, W or both must be bound according to Ex. 1d. The iteration terminates when a list shrinks to empty, that is, there exists a termination restraint, $length(L) \geq 0$, for any list L. □

4. Evaluation of Linear Recursions with List Functions

In this section, we examine the evaluation of compiled linear recursions with list functions. Since a linear recursion with list functions can be rectified into a function-free linear recursion and compiled into a chain form or a bounded form, the previously developed function-free recursive query evaluation techniques [2] are generally applicable to the compiled programs. However, since list and other functions are usually defined on infinite domains, more powerful techniques should be developed for their efficient evaluation. Three techniques, *chain-split, existence checking* and *constraint-based evaluation*, are examined in this section.

4.1. Traditional chain evaluation techniques and chain-split evaluation

A single-chain recursion can be evaluated by a partial transitive closure algorithm, and a multi-chain recursion by the Counting or Magic Sets method [2]. These methods, though developed for function-free recursions, can be applied equally well to compiled functional linear recursions if every predicate in a chain generating path is **immediately evaluable** for the query, that is, *finitely evaluable based on the current available bindings*.

Example 3. The recursion *length* defined by $(2a)$ and $(2b)$ can be rectified into $(2a')$ and $(2b')$ and compiled into a double-chain recursion $(2c)$.

$(2a)$ $length([], 0)$.

$(2b)$ $length([X \mid L_1], succ(N_1)) :- length(L_1, N_1)$.

$(2a')$ $length(L, N) :- L = [], N = 0$.

$(2b')$ $length(L, N) :- length(L_1, N_1), cons(X, L_1, L), succ(N_1, N)$.

$(2c)$ $length(L, N) = \bigcup_{i=0}^{\infty} (cons^i(X_i, L_i, L_{i-1}), succ^i(N_i, N_{i-1}), L = L_0, N = N_0, L_i = [], N_i = 0)$.

A query with the adorned predicate $length^{bf}$, such as "$? - length([a, b, c], N)$.", can be evaluated by the Counting method [1]. Starting at $L_0 = L = [a, b, c]$, the *cons*-predicate is evaluated which derives $L_1 = [b, c]$, and a variable *count* (for the implementation of Counting) is incremented by 1. The evaluation of the *cons*-chain terminates when $L_i = []$ (where $i = 3$). Then $N_i = 0$ initiates the *succ*-chain, which is evaluated *count* times and derives the length of the chain, $N = N_0 = 3$. □

However, depending on the recursions and the available query bindings, *some* functional predicates in a chain generating path may not be immediately evaluable. In this case, a chain generating path should be partitioned into two portions: *immediately evaluable portion* and *buffered portion*. The former is evaluated but the latter is buffered until the *exit portion* (the expression which corresponds to the body of the exit rule) is evaluated. Then the buffered portion obtains sufficient binding information for evaluation (otherwise, the query is not initely evaluable), and the evaluation proceeds in a way similar to the evaluation of multi-chain recursions, except that the corresponding buffered values should be patched in the evaluation. Such an evaluation technique is called the **chain-split evaluation** [9].

Example 1f. Queries with the adorned predicate $append^{bfb}(U,V,W)$, such as "$? - append([a,b],V,[a,c,d])$.", can be evaluated by a typical partial transitive closure evaluation algorithm without chain-split.

However, a chain-split evaluation technique should be applied to the queries with the adorned predicate $append^{ffb}$, such as "$? - append(U,V,[a,b])$". The chain generating path "$cons(X_i,U_i,U_{i-1}), cons(X_i,W_i,W_{i-1})$" is partitioned into two portions: the U-predicate "$cons(X_i,U_i,U_{i-1})$", and the W-predicate "$cons(X_i,W_i,W_{i-1})$". As shown in Fig. 1, when $i = 0$, the form contains no $cons$-predicate, and the evaluation derives the first set of answers: $U = U_0 = []$ and $V = W_0 = W = [a,b]$. When $i = 1$, the U-predicate is not immediately evaluable. The evaluation proceeds along the W-predicate only, which derives $W_1 = [b]$ and $X_1 = a$ from $W_0 = W = [a,b]$. X_1 is buffered, and W_1 is passed to the exit expression, making $V = W_1 = [b]$ and $U_1 = []$. Then the U-predicate is evaluable since X_1 and U_1 are available. It derives $U = U_0 = [a]$ from $cons(X_1,U_1,U_0)$. Thus the second set of answer is $\{U = [a], V = [b]\}$. Similarly, the evaluation may proceed on the W-predicate further, which derives $W_2 = []$ and $X_2 = b$ from $W_1 = [b]$. X_2 is buffered, and W_2 is passed to the exit expression, making $V = W_2 = []$ and $U_2 = []$. Then the U-predicate is evaluable, which derives $U = U_0 = [a,b]$ from $cons(X_1,U_1,U_0)$ and $cons(X_2,U_2,U_1)$. Thus the third set of answer is $\{U = [a,b], V = []\}$.

Similarly, a query with adorned predicate $append^{bbf}$, such as "$? - append([a,b],[c,d],W)$." can be evaluated by buffering the X_i's in the evaluation of the U-predicate, passing through the exit portion, and patching the buffered X_i's in the evaluation of the W-predicate. □

Algorithm 2. *Chain-split evaluation of a single-chain recursion.*

Input. A query and a compiled functional single-chain recursion.

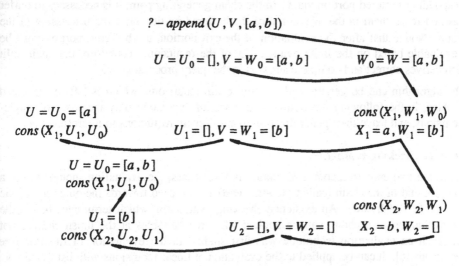

$? - append(U,V,[a,b])$

$U = U_0 = [], V = W_0 = [a,b]$ $W_0 = W = [a,b]$

$U = U_0 = [a]$
$cons(X_1,U_1,U_0)$ $U_1 = [], V = W_1 = [b]$ $cons(X_1,W_1,W_0)$
$X_1 = a, W_1 = [b]$

$U = U_0 = [a,b]$
$cons(X_1,U_1,U_0)$

$U_1 = [b]$ $cons(X_2,W_2,W_1)$
$cons(X_2,U_2,U_1)$ $U_2 = [], V = W_2 = []$ $X_2 = b, W_2 = []$

Figure 1. Evaluation of the query, "$? - append(U,V,[a,b])$".

Output. A query evaluation plan which applies the chain-split evaluation.

Method.

If every predicate in the chain generating path is immediately evaluable based on the available query bindings, the query can be evaluated without chain-split evaluation.

Suppose the chain generating path of the single-chain recursion is partitioned into two portions according to the available query bindings: an *immediately evaluable portion* p and a *buffered portion* q. Suppose in the i-th chain generating path of the compiled form, p and q share a variable X_i, p shares a variable U_i with the $(i+1)$-th p, and q shares a variable W_i with the $(i+1)$-th q.

1. First, the query instantiates U_0, the immediately evaluation portion. At the i-th iteration, based on the available binding U_{i-1}, p is evaluated which derives U_i and buffers the corresponding X_i value. The iteration terminates when it satisfies the termination condition (e.g., when the list shrinks to empty). Suppose that it terminates at the k-th iteration.

2. Evaluate the exit portion of the compiled form.

3. Pass the bindings obtained in the processing of the exit portion to q. Based on the available binding W_i and the buffered X_i, p is evaluated which derives W_{i-1} at the $(k-i)$-th iteration. The evaluation terminates at the k-th iteration or when there is no W_{i-1} derived at some iteration. □

Theorem 2. *The chain-split evaluation performed by Algorithm 2 correctly evaluates the compiled single-chain recursion.*

Proof.

The algorithm is similar to the Counting method [1] except that the values of variable X_i's are buffered in the processing of the immediately evaluable portion of a chain generating path and reused in the processing of its buffered portion. Notice that if there were no X_i linking the two portions in the recursion, there would be two chains in the compiled recursion to which the Counting method applies. Since the immediately evaluable portion is linked to the corresponding buffered portion via X_i in the chain generating path, it is necessary to buffer X_i values and reuse them in the evaluation of the buffered portion after the processing of the exit portion. Notice that after the evaluation of the exit portion, the buffered portion must be finitely evaluable based on the finite evaluability of the recursion. Therefore, the chain-split evaluation derives correct and complete answers in the query processing. □

The algorithm can be generalized to multi-chain recursions, which is left to interested readers. Also, in the following discussion in this section, we study only the cases of single-chain recursions, and leave their generalization to multi-chain recursions to interested readers.

4.2. Existence checking evaluation

There are two ends in a compiled chain. In most cases, the evaluation should start at a more selective end of the chain (called the **start end**) and proceed towards the other end of the chain (called the **finish end**). An existence checking evaluation, which terminates before the complete evaluation of a chain, can be applied when the variables at the finish end are not inquired. Such an evaluation technique was first studied in the evaluation of function-free linear recursions [6]. It can be applied to the evaluation of linear recursions with list functions.

Example 4. The recursion $member(X, L)$, defined by $(3a)$ and $(3b)$, can be rectified into $(3a')$ and $(3b')$, which is compiled into $(3c)$, a single-chain recursion.

3a) $member(X, [X | L_1])$.

3b) $member(X, [Y | L_1]) :- member(X, L_1)$.

3a') $member(X, L) :- cons(X, L_1, L)$.

3b') $member(X, L) :- member(X, L_1), cons(Y, L_1, L)$.

3c) $member(X, L) = \bigcup_{i=1}^{\infty} (cons^i(X_i, L_i, L_{i-1}), L = L_0, X = X_i)$.

A query, "$? - member([a], [b, a, c, d])$", can be evaluated by an existence checking evaluation algorithm because the instantiation at the start end of the chain is $L_0 = L = [b, a, c, d]$, while that at the finish end is $X = X_i = a$. Both ends are instantiated but not inquired. Notice that L_0 must be the start end, otherwise the $cons$-predicate is not immediately evaluable. The evaluation proceeds as follows. When $i = 1$, it derives no answer since $L_1 = [a, c, d]$, but $X_1 = b \neq X$. When $i = 2$, it evaluates to *true* since $L_2 = [c, d]$, and $X_2 = a = X$. The evaluation terminates because one *true* answer is adequate to the query. The evaluation has to proceed until $L_{i-1} = []$ only if L contains no element a. In this case, the answer to the query is *false*. □

Algorithm 3. *Existence-checking evaluation of a single-chain recursion.*

Input. A query and a compiled single-chain recursion with the chain generating path p.

Output. A query evaluation plan which applies existence-checking evaluation.

Method.

Suppose the finish end of the compiled chain is not inquired in the query. The query can be evaluated by existence checking as follows.

1. Push the query instantiations at the start end into the chain and evaluate predicate p at each iteration. If the start end is inquired in the query, treat each initial value at the start end as a source node of the chain. Otherwise, treat the whole set of the values at the start end as one source node set of the chain.

2. For each source node (or source node set) of the chain, if the chain evaluation at the current iteration validates the query (making it *true*), the evaluation for the source node (set) terminates (the source is not *active*). Otherwise, continue evaluation for the source node (set) at the next iteration.

3. The evaluation terminates if there exists no active source node (set), or it reaches the normal termination condition of a single-chain recursion. □

Theorem 3. *The existence-checking evaluation performed by Algorithm 3 correctly evaluates the compiled single-chain recursion.*

Proof.

A single-chain recursion has only one compiled chain with two ends. Suppose the query processing starts at the start end, and the finish end is not inquired in the query, that is, the variable(s) at the finish end are either constants or irrelevant to the query. If a source node (set) at the start end can derive one value satisfying the recursion, it is unnecessary to see whether it can derive more answers to the query. Therefore, the evaluation terminates when all the source nodes (or the set) are satisfied or when the evaluation reaches the normal termination conditions for the single-chain recursion [6, 24]. □

4.3. Constraint-based evaluation

Constraint-based evaluation [12, 13] is used when a query provides constraints which may help reduce the search space in the iterative evaluation. A query constraint usually instantiates or adds constraint information to an IDB predicate. In a single-chain recursion, query constraints can be enforced at both ends of a compiled chain. In most cases, the processing should choose a more restrictive end as the *start end* and proceed to a less restrictive end of the chain (the *finish end*). It is straightforward to push query constraints at the start end into the chain before the chain processing. However, care should be taken when pushing the query constraints at the finish end.

Example 5. An IDB predicate *tour* (*FnoList*, *Dep*, *Arr*, *Fare*), defined by (*4a*) and (*4b*), represents a sequence of connected flights with the initial departure city *Dep*, the final arrival city *Arr* and the total fare *Fare*, where *flight* is an EDB predicate representing the stored flight information.

(*4a*)   *tour* ([*Fno*], *Dep*, *Arr*, *Fare*) :− *flight* (*Fno*, *Dep*, *Arr*, *Fare*).

(*4b*)   *tour* ([*Fno* | *FnoList*], *Dep*, *Arr*, *Fare*) :−
$$flight (Fno, Dep, Int, F_1), tour (FnoList, Int, Arr, F_2), Fare = F_1 + F_2.$$

The recursion can be rectified into (*4a′*) and (*4b′*) and compiled into (*4c*), a single-chain recursion.

(*4a′*) $tour (L, D, A, F) :− flight (Fno, D, A, F), cons (Fno, [], L), sum (F, 0, F).$

(*4b′*) $tour (L, D, A, F) :−$
$$flight (Fno, D, I, F_1), tour (L_1, I, A, S_1), sum (F_1, S_1, F), cons (Fno, L_1, L).$$

(*4c*) $tour (L, D, A, F) = \bigcup_{i=1}^{\infty} ((flight (Fno_i, I_{i-1}, I_i, F_i), sum (F_i, S_i, S_{i-1}),$
$$cons (Fno_i, L_i, L_{i-1}))^i, D = I_0, L = L_0, F = S_0, A = I_i, L_i = [], S_i = 0).$$

Suppose a query is to *find a set of (connecting) flights from Vancouver to Zurich (Switzerland), with at most 4 hops and with the total fare between $500 to $800*, that is,

?- *tour* (*FnoList*, *vancouver*, *zurich*, *F*), $F \geq 500, F \leq 800,$
$$length (FnoList, N), N \leq 4.$$

According to the compiled form (*4c*), *D*, *L* and *F* are located at one end of the chain (called the *departure end*); while *A*, L_i and S_i are at the other end of the chain (called the *arrival end*). The information at the departure end is, (i) $D = I_0 =$ "vancouver", (ii) $500 \leq F = S_0 \leq 800$, and (iii) *FnoList* $= L_0$, *length* (*FnoList*, *N*), $N \leq 4$; while the information at the arrival end is, (i) $A = I_i =$ "zurich", (ii) $L_i = []$, and (iii) $S_i = 0$.

Since the information at the arrival end is more selective than that at the departure end, the arrival end is taken as the *start end*. Thus all the query constraints at this end are pushed into the chain for efficient processing. Notice that if query provides more selective information at the departure end, the departure end should be selected as the start end. In this case, the chain-split evaluation technique needs to be incorporated in the processing.

The query constraints at the finish end cannot be pushed into the chain in iterative evaluation without further information. For example, pushing the constraint, *Fare* ≥ 500, into the chain will cut off a promising connection whose first hop costs less than 500. On the other hand, it is clearly beneficial to push the constraint, *Fare* ≤ 800, into the chain to cut off any iopeless connections when the accumulative fare is already beyond 800. However, a constraint like $Fare = 800$ cannot be pushed into the chain directly, but a transformed constraint, $Fare \leq 800$, can be pushed in for iterative evaluation.

A systematic way to pushing query constraints at the finish end can be derived from the interactions between query constraints and monotonicity constraints. If the value (or the mapped value) of an argument in the recursive predicate monotonically increases in the evaluation, a query constraint which blocks such an increase is useful at reducing the search space in the iterative evaluation.

Based on the monotonicity constraint of the argument $Fare$, a *termination restraint template*, $Fare \not> C$, is set up, where C is a variable which can be instantiated by a *consistent* query constraint. For example, a constraint, $Fare \leq 800$, or $Fare = 800$, instantiates the template to a *concrete termination restraint*, $Fare \not> 800$. However, the constraint, $Fare \geq 500$, is not consistent with the termination restraint template. Thus it can not instantiate a termination restraint. A concrete termination restraint can be pushed into the chain for efficient iterative processing.

Similarly, a constraint, $Dep = "vancouver"$, can be used for constraint pushing if we have the airport location information and a constraint, *same flight direction*, (a monotonic constraint on flight direction). A concrete termination restraint, $longitude(Dep) \not> longitude("vancouver")$, can be derived, and the tuples generated at any iteration with the departure airports located to the west of Vancouver can be pruned in the chain processing.

For the same reason, the constraint, $"length(FnoList, N), N \leq 4"$, can be pushed into the chain for iterative evaluation.

Notice that if a constraint at the finish end or its mapping is not equivalent to its corresponding concrete termination restraint, the constraint should still be enforced at the end of the chain processing. For example, the constraint, $Dep = "vancouver"$, is mapped to $longitude(vancouver)$, which is not equivalent to its concrete termination restraint. Thus it should be used at the end of the chain processing to select those departing exactly at $vancouver$. However, it is unnecessary to use $Fare \leq 800$ again since it is the same as the termination constraint. $\square$

In general, we have

Algorithm 4. *Incorporation of query constraints in the processing of a compiled functional single-chain recursion.*

Input. A compiled functional single-chain recursion, a set of integrity constraints, a query predicate, and a set of query constraints.

Output. A query evaluation plan which incorporates the query constraints.

Method.

1. Test whether the query is finitely evaluable and terminable. If it is not, stop.

2. Determine the start end of the chain processing based on the relative selectivity of the query constraints at both ends. Apply the query constraints relevant to the start end as query instantiations to reduce the size of the initial set.

3. Instantiate termination restraint templates using the query constraints at the finish end. (Note that the termination restraint templates are derived using the monotonicity constraints at compile time). Push the instantiated termination restraints into the chain

expression for iterative chain evaluation.

4. When the iteration terminates, select the set of answers to the query using the query constraints at the finish end which are not equivalent to the instantiated termination restraints. □

Theorem 4. *Algorithm 4 correctly incorporates query constraints in the evaluation of compiled functional single-chain recursions.*

Proof.

Step 1 is necessary since a query must be finitely evaluable and terminable. The test is performed using the methods discussed in the previous two subsections. Step 2 is necessary and correct since the most selective information should be pushed into the compiled chain for initial processing [2]. Step 3 is correct since at some iteration if the value of a monotonic argument in a generated tuple cannot satisfy a termination restraint, future derivations based on it can never satisfy the termination restraint (because of the monotonicity constraint). Step 4 is obviously necessary since the remaining query constraints must be applied at the end of query processing to make the query satisfiable. The other query constraints have been used either at the beginning or during the iterative processing and do not need to be reused at the end of the chain processing. □

4.4. Chain-Based Query Evaluation Method

As a summary of the discussion in this section, we present a chain-based query evaluation algorithm which outlines a general picture on the integration of different techniques in the evaluation of a compiled functional single-chain recursion. The corresponding algorithm for a compiled functional multi-chain recursion can be derived similarly.

Algorithm 5. *Chain-based query evaluation of a compiled functional single-chain recursion.*

Input. A compiled functional single-chain recursion, a set of integrity constraints, and a query.

Output. A chain-based query evaluation plan.

Method.

1. Test whether the query is finitely evaluable and terminable. If it is not, stop.

2. Determine the start end of the chain based on the relative selectivity of the provided query constraints and constants at both ends. Push the query constraints and constants relevant to the start end into the chain as the instantiations of the chain processing.

3. If there is a portion of the chain generating path not immediately evaluable, apply the chain-split evaluation (Algorithm 2). If the finish end is not inquired in the query, apply the existence checking evaluation (Algorithm 3). If the finish end provides query constraints, and there are monotonicity constraints available, apply the constraint-based evaluation (Algorithm 4). (Notice that these evaluation algorithms can be combined, for example, a constraint-based chain-split evaluation should be applied if the query satisfies the conditions of both evaluation algorithms). □

Theorem 5. *Algorithm 5 correctly incorporates query information and constraint information in the evaluation of a compiled functional single-chain recursion.*

Proof.

Based on the proofs of Theorems 2 to 4 in this section. □

116

5. Discussion

In this section, we examine the extension of the chain-based evaluation method to more complex kinds of recursions and compare the method with other relevant methods.

5.1. Towards more complex kinds of recursions

First, we show that the chain-based evaluation method can be applied to more complex classes of functional recursions than linear ones as long as the recursions can be compiled into chain forms.

Example 6. The recursion defined by $(5a)$, $(5b)$ and $(5e)$ is a *multiple linear recursion*, a recursion consisting of multiple linear recursive rules and one or more exit rules.

$(5a)$ $delete([X|Xs],X,Ys):- delete(Xs,X,Ys).$

$(5b)$ $delete([X|Xs],Z,[X|Ys]):-X \neq Z, delete(Xs,Z,Ys).$

$(5e)$ $delete([],X,[]).$

The recursion can be rectified into $(5a')$, $(5b')$ and $(5e')$ and compiled into $(5c')$, which is still a single-chain recursion.

$(5a')$ $delete(L,X,M):-delete(L_1,X,M_1), M=M_1, cons(X,L_1,L).$

$(5b')$ $delete(L,X,M):-$

$$delete(L_1,X,M_1), cons(X_1,L_1,L), cons(X_1,M_1,M), X \neq X_1.$$

$(5e')$ $delete(L,X,M):-L=[], M=[].$

$(5c)$ $delete(L,X,M)=\bigcup_{i=0}^{\infty}((((cons(X,L_i,L_{i-1}), M_{i-1}=M_i) \cup (cons(X_i,L_i,L_{i-1}),$

$$cons(X_i,M_i,M_{i-1}), X \neq X_i))^i, L_i=[], M_i=[], L=L_0, M=M_0).$$

Since the recursion can be compiled into the chain form, queries on the recursion can be evaluated the same way as a (single) linear one. We examine the evaluation of the query, "$?-delete(a,[b,a,a,c],M).$". The chain generating path in the compiled form is the union ("or") of two subportions: (a) "$cons(X,L_i,L_{i-1}), M_{i-1}=M_i$", and (b) "$cons(X_i,L_i,L_{i-1}), cons(X_i,M_i,M_{i-1}), X \neq X_i$". From $X=a$ in (a) and $X \neq X_i$ in (b), it is clear that either (a) or (b) but not both may proceed at any iteration. When $L_0=L=[b,a,a,c]$, only the (b)-portion can proceed, and we obtain $X_1=b$, $L_1=[a,a,c]$, but $cons(X_1,M_1,M_0)$ is not immediately evaluable, and the chain generating path (b) is split with X_1 buffered. At the next iteration, only the (a)-portion can proceed with $X_2=X=a$, $L_2=[a,c]$, and $M_2=M_1$. Similarly, the third iteration makes $X_3=X=a, L_3=[c]$, and $M_3=M_2$. Finally, the fourth iteration makes $X_4=c, L_4=[]$, and $M_4=[]$. L_4 and M_4 match the exit portion, and the buffered portion can be evaluated by $cons(c,[],M_3)$, $M_1=M_2=M_3=[c]$, and $cons(b,[c],M_0)$. Therefore, the final answer to the query is $M=M_0=[b,c]$. $\square$

Previous studies show that many *multiple linear recursions* (the recursions containing multiple linear recursive rules), *nonlinear recursions* (the recursions containing some nonlinear recursive rules), mutual recursions and multiple levels of recursions can be compiled into chain forms [8,24]. Clearly, the chain-based query evaluation method is applicable to such recursions.

However, there exist complex recursions which cannot be compiled into regular chain forms. Such kind of recursions, though not frequently encountered in function-free ones, may find many examples in recursions with list functions. We present one such example.

Example 7. The recursion, *hanoi* , defined by (*6a*) and (*6b*) is a *nonlinear recursion*.

(*6a*) $hanoi(1, A, B, C, [A \ to \ B])$.

(*6b*) $hanoi(succ(N), A, B, C, Moves) :- hanoi(N, A, C, B, Ms_1),$
 $hanoi(N, C, B, A, Ms_2), append(Ms_1, [A \ to \ B \mid Ms_2], Moves).$

This rule set defines the *Towers of Hanoi* puzzle [23] which moves N discs from peg A to peg B using peg C as an intermediary. It cannot be compiled into chain forms based on the current compilation technique. Thus the chain-based evaluation method cannot be applied to this recursion. □

5.2. Strength and weakness of the chain-based evaluation method

Our chain-based query evaluation method is developed based on the previous studies on safeness, termination, compilation and efficient evaluation of recursions in deductive databases [4, 7, 15, 18-20, 22, 24]. Here we compare our approach with some relevant methods.

Linear recursions with list functions can be evaluated by Prolog implementations [23]. However, a Prolog implementation cannot guarantee the termination of an evaluation, and moreover, the processing efficiency and the use of query constraints are determined by programmers. Furthermore, the evaluation is tuple-oriented, which is inefficient in database environments.

Recent studies in deductive databases have proposed the use of the Magic Sets method in the evaluation of functional recursions [5, 24]. The method applies set-oriented processing and reduces the search space to the portion of the database relevant to a query, which improves search efficiency. However, without compiling functional linear recursions into chain forms and performing a detailed analysis of the monotonicity and finiteness behaviors of a compiled recursion, it is difficult to fully explore various kinds of constraints in query processing. For example, the existence checking evaluation of recursive queries and the push of termination constraints into chain expression for efficient processing cannot be realized in the Magic Sets evaluation.

In this sense, our study provides an efficient evaluation method on the recursions compilable to regular chain forms. The weakness of our technique is that there are complex recursions beyond linear ones which cannot be compiled into chain forms or other regular forms based on the current technology. Thus the class of recursions which can be solved by the chain-based evaluation is a subset of those which can be solved by Prolog implementations or the Magic Sets method. However, the compiled chain-based approach, though less general than the Magic Sets approach, can reduce search space more accurately for at least some interesting class of programs. Thus it is worthwhile to further explore its strength and extend its application domain to more complex kinds of recursions.

5.3. Some implementation considerations

Many logic programs frequently use a small set of list manipulation primitives, such as *member, length, append, delete, reverse, sort*, etc. It is inefficient to compile, analyze and implement these list manipulation functions from scratch, especially in large databases. Therefore, a deductive database system should provide efficient implementations of a set of frequently-used list manipulation primitives. Other functions and logic predicates can treat these primitive list manipulation functions as efficiently implemented, nondecomposable primitives. Then the compilation, analysis and evaluation of a complex deductive database program can be performed at a higher level. For example, in the query on *tour* of Ex. 5, the function *length* should be considered as a given primitive function without further analysis.

Our study has been focused on the static control of query execution [17], in which the flow of execution is predetermined at query compilation and analysis time, which is different from most AI systems which adopt dynamic control in query execution [13,18]. Although static control, exercised by a query optimizer, is suitable for finding all the answers to a query, dynamic control of the search process, exercised by the system at run time, may further reduce search space, enhance performance, and produce a few but knowledgeable answers. To facilitate the dynamic control of query execution, a *dynamic constraint enforcement* method, such as *prioritizing* query constraints and controlling the application of the constraints during query execution, has been proposed as an extension to our approach. A detailed discussion of this approach is in [10].

6. Conclusions

We studied the efficient evaluation of linear recursions with list functions in deductive databases. A chain-based query evaluation method is developed based on the compilation of functional linear recursions into chain forms. Three interesting techniques: *chain-split, existence checking* and *constraint-based evaluation*, are developed to improve the efficiency of query evaluation. Our study shows that chain-based evaluation, though less general than some traditional recursive query evaluation methods, can reduce search space more accurately for the programs compilable into regular chain forms.

A large class of recursions with list functions can be compiled into chain forms. It is an interesting research topic to explore powerful compilation techniques to compile more complex recursions into chain or other regular forms. Also, it is interesting to study the application of the evaluation techniques, such as *chain-split, existence checking* and *constraint-based evaluation*, to different classes of functional recursions not compilable into chain forms.

References

1. F. Bancilhon, D. Maier, Y. Sagiv and J. D. Ullman, Magic Sets and Other Strange Ways to Implement Logic Programs, *Proc. 5th ACM Symp. Principles of Database Systems*, Cambridge, MA, March 1986, 1–15.

2. F. Bancilhon and R. Ramakrishnan, An Amateur's Introduction to Recursive Query Processing Strategies, *Proc. 1986 ACM-SIGMOD Conf. Management of Data*, Washington, DC, May 1986, 16–52.

3. C. Beeri and R. Ramakrishnan, On the Power of Magic, *Proc. 6th ACM Symp. Principles of Database Systems*, San Diego, CA, March 1987, 269–283.

4. A. Brodsky and Y. Sagiv, On Termination of Datalog Programs, *Proc. 1st Int. Conf. Deductive and Object-Oriented Databases (DOOD'89)*, Kyoto, Japan, December 1989, 95–112.

5. D. Chimenti, R. Gamboa, R. Krishnamurthy, S. Naqvi, S. Tsur and C. Zaniolo, The LDL System Prototype, *IEEE Trans. Knowledge and Data Engineering*, 2(1), 1990, 76–90.

6. J. Han, Multi-Way Counting Method, *Information Systems*, **14**(3), 1989, 219–229.

7. J. Han, Compiling General Linear Recursions by Variable Connection Graph Analysis, *Computational Intelligence*, **5**(1), 1989, 12–31.

8. J. Han and W. Lu, Asynchronous Chain Recursions, *IEEE Trans. Knowledge and Data Engineering*, **1**(2), 1989, 185–195.

9. J. Han and Q. Wang, Evaluation of Functional Linear Recursions: A Compilation Approach, *Information Systems*, **16**(4), 1991, 463–469.

10. J. Han, Constraint-Based Reasoning in Deductive Databases, *Proc. 7th Int. Conf. Data Engineering*, Kobe, Japan, April 1991, 257–265.

11. L. J. Henschen and S. Naqvi, On Compiling Queries in Recursive First-Order Databases, *J. ACM*, **31**(1), 1984, 47–85.

12. T. Imielinski, Intelligent Query Answering in Rule Based Systems, *Journal of Logic Programming*, **4**, 1987, 229–257.

13. J. Jaffar and J. Lassez, Constraint Logic Programming, *Proc. 14th ACM Symp. Principles of Programming Languages*, Munich, 1987, 111–119.

14. B. Jiang, A Suitable Algorithm for Computing Partial Transitive Closures, *Proc. 6th Int. Conf. Data Engineering*, Los Angeles, CA, February 1990, 264–271.

15. D. B. Kemp, K. Ramamohanarao, I. Balbin and K. Meenakshi, Propagating Constraints in Recursive Deductive Databases, *Proc. 1989 North American Conf. Logic Programming*, Cleveland, OH, October 1989, 981–998.

16. R. Krishnamurthy, R. Ramakrishnan and O. Shmueli, A Framework for Testing Safety and Effective Computability of Extended Datalog, *Proc. 1988 ACM-SIGMOD Conf. Management of Data*, Chicago, IL, June 1988, 154–163.

17. R. Krishnamurthy and C. Zaniolo, Optimization in a Logic Based Language for Knowledge and Data Intensive Applications, *Proc. Int. Conf. of Extending Database Technology (EDBT' 88)*, Venice, Italy, March 1988, 16–33.

18. M. J. Maher and P. J. Stuckey, Expanding Query Power in Constraint Logic Programming Languages, *Proc. 1989 North American Conf. Logic Programming*, Cleveland, OH, October 1989, 20–36.

19. J. F. Naughton, R. Ramakrishnan, Y. Sagiv and J. D. Ullman, Efficient Evaluation of Right-, Left-, and Multi-Linear Rules, *Proc. 1989 ACM-SIGMOD Conf. Management of Data*, Portland, Oregon, June 1989, 235–242.

20. R. Ramakrishnan, F. Bancilhon and A. Silberschatz, Safety of Recursive Horn Clauses with Infinite Relations, *Proc. 6th ACM Symp. Principles of Database Systems*, San Diego, CA, March 1987, 328–339.

21. A. Rosenthal, S. Heiler, U. Dayal and F. Manola, Traversal Recursion: A Practical Approach to Supporting Recursive Applications, *Proc. 1986 ACM-SIGMOD Conf. Management of Data*, Washington, DC, May 1986, 166–176.

22. Y. Sagiv and M. Vardi, Safety of Datalog Queries over Infinite Databases, *Proc. 8th ACM Symp. Principles of Database Systems*, Philadelphia, PA, March 1989, 160–171.

23. L. Sterling and E. Shapiro, *The Art of Prolog*, The MIT Press, 1986.

24. J. D. Ullman, *Principles of Database and Knowledge-Base Systems, Vol. 2*, Computer Science Press, Rockville, MD, 1989.

Multiple Substitutability
Without
Affecting the Taxonomy*

Guido Moerkotte   *Andreas Zachmann*

Universität Karlsruhe
Fakultät für Informatik
D-7500 Karlsruhe, F. R. G.
Netmail: [moer|zachmann]@ira.uka.de

Abstract

Two areas where common object-oriented modeling power lacks the necessary expressiveness are identified. An analysis of the situation shows that there exists a single reason why the real world situations cannot be modeled adequately. What really is missing is a means to express that objects of a certain type are able to behave in a fashion objects of another type would do. To remedy this situation we introduce a single new concept, define its semantics, give a thorough analysis of its applicability in light of strong typing, and illustrate its symbiosis with inheritance and genericity. The concept is illuminated by means of several examples.

1 Introduction

Object-oriented database systems are emerging as the "next-generation" DBMSs for non-standard database applications, e.g., VLSI design, CAD/CAM, software engineering, etc. One of the key concepts to provide the necessary modeling power is the possibility to build taxonomies utilizing the *is-a* relationship including subtyping and inheritance. One consequence of a type being a subtype of another is that objects of the subtype may be substituted for objects of the supertype. Nevertheless, further substitution is not allowed.

As turned out there exist cases where this restriction unnecessarily cuts down the much-needed modeling power to provide the flexibility required by non-standard applications. More specifically, the identified situations demand objects of a certain type to be substitutable for objects of another type where these types are not necessarily related by the subtype relationship.[1] We call this feature *multiple substitutability*.

---

*This work was partially supported by the German Research Council DFG under contract number SFB 346.

[1]This is independent of the subtype relationship used. For instance applying a subtype relationship based on structural or name equivalence (see [1] and [4], resp., and [2] for a comparison) does not make any difference for the problems studied here. Both exhibit the same problems.

Multiple substitutability is a necessary means to solve modeling problems arizing if one wants to

- look at the whole object as a part, or

- look at a part of an object as a (or the) whole object.

We discuss each of these areas separately.

It is often convenient to transparently take an object for an object's part. This results in the requirement that an object understands messages understood by its components. Take a car for instance. No one would fill gasoline in the car, e.g., in the cabin. Instead the fuel is delivered to the fuel receptacle. Nevertheless it is convenient to think about a car to be refilled with gasoline. Obviously, multiple inheritance does not solve the problem since neither a car is a fuel receptacle nor vice versa.

Representative problems are characterized by the existence of a collection of objects with a single denominated representative who takes care of general duties. A typical example is a department. Despite the fact that a department is not able to read it is possible to address a letter, e.g., an order or a bill, directly to a department. Inside the department the letter will then be directed to the representative responsible to take care of the incoming mail, e.g., the secretary. Again, multiple inheritance does not solve the problem since neither a department is a person nor vice versa.

The other case arizes if one wants to select some of the object's capabilities in order to gather all the necessary features required by another type definition. As an example consider a house boat which really is not a house but a boat. (Take the mobility property.) In order to model the house capabilities of a house boat the modeler is forced to either duplicate the capability definitions or to use multiple inheritance: the former does not allow to substitute house boats for houses and the latter impacts the taxonomy in such a way that a house boat becomes a house which is an undesired effect.

As will become clear soon, all these problems can be solved if we allow multiple substitutability of objects and avoid to affect the taxonomy. Before this may be allowed the objects must be enabled to behave in a fashion objects of the type they are substituted for do. The paper introduces a single concept called *fashion* which instantiates this idea.

The rest of the paper is organized as follows. The next Section contains examples where current object-oriented models lack the required flexibility and shows how the arizing problems can be solved by utilizing the *fashion* construct. The general concept together with its syntax and semantics is introduced in Section 4. It also includes a thorough discussion of its applicability in the context of strong typing, of possibly evolving conflicts, and of its interplay with inheritance. Section 5 concludes the paper.

2 Taking the Whole for a Part

Let's put ourselves in an engineer's position: Suppose, somebody fixed the notion of a gas tank in terms of the type definition *GasTank*. Its structural description contains the attributes *volume* and *contents* to store and retrieve information about the amount of fuel filled into the receptacle. There are operations *fill* and *use* to manipulate these attributes. In GOM syntax [5] the type definition looks as follows:

```
type GasTank is
    public volume→, contents→, fill, use
    body [ volume  : float;
               contents : float; ]
    operations
        declare fill: float → void;
        declare use: float → void;
    implementation
        ...
end type GasTank;
```

Besides this assume the existence of many applications for gas tanks. For example, we modeled gas station attendants to get the possibility to refill gas tanks. Each gas station attendant understands the message *fillup*, which causes him to refill the receptacle exactly up to the point where its contents equals its volume.

```
type GasStationAttendant supertype Person is
    operations
        declare fillup: GasTank → void;
    implementation
        ...
end type GasStationAttendant;
```

Thus, we are able to carry a *GasTank* to the gas station attendant *DavidBowie* and let him refill it:

```
var gt              : GasTank;
    DavidBowie : GasStationAttendant;
begin
    gt.create;
    DavidBowie.create;
        ...
    DavidBowie.fillup( gt );
```

It is now the engineer's task to build an engine driven metal box upon wheels around a fuel receptacle. Thus, we have to model a car. Within the model of a car the gas tank will become a part of the whole, e.g., the definition of *Car* contains an attribute *gastank: GasTank*. But what happens, if we want to drive an instance of *Car*, say *myPorsche*, to the gas station? Of course, we could say

DavidBowie.fillup(myPorsche.gastank)

but this seems to be not a very natural way since the information that the gas tank is to be refilled is implicitly clear. Further, this solution exhibits another disadvantage: the existence of *gastank* has to be revealed at the interface of *Car*. There is no way to hide this information from our gas station application and to call

DavidBowie.fillup(myPorsche).

This lack of information hiding results in a major decrease of code reusability. As soon as the *Car* type is changed, e.g., the attribute *gastank* is renamed or moved further "inside" the type definition (as an attribute of a further subobject) the above piece of code has to be rewritten in every application.

What really is intended is the following: a message addressed to the enclosing whole (the car) should be automatically directed to some part (the fuel receptacle). A realization of this idea requires that cars must be substitutable for gas tanks and that the parts for which the whole may be substituted are specified. As a further requirement, the *routing* of the message to locate the right part within the object representing the whole has to be encapsulated. Our solution to the problem is given by the **fashion** clause which may be inserted into type definitions. Consider again the type *Car*. Within its type definition we include

        fashion GasTank using self.gastank;

This clause has two consequences. First it says that a *Car* is able to behave in a fashion a *GasTank* does, and can hence be substituted for a *GasTank*. Second it specifies the routing (self.gastank[2]) of a message if received when a car is looked at as being a *GasTank*. Thus substitution of a car for a gas tank is possible and the following is legal:

```
var myPorsche  : Car;
    DavidBowie : GasStationAttendant;
begin
  myPorsche.create;
  DavidBowie.create;
      ...
  DavidBowie.fillup( myPorsche );    !! fillup expects an instance of GasTank!
```

The intended characteristics of this example—taking the whole for a part—can also be examined in the following example. It belongs, to the more general class of *representative problems*.

2.1 Representative Problems

Consider modeling *Departments*. In order to model the membership of the employees to the department the type definition of *Department* contains a set-typed attribute *members: {Employee}*. Now we want to treat a *Department* as if it is a real employee. In the strict sense this is impossible but it is very convenient. For example if a meeting has to be scheduled where each department is demanded to send a representative. Normally the representative is equal to the head of the department, but for example if he gets ill the department wants to be able to select anybody else. In principle the scheduler is not interested in who represents the department but prefers to send the invitation to each department.

We have the problem to allow *Departments* to be substitutable for *Employees*. Again, **fashion** solves it:

---

[2]self is bound to the corresponding *Car* instance in this case.

```
type Department supertype ANY is
   body [ members:      {Employee};
          head:         Manager;
          representative: Employee; ]
   fashion Employee using self.representative;
   ...
end;
```

Now, each *Department* may become apparent as an *Employee* without really being one. We may insert the development department into the set of meeting participants, like this:

```
var MeetingParticipants: {Employee};
    DevelopmentDep  : Department;
    BigBoss         : Manager;
    emp             : Employee;
    ...
begin
    ...
    MeetingParticipants.insert( BigBoss );          !! no meeting without him
    MeetingParticipants.insert( DevelopmentDep ); !! they will send a representative
```

A representative will be selected via **self.**representative* each time when we access *Employee* properties of a *Department*. If we print the name of all participants—for example to get a mailing list—, the selection of the representative will be done while evaluating the expression *emp.Name*:

```
foreach (emp in MeetingParticipants)
    print( emp.Name );
```

Since the selection of the representative is hidden behind the interface of *Department*, he can be exchanged easily. For example, if the current representative gets ill, we may point out another one without the need to update the set *MeetingParticipants*.

2.2   Some Remarks

In this subsection we want to stress that it is not possible to solve the above problems by utilizing inheritance. There are three main reasons why inheritance is inappropriate:

1. Inheritance affects the taxonomy of types. In the above cases this has to be avoided since a car is not a gas tank and a department is not an employee.

2. Inheritance "clashes" identities. If a car inherits the properties of gas tank, or a department inherits the properties of an employee neither the gas tank nor the employee (representative) would have its own identity. Note that this problem is also solved by delegation (see [6]) for example.

3. Unexpected (and senseless) inheritance conflicts are possible. For example if we want both, *Departments* and *Employees* to have a *head* attribute a conflict arizes if a *Department*'s head denotes the leader of all department members and a *Person*'s head is part of the person's body.

These points remain true for subsequent examples.

3   Taking Parts for a Whole

Within the last Section we tackled problems where we wanted to take the whole for a part. Now tables are turned: We show a possibility to simulate a whole object by gluing together some selected parts. Let us demonstrate this by means of an example. A house can be (partially) characterized by the following attributes and operations:

1. number of floors,

2. a list of tenants, and

3. people can move in and out.

This is reflected in the following type definition:

```
type RealEstate is ... end;

type House supertype RealEstate is
    public no_of_floors, move_in, move_out
    body [ no_of_floors: int;
           tenants      : (Person);
           ...
         ]
    operations
        declare move_in: Person → void;
        declare move_out: Person → void;
        ...
    implementation
        ...
end;
```

With respect to these features a *house boat* is very similar to a house: It possesses all of them. We admit that a slightly different terminology is used, e.g., the *floors* of the house boat are called *decks*. Surely, nobody standing in front of a house boat would classify it as a house since there is a significant difference between a house and a house boat: A house is a *real estate* and thus per definitionem not movable while a house boat can easily change its location.

Nevertheless, there are some cases, where we want to treat the house boat like a house, e.g., a move enterprise does not make any difference between a house and a house boat.

```
type MoveEnterprise is
    ...
    operations
        declare move:   p:Person, from:House , to:House → Cost;
        ...
    end type MoveEnterprise;
```

Assume the existence of some type definition for *HouseBoat*. To perform a move from a house to a house boat some code along the lines of the following must be executed:

```
    var MoveAndSonsInc : MoveEnterprise;
        Me              : Person;
        old_residence   : House;
        new_residence   : HouseBoat;
    begin
        . . .
        MoveAndSonsInc.move( Me, old_residence, new_residence );
```

n order to support the call of *move* the house boat *new_residence* must be substitutable
or *House* objects. The usage of inheritance again leads to a conflict with the real world's
axonomy.

A better solution to the problem is provided by utilizing the *fashion* construct. We
"construct" a house as a new whole from selected parts of a house boat.

```
    type HouseBoat supertype boat is
        body [ no_of_decks : int;
               tenants      : (Person);
               . . .
             ]
        fashion House
            where no_of_floors: int is self.no_of_decks;
            where move_in: p:Person → void is self.move_in(p);
            where move_out: p:Person → void is self.move_out(p);
        operations
            declare move_in: Person → void;
            declare move_out: Person → void;
            . . .
    end type HouseBoat;
```

Within the *fashion* clause we map the properties of *HouseBoat* to the properties of *House*.
Note, that renaming of attributes—as we did for *no_of_decks*—is a special case of such a
mapping.

It is important to notice that the simulated object (here, the house) does not have its
own identifier. Instead, the identifier of the object providing the selected parts (here, the
house boat) is preserved.

4 General Syntax and Semantics

4.1 The Syntax

It is common practice to gather both, the structural and behavioral specification of a
type definition, in a type definition frame. Objects are then created by instantiating a
certain type. As seen in the above examples a type definition frame consists in GOM of
several clauses: the public, body, operations, and implementation clauses (see [5]). The
type definition frame is now enhanced by a *fashion* clause. Figure 1 shows the full type
definition frame including the fashion clause.

Each ⟨fashion construct⟩ in turn has the following syntax:

```
[persistent] type ⟨type name⟩ ⟨supertype specification⟩ is
    [public ⟨operations list⟩]
    [body ⟨type structure⟩]
    [fashion
        ⟨fashion construct⟩
        ...
        ⟨fashion construct⟩]
    [operations
        ⟨operation signature⟩
        ...
        ⟨operation signature⟩]
    [implementation
        ⟨operation implementation⟩
        ...
        ⟨operation implementation⟩]
end type ⟨type name⟩;
```

Figure 1: Type Definition Frame

```
⟨name of fashioned type⟩ [using ⟨fashion-expr⟩]
    [ where⟨operation signature⟩ is ⟨where-expr⟩;
        ...
    where⟨operation signature⟩ is ⟨where-expr⟩ ];
```

Here, ⟨name of fashioned type⟩ is a type symbol utilized in another type definition frame, ⟨fashion-expr⟩ is a GOM expression returning an object of type t, ⟨operation signature⟩ is an operation signature, i.e., the operators input and output type specification, and ⟨where-expr⟩ is a GOM expression of the specified operation signature's output type.[3] Note that the *where* and the using clause are optional and may both be missing. This is interpreted as an abbreviation of in self.

If the type definition is declared to be a subtype of another type the **fashion** clause of the supertype is inherited. Overriding, i.e., redefinition of a ⟨fashion construct⟩ for a particular type is possible by just restating a ⟨fashion construct⟩ for this type. In summary, for a type t all ⟨fashion construct⟩s (for a particular type) from clauses of supertypes of t except the redefined ones plus the explicitly defined ones are *visible* in t. Of course, conflicts may occur and must be resolved by redefinition of certain ⟨fashion construct⟩s. This is discussed in Section 4.2.3

4.2 The Semantics

The main purpose of the *fashion* construct is to *manipulate the substitutability relation*. As pointed out in [4] and [5] objects of a type T may only be substituted for objects of type S if objects of type T are at least as knowledgeable (wrt. applicable operations) as

---

[3]The *where* clause within the fashion construct is analogous to the *where* clause in [3] where it is utilized to overcome certain anomalies of standard inheritance.

objects of type S, i.e. T is a valid refinement of S. Exactly if this is the case we can write in the type definition of T

fashion S;

We say that T is fashioned as S. If this is not the case and nevertheless substitutability of objects of type T for objects of type S is wanted then we must apply certain "corrections". These can be performed utilizing *using* or *where*. The discussion of these topics is followed by a characterization of the run-time behavior of fashioned objects.

4.2.1   How *Fashion* Affects Substitutability

A regular schema without *fashion* defines a binary subtype relation $\prec_T$ on the set of all defined types. If this subtype relation is, as in GOM, based on name equivalence we have $S \prec_T T$ iff T is defined to be a supertype of S. By the inherit-all paradigm which is obligatory for strongly typed languages the objects of type S have at least all the features of objects of type T.

As a consequence of $S \prec_T T$, objects of type S are allowed to be substituted for objects of type T. Thus, substitutability may be interpreted as a binary relation $\Leftarrow$ over types, too. Up to now it is identical to $\prec_T$. It is this relation that may be altered by a *fashion* clause.

If the type definition of type T contains an entry

fashion $F \ldots$;

i.e., T is fashioned as F, the substitutability relation $\Leftarrow$ will be expanded to

$$\Leftarrow' := \Leftarrow \cup (F, T).$$

As a consequence we can substitute an object of type T for an object of type F. On the language level expressions of type F may now be replaced by expressions of type T. The most important case is to assign to a variable of type F an expression of type T:

```
var f:F;
begin
    f := T$create;    !! legal (due to fashion)
```

The assignment is legal due to the modified substitutability relation.

Of course, we cannot change the substitutability relation unseen if we want to get running code. For a type F providing an operation *op* and type T not providing *op*, with T fashioned as F, consider the following code fragment:

```
var f:F;
    t:T;
begin
    f := F$create;    !! create an object of type F
    t := T$create;    !! create an object of type T
    f.op;             !! op, associated to F, will be executed
    f := t;           !! legal (due to fashion)
    f.op;             !! FAILURE
```

The last operation fails since there is no operation *op* for objects of type T available. Thus, the first point we have to assure before changing the substitutability relation is the availability of appropriate operations and their code.

But failures may be more subtle. Let F provide an operation *op* returning a Boolean value and T an operation *op* returning an integer. It is obvious that type conflicts may occur which cannot be checked at compile time since the actual contents of (e.g.) variables is not known. Further, the types of the input parameters may differ which leads to further difficulties. In the following we first give a necessary and sufficient condition for guaranteeing type safety and then provide the means by which this condition can be satisfied.

The following heavily relies in results of [4], [5] and only the bare minimum of needed definitions is reviewed: For a type T define its type signature Σ_T as the collection of all the signatures of its operations, where for tuple types attributes are treated as operations and for set types the standard signatures for *insert* and *remove* are included.[4] Since attributes may also occur on the left hand side of an assignment two signatures have to be added for each attribute. For a type T containing an attribute A of type T_A, we have the signatures

1. $A : T \to T_A$ for reading an attribute. A is called a value-returning operation (VTO for short).

2. $A : T \leftarrow T_A$ for writing an attribute. A is called a value-receiving operation (VCO for short).

In order to guarantee type safety in the context of strong typing the following must hold:

$S \preceq_T T$ iff S is a valid refinement of T

where S is a valid refinement of T iff

- for every value returning operation *op*: $s_1, \ldots, s_n \to s_{n+1}$ in Σ_T there exists an operation *op*: $s'_1, \ldots, s'_n \to s'_{n+1}$ in Σ_S such that

  1. $s_i \leq s'_i$ for $1 \leq i \leq n$ (i.e., the input parameter types must be supertypes)
  2. $s'_{n+1} \leq s_{n+1}$ (i.e., the result type must be a subtype)

- and for every value receiving operation *op*: $s_1, \ldots, s_n \leftarrow s_{n+1}$ in Σ_T there exists a value receiving operation *op*: $s'_1, \ldots, s'_n \leftarrow s'_{n+1}$ in Σ_S such that

  1. $s_i \leq s'_i$ for $1 \leq i \leq n+1$ (all parameters can be viewed as input parameters).

Whenever T is fashioned as S and T is a valid refinement of S there exists no problem and we can include

fashion S;

into the type definition of T. If T is not a valid refinement of S we have to do some adjustments in order to guarantee type safety. The *fashion* construct provides two means for performing the necessary corrections. Roughly, we have

[4]For a formal definition of type signatures and more details on the subsequent condition see [4] or [5].

1. the **using** clause for "large scale integration" and

2. the **where** clause for "small scale surgery".

Whenever the *using* clause is utilized for fashioning T as F the ⟨fashion expression⟩ specifies a way to get an object fulfilling the requirements of type F. Thus there must exist a part of T which is a valid refinement of F. More formally, if T is fashioned as F we define a special fashion signature $\Sigma_{T,S}^{fashion}$ as follows: If **using** e is specified for an expression e of type S then

$$\Sigma_{T,F}^{fashion} := \Sigma_S$$

The fashioning of T as F is now legal if

$\Sigma_{T,F}^{fashion}$ is a valid refinement of Σ_F.

If this is not true the surgery mechanism of the *where* clause must be applied. For all operators *op* in F for which we cannot find the appropriate counterpart within $\Sigma_{T,F}^{fashion}$ one *where* clause of the form

$$\textbf{where } op: \quad p_1 : T_1, \ldots, p_n : T_n \leftrightarrow T_{n+1} \text{ is } \langle \text{where-expr} \rangle^{5\ 6}$$

which enhances $\Sigma_{T,F}^{fashion}$

$$\Sigma_{T,F}^{fashion} := \Sigma_{T,F}^{fashion} \cup \{op : T_1, \ldots, T_n \leftrightarrow T_{n+1}\}.$$

has to be provided such that the resulting fashion signature $\Sigma_{T,F}^{fashion}$ is a valid refinement of F. As we will see this condition called *validity* of a fashion construct is necessary and sufficient to guarantee type correctness of operator calls.

4.2.2 The Dynamics of Fashioned Objects

We now turn to the treatment of the dynamics of expression evaluation if fashioned objects occur. Whenever the *using* clause is utilized for fashioning T as F the ⟨fashion expression⟩ specifies a way to get an object of type F. During runtime this expression is evaluated *each time* a dereferenciation of an object of type T in the context of F to a property of F is required. As an example take some operator applied to a variable f of type F where f is currently bound to an object of type T. The result of this call is computed by first evaluating the ⟨fashion expression⟩ and then applying the operator to the result, i.e., by evaluating $f.fashion\text{-}expr.op$. In other words: evaluation of the fashion expression will be inserted between the dereferenciation of some object identifier and the selection of the operator code to be applied. The runtime consequences of the *where* clause can briefly be characterized as follows. Whenever a *where* clause is specified for an operator *op*, $f.where\text{-}expr$ is evaluated instead of $f.fashion\text{-}expr.op$.

Chains of fashioned types as well as conflicts if the same operator name is multiply used provide certain difficulties for the selection of the correct code to be executed when an expression of a fashioned type occurs. Our approach to define the selection mechanism

---

[5] ↔ means ← or → (i.e. VTO or VCO)
[6] we do allow side effects within ⟨where-expr⟩

of the correct piece of code for an operator call to an object within a certain context is as follows. We first define the notion of *behavioral origin* which is a syntactic construct which can easily be interpreted and specifies the behavior of an object within a context. In a sense the behavioral origin even specifies the objects context. We then show how a *well-typed* behavioral origin can be determined at runtime. This implies that type safety can be guaranteed at compile time. Additionally, it is a desirable feature that there exists always exactly *one* behavioral origin. Otherwise, the corresponding object's behavior would get indeterministic in the sense, that we cannot predict which of the possible choices will be taken. Section 4.2.3 treats this problem.

The first useful definition concerns the *behavioral origin* for each occurrence of an object (identifier). It tells us how to acquire the behavior expected from the referenced object in a certain context. The original behavior of an object, i.e., the operations provided by the type it is an instance of is called *domestic*.

The set BO of all *behavioral origins* for a given schema is defined inductively as follows:

1. $T_{domestic} \in BO$, if T is a type symbol. If this BO is associated with a reference to object o the domestic operations of T are applied when o is dereferenced.

2. $T_{\langle fashion\ construct\rangle} \in BO$, if T is a type symbol and $\langle fashion\ construct\rangle$ is a valid fashion construct declared in the definition of T. If a BO of this kind is associated with a reference to object o the operations of F are applied utilizing the $\langle fashion\ construct\rangle$ which was implemented with operations of T.

3. $b \circ T_{\langle fashion\ construct\rangle} \in BO$, if $b, T_{\langle fashion\ construct\rangle} \in BO$ and $\langle fashion\ construct\rangle$ is a valid fashion construct declared in the definition of T. This is the concatenation of the behavioral origins b and $T_{fashion\ F\ ...}$[7] with the intended meaning that the operations of F are applied by utilizing the fashion construct implemented with operations of T which in turn can be acquired via b.

We identify two kinds of types associated to each $b \in BO$: Each behavioral origin implements the properties of $b\_type(b)$ utilizing the resources given by $r\_type(b)$.

$b \in BO$	$b\_type(b)$	$r\_type(b)$
$T_{domestic}$	T	T
$T_{fashion\ F\ ...}$	F	T
$b' \circ T_{fashion\ F\ ...}$	F	$r\_type(b')$

Clearly, only those concatenations $b' \circ T_{fashion\ F\ ...}$ of BOs are legal where $T_{fashion\ F\ ...}$ utilizes the resources which are offered by b'. Therefore, we restrict our investigations to *well-typed* BOs. A behavioral origin $b \in BO$ is called *well-typed*, iff for some types T, F either $b = T_{domestic}$, $b = T_{fashion\ F\ ...}$ or $b = b' \circ T_{fashion\ F\ ...}$ with $b\_type(b') \preceq_T r\_type(T_{fashion\ F\ ...})$. It is easy to see that for a well-typed behavioral origin b all the properties offered at the interface of $b\_type(b)$ can really be implemented utilizing the resources offered at the interface of $r\_type(b)$. A behavioral origin b is called *consistent* for a reference to an object of type T iff b is well-typed and $T \preceq_T r\_type(b)$.

---

[7]We will write $T_{fashion\ F\ ...}$, if we are not interested in the complete fashion construct but we want to signal, that T will be fashioned as F.

For a strongly typed language, we will show how to derive a *well-typed* behavioral origin for all references to some object. Without loss of generality we restrict ourselves to references realized by variables and to only two ways to store an object reference in a variable:

- the reference is stored upon object creation:

      var s:S;
      ...
      s.create;

- the reference is distributed by assignment:

      var t:T; s:S;
      ...
      t := s;

Note, that since we consider strongly typed languages we have to examine only those assignments where $T \Leftarrow^* S$ holds.

We now show how a consistent behavioral origin can be acquired for each reference. The first case is trivial since $b = S_{domestic}$ is the only choice of associating a behavioral origin with s. The consistency of b to s is obvious.

Considering assignments, we first treat the cases, where $S \preceq_T T$ holds. Here, the behavioral origin of s is just carried over as the one of t. Obviously, it is consistent for t.

Now, only the cases remain where $S \npreceq_T T$ and $T \Leftarrow^* S$. If $T \Leftarrow S$ then (since S is not a subtype of T) there must exist a valid fashion construct "fashion $T \ldots$" within the definition of S, which fashiones S as T. If we assume b_s to be a consistent behavioral origin for s it is an easy job to get a consistent behavioral origin for t: $b_s \circ S_{fashion\,T\,\ldots}$. The general case $T \Leftarrow^* S$ is proven by induction. We omit the proof since it does not give any new insights.

The most important implication of the above is that type safety can be guaranteed at compile time. Thus, the fashion construct does not jeopardize the benefits of strong typing.

4.2.3 Conflicts

This section treats the last open question—how can the uniqueness of the behavioral origin be guaranteed. To become acquainted with the problem consider the following example. Suppose the definition of the four types A, B, C and D. B is a subtype of A, D is a subtype of C, and there exist fashion constructs to behave C as A and D as B.

      type A is ...;
      type B supertype A is ...;

      type C is
         ...fashion A ...;
      end type C;

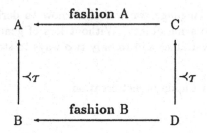

Figure 2: A typical conflict situation

```
type D supertype C is
  ...fashion B ...;
end type D;
```

The ambiguity of consistent behavioral origins arises when we want to assign a variable
of type D to a variable of type A:

```
var a:A, d:D;
begin
    d.create;    !! b_d = D_{domestic}
    a := d;      !! b_a = D_{domestic} ∘ C_{fashion A ...}  or
                 !! b_a = D_{domestic} ∘ D_{fashion B ...} ?
```

Two consistent behavioral origins exist and can be derived by the rules defined in the
previous Section: First we can interpret the object, referenced by d—an instance of D—
as an instance of C. For instances of C in turn fashioning as A is possible. In other
words, we can associate $D_{domestic} \circ C_{fashion A ...}$ as a consistent behavioral origin to the
reference a. The other possibility is $D_{domestic} \circ D_{fashion B ...}$. In this case, we use the
possibility of fashioning instances of D as instances of B. Due to the subtype relationship
of B and A, we can assign it to a. Figure 2 illustrates this conflict. Instead of giving
explicit conflict resolution strategies like precedence rules we require the programmer to
resolve the conflict. Typically the compiler detects unresolved conflicts which then can be
corrected by the programmer by rewriting his program by replacing the above assignment
by one of the following alternatives:

1.
```
        c := d;    !! b_c = D_{domestic}
        a := c;    !! b_a = D_{domestic} ∘ C_{fashion A ...}
```

2.
```
        b := d;    !! b_b = D_{domestic} ∘ D_{fashion B ...}
        a := b;    !! b_a = D_{domestic} ∘ D_{fashion B ...}
```

Now, there are no ambiguities left. To avoid the additional and unnecessary assignment,
GOM allows the usage of *type qualifications* in the form of "$\langle type\ name \rangle \$ \langle expression \rangle$".

A type qualification explicitly specifies the type of an expression. Of course, this specified type must be a supertype of the type of the expression. Thus, the above conflict may also be resolved by replacing the assignment by one of the following alternatives:

1.   a := C\$d;   !! $b\_a = D_{domestic} \circ C_{fashion\,A}\,...$

2.   a := B\$d;   !! $b\_a = D_{domestic} \circ D_{fashion\,B}\,...$

But there exist some *hopeless* cases, in which even this explicit conflict resolution is impossible. One can show that these arise only in one of the following cases:

1. if there are two **fashion** constructs defined in the same type, both fashioning another, *equal* type.

2. if there exists a **fashion** construct, fashioning a supertype of the given type or the given type itself.

These cases are detected and rejected by the compiler.

5   Conclusion

We have identified two groups of problems where the possibility to build taxonomies utilizing the *is-a* relationship including subtyping and inheritance lacks the needed modeling power. The identified groups have in common that they require objects of a certain type to be substitutable for objects of another type where the two types are not necessarily related by the subtype relationship. To overcome these problems the concept of fashioning has been introduced and illustrated by its application to several example problems. It has been shown that valid fashion clauses do not violate strong typing. Further investigations concern the interplay of the fashion construct with inheritance and genericity as well as a comparison with delegation (see [6]) which seems to be a special case of fashioning.

6   Acknowledgements

The authors gratefully acknowledge the helpful comments of the anonymous referees.

References

[1] L. Cardelli and P. Wegner. On understanding types, data abstraction, and polymorphism. *ACM Computing Surveys*, 17(4):471–522, Dec 1985.

[2] J. A. Goguen and D. Wolfram. On types and FOOPS. In *Proc. IFIP TC-2 Conf. on Object-Oriented Databases*, Windermere, UK, Jun 90.

[3] A. Kemper and G. Moerkotte. Correcting anomalies of standard inheritance — a constraint-based approach. In *Proc. Int. Conf. on Database and Expert Systems Applications (DEXA)*, pages 49–55, 1990.

[4] A. Kemper and G. Moerkotte. A framework for strong typing and type inference in (persistent) object models. In *Proc. Int. Conf. on Database and Expert Systems Applications (DEXA)*, 1991.

[5] A. Kemper, G. Moerkotte, H.-D. Walter, and A. Zachmann. GOM: a strongly typed, persistent object model with polymorphism. In *Proc. of the German Conf. on Databases in Office, Engineering and Science (BTW)*, pages 198–217, Kaiserslautern, Mar 1991. Springer-Verlag, Informatik Fachberichte Nr. 270.

[6] L. Stein. Delegation is inheritance. In *Proc. of the ACM Conf on Object-Oriented Programming Systems and Languages (OOPSLA)*, 1987.

A View Mechanism for Object-Oriented Databases

Elisa Bertino *
Dipartimento di Matematica - Universita' di Genova
Via L.B. Alberti 4, 16132 Genova (Italy)

Abstract

In this paper, we present a view model for object-oriented databases that extends
in various directions view models typical of relational databases. In particular, the
definition language allows views to be defined that augment class definitions (by
adding properties and methods), and that support a wide spectrum of schema modifications. Therefore, views represent a unified mechanism able to provide several
functions, such as query shorthand, definitions of dynamic sets and partitions of
classes, authorizations, schema changes and versions, object perspectives.

1 Introduction

In the relational data model, a view is defined as a *virtual relation* derived by a query on
one or more stored relations. The relational operations join, select, and project may be
used to define a view. Views can be used in (almost) any query where a relation can be
used. Furthermore, authorizations may be granted and revoked on views as on ordinary
relations. This possibility allows content-based authorization [Bert 88] to be granted on
stored relations. Therefore, views can be used for two reasons: data protection and user
convenience (see the concepts of *protection view* and *shorthand view* in [Bert 88]). Another
important usage of views in databases is to support a (limited) form of external schemas,
since a view mechanism allows views to be defined with a subset of the properties of a
base relation, or a view obtained as a combination of several base relations (i.e. it allows
relation merging).

An important question is whether the concept of views in object-oriented databases
is still useful, or other mechanisms such as inheritance to some extent obviates the need
for views as used in relational databases. A first reason for defining different views on a
class is to allow different interpretations of the class instances. For example, a group of
users may be interested in seeing the class Student through two views, UnderGraduate
and Graduate, while another group of users may be interested in the views ForeignStu-
dent and DomesticStudent. If we define each of these views as a subclass of the class
Student, all the instances should belong to the subclasses. However, these views do not
constitute a partition of the class Student, since a foreign student can be also a graduate

---

*The work reported in this paper has been partially supported by the Consiglio Nazionale delle
Ricerche under the project Progetto Finalizzato Sistemi Informatici e Calcolo Parallelo - Sottoprogetto
5 (Sistemi Evoluti per Basi di Dati

student. Therefore, we must define all combinations of these subclasses (i.e. Foreign-Graduate, ForeignUndergraduate, etc.). The view mechanism appears useful in allowing different interpretations of the same class, without complicating the class hierarchy organization. Moreover, the fact that views are defined by queries allows subsets of classes to be dynamically defined based on constraints over the class instances. For example, a view ExcellentStudent could be defined on the class Student by selecting all students having the mark *A* in all exams.

The need of different interpretations for the same object is also found in object-oriented programming languages, office models, and software information bases. For example, the concept of a *perspective* [Stef 86] allows different views of the same conceptual entity to be defined. In certain cases, as in LOOPS, each perspective of an object can have different instance variables and methods. Therefore, a view mechanism, if properly enhanced, could provide the equivalent of a perspective in object-oriented databases. The need of supporting multiple views of the same class has also been recognized as an important requirement in supporting large software bases [Shil 89].

As in relational databases, views are a powerful mechanism to provide authorization based on database contents. An authorization models for object-oriented databases have been defined in [Rabi 91] and [Thur 89]. The model defined in [Rabi 91] is a discretionary model and supports different levels of granularity (class, attribute, instance). The model described in [Thur 89] considers mandatory access control. However, both models do not support authorizations that dynamically depend on object contents. A way to provide a content-based access control on instances of a class is to define views containing predicates on the values of some specific attributes of the class. Therefore, only the objects that meet the specified conditions are visible through the view. If authorizations are granted on the view and not on the class, the access is restricted to the class instances that are not filtered out by the view.

Finally, we note that a view mechanism would allow one form of schema evolution [Bane 87, Penn 87]. The possibility of dynamically modifying a database schema but yet retaining its older versions is very important for advanced applications, like CAD/CAM, multimedia documents, software engineering, where defining the structure and the behavior of objects is a crucial activity. In particular, we will show in this paper how the view mechanism can be extended to support schema versions and to experiment with schema changes before actually executing them. Therefore a view mechanism in object-oriented databases is useful for: user convenience as shorthand, definition of dynamic sets and partitions of classes, authorization, schema changes and versions.

The remainder of this paper is organized as follows. Section 2 describes a simple definition language for views and discusses the different types of views that can be created by using this language. Section 3 discusses how views are used to simulate both primitive [Bane 87] and complex schema changes. Finally, Section 4 summarizes the paper.

2 View Definition and Semantics

In this section, we first review some concepts concerning object-oriented data models and we briefly survey the object-oriented query language which is used to define views. We

hen present the view definition language. By using this language we will show different
usage of views.

2.1 Object-oriented data models

The object-oriented paradigm is based on a number of basic concepts [Bert 91, Stef 86].
Here, we only describe those concepts that are relevant to the subsequent discussion.

Objects Any real-world entity is represented by only one modeling concept: the object.
Each object is uniquely identified by a system-defined identifier (called here object
identifier, or OID). The state of an object is defined at any time by the value of
its *properties* (called attributes, or instance variables, elsewhere). Properties can
have as values both primitive objects, such as strings, integers or booleans, and
non-primitive objects. The behavior of an object is specified by the *methods* that
operate on the object state.

Classes Objects with the same properties and behavior are grouped in *classes*. Objects,
instances of a given class, have a value for each property defined for the class, and
they respond to all messages that invoke methods defined for the class. We assume
that properties at class level are typed, i.e. a domain is associated with each property
specifying the class of the possible objects that can be assigned to the property
when the class is instanciated. The fact that a class is domain of a property of
another class establishes a relationship, called *aggregation relationship*, between the
two classes. Aggregation relationships among classes in an object-oriented database
organize classes in an *aggregation graph*. In addition to the intensional notion, we
make the assumption that the concept of class has the extensional notion of the set
of objects sharing a common definition. In this case, the class provides the basis
for formulating queries. In fact, queries are meaningful only if applied to sets of
objects.

Inheritance Classes are also organized in an *inheritance* hierarchy, orthogonal to the
aggregation hierarchy. Inheritance allows a class, called subclass, to be defined as
a specialization of some other existing class, called superclass. A subclass inherits
properties and methods from its superclass, and may have specific properties and
methods. Most models support, however, the overriding of inherited properties and
methods. Therefore, the inheritance mechanism allows a class to specialize another
class by *additions* and *substitutions*.

An object oriented database can be represented as a graph. In this representation,
a node (denoted by a box) represents a class. A class node contains the names of all
instance properties and methods. Nodes can be connected by two types of arc. An arc
from a class C to C' indicates different relationships between the two classes depending
on the arc type. A normal arc (i.e. non-bold) indicates that C' is domain of a property of
C, or that C' is the domain of the results of a method of C. A bold arc indicates that C
is a superclass of C'. The '*' symbol following a property name denotes that the property
is multivalued. An example is presented in Figure 1.

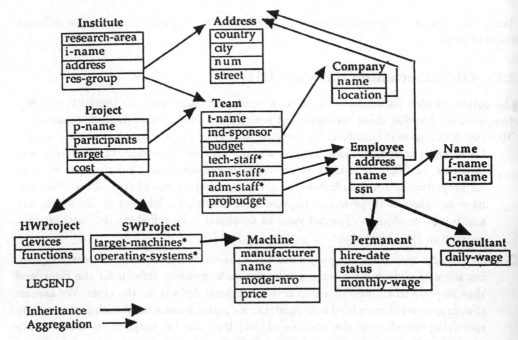

Figure 1: Database schema example

2.2 Review of the query language

[Bert 91a] describes a model of object-oriented queries. The language has been defined as an extension of a predicate calculus language. A query in OOPC (object-oriented predicate calculus) consists of three clauses:

1. **Target clause.** It specifies what must be retrieved by the query. It is possible to retrieve objects from a single class, or from a union (denoted by ∨) of classes, or from the classes in an inheritance hierarchy (* operator). Moreover, it is possible to retrieve only some properties from the queried objects (i.e., projections are supported).

2. **Range clause.** It contains a list of quantified variables, denoting objects, bound to classes or collections of objects. This clause specifies the variable declarations for classes to which the query applies.

3. **Qualification clause.** It is a well-formed formula, defined as a boolean combination of simple predicates. Among the predicates, we mention the *alternative predicate* used to formulate different conditions on different subclasses in a given inheritance hierarchy.

An example of the query against the schema of Figure 1 is

Retrieve the last names of all permanent employees and consultants living in Rome, working in the technical staff of a team sponsored by a company located in Turin, and such that if they are permanents their salary is higher than

140

4,000, if they are consultants their daily wage is higher than 500.

Ths previous query is expressed in OOPC as follows:

target   x.name.l-name;
range   x/ (Permanent ∨ Consultant)
qualification   (∃t/Team) (x.address.city = 'Rome' ∧
t.ind-sponsor.location.city = 'Turin' ∧ x ISIN t.tech-staff ∧
CLASS_OF (x) = [Permanent: x.monthly-wage > 4000; Consultant: x.daily-wage> 500]).

The previous query shows many characteristics of the query language. The last predicate in the query is an example of alternative predicate. The alternative predicate is expressed as a case on the classes to which the variable x is bound. In the previous query, the variable x is bound to two classes Permanent and Consultant. The alternative predicate contains two cases, one for each of those two classes. In the alternative predicate, the name of a class is followed by the predicate to be used when a particular instance belongs to that class. A sequence of property names following a variable, such as 'x.address.city', is called *path-expression* and is used to denote a nested property of the object denoted by the variable. Path-expressions do not increase the expressive power of queries. However, they represent a convenient and natural way to express queries based on navigation along the aggregation hierarchy. Path-expressions can be used in the target clause to retrieve the values of object nested properties. The predicate 'x ISIN t.tech-staff' is an example of *set membership* predicate. The predicate is true if the object, denoted by variable x, belongs to the set of objects, values of the multi-valued property 'tech-staff', of the object denoted by variable t.

2.3   Organization of an Object-Oriented Schema with Views

As we discussed earlier, an object-oriented schema is organized along two dimensions (i.e. aggregation and inheritance). An important question is whether the organization of an object-oriented schema is to be extended when views are introduced. In the approach we propose, the schema is extended by introducing a new dimension, called *view derivation*. A view derivation relationship between a class C and a view V denotes that V is defined "on top of" C, that is, C is a *base class* of V. The view derivation hierarchy is different from a class hierarchy. A view derived from a class may have fewer properties than the class and additional methods. Therefore, the view cannot be a subclass of the class from which is derived (since it has fewer properties), and vice versa (since it has more methods). In this case, it is not possible to use the class hierarchy to represent the relationship between the class and the view. In [Scho 90] an approach is described where views are inserted in the inheritance hierarchy, that is, a view is handled as a subclass or a superclass of some existing class(es). This approach has the major problem that gives rise to inheritance hierarchies quite complex, often containing classes that are not semantically meaningul for the users. We have introduced the possibility of defining a view as subview of other views. The reason is to allow the user to re-use a method definition, associated with a view, in defining another view. As we will see in the following section, a view can have its own methods in addition to these obtained from its base class(es).

2.4 View definition language

In our model a view is defined by a query (*view-query*), as in relational systems [Bert 88], on top of one or more classes, called *base class (es)* of the view. However, in order to be suitable for usage in object-oriented databases, this model must extended along several directions. First, the possibility of views with *additional properties* has been introduced. Additional properties are not derived from the base classes. This allows views to be defined that augment the definition of the base classes. Their more important usage is in supporting schema changes. Second, the view model we define is not only a structural model but it has also behavioral features, that is, a view may have methods. Finally, a view, like a class, may be defined as subview of other views.

The view definition statement has the following format:

create-view Viewname   [properties ListofPropertyNames]
                          [view-query query]
                          [additionalproperties ListofProperties]
                          [methods ListofMethodSpecifications]
                          [superviews ListofViews]
                          [OID TrueOrFalse]
                          [identityfrom ListofClassNames]

Viewname is the name of the view. A view must have a name which is different from the names of other views and classes. The parameters associated with each keyword are described as follows:

properties The ListofPropertyNames associated with this keyword specifies the names of the view properties and possibly default values for the properties. However, no domain must be specified for these properties since they are deduced from the target clause of the query. If no property names for the view are specified, the names are equal to the names of the corresponding properties of the base class(es). In general specifying property names for a view is not mandatory, unless the view is defined on two or more classes that have the same name for their properties and these properties are included in the query target. The default value of a property in the view may be different from the default value of the corresponding property in the base class. Therefore, when an instance is created through a view and no value is specified for a property, the default value in the view will be assumed for this property. If no default value is specified in the view, the property will take the default value specified in the base class.

view-query This keyword is followed by the query expression that defines the view. Any query expression defined according to the query language described in [Bert 91a] can be used in the view definition.

additionalproperties The ListofProperties associated with this keyword provides a specification of the view properties that are not derived from the class(es) on which the view is defined. A property specification is very similar to a property specification in a class definition. It consists of the property name and the domain. The domain can be a class or a view.

methods This keyword is followed by the specifications of the view methods. A method specification can be one of the following:

1. MethodName [of ClassName]
2. MethodName1 as MethodName2 [of ClassName]
3. MethodName MethodImplementation
4. **AllMethods** [of ListofClassNames].

When only the method name is specified (case (1) above), the view receives the corresponding method (i.e the method with the same name) from the base class. Optionally, a class name may be specified (parameter ClassName). This is mandatory if the view is defined on several base classes having methods with the same name. Moreover, this feature is useful for schema changes where the inheritance of a method is changed. In this case, the name of the class indicates one of the superclasses of the view base class. The second alternative for method specification allows the renaming of a method which is received from a base class. Therefore, the view has a method MethodName1 that has the same parameters and implementation of MethodName2 of the base class. A class name may be specified. This is mandatory if the view is defined on several base classes having methods with the same name. The third alternative defines new methods for the view. This is useful for augmenting a class definition by adding new methods, and for providing different implementations of the base class method. In the latter case, the method name would be that of the method in the base class, but the implementation would be different; this is analogous to method overriding in subclass definitions.

A view does not automatically receive the methods of its base class(es). The reason for this is that the view definition may contain only a subset of the properties defined for the base class(es). Therefore, some methods may not be valid for the view. In order to determine which methods are applicable to the view, the system should determine the properties used in each method implementation. Therefore, we have taken the option that no methods from the base class(es) are associated with the view, unless explicitly included by the user. However, in cases where the user wishes to associate all methods from the base class(es) with the view definition, we provide the keyword **AllMethods**. This keyword is a shorthand. It can be followed by one or more class names for cases where there is more than one base class.

superviews Since a view may contain additional properties and methods other than those derived from the base class(es), it is convenient to allow an existing view definition to be re-used in the specification of a new view. This clause specifies the view(s) which will become the superviews of the newly created view.

OID This keyword may have the value True or False, indicating whether persistent identifiers must be provided for the view instances. The default value is True. In general, supporting identifiers for view instances involves allocating and maintaining some storage structures. A possible approach is discussed in [Bert 91b]. Therefore, in all cases where there is no need to reference a view instances, the user can declare this by using this keyword. An example is a view defined only to be used as a shorthand in queries. If, however, the view has additional properties the keyword OID must have the value True.

identityfrom This clause is used for views, whose view-queries contain joins, to define a subset of the base classes on which the view instances depend for identity. This influences the way updates on the view are propagated on the underlying classes.

In our model, a view can be defined in terms of other views. Therefore, a view can appear as the target of the view-query in a view definition. Moreover, a view can be used as the domain of an additional property in the definition of another view.

An example of view definitions is the following. Let us consider the class Machine in Figure 1. Suppose that this class must be partitioned into two sets depending on whether a machine is manufactured by an Italian company or not. These partitions can be defined by the following views:

EX1 **create-view** ItalianMachine

    view-query x; x/Machine; x.manufacturer.location.country = 'Italy'

    create-view ForeignMachine

    view-query x; x/Machine; x.manufacturer.location.country $\neg$ = 'Italy'

In this case the views have the same properties of the class Machine. More complex view definitions will be presented in the following section to illustrate how schema changes are performed by using the view mechanism.

3 Views for Schema Evolution

The application environments that are expected to use an OODBMS require mechanisms to support schema changes. These applications are very often evolutionary and characterized by the fact that schema modifications are a rule, rather than an exception. For example, it is common that during a design application, the ways of classifying objects and their interrelationships evolve. To support those applications, most OODBMSs provide schema modification primitives [Bane 87, Penn 87]. Some of those primitives, however, when executed cause loss of information. For example if a property is dropped from a class definition, all instances of the class lose the values of that property. Those values cannot be recovered later on, if the user decides to revert the change (unless the user has somehow saved them). Moreover, once a user executes a schema change, all the other users must use the modified schema, that is, it is not possible to isolate the modifications. Views represents a mean to overcome those problems, since they allow users to experiment with schema changes before executing them. Moreover, since the definition of a view does not impact the definition of the underlying classes, it is possible for a user to define his own modified schema without affecting other users.

A possible classification of *basic changes* is: changes to a class content, and changes to the class inheritance hierarchy [Bane 87]. We discuss now how some of these schema changes are supported by our view mechanism.

Changes to the definition of a class

- Adding a property to a class is supported by defining a view with an additional property.

- Dropping a property from a class is simply supported by a view whose view-query does not include in the target list the property to be dropped.

- Changing the name of a property is accomplished by defining a view which renames in the clause **properties** the name of this property.

- Changing the domain of a property of a class is accomplished by defining a view which projects out the property from the target clause of the view-query and which has an additional property with the same name and the desired domain.

- Inheriting a property from another superclass C is accomplished as in the previous case. A view is defined which projects out this property from the base class and which has an additional property whose domain is the same of the superclass C.

- Changes to the methods are directly supported by the view definition mechanism, since the user explicitly specifies which methods the view should receive from the base class. It is also possible to define additional methods or define a different implementation for a given method (cf. Section 2).

The following examples illustrate the usage of the view definition language to support some of the previous schema changes,

EX2 As we mentioned in the previous Section, a view may be defined as a projection of some class. This feature can be used to simulate schema changes where a property is dropped. Suppose that we wish to remove the property 'model-nro' from the class Machine. A view accomplishing this change is defined as follows:

create-view NewMachine
view-query x.manufacturer, x.name, x.price; x/Machine;

(the query in the previous view definition does not contain the qualification clause, since it is a projection.)

EX3 Suppose that a machine produced in a country different from Italy costs less if bought directly in the country where it is produced. The property 'price' in the definition of Machine refers to the price in Italy. Suppose that we wish to define a view like the view ForeignMachine (defined in example EX1), which contains for each foreign machine the price in the country where the machine is produced. This new property is called 'fprice'. A view containing this additional property is defined as follows:

create-view ExtForeignMachine
view-query x; x/Machine; x.manufacturer.location.country $\neg=$ 'Italy'
additionalproperties (fprice: **numeric**)

The user can then modify the additional property of the view by providing the appropriate value. The view resulting properties are: 'manufacturer', 'name', 'model-nro', 'price' (which are received from the base class), 'fprice' (which is an additional property)

EX4 Suppose that if a machine is produced in the USA, the price is 20% less there than the price in Italy; while for the other countries is 10% less. In this case, the foreign price can be determined from the price in Italy. Therefore, instead of defining the foreign price as an additional property (as we did in example EX3), we define it as a method. Therefore, the view definition is as follows:

create-view ExtForeignMachine
view-query x; x/Machine; x.manufacturer.location.country $\neg=$ 'Italy'
Methods (fprice () $\rightarrow$ numeric)) [1]

This example shows a view with an additional method.

Changes to the inheritance hierarchy

Primitives for modifying the inheritance hierarchy include the addition, and removal of a superclass of a given class; and the permutation of the superclass order. The first two primitives have the effect of making a class to acquire properties and/or methods (the addition primitive), or to loose some properties and/or methods (the removal primitive) [2]. When the order of superclasses is changed, instead, the class may change the inheritance of some properties and methods. The removal of a superclass C' from the list of superclasses of a class C may be simulated by a view defined on C that projects out all properties and methods inherited from C'. The addition of a superclass to a class C is simulated by a view with additional properties and methods. The permutation of superclasses may be simulated by a view that filters out some properties and methods, and has some additional properties and methods.

In addition to above change primitives, some *complex changes* can be devised. They are complex since they can be implemented by using the basic modification primitives. Complex schema changes are discussed in [Motr 87] and [Li 89]. Examples of complex schema changes include the merge of the classes in an inheritance hierarchy, and the modification of the aggregation hierarchy. Some of those changes may not be implemented in systems not supporting object migration among classes. Views may therefore be a way to support some complex schema modification primitives in those systems. In the remainder, we discuss these schema changes and we illustrate them using some example.

3.1 Merge of classes in an inheritance hierarchy

As we discussed previously it is possible to define views with additional properties other than those derived from the base class(es). This simulates the creation of subclasses and therefore the refinement of an inheritance hierarchy. Now, we discuss the inverse operation (*merge*), which allows the classes in a given inheritance hierarchy to be compacted in a single class. This modification could be accomplished by moving all instances of classes in the inheritance hierarchy into the class which is the root of the inheritance hierarchy to be compacted, and then by eliminating all classes in the inheritance hierarchy, except the root. However, this may not be possible if object migration among classes is not supported.

---

[1] Methods are defined by providing their signatures (consisting of the method name, the input parameters enclosed among brackets, and the output parameter following the $\rightarrow$ symbol), and their implementations. The method in example EX4 does not have input parameters. The implementation of the method is omitted for brevity.

[2] When a superclass is removed from the list of a superclasses of a class C, C looses all properties and methods inherited by the removed class, except for the properties and methods that are present in other superclasses

As an example we define a view that merges all classes in the inheritance hierarchy rooted at class Employee. The view definitions is as follows:

EX5 create-view NewEmployee
   view-query x; x/Employee *;

In the previous view-query, the operator '*' indicates that the query applies to all classes in the inheritance hierarchy rooted at class Employee [3]. Since the qualification clause of the query is empty, all instances of Employee and of all its subclasses are retrieved by the query.

When a view is defined against an inheritance hierarchy, its instances are derived from instances of classes that may have additional properties with respect to the root of the hierarchy. In the previous view, for example, some instances have the property monthly-wage while others have the property daily-wage. One question is whether, given a view-query on an inheritance hierarchy, there would result a single view, or a hierarchy of views (one for each base class). We take the first position; that is, the result is a single view and the view structure is equal to the structure of the root class of the hierarchy, unless a list of properties is explicitly provided in the target clause of the view-query. The reason for this is that if the user defines a view on an inheritance hierarchy rooted at a class C, the user is interested in seeing the objects through the structure of the class C. Therefore, it makes sense to define the view with the structure of C. In the case of the previous view, the class definition does not contain any wage information, and so the view.

However, in certain cases subclasses of a given class have properties which are equivalent. For example, the property daily-wage of the class Consultant multiplied by a given factor may represent the equivalent of the monthly-wage of the class Permanent. Therefore, we may want to merge the classes in an inheritance hierarchy by defining correspondences among the subclass properties. One way to define more complex correspondence is the use of methods (*mapping methods*). For example, we could define a view with a method named 'wage'. The view definition is as follows:

EX6 create-view NewEmployee
   view-query x; x/Employee *;
   Methods (wage() $\rightarrow$ numeric))

A toy implementation of the method 'wage' is illustrated in Figure 2 by using a simple language. In the language, *self* is used to denote the object to which the message invoking the method has been sent (i.e. a view instance). Sending a message m to an object O is denoted as '$O \leftarrow m$'. For example, 'self $\leftarrow$ baseobject' denotes sending the message 'baseobject' to the object to which the method 'wage' has been applied. In the implementation of the method 'wage', it is necessary to determine the base instance from which a given view instance is derived. In fact, depending on the class of the base instance different actions need to be executed. To accomplish this, the system method 'baseobject' is provided which given a view instance returns the identifier(s) of the base instance(s).

---

[3] As in [Bert 91], we distinguish between the notion of *being instance* of a class and *being member* of a class. An object is an instance of a class C if C is the most specific class, in an inheritance hierarchy, associated with the object. An object is member of a class C if the object is an instance of C or is instance of a subclass of C. A query usually applies only to the instances of a class. If, however, the '*' operator follows the class name, the query applies to all members of the class.

```
wage() → numeric
Begin
E: Employee;
N: string;
E := self ← baseobject;
N := E ← classof;
if N == "Permanent" then return(E.monthly-wage)
else (if N == "Consultant" then return(20*E.daily-wage)
else return(nullvalue))
End
```

Figure 2: Toy implementation of method 'wage'

The implementation of this method is described in [Bert 91b]. Moreover, in the example, we make the assumption that the method 'classof' applied to an object returns the name of the class of which the object is instance [Bert 91a].

Therefore in an object-oriented database extended with views, there are two types of derivation relationships. The first is between a view and a class (or another view). There is a derivation relationship from a view V to a class C (or view V') if V is defined by a view-query on the class C (or view V'). The second type of derivation relationship is between an instance of a view and an instance of a class. There is a derivation relationship from an instance I of a view to an instance I' if I has been obtained from I' by applying the transformation defined by the view. The correspondance between the instances of views and the instances of the base classes is maintained by a special structure described in [Bert 91b]. The method 'baseobject' uses this structure to determine the instances from which a given instance of a view has been derived.

When a view, defined for a merge operation, contains mapping methods for all properties of all classes to be merged, the view represents the "union" of all properties of these classes. Such a view provides an operation similar to the *fold* operation defined in [Motr 87]. The fold operation allows a class C to be absorbed into its superclass S. The superclass S is modified to contain the properties of subclass C, in addition to its own properties. The difference is that in our approach the usage of methods allows complex mappings to be defined among the classes properties, while in the approach defined in [Motr 87], the instances of the superclass receive a null value for the properties that class S has acquired from the subclass C.

3.2 Modifications to aggregation hierarchies

A basic concept in object-oriented data models is that each real-world entity is represented by an object. However, in certain cases, some properties of an entity may be stored as different objects. As an example, in the schema of Figure 1, the properties containing information about the addresses of employees have been organized as a different class, i.e. Address. We note that another possible organization would have consisted of including all properties of the class Address directly as properties of the class Employee. This operation, called *telescope* in [Motr 87], may be easily accomplished by a view definition that selects the properties of a base class C, and in addition, the properties of a class C' to be included into C. For example, suppose that we wish to include all properties of the class Address into the class Employee. This is accomplished by the following view:

EX7 create-view NewEmployee
    properties (name, ssn, country, city, num, street)
    view-query x.name, x.ssn,
    x.address.country, x.address.city, x.address.num, x.address.street; x/Employee;

The previous view definition contains a view-query that selects some nested properties of the class Employee. The nested properties are those referenced through the property 'address'.

More complex modifications are, however, possible. As an example, consider again the classes Employee and Address. Suppose that in most queries the nested property 'city' of Employee is often referenced together with the non-nested properties of Employee. Suppose that we wish re-organize the aggregation hierarchy so that the class Employee contains the city where the employees live, while another class contains the rest of the address. This schema change can be simulated by using the following views:

EX8 create-view NewAddress
    view-query x.country, x.num, x.street; x/Address;

    create-view NewEmployee
    properties (name, ssn, city)
    view-query x.name, x.ssn, x.address.city; x/Employee;
    additionalproperties (complete-address: NewAddress **connection** address)

The schema changes previously described are simulated by defining a view, NewAddress, which contains all properties of class Address, except the property 'city'. Then another view, NewEmployee, is defined which contains all properties of class Employee (except the property 'address'), and the nested property 'address.city' of Employee, and which has an additional property, 'complete-address', having as domain the view NewAddress.

View NewEmployee of example EX8 illustrates the specification of aggregation relationships among view instances through the special keyword **connection**. This keyword is followed by a property of the base class from which the view is derived. In the example, given an instance N of the view NewEmployee, the property 'complete-address' of N has as value the OID of an instance of the view NewAddress. This OID must be the identifier of an instance N of NewAddress which is derived from an instance A of the class Address, such that A is the value of the property 'address' of the instance of Employee from which N is derived. In this way, aggregation relationships are propagated through views. Figure 3 illustrates the discussion by considering two instances of classes Employee and Address and the corresponding derived instances of views NewEmployee and NewAddress.

Another useful transformation for aggregation hierarchies consists in splitting a class into several classes. For example, suppose that we wish to remove the information about the staff from the class Team and store them as a separate class. To simulate this change, we define two views: the first containing all information about the teams, except the staff; the second containing only information about the staff.

The views are defined as follows:

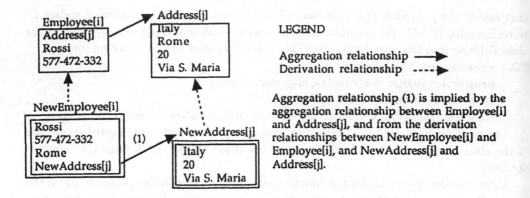

Figure 3: Derived aggregation relationships

EX9 create-view TeamStaff
    view-query x.tech-staff, x.man-staff, x.adm-staff; x/Team;

    create-view NewTeam
    view-query x.tname, x.ind-sponsor, x.budget; x/Team;
    additionalproperties (staff-info: TeamStaff **connection by base-instance** Team)
    methods (projbudget of Team)

View NewTeam shows another example of the definition of aggregation relationship between instances of different views. In this case, the aggregation relationhip is implied by the fact that both instances are derived from the same base instance of the class Team. In this example, an instance N of view NewTeam has the OID of an instance T of view TeamStaff as value of property 'staff-info', where both N and T are derived from the same base-instance of class Team. This is specified by using the keyword *connection by base-instance* followed by the name of the base class from which both views are derived (the name of the base class can be omitted when both views are derived from a single class). Figure 4 illustrates the discussion by considering an instance of the class Team and the corresponding derived instances of view TeamStaff and NewTeam.

4 Conclusions and Future Work

In this paper, we have first discussed the usage of views in object-oriented databases. We have mentioned that views can be used for authorization and shorthand, as in relational databases. In addition, we have discussed other usages of views, such as the support of schema changes. We have then presented a view definition language, which illustrates the possible usages of views. In particular, this language allows views to be specified that augment the definitions of base classes, by adding properties and methods. Using this language, we have illustrated how views can be used to perform various modifications on an object-oriented database schema. Therefore, views represent a unified mechanism providing a large number of functions, such as shorthand, authorization, schema changes, object perspectives.

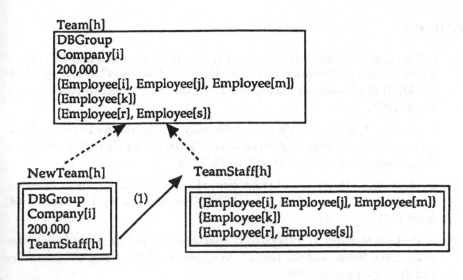

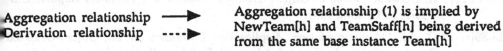

LEGEND

Aggregation relationship ——▶
Derivation relationship ----▶

Aggregation relationship (1) is implied by
NewTeam[h] and TeamStaff[h] being derived
from the same base instance Team[h]

Figure 4: Derived aggregation relationships

An important issue concerns how to support OIDs for view instances. In relational systems, tuples of a view are always accessed through a query on the view. Therefore, the system does not have to provide the equivalent of tuple identifiers (tids) for view tuples. In object-oriented databases, however, when a query is executed on a view, the system returns a set of OIDs of the view instances that satisfy the query. The user can then send messages to the selected instances. Therefore, a major issue in views for object-oriented databases whether object identifiers of view instances must be provided so that messages can be sent to those instances even after the program that issued the query has terminated. Providing persistent OIDs for view instances is crucial if views are to be used as classes. In object-oriented databases accesses are both associative, through queries, and navigational, through object identifiers. Not providing persistent OIDs for view instances would severely restrict the usage of views. In practice, they could be used only as shorthand in queries. Moreover, views with additional properties could not be supported and views could not be used as domain of other views properties. Therefore, the advantages of views in supporting schema changes would be lost. However, since supporting identifiers for view instances may involve the allocation and maintenance of some data structures, we have elected to let the user define whether OIDs must be provided for view instances. A preliminary approach is presented in [Bert 91b].

Future work includes the investigation of the view update problem and of the usage of this view mechanism for the integration of semantically heterogeneous database schemas, as in [Motr 87]. Moreover, the usage of views in methodologies for object-oriented database design based on rapid prototyping will be addressed.

References

[Bane 87]   J. Banerjee, W. Kim, H.K. Kim, and H. Korth, "Semantics and Implementation of Schema Evolution in Object-Oriented Databases", *Proc. of ACM-SIGMOD Conference on Management of Data*, San Francisco (Calif.), May 27-29, 1987.

[Bert 88]   E. Bertino, L.M. Haas, "Views and Security in Distributed Database Management Systems" *Proc. of International Conference on Extending Data Base Technology*, Venice (Italy), March 14-18, 1988.

[Bert 91]   E. Bertino, L. Martino, "Object-Oriented Database Management Systems: Concepts and Issues", *Computer* (IEEE Computer Society), Vol.24, No.4, April 1991, pp. 37-47.

[Bert 91a] E. Bertino, M. Negri, G. Pelagatti, L. Sbattella, "Object-Oriented Query Languages: the Notion and the Issues", to appear in *IEEE Trans. on Knowledge and Data Engineering*, 1990.

[Bert 91b] E. Bertino, "Views in Object-Oriented Databases", Technical Report, University of Genova, 1991.

[Li 89]   Q. Li, "Accommodating Application Dynamics in an Object-Oriented Database System", *Proc. of Advanced Database System Symposium*, Kyoto (Japan), December 7-8, 1989.

[Motr 87]   A. Motro, "Superviews: Virtual Integration of Multiple Databases", *IEEE Trans. on Software Engineering*, Vol.SE-13, No.7, July 1987, pp. 785-798.

[Penn 87]   D.J. Penney, and J. Stein, "Class Modification in the GemStone Object-Oriented DBMS", *Proc. of Object-Oriented Programming Systems, Languages, and Applications Conference (OOPSLA)*, Orlando (Florida), October 4-9, 1987.

[Rabi 91]   F. Rabitti, E. Bertino, W. Kim, D. Woelk, "A Model of Authorization for Next-Generation Database Systems", *ACM Trans. on Database Systems*, Vol.16, No.1, March 1991, pp. 88-131.

[Scho 90]   M. Scholl, C. Laasch, M. Tresch, "Views in Object-Oriented Databases", *Proc. of Second Workshop on Foundations of Models and Languages for Data and Objects*, Aigen (Austria), Sept.1990.

[Shil 89]   J. Shilling, and P. Sweeney, "Three Steps to Views: Extending the Object-Oriented Paradigm", *Proc. of Object-Oriented Programming, Languages, Systems and Applications Conference (OOPSLA)*, New Orleans (Louisiana), October 1-6, 1989.

[Stef 86]   M. Stefik, and D. Bobrow, "Object-Oriented Programming: Themes and Variations", *The AI Magazine*, January 1986, pp.40-62.

[Thur 89]   M.B. Thuraisingham, "Mandatory and Discretionary Security Issues in Object-Oriented Database Systems", *Proc. of Object-Oriented Programming, Languages, Systems and Applications Conference (OOPSLA)*, New Orleans (Louisiana), October 1-6, 1989.

Theoretical Aspects of Schema Merging *

P. Buneman, S. Davidson and A. Kosky
Department of Computer and Information Sciences
University of Pennsylvania
Philadelphia, PA 19104-6389

Abstract

A general technique for merging database schemas is developed that has a number of advantages over existing techniques, the most important of which is that schemas are placed in a partial order that has bounded joins. This means that the merging operation, when it succeeds, is both associative and commutative, *i.e.*, that the merge of schemas is independent of the order in which they are considered — a property not possessed by existing methods. The operation is appropriate for the design of interactive programs as it allows user assertions about relationships between nodes in the schemas to be considered as elementary schemas. These can be combined with existing schemas using precisely the same merging operation.

The technique is general and can be applied to a variety of data models. It can also deal with certain cardinality constraints that arise through the imposition of keys. A prototype implementation, together with a graphical interface, has been developed.

1 Introduction

The desire to provide user views that combine existing databases, and to combine user views during the design process of new databases, leads directly to the problem of schema merging — a problem that has been present in the database literature for at least ten years and to which a variety of sophisticated techniques have been applied. At one end of the spectrum, the user is provided with a set of tools for manipulating two schemas into some form of consistency [1, 2]; at the other end, algorithms have been developed that take two schemas, together with some constraints, and create a merged schema [3]. In general, one will want to use a method that lies somewhere between these two extremes; a number of such variations have been explored, and are surveyed in [4]. It appears that some user manipulation of the given schemas is essential — especially to introduce consistent names — but that a merging algorithm can also be very useful, especially when large schemas are involved.

To the best of our knowledge, the question of what meaning or semantics this merging process should have has not been explored. Indeed, several of the techniques that have

---

*This research was supported in part by ARO DAAL03-89-C-0031PRIME and NSF IRI 8610617, Peter Buneman was also supported by a UK SERC funded visit to Imperial College, London.

been developed are *heuristics*: there is no independent characterization of what result they should produce. One would like to have some semantic basis for a merge that would characterize it with some notion of consistency with the associated data. This semantic basis should be related to the notion of an instance of a schema, and is discussed in [5]. In this paper, we shall develop a simple and general characterization of database schemas that allows us to give natural definitions of what a merge is in terms of the informational content of the schemas being merged. In particular we shall define a merge which takes the union of all the information stored in a collection of database schemas, and, when possible, forms a schema presenting this but no additional information. We shall be able to define a binary merging operator that is both commutative and associative, which means that if two or more schemas are merged, the result is independent of the order in which the merges are performed. Existing techniques do not have this property. Worse still, lack of associativity is endemic to the data models against which the merging process is commonly defined, such as the Entity-Relationship (ER) model.

Using a more general formalism, we will be able to rescue this situation by introducing special, additional information during the merging process. The additional information describes its own origin, and can be readily identified to allow subsequent merges to take place. In addition, our new schema merging technique may be applied to other, existing models, such as the ER-model, by first translating the schemas of these models into our model, then carrying out the merge, and finally translating back into the original model. It is possible to show that, if such an approach is used, then the merging process respects the original model.

The paper is organized as follows: we shall first describe a general data model that sub-sumes, in some sense, data models such as relational, entity-relationship and functional. We then observe that even in this general model, we cannot expect to have associative merges. We relax the constraints on our model to produce a still more general formulation of a *weak* schema for which the merging process is well behaved, and then show how to convert these weak schemas back into our original schemas. We also show that certain common forms of constraints on the schemas, such as key constraints and some cardinality constraints, can be handled in the same framework. Finally we shall indicate how these methods could be used equally well to give definitions of alternative merge, and, in particular, describe how we could form *lower merges* representing the intersection of the information represented by a collection of schemas.

2   The Model

We represent a schema as a directed graph, subject to certain restrictions, whose nodes are taken from a set $\mathcal{N}$ of *classes*, and with two kinds of edges that are used to represent "attribute of" relationships or "specialization of" relationships between classes. Attribute edges have labels taken from a set $\mathcal{L}$, so that we represent the attribute-of edges by a relation $\mathcal{E} \subseteq \mathcal{N} \times \mathcal{L} \times \mathcal{N}$. If $(p, a, q) \in \mathcal{E}$ then we write $p \xrightarrow{a} q$, with the meaning that any instance of the class p must have an a-attribute which is a member of the class q. Since in some data models, like the ER data model, the term "attribute" is used to designate a certain kind of node in a schema, we shall use the neutral term *arrow* to refer to these labeled relationships, and say for $p \xrightarrow{a} q$ that p *has an a-arrow to class q*. The specialization edges are represented by a relation $\mathcal{S}$ on classes; we use the notation

$p \Longrightarrow q$ and say that p is a *specialization* of q when $(p,q) \in S$. This indicates that all the instances of p are also instances of q. Formally, a schema over $\mathcal{N}, \mathcal{L}$ is a triple $(\mathcal{C}, \mathcal{E}, \mathcal{S})$ where $\mathcal{C} \subseteq \mathcal{N}$ is a finite set of classes, S is a partial order (a reflexive transitive and antisymmetric relation on $\mathcal{C}$), and $\mathcal{E}$ is a subset of $\mathcal{C} \times \mathcal{L} \times \mathcal{C}$ satisfying

1. If $p \xrightarrow{a} q_1$ and $p \xrightarrow{a} q_2$ then $\exists s \in \mathcal{C} . s \Longrightarrow q_1$ and $s \Longrightarrow q_2$ and $p \xrightarrow{a} s$.

2. If $p \Longrightarrow q$ and $q \xrightarrow{a} r$ then $p \xrightarrow{a} r$.

3. If $p \xrightarrow{a} s$ and $s \Longrightarrow r$ then $p \xrightarrow{a} r$.

for all $a \in \mathcal{L}$ and $p, q, r, s \in \mathcal{C}$

The first constraint says that if p has an a-arrow, then there is *least* class s (under the ordering S) such that p has an a-arrow to class s. Such a class is said to be the **canonical class** of the a-arrow of p. The second constraint says that, if q has an a-arrow to class r and p is a specialization of q, then p must also have an a-arrow to class r. The third constraint says that, if p has an a-arrow to class s and s is a specialization of r, then p also has an a-arrow to class r, so constraints 2 and 3 together mean that arrows are, in some sense, preserved by specialization. It is worth remarking that we could equally well have defined the arrows as partial functions from classes to classes, which is how they are expressed in the definition of a functional schema in [2]. If we write $p \xrightarrow{a} q$ when p has an a-arrow with canonical class q, we have the equivalent conditions

D1. If $p \xrightarrow{a} q_1$ and $p \xrightarrow{a} q_2$ then $q_1 = q_2$

D2. If $q \xrightarrow{a} s$ and $p \Longrightarrow q$ then $\exists r \in \mathcal{C}.r \Longrightarrow s$ and $p \xrightarrow{a} r$

Also, given any $\xrightarrow{}$ satisfying conditions D1 and D2, if we define the relation $\longrightarrow$ by $p \xrightarrow{a} q$ iff there exists a $s \in \mathcal{C}$ such that $s \Longrightarrow q$ and $p \xrightarrow{a} s$, then $\longrightarrow$ will satisfy conditions 1, 2 and 3 above. Conditions D1 and D2 are those given for the arrow in [2] and are also given by Motro [1] as axioms for functional schemas (the latter uses unlabeled arrows).

For example, the ER diagram shown in figure 1 corresponds to the database schema shown in figure 2, where single arrows are used to indicate edges in $\mathcal{E}$ and double arrows are used to represent pairs in S (double arrows implied by the transitivity and reflexivity of S are omitted). In all the subsequent diagrams, edges in $\mathcal{E}$ implied by constraint 2 above, will also be omitted.

Suitable restrictions of such graphs may be used to describe instances of a variety of data models: relational, entity-relationship and functional. For a relational instance, we stratify $\mathcal{N}$ into two classes $\mathcal{N}_R$ and $\mathcal{N}_A$ (relations and attribute domains), disallow specialization edges, and restrict arrows to run labeled with the name of the attribute from $\mathcal{N}_R$ to $\mathcal{N}_A$ (first normal form), while, for the E-R model, we stratify $\mathcal{C}$ into three classes (attribute domains, entities and relationships) and again place certain restrictions on the edges. Moreover, it can be shown that the merging process described in section 4 preserves these restrictions, so that we can merge schemas from other models by first translating them into our model, then merging them, and finally translating them back into the original data model (see [5] for details). By a less constrained process we can describe instances of the functional model [6, 2, 1]. The graphs are also general enough to represent databases with higher order relations (that is, relationships between relationships),

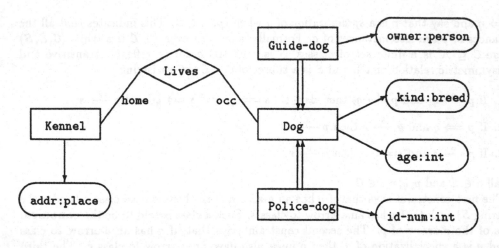

Figure 1: An ER-diagram with "isa" relations

and complex data structures (such as circular definitions of entities and relationships), features that are commonly found in object-oriented data models. Consequently, despite its apparent simplicity, the generality of the model makes it a good candidate for schema merging. One should note, however, that further adornment of these graphs is needed to describe instances of sophisticated data models such as those proposed in [7] and [8], which contain constructors for sets and variants.

3   Problems with finding merges of schemas

The first problem to be resolved when forming a common merged schema for a number of distinct databases is to state the correspondences between the classes and correspondences between the arrow labels of the various databases. This problem is inherently *ad hoc* in nature, and depends on the real-world interpretations of the underlying databases. Therefore, the designer of the system must be called upon to resolve naming conflicts, whether homonyms or synonyms, by renaming classes and arrows where appropriate. The interpretation that the merging process places on names is that if two classes in different schemas have the same name, then they are the same class, regardless of the fact that they may have different arrow edges. For example, if one schema has a class Dog with arrow edges License#, Owner and Breed, and another schema has a class Dog with arrow edges Name, Age and Breed, then the merging process will collapse them into one class with name Dog and arrow edges License#, Owner, Name, Age, and Breed. It is also possible to constrain the merging process by introducing specialization relations $a_1 \implies a_2$ between nodes a_1 in schema $\mathcal{G}_1$ and a_2 in schema $\mathcal{G}_2$. We can treat $a_1 \implies a_2$ as an atomic schema that is to be merged with $\mathcal{G}_1$ and then with $\mathcal{G}_2$. Because our schema merge is associative and commutative, the result is well-defined; indeed an arbitrary set of constraints can be added in this fashion.

For the remainder of this section and the following section, we will consider the merge of a collection of schemas to be a schema that presents all the information of the schemas being merged, but no additional information (although in Section 6, we will indicate that

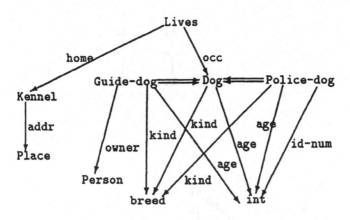

Figure 2: A database schema with "isa" relations

there may be other, equally valid interpretations of what the merge should be). Hence what we will consider to be the merge is the "least upper bound" of the database schemas under some sort of information ordering.

One of the first problems we notice in looking for a suitable definition of merge is that the merge of two schemas may contain extra *implicit* classes in addition to the classes of the schemas being merged. For example, figure 3 shows two schemas being merged. The first schema asserts that the class C is a subclass of both the classes A1 and A2. The second schema asserts that the classes A1 and A2 both have a-arrows, of classes B1 and B2 respectively. Combining this information, as we must when forming the merge, we conclude that C must also have an a-arrow, and that this arrow must be of both the class B1 and B2. Consequently, due to the restrictions in our definition of database schemas in Section 2, the a-arrow from the class C must point to class which is a specialization of both B1 and B2 and so we must introduce such a class into our merged schema.

When we consider these "implicit" classes further we find that it is not sufficient merely to introduce extra classes into a schema with arbitrary names: the implicit classes must be treated differently from normal classes. Firstly, if we were to give them the same status as ordinary classes we would find that binary merges are not associative.

For example consider the three simple schemas shown in figure 4. If we were to first merge the schemas G1 and G2 we would need to introduce a new implicit class (X?) below D and E, and then merging with G3 would make us introduce another new class below X? and F, yielding the first schema shown in figure 5. On the other hand, if we were to merge G1 with G3 and then merge the result with G2, we would first introduce an implicit class below E and F, and then introduce another one below this one and D. Clearly what we really want is *one* implicit class which is a specialization of all three of D, E and F.

Another problem is that it is possible for one schema to present more 'information than another without containing as many implicit classes. Intuitively, for one schema to present all the information of another (plus additional information) it must have, at least, all the normal classes of the other. However let us consider the two schemas shown in figure 6. We would like to assert that the schema G3 shown in figure 7 is the merge of

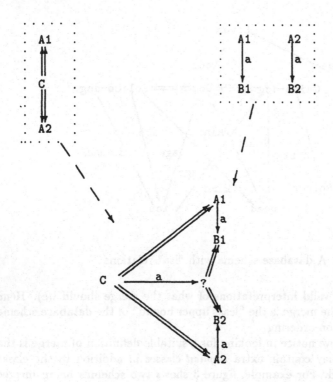

Figure 3: Schema merging involving implicit classes

the two schemas, G1 and G2, but the schema G4 also presents all the information of G1 and G2, and in addition contains fewer classes than G3. The point is that G4 asserts that the a-arrow of F has class E, which may have restrictions on it in addition to those which state that it is a subclass of both C and D, while G3 only states that the a-arrow of F has both classes C and D.

4   Merging Database Schemas

In order to avoid the complexities of introducing implicit classes, we will weaken our definition of database schemas so that implicit classes become unnecessary. We then define an information ordering on these *weak schemas*, such that binary joins do exist and are associative, and form the weak schema merge. Finally we convert the merged weak

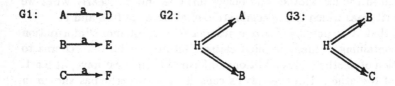

Figure 4: Some simple schemas

Merge(Merge(G1, G2), G3):   Merge(Merge(G1, G3), G2):

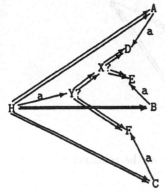
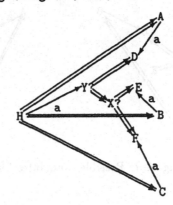

Figure 5: An example of non-associative merging

G1:   G2:

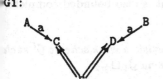
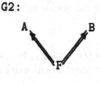

Figure 6: Yet more schemas

schema into a proper schema by introducing additional implicit classes (we will refer to the schemas satisfying the conditions in section 2 as *proper schemas*.)

4.1 Weak Schemas

A **weak schema** is a schema in which we no longer require that if class p has an a-arrow, then the a-arrow has a canonical class (condition 1 of proper schemas). Formally, a weak schema over $\mathcal{N}, \mathcal{L}$ is a triple $(\mathcal{C}, \mathcal{E}, \mathcal{S})$ where $\mathcal{C} \subseteq \mathcal{N}$ is a set of classes, $\mathcal{S}$ is a partial order (a reflexive transitive and antisymmetric relation on $\mathcal{C}$), and $\mathcal{E}$ is a subset of $\mathcal{C} \times \mathcal{L} \times \mathcal{C}$ satisfying

W1. If $p \Longrightarrow q$ and $q \xrightarrow{a} r$ then $p \xrightarrow{a} r$.

W2. If $p \xrightarrow{a} s$ and $s \Longrightarrow r$ then $p \xrightarrow{a} r$.

for all $a \in \mathcal{L}$ and $p, q, r, s \in \mathcal{C}$
The ordering on weak schemas is defined in the obvious way: Given two weak schemas $\mathcal{G}_1 = (\mathcal{C}_1, \mathcal{E}_1, \mathcal{S}_1)$ and $\mathcal{G}_2 = (\mathcal{C}_2, \mathcal{E}_2, \mathcal{S}_2)$, we write $\mathcal{G}_1 \sqsubseteq \mathcal{G}_2$ iff

1. $\mathcal{C}_1 \subseteq \mathcal{C}_2$

2. $\mathcal{E}_1 \subseteq \mathcal{E}_2$

G3:

G4:

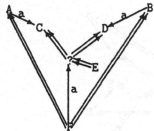
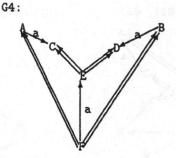

Figure 7: Possible candidates for the merges of the schemas

3. $\mathcal{S}_1 \subseteq \mathcal{S}_2$

That is, every class in $\mathcal{G}_1$ appears in $\mathcal{G}_2$, every a-arrow edge in $\mathcal{G}_1$ appears in $\mathcal{G}_2$, and every specialization edge in $\mathcal{G}_1$ appears in $\mathcal{G}_2$.

It is clear that $\sqsubseteq$ is a partial ordering on weak schemas; it is also bounded complete, as shown in the following proposition.

Proposition 4.1 *For any weak schemas $\mathcal{G}_1$ and $\mathcal{G}_2$, if there exists a weak schema $\mathcal{G}'$ such that $\mathcal{G}_1 \sqsubseteq \mathcal{G}'$ and $\mathcal{G}_2 \sqsubseteq \mathcal{G}'$ then there is a least such weak schema $\mathcal{G}_1 \sqcup \mathcal{G}_2$.*

Proof: Given weak schemas $\mathcal{G}_1$ and $\mathcal{G}_2$ as above, define $\mathcal{G} = (\mathcal{C}, \mathcal{E}, \mathcal{S})$ by

$$\mathcal{C} = \mathcal{C}_1 \cup \mathcal{C}_2$$
$$\mathcal{S} = (\mathcal{S}_1 \cup \mathcal{S}_2)^*$$
$$\mathcal{E} = \{p \xrightarrow{a} s \in (\mathcal{C} \times \mathcal{L} \times \mathcal{C}) \mid \exists q, r \in \mathcal{C} \cdot p \Longrightarrow q \in \mathcal{S}, \ r \Longrightarrow s \in \mathcal{S},$$
$$\text{and } q \xrightarrow{a} r \in (\mathcal{E}_1 \cup \mathcal{E}_2)\}$$

(where $(\mathcal{S}_1 \cup \mathcal{S}_2)^*$ denotes the transitive closure of $(\mathcal{S}_1 \cup \mathcal{S}_2)$, and $\mathcal{E}$ adds edges to $\mathcal{E}_1 \cup \mathcal{E}_2$ necessary for conditions W1 and W2 to hold). It is clear that, if $\mathcal{G}$ is a weak schema, then it is the least weak schema such that $\mathcal{G}_1 \sqsubseteq \mathcal{G}$ and $\mathcal{G}_2 \sqsubseteq \mathcal{G}$. Hence it is sufficient to show that, if there is a weak schema, $\mathcal{G}' = (\mathcal{C}', \mathcal{E}', \mathcal{S}')$, such that $\mathcal{G}_1 \sqsubseteq \mathcal{G}'$ and $\mathcal{G}_2 \sqsubseteq \mathcal{G}'$, then $\mathcal{G}$ is indeed a weak schema. The only way that $\mathcal{G}$ can fail to be a weak schema is if the relation $\mathcal{S}$ fails to be antisymmetric, so the result follows from the fact that, for any suitable $\mathcal{G}'$ as above, we must have $\mathcal{S} \subseteq \mathcal{S}'$, and so if $\mathcal{S}'$ is antisymmetric then so is $\mathcal{S}$. ∎

We say a finite collection of weak schemas, $\mathcal{G}_1, \ldots, \mathcal{G}_n$, is **compatible** if the relationship $(\mathcal{S}_1 \cup \ldots \cup \mathcal{S}_n)^*$ is anti-symmetric (where $\mathcal{S}_1, \ldots, \mathcal{S}_n$ are the specialization relations of $\mathcal{G}_1, \ldots, \mathcal{G}_n$ respectively). Consequently we have, for any finite compatible collection of proper schemas, $\mathcal{G}_1, \ldots, \mathcal{G}_n$, there exists a *weak schema merge* $\mathcal{G} = \bigsqcup_{i=1}^{n} \mathcal{G}_i$. Furthermore, since we define $\mathcal{G}$ as the least upper bound of $\mathcal{G}_1, \ldots, \mathcal{G}_n$, the operation is associative and commutative.

For example, the schemas G1 and G2 in figure 6 are compatible, and their weak schema merge is shown in figure 8.

G1 ⊔ G2:

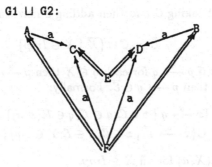

Figure 8: The least upper bound of two schemas

4.2 Building proper schemas from weak schemas

We now must pay the price for our use of weak schemas: we must provide a way of introducing implicit classes into a weak schema $\mathcal{G}$, in order to form a proper schema $\overline{\mathcal{G}}$, such that if there are any proper schemas greater than $\mathcal{G}$ then $\overline{\mathcal{G}}$ is such a schema.

First we introduce some new notation. For any $p \in \mathcal{C}$ and any $a \in \mathcal{L}$, we write $\mathcal{R}(p,a)$ to denote the set of classes reachable from p via a-arrows

$$\mathcal{R}(p,a) = \{q \in \mathcal{C} \mid p \xrightarrow{a} q\}$$

Further, for any set $X \subseteq \mathcal{C}$, we use $\mathcal{R}(X,a)$ to denote the set of classes reachable from classes in X via a-arrows

$$\mathcal{R}(X,a) = \{q \in \mathcal{C} \mid \exists p \in X \cdot p \xrightarrow{a} q\}$$

We define the function $Min_{\mathcal{S}} : \mathcal{P}(\mathcal{N}) \to \mathcal{P}(\mathcal{N})$ so that, for any set $X \subseteq \mathcal{N}$, $Min_{\mathcal{S}}(X)$ is the set of minimal elements of X under the ordering $\mathcal{S}$. That is

$$Min_{\mathcal{S}}(X) = \{p \in X \mid \forall q \in X \cdot \text{if } q \Longrightarrow p \text{ then } q = p\}$$

where $\mathcal{P}(A)$ denotes the power set of the set A.

We now proceed to build a proper schema $\overline{\mathcal{G}} = (\overline{\mathcal{C}}, \overline{\mathcal{E}}, \overline{\mathcal{S}})$ from $\mathcal{G}$ as follows:

1. First we will construct a set, $Imp \subseteq \mathcal{P}(\mathcal{N})$, of sets of classes, corresponding to our implicit classes. We will construct Imp via a series of auxiliary definitions as follows:

$$\begin{aligned} I^0 &= \{\{p\} \mid p \in \mathcal{C}\} \\ I^{n+1} &= \{\mathcal{R}(X,a) \mid X \in I^n, a \in \mathcal{L}\} \\ I^\infty &= \bigcup_{n=1}^{\infty} I^n \\ Imp &= \{Min_{\mathcal{S}}(X) \mid X \in I^\infty \text{ and } |Min_{\mathcal{S}}(X)| > 1\} \end{aligned}$$

Intuitively, Imp is the set of all sets of minimal classes which one can reach by following a series of arrows from some class in $\mathcal{C}$, with cardinality greater than 1. Note that the process of forming Imp will halt since there are a finite number of subsets of $\mathcal{P}(\mathcal{N})$.

2. We define $\overline{C}$ by first taking C and then adding a new class $\overline{X}$ for every $X \in Imp$. That is

$$\overline{C} = C \cup \{\overline{X} \mid X \in Imp\}$$

3. We define $\overline{\mathcal{E}}$ so that if $p \xrightarrow{a} q$ for each $q \in X$ then $p \xrightarrow{a} \overline{X} \in \overline{\mathcal{E}}$, while if there is a q such that $p \xrightarrow{a} q$ then $p \xrightarrow{a} q \in \overline{\mathcal{E}}$. Formally:

$$\overline{\mathcal{E}} = \{x \xrightarrow{a} q \mid x \in \overline{C}, a \in \mathcal{L}, q \in \mathcal{R}(x,a)\}$$
$$\cup \{x \xrightarrow{a} \overline{Y} \mid x \in \overline{C}, a \in \mathcal{L}, Y \in Imp, Y \subseteq \mathcal{R}(x,a)\}$$

where $\mathcal{R}(\overline{X},a) = \mathcal{R}(X,a)$ for all $X \in Imp$.

4. We define $\overline{S}$ by first taking S and then adding every $\overline{X} \Longrightarrow \overline{Y}$ such that every class in Y has a specialization in X; every $\overline{X} \Longrightarrow p$ where p has a specialization in X; and every $p \Longrightarrow \overline{X}$ where p is a specialization of every class in X.

$$\overline{S} = S \cup \{\overline{X} \Longrightarrow \overline{Y} \mid X, Y \in Imp, \forall p \in Y \cdot \exists q \in X \cdot q \Longrightarrow p \in S\}$$
$$\cup \{\overline{X} \Longrightarrow p \mid X \in Imp, p \in C, \exists q \in X \cdot q \Longrightarrow p \in S\}$$
$$\cup \{p \Longrightarrow \overline{X} \mid p \in C, X \in Imp, \forall q \in X \cdot p \Longrightarrow q \in S\}$$

For example, the effect on the schema shown in figure 8 would be to introduce a single implicit class, $\{C, D\}$, thus forming the schema G3 shown in figure 7 with the class ? replaced by $\{C, D\}$.

It can be shown that for any weak schema $\mathcal{G}$, $\overline{\mathcal{G}}$ is a weak schema and $\mathcal{G} \sqsubseteq \overline{\mathcal{G}}$. Furthermore, $\overline{\mathcal{G}}$ can be shown to respect condition 1 of the definition of a proper schema, and is therefore also a proper schema.

We would like to be able to show that $\overline{\mathcal{G}}$ is the least proper schema greater than $\mathcal{G}$. However there are two minor problems with this: first, it is possible to form other similar proper schemas by using different names for the implicit classes (compare this to alpha-conversion in the lambda calculus); second, for any two sets $X, Y \in Imp$, if every class in Y has a specialization in X then our method will include the pair $(\overline{X}, \overline{Y})$ in $\overline{S}$. However it is not necessarily the case that this specialization relation is required, and it might be safe to omit it. We could attempt to modify our method so that such pairs are only introduced when required. Instead we will argue that, since the implicit classes have no additional information associated with them, it follows that these specialization relations do not introduce any extra information into the database schema, and so, since they seem natural, it is best to leave them there. Consequently we feel justified defining the **merge** of a compatible collection of database schemas, $\mathcal{G}_1, \ldots, \mathcal{G}_n$, to be the database schema $\overline{\mathcal{G}}$, where $\mathcal{G} = \bigsqcup_{i=1}^{n} \mathcal{G}_i$.

Of course, not every merge of a collection of compatible schemas makes sense. That is, the new classes introduced may have no correspondence to anything in the real world. To capture this semantic aspect of our model, we would need to introduce a "consistency relationship" on $\mathcal{N}$, and require that, for every $X \in Imp$ and every $p, q \in X$, the pair (p, q) is in the consistency relationship. If this condition were violated, the schemas would be **inconsistent**, and $\overline{\mathcal{G}}$ would not exist. Note that checking consistency would be very efficient, since it just requires examining the consistency relationship. However, while the idea is interesting, it is beyond the scope of this paper. Suffice it to say that if the merge of $\mathcal{G}_1, \ldots, \mathcal{G}_n$ fails, either because $\mathcal{G}_1, \ldots, \mathcal{G}_n$ are *incompatible*, or because they are *inconsistent*, the merge should not proceed, and the user must re-assess the assumptions that were made to describe the schemas.

5 Cardinality Constraints and Keys

The model we have used so far concentrates on the semantic relationships between classes via specialization and arrow edges, but does not further describe arrows as participating in keys or having associated cardinality constraints. Cardinality constraints in the ER model are typically indicated on the edges between a relationship and an entity by labeling them "many" (or "N", indicating unrestricted upper bounds), or "1" (sometimes indicated by an arrow pointing into the entity set).[1] For example, consider the Advisor relationship between Faculty and GS in Figure 9, and for the moment interpret this schema as an ER diagram. As drawn, Advisor is a "many-many" relationship, typically indicated by labeling the faculty and victim edges "N": a graduate student may be advised by several faculty members, and each faculty member can advise several different graduate students. If we decided to restrict Advisor to indicate that a graduate student can be advised by at most one faculty member, the faculty edge from Advisor to Faculty would be relabeled "1".

As it stands, however, our model has no way of distinguishing these different edge semantics. Using the example of the previous paragraph, labeling the faculty edge in the Advisor relationship "1" rather than "N" could result in the same graph in our model, *i.e.* the graph in Figure 9.[2] In this section, we will capture such constraints by introducing "key constraints" on nodes, and argue that in some sense they are more general than the cardinality constraints typically found in ER models.

Key constraints, which indicate that certain attributes of an entity form a *key* for that entity, are another common form of assertions found in database models. As an example, in the ER and relational models, for the entity set Person(SS#, Name, Address), we might claim that there are two keys: {SS#} and {Name, Address}. The intuition behind this statement is that if two people have the same social security number, or the same name and address, then they are the same person. Generalizing, one could claim that a set of *edges* of a relationship form a key for that relationship. As an example, for the Advisor relationship in which the faculty edge was labelled with a "1" and the victim edge was labelled with a "N", we could claim that the victim edge forms a key. In the terminology of proper schemas, we capture such key constraints by asserting that $\{a_1, a_2, ..., a_n\}$ form a key for p, where each a_i is the label of some arrow out of p.

In many established data-models it is required that every class has at least one key, so that the set of all the arrows of a class forms a key if no strict subset of the arrows does. By relaxing this constraint, so that a class may have no key at all, we can capture models in which there is a notion of object identity. A *superkey* of a class is any superset of a key. We may therefore think of the set of superkeys for a class p, $\mathcal{SK}(p)$, as a set of

---

[1] It is worth noting that there is little agreement on what edge labels to use, and what they mean in ER digrams, especially for ternary and higher degree relationships. No semantics are given in [9]. Introductory textbooks on databases avoid the question and merely give examples of binary relationships [10, 11, 12]; [13] is slightly more honest and says that "the semantics of ternary and higher-order relationship sets can become quite complex to comprehend." Varying interpretations can be found in [14, 15, 3].

[2] Of course, one might eliminate the Advisor node entirely, and draw a single Advisor-edge from GS to Faculty, but this reasoning does not extend to ternary and higher degree relationships.

sets of labels of arrows out of p. $\mathcal{SK}(p)$ has the property that it is "upward closed", *i.e.* if $s \in \mathcal{SK}(p)$ and $s\prime \supseteq s$, then $s\prime \in \mathcal{SK}(p)$.

We now have the constraint on specialization edges that if $p \Longrightarrow q$ then $\mathcal{SK}(p) \supseteq \mathcal{SK}(q)$, *i.e.* all the keys for q are keys (or superkeys) for p. For example, the specialisation `Advisor` $\Longrightarrow$ `Committee` in the schema shown in figure 9 asserts that the advisor of a student must also be a member of the thesis committee for that student.

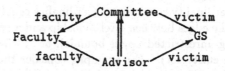

Figure 9: "Isa-A" Relation Between Relationships

Since the committee for a student consists of several faculty members, and each faculty member can be on several thesis committees, the set of keys for `Committee` is {{`faculty`, `victim`}}. However, since each student has at most one advisor, but that each faculty member can be the advisor of several students, the set of keys for `Advisor` is {{`victim`}}. This is equivalent to having cardinality constraints asserting that the relation `Advisor` is "one-to-many" while `Committee` is "many-to-many". Note that {{`victim`}, {`faculty`, `victim`}} $\supseteq$ {{`faculty`, `victim`}}, thus the merged schema satisfies our constraint.

Our task now becomes to derive keys in the merged schema subject to this constraint.

Suppose schema $\mathcal{G}$ is the proper schema merge of $\mathcal{G}_1$ and $\mathcal{G}_2$. Each class p in $\mathcal{G}$ appears at most once in each of $\mathcal{G}_1$ and $\mathcal{G}_2$, with key assignments $\mathcal{SK}_1(p)$, $\mathcal{SK}_2(p)$ respectively (when defined). We define $\mathcal{SK}$ to be a *satisfactory assignment* of keys to classes if

1. $\mathcal{SK}_1(p) \subseteq \mathcal{SK}(p)$, if $p \in \mathcal{C}_1$; and

2. $\mathcal{SK}_2(p) \subseteq \mathcal{SK}(p)$, if $p \in \mathcal{C}_2$; and

3. $\mathcal{SK}$ satisfies the condition that $\mathcal{SK}(p) \supseteq \mathcal{SK}(q)$ whenever $p \Longrightarrow q$.

It is readily checked that if $\mathcal{SK}$ and $\mathcal{SK}\prime$ are satisfactory assignments, then so is $\mathcal{SK} \cap \mathcal{SK}\prime$, defined by $(\mathcal{SK} \cap \mathcal{SK}\prime)(p) = \mathcal{SK}(p) \cap \mathcal{SK}\prime(p)$. Thus there is a unique minimal satisfactory assignment of keys to classes.

We can see that key constraints are sufficient to capture the kinds of cardinality constraint most commonly found in the ER literature, namely the restriction of attributes or relations to being "many-to-many", "many-to-one" and so on, at least in the case of binary relationships where their meaning is clear. However they are not capable of representing the participation constraints, representing total versus partial participation of an entity set in a relationship, found in some models (see [3]): for example, we cannot use key in our schemas to specify that each graduate student *must* have a faculty advisor, but that not every faculty member must necessarily advise some student. On the other hand, cardinality constraints cannot capture all key assertions: For example, consider the relationship `Transaction` in Figure 10. The statement that `Transaction` has two keys, one being {`loc`, `at`}, the other being {`card`, `at`}, has no correspondence in terms of labeling edges.

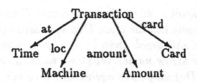

Figure 10: A Class with Multiple Keys

Keys can also be used to determine when an object in the extent of a class in an instance of one schema corresponds to an object in the extent of the same class in an instance of another schema. For example, if Person is a class in two schemas, $\mathcal{G}_1$ and $\mathcal{G}_2$, which are being merged, and both schemas agree that {SS#} is a key for Person, then an object in the extent of Person in an instance of $\mathcal{G}_1$ corresponds to an object in the extent of Person in an instance of $\mathcal{G}_2$ if they have the same social security number. However, suppose that $\mathcal{G}_1$ claims that {SS#} is a key for Person, and $\mathcal{G}_2$ has an SS#-arrow for Person but does *not* claim that it is a key. Since {SS#} is a key for Person in the merged schema, an additional constraint has been placed on the extents of $\mathcal{G}_2$: two objects in the extent of Person are the same if they have the same social security number, no matter whether both are from an instance of $\mathcal{G}_1$, both are from an instance of $\mathcal{G}_2$, or one is from an instance of $\mathcal{G}_1$ while the other is from an instance of $\mathcal{G}_2$. Furthermore, if $\mathcal{G}_1$ claims that {SS#} is a key for Person but $\mathcal{G}_2$ does *not have* an SS#-arrow for Person, then there is not way to tell when an object from the extent of Person in an instance of $\mathcal{G}_1$ corresponds to an object from the extent of Person in an instance of $\mathcal{G}_2$.

6 Lower Merges

In Section 4 we defined the merge of a collection of schemas as their *least upper bound* under an information ordering. A consequence of this is that, if we merge a number of schemas, then any instance of the merged schema can be considered to be an instance of any of the schemas being merged. In some cases, however, it is desirable to find the *greatest lower bound* of a collection of schemas and use that as the merge. In this case any instances of the schemas being merged would also be instances of the merged schema, and, further, we would expect to be able to coalesce or take the union of a number of instances of the collection of schemas and use that as an instance of the merged schema. This kind of merge is likely to arise in, for example, the formulation of federated database systems.

We will refer to the merges defined in section 4 as **upper merges**, and, in this section, we will discuss the formulation of **lower merges**, representing the greatest lower bound of a collection of schemas. It could legitamately be argued that lower merges are of primary importance and should have been introduced first. However we introduced upper merges as our primary concept of a merge because they are inherently simpler and more natural to formulate. There are a number of complications involved in giving a formal definition of lower merges. For a detailed treatment of the problems involved see [5].

As it stands, taking the lower bound of a collection of schemas using our information ordering is clearly unsatisfactory: any information on which two schemas disagree on is lost. For example if one schema has the class *Dog* with arrows *name* and *age*, and another has *Dog* with arrows *name* and *breed*, then in the lower bound of the two schemas the class *Dog* will only have the arrow *name*. What we want, however, is some way of saying that instances of the class *Dog* may have *age*-arrows and *may* have *breed*-arrows, but are not necessarily required to do so. Worse still, if one schema has the class *Guide-Dog* and another does not, then the lower bound of the two schemas will not. The second problem can be dealt with easily by adding all classes involved in other schemas to each schema in a collection before proceeding with the construction of the lower merge. The first problem, however, is more difficult and requires us to extend our definition of (weak) schemas.

We define the semi-lattice of **participation constraints**, ordered by $\leq$, to be as shown in figure 11. We will extend the definition of (weak) schemas by associating a participation

Figure 11: The semi-lattice of participation constraints

constraint with each arrow of a schema via a mapping $\mathcal{K} : \mathcal{E} \rightarrow \{0, 0/1, 1\}$. The idea is that, if a class p has an a-arrow of class q, then if the arrow has participation constraint 1 then every instance of class p *must* have a an a-arrow to an instance of class q; if the arrow has participation constraint $0/1$ then an instance of p *may* have an a-arrow of class q; and if the arrow has constraint 0 then an instance of p *may not* have an a-arrow of class q. We adopt the convention of not drawing arrows with the participation constraint 0 in our diagram, and, further, assume that a schema which does not have some arrow $p \xrightarrow{a} q$ is equivalent to the same schema but with the arrow $p \xrightarrow{a} q$ with participation constraint 0.

Now, if one schema has an arrow which is not included in another, then we can assume that the second schema also has the arrow, but with participation constraint 0, and we can take the greatest lower bound of the participation constraints (under the ordering $\leq$) to be the participation constraint of the arrow in the merged schema.

Hence, with the addition of participation constraints, we can form the *weak lower merge* of a collection of schemas in a similar manner to that used to construct the *weak upper merges* in section 4. We can also build a proper schema from a weak lower merge using an algorithm similar to that in section 4, except that that the implicit classes are introduced above, rather than bellow, the sets of proper schemas that they represent.

It is worth noting that, while upper and lower merges represent two extreme views of what the merge of a collection of schemas should be, there may well be valid and useful concepts of merges lying inbetween the two. However the authors believe that, in order for a concept of a merge to be valid and well defined, it should have a definition in terms of an information ordering similar to the ones given here.

7 Conclusions

Using a simple but general formalism, we have characterized the *weak schema merge* of a collection of schemas as their least upper bound. The *merge* of these schemas is then defined by translating the weak schema merge to a *proper* schema. The translation introduces new "implicit" classes as required, and identifies their origin in their name. Although not discussed in detail in this paper, the "real-world" validity of an implicit class can be efficiently checked by consulting a consistency relationship between the classes from which the implicit class was formed.

Despite the simplicity of our mathematical construction, we believe that using an information ordering is the right way of describing the merge of schemas: it has a well-defined result, and the merge operation is associative and commutative. Thus user assertions about the relationships between schemas can be thought of as real assertions rather than "guiding heuristics" since the merge is independent of the order in which the assertions are stated. The approach in this paper focused on the upper merge of schemas, which seems to be the most natural concept of a merge. Other kinds of merge can be defined, including the lower merge, by varying the information ordering used.

The approach presented in this paper can be generalized to describe the merge in a number of other data models by representing schemas in other data models as "restricted" instances of schemas in our general model (*i.e.* stratifying classes in terms of their meaning in other models), and finding their proper schema merge. Our merge can be shown to "preserve strata", guaranteeing that the result will an instance of the original model; a proof of this with full details can be found in [5].

To use this approach as a practical schema merging tool, several issues should be addressed. Firstly, more attention should be paid to how cardinality constraints should be encorporated. While our preliminary approach has been to use a notion of keys, other ideas include allowing arrows to be "multivalued functions" as in [2]; [5] shows how this idea can be extended to our model. Secondly, some form of assistance should be given for "restructuring" schemas to obtain a better merge. Not only can "naming" conflicts occur (such as homonyms and synonyms), but "structural" conflicts can occur. For example, an attribute in one schema may look like an entity in another schema, or a many-one relationship may be a single arrow in one schema but introduce a relationship node in another schema. In these cases, the merge will not "resolve" the differences but present both interpretations. To force an integration, we need some kind of "normal form". Thirdly, we need to evaluate how many implicit classes can be introduced in the merge. Although in the examples we have looked at this number has been small, it may be possible to construct pathological examples in which the number of implicit classes is very large; however, we do not think these are likely to occur in practice. Fourthly, we must discuss how to merge instances; for a discussion of the problems involved, see [16].

We have found that the simplicity of the method and presence of strong theoretical underpinnings have made extensions of the technique very easy to develop. In addition, we have been able to rapidly prototype the method, together with a graphical interface for creating and displaying schema graphs.

References

[1] A. Motro, "Superviews: Virtual Integration of Multiple Databases," *IEEE Transactions on Software Engineering*, vol. SE-13, pp. 785–798, July 1987.

[2] J. Smith, P. Bernstein, U. Dayal, N. Goodman, T. Landers, K. Lin, and E. Wong, "Multibase– Integrating Heterogeneous Distributed Database Systems," in *Proceedings of AFIPS*, pp. 487–499, 1981.

[3] S. Navathe, R. Elmasri, and J. Larson, "Integrating User Views in Database Designs," *IEEE Computer*, pp. 50–62, January 1986.

[4] C. Batini, M. Lenzerini, and S. Navathe, "A Comparative Analysis of Methodologies for Database Schema Integration," *ACM Computing Surveys*, vol. 18, pp. 323–364, December 1986.

[5] A. Kosky, "Modeling and Merging Database Schemas," Tech. Rep. MS-CIS-91-65, University of Pennsylvania, 1991.

[6] D. Shipman, "The Functional Data Model and the Data Language DAPLEX," *ACM Transactions on Database Systems*, vol. 6, pp. 140–173, March 1981.

[7] R. Hull and R. King, "Semantic Database Modeling: Survey, Applications, and Research Issues," *ACM Computing Surveys*, vol. 19, pp. 201–260, September 1987.

[8] A. Ohori, "Semantics of Types for Database Objects," *Theoretical Computer Science*, vol. 76, pp. 53–91, 1990.

[9] P. Chen, "The Entity-Relationship Model: Towards a Unified View of Data," *TODS*, vol. 1, no. 1, pp. 9–36, 1976.

[10] J. Ullman, *Principles of Database and Knowledge-Base Systems*. Vol. 1, Computer Science Press, 1988.

[11] H. Korth and A. Silberschatz, *Database System Concepts*. McGraw Hill, second ed., 1991.

[12] R. Elmasri and S. Navathe, *Fundamentals of Database Systems*. Benjamin/Cummings, 1989.

[13] D. Tsichritzis and F. Lochovsky, *Data Models*. Prentice-Hall, 1982.

[14] T. Teory, D. Yang, and J. Fry, "A Logical Design Methodology for Relational Databases Using the Entity-Relationship Model," *ACM Computing Surveys*, vol. 18, pp. 197–222, June 1986.

[15] M. Lenzerini and G. Santucci, "Cardinality Constraints in the Entity Relationship Model," in *The Entity-Relationship Approach to Software Engineering*, pp. 529–549, North-Holland, 1983.

[16] S. Widjojo, R. Hull, and D. Wile, "Distributed Information Sharing Using WorldBase," in *A Newsletter of the Computer Society of IEEE*, pp. 17–26, August 1989.

Towards a logical-object oriented programming language for databases

Elisa Bertino[1], Danilo Montesi[2]

1) Dipartimento di Matematica	2) Dipartimento di Informatica
Università di Genova	Università di Pisa
via L.B. Alberti 4, 16132 Genova	Corso Italia 40, 56125 Pisa
bertino@igecuniv.bitnet	montesi@dipisa.di.unipi.it

Abstract

This paper presents an approach for the integration of logic and object-oriented paradigms. A hierarchy of languages is defined starting from a logical notion of object, based on the concept of evolving theory. They are based on $\mathcal{LDL}$ language, which captures the notion of state evolution. In order to achieve the mapping from object-oriented paradigm to a logical-object oriented programming language, the notions of object, message passing, class and inheritance are reinterpreted in the context of logic programming.

1 Introduction

The logic programming paradigm is becoming the basis of real implementation languages also for large applications. Since the beginning, the scientific community interested in logic programming recognized that a major problem for the possibility of using these languages to write large programs was the lack of modularity and the possibility of programming in the large. What is needed is very similar to what has already been proved very useful in many other different languages (imperative and functional), i.e. the possibility to give a structure to the program, the possibility to reuse different pieces of programs, the ability to perform cooperation, the ability to hide, and many other features. Recently, there have been many proposals trying to fill this gap among them [2,4,6,7,17,19,23]. Some of these approaches are oriented towards the metaprogramming [7]. Here we will address another approach based on the object-oriented paradigm.

Object-oriented programming paradigm is primarily a system-building tool because it emphasizes reusability as the center of the software development process, making reusability the usual way to build new components. These reusable components, called Software-ICs in [11], emphasize the parallel with the way hardware engineers build circuits from a stockroom of generic, reusable silicon chips. A Software-IC implements an object which is the unit of modularity in an object-oriented system. It is a package of programming effort that is independent of the specific job at hand highly reusable in future jobs. Even, programmers seldom create new Software-ICs from first principles. They develop new, specialized ICs by describing only how they differ from older, generic ones from the stock- room. In addition object-oriented tools help to produce software that is far more tolerant of changes. We note that the logic and object-oriented paradigms have started being widely applied in different areas of computer science such as programming languages, software engineering, databases and expert systems. Therefore, most database systems currently developed are organized around logic languages such as Datalog [21] and $\mathcal{LDL}$ [20] or around procedural object-oriented languages such as Iris [12], ORION [14] and O_2 [13]. However, no one of them provides all the features required by advanced applications such as declarativeness and modularity. Therefore research efforts are ongoing to investigate the integration of logic and object-oriented paradigms. It is believed that new generation languages will inherit features from both paradigms [1].

In this paper, we intend to study the basic principles for integrating the logic and object-oriented paradigms for database systems. Such paradigms have important features. The former paradigm has its peculiarity in the declarativeness and uniformity of language. On the semantics side, there is a well founded semantics and a rich literature. The later paradigm provides structuring and reusability of software even if it has not a solid underlying theory. In addition, it is based on objects and reflects a natural view of the world we are modeling. These facts are obviously very interesting, since an enormous amount of results and techniques for logic and object-oriented paradigms can be exploited in the framework of a logical language for object-oriented programming. Therefore, our aim is to define a logical-object oriented programming language for databases. In doing so we would like to capture the relevant features of logic programming languages and object-oriented programming languages. From the logic paradigm, we expect to have the declarativeness and uniformity of language for describing data, programs, queries, views and integrity constraints. From the object-oriented paradigm we want to have the powerful structuring and reusability aspects. In addition as in the relation model, there is a clear separation between the notions of instance and schema. The schema not only contains the information on the *structure of data* but also on the *behavior of data*. We believe that the object oriented paradigm can be added to any conventional programming language, i.e. imperative, logic and functional by grafting a number of new syntactic features alongside the existing capabilities of the language obtaining an imperative object-oriented language, a functional object-oriented language and a logical-object oriented language. From a semantics point of view the perspective is more complex. The integration of logic and object-oriented paradigms shows fundamental differences between these paradigms such as the notion of state evolution and the structuring mechanism which are embodied into the object-oriented paradigm but are not into the logic programming. Furthermore, we have to investigate how to map the key concepts of object-oriented paradigm into the logic programming.

To do that, a minimal prerequisite is a logical notion of object. Almost all approaches we have seen can be classified with respect to the "logical notion of object". An object can be seen as a "term" or as a "theory". This is called the *granularity* of the object. Furthermore, another classification can be used to characterize the proposals in literature (see Section 4); the *state evolution* of objects in order to support "static" objects or "dynamic" ones. In our approach we choose the granularity of object, which seems close to our intuition i.e. a theory which can also be seen as a deductive database and therefore optimization's techniques from the database area can be used. Therefore, we have to reinterpret the main notions of the object-oriented paradigm such us what is an object, a class, the inheritance and the message passing mechanism in the context of logic programming (possibly extended). We will take an approach similar to the one shown in [17] where the natural analogue of an *object* in the context of logic programming is the concept of a *theory* - the set of all atomic consequences known "about" an object determines the object. In logic programming we usually have a theory T which is a logic program (database) and a formula F which is a goal (query) and a provability relation "⊢"which says if the atomic formula F is provable from T, shortly $T \vdash F$. We consider an extension of the theory considering also the notion of state evolution of the theory. We will follow the schema that the cooperation among objects is performed through message passing modeling a uniform communication mechanism. A class template notion is introduced to provide the description of several evolving theories within one system and to describe relationships between these theories. Therefore a class can be seen as an object factory which defines constraints on the structure and on the behavior of the objects of that class. Furthermore, class inheritance is also presented for the structural and behavioral parts.

The paper is organized as follows. In the remainder of this section, we summarize some preliminaries concepts. Next section is an outline of a subset of $\mathcal{LDL}$ w.r.t. actions and deductions. Section 3 will relate the key concepts from the object-oriented paradigm to an extended logic programming language and therefore proposes a "logical object-based programming language". A "logical class-based programming language" is defined adding the notion of class template. Adding the notion of inheritance a "logical object-oriented programming language" is defined starting from the previous one. Section 4 discusses related works aiming to integrate the logic and object-oriented paradigms. Finally, section 5 is devoted to some conclusion remarks and to future work.

1.1 Preliminaries

The reader is assumed to be familiar with the terminology and the basic definitions of logic programs [21] and the notions of object-oriented programs [22,10]. Let $Pred$ be a finite set of *predicates symbols*, Var a denumerable set of *variable symbols* and $Term$ the set of terms built on $Const$ and Var. The notation $\tilde{t}$ will be used to denote a tuple of terms. A substitution is a mapping $\vartheta : Var \rightarrow Term$. An atom is an object of the form $p(t_1, \ldots, t_n)$ where $p \in Pred, t_1, \ldots, t_n \in Term$. A *literal* is an atom or the negation of an atom. A *rule* is a formula of the form $H \leftarrow L_1, \ldots, L_n$, where H (the *head*) is an atom and $L_1, \ldots, L_n$ (the *body*) are literals. "←" and "," denote logic implication and conjunction respectively; all variables are universally quantified. We denote $L_1, \ldots, L_n$ by $BODY$. If the body is empty the rule is a *fact*. A *program* P is a set of rules. A *goal* is a rule without head.

2 Actions and Deductions in logic programming

Programs and databases are models of some reality and therefore we can see a database as a snapshot of a world and since change is an integral part of the natural order of things, we have to change our descriptions to keep them consistent with reality. However, accommodating updates in database systems remains a hard research problem. A considerable research effort has been devoted in this area but some difficult questions remain to be solved. Traditional database languages usually separate the function of querying and updating the database. In $\mathcal{LDL}$ [20] and RDL1 [16] both functions are integrated. So rather than having to specify updates in some other language or facility meant specifically for this purpose, we use $\mathcal{LDL}$ for both purposes. The key idea is to combine the *actions* and *deductions* in a single framework [19]. Actions allow base relations to be inserted or deleted from a state and take place on some world, modifying one state of affair to another. The notion of state is introduced as a set of base relations. At any time between occurrences of actions, it is possible to perform deductions on the current state of affairs. We will start by a subset of $\mathcal{LDL}$ (*legal programs*) [20] and we will provide it with an object-oriented extension. $\mathcal{LDL}$ extends the set of predicates that can occur in the body of a rule by allowing *update predicates* of the form $\alpha p(t_1, \ldots, t_n)$, called update predicates. The intuitive meaning of an update predicate such us $+p(t_1, \ldots, t_n)$ is to insert the tuple $(t_1, \ldots, t_n)$ into the base relation p; correspondingly, the intuitive meaning of $-p(t_1, \ldots, t_n)$ is to delete the tuple $(t_1, \ldots, t_n)$ from the base relation p. Note that a set of ground base relations define the state of the database.

Example 2.1 *Let us consider the following program P where student(N) denotes the student with name N, add(N, A) defines that the student with name N has address A.*

> student(bob).
> add(bob, boston).
> chaA(N, A, NewA) ← −add(N, A), +add(N, NewA).

A change operation can be specified as a delete followed by an insertion operation as shown in the program above. The goal ?student(X) computes the substitution {X/bob}. ?chaA(bob,boston,rome) performs a state transition from the state {student(bob), add(bob,boston)} to the state {student(bob), add(bob,rome)}. The goal ?+student(tom) performs a state transition from {student(bob), add(bob,rome)} to {student(bob), add(bob,rome), student(tom)}. The goal ?student(X) computes {X/bob} and {X/tom}. ◊

Note that the changes of states are performed as side-effect of the refutation process. The semantics of the updates to base relations have been given for logic programs augmented with simple update operations based on Dynamic Logic [20] in term of declarative semantics and equivalent constructed model semantics.

3 Notions of the object-oriented approach in logic programming

We will attempt here to relate some of the key concepts from object-oriented paradigm to an extended logic programming language. We will use the definitions proposed by Wegner [22]

object-oriented = objects + classes + inheritance + {message passing}

extended with the notion of message passing. The notion of message passing has been introduced to emphasize the cooperation among objects. The above definition can not be regarded as "the definition" of object-oriented paradigm but as a framework to propose our approach. In addition the main feature of this framework is to describe a hierarchy of languages which will allow us to give an incremental definition starting from a "logical-object based language" (which is a proper subset of a logical-class based language), next a "logical-class based language" (which is a proper subset of a logical-object oriented language) and finally a "logical-object oriented language". The other "dimensions" of language design, such us data abstraction, strong typing, concurrency and persistence, are not considered here.

3.1 Objects and message passing in logic programming

An object should provide an *encapsulation* mechanism and the *state evolution*. In order to achieve these features a labeled evolving theory is defined. A labeled *evolving theory* has the form $t_h : \{B, R\}$, where t_h is a theory name, B is a finite set of facts $\{fact_1, \ldots, fact_e\}$ and R is a finite set of rules $\{head_1 \leftarrow BODY_1, \ldots, head_f \leftarrow BODY_f\}$. We group together the facts and rules which relate to each individual theory and enclose them into a pair of $\{\}$'s and associate an identifying term or label. Rules can have in their bodies literals $p(\hat{t}), \neg p(\hat{t})$ and action atoms $\alpha p(\hat{t}), \alpha = \{-, +\}$. Literals are built starting from deduction predicate symbols $Pred^d$ and action atoms are built from action predicate symbols $Pred^a$. Action predicate symbols have the form $Pred^a = \{\ldots, -p, +p, -q, +q, \ldots\}$. The set of *general predicate symbols*, $Pred$ can be partitioned into the set of deduction predicate symbols $Pred^d = \{p_1^d, \ldots, p_s^d\}$ and the set of action predicate symbols $Pred^a = \{p_1^a, \ldots, p_r^a\}$ such that and $Pred^a \cap Pred^d = \emptyset$. Note that $\forall p, \neg p, p \in Pred^d$. Therefore, a labeled evolving theory has the form

$$theory_h : \{ \quad fact_1 \ldots fact_e.$$
$$head_1 \leftarrow BODY_1.$$
$$\vdots$$
$$head_f \leftarrow BODY_f.\}$$

which can change over time.

A goal $\hat{g}$, for a labeled evolving theory t_h, is a conjunction of literals $\hat{g} =?g_1, \ldots, g_n$ where the predicate symbol of g_i is in $Pred^d, i = 1 \ldots n$. Note that we do not allow action atoms in goals. We want the set of all the possible actions to be "stored" in our program.

Example 3.1 *Let us consider a program* $P = \{Tom\}$ *which defines information for the labeled evolving theory Tom.*

$$Tom : \{ \quad marTo(tom, sue).$$
$$wifeOf(W, M) \leftarrow marTo(M, W).$$
$$toMarry(M, W) \leftarrow \neg marTo(M, W), +marTo(M, W). \}$$

The goal ?wifeOf(X, Y) computes {X/sue, Y/tom}. ?toMarry(john, mary) performs a state transition. ◇

The notion of labeled evolving theory has the basic features of an object, an encapsulation mechanism and provides the state evolutions. However, it can not still be considered as a logical object because there is no mechanism for cooperation among evolving theories which we will see in the following. Note that normally any facts and rules in a logic program can be used in a deduction step; however, since we are dealing with potentially more than one set of facts and rules collected into several theories, we are required to be more specific as to which theory each rule comes from in each deduction step. We do this by implicitly (and sometimes explicitly) associating a label with every condition in the query.

A program is now a set of labeled evolving theories $P = \{t_1, \ldots, t_p\}, t_h \in T, h = 1 \ldots p$. A computation can be performed evaluating a goal of the form $?G_r, \ldots, G_k$, $(r \neq k, r, k \leq p)$. Where each G_k is a couple $t_k : \hat{g}_k$, which states where the refutation (t_k)starts for the subgoal $\hat{g}_k$ (by $\hat{g}_k = g_{k1_1}, \ldots, g_{kn_k}$ we mean a conjunction of literals) with the predicate symbols of the literals $g_{kj} \in Pred^d, j = 1_1 \ldots n_k$. Therefore the general form of a goal for a program P is $?t_1 : \hat{g}_1, \ldots, t_k : \hat{g}_k$.

Example 3.2 *Let us consider a program $P = \{Tom, John\}$ made of the labeled evolving theories Tom and John.*

    Tom : { name(tom).
             marTo(tom, sue).
             wifeOf(W, M) ← marTo(M, W).
             toMarry(M, W) ← ¬marTo(M, W), +marTo(M, W). }

    John : { name(john).
              marTo(john, mary).
              wifeOf(W, M) ← marTo(M, W).
              toMarry(M, W) ← ¬marTo(M, W), +marTo(M, W). }

The goal ?Tom : wifeOf(X, Y), John : wifeOf(Z, V) computes {X/sue, Y/tom} and {Z/mary, V/john}. ?Tom:name(X), marTo(tom, Y) computes {X/tom, Y/sue}. ◇

Since we have prefixed in the first goal the *name(.)* and *marTo(.)* conditions with the *Tom* label, only those facts and rules which are in *Tom* will be used to solve them; moreover, in order to actually solve the *name(.)* and *marTo(.)* conditions it might be necessary to invoke predicates defined in other theories. The query can also be interpreted as sending the *name(.)* and *marTo(.)* messages to the *Tom* theory. The *Tom* theory responds to this by attempting the relevant proofs for *name(.)* and *marTo(.)*. A successful completion of those proofs corresponds to the successful "handling" of the messages by the *Tom* theory. The previous example shows that a goal can trigger more than one theory. Now we want to model a notion of cooperation based on message passing defining a way to drive the refutation process through the theories. Message passing between objects achieves the computation in the object-oriented model. A message sent to an object is interpreted as a request to execute one of its methods. In logic programming computation is achieved by deduction: typically by reducing a goal to the empty goal. In a logical-object based programming language the computation is achieved by means of actions and deductions. In our approach, the actions are performed as side-effect of the deduction process and, therefore, we only have to model the deduction process. The computation, triggered by a goal can be performed into a theory as a stand alone unit, as in the above example, where the refutation is completed into a theory or the theory can cooperate with other theories to perform the task (the refutation can go through several theories) and therefore message passing can be used to drive the refutation process.

We extend the approach of evolving theory allowing labeled conjunctions of literals in the bodies of the rules of the theories and therefore we define a *(cooperating) object* as $o_h : \{B, R^O\}$, where o_h is an object name, O is a denumerable set of object names, B is a finite set of base relations and R^O is a finite set of rules $\{head_i \leftarrow BODY_1, \ldots, head_j \leftarrow BODY_j\}$ which can have in their bodies conjunctions of literals $(\hat{p}_i^d)$ and conjunctions of action atoms $(\hat{p}_j^a)$, as for the theory defined above and labeled conjunctions of literals $o_x : \hat{p}_i^d$ with $o_x \in O$. A method of an object in the object-oriented paradigm can be seen in a logical-object based language as a rule. A message $o_x : \hat{p}_i^d$, interpreted in the object-oriented paradigm, as a request to perform one of its methods, can be seen in this context, as the request to find a refutation for a conjunction of literals $\hat{p}_i^d$ in the object o_x. Note that the label of an object, is the counterpart of the object identifier in the object-oriented paradigm which must be unique over the program. Therefore, an object has the form

$$o_h : \{ \quad fact_1 \ldots fact_e.$$
$$head_1 \leftarrow \hat{p}_1^d, \hat{p}_2^a, o_u : \hat{p}_3^d, \ldots o_v : \hat{p}_4^d.$$
$$\vdots$$
$$head_j \leftarrow \hat{p}_5^d, \hat{p}_6^a, o_z : \hat{p}_7^d, \ldots o_t : \hat{p}_8^d. \}$$

The object can cooperate through $\{< o_x : \hat{p}_i^d >| \forall r \in R^O, o_x \in O, < o_x : \hat{p}_i^d > \in Body(r)\}$ with other objects. *Body* is a function which given a rule returns the set of labeled conjunction of literals $< o_x : \hat{p}_i^d >$ which are in the body of a rule r. A program is a set of cooperating objects $P = \{o_1, \ldots, o_p\}, o_h \in O, h = 1 \ldots p$. A computation can be performed evaluating a goal of the form $?G_r, \ldots, G_k$ as for the evolving theories.

Example 3.3 *Let us consider a program* $P = \{Tom, John\}$ *where the object John cooperates with the object Tom through* $\mathbf{Tom : wifeOf(W, M)}$ *and the object Tom does not cooperate with the object John.*

$$Tom : \{ \quad name(tom).$$
$$marTo(tom, sue).$$
$$wifeOf(W, M) \leftarrow marTo(M, W).$$
$$toMarry(M, W) \leftarrow \neg marTo(M, W), +marTo(M, W). \}$$

$$John : \quad \{ \quad name(john).$$
$$marTo(john, mary).$$
$$wifeOf(W, M) \leftarrow marTo(M, W).$$
$$wifeOf(W, M) \leftarrow \text{Tom} : \textbf{wifeOf}(\textbf{W}, \textbf{M}).$$
$$toMarry(M, W) \leftarrow \neg marTo(M, W), +marTo(M, W). \}$$

The goal *?John: wifeOf(X, Y)* computes $\{X/mary, Y/john\}$ and $\{X/sue, Y/tom\}$.
The goal *?Tom: wifeOf(X, Y)* computes the substitution $\{X/sue, Y/tom\}$. ◇

Tom : **wifeOf(W, M)** can be seen as the message, $wifeOf(W, M)$ sent to the object *Tom*. The idea is that the object *John* asks the object *Tom* to find a refutation for $wifeOf(W, M)$. The above example shows the cooperation between the objects *Tom* and *John* through $Tom : wifeOf(W, M)$ when the goal $?John : wifeOf(X, Y)$ computes $\{X/sue, Y/tom\}$.

Miming the classification of languages given in [22] and previously extended we claim that the language defined so far is a "logical-object based language" because it support objects and message passing as language features. Note that the approach followed to model cooperation among objects through message passing is close to the open program presented in [5] in the case of definite pure logic programs.

3.2 Classes in logic programming

The previous example has shown that the objects can change state and cooperate. The object *Tom* held information about himself such as name, wife and so on. Analogously, the object *John*. In order to describe objects which have uniform structure and behaviour we introduce the notion of class as a collection of objects. A class must provide functions of a *specification* and of an *object factory*. As a specification the notion of class gives us constraints on the structure and behaviour of the instances of a class, the objects. As an object factory we can generate and destroy objects as we need. We start defining a *class (template)* as $c_h(t_1, \ldots, t_n) : \{B(t_1, \ldots, t_n), R^C\}$. c_h is a class name, C is a finite set of class names, the tuple $t_1, \ldots, t_n$ defines the parameters of the class, $B(t_1, \ldots, t_n)$ denotes a finite set of base relations which have as terms a subset of the terms of the tuple $t_1, \ldots, t_n$ denoted by w_j (see below) and R^C is a finite set of rules as for the definition of object, where the label are now taken from the set C. The set of facts and rules of a class is called *class body*. A class has a tuple of terms as parameters which allow objects to be specified when they are created. The predicate $new(c_h, t_1, \ldots, t_n, o_j)$ creates a new object from c_i with parameters $t_1, \ldots, t_n$ and returns $o_j \in O$ which can be seen as the object identifier in the object-oriented paradigm. From now on $O = \{0, s(0), s(s(0)), \ldots\}$ is a denumerable set of object identifiers built with the function *successor* and thus is a subset of the set of natural numbers. Note that $O \cap C = \emptyset$. The predicate *new* is predefined and can be seen as a system predicate into a goal and will always succeed given the arguments c_h and $t_1, \ldots, t_n$ if c_h is defined. Therefore, a class has the form

$$class_h(t_1,\ldots,t_n): \quad \{ \quad fact_1(w_1) \;\ldots\; fact_e(w_e).$$
$$head_1 \leftarrow \hat{p}_1^d, \hat{p}_2^a, class_u : \hat{p}_3^d, \ldots class_v : \hat{p}_4^d.$$
$$\vdots$$
$$head_f \leftarrow \hat{p}_5^d, \hat{p}_6^a, class_x : \hat{p}_7^d, \ldots class_t : \hat{p}_8^d. \quad \}$$

where $w_j \in \{(t_{i_1},\ldots,t_{i_k}) \mid 1 < i_1,\ldots, < i_k < n \wedge k \leq n\}, j = 1\ldots e$. Note that the variables in $t_1,\ldots,t_n$ are universally quantified over all the facts and rules in a class as shown in the example below.

Example 3.4 *The following notations are equivalent.*

$$person(M, A). \quad \{ \quad name(M).$$
$$add(A).$$
$$chaA(Y, NewY) \leftarrow -add(Y), +add(NewY).\}$$

$$\forall M, \forall A \; person(M, A): \quad \{ \quad name(M).$$
$$add(A).$$
$$chaA(Y, NewY) \leftarrow -add(Y), +add(NewY).\}$$

$\diamond$

A logical-class based program is $P = \{c_1(t_{1_1},\ldots,t_{n_1}),\ldots,c_p(t_{1_p},\ldots,t_{n_p})\}$ which is a set of class definitions with parameters, $c_h \in C, h = 1\ldots p$ and $t_j \in Term, j = 1_1 \ldots n_p$. A computation can be performed evaluating a goal of the form $?G_r,\ldots,G_k$, where G_k is a couple $o_k : \hat{g}_k$ or one of the system predicates. o_k is the label of an object or of a class i.e. $o_k \in C \cup O$, and $\hat{g}_k$ is as introduced before a conjunction of deduction predicates. Note that the set of *predicate system symbols* $Pred^s$ contains other two predefined predicates *remove* and *isa*, therefore $Pred^s = \{new, remove, isa\}$. *remove(.)* has a complementary meaning of *new(.)*, while *isa(.)* which takes the parameter Oid, checks the membership of the object Oid and returns the class to which it belongs and the parameters.

Example 3.5 *Let us consider a program* $P = \{person(M, A), student(N, D)\}$.

$$person(M, A): \quad \{ \quad name(M).$$
$$age(A).$$
$$chaA(Y, NewY) \leftarrow -age(Y), +age(NewY).\}$$

$$student(N, D): \quad \{ \quad name(N).$$
$$dep(D).$$
$$age(Y) \leftarrow \textbf{person}: \textbf{age}(Y).$$
$$chaD(Y, NewY) \leftarrow -dep(Y), +dep(NewY).\}$$

and the follwing sequence of goals.

$G_1 = ?new(person, john, 25, Oid)$ $G_5 = ?0: age(X)$

$G_2 = ?new(person, john, 26, Oid)$ $G_6 = ?isa(X_1, X_2, X_3, 0)$

$G_3 = ?new(person, bob, 26, Oid)$ $G_7 = ?0: chaA(25, 26)$

$G_4 = ?person: age(X)$ $G_8 = ?person: chaA(26, 27), name(john)$

The goals (1), (2) and (3) create three new objects and compute their object identifiers through the substitution $\{Oid/0\}, \{Oid/s(0)\}$ and $\{Oid/s(s(0))\}$. The goal (4)
computes the substitutions $\{X/25\}$ and $\{X/26\}$. The goal (5) computes the substitution
$\{X/25\}$ because 25 is the age for the object 0. The goal (6) computes the substitution
$\{X_1/person, X_2/john, X_3/25\}$ giving the membership and the information on the object 0. The goal (7) succeeds in producing a state transition for the object 0 from
$\{name(john), age(25)\}$ to $\{name(john), age(26)\}$. The goal (8) succeeds in producing
a state transition for all objects of the class person with name john i.e. 0 and $s(0)$.

◇

Following the classification of languages previously extended we claim that the
language defined so far is a "logical-class based language" because every object has a
class and can cooperate through message passing.

3.3   Class inheritance in logic programming

The previous example has shown that classes can be defined. However, we note that
another way of structuring information into classes is through specialization. For example, w.r.t. the previous example we want to describe students as a specialization
of persons. It would be very convenient if we could directly express this information
in a simple way. The logical equivalent of specialization is *inheritance*. When we
say that a student is a special case of person we are stating that whatever is true of
persons is also true of students. Class inheritance is the most innovative part of the
object-oriented paradigm and has been investigated in the pure logic programming
and a model theoretic and fixpoint semantics have been given through meta-level operators [6]. We now want to model class inheritance of both the *structure* and the
behaviour of class. The structural inheritance is achieved extending the previous class
definition. Therefore the definition of a *class (with inheritance of the structure)* is
$c_i(t_1, \ldots, t_n) :< \{B(t_1, \ldots, t_n), R^C\}$ c_i Op c_j. c_i, c_j are class names, $C, t_1, \ldots, t_n$ and
$\{B(t_1, \ldots, t_n), R^C\}$ are defined as for the previous definition of class. c_i Op c_j states
that $c_i \in C$ is structurally a subclass of $c_j \in C$. Intuitively speaking, a structural
hierarchical relation between two classes states that the base relations of $B(t_1, \ldots, t_n)$
contained in a superclass are inherited by, i.e. become visible to, a subclass which

is hierarchically linked to the former. Typically, an exception mechanism is adopted, which states that the subclass inherits from the superclass everything but what itself redefines. In the following, given two classes c_i and c_j, $preds_{ij}$ will stand for the set of predicates which are defined in both classes. Two kind of operators are introduced in order to model hierarchical relationship between c_i and c_j for the *extended* and *overriding* mode.

- $c_i <= c_j$, with c_i subclass and c_j superclass, states that the facts in the class identified by c_j are also in class c_i. c_i contains, in addition to its predicates, the definitions of predicates occurring in c_j only.

- $c_i \ll c_j$, with c_i subclass and c_j superclass, states that c_i contains the intersection of the definitions of the predicates in $preds_{ij}$ and inherits the definitions of the predicates occurring in c_j only.

Therefore, a class with inheritance on the structure has the form

$$c_i(t_1, \ldots, t_n) : \quad \{ \quad fact_1(w_1). \ldots fact_e(w_e).$$
$$rule_1 \ldots rule_f \}$$
$$c_i \; Op \; c_j$$

where $rule_x, x = 1, \ldots f$ denotes $head_x \leftarrow BODY_x$. We assume that class hierarchies are organized into trees, i.e. each class can have at most one direct superclass and several subclasses. Classes are statically defined, as opposed .to instances that can be dynamically created. A logical-object oriented program is still $P = \{c_1(t_{1_1}, \ldots, t_{n_1}), \ldots, c_p(t_{1_p}, \ldots, t_{n_p})\}$. The predicate $new(c_i, t_1, \ldots, t_k, o_h)$ creates now a new object from c_i with parameters $t_1, \ldots, t_k$ which are a superset of the parameters used to define c_i. This allow us to model the structural inheritance by means of $new(.)$ which creates an object in the subclass c_i which is also partially visible from the superclass c_j. Note that an instance of a subclass can not be created without the parameters for the superclass as shown by the following example.

Example 3.6 *Let us consider the following class definitions with class inheritance in extended mode*

$$person(M, A) : \quad \{ \quad name(M).$$
$$age(A).$$
$$chaA(Y, NewY) \leftarrow -age(Y), +age(NewY).\}$$

$$student(D) : \quad \{ \quad dep(D).$$
$$chaD(Y, NewY) \leftarrow -dep(Y), +dep(NewY).\}$$
$$student <= person$$

The class student extends the structural part consisting of dep(D) with the structural part consisting of name(M) and age(A) of the class person obtaining name(M), dep(D) and age(A). Consider the following sequence of goals.

$G_1 = ?new(student, tom, history, 28, Oid)$ $G_3 = ?person: name(X)$
$G_2 = ?new(student, tom, computer, 24, Oid)$

The goals (1) and (2) create two new objects in the class student $\{Oid/0\}$ and $\{Oid/s(0)\}$. The goal (3) succeeds in computing the substitution $\{X/tom\}$.   ◇

Note that *age(.)* and *name(.)* are inherited from the class person and they are visible to class student. Thus to model that a student is also a person the predicate *new(.)* takes also the term of the predicates *age* and *name*. If the class rule is empty, then the class with inheritance of the structure is a class template.

Example 3.7 *Let us consider the following class definitions with class inheritance in overriding mode*

$person(M, A):$ $\{name(M).$ $adult(X):$ $\{age(X) \leftarrow X > 17.$
                $age(A).\}$ $\}$
          $adult \ll person$

The structural part of adult contains the definition for age(X) given in adult. Lets us consider the following sequence of goals.

$G_1 = ?new(person, bob, 25, Oid)$ $G_3 = ?person: age(X)$
$G_2 = ?new(person, tom, 11, Oid)$ $G_4 = ?adult: age(X)$

The goals (1) and (2) create two new objects $\{Oid/0\}$ and $\{Oid/s(0)\}$. The goal (3) succeeds in computing $\{X/25\}$ and $\{X/11\}$. The goal (4) succeeds in computing $\{X/25\}$.   ◇

Following the classification of languages previously extended we claim that the language defined so far is a "logical-object oriented language" because its objects, co-operating through message passing, belong to classes and class hierarchies may be incrementally defined by an inheritance mechanism. The previous examples have shown that inheriting the structure is useful but we also want a way to manipulate the inherited structure.

The fact *age(.)* inherited saves us from defining it again in the class student, but we also want a way to act on this fact using for example the rule *chaA(.)* $\leftarrow$ $-age(.), +age(.)..$

We want thus to model also inheritance of the behaviour. The class with inheritance of structure and behaviour is an extension of the class with inheritance of structure seen above. The definition of a *class (with inheritance of structure and behaviour)* is $c_i(t_1, \ldots, t_n) : \{B(t_1, \ldots, t_n), label_x : r_1, \ldots, label_y : r_f\} c_i$ Op c_j, where $c_i(t_1, \ldots, t_n)$ defines the name and parameters of the class, $B(t_1, \ldots, t_n)$ denotes a finite set of base relations which have as terms a subset of the terms of the tuple $t_1, \ldots, t_n$ denoted by w_j as introduced before. $LABEL$ is a finite set of label names, $r_j \in R^C, (j = 1 \ldots f)$

is a rule. Behavioural inheritance between classes is defined through labels. Note that $O \cap C \cap LABEL = \emptyset$. Therefore, a class with inheritance of structure and behaviour has the form

$$c_i(t_1, \ldots, t_n) : \{ \quad fact_1(w_1) \ldots fact_e(w_e).$$
$$label_x : rule_1 \ldots label_y : rule_f \}$$
$$c_i \; Op \; c_j$$

Note that within a class definition, a label can be used only once. Therefore, there are no rules, in a class definition, with the same label. Rules of different classes can have the same label and this will be used to have class with inheritance of behaviour. Given two classes c_i and c_j

$$c_i(\ldots) : \{ \quad \ldots label_x : head_a \leftarrow BODY_a \ldots \}$$
$$c_i \; Op \; c_j$$

$$c_j(\ldots) : \{ \ldots label_y : head_b \leftarrow BODY_b \ldots \}$$

we define by cases the intuitive meaning of behavioural inheritance depending on the labels.

- $label_x = label_y$. If the heads of the rules have the same predicate symbol p, ($head_a = p(\tilde{t})$ and $head_b = p(\tilde{u})$) then the rule obtained by inheritance is $(p(\tilde{u}))\theta \leftarrow (BODY_a, BODY_b)\theta$ with $\theta = mgu((\tilde{t}), (\tilde{u}))$, thus $(\hat{p}_1^d, \hat{p}_2^a, class_u : \hat{p}_3^d, \ldots class_v : \hat{p}_4^d)\theta = \hat{p}_1^d, \hat{p}_2^a\theta, class_u : \hat{p}_3^d, \ldots class_v : \hat{p}_4^d\theta$. If the heads of the rules do not have the same predicate symbol ($head_a = p(\tilde{t})$ and $head_b = q(\tilde{u})$) then the rule obtained by inheritance is $head_b \leftarrow BODY_b$ which overrides $head_a \leftarrow BODY_a$.

- $label_x \neq label_y$. The rules obtained by inheritance are the two rules $rule_a$ and $rule_b$ independently from the heads of the rules.

Note that behavioural inheritance is independent from the mode of structural inheritance. The mode of behavioural inheritance is defined through the labels while the mode of structural inheritance is defined through Op. Note that if the labels are equal and the heads of rules are also equal we perform a kind of refinement of the behaviour defined by the rule with label $label_a$ in c_i by means of the rule in c_j with label $label_b$.

Example 3.8 *Let us consider the following class definitions with structural and behavioural inheritance*

$$person(M, A) : \{ \quad name(M).$$
$$age(A).$$
$$CA : chaA(Y, NewY) \leftarrow -age(Y), +age(NewY).\}$$

$$student(D): \{\quad dep(D).$$
$$CD: chaD(Y, NewY) \leftarrow -dep(Y), +dep(NewY).\}$$
$$student <= person$$

The class student extends its structural part consisting of dep(D) with the structural part consisting of name(M) and age(A) of the class person obtaining name(M), dep(D) and age(A). The rules labeled CA and CD are obtained by behavioural inheritance. Consider the following sequence of goals.

$$G_1 = ?new(student, john, computer, 26, Oid) \quad G_2 = ?student: chaA(26, 27)$$

The goal (1) creates a new object $\{Oid/0\}$ in the class student. The goal (2) succeeds because the rule labeled CA is visible in student through the behavioural inheritance and produces a state transition for the object 0 from $\{name(john), age(26)\}$ to $\{name(john), age(27)\}$. ◊

4 Related Works

Below we classify the approachs to the integration between the logic and the object-oriented paradigms w.r.t. state evolution of objects and of the granularity of objects.

Evolution/Granularity	Term	Theory
No		[17,19,15,18]
Yes	[2,3,4,8,9,10,23]	

Almost all proposals in the above table fail in some way in the integration of logic and object-oriented paradigms w.r.t. to the basic notions of the object-oriented paradigm. Some of them do not provide classes, inheritance, objects, message passing or state evolution. The approaches [2,8] are "data model" driven in the sense that the perspective from which they start is rather different from the others. These approaches are based on a "object-based data model" which usually supports complex objects, i.e. an object can be composed starting from other objects. The other approaches attempt to integrate the logic and object-oriented paradigms providing state evolution only within the granularity of terms or without state evolution within granularity of theories.

5 Conclusion and future work

We have seen a hierarchy of languages, a logical-object based language, a logical-class based language and a logical-object oriented language. They are build starting from the notion of object seen as a cooperating evolving theory. A mechanism of message passing uniform w.r.t. the goal is also provided. It provides the cooperation for the actions and deductions among objects. A notion of class template with inheritance on the structure and on the behaviour is also given. This approach provides the traditional dynamic property of the object-oriented paradigm, the controlled state evolution of objects and their creation/destruction. Moreover it seems promising with respect to the semantics. In particular the semantics for the logical-object based language can be derived from [17] for a logical-object based language without actions. Note that when actions occur, as pointed out before, they are performed as side-effects of the refutation process and they are performed into an object without outside knowledge of this. Within an object the semantics for actions and deductions can be given as for the $\mathcal{LDL}$ language. The perspective is more difficult when we consider a logical-class based language and a logical-object oriented language. Therefore our directions for future research are:

- to investigate the semantics relationship between the Ω-open program [5] and a logical language providing actions e.g. $\mathcal{LDL}$ in order to model a compositional semantics

- to characterize the semantics of class template and their operations

- to study the addition of integrity constraints to classes and to investigate query optimization

- to investigate the semantics of inheritance and multiple inheritance mechanism for the structural and behavioural parts.

Acknowledgments: The authors wish to thank Prof. Maurizio Martelli who suggested several relevant bibliographic references and carefully reviewed earlier versions of this manuscript by making many constructive comments.

References

[1] S. Abiteboul. Towards a Deductive Object-Oriented Database Language. In W Kim et al., editor, *Proc. First Int'l Conf. on Deductive and Object-Oriented Databases*, pages 419–438, 1989.

[2] S. Abiteboul and P. Kanellakis. Object Identity as a Query Language Primitive. In *Proc. Int'l Conf. ACM on Management of Data*, pages 159–173, 1989.

[3] H. Ait-Kaci and R. Nasr. Login: a Logic Programming Language With Built-In Inheritance. *Journal of Logic Programming*, 3:185–215, 1986.

[4] J. M. Andreoli and R. Pareschi. LO and behold! Concurrent Structured Processes. In N. Meyrowitz, editor, *Proc. Int'l Conf. on Object-Oriented Programming: Systems, Languages, and Applications*, pages 1–13, 1990.

[5] A. Bossi, M. Gabbrielli, G. Levi, and M. C. Meo. Contributions to the Semantics of Open Logic Programs. Technical Report TR 17/91, Dipartimento di Informatica, Università di Pisa, 1991.

[6] A. Brogi, P. Mancarella, F. Turini, and D. Pedreschi. Composing Operators for Logic Theories. In J. W. Lloyd, editor, *Computational Logic*, pages 117–134. Springer-Verlag, Berlin, 1990.

[7] A. D. Burt, P. M. Hill, and J. W. Lloyd. Preliminary Report on the Logic Programming Language Gödel. Technical Report TR 90-02, Computer Science Department, Univeristy of Britstol, 1990.

[8] F. Cacace, S. Ceri, S. Crespi-Reghizzi, L. Tanca, and R. Zicari. The Logres project: Integrating Object-Oriented Data Modelling with a Rule-Based Programming Paradigm. Technical Report TR 89-039, Politecnico di Milano, 1989.

[9] W. Chen and D. S. Warren. Objects as Intensions. In R.A. Kowalski and K.A. Bowen, editors, *Proc. Fifth Int'l Conf. on Logic Programming*, pages 404–419. The MIT Press, Cambridge, Mass., 1988.

[10] J. S. Conery. Logical Objects. In R.A. Kowalski and K.A. Bowen, editors, *Proc. Fifth Int'l Conf. on Logic Programming*, pages 420–434. The MIT Press, Cambridge, Mass., 1988.

[11] B. J. Cox. *Object-Oriented Programming*. Addison-Wesley, 1986.

[12] D. H. Fishman et al. Overview of the Iris DBMS. In W. Kim and F. H. Lochovsky, editors, *Object-Oriented Concepts, Databasases, and Applications*, pages 219–250. Addison-Wesley, 1989.

[13] Deux et al. The Story of O_2. *IEEE Tran. on Knowledge and Data Eng.*, 2(1):91–108, 1990.

[14] W. Kim et al. Features of the ORION Object-Oriented Database System. In W. Kim and F. H. Lochovsky, editors, *Object-Oriented Concepts, Databasases, and Applications*, pages 251–282. Addison-Wesley, 1989.

[15] E. Laenens, D. Saccà, and D. Vermeir. Extending logic programming. In *Proc. Int'l Conf. ACM on Management of Data*, pages 184–193, 1990.

[16] C. Maindreville and E. Simon. Modelling Non Detrministic Queries and Updates In Deductive Databases. In F. Bancilhon and D. J. DeWitt, editors, *Proc. Fourteenth Int'l Conf. on Very Large Data Bases*, pages 395–406, 1988.

[17] F.G. McCabe. *Logic and Objects*. PhD thesis, University of London, November 1988.

[18] D. Miller. A Theory of Modules for Logic Programming. In *Proc. IEEE Symposium on Logic Programming*, pages 106–114, 1986.

[19] L. Monteiro and A. Porto. Objects as Situated Theories. Technical report, Esprit, 1990. Basic Research Action n. 3020.

[20] S. Naqvi and S. Tsur. *A Logical Language for Data and Knowledge Bases*. Computer Science Press, 1989.

[21] L. Tanca S. Ceri, G. Gottlob. *Logic Programming and Databases*. Springer-Verlag, Berlin, 1990. Second edition.

[22] P. Wegner. Dimensions of Object-Based Language Design. In L. Power and Z. Weiss, editors, *Proc. Int'l Conf. on Object-Oriented Programming: Systems, Languages, and Applications*, pages 168–182, 1987.

[23] C. Zaniolo. Object Identity and Inheritance in Deductive Databases - an Evolutionary Approach. In W Kim et al., editor, *Proc. First Int'l Conf. on Deductive and Object-Oriented Databases*, pages 106–114, 1989.

Supporting Access Control in an Object-Oriented Database Language

Rafiul Ahad, James Davis, Stefan Gower
Peter Lyngbaek, Andra Marynowski and Emmanuel Onuegbe

Hewlett-Packard Company
Cupertino, California, USA

In memory of Peter Lyngbaek
March 9, 1955 - October 13, 1991

Abstract

This paper presents an approach for providing access control in OSQL, an object-oriented database language that supports, among others, user-defined abstract data types, multiple inheritance, and late binding. The authorization scheme is based on a single concept: that of controlling function evaluation. The paper discusses how the authorization model can be realized using existing OSQL mechanisms, i.e. subtyping, user-defined operations, and function resolution. It also presents two novel constructs: guard functions and proxy functions, which are useful in providing database security in a flexible and non-invasive manner. Various issues related to the language semantics are examined.

1 Introduction

One of the functions of a database management system (DBMS) is access control. A DBMS must prevent unauthorized access to data stored in the database. Although commercially available DBMSs do have security subsystems that support access control, support for authorization in object-oriented and functional database systems has not yet been fully addressed. In such systems, authorization features must interact with advanced model and language features such as user-defined operations, encapsulation, multiple inheritance, generic operations, and late binding.

This paper addresses some of the problems that arise when an authorization mechanism is added to an object-oriented database language that supports polymorphism. In particular, an authorization model for OSQL [14] is presented. OSQL is an object-oriented database language for the Iris DBMS prototype developed at HP Labs [8,7,22].

Object-oriented languages inherently provide some form of access control in the way abstract data types encapsulate private state information [16]. Although the abstract data types provide support for access control at the implementation level, there still remains the need for protection of data at the organizational level.

The authorization model of OSQL is based on the notion of controlling function evaluation. Only a single privilege, i.e. the privilege to call functions, is necessary to support an authorization model that is more powerful, more flexible, and has finer levels of access granularity than the traditional authorization model of relational databases [11]. The paper shows how the granularity of access can be controlled using existing OSQL mechanisms, i.e. subtyping, user-defined operations, and function resolution. It also illustrates how two new OSQL mechanisms, i.e. guard functions and proxy functions, can be used to support authorization in a flexible and non-invasive manner. Various issues related to the language semantics are examined.

The remainder of the paper is organized as follows. Section 2 summarizes the standard features of an authorization model for relational database systems. Section 3 provides an overview of the OSQL language. Section 4 presents a model of access control for OSQL. Justifications for this model are provided and various semantics tradeoffs are described. Section 5 discusses various techniques for realizing the access control model using existing as well as some new OSQL mechanisms. Functionality and performance tradeoffs for each of the techniques are discussed. Section 6 provides a review of related work. Finally, Section 7 contains some concluding remarks.

2 The Authorization Model of Relational Systems

The basic authorization model of standard SQL [4] can be characterized by a matrix captured by a relation schema (S,O,M). S is the domain of all subjects that access the database system (users, processes), O is the domain of objects (base relations and views), and M is the domain of access operations (SELECT, INSERT, DELETE, UPDATE, and ALTER).

Most RDBMS implementations support the notion of ownership. Each database schema has a designated system administrator, database administrator, or database creator that is the *owner* of all objects created in that schema. Furthermore, when a user creates an object, he becomes the owner of the object. In general, the owner of an object holds all privileges on that object.

An owner may grant access to his objects to other users. Commercial systems implement mechanisms that allow the owner to selectively grant SELECT, INSERT, DELETE, UPDATE, and ALTER privileges on objects to other users. Furthermore, an owner of an object may grant a GRANT privilege on the object, thereby enabling other users to further grant privileges on the object.

Many of the concepts developed for relational database authorization are fundamental in nature and are applicable to other technologies as well, e.g. object-oriented DBMSs. These fundamental concepts include the notion of ownership, users and groups, privileges, and granting and revoking privileges. Section 4 discusses how the fundamental concepts from relational database authorization have been adopted by the more powerful and flexible authorization model of OSQL. However, first an introduction to OSQL is provided.

3 OSQL: An Object-Oriented Database Language

OSQL (Object SQL) is a high-level language for developing object-oriented database applications. A fundamental goal of OSQL is to provide a database interface with modeling constructs that closely match real-life situations and the needs of business and technical applications. OSQL is a functional language with special syntactic forms, resembling those of SQL, for common database functionality. This paper limits its focus to the functional aspects of OSQL.

The design of OSQL is influenced by pioneering work on semantic and functional database languages, notably the functional data language Daplex [19] and the language Taxis [17] for designing interactive information systems. As mentioned above, OSQL also has similarities to SQL [2,4]. The OSQL effort was started in the late 1986 at HP Labs as part of the Iris project [8,7,22]. Iris is a research prototype of an object-oriented database management system based on the Iris Data Model [15].

Functional programming and *abstract data types* are the fundamental concepts of the OSQL programming paradigm. All OSQL objects are instances of abstract data types. Objects (and their data) are encapsulated by a set of functions. To access an object, users call the appropriate functions; they need not be directly concerned with the structural layout of data. Objects, types, and functions provide the framework supporting the OSQL abstract data type paradigm. These are briefly introduced below. A full description of OSQL can be found in [14].

3.1 Objects

Objects represent entities and concepts from the application domain being modeled. Some objects such as integers and character strings are self identifying. These are called *literal* objects. Other objects are represented by system-generated, unique, immutable *object identifiers* or OIDs. These are called *surrogate* objects. Examples of surrogates are objects representing persons, employees, departments, and vehicles in the database. Surrogate objects may also represent entities used by the system. For example, types and functions are represented by surrogates. Surrogates must be explicitly created and deleted either by the system (for system-defined objects) or by the user (for user-defined objects).

Literal objects are identified by their external representation. There is a fixed set of literal objects. Examples include integers, reals, dates, and character strings.

OSQL also supports aggregate objects. Such objects may be composed of other objects. An object of type Set or Bag is an unordered collection of objects. Sets contain no duplicate elements. Bags may contain duplicates. Sets are subtypes Bags. An object of type List is an ordered collection of objects that may contain duplicates. An object of type Tuple is an ordered, fixed-sized collection of objects.

3.2 Types

Objects are classified by types. A type is used to characterize objects in terms of the functions that can be applied to the objects. The *extension* of a type is the set of objects of that type. Objects in the extension of a type are called *instances* of that type. Some types have pre-defined extensions, such as Integer. Other types have extensions that may change over time. The extensions of surrogate types, e.g. Person, may change when surrogate objects are explicitly created, deleted, added to a type, or removed from a type.

Types are related in a subtype/supertype hierarchy, known as the type hierarchy. The type hierarchy is a directed acyclic graph, rooted in the type Object. The type hierarchy models type containment. If an object is an instance of a type it is also an instance of all the type's supertypes. Suppose for example that the type Student is a subtype of type Person. Then every object that is an instance of Student is also an instance of Person. OSQL allows a given type to have multiple supertypes.

Anywhere an instance of a type can be used, an instance of a subtype can also be used. In other words, a function defined on a given type is implicitly defined on, or inherited by, all the type's subtypes. An example type hierarchy is shown in Figure 1. The type Person is a user type. It has two subtypes, Student and Employee. Employee

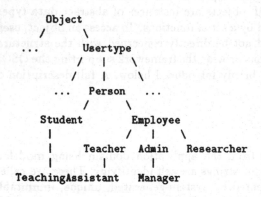

Fig. 1. Example Type Graph

is the supertype of Teacher, Admin, and Researcher. The type TeachingAssistant, a subtype of Student as well as Teacher, is an example of a type with multiple supertypes. The type Manager is a subtype of Admin.

Objects may belong to multiple types even if the types are not related by a subtype/supertype relationship.

A type has an associated *type predicate function* which takes an object of the type Object and returns true if and only if the object belongs to the extension of that type. It can be used to check if a given object has a given type. A type also has an associated *type extension function* which takes no arguments and returns the set of all objects belonging to the extension of the type.

3.3 Functions

Functions describe attributes of objects, relationships among objects, and operations on objects.

An OSQL function may take an object as an argument and may return an object as a result. The argument object must be an instance of the argument type specified for the function. It can return results only of the specified result type. Both the argument and the result may be aggregate objects. A function returning a bag, set or list object can be thought of as a many-valued function.

Functions may change the state of the database as a side-effect of their execution. Functions perform database updates by updating other functions. Functions that perform updates are said to have *side-effects*.

Similar to types, functions have *extensions*. The extension of a function defines the mapping between its arguments and results. Function extensions may be explicitly stored or may be computed. The function Birthdate would have a stored extension, but arithmetic functions, such as Plus and Minus, have computed extensions.

A distinction is made between a function's *declaration* and its *implementation*. The declaration defines the signature of the function and the constraints on its extension. The implementation defines the behavior of the function. The implementation of a function may be changed without impacting the applications that call the function. This provides a degree of data independence. A function is implemented by specifying its body. This can be done by specifying the implementation to be *stored*, or by defining the body by an OSQL program (this is called a *derived* function), or by providing a non-OSQL program for the body (this is called an *external* function).

The extension of a function may change with time. This can be accomplished by executing an associated update function. This has the side-effect of updating the underlying storage structures used to maintain the functions' extensions. The system may automatically generate the update functions for stored and certain derived functions. The user could also explicitly assign an update function to a given function.

3.4 Function Evaluation as Execution Paradigm

The execution paradigm of OSQL is that of function evaluation. The fundamental OSQL primitive is the *function call*. Features and functionality of OSQL, e.g. capabilities for data definition, data manipulation, and queries are provided by a set of built-in functions. For example, the TypeCreate function creates new types and the Select function performs a set-oriented database query. Special operators in the OSQL language, such as the arithmetic operators, are also provided by a set of built-in functions. For example, the type graph shown in Figure 1 could be extended with a new type ResearchAsst by the following call:

```
TypeCreate('ResearchAsst', {'Student', 'Researcher'});
```

The new type ResearchAsst becomes a subtype of Student and Researcher. The call to TypeCreate returns an object of type Type representing the new type.

3.5 Function Overloading and Resolution

Functions may be overloaded. That is, a *generic function* may have a set of associated *specific functions* that are defined on different types. A generic functions and its associated specific functions have identical names. When a generic function call is issued, a specific function is selected for invocation. This selection, also called *function resolution*, is based on the type of the argument object in the actual call. The function defined on the most specific type of the actual argument is chosen for invocation. In general, function resolution supports *late binding semantics*. With late binding semantics, a specific function to be invoked is selected based on the type of the actual argument at the time the function is executed. This has implications for functions defined in terms of other functions. If overloaded function names are used in the bodies of such functions resolution will not be performed until the functions are called.

Figure 2 shows an example where the function **Salary** is overloaded.

```
Employee subtype of Person
    FixedSalary
    Salary = FixedSalary

Admin subtype of Employee
    OvertimePay
    Salary = FixedSalary + OvertimePay

Researcher subtype of Employee
    ContractPay
    Salary = FixedSalary + 1/12 * ContractPay

Manager subtype of Admin
    Bonus
    Salary = FixedSalary + Bonus

TeachingAssistant subtype of Student, Teacher
    UnitsTaught
    Salary = UnitsTaught * UnitPay
```

Fig. 2. Payroll Application Using Overloaded Function Names

A payroll application can now apply the generic **Salary** function to any **Employee** object and obtain the correct amount of pay without any knowledge of the specific kind of employee.

In some cases, the mapping from a generic function to a specific function is ambiguous. That happens when there is more than one specific function corresponding to a given function call. OSQL does not prescribe default semantics for choosing a specific function in case of ambiguities; it instead reports an error. However, a *type-specific* function reference can be used to unambiguously identify a specific function. For example, the reference **Salary.Admin** denotes the **Salary** function defined on type **Admin**. Type-specific references can be resolved at compile-time which may give them a performance advantages over generic references.

4 Authorization in OSQL

The authorization model of OSQL borrows several fundamental concepts from SQL. These concepts include the notion of users, groups, ownership, privileges, and granting and revoking privileges. In addition, some new concepts related to derived function and function resolution are introduced. This section describes the OSQL authorization model and examines how it interacts with existing OSQL concepts such as derived functions, late binding, and function resolution.

4.1 The Call Privilege

In OSQL, a user who has a *call privilege* on a given function is authorized to evaluate the function. The assignments of call privileges can be modeled by the function:

```
CanCall(User, Function, Object) -> Boolean
```

where `Object` is the type of the argument to the function. The predicate is true for a given user, function, and arguments if the user is authorized to call the function with the specified arguments.

As mentioned in Section 2, the authorization model of SQL introduces insert, delete, update, and alter privileges. Such privileges are not necessary here, since all updates to an OSQL database are performed by evaluating functions. Therefore, in order to prevent a user from performing a certain update, he must be prevented from invoking the functions that can perform the update. This can be accomplished by not granting him call authorization on the functions. Notice that schema definition and schema modification in OSQL are also done by evaluating functions. Therefore, support of access control in OSQL extends to the data definition in addition to data manipulation.

4.2 Users, Groups, and Owners

Users are modeled by the OSQL type `User` which is characterized by a set of functions that create and destroy `User` objects, return valid user names, and match passwords. For example, the function:

```
UserCreate(Char) -> User
```

creates a new user.

Users may be classified by *groups*. Privileges can be granted to a group in which case they apply to each user in the group. Typically, users are classified based on their roles [6,9,13]. A user may belong to multiple groups, that way accumulating the privileges from each individual group. Furthermore, groups may be nested. A nested group inherits the privileges of the nesting groups similar to the way functions are inherited by a subtype from a supertype. The group hierarchy of OSQL is similar to the group hierarchy of the Orion object-oriented database system [18].

Groups are modeled by the OSQL type `Group`. Group members are either individual users or other groups and are modeled by the type `Subject` which is the supertype of `User` and `Group`. Typical functions defined on `Group` and `Subject` include functions for creating and deleting groups, for adding and removing subjects, for returning group members, and for granting and revoking call privileges. For example the function:

```
GroupMember(Group) -> { Subject }
```

return the set of members of a group.

The user who creates a given function is said to be the *owner* of the function. Function ownership can be modeled by the function:

```
Owns(User) -> { Function }
```

The owner of a function automatically has a call privilege on the function. Furthermore, the owner can grant call privileges on the function to other users using the function **Grant** as illustrated in Section 4.3.

The group hierarchy is rooted in the group **Public** which has call authority on common system functions such as **Connect** and **Select**. Every authenticated user by default belongs in Public.

Database Administrators (DBAs) are special users with more privileges than ordinary users. For example, DBAs have all the privileges implied by ownership of functions, e.g. grant authority on every function. The concept of database administrators is captured by the group **DBA**.

4.3 Granting and Revoking Privileges

Call privileges can be granted and revoked on a per-group basis and a per-user basis. This is modeled as follows:

```
Grant(Subject, Function, Object) -> Boolean
Revoke(Subject, Function, Object) -> Boolean
```

Notice that OSQL's authorization model does not have to introduce an explicit *grant privilege* as seen in SQL's authorization model. Rather, grant authority can be supported by applying the concept of call authority to the function **Grant**. For example, the following assertion:

```
CanCall(John, Grant, <Admin, Salary, Sue>) = true
```

models the fact that the user **John** can grant call authority on the function **Salary** with argument **Sue** to the group **Admin**.

The concept of a *grant privilege with grant option*, i.e., the privilege that allows a user to grant another user the right to grant a call authority on a function, can also be modeled by by applying call authority on the function **Grant**. For example, the following assertion:

```
CanCall(Ed, Grant, <Manager, Grant, <Admin, Salary, Sue>>) = true
```

models the fact that the user **Ed** can grant call authority to the group **Manager** on the function **Grant** when applied to the group **Admin** and the function **Salary** with argument **Sue**.

4.4 Static and Dynamic Authorization of Derived Functions

Since derived functions are defined in terms of other functions, it is necessary to address whether call authority on a derived function is sufficient to successfully evaluate the derived function (called *static authorization*), or whether the caller needs call authority on individual functions that are actually evaluated by the derived function (called *dynamic authorization*).

We contend that both mechanisms are useful. With static authorization, derived functions can be used as a mechanism for information hiding. Consider, for example, the function Salary. Some users may be able to see the salary of all employees, but other users may be restricted to see their own salary. In such a case one can create a function SelfSalary which calls Salary with the caller of SelfSalary as an argument. Users would not have call authority on the general function Salary, but they could be granted call authority on the derived function SelfSalary. Clearly, call authority on SelfSalary should not imply call authority on Salary regardless of the fact that Salary is called during the evaluation of SelfSalary.

When derived functions are used as a mechanism for providing procedural abstractions in order to modularize functions and programs, dynamic authorization applies. With dynamic authorization, a user can call a derived function only if he has call authority on all the underlying functions that are called during the evaluation of the derived function. As an example, consider again the function Salary. A derived function, OrderedSalary, defined in terms of Salary is also provided. OrderedSalary returns a list of all employees with their salaries ordered by increasing salary. Clearly, if a user is not authorized to call Salary he should not be allowed to call OrderedSalary either. Dynamic authorization will enforce that. Functions with dynamic authorization may be executed less efficiently than similar functions with static authorization. This is because there are more checks to be performed at run-time.

When creating derived functions, a user must specify whether the authorization of the defining functions are to be checked statically or dynamically. In either case, the function creator must have call authority on all the underlying functions. If the creator of the function specifies that the function is to have dynamic authorization, he is free to grant call authority on the function to other users. If the creator of the function specifies that the function is to have static authorization, he cannot grant call authority on the function to other users unless he has grant authority on all the underlying functions. Otherwise, existing security constraints could be violated. Special users, e.g. a DBA administering security policies, must be able to grant call authority on functions with static authorization to selected users.

4.5 The Interaction of Authorization and Function Resolution

OSQL supports dynamic function resolution as described in Section 3.5. When a user calls a generic function, a specific function is selected for execution at run-time based on the actual arguments supplied in the call. In this section, we discuss how OSQL's function resolution paradigm interacts with the proposed authorization model.

The first question to answer is whether function call authority should be specified for generic or specific functions. Below, we argue that both approaches are useful. One way to think of a generic function is that it represents a single service that possibly has many different implementations. This is the way virtual function of C++ [21] and abstract methods of Smalltalk [10] are used. An example is the salary service represented by the generic function **Salary** and its associated specific functions. If security policies refrain certain users from using a generic service altogether, it makes sense to specify call authority at the generic function level. For example, users who are not supposed to see the salary of any employee should not have call authority on the generic function **Salary**. If a user attempts to call a generic function on which he has no call authority, an appropriate action for security violation is taken (see Section 4.6). The same is true if he calls one of the specific functions associated with the generic function. On the other hand, if the user is permitted to evaluate a generic function, it implies that he/she has the permission to evaluate all specific functions of that generic function. This approach is called *generic function authorization*. One of its advantages is that specific functions can be modified and new ones added without impacting authorization. Another advantage is that authorization checks can be done at compile time.

However, there are also cases where it makes sense to allow users to make partial use of a generic service. For example, some users might be authorized to see the salary of managers, but not the salary of employees in general. To support such cases, call privileges must be specified for specific functions. When a user attempts to evaluate a generic function, function resolution takes place in order to select a specific function. The specific function is invoked only if the user has the appropriate call authority. In this approach, called *specific function authorization*, there is a number of ways the function resolution process can select the specific function to be executed. One way is to perform the resolution without taking authorization into account. Once a specific function has been selected, the authorization is checked. This approach is called *authorization-independent resolution*. It cleanly separates the two orthogonal aspects of application semantics and access control, i.e., security policies can be changed without affecting the result returned by a generic function invocation.

Another approach is to take the user into account and appropriately resolve the function so that the resolver only sees the functions the user is authorized to call. That way, the user ends up executing the most specific function that he is authorized to evaluate. This approach is called *authorization-dependent resolution*. It supports access control policies that allow a given function invocation to return different results depending on the identity of the invoker. This has some usability advantages, e.g., it is better to return something than nothing. However, in situations where query semantics are not to depend on authorization policies, this can be seen as a major disadvantage.

The added flexibility provided by specific function authorization comes at an extra cost in space and time. For example, call authority cannot be checked at compile-time, but must be performed at run-time.

Notice that specific function authorization can emulate generic function authorization, and both generic and specific function authorization approaches can be supported simultaneously. One possible semantics of a call to a generic function would be as follows: If the user has call authority on the generic function, function resolution takes place as usual. The selected specific function is evaluated only if the user has call authority on it; otherwise an action for security violation is taken (see Section 4.6). If the user does not have call authority on the generic function, an action for security violation is taken.

4.6 Action for Security Violation

When a user tries to evaluate a function that he is not authorized to evaluate, what action should the system take? An obvious answer is to abort the request and issue an authorization error. This approach, called the *termination* approach, works fine if all authorization checks can be performed before any results are returned to the caller. However, that is not always the case. The user may end up with partial results before an authorization violation is detected. This situation could be caused by a query. In a query, call authority is needed for every function referenced in the query. Sometimes the specific functions referenced cannot be determined at the time the query is compiled. If specific function authorization semantics is adopted, some queries will compile correctly, but may fail authorization checks at run-time. If a user opens a cursor on such a query, he may retrieve partial results before an access control violation is discovered. At that time, the cursor will be closed. Termination semantics cleanly separates application semantics and access control as orthogonal aspects.

Another approach would be to adopt the following semantics: If a user is not authorized to evaluate a function for certain arguments, the function is undefined for those argument objects. This is called the *cover story* approach. Since, in OSQL, a single-valued function is null if it is undefined, and a set-valued function is empty if it is undefined, those are the valid responses for authorization violation. Therefore, if a user is not authorized to evaluate a function, he gets a null or an empty set depending on whether the function is single-valued or multi-valued, respectively. Now, this returned value is not distinguishable from the case where the user has the call authority on the function but the function is not defined for the argument. If cover story semantics were adopted the cursor problem discussed above would be solved by returning null values when access control violations are detected instead of closing the cursor. With cover story semantics, the results of derived functions and querys may become dependent on authorization policies. As a result it is possible to implement a security policy that allow a given function invocation to return different results depending on who makes the call. This has certain usability advantages.

The problem discussed here is not present in SQL's authorization model where all authorization checks can be performed at compile-time.

5 Techniques for Realizing the OSQL Authorization Model

This section describes a number of techniques that are useful for realizing the authorization model introduced above. An obvious implementation technique would be to maintain the predicate CanCall as a stored function. Alternatively, the logical compliment, CannotCall, could be maintained. Those functions realize OSQL's access control matrix. Each time a user attempts to evaluate a function, the system evaluates CanCall (or CannotCall) to check that the user has the privilege to call the function with the specified arguments. The Grant and Revoke operations could easily be defined in terms of the update functions associated with CanCall (or CannotCall).

However, the predicates CanCall and CannotCall may have infinite extensions since the set of all possible arguments for a function may be infinite (e.g., the multiply function). Therefore, rather than storing individual argument values, some form of encoding in terms of expressions could be adopted. For example, a * could be introduced to specify any possible argument value. Likewise, ranges of values could be specified using comparison operators. With such encodings, however, the evaluation of CanCall would be slower.

Below we discuss how *subtyping, derived functions, guard functions*, and *proxy functions* can be used to realize the OSQL authorization model. These techniques are not mutually exclusive, but may be useful in a combination. Furthermore, any one technique individually may not be complete. We discuss the functionality and performance tradeoffs of each technique.

5.1 Subtyping

In this technique, the function CanCall without the argument type, i.e., CanCall(User, Function) is implemented as a stored function. The function in the argument to CanCall is a specific function. Subtyping is used to achieve finer granularity of control.

A function whose argument type is T can be called with any argument object that has type T. Sometimes, a user may wish to restrict the evaluation of this function so that certain users may evaluate it for certain subset of the valid argument objects only. Subtyping, in combination with specific function authorization semantics, can be used for such a purpose. In the extreme case a subtype with just a single object instance could be defined.

The effect of granting and revoking argument-specific call privileges can be obtained by adding and removing objects to types. The normal action taken for security violation in this approach is termination.

Subtyping may not always be an good way to refine access control. In general, subtyping should be used for the purpose of access control only if the security requirements fits naturally with the application semantics.

5.2 Derived Functions

Derived functions, which are defined by OSQL programs, can be used to encapsulate other functions. The OSQL language is computationally complete and supports external functions. Therefore, any security policy can be implemented by derived functions. Typically, security policies can be implemented by checking argument and result parameters and the identity of the user calling the function.

As an example of the use of derived functions for the purpose of information hiding, consider an application that requires every employee to be able to see his/her salary and the salaries of those he/she manages directly or indirectly. The function RestrictedSalary illustrated in Figure 3 accomplishes this goal. Any user may call RestrictedSalary[1] and no user can call Salary or FixedSalary functions directly.

The system function CurrentUser used in the body of RestrictedSalary returns

---

[1] It would be more intuitive to switch the names of the functions RestrictedSalary and Salary so that the original function Salary becomes a restricted salary function that no user has direct access to.

```
Create function RestrictedSalary(Employee e) -> Integer static as
  Select Salary(e)
  where e = CurrentUser() or
        e in TClose(Manages, CurrentUser());
```

Fig. 3. Restricted Salary Function Definition

the current user object [2] The system function **TClose** returns the transitive closure of the function **Manages** starting from the current user.

The advantage of derived function is that the static authorization check is amenable to compile-time type checking. This is so because the derived function takes care of checking which users can call the function for which arguments. It is equivalent to views in SQL.

The disadvantage of derived function is that the function implementation becomes more complicated and unnatural because of the embedded authorization checks; authorization is no longer orthogonal to the semantics of the function. Furthermore, if the users security needs change, it is more difficult to change the implementation of the derived function.

5.3 Guard Functions

Guard functions serve to restrict the evaluation of other functions and, in this sense, are used to implement security-motivated preconditions on the functions. The function that is protected by a guard and is the subject of access control is called the target function. A guard function does not modify the source code of the application calling the target function; nor does it modify the source of the target function. Hence, any guard function can be installed at any time without disrupting the system.

Whenever the target is invoked, its guard is evaluated first. Informally, evaluating a target function f_t with a guard function f_g is equivalent to executing the expression **if** f_g **then** f_t .

Since the target function is not evaluated if the precondition fails, guards enforce the termination semantics discussed earlier. A system that implements guards can also support cover story semantics in a limited sense. Rather than terminating, the system could return a null value if the precondition fails. Conceptually, this equivalent to executing the expression **if** f_g **then** f_t **else return null** .

One concern with guards is their safety - the guarantee that expressions formed out of guards will terminate. In order to avoid unnecessary circularity and infinite loops, some restrictions must be imposed:

1. A guard function cannot itself be guarded. This is equivalent to granting call privilege to the guard with static authorization to the group **Public**.

---

[2] In OSQL, any surrogate object may be given any user-defined type. In this example, we are assuming that employee objects are also given the type User; i.e., some members of type User are employees.

2. The guard function should not have side-effects on persistent data.

To illustrate the utility of a guard function, assume that **TeacherSalary** defined in Figure 4 is used in an application that a university has installed. Later the university decides that employees who have not completed 90 days of teaching should not be allowed to see any salary at all. A function that checks if the caller has been employed at least 90 days needs to be created and attached to the target **TeacherSalary** as a guard. This is illustrated in Figure 4.

```
Create function TeacherSalaryGuard(Teacher t) -> Boolean as
   select b
   for each Boolean b
   where b = (CurrentDate() - DateOfHire( CurrentUser()) > 90);

AttachGuard(TeacherSalary, TeacherSalaryGuard);
```

Fig. 4. A Guard for TeacherSalary

Grant and revoke operations are extended to take the guard function as one of its arguments. The effect of having a target function without an attached guard is the same as having granted the function for any argument.

A main advantage of guards is that they can be installed as security attachments to an existing schema design, thus providing a clean separation between application semantics and security considerations.

Since guards implement preconditions, guard functions can only be used to restrict access to the target function. If a guard is to reject the invocation of a target function depending on the value the target function would return (i.e., there is a post condition on the target function), the guard must evaluate the target function. With guards, the application semantics cannot be changed on a per user or per group basis as it can be done with derived functions. However, proxy functions discussed next, provide the advantages of security attachments and user-based application semantics.

5.4 Proxy Functions

Proxy functions support a special kind of overloading that is an extension to the existing function overloading mechanism in OSQL. Proxy functions essentially provide different implementations of specific functions for different users. A given specific function can have numerous associated proxies, the proxies being applicable to different groups of users.

When the function is invoked, the OSQL system must execute the proxy rather than the original function. The resolution of a specific function into one of its proxies is similar to the resolution of a generic function into one of its specific functions. The difference is that it is the user calling the function, rather than the type of the actual argument parameter, that is used as the discriminant in the resolution to proxies. In this sense,

198

the authorization in OSQL is an extension of the function resolution paradigm. This is illustrated in Figure 5.

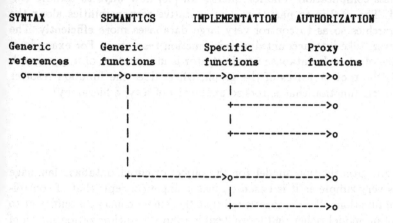

Fig. 5. Resolution With Proxy Functions

The proxy approach, like the guard approach, does not explicitly provide support for the grant and revoke operations. However, the effect can be obtained by attaching and detaching proxies or by changing the definition of the proxy functions.

Proxies have the same major advantages as guard functions. Security policies can be implemented without any impact to an application and its OSQL schema. Furthermore, the approach is very general and flexible since the OSQL language used to define proxies is computational complete and support external functions. In addition, proxy functions allow security policies to be supported on a per user basis. A major disadvantage is that the approach adds a significant amount of overhead to the resolution process. However, clever implementation techniques could take advantage of the fact that the user remains the same throughout the execution of an application.

6 Related Work

[18] presents a conceptual framework for authorization in object-oriented and semantic database models. This framework uses the same concepts as access control matrixes, but seeks to minimize storage requirements of the authorization system data by improving on implicit authorizations introduced earlier in [6]. The concept of inheritance, both function inheritance (through the type/subtype hierarchy) and inheritance of privileges (through group nesting) and the partial ordering of privilege modes (for example, update privilege on an object implies a read privilege on the same object) are all used in determining the implicit authorization on objects and in defining exceptions to the grants. [5] contains an authorization model for structural object-oriented systems that also seeks efficiency through implicit and negative authorizations. Concerns for storage requirements are not

completely shared in [18] which, presents efficient transitive closure methods for processing nested groups based on the assumption that, since updates to the authorization system data are rare, it is better to use up more storage by maintaining the transitive closure and use up less computation time for queries. In [20] new ways to achieve efficiency are presented. The goal is to partition administrative responsibilities along the line of the type hierarchies so as to control very large databases more efficiently. The work does not, however, take into account dynamic function resolution. For example, if the sphere of influence of a user's database administrator is in a portion of a type graph that neither includes the root or leaves of the graph, where does the function resolver begin to resolve a generic function that is rooted at the top of a type hierarchy?

7 Conclusions

We have presented an authorization model for the object-oriented database language OSQL. The model is very simple as it is based on just a single concept: that of controlling the invocation of functions. We demonstrated that this single concept is sufficient to provide an authorization model richer and more flexible than the authorization model of SQL which is based on privilege types for every kind of operation (SELECT, UPDATE, INSERT, DELETE, ALTER, and GRANT). For example, the OSQL authorization model allows access control to be specified uniformly for functions that implement schema definition and data manipulation. The interaction between the proposed OSQL authorization model and existing OSQL concepts, e.g., derived functions, late binding, and function resolution, were examined and a number of userful semantics were identified, i.e., static authorization, dynamic authorization, generic function authorization, specific function authorization, authorization-dependent resolution, authorization-independent resolution, termination semantics, and cover story semantics. These semantics provide a very flexible and powerful authorization model. The authorization model was described in terms of the OSQL model constructs (objects, types, functions). Various techniques for realizing the model were described. Some techniques are based on existing OSQL functionality, e.g., subtyping, function resolution, derived functions. Other techniques are based on two novel constructs, i.e., guard functions and proxy functions. These constructs are flexible and non-invasive in that they allow security policies to be implemented for a given database after the database schema has been defined.

References

1. American National Standards Institute. *Database Language SQL*, 1986. ANSI X3.135-1986.
2. M. M. Astrahan and D. D. Chamberlin. Implementation of a structured English Query Language. *Communications of the ACM*, 18(10), October 1975.
3. E. F. Codd. A Relational Model of Data for Large Shared Data Banks. *Communications of the ACM*, 13(6):377–387, June 1970.
4. C. J. Date. *A Guide to the SQL Standard*. Addison-Wesley Publishing Company, 1987.
5. K. R. Dittrich, M. Hartig, and H. Pferfferle. Discretionary Access Control in Structurally Object-Oriented Database Systems. In *Proceedings of the 2nd IFIP Workshop On Database Secuirty*, October 1988.

6. E. B. Fernandez, R. C. Summers, and C. D. Coleman. An Authorization Model For A Shared Database. In *Proceedings of the ACM SIGMOD International Conference*, 1975.
7. D. H. Fishman, D. Badal, D. Beech, E. C. Chow, T. Connors, J. W. Davis, C. G. Hoch, W. Kent, P. Lyngbaek, B. Mahbod, M. A. Neimat, T. A. Ryan, M. C. Shan, and W. K. Wilkinson. Overview of the Iris DBMS. In W. Kim and F. H. Lochovsky, editors, *Object-Oriented Languages, Applications, and Databases*. Addison-Wesley Publishing Company, 1989.
8. D. H. Fishman, D. Beech, H. P. Cate, E. C. Chow, T. Connors, J. W. Davis, N. Derrett, C. G. Hoch, W. Kent, P. Lyngbaek, B. Mahbod, M. A. Neimat, T. A. Ryan, and M. C. Shan. Iris: An Object-Oriented Database Management System. *ACM Transactions on Office Information Systems*, 5(1), January 1987.
9. R. Gigliardi, G. Lapis, and B. Lindsay. A Flexible and Efficient Database Authorization Facility. Technical report, IBM, November 1989. IBM Research Report 6826 (65360).
10. A. Goldberg and D. Robson. *Smalltalk-80: The Language and its Implementation*. Addison-Wesley, 1983.
11. P. P. Griffiths and B. W. Wade. An Authorization Mechanism For Relational Database Systems. *ACM Transactions on Database Systems*, 1(3), September 1976.
12. B. W. Lampson. Protection. *ACM Operating Systems Review*, 8(1), January 1974.
13. J. A. Larson. Granting and Revoking Discretionary Authority. *Info Systems Journal*, 8(4), 1983.
14. P. Lyngbaek. OSQL: A Language for Object Databases. Technical report, HP Labs, January 1991. HP Labs Technical Report HPL-DTD-91-4.
15. P. Lyngbaek and W. Kent. A Data Modeling Methodology for the Design and Implementation of Information Systems. In *Proceedings of 1986 International Workshop on Object-Oriented Database Systems*, Pacific Grove, California, September 1986.
16. J. H Morris. Protection in Programming Languages. *Communications of the ACM*, 16(1), January 1973.
17. J. Mylopoulos, P. A. Bernstein, and H. K. T. Wong. A Language Facility for Designing Database-Intensive Applications. *ACM Transactions on Database Systems*, 5(2), June 1980.
18. F. Rabitti, E. Bertino, W. Kim, and D. Woelk. A Model Of Authorization For Next-Generation Database Systems. *ACM Transactions on Database Systems*, 16(1):88–131, March 1991.
19. D. Shipman. The Functional Data Model and the Data Language DAPLEX. *ACM Transactions on Database Systems*, 6(1), September 1981.
20. H. Song, E. B. Fernandez, and E. Guides. Administrative Authorization In Object-Oriented Database. In *Proceedings of the EISS Workshop On Database Secuirty*, European Institute For System Security, Karlsruhe, W. Germany, April 1990.
21. B. Stroustrup. *The C++ Programming Language*. Addison-Wesley, Reading, Massachusetts, 1986.
22. K. Wilkinson, P. Lyngbaek, and W. Hasan. The Iris Architecture and Implementation. *IEEE Transactions on Knowledge and Data Engineering*, 2(1), March 1990.

This article was processed using the LaTeX macro package with LMAMULT style

CQL++: A SQL for the Ode Object-Oriented DBMS

S. Dar
N. H. Gehani
H. V. Jagadish

AT&T Bell Laboratories
Murray Hill, New Jersey 07974

ABSTRACT

CQL++ is a declarative front end to the Ode object-oriented database. It combines a SQL-like syntax with the C++ class model. CQL++ provides facilities for defining classes, and for creating, querying, displaying, and updating objects. Classes and objects created using CQL++ can freely be intermixed with those created using O++, the primary programming language of Ode. CQL++ gives its users a relatively straightforward interface, by hiding from them such O++ details as object-ids, public and private members of objects, and the implementations (bodies) of member functions.

CQL++ is based on an object algebra that preserves the closure property of SQL. CQL++ queries operate upon sets of objects and return sets of objects. CQL++ supports a rich collection of set types to maximize functionality and expressive power. CQL++ allows the user to define new classes, which can include computed attributes and make use of multiple inheritance. The user can supply default and null values for attributes, and indicate how class objects are to be displayed.

1. INTRODUCTION

Ode is a database system and environment based on the object paradigm. It offers an integrated data model for both database and general purpose manipulation [2, 3]. The database is defined, queried, and manipulated in the database programming language O++ which is based on C++ [26]. O++ borrows and extends the object definition facility of C++, called the class. O++ provides facilities for creating and manipulating persistent objects, defining sets, and iterating over sets and clusters of persistent objects. It also provides facilities for specifying constraints and triggers.

CQL++ is an adaptation of SQL [19] to the Ode object-oriented model. We were motivated to design a SQL-like interface to Ode because SQL is by far the most popular database interface. Typical database users are not likely to use a programming language such as O++. A declarative interface to Ode based on SQL would appeal to such users.

Several designs have been proposed for adapting a relational language such as SQL to nested and recursive data models [20, 22, 24]. A major strength of these proposals is that they are based on well defined data models. These models, like the relational model itself, comprise a formal description of the data structures of the database and the algebraic operations on these structures. In contrast, object-oriented languages [5-7, 12, 14, 16, 18, 23] are usually defined "operationally" rather then algebraically or axiomatically. CQL++ strives to combine the advantages of the structural and operational models. It is based on an object algebra that preserves the closure property of SQL, and applies uniformly to sets of objects, regardless of their type. Orthogonally, type specific operations are used to construct new objects and to display existing objects. These operations are specified by the user, as part of the class definition.

CQL++ provides facilities for creating, querying, displaying, and updating objects. CQL++ queries operate upon sets of objects and return sets of objects. Various types of sets are supported: clusters and cluster hierarchies are collections of persistent objects, while temporary clusters are used to store objects for the duration of a session. In addition to views, CQL++ introduces object and set variables as handles for manipulation of objects or sets of objects. CQL++ allows users to define new classes and supports the definition of computed attributes and the use of multiple inheritance. The user can supply default and null values for class attributes, specify constraints, and indicate how class objects are to be displayed.

An important goal in the design of CQL++ is to ensure its integration with O++. Although, CQL++ does not support the full definitional capabilities of O++, it can be used to formulate queries against a database defined and populated using O++. Similarly, O++ users can manipulate objects of classes defined using CQL++. CQL++ tries to minimize the details of the Ode object model users must know, while maximizing the functionality of O++ available to them. It hides from users such programming language details as object-ids, public and private members of objects, and the implementation (bodies) of member functions. See [8] for more detail.

2. BACKGROUND

The object model of Ode is based on C++ [26]. The database schema is a set of *classes*. A class is similar to an *abstract data type*: it has *public* members (components), which represent the interface to the class, and *private* members, which represent the implementation of the class. The members of the class can be data items or functions (methods). Instances of a class are called *objects*. Two special categories of member functions are *constructors*, used to create and initialize objects, and *destructors*, used to delete class objects. As an example, we give below the definition of class person in O++. (We have omitted some definitions, such as those for types Name and Address, and the bodies of member functions).

O++ extends the C++ object model by allowing objects to be *persistent*. Every persistent object has an *object-id* that uniquely identifies it. We also refer to this object-id as a *pointer to a persistent object*. Each class has an associated *cluster* in which its persistent instances reside. Clusters can be partitioned into *subclusters*.

```
class Person {
    int ssn;    // social security number
    Date birth_date;
public:
    Name name;
    char sex;
    Address addr;
    persistent Person *kids[[MAX_CHILDREN]]; // a set

    Person(Name n, char s, int snum); // a constructor
    int ssnum() const { return ssn; }
    int age() const
        { return (today().year - birth_date.year); }  // a computed attribute
    virtual void print()
        { cout << ssnum() << ", " << name << ", " << sex; }
    virtual void identify() { cout << name; }
};
```

O++ introduces sets as a general type constructor. A declaration of the form

type variable [[*size*]]

declares *variable* to be a set of elements of type *type* with space to be allocated initially for *size* elements. For example, in class `Person`, `kids` is a set of pointers to persistent `Person` objects.

By convention, for objects of classes defined in O++ to be displayed in an explicitly specified manner in CQL++, two special functions, `print` and `identify`, must be defined. These functions display an object in long and short forms, respectively. We will illustrate the use of these functions in Section 4. For now it suffices to note that a `person` object is identified by name, and printed using his/her social security number, name, and sex.

O++ supports multiple inheritance. A derived class inherits all the data items and functions of its base class(es). If an inherited function is declared *virtual* in the base class, then it can be redefined in the subclass, thus overriding the default inheritance mechanism. Here is how `Employee` can be derived from `Person`:

```
class Employee: public Person {
    int sal;
public:
    persistent Department *dept; //pointer to Department object
    Employee(Name n, char s, int snum, Date bday,
             persistent department *d);
    int salary();
    void update_salary(int new_salary);
    virtual void print();
    virtual void identify();
};
```

The `Department` class referenced by `Employee` is defined as follows:

```
class Department {
    int budget;
public:
    char dname[20];
    int dno;
    Address location;
    persistent Employee *mgr;
    persistent Employee *emps[[DEPT_EMPS]];
    Department(char nam[20], Address loc, persistent Employee *m,
        persistent Employee *es[[DEPT_EMPS]]);
    virtual void print();
    virtual void identify();
};
```

O++ provides a high-level iteration facility for accessing objects in a set or a cluster. For example,

```
for e in Employee suchthat(e->salary() > 50000) by(e->age()) {
    cout << "Name: " << e->name;
    cout << " Age: " << e->age();
    cout << " Salary: " << e->salary() << endl;
}
```

prints the name, age, and salary of all employees who make more than 50K. This information is printed in order of increasing age (as specified in the by clause).

The bodies of the print and identify functions of Employee are

```
void Employee::print()   {
    cout << ssnum() << ", " << name << ", " << dept->dname; }
void Employee::identify()   { cout << name; }
```

O++ also provides facilities for creating versions of objects [4] and for associating constraints and triggers with objects [13].

3. DESIGN GOALS

CQL++ is designed to allow SQL users a smooth transition from a relational database to the object-oriented database Ode. Here are the specific design goals we had for CQL++:

1. CQL++ should "look and feel" like SQL as much as possible.
2. CQL++ and O++ should coexist with each other since they both represent interfaces to Ode. A CQL++ user should be able to query and update a database defined and populated by an O++ program, and in particular should be able to invoke functions and triggers defined using O++. Public/private encapsulation of data defined in O++ must be respected, but the CQL++ user should not have to be aware of it.
3. The distinction between objects and object-ids in object-oriented database programming languages, such as O++, should be blurred as far as possible. CQL++ should perform object id "dereferencing" when necessary in a manner transparent to the user.
4. CQL++ should have the closure property; i.e., it should be possible to use the result of one query in another query.
5. A CQL++ user should have the ability to define new classes (types).

4. THE DATA MODEL

The Ode database model makes a sharp distinction between *persistent* store (the database) and *working* store (volatile memory). In contrast, the relational model, and SQL in particular, has no such distinction. CQL++ keeps the distinction between persistent and working store. Persistent (permanent) objects reside in the database and are grouped into clusters. Such objects persist until they are explicitly removed from the database. Temporary objects reside in working memory. Usually they exist only for the duration of a query. However, their longevity can be extended by placing them in "temporary" clusters.

In an object-oriented database, the basic unit of data storage and manipulation is the "object." To the object manager, an object consists of an *<object id, state>* pair where the object id is a unique "handle" for the object and the state is an aggregate value representing the object data. In O++, the object-id is explicitly used to manipulate an object. CQL++ provides a higher level interface to Ode in which users manipulate objects directly without the explicit use of object ids. The CQL++ user is presented with a view of an object which consists of a set of "visible" attributes, and functions that can be invoked on the object. These three views of an object are depicted in Fig. 1.

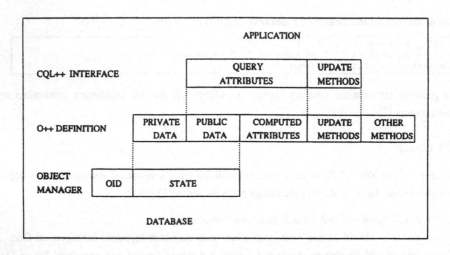

Figure 1. Three Views of an Object

CQL++ is based on a type-generic *object algebra* [8] that has the closure property over sets of objects. This closure property allows CQL++ queries to be nested. While this algebra provides a foundation for the language, CQL++ facilities, as we shall see, go beyond the algebra. In particular, objects can be manipulated by type-specific functions and operators defined for the object's type.

5. LANGUAGE CONSTRUCTS

We now describe CQL++ facilities and illustrate their use with examples.

5.1 Queries

A CQL++ query takes as its input one or more sets of objects and returns as its output a set of objects. Input sets can (interchangeably) be clusters, temporary clusters, or CQL++ sets. Queries are specified using the SELECT statement, which has the form

```
SELECT projection-list
FROM cluster-or-set-expression₁ r₁, cluster-or-set-expression₂ r₂, ..., cluster-or-set-expressionₘ rₘ
WHERE search-expression
```

The *range variables* r_i associated with the search operands *cluster-or-set-expression$_i$* are optional. The *projection-list* is a comma-separated list of expressions, which may refer to attributes of the operand objects. Expressions can involve the standard set of aggregate functions. A "null" projection can also be specified (see below).

The SELECT statement returns a set of objects each of which is constructed from a combination of objects in *cluster-or-set-expression$_1$*, *cluster-or-set-expression$_2$*, ..., *cluster-or-set-expression$_m$* (the "cross product") that satisfy the search expression. Components of the objects returned have values corresponding to the expressions in *projection-list*.

As an example, consider the following SELECT statement that prints the name, age, and department name for each employee who makes more than 50K a year:

```
SELECT E.name, E.age(), E.dept.name
FROM Employee E
WHERE E.salary > 50000
```

As in SQL, a cluster name can serve as a default range variable. Also, in the absence of an ambiguity, it is not necessary to qualify the attribute names in the SELECT statement with the cluster name (E in this case).

5.1.1 Anonymous Classes: When the projection list includes exactly one expression, the objects returned by the SELECT statement have a known (existing) type. But if the projection list includes more than one expression, the objects returned by the query are of an *anonymous* class (type) i.e., a *tuple*, formed by concatenating the types of the expressions in the projection list.

For example, the query above returns as its result a set of objects belonging to an anonymous class with three attributes: the first has the same type as Employee.name, the second has the same type as the return type of Employee.age(), and the third has the same type as Dept.name. Note that the second attribute (age) is a data member of the new class rather than a member function (computed attribute).

5.1.2 Displaying the Result of a Query: If a query is not nested within another query it is called a *display query.* The set of objects returned by the query is displayed using the print function associated with the object type, as follows:

1. If only one expression is specified in the projection list, then the objects returned by the query are of a known (named) type, and the print function associated with that type is used. If that type is a class that does not specify a print function then objects of that class is displayed in some (implementation-dependent) default manner. In our implementation, the default print function invokes the print function for every public data member.

2. If more than one expression is specified in the projection list, then the objects returned by the query are of anonymous type. The print function associated with the anonymous type invokes the print function for each data member, i.e., for each expression in the projection list.

3. The print function associated with sets invoke the print function for each element in the set (perhaps up to some limit). The print function associated with a built-in type object simply prints its value.

4. The modifier IDENTIFY can be used to override the default use of print: qualifying the expression *e* with IDENTIFY in the projection list forces the invocation of the identify function. The default identify function in our implementation invokes the identify function for every public data member that is not a set or an object reference. The identify function associated with sets invokes the identify function for each element. The identify function associated with a built-in type object simply prints its value.

The following join query retrieves employees who live in the city where the computer science (CS) department is located. For each such employee, it prints detailed information (social security number, name, department name), prints the salary, and also prints identifying information (the name) of each child.

```
SELECT Employee, Employee.salary(), IDENTIFY Employee.kids
FROM Employee, Department
WHERE Employee.addr.city = Department.location.addr.city
      AND Department.name = 'CS'
```

5.1.3 Queries on a Set-Valued Attribute: A set-valued attribute can be an operand to a query. To allow this, CQL++ permits operands to the query to be inter-dependent. The following query prints the names of all employees in the CS department who are more than 10 years older than their manager:

```
SELECT E.name
FROM Department D, D.emps E
WHERE E.age() > D.mgr.age() + 10
AND D.dname = 'CS'
```

When a query operand *Y* is dependent on another operand *X*, the binding of *X* must precede the binding of *Y*. In the query above, for each value of the range variable *D*, the range variable *E* is bound to the set of employees for the corresponding department.

5.1.4 Hierarchical Queries: The set of objects in a specified class and all classes derived from it can serve as an operand to a query by preceding the name of the base class with the keyword EVERY, as follows:

```
SELECT projection-list
FROM EVERY cluster
WHERE search-expression
```

We call such a query a *hierarchical query*, and the set of clusters in which the objects reside, a *cluster hierarchy*. Although the objects manipulated by such a hierarchical query are of different types [14], the types are related in that they are derived from the same base type and they share the attributes of the base type. Only the shared attributes of the base class can be referenced in the projection list and in the search expression. A null projection will cause the query to return a homogeneous set of objects, with objects of derived types being coerced into the base type.

Suppose classes Student and Employee derived from Person. Here is an example of a hierarchical query that lists the addresses of all persons, including students and employees, named Smith:

```
SELECT addr
FROM EVERY Person
WHERE Person.name = 'Smith'
```

5.1.5 Grouping and Ordering Objects: The set of objects returned by a query can be grouped for aggregate computation or ordered for display by using the GROUP BY and ORDER BY clauses, respectively:

```
SELECT projection-list
FROM cluster-or-set-expression₁, cluster-or-set-expression₂, ..., cluster-or-set-expressionₘ
WHERE search-expression
ORDER BY s₁, s₂, ..., sₘ
GROUP BY g₁, g₂, ..., gₙ
```

In hierarchical queries, the "attribute" CLASS can be used in place of a grouping or an ordering expression for grouping and ordering objects according to their class. This query that prints the average age separately for students, employees, and persons who are neither students or employees:

```
SELECT AVG(age())
FROM EVERY Person
GROUP BY CLASS
```

5.2 Clusters

When a class is defined, a default cluster with the same name as the class is created automatically. New instances of the class are placed in this cluster by default.

Objects returned by a query can be stored for later reference, without having to make these objects persistent. Such objects are stored in *temporary* clusters where they reside until the end of the current session. (A *session* is a CQL++ program, or an invocation of CQL++ in interactive mode. A session starts when CQL++ is invoked and terminates when CQL++ is exited). A temporary cluster is defined with the CREATE TEMP statement. For instance,

```
CREATE TEMP Person::Parents
```

creates a temporary cluster, called Parents, for objects of type Person.

5.3 Updates

CQL++ allows objects to be inserted into and deleted from the database, or to be updated. Inserting an object into a cluster (permanent or temporary) creates a new object. Deleting an object from a cluster causes the object to disappear.

5.3.1 Inserting Objects Into a Cluster: Objects are created using the INSERT statement, which has two forms. The first form uses the VALUES clause to specify the initial values for a single new object:

```
INSERT INTO cluster
VALUES (e₁, e₂, ..., eₙ)
```

The new object is initialized by invoking a constructor for the class associated with the specified cluster. The constructor selected depends upon the number and type of values specified; the list of values specified must correspond to the argument list (signature) of exactly one constructor.

Here is an example:

```
INSERT INTO Department
VALUES ('widget', 'New York',
        SELECT * FROM Employee WHERE name.first = 'Jane' AND name.last = 'Doe',
        SELECT * FROM Employee WHERE dept.dname = 'sprocket')
```

This statement creates a new Department object with a department name "widget", and location "New York". The manager is specified is an Employee object with a first name "Jane" and a last name "Doe" (there should be exactly one such employee), and the employee set is initialized to the employees of the "sprocket" department.

Specifying set-valued attribute values using embedded queries may be cumbersome. In Section 5.4 we suggest a more convenient way of specifying such values, using *object and set variables*.

The second form of the INSERT statement allows the creation and insertion of a set of objects into a cluster specified using a SELECT query. Such a SELECT query is called a *storage query*, since the set of objects returned by it is stored in a cluster.

The following INSERT statement will add to the temporary cluster, Person::Parents, objects that are copies of all employees whose have children:

```
INSERT INTO Person::Parents
SELECT name, sex, ssnum()
FROM Employee
WHERE EXISTS (SELECT * FROM kids)
```

5.3.2 Deleting Objects: Objects are deleted from a cluster using the DELETE statement which has the form

```
DELETE cluster-or-set-expression
WHERE search-expression
```

For example, to delete the sprocket department, we issue the statement

```
DELETE Department
WHERE dname = 'sprocket'
```

5.3.3 Updating Objects: Objects are updated using the UPDATE statement, which has the form

```
UPDATE cluster-or-set-expression
SET update₁, update₂, ..., updateₙ
WHERE search-expression
```

Each object from the specified set that satisfies the search expression is updated according to the update clauses *update ᵢ*, which have two permissible forms:

attribute = *expression*
function(arguments)

The first form is used to set the value of a public data member directly. The second form is used to invoke a public member function (which may have the side effect of updating the object).

The next statement sets the dept attribute of the employees of the new widget department to that department. It also gives them a 10% raise:

```
UPDATE Employee
SET dept = (SELECT * FROM Department WHERE dname = 'widget'),
    update_salary(1.1 * salary())
WHERE Employee IN (SELECT emps FROM Department WHERE dname = 'widget')
```

5.4 Set and Object Variables

Set and object variables are used as symbolic names for referencing objects (which reside in clusters). Set and object variables facilitate the manipulation, across query boundaries, of a single object or a set of objects.

5.4.1 Set Variables: Set variables are defined using the DEFINE SET statement, which has the form

```
DEFINE SET set
AS cluster-or-set-expression
WHERE search-expression
```

The DEFINE SET statement declares a set variable that is attached to (or associated with) a specified set of objects for the duration of the current session. CQL++ set variables are "static" in that updates to the underlying database do not alter the composition of an existing set. But updates to an object belonging to a set will be visible regardless of whether the object is selected from the set or from a cluster.

Here is an example of a set variable that is associated with all objects of type Person whose age attribute has a value less than 30:

```
DEFINE SET young
AS Person
WHERE age() < 30
```

Contrast this statement with the insertion of new copies of objects into the temporary cluster Person::'parents' in Section 5.3.1. The DEFINE SET statement does not create any new objects, nor does it copy any existing objects. The set variable young is simply associated with a collection of existing objects, and can be used from this point on to denote this collection.

Set variables can be used in queries wherever a set or cluster can be used. For example, the following query finds all employees in the set young who have exactly two girls:

```
SELECT *
FROM young y
WHERE (SELECT COUNT (*) FROM y.kids k WHERE k.sex = 'F') = 2
```

The INSERT, DELETE, and UPDATE operators can be applied to objects associated with a set variable. INSERT causes the creation of a new object, and its insertion in the associated cluster. In addition, the set variable now includes the new object. UPDATE modifies the values of objects in the database that are associated with the set variable and satisfy the specified search expression. DELETE causes the deletion of objects satisfying the search expression both from the set and from the associated cluster.

Existing objects can be added to and removed from a set without affecting the database using the ADD and REMOVE statements described below.

5.4.2 Adding Objects To a Set Variable: The ADD statement has the form

```
ADD TO set
set-expression
```

where *set-expression* is an expression (or query) that evaluates to a set.

In the following example the set variable good_person is associated with objects representing people between the ages of 30 and 40, or employees whose name is "Brown".

```
DEFINE SET good_person
AS Person
WHERE age() < 40
AND age() >= 30

ADD TO good_person
SELECT *
FROM Employee
WHERE name = 'Brown'
```

5.4.3 Removing Objects From a Set Variable: The REMOVE statement has the form

```
REMOVE FROM set
WHERE search-expression
```

The following example removes persons between 35 and 37 years of age from set good_person.

```
REMOVE FROM good_person
WHERE age() < 37
AND age() >= 35
```

5.4.4 Object Variables: Object variables are defined using the DEFINE OBJECT statement, which has the form

```
DEFINE OBJECT object
AS cluster-or-set-expression
WHERE search-expression
```

The search expression must be satisfied by *exactly* one object; otherwise an error is flagged.

Here is an example of an object variable:

```
DEFINE OBJECT Joe
AS Employee
WHERE name.first = 'Joe' AND name.last = 'Polansky'
```

An object variable is like a set variable that is associated with one object: it can be used wherever a set variable can be used. For example,

```
SELECT age(), address
FROM Joe
```

When a new object or set of objects is created, we can attach an object or set variable to it as part of the INSERT statement, i.e.,

```
INSERT INTO cluster
...
AS object-or-set variable
```

Set and object variables are particularly useful for supplying (initial) values to attributes whose type is a set of (references to) objects or a single object. Here is how the INSERT, DELETE, and UPDATE sequence of Section 5.3 could be written using object and set variables:

```
DEFINE OBJECT sprocket_dept
AS Department
WHERE dname = 'sprocket'

DEFINE OBJECT widget_mgr
AS Employee
WHERE name.first = 'Jane' AND name.last = 'Doe'

DEFINE SET widget_emps
AS Employee
WHERE dept = sprocket_dept

INSERT INTO Department
VALUES ('widget', 'New York', widget_mgr, widget_emps)
AS widget_dept

UPDATE Employee
SET dept = widget_dept
    update_salary(1.1 * salary())
WHERE Employee IN widget_dept.emps

DELETE sprocket_dept
```

These statements create a widget department, headed by Jane Doe, with the employees of the sprocket department. The new sprocket department employees are set to reference their new department, and the old sprocket department is deleted. Note how an object variable, widget_dept, is attached to the new widget department object as it is created.

5.5 Views:

CQL++ supports the definition and use of views, much like SQL. For example, to create a view of all employees who live in New York, we can write

```
CREATE VIEW new_york_emps AS
SELECT *
FROM Employee
WHERE addr.city = 'New York'
```

There is some similarity between set and object variables and views, but there are significant differences. The most important difference is that set and object variables have *static* (immediate) binding — they are bound when they are defined. Views have *dynamic* (deferred) binding — they are bound when they are used. The definition of a set variable can be thought of as an initialization. Elements can be added to or deleted from the set later on. The elements of a set can be arbitrary, and need not have anything in common. In contrast, the set of objects bound to a view must satisfy the search expression specified in the view definition. View maintenance is a hard problem, and a topic for continuing research. Set variables, on the other hand, are easy to implement, since they are statically defined. For instance, we can keep a list of object identifiers for the objects in a set.

5.6 Data Definition

The definition, creation, and manipulation of an object in an Ode database can be in either of CQL++ and O++, with free intermixing of the two being possible. We illustrate the CQL++ data definitions facilities by giving the CQL++ version of the O++ class Department shown in Section 2. See [8] for a more detailed description.

```
DEFINE CLASS Department
(
    budget INT DEFAULT 0 NULL -1,
    dname  CHAR(20) NULL '',
    dno INT NULL -1,
    location Address NULL Address(NULL,'','',NULL),
    mgr REFERENCES Employee,
    emps REFERENCES Employee[[48]] DEFAULT
          (SELECT * FROM Employee WHERE dept = NULL) ;
    IDENTIFY BY dname ;
    PRINT BY dno, dname, location, mgr.name ;
)
```

6. DISCUSSION

6.1 Model

Tuple and *relation* are central concepts of the relational model. The CQL++ model uses the more general concepts of *object* and *set of objects*. While objects, by definition, come in different types, it is possible to identify operations on objects that apply (and are required) across all types. As such, we divide the model into a type-generic part and a type-specific part.

The type-generic part includes the operations that can be performed on sets of objects. This allows us to define an algebra that applies uniformly to sets of objects, regardless of their type. The algebra extends relational algebra by making explicit the distinction between persistent and working memory, and by providing support for versions. The type-specific part of the model includes user-defined member functions, and also the mapping between the CQL++ interface and the object manager (see Figure 1).

6.2 Displaying an Object

Unlike relational database, in an object-oriented database the display of objects in a standard format, is not possible. This is because the structure of an object, and even an attribute of an object, can be arbitrarily complex. In addition, in languages such as O++ that support information hiding, some attributes of a class may be private. Our solution to the problem is to delegate the display of objects to the class designer. We exploit the fact that objects can have methods associated with them, and employ a standard display function print for each class.

A related issue is how to display references to objects. Assume object obj_1 of class $class_1$ has a reference to obj_2 as the value of attribute *attr*. If the user wishes to display the *attr* value of obj_1, we could

1. print the reference value, i.e., the id of obj_2,
2. flag an error, or
3. print some "identifying information" about obj_2.

The first solution is unacceptable because an object-id is a transparent, system-generated value that is meaningless to the user. The second solution is too restrictive. We therefore adopted the third solution. Let $class_2$ be the class of obj_2. We could use the print function of $class_2$ if one exists, but in general it will provide too much information. We therefore allow $class_2$ to define another function, called identify, and invoke that function with obj_2 as argument. The identifying information need not be unique, that is, it doesn't have to be a candidate key for the object. For example, in a SQL Person relation the social security number would serve as the primary key, while in a CQL++ Person class, the name attribute might be a better identifier for a Person object.

6.3 Information Hiding

An O++ class can have public and private members. The provision of privacy is crucial to the concept of encapsulation, which in turn is a cornerstone of object-orientation. CQL++ respects this concept of privacy. The user cannot reference private attributes or member functions by name: private attributes can be accessed only by calling public member functions (as in C++ and O++).

The complete object, including all private members, is retrieved when a null projection is performed. Consider, for example, the query:

```
SELECT *
FROM Employee
WHERE ...
```

Whether this query is a display, storage, or nested query, the null projection returns "complete" employee objects, including the private attributes ssn, birth_date and salary. However, if this is a display query then, as explained in Section 5.1.3, the print function of Employee is invoked, and would display each employee's social security number, name and department name. The display of the social security number is permitted in this case, since print is a public member function, and has access to the private members of Employee.

The print and identify functions can be used to exercise a finer degree of protection. For example, they could check the user's id and decide how much information to show accordingly.

7. RELATED WORK

Previous work extending SQL or QUEL beyond the relational model can be roughly classified into *structural* vs. *operational* extensions. Structural extensions include support for NF^2 relations [22, 24] and more general schemas allowing recursive and/or nested type definitions [20, 21, 25]. These proposals are intended to support complex (i.e., user-defined type) objects, and do not capture the operational aspects of the object model. In particular, functions (methods) cannot serve as attributes in these models.

Several operational extensions are designed around the notion of abstract data types. Two SQL extensions in this category are Object-SQL [12] and HDBL [18]. They both support user-defined data types, structured complex objects, and methods. Object-SQL also supports inheritance. Functions (methods) are written in a general purpose programming language, for example LISP or C for Object-SQL, and PASCAL/R for HDBL. Similar operational extensions have been developed for the QUEL language [7, 23]. The languages in this group follow the "evolutionary approach" of extending the relational model with object-oriented functionality.

There are some recent SQL extensions that, like CQL++, are based on C++. Ontologic's SQL [1] is an extension of SQL embedded in C++; an interactive version of it is under development. The design goals of Ontologic's SQL are similar to ours, however the language is quite restricted. It particular, updates are not allowed, storing query results is not addressed, and it is unclear if normal (value based) joins can be used. Other OODBMS companies are embarked on similar paths [9, 10].

When object-ids are added to the picture, the semantics of the corresponding language become more difficult to define. OSQL [6], developed as part of the Iris project [11], takes a functional view of objects and object-ids. An object-id is not simply a handle to an object, but an intrinsic property of the object that never changes. Attributes are modeled as functions applied to object-ids. True functions, in the programming language sense, are not supported however, except for the definition of computed attributes.

In ORION [14, 15], a query returns the id's of the objects in the result. The application must then make explicit requests for the actual instances. In a single-operand query with projection, the projected attribute values may also be returned. In a multiple-operand query, the application must return the list to the database and have it perform the join and return the concatenated values. The argument given against returning concatenated values is that the database must then incur the overhead of generating object id's for the values. However this happens because the query result is a set of objects. We avoid this difficulty by making the distinction between temporary and persistent objects. Indeed, we feel such a distinction implicitly exists in SQL, where a query result must explicitly be stored in order to be made persistent.

8. CONCLUSIONS

CQL++ is a declarative front end to the Ode object-oriented database. It combines a SQL-like syntax with the C++ class model. CQL++ is based on a type-generic object algebra that preserves the closure property of SQL. CQL++ queries operate upon sets of objects and return sets of objects. A rich variety of set construction mechanisms is used to provide expressive power while keeping the algebra simple.

CQL++ provides facilities for defining classes, and for creating, querying, displaying, and updating objects. Classes and objects created using CQL++ can freely be intermixed with those created using O++, the primary programming language interface to Ode. CQL++ hides from the user such O++ details as object-ids, public and private members of objects, and the implementations (bodies) of member functions. At the same time, it supports most O++ facilities, including iteration over a class or a class hierarchy, version manipulation, and the ability to define new object types.

We are currently working on an implementation of CQL++ [8]. While many of the standard optimization techniques carry over if we consider an object like a tuple, and a cluster like a relation, we are currently studying optimization issues and opportunities peculiar to CQL++. As a first step in this direction, we are currently implementing some of the ideas in [17].

We hope that the combination of a familiar interface and increased functionality will encourage SQL users to utilize object-oriented database technology.

ACKNOWLEDGMENTS

We are very grateful to Rick Greer for his comments and suggestions.

216

REFERENCES

[1]   "Ontos Object Database SQL Command Reference", Ontologic, Inc., Burlington, MA, Nov. 1989.

[2]   R. Agrawal and N. H. Gehani, "Rationale for the Design of Persistence and Query Processing Facilities in the Database Programming Language O++", *2nd Int'l Workshop on Database Programming Languages*, Portland, OR, June 1989.

[3]   R. Agrawal and N. H. Gehani, "Ode (Object Database and Environment): The Language and the Data Model", *Proc. ACM-SIGMOD 1989 Int'l Conf. Management of Data*, Portland, Oregon, May-June 1989, 36-45.

[4]   R. Agrawal, S. J. Buroff, N. H. Gehani and D. Shasha, "Object Versioning in Ode", *Proc. IEEE 7th Int'l Conf. Data Engineering*, Tokyo, Japan, Feb. 1991.

[5]   A. M. Alashqur, S. Y. W. Su and H. Lam, "OQL: A Query Language for Manipulating Object-Oriented Databases", *Proc. 15th Int'l Conf. Very Large Data Bases*, Amsterdam, The Netherlands, Aug. 1989, 433-442.

[6]   D. Beech, "A Foundation for Evolution from Relational to Object Databases", *Proc. of Int'l Conf. on Extending Database Technology*, March 1988.

[7]   M. J. Carey, D. J. DeWitt and S. L. Vandenberg, "A Data Model and Query Language for EXODUS", *Proc. ACM-SIGMOD 1988 Int'l Conf. on Management of Data*, Chicago, Illinois, June 1988, 413-423.

[8]   S. Dar, N. H. Gehani and H. V. Jagadish, "CQL++: An SQL for a C++ Based Object-Oriented DBMS", AT&T Bell Labs Technical Memorandum, 1991.

[9]   O. Deux, "The O_2 Database Programming Language", *Communications of the ACM*, Sep. 1991.

[10] P. Dewan, A. Vikram and B. Bhargava, "Engineering the Object-Relation Model in O-Raid", *Proceedings Of The International Conference on Foundations of Data Organization and Algorithms*, June 1989, 389-403.

[11] D. H. Fishman, J. Annevelink, E. C. Chow, T. Connors, J. W. Davis, W. Hassan, C. G. Hoch, W. Kent, S. Leichner, P. Lyngback, B. Mahbod, M. A. Neimat, T. Risch, M. C. Shan and W. K. Wilkinson, "Overview of the Iris DBMS", Technical Report HPL-SAL-89-15, HP Labs, Jan. 1989.

[12] G. Gardarin, J. P. Cheiney, G. Kiernan, D. Pastre and H. Stora, "Managing Complex Objects in an Extensible Relational DBMS", *Proc. 15th Int'l Conf. Very Large Data Bases*, Amsterdam, The Netherlands, Aug. 1989, 55-65.

[13] N. H. Gehani and H. V. Jagadish, "Ode as an Active Database: Constraints and Triggers", *Proc. 17th Int'l Conf. Very Large Data Bases*, Barcelona, Spain, 1991, 327-336.

[14] W. Kim, "A Model of Queries for Object-Oriented Databases", *Proc. 15th Int'l Conf. Very Large Data Bases*, Amsterdam, The Netherlands, Aug. 1989, 423-432.

[15] W. Kim, N. Ballou, H. Chou, J. F. Garza and D. Woelk, "Features of the Orion Object Database System", in *Object-Oriented Concepts and Databases*, W. Kim and F.H. Lochovsky (ed.), Addison-Wesley, 1989, 251-282.

[16] C. Lecluse, P. Richard and F. Velez, "O_2, an Object-Oriented Data Model", *Proc. ACM-SIGMOD 1988 Int'l Conf. on Management of Data*, Chicago, Illinois, June 1988, 424-433.

[17] D. Lieuwen and D. DeWitt, "Optimizing Loops in Database Programming Languages", *3rd Int'l Workshop on Database Programming Languages*, Nafplion, Greece , Aug. 1991.

[18] V. Linnemann, K. Kuspert, P. Dadam, P. Pistor, R. Erbe, A. Kemper, N. Sudkamp, G. Walch and M. Wallrath, "Design and Implementation of an Extensible Database Management System Supporting User Defined Data Types and Functions", *Proc. 14th Int'l Conf. Very Large Data Bases*, Los Angeles, California, Aug.-Sept. 1988, 294-305.

[19] J. Melton, (ed.), "(ISO-ANSI Working Draft) Database Language SQL2 and SQL3", ANSI X3H2-90-001, Dec. 1989.

[20] P. B. Mitschang, "Extending the Relational Algebra to Capture Complex Objects", *Proc. 15th Int'l Conf. Very Large Data Bases*, Amsterdam, The Netherlands, Aug. 1989, 297-305.

[21] P. Pistor and F. Andersen, "Designing A Generalized NF2 Model With an SQL-Type Interface", *Proc. 12th Int'l Conf. on Very Large Databases*, Kyoto, Japan, Aug. 1986, 278-285.

[22] M. A. Roth, H. F. Korth and D. S. Batory, "SQL/NF: A Query Langage For ¬1NF Relational Databases", *Information Systems 12*, 1 (1987), 99-114.

[23] L. A. Rowe and M. R. Stonebraker, "The POSTGRES Data Model", *Proc. 13th Int'l Conf. Very Large Data Bases*, Brighton, England, Sept. 1987, 83-96.

[24] H. J. Schek and M. Scholl, "The Relation Model with Relation-Valued Attributes", *Information Sys. 11*, 2 (1986), .

[25] D. L. Spooner, M. Hardwick and G. Samaras, "Some Conceptual Ideas For Extending SQL For Object-Oriented Engineering Database Systems", *Proc. IEEE 1st International Conference on Data and Knowledge Systems for Manufacturing and Engineering*, Oct. 1987, 163-169.

[26] B. Stroustrup, in *The C++ Programming Language (2nd Ed.)*, Addison-Wesley, 1991.

Retrieval of Complex Objects

W. Bruce Croft[1] and Howard R. Turtle[2]

[1] Computer Science Department
University of Massachusetts
Amherst, MA 01003

[2] West Publishing Company
50 West Kellogg Blvd.
St. Paul, MN 55164

Abstract

Many databases consist of large collections of "objects" that have complex structure and contain a wide variety of data such as text, numbers, and images. Current database systems can represent objects such as these only with difficulty, and often restrict the type of data that can be stored. In response to these shortcomings, object-oriented database systems have been designed specifically to represent complex objects and accommodate user-defined extensions such as new data types. One of the most important functions that a database system provides is to help users find data with particular characteristics. In object-oriented database systems, this content-based retrieval capability is typically limited to selection from a set of objects based on Boolean combinations of simple predicates. In this paper, we describe a retrieval model based on probabilistic inference that appears to provide the basis of a general retrieval model for complex objects. In particular, it can describe how the meanings of objects are related, including objects in composite object hierarchies, objects referred to by other objects, and multimedia objects.

1 The Problem

Many databases consist of large collections of "objects" that have complex structure and contain a wide variety of data such as text, numbers, and images. An obvious example is a database of scientific articles and reports, where the objects represent documents and parts of documents such as paragraphs, figures, tables, and references. Current database systems, such as those based on the relational model, can represent objects such as these only with difficulty, and often restrict the type of data that can be stored in an object. In response to these shortcomings, object-oriented database systems have been designed specifically to represent complex objects and accommodate user-defined extensions such as new data types [21]. In addition, these systems provide robust, long-term storage of objects and maintain the validity of the data through recovery and concurrency control mechanisms. These functions are important for any database system, but it is also important to provide functions that help users find data with particular characteristics. In object-oriented database systems, this content-based retrieval capability is typically limited to selection from a database of objects using Boolean combinations of simple predicates (for example, [10, 1]), although it is in general possible to define additional predicates for specific data types.

Given the importance of the retrieval function, it is appropriate to consider more general models of retrieval for complex, multimedia objects. What would be the characteristics of such a model? Part of the answer to this question may be found in the field of information retrieval (IR). IR deals with the retrieval of text which, although not the dominant data type in some scientific databases, is very common and is often used to describe a variety of other types of data, such as graphs, video, or the output of experiments. In addition, IR has for some time been investigating retrieval models for situations where queries are difficult to express, objects are difficult to describe, and the comparison of queries and objects must be more sophisticated than searching for exact matches.

Some recent retrieval models have emphasized the role of probabilistic inference, where multiple sources of evidence are used to assess the likelihood that an object satisfies the user's information need [4, 17, 18]. These models have not only been shown to be very effective for retrieving simple text-based objects, such as abstracts or documents [19], but they also appear to provide the basis of a general retrieval model for complex objects. In particular, models based on probabilistic inference can describe how the meanings of objects are related, including objects in composite object hierarchies, objects referred to by other objects, and multimedia objects. A probabilistic inference model also allows for a great deal of flexibility in formulating a query and relating the query concepts to the concepts used to describe objects.

In this paper, we address two major issues in the integration of probabilistic retrieval models and object-oriented databases. These are:

1. **Retrieval of objects in composite hierarchies:** In many databases, complex objects are described using composite or **part-of** hierarchies (e.g. [1]). In Figure 1, object A has components B, C, and D, and object C has components E and F. An example of such a composite object would be a scientific journal article, where the components would be sections, paragraphs, figures, etc. A retrieval model for composite objects should allow the user to retrieve objects from any level of the hierarchy, and should specify how the retrieval of objects depends on the other objects in the hierarchy. For example, in the case of the journal articles, users may want to retrieve whole articles or just specific sections or paragraphs that address the information need. If whole articles are to be retrieved, the extent to which an article satisfies the information need will be determined by the extent to which the sections and subsections satisfy that need. Our current ideas on the mechanism for incorporating composite objects into a probabilistic inference model are described in the next section.

2. **Retrieval of multimedia objects:** Many objects in a scientific database will be difficult to search directly. Images, digitized outputs of experiments, and graphs are all examples of data types where it is extremely difficult to define comparison operators. In many cases, these objects will be part of composite objects or will be referred to by other objects. For example, in Figure 1, object F could be a graph that is part of a section of document A. A retrieval model for multimedia objects should specify how these objects "inherit" meaning from related objects. This is different from the situation described with composite hierarchies, where the meaning of an

object is determined by the meaning of its subobjects. Instead, we can think of the objects that refer to a multimedia object as defining "contexts" that can be used for retrieval. The first context could be defined as the set of objects which directly refer to the multimedia node or are siblings in the composite hierarchy. In our example, this would mean that the first context for graph object F is E, which could be a caption. We could then define the next context as the set of objects which refer to objects in the first context or which are siblings to the parent object in the composite hierarchy. This would bring in objects B and D, which in a journal article could be paragraphs that referred to the graph or in the same document section as the graph. In section 3, we will discuss how contexts are used in a probabilistic inference model.

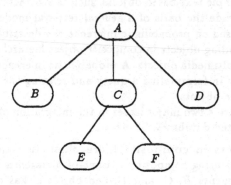

Fig. 1. A composite object hierarchy

By addressing these two issues, we are not solving the problem of complex object retrieval. There remains many other issues, such as integration with a complete query language, integration with "structural" search (e.g. [3]), query optimization, and interface design. Some of these issues are discussed briefly in later sections. The purpose of this paper is to describe the type of model that is needed for effective performance in one of the central aspects of the retrieval process, namely retrieval by content.

In the next section, we present a probabilistic text retrieval model based on inference nets [17, 19]. This model has been shown experimentally to be an effective basis for text retrieval, and appears to have the characteristics, described above, of a general model for complex object retrieval. In the third section, we show how this model can be extended for complex object retrieval and, specifically, retrieval in composite object hierarchies. In section 4, we discuss related work and possibilities for integration into a complete system.

Finally, in section 5, implementation aspects of the probabilistic object retrieval model are discussed.

2 The Inference Network Model for Text Retrieval

Text representation is inherently an uncertain process. Consider a document that contains the string "oil prices." The presence of this string does not guarantee that the document should be retrieved in response either to a query about "causes of recent increases in oil prices" or to more general queries such as "energy costs". Instead, the presence of the string is evidence that the content of the document may be related to those information needs. Statistical IR has addressed this problem by introducing models of *probabilistic indexing* (e.g. [6]). These models express the probability that a text document D will satisfy an information need I $(P(I|D))$ in terms of probabilities $P(I|R)$ and $P(R|D)$. $P(I|R)$ is the probability that an information need is satisfied given a particular text *representation* (R), and $P(R|D)$ is the probability that a particular representation holds for a document D. In implementations of probabilistic models, documents are ranked according to estimates of these probabilities for particular queries [20].

The inference network model of text retrieval is closely related to probabilistic indexing and retrieval models but places more emphasis on combining multiple sources of evidence. A number of approaches to evidential reasoning, such as the Dempster-Shafer theory of evidence [5, 16], could be adapted to the text retrieval problem but the model we present here is based on Bayesian inference networks [14, 9]. This choice was made primarily because of the similarity to probabilistic dependency networks used previously in statistical IR [20].

A Bayesian inference network is a directed, acyclic dependency graph (DAG) in which nodes represent propositional variables or constants and edges represent dependence relations between propositions. The collection of nodes in the network define an event space and this allows us to associate probabilities or beliefs with nodes. If a proposition represented by a node p "causes" or implies the proposition represented by node q, we draw a directed edge from p to q. The node q contains a specification of the conditional probability associated with the node given the state of node p $(P(q|p))$. This information is captured in a *link matrix*. In the case where each node has two states (*true* and *false*), the matrix has two rows and two columns that specify $P(q = true|p = true)$, $P(q = true|p = false)$, $P(q = false|p = true)$, and $P(q = false|p = true)$. When a node has multiple parents, the matrix specifies the dependence of that node on the set of parents and characterizes the dependence relationship between that node and all nodes representing its potential causes. Given a set of prior probabilities for the roots of the DAG, these networks can be used to compute the probability or degree of belief associated with all remaining nodes.

The basic inference network used for text retrieval, illustrated in figure 2, consists of two component networks: a document network and a query network [3]. The document network contains the representations of the text documents in the database. In the basic model, documents are treated as simple objects that contain only text and do not refer to other objects. The document network is built once for a particular database and its

---

[3] A detailed description of the inference net model of retrieval can be found in [17].

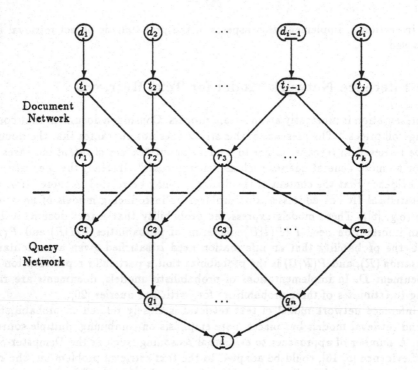

Fig. 2. Basic document inference network

structure does not change during query processing. The query network consists of a single node which represents the user's information need and one or more query representations which express that information need. A query network is built for each information need and is modified during query processing as existing queries are refined or new queries are added in an attempt to better characterize the information need. The document and query networks are joined by links between representation concepts and query concepts.

2.1 The document network

The document network consists of document nodes (d_i's), text nodes (t_j's), and concept nodes (r_k's). Each document node represents an actual document in the database and corresponds to the event associated with the occurrence of that document (i.e. selecting this document out of all documents in the database). The dependence of a text node upon the document is represented in the network by an arc from the document node to the text node. The assignment of a specific representation concept to a document is represented by a directed arc to the concept node from each text node corresponding to a document to which the concept has been assigned.

Document nodes correspond to abstract documents rather than their physical representations. A text node corresponds to the event that a particular text has occurred.

The original distinction between text and document nodes was made to simplify computations in the network, and to anticipate the situation, addressed in this paper, where documents have complex structure and multimedia content. In the next section, we will discuss the use of this part of the network for complex object retrieval, but for the time being, we assume a one-to-one correspondence between documents and texts.

Each document node has a prior probability associated with it that describes the probability of the document "event"; this prior probability will generally be set to 1/(database size) and will be small for typical databases. Each text node contains a specification of its dependence upon its parent; by assumption, this dependence is complete, a text node occurs ($t_i = true$) exactly when its parent document occurs ($d_i = true$). The link matrix associated with representation concept nodes specifies the conditional probabilities that are used in probabilistic indexing.

2.2 The query network

The query network is an "inverted" DAG with a single leaf that corresponds to the event that an information need is met and multiple roots that correspond to the concepts that express the information need. As shown in figure 2, a set of intermediate query nodes may be used in cases where multiple queries are used to express the information need.

The roots of the query network are the primitive concepts used to express the information need. A single query concept node may have several representation concept nodes as parents. A query concept node contains a specification of the probabilistic dependence of the query concept on its set of parent representation concepts. The query concept nodes define the mapping between the concepts used to represent the document database and the concepts used in the queries. In the simplest case, the query concepts are constrained to be the same as the representation concepts and each query concept has exactly one parent concept node.

The attachment of the query concept nodes to the document network has no effect on the structure of the document network. None of the existing links need change and none of the conditional probability specifications stored in the nodes are modified.

When the query network is first built and attached to the document network we compute the belief associated with each node in the query network. The initial value at the node representing the information need is the probability that the information need is met given that no specific document in the database has occurred and all documents are equally likely (or unlikely). If we now attach evidence to the network asserting that a particular document has occurred (i.e. $d_i = true$), we can compute the probability that the information need is met. This probability is used to rank the document during retrieval.

The basic inference network model has been used for text retrieval experiments on databases of up to 250 MBytes and has proved to be both effective and efficient [18]. In the next section, we describe extensions to this model for complex object retrieval.

3 Extensions for Complex Object Retrieval

In this paper, we are interested in two specific extensions to the inference network model for complex object retrieval. These are retrieval of objects that are part of a composite hierarchy and retrieval of multimedia objects.

Retrieval of composite objects

To apply the inference net model to the retrieval of composite objects we must specify how the meanings of an object and its subobjects are related. We must also specify how the composite object hierarchy is related to the document, text and concept nodes in the inference net. The first step in this process is to define our complex object terminology more precisely. In an object-oriented database, a composite object (such as that shown in Figure 1) is an instance of an object class. The definition for that class of objects will be part of the *class hierarchy* for that system and application. That is, a class definition will inherit *instance variables* and *operations* from its superclass(es) in the class hierarchy. The instance variables for a class may contain references to objects. These objects may be instances of a number of classes, and may in turn contain references to other objects. In some systems [1], composite object operations are given a special semantics to represent the notion that subobjects belong exclusively to a particular parent object. This is appropriate for our complex document examples, but the distinction is not important for the model presented in this section.

As part of specifying a query for complex object retrieval, users should be able to indicate the required object class. That is, any object class whose instances can be part of a composite object is a valid result. In the case of journal articles, for example, users could specify whether they wanted to retrieve articles, sections, paragraphs, figures or tables. Objects that are instances of the specified class should also be able to be retrieved based on their own content (that is, the values of the instance variables that refer to *primitive objects*, such as numbers and strings). Alternatively, their retrieval could be partially based on the content of their subobjects. These observations, taken together, suggest the following inference net representation for composite objects:

1. There is a one-to-one mapping between object instances and root nodes in the inference net. That is, each object in a composite object hierarchy will be represented as a root in the inference net. The database, instead of being represented as a set of document (d_i) nodes, will be represented as a set of object nodes which correspond to all object instances in the current database. An object node represents the proposition that a given object has occurred and has the values *true* or *false*. The only case in which an object is not represented by a node in the inference net is when the object's instance variables contain only references to other, non-primitive objects. That is, objects with no "content" of their own. These objects would be retrieved by instantiating the component objects, as described below.

   Each object node in the inference net is connected to a set of nodes that are similar to the text (t_i) nodes in the basic network. We refer to these nodes as "content" nodes. Content nodes correspond to the occurrence of particular object contents (instance variables containing primitive objects) and have the values *true* or *false*. Many of these nodes will be used to represent the text content of objects, as in the basic network. Other nodes will represent instance variables containing other classes of objects, such as author names, dates or figures in a journal article. By separating content nodes from object nodes, we can model shared contents and uncertain data. A node representing content shared between two or more objects will have more than one parent in the network. Uncertain data [8] can be represented using the probabilities $P(t_i|o_j)$ and $P(r_k|t_i)$ (see next section).

2. The references to subobjects that make up the composite object are not represented explicitly in the inference net. Although these links could be interpreted in the inference net model as the probability of a subobject occurring given that a parent object has occurred, we believe that this would lead to unnecessary computational problems. Instead, the the composite hierarchy relationships should be used at search time as described below.

3. Object nodes can be linked via content nodes to concept nodes in order to represent their meaning. As in the basic inference net model, some content nodes (such as the nodes representing text) will be linked to concept nodes. These nodes can be viewed as an additional level of description of the content of objects. Concept nodes are particularly important for text, but could also be an important part of multimedia object retrieval. Objects with image or video content, for example, could be described by assigning concept nodes either manually or automatically through a feedback process. Content nodes representing instance variables whose values are well-defined (such as *author = Fred Jones*) do not need to be linked to concept nodes and can be referred to directly in the query network.

By structuring the inference net in this way, objects can be retrieved independently of each other. We could, for example, specify that only objects from the class representing single paragraphs be retrieved. In that case, each o_i node associated with the instances of the specified class of objects is asserted to be *true* (one at a time), and the objects can be ranked according to their probability of satisfying the information need. In most cases, we want the retrieval of composite objects to be influenced by the content of subobjects. To accomplish this in the inference net, we can use a form of the model that has been shown to be effective in describing citation relationships between documents [4, 17].

Figure 3 shows an example of this extended form of the network. For simplicity, we do not show content nodes. In this network, object o_1 has been instantiated. All remaining objects in the network are set to *false*, except those objects that are subobjects of o_1. We assume that all subobjects (i.e. the transitive closure) have evidence attached to them in this way, and that each subobject is set to *true* (the strongest form of evidence) because of the nature of the composite object hierarchy. This means that when an object occurs, all of its subobjects occur, with certainty, at the same time. The effect of this evidence is to raise the belief in all representation concepts that describe subobjects. This effectively adds concepts to o_1's representation and reinforces belief in concepts that are used to describe both the parent object and subobjects. In the example, object o_3 is a subobject of o_1 and has been instantiated along with o_1. The addition of o_3 adds concepts r_3 and r_4 to o_1's representation, strengthens belief in r_2 given o_1, and leaves belief in r_1 unchanged.

The effectiveness of this model with real databases will depend to some extent on whether the statistical information extracted from small text objects will be as reliable as that from large text objects. There has been some work done in this area [13], but the model presented here approaches the problem from a broader perspective. Consider a single large text object. This object will be represented by a set of concept nodes and the associated probabilities $P(r_k|t_i)$. These probabilities are estimated using a *tf.idf* formula [15, 17], where the *tf* component is based on the frequency of a word in the text object, and the *idf* component is based on the frequency of the word in the collection

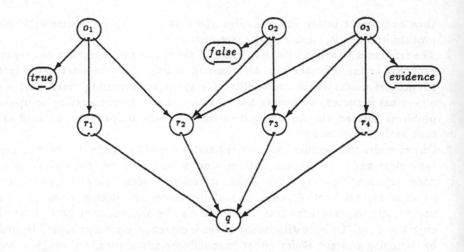

Fig. 3. The extended model for composite objects

of text objects. These probabilities are in turn used to estimate the probability of the information need being satisfied by the text object. If this text object is now broken into a number of smaller text objects, the probability estimates may change. Using the model presented in this section, all objects that are components of the original object will be instantiated. In general, this will mean that belief will propagate to the same set of concept nodes for the single large object or the collection of smaller objects. Whether the belief estimates at this point are the same, however, depends on a number of factors such as the form of the *tf.idf* function and the way beliefs are combined when multiple parent objects are instantiated. It is not even clear that we want the belief estimates to be exactly the same. These issues must be resolved by retrieval experiments.

Retrieval of multimedia objects

We can also use this extended form of the inference net model to describe retrieval of multimedia objects. In this case, we instantiate a set of objects that are related to the multimedia object (the "contexts" discussed in the first section) in order to determine the probability of satisfying the information need. In this more general form of the extended model, the belief accorded to the objects related to the multimedia object could be based on the type and strength of the relationship.

The context of a multimedia object is a set of sets of objects. Each member of the context set consists of the objects that refer to the objects in the previous member of the set. The semantics of "refer to" depends on the type of system being used. In the object-oriented systems discussed here, this could be either the *part-of* relationship or simple object reference. Different contexts could be distinguished by the types of relationships used to generate them. Retrieval of a multimedia object consists of choosing a particular subset of the context and instantiating all the objects in that subset.

As an example, suppose that a user wants to retrieve all figures that satisfy a particular information need. The figure may have a caption, in which case this could be used to retrieve them independently of other objects. In the case where there is no caption, or when the caption is not sufficiently informative, we can instantiate objects that represent other parts of the article, and this instantiation can be done in progressively wider contexts. We could initially instantiate objects representing paragraphs in the same section of the document as the figure. If this did not produce satisfactory results, we could widen the context until the whole document is being used to determine the "meaning" of the figure. Note that this instantiation of objects is going in the opposite direction to the instantiation of subobjects for composite object retrieval, and the evidence attached to objects from wider contexts may be weaker than that attached to objects that are very "close" to the figure.

Another example of multimedia object retrieval could occur in a hypermedia environment where objects are connected by links of different types. The extended model provides a mechanism for multimedia objects to be retrieved using the content of related objects, and for the type of the link to determine how much evidence should be attached to the related object [4].

4 Related Work

The object retrieval model is related to work in both database systems and information retrieval, but is primarily based on IR. Much of this work has been referred to in earlier sections, but we should also mention Fuhr's paper on a probabilistic database incorporating relevance feedback [7]. Our work differs from Fuhr's (which is also based on IR models) in the use of the inference net to model composite object and multimedia object retrieval.

In the database community, the related research has been done in the general area of uncertainty in databases. Examples of this type of work are systems that deal with extensions to the relational model to handle uncertain data [8] and uncertain queries [11]. The inference net model described here can address both of these types of uncertainty through the various probabilities represented. Garcia-Molina and Porter [8] discuss a probabilistic relational data model where probabilities are associated with the values of attributes. In the inference net model, these attribute probabilities can be represented by $P(t_i|o_j)$. In addition, the probabilities $P(r_k|t_i)$ are used to capture the uncertainty of representation of text and other complex data types. Uncertainty in the query is represented through the probabilities $P(I|q_n)$ and $P(q_n|c_m)$.

The probabilistic relational model and related work [2] suggest an approach to integrating the inference net model with a complete query language. The inference net model could be viewed as defining a *select* operator on collections of complex objects. The result of this *select* is a set of objects with associated probabilities (the probability of satisfying the information need). What is then needed is a query algebra that can manipulate this set, combine it with other sets, and preserve the semantics of the probabilities. This is essentially what is done for the relational algebra in [8], although there is no direct representation of the probability associated with the result of the *select*. For the inference net model described here, a probabilistic *object-oriented algebra* is needed.

5 Implementation of the Network

The implementation of the basic retrieval model is described in [18]. By using inverted files to represent the static part of the inference net (i.e. the object nodes and the associated concept nodes), the retrieval system based on this model has been shown to provide efficient access to databases of more than 1 gigabyte of text. The inference nets for these databases contain hundreds of thousands of nodes corresponding to paragraph-level objects and concepts. In this section we outline the principal extensions required for implementing an inference net for complex objects.

By choosing not to represent the object hierarchy directly in the inference net, we avoid two main problems. First, we avoid dealing with multiply connected inference networks. Multiply connected networks arise when more than one path exists between two nodes in the network and require special handling (see [14] or [12] for a discussion of these techniques). Since a single content node can be shared by a multiple object nodes and a single representation concept node can be shared by multiple content nodes, these multiple connections are common in an uninstantiated inference network. However, since all object nodes are instantiated during evaluation, propagation of evidence through the roots is blocked, which effectively disconnects the network and avoids a substantial computational burden each time the object hierarchy is updated.

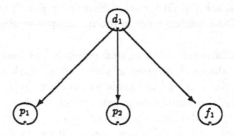

Fig. 4. Dependent sibling objects

Second, modelling all of the containment relationships present in the object hierarchy as conditional probabilities would make it difficult to compute the desired probabilities for individual object types. If, in figure 4 we model two paragraphs (p_1 and p_2) and a figure (f_1) as *part-of* document d_1 we cannot easily compute beliefs for individual paragraphs since instantiating p_1 influences our belief in its siblings (and also renders the network multiply connected if any of the siblings share representation concepts). Since we are interested in retrieving objects of arbitrary type we have chosen to represent objects independently and to incorporate the effect of structural relationships during query evaluation. To do this, we must still 1) determine the set of objects to be instantiated and 2) determine the strength of the evidence to be attached to each member of this set.

The set of objects to be instantiated when computing belief for an object can be determined directly from the object hierarchy. To model structural relationships we will fully instantiate all objects that are contained in each object of interest. In the case of multimedia objects we will instantiate objects in the context. The strength of evidence attached to these nodes will decrease with distance from the original node and will depend on the object types involved.

Techniques for combining beliefs for subobjects and instance variables to arrive at an overall belief for an object will require further study. While we have experience with "generic" combining functions useful for text retrieval, the function used should probably depend on the object types involved.

6 Conclusion

We have described a probabilistic inference model that can provide a general framework for the retrieval of complex objects. The framework was used to describe a new approach to retrieving composite and multimedia objects. Our experience with text databases suggests that the probabilistic framework will be essential for effective retrieval in applications that deal with unstructured, multimedia data. The retrieval techniques discussed here can be implemented efficiently, although their impact on the overall query optimization process has not been considered. We have also not yet integrated this framework into a complete query language, and more work needs to be done on probabilistic object algebras.

We are currently implementing a very basic approach to the integration of an object-oriented database system and the inference net model. In this approach, we have stored complex documents, such as Ph.D. dissertations, in an object-oriented database system and have then stored surrogates for the textual part of these objects in an inference net-based retrieval system. Queries that refer to textual or multimedia (i.e. tables and figures) content are referred to the text retrieval system. This system retrieves ranked lists of OIDs that refer to objects in the database system. Although simple, this system will allow us to do some preliminary experiments with the algorithms for composite object and multimedia retrieval presented in this paper.

Acknowledgments

This work was supported in part by NSF Grant IRI-8814790, by the Air Force Office of Scientific Research under contract 91-0324, and by Hewlett-Packard.

References

1. J. Banerjee, H. Chou, J.F. Garza, W. Kim, D. Woelk and N. Ballou, "Data Model Issues for Object-Oriented Applications", *ACM Transactions on Office Information Systems*, 5, 3-26, (1987).

2. R. Cavallo and M. Pittarelli, "The Theory of Probabilistic Databases", Proceedings of VLDB 87, 71-81, (1987).
3. M.P. Consens and A.O. Mendelzon, "Expressing Structural Hypertext Queries in GraphLog", Proceedings of Hypertext 89, 269-292, (1989).
4. W.B. Croft and H.R. Turtle, "A Retrieval Model Incorporating Hypertext Links", Hypertext '89 Proceedings, 213-224, (1989).
5. A. P. Dempster, "A Generalization of Bayesian Inference", *Journal of the Royal Statistical Society B*, 30, 205-247, (1968).
6. N. Fuhr, "Models for Retrieval with Probabilistic Indexing", *Information Processing and Management*, 25, 55-72, (1989).
7. N. Fuhr, "A Probabilistic Framework for Vague Queries and Imprecise Information in Databases", Proceedings of VLDB 90, 696-707, (1990).
8. H. Garcia-Molina and D. Porter, "Supporting Probabilistic Data in a Relational System", Proceedings of EDBT, 60-74, (1990).
9. S. L. Lauritzen and D. J. Spiegelhalter, "Local Computations with Probabilities on Graphical Structures and their Application to Expert Systems", *Journal of the Royal Statistical Society B*, 50, 157-224, (1988).
10. D. Maier and J. Stein, "Development and Implementation of an Object-Oriented DBMS", in *Research Directions in Object-Oriented Programming*, B. Shriver and P. Wegner (eds.), MIT Press, 355-392, (1987).
11. A. Motro, "VAGUE: A User Interface to Relational Databases that Permits Vague Queries", *ACM Transactions of Office Information Systems*, 6, 187-214, (1988).
12. R.E. Neapolitan, *Probabilistic Reasoning in Expert Systems*, Wiley Interscience, (1990).
13. J. O'Connor, "Retrieval of Answer Sentences and Answer Figures by Text Searching", *Information Processing and Management*, 11, 155-164, (1975).
14. J. Pearl, *Probabilistic Reasoning in Intelligent Systems: Networks of Plausible Inference*, Morgan Kaufmann, (1988).
15. G. Salton and M. McGill, *Introduction to Modern Information Retrieval*, McGraw-Hill, (1983).
16. G. Shafer, *A Mathematical Theory of Evidence*. Princeton University Press, 1976.
17. H.R. Turtle, "Inference Networks for Document Retrieval", Ph.D. Thesis, Computer Science Department, University of Massachusetts, Amherst, (1990).
18. H.R. Turtle and W.B. Croft, "Efficient Probabilistic Inference for Text Retrieval", Proceedings of RIAO 3, 644-661, (1991).
19. H.R. Turtle and W.B. Croft, "Evaluation of an Inference Network-Based Retrieval Model", *ACM Transactions on Information Systems*, (to appear).
20. C. J. Van Rijsbergen, *Information Retrieval*. Butterworths, (1979).
21. S.B. Zdonik and D. Maier, *Reading in Object-Oriented Database Systems*. Morgan Kaufmann, San Mateo, (1990).

This article was processed using the LaTeX macro package with LMAMULT style

EVOLUTION OF KNOWLEDGE BASES

D. Sacca

Dipartimento di Sistemi, University of Calabria
Arcavacata, I-87036 Rende (CS), Italy
2101SAC@ICSUNIV.BITNET

B. Verdonk

Research Center Alcatel-Bell
F. Wellesplein 1, B2018 Antwerp, Belgium
bver@ra.alcbel.be

D. Vermeir

Dept. of Mathematics and Computer Science, University of Antwerp (UIA)
Universiteitsplein 1, B2610 Wilrijk, Belgium
vermeir@ccu.uia.ac.be

Abstract

In the present work we introduce a simple yet powerful formalism to model the evolution of knowledge bases. The semantics are based on the fundamental intuition that more recent information overrides previous knowledge, insofar as keeping the old knowledge would lead to inconsistencies. Combining this with the techniques from logic programming and ordered logic semantics yields a notion of model that nicely extends the semantics of ordinary logic programming. Our approach extends existing ones in that we model updates that contain simple facts as well as intentional information using a uniform declarative formalism that also supports what-if reasoning and transactions.

1. Introduction

Recently, a considerable amount of research[Man89a, Naq88a, Via87a, Via88a, Abi88a, Man87a] has been done in the area of updates for logic programs. We refer to[Man89a] and[Abi88a] for an excellent survey of the results obtained so far.

In the present work, we take the view that a knowledge base not only describes the present state of affairs but also its possible evolution. This is achieved by interpreting atoms not just as having a truth value in the present state, but also after performing some updates to the knowledge base. This gives rise to the notion of "what-if" queries. In addition, by considering atoms that become true only if a certain sequence of updates are performed, we introduce the concept of transaction.

One of the novelties of our approach is that we see update as what it fundamentally is: a revision of the theory (program). This allows one to specify updates which add clauses to the program. There are some obvious advantages to this generality: it often allows for a more efficient storage of massive updates and supports updates which are hard to formulate if one is restricted to the update of factual information only. Our approach contrasts with most approaches to the theory of updates[Man89a, Naq88a] in knowledge- and databases where the possible evolution of the knowledge base is restricted to the addition or removal of simple facts. Such an approach is rather simple, as, since there is no need to change the program, the semantics can be provided by defining a Kripke-like structure of states [Kri63a], together with an accessibility relation between them that models the possible update transitions.

Our approach provides a simple and uniform declarative formalism to express the semantics of transactions, what-if queries as well as rule updates. It is based on the fundamental intuition that more recent information may override previous knowledge, insofar as keeping the old knowledge would lead to inconsistencies. Combining this with the techniques from logic programming and ordered logic[Lae90a] semantics, yields a notion of model that nicely extends the semantics of ordinary logic programming.

The paper is organized as follows. In section 2 we introduce the concept of dynamic program while in section 3 we define its semantics. Section 4 illustrates the power of our model with additional examples. Some conclusions are formulated in section 5.

2. Dynamic Programs

Our starting point is that any update of a knowledge base, i.e. a logic program, can be modeled by adding a set of facts and/or rules to it. In order to make this true two requirements should clearly be satisfied. First, negation in the head of rules must be allowed in order to model deletion/modification of information. Second, since adding negative information to the knowledge base may lead to inconsistencies, the semantics of update should be such that more recent information gets priority, overruling previous knowledge. Consider the following simple example, where the original knowledge base consists of a number of employee-salary facts.

Example 1.

$$P_0 = \{\ empSal(john,100).$$
$$empSal(peter,120).$$
$$...\ \}$$

We can model an increase of john's salary by 10%, by adding the following program to the knowledge base:

$$P_1 = \{\ empSal(john,110).$$
$$\neg\ empSal(john,100).\ \}$$

In order to resolve the inconsistency between $empSal(john,100)$ and

¬empSal(john,100), the semantics will take into account that the knowledge in P_1 is more recent than the information in P_0. We say that ¬empSal(john,100) *overrules* empSal(john,100). Obviously, the semantics should also be such that any information in the original knowledge base which is not overruled by new information still remains valid after the update. Therefore, the updated knowledge base essentially consists of $P_1 \cup P_0$, taking into account that P_1 is more recent than P_0 in order to be able to resolve possible inconsistencies. This will be formalized in the next section.□

Applying the same idea repeatedly, it is easy to model consecutive updates of a knowledge base.

Example 2. If after increasing john's salary (cfr. Example 1) we also want to increase peter's salary, the updated knowledge base would be given by $P_2 \cup P_1 \cup P_0$ where P_2 is given by

$$P_2 = \{ \; empSal(peter,132).$$
$$\quad \neg \; empSal(peter,120). \; \}$$

and taking into account that P_2 is more recent than P_1 which in its turn is more recent than P_0. Because P_2 is more recent than P_0, ¬empSal(peter,120) in P_2 will overrule empSal(peter,120) in P_0 such that after the update the salary of peter will indeed have been increased by 10%. Also, empSal(john,110) in P_1 will continue to hold in the updated knowledge base.□

Abstracting away from the above example, it is clear that any sequence of updates to a knowledge base can be modeled by a sequence of logic programs, where the original theory is the first element in the sequence, while the last element in the sequence represents the most recent information added to the knowledge base. More formally, the evolution of a knowledge base can be described by a sequence of *update events* (or *events* for short). An *event* is a term $e(\vec{X})$ where e is a special function symbol, called an *event* symbol, and $\vec{X}$ is a list of arguments. The 'effect' of an event $e(\vec{X})$ is completely determined by the (negative) logic program associated with it. Throughout this section we will use $P_{e(\vec{X})}$ to denote the (negative) logic program associated with the specific event $e(\vec{X})$, as can be seen in the following example.

Example 3. We can rewrite Examples 1 and 2 by introducing two events *init* and *modify*$(\vec{X})$ and by defining the logic programs associated with these events as follows:

$$P_{init} = \{ \; empSal(john, 100).$$
$$\quad empSal(peter, 120).$$
$$\quad ... \; \}$$

$$P_{modify(Empl,OldSal,NewSal)} = \{$$
$$\quad \neg \; empSal(Empl, OldSal).$$
$$\quad empSal(Empl, NewSal). \; \}$$

The state of the knowledge base as in Example 2 can then be characterized by the sequence of events <*init*,*modify*(john,100,110),*modify*(peter,120,132)>. □

In general, if e_i $(i=0,...,n)$ are events, then $<e_j,e_l,...,e_k>$ with $0 \leq j,l,k \leq n$, will denote the sequence of events e_j followed by e_l, ..., followed by e_k. A sequence of events may also contain variables, as placeholder for one or more consecutive events. An event $e(\vec{X})$ is said to be *fully generic* if all arguments in $\vec{X}$ are variables. On the other hand, an *actual event* is a ground instance of a fully generic event.

Given an initial knowledge base K, i.e. a logic program, a *history* $<h>$ of K is a sequence of actual events $<e_0,...,e_n>$ such that the logic program associated with the first event in the sequence, namely e_0, is precisely the initial knowledge base K. In other words, there is a one-to-one mapping between the set of histories $<h>$ of K and the set of states in the (possible) evolution of the knowledge base K. The length $|<h>|$ of a history is the number of events in the sequence. Note that if a history $<h>$ of K has length 1, it corresponds to the initial knowledge base itself (no updates).

As pointed out in the introduction and as should be clear from the above, we do not restrict new information to consist solely of facts. Indeed, the logic program associated with any update event can also contain arbitrary clauses. There are obvious advantages to this generality, since adding clauses to the theory makes it possible to revise the theory, instead of being restricted to the addition of a number of facts. Irrespective of the type of information added to the knowledge base, whether simple facts or complex rules, it may be the case that current decisions depend on the newly added information, for instance when dealing with what-if queries or hypothetical reasoning. In order to be able to also model such what-if queries, we need a way to refer to future states of the knowledge base. We therefore define an *atom* to be of the form $<\alpha>p$ where $<\alpha>$, called the *future*, is a sequence of events and p is a classical atom. If $<\alpha>$ is empty, it can be dropped from the notation. An atom is *ground* if no variables occur in either $<\alpha>$ or p. A *literal* is an atom $<\alpha>p$ or its negation, which is denoted $<\alpha>\neg p$. An atom and its negation are called *complementary* and we will assume that $\neg\neg p$ is equal to p.

Intuitively, a ground literal $<\alpha>p$ can be read as "p holds after the occurrence of the sequence of events $<\alpha>$".

Example 4. Consider the events *init* and *raise* and their associated logic programs:

$P_{init} = \{$
   happy(Y):- manager(Y,M), sal(M, SM), <raise>sal(Y,S), S $\geq$ SM .
   salary(john,100).
   salary(bill,170).
   salary(peter,120).
   manager(john, bill).
   manager(peter, bill). $\}$

$P_{raise} = \{ \neg salary(john,100).$
      salary(john,200). $\}$

and let P_{init} be the initial knowledge base. The rule in P_{init} is an example of hypothetical reasoning: it states that an individual Y is happy if Y will earn more than his manager currently earns, once his salary is raised (i.e. after the occurrence of the *raise* event). Without having to actually execute the *raise* update, the atom *<raise>sal (Y,S)* lets us refer to the value of *sal (Y,S)* after the occurrence of the *raise* event. Therefore, *happy (john)* will be true in the initial knowledge base (described by the history *<init>*) if in the updated knowledge base, described by the *<init,raise>* history, *salary (john ,S)* is true and $S \geq 170$. This is clearly the case. On the other hand, since in the updated *<init,raise>* knowledge base *salary (peter ,120)* remains true (there is no new information regarding the salary of peter in the *raise* event), we can not deduce that *happy (peter)* is true in the initial state of the knowledge base.□

Atoms of the form *<α>p* where *<α>* is a non-empty sequence of events can also occur in rule heads. As such they allow assertions about the future (after the occurrence of the sequence of events *<α>*), i.e. transactions.

Example 5. Consider the events *init*, *switchOn(S)*, *switchOff(S)* and *breakdown* and their associated logic programs:

P_{init} = {
        <switchOn(S)> turnedOn(S):- ¬ on(S).
        <switchOff(S)> turnedOff(S):- on(S).
        ¬ on(s₁).
        ¬ on(s₂). }

$P_{switchOn(S)}$ = { *on(S).* }

$P_{switchOff(S)}$ = { *¬ on(S).* }

$P_{breakDown}$ = {
        ¬turnedOn(S).
        ¬turnedOff(S). }

The events model a system of two on-off switches, where P_{init} is the initial knowledge base. The first rule in P_{init} states that, if at any time a switch s_i is not on, then after the execution of the *switchOn(s_i)* event, *turnedOn(s_i)* will be true (and similarly for the second rule in P_{init}). In other words, the first rule in P_{init} can be read as "in order to achieve *turnedOn(S)*, the condition *¬on(S)* should be established and the event *switchOn(S)* should be executed".

Notice that the occurrence of a *breakDown* event will disallow *turnedOn* and *turnedOff* for all installed switches until after a new *init* event happens. Also, the *breakDown* event adds non-ground rules, thus illustrating the power of the formalism to cope also with update of intentional information. In this case this feature is particularly useful as *breakDown* will affect all installed switches.

If we update the initial knowledge base with the events *switchOn(s₁)* and *switchOn(s₂)*, we reach a new state of the knowledge base described by the history *<h>* = *<init ,switchOn(s₁),switchOn(s₂)>*. The rules available in this updated state *<h>* of the knowledge base are all the rules in the update events making up the history *<h>*. Again, we must take the relative priority of the rules into account to resolve inconsistencies. Doing so we find that both *on(s₁)* and *on(s₂)* will be true in the updated knowledge base $<h>$. $\square$

We will continue with Example 5 after we have given some formal definitions. A *rule* is of the form

$$A :\!-C$$

where A is a literal, called the *head* of the rule and C is the *body*, which consists of a (possibly empty) conjunction of literals. In general we will denote the head of a rule r by $H(r)$ while $B(r)$ will denote the set of literals in the body of r. A *program* is a (possibly empty) set of rules.

A *dynamic program* is a tuple $\mathbf{P} = (P,(init,kb))$ where P is a mapping

$$P : e(\vec{X}) \rightarrow P_{e(\vec{X})}$$

from a (finite) set G of fully generic events to a set of programs, with the event $init \in G$ mapped to the initial knowledge base kb. P extends to all actual events by applying the same variable substitution throughout $e(\vec{X})$ and $P_{e(\vec{X})}$. Formally, if $e(\vec{x}) = e(\vec{X})\sigma$ for some ground substitution σ, then $P_{e(\vec{x})} = \{r\sigma \mid r \in P_{e(\vec{X})}\}$. Intuitively, $P_{e(\vec{x})}$ interprets an actual event $e(\vec{x})$ as the new information that becomes available upon the occurrence of $e(\vec{x})$. A dynamic program is "dynamic" because it allows the description not only of what is true in the present state, but also what may be true in the future, i.e. after the occurrence of any sequence of events.

A *history* $<h>$ of a dynamic program $\mathbf{P} = (P,(init,kb))$ is a sequence $<e_0, e_1, ..., e_n>$ of actual events such that

(i) $e_0 = init$ with $P_{init} = kb$

(ii) no consecutive subsequences of $<e_0, e_1, ..., e_n>$ are identical.

The last condition refines the previously introduced notion of history to take into account that those states in the (possible) evolution of the knowledge base which result from consecutive identical updates need not be considered. Indeed, it should be clear that e.g. $<e_0, e_1, e_2, e_1, e_2>$ and $<e_0, e_1, e_2>$ correspond to semantivally equivalent states of the knowledge base. Hence we can restrict ourselves to finding the model of the latter state (history) to be able to infer what is true in the former.

The *Herbrand universe* $U_{\mathbf{P}}$ of a dynamic program $\mathbf{P}$ consists of all constants which appear in any of the programs $P_{e(\vec{X})}$. Let E denote the set of all actual events that can be obtained from the set G of fully generic events using $U_{\mathbf{P}}$ for variable substitution. Then, E^*, where $*$ is Kleene's operator, denotes the set of all sequences of actual events. The *historic universe* $H_{\mathbf{P}}$ is the subset of E^* containing all histories of $\mathbf{P}$, i.e. $<h> \in E^*$ and $<h>$ satisfies the two conditions given above. Note that because of condition (ii) the set $H_{\mathbf{P}}$ is finite. The *historic Herbrand base* of $\mathbf{P}$, denoted $B_{\mathbf{P}}$, is the set of all ground atoms $<h>p(\vec{x})$ where $<h>$ is a history in $H_{\mathbf{P}}$, p is a predicate symbol in the language and $\vec{x}$ is a list of arguments from $U_{\mathbf{P}}$. $\neg B_{\mathbf{P}}$ contains all complements of the elements in $B_{\mathbf{P}}$.

Let r be a rule in P_e for some actual event $e \in E$. A ground instance of r is obtained by applying an appropriate ground substitution of all variables in r by members of $U_{\mathbf{P}}$ or E^*. We denote the set of all ground instances of rules in P_e, $e \in E$, by $ground(P_e)$.

Remember that to infer something in a state $<h>$ of the knowledge base, the rules in $ground(P_e)$, for each event e in the history $<h>$, can be used. In order to make this explicit, we will copy the rules from each $ground(P_e)$, prefixing the literals in the head and the body of each rule by $<h>$. Moreover, in order to resolve possible inconsistencies we give each such copied rule an age: the later the event e occurs in the history $<h>$, the younger the rules copied from $ground(P_e)$. Given a history $<h>$, we therefore define the set $V_{<h>}$ containing the rules "visible" in the state $<h>$ as follows. With each rule

$$<\alpha>p :- <\beta_1>q_1, ..., <\beta_k>q_k$$

in $ground(P_e)$, where e is the ith event in the history $<h>$ of length n, we form the tuple

$$(<h\,\alpha>p :- <h\,\beta_1>q_1, ..., <h\,\beta_k>q_k, \; age = n-i)$$

and add it to $V_{<h>}$. The first argument in this tuple is a copy of a rule in P_e, the second argument is the age of the copied rule. In this way all the rules in $V_{<h>}$ have an age indicating their relative priority. Note that not all rules r in $V_{<h>}$ are such that $H(r)$ is of the form $<h>p$. Some rules in $V_{<h>}$ refer to states subsequent to $<h>$.

Example 5b. Continuing Example 5, we find that for the history $<h> = <init, switchOn(s_1), switchOn(s_2)>$ of length 3, the rules in the ith event of $<h>$, ($i=1,2,3$) are copied and given age $3-i$ and all literals in the body and the head of the rules are preceded by $<h>$. By convention, the history $<h>$ followed by a sequence of events $<\alpha>$ will be denoted by $<h, \alpha>$. In this example, the set $V_{<h>}$ is therefore given by:

$$
\begin{aligned}
V_{<h>} = \{ \quad & \\
& (<h, switchOn(S)>\, turnedOn(S):- <h> \neg\, on(S)., age = 2) \\
& (<h, switchOff(S)>\, turnedOff(S):- <h>\, on(S)., age = 2) \\
& (<h> \neg\, on(s_1)., age = 2) \\
& (<h> \neg\, on(s_2)., age = 2) \\
& (<h>\, on(s_1)., age = 1) \\
& (<h>\, on(s_2)., age = 0) \; \}
\end{aligned}
$$

where, for conciseness, we have not written down the ground instances of the rules but the uninstantiated rules themselves. Note that the reference to the future in the rules in P_{init} is now expressed relative to the current state $<h>$ of the knowledge base. This has important implications. Indeed, we pointed out above that the rule

$$<switchOn(S)>\, turnedOn(S):- \neg on(S).$$

in P_{init} means "in order to achieve $turnedOn(S)$, the condition $\neg on(S)$ should be established and the event $switchOn(S)$ should be executed". However, even though we executed the events $switchOn(s_1)$ and $switchOn(s_2)$ in $<h>$, we can not establish the validity of the literals $<h>turnedOn(s_1)$ nor $<h>turnedOn(s_2)$ using the rules in $V_{<h>}$. We will need to consider the rules in previous theories $V_{<init>}$ and $V_{<init, switchOn(s_1)>}$:

$V_{<init>} = \{$

      $(<init, switchOn(S)> turnedOn(S):- <init> \neg on(S)., age = 0)$

      $(<init, switchOff(S)> turnedOff(S):- <init> on(S)., age = 0)$

      $(<init> \neg on(s_1)., age = 0)$

      $(<init> \neg on(s_2)., age = 0) \}$

$V_{<init, switchOn(s_1)>} = \{$

      $(<init,switchOn(s_1), switchOn(S)> turnedOn(S):-$

               $<init,switchOn(s_1)> \neg on(S)., age = 1)$

      $(<init,switchOn(s_1), switchOff(S)> turnedOff(S):-$

               $<init,switchOn(s_1)> on(S)., age = 1)$

      $(<init,switchOn(s_1)> \neg on(s_1)., age = 1)$

      $(<init,switchOn(s_1)> \neg on(s_2)., age = 1)$

      $(<init,switchOn(s_1)> on(s_1)., age = 0) \}$

The first two rules in both $V_{<init>}$ and $V_{<init,switchOn(s_1)>}$ refer to states of the knowledge base which are subsequent to $<init>$ and $<init,switchOn(s_1)>$. In other words, they contain rules with which it is possible to infer information about future states of $<init>$ and $<init,switchOn(s_1)>$, in casu $<h>$. For example, we can conclude $<h>turnedOn(s_2)$ by applying the first rule in $V_{<init,switchOn(s_1)>}$ with $S=s_2$. Still, there is no rule to infer $<h>turnedOn(s_1)$. However, there is a rule in $V_{<init>}$ whose head is of the form $<h_1>turnedOn(s_1)$ where $<h_1> = <init,switchOn(s_1)>$ is an initial subsequence of $<h>$. This rule permits to establish the truth of $turnedOn(s_1)$ in $<h_1>$. We believe that, unless new information overrules the application of this rule, it should also enable us to infer the truth of $turnedOn(s_1)$ in states subsequent to $<h_1>$□

We formalize this as follows. For each history $<\eta>$ representing a state prior to $<h>$ and for each tuple in $V_{<\eta>}$ of the form

$$(<\eta\alpha>p :- <\eta\beta_1>q_1, ..., <\eta\beta_k>q_k, age = j)$$

where $<h> = <\eta\alpha\gamma>$, we extend the sequence of events in the head and the body of the rule with the sequence of events $<\gamma> \in E^*$ to obtain the tuple

$$(<h>p :- <\eta\beta_1\gamma>q_1, ..., <\eta\beta_k\gamma>q_k, age = j+|<\gamma>|)$$

The literals in the body of the rule are extended with the sequence of events $<\gamma>$ in order to make sure that the new rule only be applicable if $<\gamma>$ does not introduce contradicting information. Also, the age of the new rule equals the age of the original rule incremented by the length of $<\gamma>$. The point of generating these new rules is to make sure that rules operational in a particular state remain operational in any subsequent state. All rules generated in this way are grouped in the set $C_{<h>}$. Note that all rules in $C_{<h>}$ refer to the state $<h>$.

Example 5c. Continuing Example 5, one of the rules in $C_{<h>}$ where $<h> = <init,switchOn(s_1),switchOn(s_2)>$, is constructed from the first rule in $V_{<init>}$:

$$(<init,switchOn(s_1)> turnedOn(s_1) :- <init> \neg on(s_1)., age = 0)$$

yielding

$$(<init, switchOn\,(s_1), switchOn\,(s_2)>turnedOn\,(s_1) :-$$
$$<init, switchOn\,(s_2)> \neg on\,(s_1)., age = 1)$$

from which $<h>turnedOn\,(s_1)$ can be inferred (since there are no overrulers in this case). □

All the rules in $\cup_i V_{<h_i>}$, together with all the rules in $\cup_i C_{<h_i>}$, $<h_i> \in H_P$, will determine what is true in any history $<h>$, where $<h>$ reflects a sequence of consecutive updates of the initial knowledge base kb. We will denote the subset of rules which refer to the state $<h>$ by

$$R_{<h>} = \{r \mid H(r)=<h>p \text{ and } r \in \cup_i V_{<h_i>} \cup C_{<h>}\}$$

3. Semantics of dynamic programs

Given a particular history $<h>$, let $L_{<h>}$ be the subset of $B_P \cup \neg B_P$ containing all ground literals of the form $<h>p$ referring to the state $<h>$. An *interpretation* of a dynamic program P is a function

$$I : <h> \rightarrow I\,(<h>) \subseteq L_{<h>}$$

that associates with each history $<h>$ in H_P a set $I\,(<h>)$ of ground literals in $L_{<h>}$.

In order for $I\,(<h>)$ to correctly reflect what is true in the state $<h>$ of the dynamic program P all rules in $R_{<h>}$ should be satisfied in I. In traditional logic programming, the term "satisfied" means "every applicable rule is applied". In dynamic programming this is only partially true because negation in the head is allowed and possible inconsistencies must be resolved. This can be done by introducing a preference order among rules[Lae90a, Lae90b, Lae91a] such that possible contradictions are resolved using the chosen preference criterion. As illustrated in the examples above, we use the age of a rule as preference criterion by accepting the following natural assumption: younger rules are more up to date and, therefore, they may make obsolete the contribution of older ones. In order to deal with this additional aspect of preference among rules we need the following concepts[Lae90a, Lae90b, Lae91a].

Let I be an interpretation of a dynamic program P and $<h>$ a history. A rule r in $R_{<h>}$ is said to be

- *applicable* in I if for each $<\beta>q \in B\,(r)$, $<\beta>q \in I\,(<\beta>)$
- *applied* in I if r is applicable in I and $H\,(r) \in I\,(<h>)$
- a *competitor* for another rule r' if $H\,(r)=\neg H\,(r')$ and $age\,(r) \leq age\,(r')$
- *defeated* in I if there exists an applicable competitor $\hat{r}$ of r in $R_{<h>}$
- *defeasible* in I if there exists a competitor $\hat{r}$ of r in $R_{<h>}$ such that $B\,(\hat{r})$ contains no unfounded literals w.r.t. I.

Intuitively, the notion of defeasible relaxes the notion of defeated: instead of demanding that a rule's competitor be applicable, defeasible only requires that the literals in the body of the competitor are not "unfounded" [Gel88a, Lae90a]. A literal is said to be unfounded w.r.t. an interpretation I if it is neither true nor undefined [Ben00a, You90a] w.r.t. the interpretation. More formally, a non-empty subset X of $B_P \cup \neg B_P$ is an *unfounded set* w.r.t. an interpretation I if for each $<h>p$ in X, it holds that every rule r in $R_{<h>}$ with $H(r)=<h>p$ either is defeated in I or has $B(r) \cap X \neq \varnothing$.

The *greatest unfounded set* of P with respect to an interpretation I, denoted $U(I)$, is the union of all unfounded sets of P w.r.t. I.

We will illustrate these concepts with the following example.

Example 6.

$P_{init} = \{$
    $empSal(x_1, s_1).$
    $empSal(x_2, s_2).$
    ...
    $<raise(R), confirm> raiseAll(R) :- R \geq 0.$
$\}$

$P_{raise(R)} = \{$
    $<confirm> empSal(X,NS) :- empSal(X,S), NS = S + R * S.$
    $<confirm> \neg empSal(X,S) :- empSal(X,S).$
$\}$

$P_{confirm} = \{\}$

In the *raise* event, new information is asserted "in the future", i.e. after the occurrence of the *confirm* event. Note that this dynamic program emulates primitive update specifications as defined in [Man89a] without using special symbols to denote the previous and new literals. In fact, a same effect is achieved through the combination of the *raise* and *confirm* events. The different sets $V_{<h>}$, $C_{<h>}$ and $R_{<h>}$ for the history $<h> = <init, raise(0.1), confirm>$ and its initial subsequences are given below. For conciseness, we have written down the rules themselves instead of their ground instances.

$V_{<init>} = \{ (<init> empSal(x_1, s_1)., age = 0)$
    $(<init> empSal(x_2, s_2)., age = 0)$
    ...
    $(<init, raise(R), confirm> raiseAll(R) :- <init> R \geq 0., age = 0) \}$
$V_{<init, raise(0.1)>} = \{ (<init, raise(0.1)> empSal(x_1, s_1)., age = 1)$
    $(<init, raise(0.1)> empSal(x_2, s_2)., age = 1)$
    ...
    $(<init, raise(0.1), raise(R), confirm> raiseAll(R) :-$
        $<init, raise(0.1)> R \geq 0., age = 1)$
    $(<init, raise(0.1), confirm> empSal(X,NS) :-$
        $<init, raise(0.1)> empSal(X,S),$
        $<init, raise(0.1)> NS = S + R * S., age = 0)$
    $(<init, raise(0.1), confirm> \neg empSal(X,S) :-$
        $<init, raise(0.1)> empSal(X,S)., age = 0) \}$

$V_{<h>} = \{\ (<h> \ empSal(x_1,s_1)., age = 2)$
$\quad\quad (<h> \ empSal(x_2,s_2)., age = 2)$
$\quad\quad ...$
$\quad\quad (<h, raise(R), confirm> \ raiseAll(R) \ :- \ <h> \ R \geq 0., age = 2)$
$\quad\quad (<h, confirm> \ empSal(X,NS) \ :-$
$\quad\quad\quad\quad\quad\quad <h> \ empSal(X,S),$
$\quad\quad\quad\quad\quad\quad <h> \ NS = S + R * S., age = 1)$
$\quad\quad (<h, confirm> \ \neg empSal(X,S) \ :-$
$\quad\quad\quad\quad\quad\quad <h> \ empSal(X,S)., age = 1) \ \}$

$C_{<h>} = \{$
$\quad\quad (<h> \ empSal(x_1,s_1)., age = 2)$
$\quad\quad (<h> \ empSal(x_2,s_2)., age = 2)$
$\quad\quad ... \ \}$

$R_{<h>} = \{$
$\quad\quad (<h> \ raiseAll(0.1) \ :- \ <init> \ 0.1 \geq 0., age = 0)$
$\quad\quad (<h> \ empSal(X,NS) \ :-$
$\quad\quad\quad\quad <init, raise(0.1)> \ empSal(X,S),$
$\quad\quad\quad\quad <init, raise(0.1)> \ NS = S + R * S., age = 0)$
$\quad\quad (<h> \ \neg empSal(X,S) \ :-$
$\quad\quad\quad\quad <init, raise(0.1)> \ empSal(X,S)., age = 0)$
$\quad\quad (<h> \ empSal(x_1,s_1)., age = 2)$
$\quad\quad (<h> \ empSal(x_2,s_2)., age = 2)$
$\quad\quad ... \ \} \cup C_{<h>}$

Note that the third rule in $R_{<h>}$ is a competitor of the facts in $R_{<h>}$ since its age is smaller. A possible interpretation of this dynamic program would map the history $<h>$ to the set of literals

$$I(<h>) = \{\ <h> \ empSal(x_1,s_1), \ <h> \ empSal(x_2,s_2*1.1),$$
$$<h> \ \neg empSal(x_2,s_2), \ <h> \ empSal(x_1,s_1*1.21) \ \}$$

Given an interpretation I, a rule r in $R_{<h>}$ is *satisfied* in I if r is either applied in I, not applicable in I or defeasible in I. Note that whether or not a rule r in $R_{<h>}$ is satisfied in I, depends not only on the set $I(<h>)$ but also on sets $I(<h_1>)$, where $<h_1>$ is another history (reflecting postconditions and hypothetical reasoning).

An interpretation M for a dynamic program $\mathbf{P}$ is said to be a *model* for $\mathbf{P}$ if for each history $<h>$, $M(<h>)$ is a consistent set of literals (i.e. it contains no two complementary literals) and each rule $r \in R_{<h>}$ is satisfied in M.

Example 7. The interpretation I where $I(<init, raise(0.1), confirm>)$ is as in Example 6 and where

$$I(<init, raise(0.1)>) = \{ <init, raise(0.1)> empSal(x_1, s_1),$$
$$<init, raise(0.1)> empSal(x_2, s_2) \}$$

does not satisfy the definition of model. Indeed, the second and third rule in $R_{<h>}$ with $X = x_1$ and $S = s_1$ are applicable but not applied nor defeasible in I. In order for I to become a model M these rules have to be applied in M (neither of the rules can be defeasible in M since they have no competitors) and hence $<h>empSal(x_1, s_1 * 1.1)$ and $<h>\neg empSal(x_1, s_1)$ must be in $M(<h>)$. As a consequence, $<h>empSal(x_1, s_1)$ must be removed from the interpretation $I(<h>)$. Note that the fact $<h>empSal(x_1, s_1)$ is defeasible in M. A possible model M therefore maps the history $<h> = <init, raise(0.1), confirm>$ to

$$M(<h>) = \{<h> empSal(x_1, s_1 * 1.1), <h> empSal(x_2, s_2 * 1.1),$$
$$<h> \neg empSal(x_2, s_2), <h> \neg empSal(x_1, s_1),$$
$$<h> empSal(x_1, s_1 * 1.21) \}$$

Intuitively, a model M of a dynamic program $\mathbf{P}$ guarantees that there are no rules which definitely should, and are not applied in M. However, a model may not correctly reflect what is true in that it may contain literals that cannot be actually inferred. In order to formalize this intuition, we introduce the notion of assumption set[Lae90a].

Let $\mathbf{P}$ be a dynamic program and M a model of $\mathbf{P}$. A subset X of $\cup_{<h>} M(<h>)$ is said to be an *assumption set* of $\mathbf{P}$ w.r.t. M if for each $<h>p$ in X, every rule in $R_{<h>}$ with $H(r) = <h>p$ satisfies one of the following conditions:

- r is non-applicable in I, or
- r is defeated in I, or
- r is defeasible in I, or
- $B(r) \cap X \neq \varnothing$.

The *greatest assumption set* of $\mathbf{P}$ with respect to a model M, denoted $A(M)$, is the union of all assumption sets of $\mathbf{P}$ w.r.t. M. An element of $A(M)$ is said to be an *assumption*. M is said to be assumption free iff $A(M) = \varnothing$.

It seems natural to restrict our attention to assumption free models only, since models with assumptions do not correctly reflect the meaning of the dynamic program.

Extending the result of [Lae90a, Lae91a] it can be shown that an assumption free model of a dynamic program $\mathbf{P}$ always exists, and that, if several such assumption free models exist, there is always a smallest model according to the $\subseteq$ partial order. The intended meaning of a dynamic program $\mathbf{P}$ is correctly reflected by this smallest assumption free model, also called *well-founded* (partial) model. The well-founded model can be computed using the fixpoint operator $W_{\mathbf{P}}$ defined by $W_{\mathbf{P}}(I) = \{<h>p \mid \exists$ rule r in $R_{<h>}$ such that $H(r) = <h>p$, r is applicable in I and non-defeasible in $I\}$.

We can show that $W_{\mathbf{P}}(\varnothing)$ is exactly the well-founded model of $\mathbf{P}$.

Example 8. The model given in Example 7 above contains the assumption $<h>empSal(x_1, s_1 * 1.12)$. The well-founded model of the dynamic program maps

$<h> = <init, raise\ (0.1), confirm>$ to

$$M(<h>) = \{<h>\ empSal(x_1, s_1 * 1.1),\ <h>\ empSal(x_2, s_2 * 1.1),$$
$$<h>\ \neg empSal(x_2, s_2),\ <h>\ \neg empSal(x_1, s_1)\ \}$$

4. Evolution of Dynamic Programs

Up to now, the semantics of dynamic programs enable us to pose "what-if" queries such as $<\eta>p$, i.e. "will p hold if the events in the history $<\eta>$ were to occur?".

In the present section, we describe how the actual evolution of a dynamic program can be specified. To this end, we introduce a function called *assert* which takes a dynamic program P, a history $<\eta>$ of P and a sequence of events $<\gamma>$ as input, yielding a new state of the dynamic program $<\eta\gamma>$. In a sense, an application of *assert* $(P, <\eta>, <\gamma>)$ corresponds to singling out the evolution indicated by $<\gamma>$ and to remove all alternatives, thus freezing part of the future of P (see Figure 1).

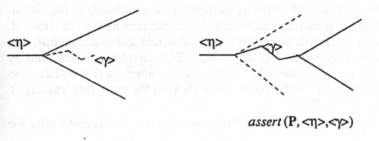

$$assert\ (P, <\eta>, <\gamma>)$$

Figure 1.

The above function is defined for any sequence of actual events $<\gamma> \in E^*$, which is to be provided ad hoc by the user. However, the user can also let a dynamic program evolve by using its rules, thus allowing only those evolutions that are sanctioned by the program. This may be useful, as the rules can be designed in such a way so as not to violate certain (static or dynamic) integrity constraints. Indeed, a rule $<\alpha>t :- C$ at an actual event $e \in E$ can intuitively be interpreted as "t will hold if the program is subjected to the sequence of events $<\alpha>$ and moreover, C holds". (Note that literals in C may refer to the present or future situations). Thus classical literals t that appear in (the head of) rules of the form $<\alpha_i>t :- C_i$ may be regarded as *transactions* whose possible effects are determined by the futures $<\alpha_i>$. The next example shows an interesting use of nondeterministic transactions.

Example 9. Consider the dynamic program of Example 5, where the *init* event is extended with the rule

$$<switchOn\ (S)>\ moreLight\ :-\ \neg on\ (S).$$

By querying $?\ <X>\ moreLight$ one of the switches that were off will be turned on and

$<X>$ will be bound to either $<init,switchOn(s_1)>$ or $<init,switchOn(s_2)>$. Note that the nondeterminism is restricted since only minimal, w.r.t. the lexicographical ordering on histories, solutions will be returned.□

Example 10. As another example of nondeterminism, consider the classical problem of graph orientation, which is solved by the following dynamic program.

$P_{installGraph}$ = {
    arc(a,b).
    ... }
$P_{removeArc(X,Y)}$ = { ¬ arc(X,Y). }
P_{init} = {
    ¬moreDoubleArcs.
    moreDoubleArcs :- arc(X,Y), arc(Y,X).
    <removeArc(X,Y),H> orientGraph :-
        arc(X,Y), arc(Y,X), <removeArc(X,Y), H > orientGraph.
    orientGraph :-
        ¬moreDoubleArcs.
    }

In P_{init}, *moreDoubleArcs* is non-inferrable since there is a contradicting fact for it. Similarly ¬ *moreDoubleArcs* is non-inferrable until all double arcs have been removed. At that time ¬ *moreDoubleArcs* will be the only applicable rule and hence be true. The first rule for *orientGraph* may seem circular at first. This circularity is removed by keeping in mind that the rule is still valid after any update, so *<removeArc(x,y),H>orientGraph* in the body will unify with the same rule, causing H to unify with *<removeArc(X,Y),H'>*.

Note that in[Abi90a] an explicit nondeterministic "witness" operator is needed to solve the above problem.□

5. Conclusion

In this paper we have presented the basic properties of a simple yet powerful formalism for modeling the evolution of knowledge bases. The semantics are based on the fundamental intuition that more recent information overrides previous knowledge. Combining this with the techniques from logic programming and ordered logic semantics, yields a notion of model that nicely extends the semantics of ordinary logic programming and supports both what-if reasoning and transactions. Current work is devoted to designing effective algorithms, including a top-down procedure for computing the well-founded model, as well as plans for reaching desirable states. Moreover, the formalism can be extended to capture also parallel execution of updates. Finally, we point out that the algorithms for finding the well-founded model of particular classes of dynamic programs are currently being implemented as part of the LOCO [Lae90c] language within the framework of the KIWIS project.

244

References

Abi90a.
S. Abiteboul, E. Simon, and V. Vianu, "Non-deterministic Languages to express Deterministic Transformations," in *Proc. of the Symposium on Principles of Database Systems*, pp. 218-230, 1990.

Abi88a.
S. Abiteboul, "Updates, a New Frontier," in *Proc. of the 2nd International Conference on Database Theory*, pp. 1-18, 1988.

Ben00a.
M. Ben-Jacob and M. Fitting, "Stratified and three-valued logic programming semantics," in *Proc. 5th Int. Conf. and Symp. on Logic Programming*, pp. 1054-1068, 1988.

Gel88a.
A. Van Gelder, K. Ross, and J. S. Schlipf, *The Well-Founded Semantics for General Logic Programs*, 1988. UCSC-CRL-88-16

Kri63a.
S. Kripke, "Semantic analysis of modal logic I, normal propositional calculi," *Zeitschrift fur mathematische Logik und Grundlagen der Mathematik*, vol. 9, pp. 67-96, 1963.

Lae91a.
E. Laenens and D. Vermeir, "On the Relationship between Well-Founded and Stable Partial Models," in *Proc. of the Mathematical Fundamentals of Database and Knowledge Base Systems*, 1991.

Lae90c.
E. Laenens, B. Verdonk, D. Vermeir, and D. Sacca, "The LOCO language: towards an integration of logic and object oriented programming," *Proc. of the Workshop on Logic Programming and Non-Monotonic Reasoning*, pp. 62-73, Austin, Texas, 1990.

Lae90a.
E. Laenens, *Foundations of Ordered Logic*, 1990. Ph.D. Thesis, University of Antwerp UIA

Lae90b.
E. Laenens, D. Sacca, and D. Vermeir, "Extending logic programming," in *Proc. of the ACM-SIGMOD conference*, pp. 184-193, 1990.

Man89a.
S. Manchanda, "Declarative Expression of Deductive Database Updates," in *Proc. of the 1989 Symposium on Principles of Database Systems*, pp. 93-100, 1989.

Man87a.
S. Manchanda and D. S. Warren, "A Logic-based Language for Database Updates," in *Deductive Databases and Logic Programming*, pp. 363-394, 1987.

Naq88a.
S. Naqvi and R. Krishnamurthy, "Database Updates in Logic Programming," in *Proc. of the Symposium on Principles of Database Systems*, pp. 251-262, 1988.

Via87a.
V. Vianu, "Dynamic functional dependencies and database aging," *Journal of the ACM*, vol. 34, no. 1, pp. 28-59, 1987.

Via88a.
V. Vianu, "A Dynamic Framework for Object Projection Views," *ACM Transactions on Database Systems*, vol. 13, no. 1, pp. 1-22, 1988.

You90a.
Jia-Huai You and Li Yan Yuan, "Three-Valued Formalization of Logic Programming: Is It Needed?," in *Proc. of the Symposium on Principles of Database Systems*, pp. 172-182, 1990.

The Events Method
for View Updating in Deductive Databases

Ernest Teniente   Antoni Olivé
Universitat Politècnica de Catalunya
Facultat d'Informàtica
Pau Gargallo 5
E-08028 Barcelona - Catalonia

Abstract

We propose a new method for view updating in deductive databases. The method is based on events and transition rules, which explicitly define the insertions and deletions induced by a database update. Using these rules, an extension of the SLDNF procedure allows us to obtain all valid translations of view update requests. The main advantages of the method are its simplicity, the uniform treatment of insert and delete requests and the integration of integrity checking during the derivation process. The method has the full power of the methods developed so far, without some of their limitations.

1. Introduction

The view update problem of relational and deductive databases has attracted a lot of research during the past years [1,2,5,6,7,8,9,11,13,16]. The aim is to provide effective methods for translating view updates into (correct) database updates.

Two basic approaches have been proposed to solve the problem. The first suggests treating views as **abstract data types**, so that the definition of a view includes all permissible view updates together with their translation. The second approach is to define a general translation procedure (a translator). Inputs to the translator are a view definition, a view update and the current database, and the output is a database update that translate the view update, satisfying some properties [7]. In this paper, we follow the translator approach.

Bancilhon and Spyratos [2] proposed an elegant method for defining translators in the context of relational databases. In their approach, a translator is a mapping that associates with each view update a unique database update called a "translation". The translation takes the database to a state mapping onto the updated view, and leaving invariant the information not visible within the view.

Tomasic's method [16] deals with view updates in definite deductive databases. He proposes procedures based on SLD-resolution for computing translations. These procedures provide a basis for methods which reduce the number of translations.

Decker's method [6] deals with view updates in deductive databases. In this method, updates for delete requests are drawn from SLDNF derivations. For insert requests, not all possible updates that satisfy a view update request may be obtained using SLDNF resolution, thus the method defines "view updates trees", from which a complete set of database updates can be drawn. However, completeness of such updates is relative, in the sense that valid database updates which are not obtained by the method may exist.

Kakas and Mancarella's [11] method deals also with view updates in deductive databases. The problem is approached by casting it into an abductive framework. A common procedure for insert and delete update requests is defined, and its correctness and completeness is investigated.

Guessoum and Lloyd's [8,9] method provides another approach to view updating. In the first version of the method [8], procedures for deleting an atom from a normal program and inserting an atom into a normal program are presented. Various properties of these procedures included their correctness are proved. In a later version [9], these procedures are generalized such that the deletion procedure calls the insertion procedure and the insertion procedure calls the deletion procedure, thus providing mutually recursive versions of the update procedures. The intensional database must satisfy a "strictness" condition in order to avoid the problem of solutions invalidated due to negation. Moreover, valid solutions which are not obtained by the method may exist.

We propose here a new method for view updating in deductive databases, which we call the Events Method. The method is an application of an approach developed [14] for the design of information systems from deductive conceptual models. A different application to integrity checking in deductive databases is presented in [15]. The database is augmented with a set of rules, called transition and events rules, which explicitly define the insertions and deletions (view updates) induced by a database update. SLDNF resolution can then be used to translate a view update into database updates.

The paper is organized as follows. The next section reviews basic concepts of deductive databases. Section 3, which is based on [15], reviews the key concept of event, and the method for deriving transition and events rules. Section 4 discusses the application of these rules in the view update problem. In section 5 other features of the method are presented. In Section 6, we compare our method with some of the above methods. Finally, in Section 7 we present our conclusions. We assume the reader is familiar with logic programming.

2. Deductive Databases

A deductive database D consists of three finite sets: a set F of facts, a set R of deductive rules, and a set I of integrity constraints. A relational database is a deductive database without deductive rules. A fact is a ground atom. The set of facts is called the *extensional* database (EDB), and the set of deductive rules is called the *intensional* database (IDB).

We assume that database predicates are partitioned into view (derived) predicates and base predicates. A base predicate appears only in the EDB and (eventually) in the body of deductive rules. A view predicate appears only in the IDB. Every database can be defined in this form [3].

2.1 Deductive rules

A deductive rule is a formula of the form:
$$A \leftarrow L_1 \wedge ... \wedge L_n \quad \text{with } n \geq 1$$
where A is an atom and the L_1 ,..., L_n are literals (that is, atoms or negated atoms). Any variables in A, L_1 ,..., L_n are assumed to be universally quantified over the whole formula. A is called the *conclusion* of the rule and the L_1 ,..., L_n the *conditions*. The terms in the conclusion must be distinct variables, and the terms in the conditions must be variables or constants.

As usual [6], we require that the database before and after any updates is allowed, that is any variable that occurs in a deductive rule has an occurrence in a positive condition of the rule. This ensures that all negative conditions can be fully instantiated before they are evaluated by the "negation as failure" rule.

2.2 Integrity constraints

An integrity constraint is a closed first-order formula that the database is required to satisfy. We deal with constraints that have the form of a *denial*:

$$\leftarrow L_1 \wedge \ldots \wedge L_n \quad \text{with } n \geq 1$$

where the L_i are literals and variables are assumed to be universally quantified over the whole formula. For the sake of uniformity, we (as in [12]) associate to each integrity constraint an inconsistency predicate Icn, and thus it has the same form as the deductive rules. We call them *integrity rules*. The above denial would be rewritten as $Ic1 \leftarrow L_1 \wedge \ldots \wedge L_n$

3. Transition and Events Rules

In this section, we shortly review the concepts and terminology of events, transition and events rules, as presented in [15]. In next section we will apply them to develop a new method for view updating.

3.1 Events

Let D be a database, P a predicate in D, T a transaction, D' the updated database and P' the predicate P evaluated in D'. The application of T to D produces D'. We say that T induces a transition from D to D'. In general, the application of T will change the extension of database predicates. We formalize these changes with the concept of event.

For each database predicate P we define two meta predicates ιP and δP, called insertion (event) predicate and deletion (event) predicate, respectively, defined as:

(1) $\forall x(\iota P(x) \leftrightarrow P'(x) \wedge \neg P(x))$

(2) $\forall x(\delta P(x) \leftrightarrow P(x) \wedge \neg P'(x))$

where x is a vector of variables. From the above, we have:

(3) $\forall x(P'(x) \leftrightarrow (P(x) \wedge \neg \delta P(x)) \vee \iota P(x))$

(4) $\forall x(\neg P'(x) \leftrightarrow (\neg P(x) \wedge \neg \iota P(x)) \vee \delta P(x))$

If P is a base predicate, then ιP and δP facts represent insertions and deletions of base facts, given by T. If P is a derived predicate, then ιP and δP facts represent insertions and deletions induced by T. Finally, if P is an inconsistency predicate, then ιP facts represent violations of its integrity constraint (for inconsistency predicates, δP is not defined).We say that an insertion ιP or deletion δP predicate is base (resp. derived) if P is base (resp. derived).

3.2 Transition rules

Let us take a derived or inconsistency predicate P of the database. The definition of P consists of the rules in the database having P in the conclusion. Assume that there are m (m$\geq$ 1) such rules. For our purposes, we rename predicate symbols in the conclusions of the m rules by $P_1, \ldots, P_m$, and add the set of clauses:

(5) $P \leftarrow P_i \qquad i = 1 \ldots m$

Consider now one of the rules $P_i(x) \leftarrow L_1 \wedge \ldots \wedge L_n$. When the rule is evaluated in the new state, its form is $P'_i(x) \leftarrow L'_1 \wedge \ldots \wedge L'_n$. If we replace each literal in the body by an equivalent expression in terms of the old state and the events, we get a new rule, called a *transition rule*, which defines the new state predicate P'_i in terms of the old state predicate P_i and events predicates.

More precisely, if L'_j is a positive literal $Q'_j(x_j)$ we apply (3) and replace it by:

$$(Q_j(x_j) \wedge \neg \delta Q_j(x_j)) \vee \iota Q_j(x_j)$$

and if L'_j is a negative literal $\neg Q'_j(x_j)$ we apply (4) and replace it by:

$$(\neg Q_j(x_j) \wedge \neg \iota Q_j(x_j)) \vee \delta Q_j(x_j)$$

After distributing $\wedge$ over $\vee$, we get the set of transition rules for P'_i.

Example: Let the rule $P_1(x) \leftarrow Q(x) \wedge \neg R(x)$. Replacing $Q'(x)$ and $\neg R'(x)$ by their equivalent expressions given by (3) and (4) we get:

$$P'_1(x) \leftarrow [(Q(x) \wedge \neg \delta Q(x)) \vee \iota Q(x)] \wedge [(\neg R(x) \wedge \neg \iota R(x)) \vee \delta R(x)]$$

which is transformed into:

$$P'_{1,1}(x) \leftarrow Q(x) \wedge \neg \delta Q(x) \wedge \neg R(x) \wedge \neg \iota R(x)$$
$$P'_{1,2}(x) \leftarrow Q(x) \wedge \neg \delta Q(x) \wedge \delta R(x)$$
$$P'_{1,3}(x) \leftarrow \iota Q(x) \wedge \neg R(x) \wedge \neg \iota R(x)$$
$$P'_{1,4}(x) \leftarrow \iota Q(x) \wedge \delta R(x)$$

with: $\quad P'_1(x) \leftarrow P'_{1,j}(x) \quad j = 1..4$

In general, if the body of the P_i rule has n literals we get 2^n transition rules for P_i.

3.3 Insertion events rules

Let P be a derived or inconsistency predicate. Insertion predicates ιP were defined in (1) as:

$$\forall x(\iota P(x) \leftrightarrow P'(x) \wedge \neg P(x))$$

If there are m rules for predicate P, then by (5) $P'(x) \leftrightarrow P'_1(x) \vee ... \vee P'_m(x)$, and replacing $P'(x)$ we obtain: $\quad \iota P(x) \leftarrow P'_i(x) \wedge \neg P(x) \quad i = 1 ... m$

and replacing again $P'_i(x)$ by its transition rules we get:

(6) $\quad \iota P(x) \leftarrow P'_{i,j}(x) \wedge \neg P(x) \qquad i = 2 ... m, \quad j = 1 ... 2^n$

The set of rules (6) above is called the *insertion events rules* for predicate P. They allow us to deduce which ιP facts (induced insertions) happen in a transition. Rules (6) can be simplified in several ways. We refer the reader to [15]. Note that in particular we ommit insertion rules corresponding to j=1. The reason is that they can not produce ιP facts (see [15]).

3.4 Deletion events rules

Let P be a derived predicate. Deletion predicates δP were defined in (2) as:

$$\forall x(\delta P(x) \leftrightarrow P(x) \wedge \neg P'(x))$$

If there are m rules for predicate P, we then have:

$$\delta P(x) \leftarrow P_i(x) \wedge \neg P'(x) \qquad i = 1 ... m$$

and replacing $P'(x)$ by its equivalent definition given in (5) we obtain:

(7) $\quad \delta P(x) \leftarrow P_i(x) \wedge \neg P'_1(x) \wedge ... \wedge \neg P'_i(x) \wedge ... \wedge \neg P'_m(x) \quad$ for $i = 1 ... m$

In [15] we show how rules (7) can be simplified in the general case. Here, we are mainly interested in the case when all variables appearing in the conditions of the rule $P_i(x) \leftarrow L_1 \wedge ... \wedge L_n$ are a subset of x. In this case, rules (7) are equivalent to:

(8) $\quad \delta P(x) \leftarrow L_1 \wedge ... \wedge L_{j-1} \wedge [\delta L_j | \iota L_j] \wedge L_{j+1} \wedge... \wedge L_n \wedge$
$$\neg P'_1(x) \wedge ... \wedge \neg P'_{i-1}(x) \wedge \neg P'_{i+1}(x) \wedge... \wedge \neg P'_m(x)$$
$$\text{for } i = 1 ... m, \text{ and } j = 1 ... n$$

where the first option (δL_j) is taken if L_j is positive, and the second one (ιL_j) if negative

This set of rules is called the *deletion events rules* for predicate P. They allow us to deduce which δP facts (induced deletions) happen in a transition.

Example: Let the only rule for P be P(x) ← Q(x)∧¬R. Then, the deletion rules for P are:

$$\delta P(x) \leftarrow \delta Q(x) \wedge \neg R$$
$$\delta P(x) \leftarrow Q(x) \wedge \iota R$$

4. View Updating

4.1 Our approach

We now focus on the problem of view updating in deductive databases. This problem is a generalization of the view update problem of relational databases, which is concerned with determining how a request to update a view can be appropriately translated into an update of the underlying relations (see [1,2,5,7]).

Usually, there are several ways of satisfying an update request. Our approach consists in generating all possible minimal translations for a given update request. We consider only translations that consist of insertions and deletions of ground facts of base predicates. For this reason, updates on the intensional database (deletion, insertion or modification of rules, insertion of ground facts of view predicates, etc) are not considered here. There are several reasons that motivate why a view update request should be effected by changing the extensional database only: see for example [6,11]. We require the solutions to be minimal in the sense that no proper subset of them is itself a solution. Several different minimal solutions may exist to satisfy an update request. The problem of how to choose between them will not be addressed in this paper. Some comments can be found in [10,11].

For simplicity of presentation we assume that a view update request is either an insert request or a delete request. In our method, an insert (resp. delete) request u corresponds to a fact ιP(K) (resp. δP(K)), where P'(K) is the fact that must hold (resp. must not hold) in the new database. A translation of u, denoted T, defines a set of insertions and/or deletions of base facts such that if u is an insert request ιP(K) (resp. delete request δP(K)), P'(K) is (resp. is not) a logical consequence of the completion of the database updated according to T.

Let D be a database and let us denote by A(D) the augmented database consisting of the database D and its transition and events rules. Let T be a translation consisting on a set of base events. Using SLDNF proof procedure, T satisfies the update request u if the goal {←u} succeeds from input set A(D) ∪ T. A translation T can be obtained by having some failed derivation of A(D) ∪ {←u} succeed. This is effected by including in the input set of clauses a ground instance of each literal corresponding to a positive base event selected during the derivation. T will contain these selected base events. The following examples illustrate our approach. We give the formal definition of the method in section 4.4.

4.2 A first example

Let D be a database containing the following facts, deductive rules and integrity constraints (where Q, R, S and T are base predicates):

F.1	S(B)	
F.2	T(C)	
DR.1	P(x) ← Q(x) ∧ ¬R(x)	
DR.2	P(x) ↤ S(x)	
IC.1	Ic1 ← Q(C) ∧ T(C)	

The transition, insertion and deletion events rules associated to this database are:

T.1 $P'_{1,1}(x) \leftarrow Q(x) \wedge \neg\delta Q(x) \wedge \neg R(x) \wedge \neg\iota R(x)$

T.2 $P'_{1,2}(x) \leftarrow Q(x) \wedge \neg\delta Q(x) \wedge \delta R(x)$

T.3 $P'_{1,3}(x) \leftarrow \iota Q(x) \wedge \neg R(x) \wedge \neg\iota R(x)$

T.4 $P'_{1,4}(x) \leftarrow \iota Q(x) \wedge \delta R(x)$

T.5 $P'_{2,1}(x) \leftarrow S(x) \wedge \neg\delta S(x)$

T.6 $P'_{2,2}(x) \leftarrow \iota S(x)$

T.7 $Ic1'_{1,1} \leftarrow Q(C) \wedge \neg\delta Q(C) \wedge T(C) \wedge \neg\delta T(C)$

T.8 $Ic1'_{1,2} \leftarrow Q(C) \wedge \neg\delta Q(C) \wedge \iota T(C)$

T.9 $Ic1'_{1,3} \leftarrow \iota Q(C) \wedge T(C) \wedge \neg\delta T(C)$

T.10 $Ic1'_{1,4} \leftarrow \iota Q(C) \wedge \iota T(C)$

I.1...3 $\iota P(x) \leftarrow P'_{1,j}(x) \wedge \neg P(x)$ $j = 2 ... 4$

I.4 $\iota P(x) \leftarrow P'_{2,j}(x) \wedge \neg P(x)$ $j = 2$

I.5...7 $\iota Ic1 \leftarrow Ic1'_{1,j}$ $j = 2 ... 4$

D.1 $\delta P(x) \leftarrow \delta Q(x) \wedge \neg R(x) \wedge \neg P'_{2,1}(x) \wedge \neg P'_{2,2}(x)$

D.2 $\delta P(x) \leftarrow Q(x) \wedge \iota R(x) \wedge \neg P'_{2,1}(x) \wedge \neg P'_{2,2}(x)$

D.3 $\delta P(x) \leftarrow \delta S(x) \wedge \neg P'_{1,1}(x) \wedge \neg P'_{1,2}(x) \wedge \neg P'_{1,3}(x) \wedge \neg P'_{1,4}(x)$

Let the view update request be the derived event $\iota P(A)$. This means that $P'(A)$ must be true in the new database. Possible view updates that satisfy the update request are insert($Q(A)$) and insert($S(A)$). Each of these updates can be obtained from the tree of $A(D) \cup \{\leftarrow \iota P(A)\}$ shown below:

Translations for the update request $\iota P(A)$ are obtained by having some failed derivation in the SLDNF-tree of $A(D) \cup \{\leftarrow \iota P(A)\}$ succeed. Let us consider all derivations of this tree.

Left branch reaches the goal $\leftarrow Q(A) \wedge \neg\delta Q(A) \wedge \delta R(A)$, from where the literal $Q(A)$ is selected. This goal fails because there is no clause in $A(D)$ to be unified with $Q(A)$ (fact $Q(A)$ does not hold in the current database).

As it is not possible to get a success from this branch, no translation can be obtained from it. Selecting clause I.3 in step 1, we obtain a failed derivation that can not be succeeded (this derivation is not shown in the tree above).

Steps 1 to 4 in the central derivation are SLDNF-resolution steps. After step 4 we get the goal $\leftarrow\iota Q(A)\wedge\neg\iota R(A)$ that can be satisfied if $\iota Q(A)$ is included in the input set and $\iota R(A)$ is not included in it. In general, a translation T contains a ground instance of each literal corresponding to a positive base event selected during the derivation and, thus, $\iota Q(A)$ must be included in it (this is done in step 5).

In order to get success for this branch, $\leftarrow\iota R(A)$ must fail. This implies that event $\iota R(A)$ must not belong to T. We use a condition set C to check that later on, during the derivation process, the event $\iota R(A)$ will not be included in T. In general, a condition set C contains base events that can not be included in the translation T in order to ensure that T satisfies the update request. C will also be obtained during the derivation process and it will contain the atoms corresponding to the selected negative base events. Thus, in step 6 $\iota R(A)$ is included in C.

Due to the opposite meaning of T and C, before including a base event in T (resp. in C) it must be checked that it does not belong to the subset of C (resp. of T) already determined. If it does, we get a contradiction for the current branch and then, no valid translation can be obtained from it. In the above example, no contradiction is found when including base events in T nor in C.

Once we get the empty clause, the process finishes, and the set T gives the base events that produce the desired effect. Updating the extensional database with these base events the update request will be satisfied. In the central derivation of the example we have obtained $T_1=\{\iota Q(A)\}$. Then, the view update can be achieved by inserting Q'(A) into the database.

In a similar way, right derivation reaches the goal $\leftarrow\iota S(A)$, that can be succeeded by including $\iota S(A)$ in the input set (step 4). Thus, another possible translation is $T_2=\{\iota S(A)\}$, that is, P'(A) can be also deduced in the updated database if we insert S'(A).

4.3 A second example

Delete requests are handled in the same way as insert requests. Consider again the database presented in the previous example and let the update request be the deletion of P(B). This delete request corresponds to a fact $\delta P(B)$. Possible solutions will be obtained by having some failed derivations of A(D) $\cup\{\leftarrow\delta P(B)\}$ succeed. We proceed in the same way as we did in the previous example.

$$\leftarrow \delta P(B)$$
$$1 \quad \Big| \quad (D.3)$$
$$\leftarrow \delta S(B) \wedge \neg P'_{1,1}(B) \wedge \neg P'_{1,2}(B) \wedge \neg P'_{1,3}(B) \wedge \neg P'_{1,4}(B)$$
$$2 \quad \Big| \quad T = \{\delta S(B)\}$$
$$\leftarrow \neg P'_{1,1}(B) \wedge \neg P'_{1,2}(B) \wedge \neg P'_{1,3}(B) \wedge \neg P'_{1,4}(B)$$
$$T = \{\delta S(B)\}$$

Selecting clauses D.1 and D.2 in step 1 we obtain failed derivations that can not be succeeded. These derivations are not shown in the tree above. Selecting clause D3 we reach the goal $\leftarrow\neg P'_{1,1}(B)\wedge\neg P'_{1,2}(B)\wedge\neg P'_{1,3}(B)\wedge P'_{1,4}(B)$. This goal can be satisfied if we check that the subsidiary tree associated to each negative literal $\neg P'_{1,j}(B)$, $j=1...4$, fails finitely.

$$T= \{\delta S(B)\} \qquad\qquad\qquad\qquad T= \{\delta S(B)\}$$

$$\leftarrow P'_{1,1}(B) \qquad\qquad\qquad\qquad \leftarrow P'_{1,3}(B)$$

$$1 \;\big|\; (T.1) \qquad\qquad\qquad\qquad 1 \;\big|\; (T.3)$$

$$\leftarrow \underline{Q(B)} \wedge \neg\delta Q(B) \wedge \neg R(B) \wedge \neg \iota R(B) \qquad \leftarrow \iota Q(B) \wedge \underline{\neg R(B)} \wedge \neg \iota R(B)$$

$$2 \;\big|\; \qquad\qquad\qquad\qquad\qquad 2 \;\big|\; (\leftarrow R(B) \text{ fails})$$

$$\text{fails} \qquad\qquad\qquad\qquad\qquad \leftarrow \iota Q(B) \wedge \neg \iota R(B)$$

$$T_1 = \{\delta S(B)\} \qquad C_1 = \{\iota Q(B)\}$$

$$T_2 = \{\delta S(B),\ \iota R(B)\}$$

On the left tree, the goal $\leftarrow Q(B) \wedge \neg\delta Q(B) \wedge \neg R(B) \wedge \neg \iota R(B)$ is reached. As it is not possible to unify the selected literal $Q(B)$ with any clause of the database, the derivation fails. Derivation trees associated to $\neg P'_{1,2}(B)$ and to $\neg P'_{1,4}(B)$ (not shown in the example) fail in a similar way.

On the right tree, all possible ways in which the reached goal $\leftarrow \iota Q(B) \wedge \neg \iota R(B)$ can fail must be explored. We will obtain as many translations as different ways to make this goal fail.

There are two possible ways to ensure failure for the conjunction $\leftarrow \iota Q(B) \wedge \neg \iota R(B)$: including $\iota R(B)$ in the input set or assuming that $\iota Q(B)$ will not be included in it. Then, two different translations will be obtained. Considering the second possibility, the inclusion of the base event $\iota Q(B)$ in the condition set C_1 ensures that $\iota Q(B)$ will not be included in T. Then, a possible view update is $T_1 = \{\delta S(B)\}$. The deletion of the fact $S(B)$ will satisfy the request for deleting $P(B)$.

The addition of $\iota R(B)$ to the input set is effected by including it in T. Thus, another possible view update is $T_2 = \{\delta S(B), \iota R(B)\}$. That is, the update request will also be satisfied if the fact $S(B)$ is deleted from the database and the fact $R'(B)$ is inserted into it. Notice that T_2 is not a minimal solution because there is a subset of it (i.e. T_1) that is itself a solution. As we consider only minimal solutions, T_1 would have to be applied.

4.4 The Events Method

As we have seen in the previous examples, our method is an interleaving of two activities: 1) satisfying the update request by including base events in the translation set and 2) checking if the view updates induced by these base events are contradictory with the requested update. In order to simplify the presentation, we will define first in this section a restricted form of the method where only base events are included in the condition set. In next section we explain how to deal with more complex conditions.

Predicates in the augmented database A(D) may be (we include examples from previous section):
- old (state) base predicates (S,T)
- old (state) derived predicates (P)
- base events (δS, ιT)
- derived events (δP, ιP)
- new (state) predicates ($P'_{1,1}$, $Ic1'_{1,1}$)

Base events represent the actions that can be performed on base predicates of the database, so ιT, being T a base predicate, represent the insertion of T, while δT represents the deletion of T. Derived events represent the induced updates on the derived predicates that happen during the transition. New predicates represent the evaluation of the predicate with the same name on the updated database, i.e. P' denotes the evaluation of the derived predicate P on the updated database.

A **constructive** derivation from $(G_1 \ T_1 \ C_1)$ to $(G_n \ T_n \ C_n)$ via a safe selection rule R is a sequence: $(G_1 \ T_1 \ C_1), (G_2 \ T_2 \ C_2),..., (G_n \ T_n \ C_n)$
such that for each $i>1$, G_i has the form $\leftarrow L_1,...,L_k$, $R(G_i) = L_j$ and $(G_{i+1} \ T_{i+1} \ C_{i+1})$ is obtained according to one of the following rules:

A1) If L_j is positive and it is not a base event then $G_{i+1}= S$, $T_{i+1}= T_i$ and $C_{i+1}= C_i$, where S is the resolvent of some clause in A(D) with G_i on the selected literal L_j.

A2) If L_j is a positive base event "ιP" (resp. "δP"), $L_j \notin C_i$ and fact P does not (resp. does) hold in the old database then $G_{i+1} = \leftarrow L_1,..., L_{j-1},L_{j+1},...,L_k$, $T_{i+1}=T_i \cup \{L_j\}$ and $C_{i+1}= C_i$.

A3) If L_j is a negative old base or derived predicate "$\neg P$", then $G_{i+1} = \leftarrow L_1,...,L_{j-1}, L_{j+1},...,L_k$, $T_{i+1}=T_i$ and $C_{i+1}=C_i$, if the goal " $\leftarrow \neg P$" succeeds. "$\leftarrow \neg P$" *succeeds* if the goal $\leftarrow P$ fails finitely, i.e., if for some computation rule R' the SLDNF-search space for A(D) $\cup \{\leftarrow P\}$ fails finitely.

A4) If L_j is a negative base event "$\neg \iota P$" (resp. "$\neg \delta P$"), $\iota P \notin T_i$ (resp. $\delta P \notin T_i$) and fact P does not (resp. does) hold in the current database then $G_{i+1}=\leftarrow L_1,...,L_{j-1},L_{j+1},...,L_k$, $T_{i+1}=T_i$ and $C_{i+1}= C_i \cup \{\iota P\}$ (resp. $C_{i+1}= C_i \cup \{\delta P\}$).

A5) If L_j is a negative, new or derived event, predicate "$\neg P$" and there exists a consistency derivation from $(\{\leftarrow P\} \ T_i \ C_i)$ to $(\{\} \ T' \ C')$ then $G_{i+1} = \leftarrow L_1,...,L_{j-1}, L_{j+1},...,L_k$, $T_{i+1}= T'$ and $C_{i+1}= C'$.

Steps A1) and A3) are SLDNF resolution steps. In step A2) base events are added to the translation set. This is done in order to have a failed derivation of A(D)$\cup\{\leftarrow u\}$ succeed. In step A4) base events are added to the condition set in order to ensure that they will not be included in the translation set afterwards. In step A5) the induced view updates are checked for consistency with the update request. This may require in some cases the inclusion of more base events to T and/or to C.

Definition: *fair selection rule*

A fair selection rule R is a function which, given a goal $\leftarrow L_1,...,L_k$, $k\geq 1$, returns an atom L_i, $i=1...k$, such that selects base and derived predicates (positives or negatives and ground), positive new predicates and positive derived events predicates with priority. Selecting literals in a fair manner never conflicts with the requirement of safe selection [4].

A **consistency** derivation from $(F_1 \ T_1 \ C_1)$ to $(F_n \ T_n \ C_n)$ via a fair selection rule R is a sequence: $(F_1 \ T_1 \ C_1), (F_2 \ T_2 \ C_2),..., (F_n \ T_n \ C_n)$
such that for each $i>1$, F_i has the form $\{\leftarrow L_1,...,L_k\} \cup F'_i$ and *for some* $j=1...k$ $(F_{i+1} \ T_{i+1} \ C_{i+1})$ is obtained according to one of the following rules:

B1) If L_j is positive and it is not a base event then $F_{i+1}= S' \cup F'_i$ where S' is the set of all resolvents of clauses in A(D) with $\leftarrow L_1,...,L_k$ on the literal L_j, and $[] \notin S'$, $T_{i+1}= T_i$ and $C_{i+1}= C_i$.

B2) If L_j is a positive base event and $L_j \in C_i$, then $F_{i+1} = F'_i$, $T_{i+1}= T_i$ and $C_{i+1}= C_i$.

B3) If L_j is a positive base event, $L_j \in T_i$, $L_j \notin C_i$ and $k>1$, then $F_{i+1}=\{\leftarrow L_1,...,L_{j-1},L_{j+1},...,L_k\} \cup F'_i$, $T_{i+1}= T_i$ and $C_{i+1}= C_i$.

B4) If L_j is a positive base event "ιP" (resp. "δP"), $L_j \notin T_i$, $L_j \notin C_i$, and fact P does not (resp. does) hold in the current database then $F_{i+1} = F'_i$, $T_{i+1}= T_i$ and $C_{i+1}= C_i \cup \{L_j\}$.

B5) If L_j is a negative old base or derived predicate "$\neg P$", then $F_{i+1}=\{\leftarrow L_1,...,L_{j-1}, L_{j+1},...,L_k\} \cup F'_i$, $T_{i+1}= T_i$ and $C_{i+1}= C_i$, if the goal "$\leftarrow \neg P$" succeeds. "$\leftarrow \neg P$" *succeeds* if the goal $\leftarrow P$ fails finitely, i.e., if for some computation rule R' the SLDNF-search space for A(D) $\cup\{\leftarrow P\}$ fails finitely.

B6) If L_j is a negative base event, and $\neg L_j \in T_i$, then $F_{i+1} = F'_i$, $T_{i+1}= T_i$ and $C_{i+1}= C_i$.

B7) If L_j is a negative base event, $\neg L_j \in C_i$ and $k>1$, then $F_{i+1} = \{\leftarrow L_1,...,L_{j-1}, L_{j+1},...,L_k\} \cup F'_i$, $T_{i+1} = T_i$ and $C_{i+1} = C_i$.

B8) If L_j is a negative base event "$\neg \iota P$" (resp. "$\neg \delta P$"), $\iota P \notin C_i$ (resp. $\delta P \notin C_i$), $\iota P \notin T_i$ (resp. $\delta P \notin C_i$) and fact P does not (resp. does) hold in the current database then $F_{i+1} = F'_i$, $T_{i+1} = T_i \cup \{\iota P\}$ (resp. $T_{i+1} = T_i \cup \{\delta P\}$) and $C_{i+1} = C_i$.

B9) If L_j is a negative, new or derived event, predicate "$\neg P$", and there exists a constructive derivation from $(\{\leftarrow P\}\ T_i\ C_i)$ to $([]\ T'\ C')$ then $F_{i+1} = F'_i$, $T_{i+1} = T'$ and $C_{i+1} = C'$.

Once a goal that includes only events predicates and new predicates has been reached, all possible ways in which it can fail must be explored. A fair selection rule ensures that a goal like this is reached after processing base and derived predicates. Steps B1) and B5) are SLDNF resolution steps. In case B2 (resp. B6) the current branch is dropped from the consistency derivation because the subset of C (resp. of T) already determined ensures failure for this branch. In case B3 (resp. B7), the selected literal is removed from the goal because it already belongs to the translation set (resp. to the condition set). In case B4 (resp. B8) new base events are added to C (resp. to T). They correspond to the different ways in which the goal can fail. In both cases the current branch can be dropped because failure for it is ensured. In case B9) the current branch will be dropped if there exists a constructive derivation for the selected literal.

Let u be an update request. T will be a translation of u if there exists a constructive derivation from $(\leftarrow u\ \{\}\ \{\})$ to $([]\ T\ C)$. When no such derivation exists, the update request can not be satisfied by changing only the extensional database. The base events contained in the translation set T correspond to the updates (insertions and/or deletions) that must be performed on the current database in order to satisfy the update request.

Our method also deals with **mixed multiple updates** because we handle insert and delete requests in the same way. Thus, a mixed multiple update of the form: insert(P_1) and ... and insert(P_n) and delete (Q_1) and ... and delete(Q_m) will correspond to a root goal $\leftarrow \iota P_1 \wedge ... \wedge \iota P_n \wedge \delta Q_1 \wedge ... \wedge \delta Q_m$. View updates for a mixed multiple update request will be obtained as explained above.

4.5 Integrity constraints satisfaction

Some of the obtained translations could be invalidated by integrity constraints. That is, they may include some base events such that some ιIcn becomes true in the transition from the old state of the database to the updated database. In our method, integrity checking can be carried out dynamically during the derivation process, so that translations that satisfy both the update request and the integrity constraints will be obtained.

The root goal must be modified in order to incorporate integrity constraints into the update request. The root goal is now defined as $\{\leftarrow u \wedge \neg \iota Ic\}$, where u is the update request and $\neg \iota Ic$ indicates that all integrity constraint must be satisfied. The predicate ιIc is defined as $\iota Ic \leftarrow \iota Ic1, ..., \iota Ic \leftarrow \iota Icn$, where n is the number of integrity constraints in the database and each ιIcj has its respective arguments.

The method for finding all possible translations that satisfy the update request and the integrity constraints is exactly the same defined in the previous section. During the *constructive derivation*, the literal $\neg \iota Ic$ will be selected. As it corresponds to a negative derived event predicate (case A5), next step of the constructive derivation is reached if there exists a *consistency derivation* from $(\{\leftarrow \iota Ic\}\ T\ C)$ to $(\{\}\ T'\ C')$, where T and C are the sets of translations and conditions already determined when the literal $\neg \iota Ic$ is selected. Ensuring finitely failure for this consistency derivation is equivalent to ensure that no insertion of integrity constraint is induced when performing the view update. In this way, integrity checking is included as a part of the existing consistency derivation.

Consider again the example database given in section 4.2. Ic1 would be violated if both Q'(C) and T'(C) are true in the new state. We define the predicate ιIc as ιIc←ιIc1 because there is only one integrity constraint in the database. Note that ιIc1 represent violations of Ic1 originated in te transition. The constructive derivation for the update request ← ιP(C)∧¬ιIc is shown below:

$$← \underline{ιP(C)} ∧ ¬ιIc$$

1 | (I.2)

$$← P'_{1,3}(C) ∧ \underline{¬ P(C)} ∧ ¬ιIc$$

2 | (← P(C) fails)

$$← \underline{P'_{1,3}(C)} ∧ ¬ιIc$$

3 | (T.3)

$$← ιQ(C) ∧ \underline{¬ R(C)} ∧¬ιR(C)∧ ¬ιIc$$

4 | (← R(C) fails)

$$← \underline{ιQ(C)} ∧¬ιR(C)∧ ¬ιIc$$

5 | T= {ιQ(C)}   C=∅

$$← \underline{¬ιR(C)} ∧ ¬ιIc$$

6 | T= {ιQ(C)}   C= {ιR(C)}

$$← ¬ιIc$$

T = {ιQ(C)}   C = {ιR(C)}

Steps 1 to 4 are SLDNF-resolution steps (corresponding to cases A1) and A3)). In step 5, the selected literal ιQ(C) corresponds to a positive base event that does not belong to T nor to C, and then, case A2) applies. The literal is removed from the current goal and it is included in the translation set T. Step 6 corresponds to case A4). The treatment is similar to the one of the previous step, with the difference that the selected literal is included in the condition set. When ¬ιIc is selected, its associated consistency derivation must be taken into account (step A5).

The derivations resulting of selecting clauses I.1 and I.3 in step 1 of the constructive derivation are not shown in the example because no other translations can be obtained from them. The consistency derivation for ←ιIc is shown below:

$$← \underline{ιIc} \qquad T = \{ιQ(C)\}$$
$$C = \{ιR(C)\}$$

1 |

$$← \underline{ιIc1}$$

2 (I.5) _____ 2 | (I.6) _____ 2 (I.7)

$$← \underline{Ic1'_{1,2}} \qquad\qquad ← \underline{Ic1'_{1,3}} \qquad\qquad ← \underline{Ic1'_{1,4}}$$

3 | (T.8)   3 | (T.9)   3 | (T.10)

$$← \underline{Q(C)} ∧ ¬δQ(C) ∧ ιT(C) \qquad ← ιQ(C) ∧ \underline{T(C)}∧¬δT(C) \qquad ← \underline{ιQ(C)} ∧ ιT(C)$$

4 | 4 | (F.2)   4 | (ιQ(C) ∈ T)

fails $$← \underline{ιQ(C)} ∧¬δT(C) \qquad\qquad ← \underline{ιT(C)}$$

5 | (ιQ(C) ∈ T)   5 |

$$← \underline{¬ιR(A)} \qquad\qquad\qquad fails$$

6 | T' = {ιQ(C), δT(C)}
C' = {ιR(C)}

{ }

Left derivation fails because there is no clause in the input set to unify with the selected literal Q(C). Right derivation fails in step 5 because T(C) holds in the current database. Then, none of the cases B1) to B9) can be applied for this branch.

Steps 1 to 4 in the central derivation are SLDNF-resolution steps (corresponding to cases B1) and B5)). In step 5 a positive base event that already belongs to T is selected, this corresponds to case B3). In step 6, the selected negative base event literal is included in the translation set T as explained in case B8). Notice that we must include δT(C) in T in order not to violate an integrity constraint. After this step, we have obtained a consistency derivation from({← ιIc} T C) to ({} C' T'), where T'={ιQ(C), δT(C)} and C'={ιR(C)}.

Once the derivation process has finished, the translation T={ιQ(C), δT(C)} has been obtained. Then, the view update will be performed by inserting Q'(C) in the database and deleting T(C) from it. As it can be easily seen, T is a valid translation that satisfies the request of inserting P'(C) and that satisfies all the integrity constraints of the database.

Transition integrity constraints can also be checked in our method. A transition integrity constraint is a constraint that database transitions must satisfy . An example could be that salaries can not decrease. See [15] for the details of transition and events rules in this case.

The incorporation of integrity checking into the derivation process allows us to reject potential inconsistent solutions to the request during their generation. Another important advantage of this integration is that we can obtain solutions that would not be generated considering integrity checking as an additional step independent from view updating.

As an example, considering the view update request of inserting P(C) in the previous database, we would obtain the translation T = {ιQ(C)}. Afterwards, when checking integrity constraints, this solution would be invalidated because it violates Ic1. Thus, no solution that satisfies both the update request and the integrity constraint would be obtained. However, handling integrity checking into the derivation process the valid solution T={ιQ(C), δT(C)} is obtained (as shown in the previous example) .

5. Other features

5.1 Local variables

In [15] we show how to derive insertion and deletion events rules when local variables are involved in the definition of view predicates (that is, when some body literal has a variable that does not appear in the head). In this case, our method allows the inclusion of more complex conditions in C. As an example, consider the database consisting of only one rule and two facts:

$$P \leftarrow Q(x) \wedge R(x)$$
$$Q(A)$$
$$R(A)$$

Transition and some events rules associated to this database are:

$$P'_{1,1} \leftarrow Q(x) \wedge \neg \delta Q(x) \wedge R(x) \wedge \neg \delta R(x)$$
$$P'_{1,2} \leftarrow Q(x) \wedge \neg \delta Q(x) \wedge \iota R(x)$$
$$P'_{1,3} \leftarrow \iota Q(x) \wedge R(x) \wedge \neg \delta R(x)$$
$$P'_{1,4} \leftarrow \iota Q(x) \wedge \iota R(x)$$
$$\delta P \leftarrow Q(x) \wedge \delta R(x) \wedge \neg P'_{1,1} \wedge \neg P'_{1,2} \wedge \neg P'_{1,3} \wedge \neg P'_{1,4}$$

In order to obtain translations that satisfy the request of deleting P from the above database, consistency trees associated to the literals $\neg P'_{1,j}$, j=1...4, must fail finitely. Consider for example literal $\neg P'_{1,4}$. Its associated consistency tree is shown below:

$$\leftarrow P'_{1,4}$$
$$|$$
$$\leftarrow \iota Q(x) \wedge \iota R(x)$$

Ensuring a failure for this tree requires that no individual 'x' exists such that $\iota Q(x)$ and $\iota R(x)$ are true. In this case, the condition $\neg \exists x\ (\iota Q(x) \wedge \iota R(x))$ is added to the condition set. With a simple extension, the method is able to check conditions like this when base events are selected during the derivation process.

5.2 Modification requests

While some proposals have been done in order to deal with modification requests in relational databases [5], all methods presented up to date for view updating in the deductive database field consider only two kind of requests: insertion and deletion. Our method, however, can also handle modification requests.

A *modification request* is understood as a request for replacing the value of some attribute in a view predicate by a new, different value. In fact, a modification request can be regarded as a deletion of a view fact followed by an insertion of another fact on the same view predicate, where the value has been changed for the desired attribute. The natural meaning of the events allow us to define a goal where all these actions are considered.

As an example, consider a database containing only the Employee-Department-Manager view predicate (denoted by Edm) defined as: Edm (e,d,m)←Ed(e,d)∧Dm(d,m),where Ed denotes Employee-Dept base predicate while Dm denotes Dept-Manager base predicate. Assume the database contains the facts Ed(John,D1) and Dm(D1, Mary), from where can be easily deduced that Edm(John,D1,Mary) holds in the current database.

Let the modification request be the replacement of department D1 by D3, mantaining Mary as John's manager. This replacement is a request of deleting the view fact Edm(John,D1,Mary) and inserting afterwards Edm(John,D3,Mary).

In our method, view updates that satisfy this modification request will be obtained from the constructive derivation rooted at ←δEdm(John,D1,Mary)∧ιEdm(John,D3,Mary).Translations T={δDm (D1,Mary), ιEd(John,D3), ιDm(D3,Mary)} and T={δEd(John,D1), ιEd(John,D3), ιDm(D3,Mary)} are obtained from this derivation. Notice that, in both cases, after performing the update, department D3 will substitute department D1 in the Employee -Department - Manager relation between John and Mary, that is, both translations satisfy the modification request.

6. Comparison with other methods

In this section we compare in detail our method for view updating in deductive databases with the approaches taken by some of the methods mentioned in the Introduction. All of these methods deal with the same class of databases and view update requests as our. However, they do not handle transition integrity constraints, modification requests nor prevention of side effects on other views.

6.1 Decker's method [6]

Let D be a deductive database and u an update request. In Decker's method view updates for delete requests are obtained by having each non-failed branch in an SLDNF-tree of $D\cup\{\leftarrow u\}$ fail. This is effected by deleting, for each non-failed derivation in the tree, an input clause used in that derivation or by requesting the insertion of an atom of a negative literal used as input clause (negative literals are treated as subsidiary insert requests).

View updates for insert requests are obtained by having some failed derivation of $D\cup\{\leftarrow u\}$ succeed. This is effected by inserting a ground instance of each positive literal appearing in some goal G of the derivation and by requesting the deletion of the atom of each ground negative literal in G (negative literals are treated as subsidiary insert requests)

We see three noteworthy differences between this method and the method proposed here. First, the main problem present in Decker's method is that it is possible to draw solutions that are invalidated due to negation. That is, solutions that do not satisfy the update request may be obtained. As an example, consider a database containing the following facts and deductive rules:

$$Q(A)$$
$$R(A)$$
$$P(x) \leftarrow Q(x) \wedge R(x) \wedge \neg S(x)$$
$$P(x) \leftarrow T(x)$$
$$S(A) \leftarrow Q(A)$$

and let the view update request be the insertion of P(A).

In Decker's method two different solutions would be obtained: delete(Q(A)) and insert(T(A)). However, the deletion of Q(A) does not satisfy the insert request P(A). Thus, what can be drawn from derivations in the presence of negation are *possible* updates. A possible update is a *valid* one, if the updated database satisfies the update request. This must be validated by running the request in the updated database. In our method, only one translation T={ιT(A)} would be obtained. Notice that this is the only valid solution.

A second difference is that, in some cases, Decker's method must be iterated a number of times in order to obtain all valid solutions. The problem is that, in general, it is not known how many iterations should be performed. Because of this, Decker proposes to settle with single pass runs of the method, with which it is possible that not all valid translations are obtained. Our method always gets all valid solutions.

Third, in this method integrity checking is performed as an additional step after once obtained the possible solutions. On the contrary, in our method integrity checking is carried out dynamically during the derivation process. The advantages of the latter approach have been explained in section 4.5. Finally, the different processing of insert and delete requests does not allow this method to deal with multiple update requests, while we do.

6.2 Kakas and Mancarella's method [10,11]

This method studies the view update problem within an elegant abductive approach. It distinguishes clearly two steps to obtain solutions that satisfy an update request. In the first step, the update request is translated into several sets Δ_i. Each Δ_i is a specification of a set of sufficient requirements that the extensional database, EDB, should satisfy for the original request to be effected. Thus, every set Δ_i corresponds to a valid solution. The second step of the update procedure involves solving the update problem on the EDB generated in the previous step.

A first problem of this method is that in first step it may do some unnecessary work due to the fact that it does not take into account the contents of the current database to obtain the Δ_i. Then, some Δ_i expressing requirements that the current database already satisfies may be obtained. Because of this, the number of Δ_i obtained may become very large and, thus, the amount of unnecessary work can increase. As an example, consider a simple database containing the following facts and rules:

$$Q$$
$$R$$
$$P \leftarrow Q \wedge R$$
$$P \leftarrow S \wedge T$$
$$S \leftarrow A \wedge B$$
$$T \leftarrow C \wedge D$$

and let the view update request be the deletion of P.

In this method, eight different sets Δ_i of sufficient requirements that the EDB should satisfy are obtained: $\Delta_1=\{Q^*,A^*\}$, $\Delta_2=\{Q^*,B^*\}$, $\Delta_3=\{Q^*,C^*\}$, $\Delta_4=\{Q^*,D^*\}$, $\Delta_5=\{R^*,A^*\}$, $\Delta_6=\{R^*,B^*\}$, $\Delta_7=\{R^*,C^*\}$, $\Delta_8=\{R^*,D^*\}$, where P^* denotes that fact P must not hold in the new database state. However, there are only two solutions that satisfy the update request: $\{delete(Q)\}$ or $\{delete(R)\}$. In our method, two translations would be obtained: $T_1=\{\delta Q\}$ and $T_2=\{\delta R\}$. Notice that they correspond to the valid solutions.

Another important difference is the way of handling integrity checking during the derivation process. In Kakas and Mancarella's method integrity constraints can be dynamically checked as part of the derivation performed in the first step. The problem is that perhaps not all violations of integrity constraints may be detected during this derivation. As an example, consider the database containing the following rules and integrity constraint.

$$S(x) \leftarrow Q(x)$$
$$P(x) \leftarrow Q(x)$$
$$Ic1(x) \leftarrow P(x) \wedge \neg R(x)$$

and let the view update request be the insertion of S(A). In this method a set $\Delta=\{Q(A)\}$ would be obtained. Thus, in step 2, Q(A) would be inserted in the database. Note that this solution does not satisfy the integrity constraint. In our method, we would obtain the solution $T=\{\iota Q(A), \iota R(A)\}$ which satisfies both the update request and the integrity constraint. Finally, this method does not handle transition integrity constraints, while we do.

7. Conclusions

In this paper we have presented a new method for view updating in deductive databases. The method is based on the events and transition rules, which explicitly define the insertions and deletions induced by a database update. Using these rules, a simple extension of the SLDNF procedure allows us to obtain all valid translations satisfying view update requests.

The Events Method provides a simple framework in which both insert and delete requests are handled uniformily. Complex updates, such as mixed multiple updates, can be requested. Another important feature of our method is that it incorporates integrity checking dynamically into the derivation process, and allows checking transition integrity constraints.

We have shown that our method has the power of the methods developed so far, without some of their limitations.

The main cost implied by our method is the space required to store the transition and events rules. The cost may only be important in databases with a large number of deductive rules. However, in most practical databases this number is small as compared to the number of base facts stored and, thus, the cost should not be significant. The gain is the simplicity of the method and the additional power we get.

Acknowledgments

We would like to thank Dolors Costal, Hendrik Decker, A.C. Kakas, Enric Mayol, Joan Antoni Pastor, Carme Quer, M. Ribera Sancho, Jaume Sistac and Antoni Urpí for many useful comments and discussions. This work has been partially supported by the CICYT PRONTIC program project TIC 680.

REFERENCES

1. Abiteboul, S. "Updates, a new frontier", Proc. ICDT 88, Springer, 1988, pp. 1-18.
2. Bancilhon, F.; Spyratos,N. "Update semantics of relational views", ACM TODS, Vol. 6, No. 4, December 1981, pp. 557-575.
3. Bancilhon, F.; Ramakrishnan,R. "An amateur's introduction to recursive query processing strategies". Proc. ACM SIGMOD Int. Conf. on Management of data. Washington D.C., May 1986, pp. 16-52.
4. Cavedon, L.; Lloyd, J.W. "A Completeness theorem for SLDNF-Resolution". TR87/9, Dept. of Computer Science, Univ. of Melbourne, Australia, 1987.
5. Dayal, U.; Bernstein P.A. "On the correct translation of Update Operations on relational Views" ACM TODS, Vol. 8, No. 3, 1982.
6. Decker, H. "Drawing updates from derivations". Proc. ICDT 90, Springer 1990, pp.437-455.
7. Furtado, A.L.; Casanova,M.A. "Updating relational views", In Kim,W,; Reiner, D.S.; Batory, D.S. (Eds.), "Query processing in database systems", Springer-Verlag, Berlin, 1985, pp. 127-142.
8. Guessoum, A.; Lloyd, J.W. "Updating Knowledge Bases". New Generation Computing, Vol. 8, No.1, 1990.
9. Guessoum, A.; Lloyd, J.W. "Updating Knowledge Bases II". TR-90-13. Univ. Bristol, Comp. Science. May 1990.
10. Kakas, A.C. "Belief Revision for Deductive Databases". International Workshop on the Deductive Approach to Information Sytems and Databases, Report LSI/90/30, S'Agaró, Catalonia, 1990, pp. 191-218.
11. Kakas, A.C.; Mancarella, P. "Database Updates Through Abduction". Proc. of the 16th VLDB, Brisbane 1990, pp.650-661.
12. Kowalski, R. "Logic for data description". In Gallaire,H.;Minker,J. (Eds.) "Logic and Data Bases", Plenum Press, New York, 1978, pp. 77-103.
13. Nicolas, J.; Yazdanian, K. "An Outline of BDGEN: A Deductive DBMS". Proc. IFIP 83, Elsevier 1983.
14. Olivé, A. "On the design and implementation of information systems from deductive conceptual models". Proc. of the 15th. VLDB, Amsterdam, 1989, pp. 3-11.
15. Olivé, A. "Integrity Constraints Checking in Deductive Databases". Proc. of the 17th. VLDB, Barcelona, 1991, pp.513-524.
16. Tomasic, A. "View update annotation in definite deductive databases", Proc. ICDT 88, Springer, 1988, pp. 338-352.

Implementation of Delayed Updates in Heraclitus*

Shahram Ghandeharizadeh, Richard Hull, Dean Jacobs

Computer Science Department
University of Southern California
Los Angeles, California 90089

Abstract

The Heraclitus languages are database programming languages that give prominence to "delayed updates" or *deltas*, which are first-class values representing sets of proposed updates, such as inserts and deletes, to the underlying persistent store. Deltas can be created, inspected and combined without committing to the given updates. Deltas are useful for realizing advanced database features that manipulate virtual database states in addition to the currently stored state; examples include supporting rule-based triggers, hypothetical reasoning, and concurrent transaction processing systems.

This paper introduces Heraclitus[Alg], a relational algebra extended by deltas, and the HERALD system that implements it. Heraclitus[Alg] is a low-level, internal language which will be used in the implementation of richer, calculus-style Heraclitus languages that have been previously proposed. HERALD is built on top of the Wisconsin Storage System (WiSS), and extends this system to support deltas and the various delta operators.

1 Introduction

Several advanced database capabilities, including rule-based triggers, database support for hypothetical reasoning, and some concurrent transaction processing systems, use one or more *virtual database states* in addition to a currently stored state. Research into these and related areas is on-going, and a consensus has not yet emerged as to the appropriate ways to define their semantics and to implement them. Indeed, tools are needed to enable comparisons between different proposals, and to simplify the task of experimenting with new ones.

A good illustration of this is the area of "active" databases that use a paradigm of rule-based triggers to generate automatic updates, in a manner reminiscent of expert systems. As discussed in [HJ91b] and elsewhere, each of the active systems described in the literature uses a different semantics for rule application. Some of these differences stem from the choice of underlying data model (e.g., relational or object-oriented), but the most crucial differences stem from choices concerning when rules should be fired (e.g., at transaction boundaries or within transactions), how they should be fired (e.g., in parallel or sequentially in some order), and how their effects should be combined (e.g., aborting on conflict or giving priority to insertions). This highlights the fact that the "knowledge" represented in both active and deductive databases stems from two

---

*The first author was supported in part by the NSF under grant IRI-9110522 and the USC Faculty Research and Innovation Fund under grant 22-1509-9440. The second author was supported in part NSF grant IRI-9107055 and by the Defense Advanced Research Projects Agency under DARPA grant MDA903-81-C-0335. The third author supported in part by the German Academic Exchange Service. The research of the second and third authors supported in part by AT&T, and was performed in part while they were visiting the Technische Universität Berlin.

distinct components: (a) the rule base and (b) the semantics for rule application. It appears that different rule-application semantics will sometimes be appropriate, even within a single database. This perspective is supported by the LOGRES system [CCCR+90], in which users can choose, for each requested update, from a palate of six rule application semantics. It seems unlikely that a fixed collection of choices will suffice however, especially as active databases become increasingly sophisticated. For example, there has been recent interest in developing techniques for modularizing rules, e.g., by clustering them with classes in an object-oriented system (cf. [MP90]) or with different kinds of database transactions. It seems natural that designers will require different semantics for different kinds of clusters.

The family of Heraclitus languages, introduced in [JH91], provide an important tool for manipulating virtual states. The primary novel feature of these languages is the incorporation of "delayed updates" or *deltas* as first-class values. A delta represents a set of proposed updates, such as inserts and deletes, to the underlying persistent store. Deltas can be created, inspected and combined without committing to the given updates. These capabilities permit the direct use of deltas to represent virtual states. Indeed, as illustrated in [HJ91a], the Heraclitus constructs can be used to specify a wide variety of semantics for active databases.

This paper introduces Heraclitus[Alg], a relational algebra extended by deltas, and the HERALD (HEraclitus Relational ALgebra with Deltas) system that implements it. Heraclitus[Alg] is a low-level, internal language which will be used in the implementation of the richer, calculus-style Heraclitus languages that have been previously proposed [JH91]. HERALD is built on top of the record-based Wisconsin Storage System (WiSS)[1], and extends this system to support deltas and the various delta operators by translating them into appropriate relations and relational algebra operators.

A particularly significant aspect of this translation is the treatment of the "when" operator. The expression E when D calls for the evaluation of expression E in the hypothetical state resulting from applying delta D to the current state. In order to avoid the inefficiency of actually constructing this hypothetical state, we distribute the when down to the atomic subexpressions of E. As detailed below, the treatment of nested whens is especially intricate.

Heraclitus[Alg] has allowed us to examine a variety of design and implementation issues associated with the interaction between deltas and the relational algebra, and more generally with low-level primitives for supporting deltas and their operations. A particularly interesting aspect of this study has been the extension of our previous notion of deltas to support explicit modifies along with inserts and deletes. As described in this paper, the consistency conditions needed to define these generalized deltas and the definitions of the delta operators are significantly more intricate in this context. Indeed, from this experiment we have concluded that incorporating explicit modifies at this low level is undesirable, primarily because of this intricacy. Note that this does not exclude the possibility of providing some form of modify capability at a higher level.

A brief overview of deltas and delta operators is presented in Section 2. Section 3 presents an example, using Heraclitus[Alg], of how deltas can be used in the framework of active databases. Section 4 gives a more formal description of deltas and their operators and discusses the issue of modifies. Section 5 describes the architecture and primary features of the HERALD system. Related work is described in Section 6. Brief conclusions are offered in Section 7.

Due to space limitations, the formal BNF specification of the syntax of Heraclitus[Alg], more details about the implementation of HERALD, and the proofs of theoretical results related to the semantics of the delta operators are omitted here; these may be found in [GHJL92].

---

[1]HERALD is conceptually independent of WiSS and could be ported to other relational file managers with minimal difficulty.

2 Overview of Heraclitus[Alg]

Heraclitus[Alg] is designed to be a database manipulation sublanguage embedded in a conventional imperative language; C in the case of our current implementation. C/Heraclitus[Alg] hybrid programs are translated by a preprocessor into pure C containing calls to HERALD, the Heraclitus run-time system. Bulk data facilities are provided by relation-valued variables, which may be either persistent or transient. A relational algebra is provided as part of the expression language to support queries and updates.

The primary novel feature of Heraclitus is "delayed updates", as embodied by the type delta. In the *no-modify* context introduced in [JH91], a value of this type represents a set of proposed insertions into, and deletions from, the values of relation variables. In the *modify* context introduced in this paper, a delta value may also include proposed modifies to the relation variables. Delta values are generated by evaluating delta expressions. For example, the atomic delta expression <+R($e_1, \ldots, e_n$)> produces a delta that calls for (the value of tuple expression) ($e_1, \ldots, e_n$) to be inserted into (the value of relation variable[2]) R. Similarly, the atomic delta expression <-R($e_1, \ldots, e_n$)> produces a delta that calls for ($e_1, \ldots, e_n$) to be deleted from R. Finally, the atomic delta expression <mod R($e_1, \ldots, e_n; e'_1, \ldots, e'_n$)> calls for the value of ($e_1, \ldots, e_n$) in relation R to be *replaced* with the value of ($e'_1, \ldots, e'_n$).

Two binary operators for combining deltas are provided: *Merge* (&) forms the "union" of two deltas, but produces the special delta *fail* if conflicting updates are proposed. *Smash* (!) resolves conflicting updates in favor of the second delta. For example,

- <+R(1)> & <+R(2)> produces a delta that calls for (1) and (2) to be inserted into R.

- <+R(1)> & <-R(1)> produces *fail*.

- <+R(1)> ! <+R(2)> produces a delta that calls for (1) and (2) to be inserted into R.

- <+R(1)> ! <-R(1)> produces a delta that calls for (1) to be deleted from R.

Merge implements a semantics based on "accumulation" of requested updates, while smash implements a semantic based on "overwriting" (see [HJ91b]). In general, a delta value may refer to more than one relation variable.

If δ is a delta expression, then the Heraclitus[Alg] command apply δ updates the database state according to the changes requested by δ. Heraclitus also provides two ways of accessing deltas without committing to the proposed modifications as in the command apply. The first way, called "peeking", permits the programmer to directly inspect the proposed modifications. For example, peekdel(R, δ) returns the set of tuples that are proposed by δ to be deleted from R. The second way, called "hypothesizing", permits the programmer to query the hypothetical database obtained by applying a delta to the current state. For example, the expression (cross(R,S) when δ) evaluates to the cross product of relations R and S in the hypothetical database state obtained by applying the value of delta expression δ to the current state. The semantics of delta operators are provided in detail in Section 4.

3 An Example

This section illustrates the core of Heraclitus[Alg] using an example. We reiterate that Heraclitus[Alg] is intended as a low-level, internal language upon which higher-level Heraclitus languages will be constructed; programmers will not write code directly in Heraclitus[Alg].

---

[2] Relations are viewed as sets; if ($e_1, \ldots, e_n$) is in the current value of R then applying <+R($e_1, \ldots, e_n$)> causes no change to R.

The example illustrates how Heraclitus[Alg] (in both contexts) provides the basic capabilities needed to specify the semantics of active database systems. In particular, we describe a Heraclitus[Alg] program that implements an overdraft protection service provided by a bank. With this service, a Checking account, represented as a record in Checking(ss#, CBal) relation, has a Savings account associated with it[3] Savings(ss#, SBal). If an update takes the balance of a Checking account below zero (i.e., an overdraft), the bank determines whether the associated Savings account can compensate for the overdraft. If so, the Savings balance is debited by the amount of overdraft and the Checking balance is left at zero, allowing the update to commit successfully. Otherwise, the update is aborted and the bank keeps track of the account in a Bouncer(ss#) relation.

Assume that the bank collects all updates and processes them at the end of a business day by proposing a set of updates to the balance of its Checking accounts (Δ_{prop}). The Heraclitus program described here takes the original database state and Δ_{prop} as input and outputs a new delta (Δ_{fix}) such that the smash of these two deltas (i.e., Δ_{prop} ! Δ_{fix}) implements the overdraft protection service. More formally, for each person with social security number ss, assuming that CBal (SBal) is the balance of ss's Checking (Savings) account after Δ_{prop}, Δ_{fix} will consist of a set of changes such that Δ_{prop} ! Δ_{fix} (termed Δ_{final}) will result in:

"No_Problem": if CBal $\geq$ 0, maintain the modifications requested by Δ_{prop},

"Covered": if CBal < 0, and[4] |CBal| < SBal, then Δ_{final} should modify the state so that:

- The ss tuple in Checking is (ss, 0), and
- The ss tuple in Savings is (ss, SBal + CBal).

"Must_Bounce": if CBal < 0 and |CBal| > SBal then Δ_{final} should modify the state so that:

- The ss tuple in Checking is (ss, original_balance),
- The ss tuple in Savings is (ss, original_balance), and
- Add ss to the Bouncer relation.

We first describe how this is supported in the no-modify context, and then revise it using modifies.

Algebraic expressions to construct Δ_{fix} can be written in Heraclitus[Alg]. In the code we represent Δ_{prop} using variable D_prop, and Δ_{fix} by D_fix. To begin, we evaluate a query against the hypothetical database obtained by applying Δ_{prop} to the current state, in order to compute a 3-ary relation Status_After_Prop(ss#,CBal,Sbal) consisting of a person's social_security number, and Checking and Savings balances after the proposed update[5]:

```
Status_After_Prop := join(<Checking.ss#, CBal, SBal>,
                          {Checking.ss# = Savings.ss#},
                          Checking,
                          Savings)
                    when D_prop;
```

The syntax of the join operator is as follows. The two relations to be joined are given in the third and fourth arguments. The second argument specifies the join condition, and the

---

[3]For simplicity, we assume that a person has only one checking and one savings account.
[4]Absolute value of CBal.
[5]Heraclitus[Alg] uses column indexes to refer to the attributes of a relation. This example uses column names in order to make the text more readable.

first defines the attributes projected from the relation resulting from this operation. The first argument is optional; if omitted then each tuple in the result is the concatenation of the two joining tuples from each relation.

Next, we assign `Below_Zero(ss#,CBal,Sbal)` to contain the `Checking` account tuples whose balance are below zero in the hypothetical database:

```
Below_Zero := select({Checking.CBal < 0}, Status_After_Prop);
```

The first argument of the `select` command is a condition, followed by the name of a relation.

We then construct the set `Covered(ss#,CBal,SBal)` that consists of persons whose `Savings` balance can compensate for the overdraft from their `Checking` account. In addition, we create two deltas that contain the updates needed to implement the overdraft protection service for persons in `Covered`:

```
Covered := select({-CBal <= SBal}, Below_Zero);
D_Covered_C := bulk(-Checking(ss#, CBal), Covered)
                & bulk(+Checking(ss#, 0), Covered);
D_Covered_S := bulk(-Savings(ss#, CBal), Covered)
                & bulk(-Checking(ss#, SBal + CBal), Covered);
```

The `bulk` command generates a set of updates according to the *template* given as first coordinate, one update (duplicates removed) for each tuple in the value of the second coordinate. In the no-modify context, we obtain the effect of modifies by performing a set of deletes and set of inserts. (Note that the deltas assigned to D_Covered_C and D_Covered_S are consistent, by the construction of Covered.)

Next, we construct a set `Must_Bounce(ss#,CBal)` of accounts whose `Savings` balance cannot compensate for the overdraft:

```
Must_Bounce := project(<ss#,CBal>, Below_Zero - Covered);
```

Furthermore, we compute into `Orig_Must_Bounce(ss#,CBal)` the balance of these accounts in the original database state:

```
Orig_Must_Bounce := join(<Must_Bounce.ss#, Checking.CBal>,
                         {Must_Bounce.ss# = Checking.ss#},
                         Must_Bounce,
                         Checking);
```

With the balance of the `Checking` account before Δ_{prop} and after Δ_{prop} for the "must_bounce" category, we construct $\Delta_{Must\_Bounce\_C}$ in order to propose modifications that restore the original balance of these `Checking` accounts. Furthermore, we construct $\Delta_{Must\_Bounce\_B}$ that keeps track of these accounts in the `Bouncer` relation.

```
D_Must_Bounce_C := bulk(-Checking(ss#,CBal), Must_Bounce)
                    & bulk(+Checking(ss#,CBal), Orig_Must_Bounce);
D_Must_Bounce_B := bulk(+Bouncer(ss#), Must_Bounce);
```

We now merge these deltas to construct Δ_{fix}:

```
D_fix := (((D_Covered_C & D_Covered_S) & D_Must_Bounce_C) & D_Must_Bounce_B);
```

Finally, the database is updated according to the smash of Δ_{prop} and Δ_{fix}:

```
apply (D_prop ! D_fix)
```

(We did not apply Δ_{prop} by itself because this could result in a violation of integrity constraints.)

Finally, we give an example of a "peeking" operator. Suppose that the user is interested in knowing the set of inserts to Savings that are called for by D_prop ! D_fix. This is computed into Inserted_to_Savings(ss#,SBal) by

```
Inserted_to_Savings := peekins(Savings, D_prop ! D_fix)
```

In this example, we assigned algebraic expressions to several intermediate variables to construct Δ_{fix}. Heraclitus[Alg] permits arbitrary nesting of operators, so Δ_{fix} may also be been obtained by a single expression. This is the kind of expression that would typically be generated as the result of translating an active database rule into Heraclitus[Alg].

In the modify context, under the assumption that social-security# is a key for both Checking and Savings, the assignments to variables D_Covered_C, D_Covered_S, and D_Must_Bounce_C can be sets of explicit modifies, rather than sets of inserts and deletes. In particular, the commands assigning these values can be rewritten as follows:

```
D_Covered_C := bulk(mod Checking(ss#, CBal; ss#, 0), Covered);
D_Covered_S := bulk(mod Savings(ss#, SBal; ss#, SBal + CBal), Covered);
D_Must_Bounce_C := bulk(mod Checking(ss#, Must_Bounce.ss#;
                                ss#, Orig_Must_Bounce.ss#),
                    join({Must_Bounce.ss# = Orig_Must_Bounce.ss#},
                        Must_Bounce,
                        Orig_Must_Bounce));
```

As used in this example the deltas with explicit modifies have the same effect as the corresponding deltas originally given. In general, however, the corresponding expressions are not equivalent. To see why, consider:

```
D_del_ins := <-Checking(123-45-6789, 100)> & <+Checking(123-45-6789, 200)>;
D_mod := <mod Checking(123-45-6789, 100; 123-45-6789, 200)>
```

In a database state where (123-45-6789, 100) is in Checking applying D_del_ins and D_mod have the same effect. However, in a state where (123-45-6789, 100) is not in Checking, then applying D_mod has no impact, but applying D_del_ins has the effect of inserting (123-45-6789, 200) into Checking.

4   Semantics of Deltas and Delta Operations

This section briefly describes the formal semantics of deltas and the delta operators *apply*, *merge*, *smash*, the "peeking" operators, and *when*. We give the description for both the no-modify and modify contexts in parallel, always considering the no-modify context first. The semantics for the no-modify context is essentially that of [HJ91a, JH91]; and that of the modify context involves numerous substantial extensions.

We assume here that a set $\mathbf{R} = \{R_1, \ldots, R_k\}$ of (persistent and temporary) relation variables is fixed, with associated signatures $\sigma(R_i)$ and arities $\alpha(R_i)$ for $i \in [1..k]$. A *database state* over $\mathbf{R}$ is a function DB, that assigns to each $R \in \mathbf{R}$ a relation instance with signature $\sigma(R)$. The relation associated to $R \in \mathbf{R}$ by DB is denoted $DB(R)$. Relations are sets; duplicates are not supported.

Delta expressions in Heraclitus[Alg] evaluate to *delta* (*value*)s. In the no-modify context, a *pre-delta* Δ is a function mapping each $R \in \mathbf{R}$ to a pair $(I_{\Delta,R}, D_{\Delta,R})$ of relation instances where

(i) $I_{\Delta,R}$ has signature $\sigma(R)$, (ii) $D_{\Delta,R}$ has signature $\sigma(R)$, and A *delta* is either (a) the special value *fail* or (b) a pre-delta Δ that is *consistent*, in the sense that $I_{\Delta,R} \cap D_{\Delta,R} = \emptyset$ for each relation $R \in \mathbf{R}$.

In the modify context, a *pre-delta* Δ is a function mapping each $R \in \mathbf{R}$ to a triple $(I_{\Delta,R}, D_{\Delta,R}, M_{\Delta,R})$ of relation instances where the first two coordinates are as before, and (iii) $M_{\Delta,R}$ has signature $concat(\sigma(R), \sigma(R))$. A *delta* is either (a) the special value *fail* or (b) a pre-delta that is *consistent* (defined below).

In both contexts, deltas are given a declarative interpretation in terms of the function

$$apply : state \times delta \rightarrow state$$

which applies a delta to a state to produce a new state. Intuitively, the new state is the result of the *simultaneous* application of all deletes, inserts, [and modifications] called for by Δ, where $I_{\Delta,R}$ corresponds to insertions requested for $DB(R)$; $D_{\Delta,R}$ corresponds to deletions requested for $DB(R)$; [and $M_{\Delta,R}$ corresponds to modifications requested for $DB(R)$]. As noted earlier, we view a modification mod $R(s;t)$ as calling for the *replacement* of s by t in $DB(R)$.

To motivate and define the notion of consistency for the modify context, we establish more notation. In the following, $t_1 \times t_2$ denotes concatenation of tuples, $old(M_{\Delta,R})$ denotes the projection of $M_{\Delta,R}$ onto its first $\alpha(R)$ columns, and $new(M_{\Delta,R})$ denotes the projection of $M_{\Delta,R}$ onto its last $\alpha(R)$ columns. Also, an *r-delta* (*relation-delta*) of a pre-delta Δ is $\Delta(R)$ for any $R \in \mathbf{R}$. A *subdelta* of a pre-delta Δ is a coordinate of the triplet $\Delta(R)$ for any $R \in \mathbf{R}$.

For an arbitrary pre-delta Δ, we can identify two kinds of "direct" conflict and two kinds of "subtle" conflict for the r-delta corresponding to $R \in \mathbf{R}$:

(D1) (*insert-delete*) $\exists t \in I_{\Delta,R} \cap D_{\Delta,R}$;

(D2) (*modify-modify*) $\exists s, t, t'$ such that $s \times t \in M_{\Delta,R}$, $s \times t' \in M_{\Delta,R}$, and $t \neq t'$.

(S1) (*insert-modify*) $\exists s \in I_{\Delta,R} \cap old(M_{\Delta,R})$

(S2) (*delete-modify*) $\exists t \in D_{\Delta,R} \cap new(M_{\Delta,R})$

In cases (D1) and (D2), the r-delta $\Delta(R)$ is requesting that two different things be done with the same tuple; these cases will be prohibited. The situations arising in cases (S1) and (S2) do have a natural interpretation under the assumption that all modifications in the r-delta are to be applied simultaneously to the members of $DB(R)$. To illustrate, consider the two following examples. For these examples we assume that $\mathbf{R}$ has just one relation R, and denote states DB by simply writing the set $DB(R)$. (Also, we abuse the notation here and below by denoting pre-deltas as the set of atomic updates that correspond to their subdeltas. For example, we write $\{$-R(t), -R(t'), mod R$(s;t)\}$ to denote $(\emptyset, \{t, t'\}, \{s \times t\})$.)

(i) (*delete-modify*) $apply(\{s, t\}, \{$-R(t), mod R$(s;t)\}) = \{t\}$.

(ii) (*modify-insert*) $apply(\{s\}, \{$+R(s), mod R$(s;t)\}) = \{s, t\}$.

Speaking informally, in the first case the "original" copy of t is deleted by -R(t), but s is replaced by a "new" copy of t as a result of mod R$(s;t)$. In the second case the "original" copy of s is replaced by t as a result of mod R$(s;t)$, but a "new" copy of s is inserted by +R(s). In the modify context version of Heraclitus[Alg] described here we have chosen to permit these situations to arise in deltas.

We say that a pre-delta Δ is *consistent* if no r-delta of Δ satisfies conditions (D1) or (D2) above. Consistency of a pre-delta can be checked in $O(n \log n)$ time (sort each coordinate of an r-delta, and check for violations of (D1) and (D2)).

We now return to the discussion of both contexts, and define the *apply* function for non-*fail* deltas (the *apply* function is not defined if the delta is *fail*). In the no-modify context, the mpact of applying a non-*fail* delta Δ on $DB(R)$ is:

(i) if $t \in I_{\Delta,R}$, then t is added to $DB(R)$.

(ii) if $t \in D_{\Delta,R}$, then t is deleted from $DB(R)$.

From the point of view of computation, for a non-*fail* delta Δ and for each $R \in \mathbf{R}$, it can be shown that:

$$apply(DB, \Delta)(R) = (DB(R) \cup I_{\Delta,R}) - D_{\Delta,R}$$
$$= (DB(R) - D_{\Delta,R}) \cup I_{\Delta,R}$$

In the modify context, the impact of applying a non-*fail* delta Δ on $DB(R)$ is:

(a) if $t \in I_{\Delta,R}$, then t is added to $DB(R)$.

(b) if $t \in D_{\Delta,R}$ and $\not\exists s \in DB(R)$ such that $s \times t \in M_{\Delta,R}$, then t is deleted from $DB(R)$.

(c) if $s \in DB(R)$ and $s \times t \in M_{\Delta,R}$, then t is inserted into $DB(R)$.

(d) if $s \times t \in M_{\Delta,R}$, $s \notin I_{\Delta,R}$ and $\not\exists s' \in DB(R)$ such that $s' \times s \in M_{\Delta,R}$, then s is deleted from $DB(R)$.

Of course, in general it is unlikely that a programmer will explicitly call for deltas that include occurrences of conditions (S1) and (S2); if these are not present then the above specification is equivalent to modifying each relation $DB(R)$ by

(a') inserting all tuples in $I_{\Delta,R}$;

(b') deleting all tuples in $D_{\Delta,R}$; and

(c-d') for each $s \times t \in M_{\Delta,R}$, if $s \in DB(R)$ then deleting s and inserting t.

The primary motivation for permitting conditions (S1) and (S2) to be true in deltas is so that the family of non-*fail* deltas will be closed under the smash operator. For example, if (S1) and (S2) were prohibited, then, e.g., $\{-R(s)\}$! $\{mod\ R(t; s)\}$ and $\{mod\ R(s; t)\}!\{+R(s)\}$ would evaluate to *fail*.

From the point of view of computation, for a non-*fail* delta Δ and for each $R \in \mathbf{R}$, it can be shown that:

$$apply(DB, \Delta)(R) = I_{\Delta,R} \cup (DB(R) - (D_{\Delta,R} \cup old(M_{\Delta,R})))$$

$$\cup \{s' \mid \exists s \text{ such that } s \in DB(R) \text{ and } s \times s' \in M_{\Delta,R}\}$$

Letting $n = \alpha(R)$, the last set of tuples in the above expression can also be written as:

$$\pi_{2n+1,\dots,3n}(R \bowtie_{1=n+1 \wedge \dots \wedge n=2n} M_{\Delta,R})$$

For all database states DB, $apply(DB, fail)$ is undefined (and will cause a runtime error if invoked by the system).

It is easily verified that if a delta in the modify context has no modifies, then applying that delta according to the definition for the no-modify context has the same effect as applying it according to the definition for the modify context.

As shown in [GHJL92], in either context the *apply* operator is monotonic on states, in the sense that given states DB_1, DB_2 and delta Δ, if[6] $DB_1 \subseteq DB_2$ then $apply(DB_1, \Delta) \subseteq apply(DB_2, \Delta)$.

In either context, two deltas are *equivalent* (denoted $\equiv$) if they have identical impact when applied to any database state. For example, in the modify context, if we assume that $s \neq t$, $\{\text{-R}(s), \text{+R}(t)\} \equiv \{\text{mod R}(s;t), \text{+R}(t)\}$ and $\{\text{mod R}(s;s)\} \equiv \{\}$. (Note that the behavior of equivalent deltas may differ in the context of merging, e.g., $\{\text{-R}(s), \text{+R}(t)\}\&\{\text{-R}(s)\}$ is consistent but $\{\text{mod R}(s;t), \text{+R}(t)\}\&\{\text{-R}(s)\}$ is not.) As shown in [GHJL92], two deltas Δ_1 and Δ_2 are equivalent iff they applying them yields the same result for all database states with ≤ 1 tuple in them. From this it follows that equivalence can be tested in time $O(n \log n)$.

We now turn to the merge and smash operators. Intuitively, the merge of two deltas is a delta which combines their effects, assuming that they are consistent with each other. In the no-modify context, we first define a pre-merge operation $\widehat{\&}$ on pre-deltas:

$$\Delta_1 \widehat{\&} \Delta_2(R) = (I_{\Delta_1,R} \cup I_{\Delta_2,R}, \ D_{\Delta_1,R} \cup D_{\Delta_2,R})$$

The pre-merge for the modify context is defined as:

$$\Delta_1 \widehat{\&} \Delta_2(R) = (I_{\Delta_1,R} \cup I_{\Delta_2,R}, \ D_{\Delta_1,R} \cup D_{\Delta_2,R}, \ M_{\Delta_1,R} \cup M_{\Delta_2,R})$$

In both contexts, the merge operation is now defined as follows.

$$\Delta_1 \& \Delta_2 = \begin{cases} fail & \text{if } \Delta_1 = fail, \Delta_2 = fail, \text{ or } \Delta_1 \widehat{\&} \Delta_2 \text{ is not consistent} \\ \Delta_1 \widehat{\&} \Delta_2 & \text{otherwise} \end{cases}$$

The smash of two non-*fail* deltas Δ_1 and Δ_2 will be defined to be a Δ such that for each database state DB we have

$$apply(DB, \Delta) = apply(\ apply(DB, \Delta_1), \ \Delta_2)$$

The smash is defined syntactically, without reference to database states: Given Δ_1 and Δ_2 over **R**, if either of these is *fail* then

$$\Delta_1 ! \Delta_2 = fail$$

For the smash of non-*fail* deltas we define each r-delta separately. In the no-modify context, then, $\Delta = \Delta_1 ! \Delta_2$ is defined so that:

$$I_{\Delta,R} \ = \ I_{\Delta_2,R} \cup (I_{\Delta_1,R} - D_{\Delta_2,R})$$

$$D_{\Delta,R} \ = \ D_{\Delta_2,R} \cup (D_{\Delta_1,R} - I_{\Delta_2,R})$$

In the modify context things are, to put it mildly, a bit more intricate. In particular, $\Delta = \Delta_1 ! \Delta_2$ is defined so that for each $R \in \mathbf{R}$,

$$
\begin{aligned}
I_{\Delta,R} \ = \ & I_{\Delta_2,R} \cup (I_{\Delta_1,R} - (D_{\Delta_2,R} \cup old(M_{\Delta_2,R}))) \\
& \cup \{s' \mid \exists s \text{ such that } s \in I_{\Delta_1,R} \text{ and } s \times s' \in M_{\Delta_2,R}\}
\end{aligned}
$$

$$
\begin{aligned}
D_{\Delta,R} \ = \ & [D_{\Delta_1,R} \cup (D_{\Delta_2,R} - old(M_{\Delta_1,R})) \\
& \cup \{s \mid \exists s' \text{ such that } s \times s' \in M_{\Delta_1,R} \text{ and } s' \in D_{\Delta_2,R}\}] \\
& - I_{\Delta,R}
\end{aligned}
$$

$$
\begin{aligned}
M_{\Delta,R} \ = \ & (M_{\Delta_1,R} - \{s \times s' \in M_{\Delta_1,R} \mid s' \in D_{\Delta_2,R} \cup old(M_{\Delta_2,R})\}) \\
& \cup (M_{\Delta_2,R} - \{s' \times s'' \in M_{\Delta_2,R} \mid s' \in D_{\Delta_1,R} \cup old(M_{\Delta_1,R})\}) \\
& \cup \{s \times s'' \mid \exists s' \text{ such that } s \times s' \in M_{\Delta_1,R} \text{ and } s' \times s'' \in M_{\Delta_2,R}\}
\end{aligned}
$$

---

[6] We write $DB \subseteq DB'$ if $DB(R) \subseteq DB'(R)$ for each $R \in \mathbf{R}$.

Speaking informally, in this definition the first two union terms of the $I_{\Delta,R}$ expression are quite natural, and the third term takes care of the case where Δ_1 inserts (more correctly, calls for the insertion of) a tuple and Δ_2 modifies that tuple. The third union term of the $D_{\Delta,R}$ expression takes care of the case where Δ_1 modifies a tuple and then Δ_2 deletes the modified tuple. $I_{\Delta,R}$ is subtracted in this expression because, e.g., the first union term $D_{\Delta_1,R}$ may call for the deletion of a tuple which is to be inserted by $I_{\Delta,R}$; in this case the insertion should take precedence. Turning to the $M_{\Delta,R}$ expression, the first union term corresponds to the case where Δ_1 modifies a tuple and Δ_2 doesn't change it further; the second union term to the case where Δ_1 leaves a tuple alone and Δ_2 modifies it; and the third union term to the case where Δ_1 modifies a tuple s to s', and Δ_2 modifies s' to s''.

A formal proof is given in [GHJL92] which shows that in both contexts the smash of two non-$fail$ deltas is consistent, and has the desired behavior.

Some examples of the smash are (assuming that $R = R$, where $\sigma(R) = ($int$)$):

1. $\{$mod $R(2;1)\}$! $\{$-$R(1)\} = \{$-$R(1),$ -$R(2)\}$

2. $\{$-$R(1)\}$! $\{$mod $R(2;1)\} = \{$-$R(1),$ mod $R(2;1)\}$

3. $\{$+$R(1)\}$! $\{$mod $R(1;2)\} = \{$+$R(1),$ +$R(2)\}$

4. $\{$mod $R(1;2)\}$! $\{$+$R(1)\} = \{$+$R(1),$ mod $R(1;2)\}$

Note that the output in case (2) violates (S1) from above, and the output in case (4) violates (S2).

We conclude this section by considering the semantics of "peeking" and of "hypothesizing". The commands for peeking, namely peekins, peekdel [and peekmod], permit the direct examination of a subdelta; for example, the command peekmod(R,D) returns the relation $M_{\Delta,R}$, where Δ is the current value of D.

The semantics for the when operator, which implements hypothesizing, is more complex. In both contexts the semantics for Heraclitus[Alg] a function $eval : state \times expression \rightarrow value$ that evaluates expressions relative to a given state is defined. For expressions not involving when this is defined in the usual manner. For a state DB and expression E and delta expression D,

$$eval(DB, E \text{ when } D) = eval(\ apply(DB, eval(DB, D)),\ E)$$

i.e., the result of evaluating E when D over DB is equal to the result of evaluating E over $apply(DB, eval(DB, D))$.

It can be shown that when "distributes" over the algebraic operators for relations and deltas. For example,

$$eval(DB, \text{cross}(R,S) \text{ when } D) = eval(DB, \text{cross}(R \text{ when } D,\ S \text{ when } D))$$

This transformation is necessary for implementing expressions which involve when's (see Section 5). The interaction of nested when's and $eval$ is especially interesting: for delta expressions D_1, D_2,

$$eval(DB, (E \text{ when } D_1)\text{ when } D_2) = eval(DB, E \text{ when } (\ D_2\ !\ (\ D_1 \text{ when } D_2\ )))$$

This equality is central to the implementation of nested when's in HERALD (see Section 5).

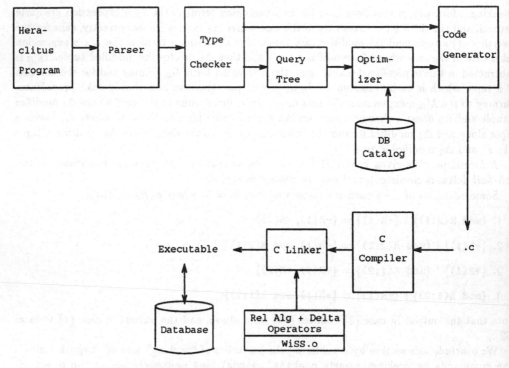

Figure 1: Building components of HERALD

5 Design of HERALD

At this time we have implemented HERaclitus ALgebra for Deltas (HERALD) to support Heraclitus[Alg] in both the no-modify and modify contexts. Essentially all of the system description presented here applies to both contexts. Indeed, the no-modify context is implemented simply by disabling the modify field of all subdeltas, and omitting all manipulations involving the modify field.

We begin by presenting a brief overview of the system architecture. Next, we describe two novel features of the system.

File services in HERALD are provided by the Wisconsin Storage System (WiSS) [CDKK85]. We are implementing relational algebra and delta operators using WiSS. HERALD is quite independent of WiSS and could be ported to other relational file systems with minimal difficulty.

In Figure 1, we present the architecture of HERALD. Given a C program with embedded Heraclitus commands, we use a parser and type checker to process each Heraclitus command to an internal *syntax tree* representation. This tree may not be directly executable due to the presence of when operator nodes (see Section 5.3). Consequently, we transform a *syntax tree* to a *query tree*. Logically, the internal nodes of a query tree are either relational algebra or delta operations. Next, an optimizer reorders the operators of this tree in order to minimize the number of disk I/Os required to execute it. This module accesses the database catalog to retrieve the required statistics to evaluate the cost of alternative execution plans for a query. Our code generation module consumes this query tree and generates the necessary function calls to our storage manager (WiSS + relational and delta operators) to implement the appropriate behavior. Thus, the code generation routine replaces a Heraclitus Query tree with appropriate

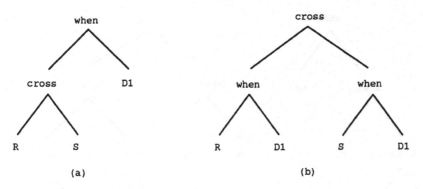

Figure 2: Transformation of a when expression

function calls, generating a C program. This C program is compiled and linked with an extended version of WiSS to generate an executable Heraclitus program that accesses and manipulates the database.

The two novel features of this implementation are: 1) extending WiSS to provide effective support for delta variables and operators, and 2) translating a parsed syntax tree into an executable query tree representation. We begin by providing a brief overview of WiSS. This is followed by a description of the techniques to support the novel features of HERALD.

5.1 Overview of Wisconsin Storage System

WiSS provides file services that include structured sequential files, byte stream files as in UNIX, B^+ indices, a Hash index, long data items, a sort utility, and a scan mechanism. A sequential file is a sequence of records. Records may vary in length (up to one page in length), and may be inserted and deleted at arbitrary locations within a sequential file. Optionally, each sequential file may have one or more associated indices. The index maps key values to the records of the sequential file that contain a matching value. Furthermore, one indexed attribute may be used as a clustering attribute for the file. The scan mechanism provided by WiSS is similar to that of System R's RSS [ABC+76].

We are using WiSS to implement relational algebra operators (select, join, project, union, difference, intersection, and aggregates) along with delta operators (apply, merge, smash, when, peekmod, peekdel, peekadd, bulkmod, and bulkdel). Below, we describe the physical representation of a delta variable.

5.2 Implementation of Deltas

Conceptually, HERALD represents a delta by storing the three sub-deltas $(I_{\Delta,R}, D_{\Delta,R}, M_{\Delta,R})$ of Δ for each variable R (see Section 4). Thus, if there are n declared internal and external relation variables in a Heraclitus[Alg] program, there can be as many as $3n$ WiSS relations used to represent a delta. In actuality, a WiSS relation is created only for those subdeltas that are nonempty (determined at run time).

The implementation of the various delta operators (e.g., apply, smash) is defined as a series of calls to relational algebra operators. This implementation follows the semantics described in Section 4.

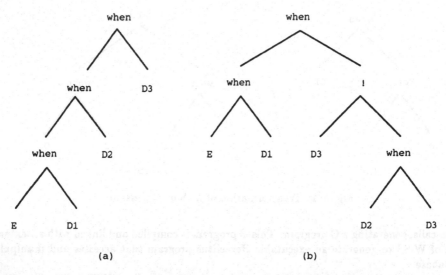

Figure 3: Translation of a nested **when** expression.

5.3 Query Tree Representation of Heraclitus[Alg] expressions

Similar to a relational system, we translate the relational and delta expressions to a tree format where each node represents an operator that manipulates one or two input sets. There are two advantages to using a query tree for executing an expression: 1) it simplifies the query optimization step, and 2) it unifies the interface for invoking relational and delta operations.

While obtaining the query tree representation of an expression with either the *smash* or *merge* operator is straightforward, that of *when* is complicated. We implement expression E **when** D by "pushing" the delta expression D to the atomic subexpressions of E. For example, given expression (cross(R,S) when D1), we transform the syntax tree of Figure 2.a into the query tree of Figure 2.b which can be executed directly.

The situation is more complex if nested **when** operators occur in a syntax tree, i.e., if the left subtree of a **when** operator is again a **when** operator (see below). Recall from Section 4 that an expression ((E **when** D1) **when** D2) can be translated to (E **when** (D2 ! (D1 **when** D2))). In order to create an executable query tree for an expression with nested **when** operators, we perform this translation step repeatedly on the tree in a top-down manner. So, for example, consider the syntax tree representation of the algebraic expression ((E **when** D1) **when** D2) **when** D3 (see Figure 3.a). In the first iteration, we perform the translation on the two **when** nodes at the root to construct the tree in Figure 3.b. We apply the translation step once again to obtain the tree in Figure 4. This tree is an executable query tree. Note that it has two common subtrees (circled with dotted lines). We detect the common subtrees at compile time and replace them with the final result of the leftmost subtree in order to avoid duplicate computations when executing the tree[7].

6 Related Work

There are two fundamental differences between differential files [SL76] and Heraclitus[Alg]: First, the main focus of Heraclitus is at the conceptual and programming level as opposed to the phys-

---

[7]We are assuming that a query tree is executed in a post-traversal order.

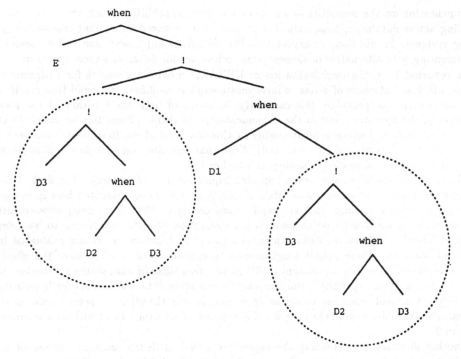

Figure 4: An executable query tree.

ical implementation level. Second, Heraclitus provides the user with constructs to manipulate one or more deltas. In particular, deltas can be used in conjunction with the relational algebra operators.

[WCL91] describes the implementation of the Starburst Rule System, which supports set-oriented production rules in Starburst [HCL+90]. The implementation uses "transition tables" that, similar to deltas, are logical tables reflecting the changes that have occurred during the successive application of rules. The transition tables support inserts, deletes and modifies, and the rule syntax supports peeking and hypothesizing based on the transition tables created during the course of rule firing. An underlying assumption in that system is that each tuple has a unique tuple identifier; as a result the operations on transition tables are less intricate than the operations for deltas with modify presented here for the "pure" relational model. Also, Heraclitus[Alg] provides constructs for creating and manipulating arbitrary deltas and our implementation accommodates this flexibility; in this sense the delta manipulation supported by Heraclitus[Alg] is richer than that of the Starburst system.

7 Conclusions and Future Research Directions

The research described here makes two fundamental contributions: (a) the development of the language Heraclitus[Alg], which incorporates deltas and delta operators into the relational algebra framework, and (b) the development of techniques for implementing deltas, their operators, and expressions using them in terms of the HERALD system. This is the first step towards implementing a rich database programming language that supports deltas and can be used for experimentation on the semantics of advanced database capabilities which use virtual states, including active databases, hypothetical databases and advanced concurrent transaction processing systems. In addition, we expect that the HERALD implementation will be useful for experimenting with alternative implementation techniques for deltas and their operators.

As reported here, the implementation of HERALD provided a vehicle for designing and implementing an extension of deltas to incorporate explicit modifies. We found that significant costs are incurred in providing this capability, in terms of both the intricacy of the logical definition of the operators, and in the implementation of them. ¿From this we conclude that it is inappropriate to include explicit modify at this low level of the Heraclitus framework (at least, if the "pure" relational model is used). Note that this does not exclude the possibility of providing some form of modify capability at a higher level.

The investigation here raises several specific topics for further research. The first of these concerns the syntax and semantics of deltas themselves. The deltas presented here incorporate inserts, deletes (and modifies) that are explicit and concrete. We are currently experimenting with an enriched mechanism which permits the evaluation of delta expressions to be *delayed* (see [GHJLL91]). This allows delta expressions to act as functions which are evaluated in a variety of contexts. These permit programmers to express updates which have the effect of "Give everybody in the Toy department a 10% raise," regardless of what state or virtual state is currently active. This capability is fundamental to providing database support for hypothetical reasoning. A second extension of deltas developed in [GHJLL91] is to permit *wild-cards* in deletes. For example, <-R(2,*)> calls for the deletion of all tuples in R with first coordinate equal to 2.

Another direction for extending the expressive power of deltas concerns the use of *variables* in atomic delta expressions. For example, if $Salary$ holds salary information, then in this richer syntax the command mod Salary(x,y;x,y*1.1) would have the effect of giving everyone a 10% raise. One price for this extension is that the family of non-*fail* deltas would no longer be closed under smash. For example, if R has signature (int,int) then mod R(1,2;1,3) ! mod R(x,2;x-5,2) cannot be expressed as a delta in this syntax. A possible solution is to go to an even richer family of deltas by using a syntax permitting expressions such as 'x /= 2', as found in the language of [AV89].

A crucial component of any system supporting deltas will be the efficiency with which delta operators and expressions are evaluated. An important task here is the development of optimization techniques for minimizing the cost of evaluating a query tree with delta operators. This is especially important because Heraclitus[Alg] can easily serve as the foundation for numerous other languages using deltas. Now that HERALD is implemented, we have begun to perform an in-depth performance analysis of the system to evaluate the tradeoffs associated with using deltas and delta operators (see [GHJLL91]).

8   Acknowledgment

We would like to thank the team of students who were involved in the implemenation of HERALD: Martha Escabar, Ching-Lan Ho, Ming-Dar Jaw, Jessie Kang, Chung-hsi Lai, Yoram Landau, Miao-Ying Liu, Junhui Luo, Prem Ranganathan, Ching-Yuan Shen, Ming-Yeh Shen, Cheng-hsiang Wan, and Paul Woo.

References

ABC+76] M. Astrahan, M. Blasgen, D. Chamberlin, K. Eswaran, J. Gray, P. Griffiths, W. King, R. Lorie, P. McJones, J. Mehl, G. Putzolu, I. Traiger, B. Wade, and V. Watson. System R: A relational approach to data base management. *ACM Trans. on Database Systems*, 1(2):97–137, June 1976.

AV89] S. Abiteboul and V. Vianu. A transaction-based approach to relational database specification. *J. ACM*, 36(4):758–789, October 1989.

CCCR+90] F. Cacace, S. Ceri, S. Crespi-Reghizzi, L. Tanca, and R. Zicari. Integrating object-oriented data modeling with a rule-based programming paradigm. In *Proc. ACM SIGMOD Symp. on the Management of Data*, pages 225–236, 1990.

CDKK85] H-T. Chou, D. DeWitt, R. Katz, and T. Klug. Design and implementation of the Wisconsin Storage System (WiSS). *Software Practices and Experience*, 15(10), October 1985.

GHJL92] S. Ghandeharizadeh, R. Hull, D. Jacobs, and J. Luo. Heraclitus[Alg]: Syntax, semantics, and implementation. Technical report, USC Computer Science Department, 1992. in preparation.

GHJLL91] S. Ghandeharizadeh, R. Hull, D. Jacobs, J. Luo, and Y. Landau. Design, implementation, and evaluation of Heraclitus[Alg]. Technical report, USC Computer Science Department, 1991. in preparation.

HCL+90] L. Haas, W. Chang, G. Lohman, J. McPherson, P. Wilms, G. Lapis, B. Lindsay, H. Pirahesh, M. Carey, and E. Shekita. Starburst mid-flight: As the dust clears. *IEEE Transactions on Knowledge and Data Engineering*, 2(1):143–160, March 1990.

HJ91a] R. Hull and D. Jacobs. Language constructs for programming active databases. In *Proc. of Intl. Conf. on Very Large Data Bases*, pp. 455-468, September 1991.

HJ91b] R. Hull and D. Jacobs. On the semantics of rules in database programming languages. In J. Schmidt and A. Stogny, editors, *Next Generation Information System Technology: Proc. of the First International East/West Workshop, Kiev, USSR, October 1990*. Springer-Verlag LNCS, Volume 504, 1991.

JH91] D. Jacobs and R. Hull. Database programming with delayed updates. In *Intl. Workshop on Database Programming Languages*, San Mateo, Calif., 1991. Morgan-Kaufmann, Inc. to appear.

MP90] C.B. Medeiros and P. Pfeffer. A mechanism for managing rules in an object-oriented database. Technical report, Altair, 1990.

SL76] D. Severance and G. Lohman. Differential files: Their application to the maintenance of large databases. *ACM Trans. on Database Systems*, 1(3):256–267, September 1976.

WCL91] J. Widom, R. Cochrane, and B. Lindsay. Implementing set-oriented production rules as an extension to Starburst. Technical Report RJ 7979 (73248), IBM Almaden Research Center, San Jose, CA (appears in *Intl. Conf. on Very Large Databases*, 1991), February 1991.

Adaptive and Automated Index Selection in RDBMS

Martin R. Frank, Edward R. Omiecinski and Shamkant B. Navathe

College of Computing, Georgia Institute of Technology, Atlanta GA 30332-0280, USA
{martin,edwardo,sham}@cc.gatech.edu

We present a novel approach for a tool that assists the database administrator in designing an index configuration for a relational database system. A new methodology for collecting usage statistics at run time is developed which lets the optimizer estimate query execution costs for alternative index configurations. Defining the workload specification required by existing index design tools may be very complex for a large integrated database system. Our tool automatically derives the workload statistics. These statistics are then used to efficiently compute an index configuration. Execution of a prototype of the tool against a sample database demonstrates that the proposed index configuration is reasonably close to the optimum for test query sets.

1 Introduction

Relational database management systems (RDBMS) are by far the most popular database systems today. Despite their known shortcomings in non-traditional applications like engineering and image processing, no clear alternatives have evolved despite substantial research. Thus RDBMS are likely to dominate the commercial arena for years to come, especially for business applications.

Relational databases use indices to provide fast access to data. The presence of an index reduces the search time for indexed data items but also complicates update operations since the tuples as well as the indices must be updated. Hence there is a tradeoff involved in selecting indices and indexing every column is rarely a good idea[1]. This tradeoff decision will be referred to as the *index selection problem* (ISP).

In the context of this paper the ISP refers to tailoring the index configuration to the database usage profile, not to selecting an index set to process a single query. The *single-relation* ISP denotes the ISP reduced to selecting an index configuration for a single relation, which is much easier than the general ISP since join queries pose the hardest problems. The *single-index* ISP refers to choosing an index configuration consisting of single indices, combined (concatenated) indices are excluded from consideration.

The decision as to which attributes to index is influenced by numerous factors, such as database usage, characteristics of the database system and the underlying operating system. Due to this complexity, it is difficult for the unassisted database administrator (DBA) to choose a good index configuration for a large integrated database. Tools were

---

[1] In the context of B-tree indices, not Grid files.

proposed which relieve some of this burden from the DBA, however even the most so-phisticated ones like DBDSGN [FST88] still require the DBA to manually specify the *workload*. The designer has to specify the workload as a small set of weighted representative queries. It is unclear how the DBA can condense the transactions on a huge DBMS (consider 100 tables and 1000 transactions per hour) to just – say – 20 representing the original workload. Hence mechanisms have to be found which derive the workload information for those tools from the database system itself.

Throughout this paper the *workload specification* (or *usage input*) denotes the part of the input for index selection tools which contains information about the workload for which the index configuration is optimized. The workload specification may consist of statistics (e.g. how often a certain column was referenced or updated during the last time period) or representative queries.

Research in the area of automated index selection has treated statistics gathering and statistics evaluation *separately*. Consequently: (1) the existing statistics gathering mech-anisms – originally intended for debugging – consume too much overhead to continuously collect usage data ,and (2) the existing index selection tools are rarely used in practice because they require hard-to-derive statistics as input. It is our belief that a successful tool must integrate both aspects.

Our tool requires no usage input specified by the designer, it derives all its input automatically during regular database usage. The output is an optimum[2] index confi-guration for the queries during the recording period in the sense that it minimizes the average query execution time.

2 Previous Research

We discuss previous work on the index selection problem (ISP) with respect to the work-load specification. The list is by no means complete. Research in the area not discussed here has been done by Palermo [Pal70], King [Kin74] and many others.

Stonebraker [Sto74] constructs a probabilistic model for database activity and solves the single-index single-relation ISP for certain special cases in polynomial time. The formalization of the index selection problem provides insight into its difficulty, but the results are valid for special cases only and there is no methodology presented for finding an index configuration for the general case. The usage input parameters are (1) the probability that a query is a non-retrieval query (Insert, Delete, Update) as opposed to a retrieval query (Select) and (2) for all columns i the probability that column c_i appears restrictively in a query. These statistics have to be specified as input to the tool. It is obvious that these statistics are not trivial to derive. There are also some general problems with analytical approaches to the ISP. First, substantial simplifications have to be made to derive an analytical solution. Second, the model becomes obsolete if there are changes to the query processing strategy or to other modeled aspects of the DBMS.

Schkolnick [Sch75] presents a more general probabilistic model and an algorithm that solves the single-index single-relation ISP significantly faster than the naive approach. As in [Sto74] a cost function is derived that gives the expected average query execution cost depending on the index configuration. An algorithm is presented that finds the optimal

---

[2] Truly optimal only for a restricted version of the index selection problem.

index configuration provided that the target function is *regular*. The usage input has a similar flavor as in [Sto74], for example the probability $\alpha_j(a)$ that column j is restricted to value a in a query. The approach does not qualify for a practical index selection tool since (1) maintaining the detailed statistics used in the cost function requires too much overhead (2) the amount of storage for these statistics is substantial (3) and the cost of the evaluation run ($O(2^{\sqrt{c}\log c})$) is still too costly even for a moderate number of columns c. There are also the general problems of analytical approaches for an index selection tool as discussed above.

Hammer and Chan [HC76] envision fully-automated index selection (single-index, single relation) but their approach is unrealistic for real-life databases in various ways. Fully automated index selection means that the system adopts the current index configuration based on automatically gathered statistics so that users do not even have to know about the concept of indices. An example for the database usage statistics used are the restrictive clauses for every query. Gathering, maintaining and evaluating such detailed statistics is clearly infeasible for an unrestricted query language.

Whang et al. [WWS81] present a single-index multiple-relation index selection method based on a set of join methods that is *separable*. This property reduces the index selection problem to finding a *locally* optimal index configuration for each relation. The set of join methods is reduced to two because these are the only ones adhering to separability. It is unclear if the advantage of a better index configuration outweighs the disadvantage of not using efficient join methods which would otherwise be available. The usage input consists of a weighted set of queries. This is an improvement over specifying statistics of the kind discussed above. The general problem with this form of usage input is that the "representative" query set might not be representative of the real workload because it has to be of moderate size for complexity reasons.

Finkelstein, Schkolnick and Tiberio [FST88] discuss the single-index multiple-relation index selection methodology used by the commercially available physical design tool RDT (Relational Design Tool) and its experimental prototype DBDSGN (DataBase DeSiGN Tool). The usage input consists of a weighted representative query set as in [WWS81]. An obstacle for its success is that the designer has to specify a set of non-intuitive parameters to reduce the run time of the tool which require insight into the internal algorithm of the tool. The designer could choose not to specify any of these parameters but then the execution time would become impractical. However, the most significant problem is – again – finding a "representative" query set for the real database usage.

3 Index Benefit Graphs

Which indices[3] are useful for a given query and how useful are they? This is the central question for any index selection tool operating on a query-by-query basis.

Our tool "converses" with the optimizer to answer this question. An example for such a dialog is shown in figure 1, it is shown in natural language for illustration only. The last response shown terminates the dialog. A special case for the optimizer's first response is that it would use a sequential scan (or that the database transaction does not require access to tables at all). Then no savings are recorded for any index.

---

[3] This includes indices which do not currently exist.

Tool: Which index would you use for query q if you could choose from a virtual index set p_1 which contains all possible indices for the database? And what is your cost estimate for executing the query using this index?

Optimizer: I would use index i_1, my cost estimate for the query using this index is c_1.

Tool: What is your index choice and cost estimate for query q when you can choose from the previous index set minus the index you just used ($p_2 = p_1 - i_1$)?

Optimizer: Then I would use index i_2, the cost estimate is c_2.

Tool: What is your index choice and cost estimate for the index set $p_3 = p_2 - i_2$?

$$\vdots$$

Optimizer: Then I would use index i_n, the cost estimate is c_n.

Tool: What is your index choice and cost estimate for the index set $p_n - i_n$?

Optimizer: Then I would not use any index at all but would rather do a sequential scan. The cost estimate for it is c_{seq}.

Fig. 1. The Dialog between Tool and Optimizer

The optimizer must provide the following functionality: presented with an SQL statement [CB74] and an index set to choose from for processing a given statement it must be able to export the index set it would choose and its cost estimate for processing the query using this set[4]:

optimizer(st: statement, presented-with: index-set) → chosen: index-set, cost: real

The difference of this requirement as compared to the existing EXPLAIN statements [FST88] is that the combined functionality of the EXPLAIN COST and EXPLAIN PLAN statements only provides for the following:

optimizer(st: statement) → chosen: index-set, cost: real

So EXPLAIN statements can only provide optimizer information based on the *currently existing* index configuration. Our tool constructs an *Index Benefit Graph* (IBG) using the information from the dialog, a simple example of such a graph is shown in figure 2. The label on an arrow is the index set the optimizer is presented with, the index set the optimizer chooses is pointed to by the arrow. These sets will be referred to as the *presented-with* and *chosen* sets. The encircled number denotes the optimizer's cost estimate for the query if the index set to its left is used. The numbers in squares provide a numbering of the nodes. This IBG corresponds to the dialog in figure 1 where $i_1 = \{b\}, i_2 = \{d\}, i_3 = \{c\}, i_4 = \{a\}, p_1 = \{a, b, c, d\}, p_2 = \{a, c, d\}, p_3 = \{a, c\}, p_4 = \{a\}, p_5 = \{\}, c_1 = 23, c_2 = 27, c_3 = 51, c_4 = 51$ and $c_{seq} = 80$.

So far we have assumed that the optimizer chooses at most one index per query. In this case constructing the IBG is straightforward. Let us now consider the general case.

---

[4] We will discuss alternative cost measures shortly, assume the cost is the execution time for the moment.

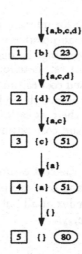

Fig. 2. A Simple Index Benefit Graph

Index *sets* are chosen to process a query. This leads to the problem of determining which subsets of the chosen set would also be beneficial, the *beneficial subsets problem*. If an index set $\{a, b, c, d\}$ is used, would the set $\{a, c, d\}$, say, also be beneficial? And what would be the execution cost when using $\{a, c, d\}$?

There is a simple way to solve the problem. Let the elements of a set be numbered in an arbitrary but consistent way (e.g. alphabetically) and let a singleton set consisting of the ith element of set C be denoted by C^i. For each node of the graph where the optimizer was presented with index set P, spawn all possible subsets of size $|P-1|$, namely $P - P^i$ for $1 \leq i \leq |P|$. We will refer to a graph built in this way as a *Brute-Force Graph* (BFG). An example for a BFG is shown in figure 3. For example, in the root node $P = \{a, b, c, d\}$ so that $|P| = 4$ subgraphs starting with $P - P^1 = \{a, b, c, d\} - \{a\} = \{b, c, d\}$, $P - P^2 = \{a, c, d\}$, $P - P^3 = \{a, b, d\}$ and $P - P^4 = \{a, b, c\}$ are spawned. This results in a graph with $2^{|P_R|}$ nodes where P_R denotes the set the optimizer is initially presented with in the root node. This graph presents the optimizer with all possible subsets of P, and will therefore contain all sets that the optimizer may choose to process the query.

Building a graph exponential in the number of potential indices for every query is infeasible. Our IBGs consist of far less nodes than corresponding BFGs on average which makes their use practical. Index Benefit Graphs are constructed in the following way. If the optimizer chose the index set C from the index set P it was presented with, then $|C|$ subgraphs starting with $P - C^i$ are spawned for $1 \leq i \leq |C|$. Figure 4 gives an example for an IBG constructed in this way. For example, in the root node $P = \{a, b, c, d\}$ and $C = \{a, b\}$, so that $|C| = 2$ subgraphs starting with $P - C^1 = \{a, b, c, d\} - \{a\} = \{b, c, d\}$ and $P - C^2 = \{a, b, c, d\} - \{b\} = \{a, c, d\}$ are spawned.

An IBG contains far less nodes than a BFG on average. Does this mean that we miss chosen sets that are contained in a BFG? In the rest of this section we prove that this cannot happen assuming that the optimizer shows reasonable ("sane") behavior. The main result is that the IBG contains the same information as the corresponding BFG if

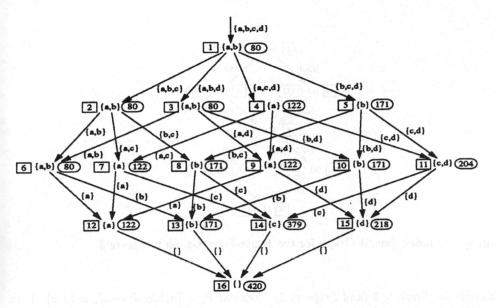

Fig. 3. A Brute-Force Graph (for the Query "select * from X, Y where X.b = Y.d and X.a = Y.c;")

the "Sanity Property" holds.

Let P_1 and P_2 denote index sets the optimizer is presented with, C_1 and C_2 are index sets the optimizer chooses for executing a given query. $P \to C$ means "presented with P the optimizer chooses C ($\subseteq P$)". Let $A \subset B$ denote that A is a *proper* subset of B. The empty set is denoted by {}.

Property 1 (The Sanity Property) *"For a given query, new indices to choose from can only affect the chosen index set when they are part of it."*

$$\forall P_1, C_1, P_2 \supset P_1, C_2 : (P_1 \to C_1 \land P_2 \to C_2) \Rightarrow (C_2 = C_1) \lor (C_2 \cap (P_2 - P_1) \neq \{\})$$

Property 2 (Derived from Property 1) *"For a given query, if some indices were chosen from a presented-with set then they will be chosen again from a subset of this set which still contains all the chosen indices."*

$$\forall P_2, C_2 : (P_2 \to C_2) \Rightarrow (\forall P_1, C_2 \subseteq P_1 \subset P_2 : P_1 \to C_2)$$

Proof of (1) ⇒ (2) (by Contradiction) Assume a violation of property 2: $\exists P_1, C_1, P_2, C_2 :$ $C_2 \subseteq P_1 \subset P_2 \land C_1 \neq C_2 \land P_1 \to C_1 \land P_2 \to C_2$. This implies: $\exists P_1, C_1, P_2 \supset P_1, C_2 :$ $P_1 \to C_1 \land P_2 \to C_2 \Rightarrow (C_2 \neq C_1) \land (C_2 \subseteq P_1 \subset P_2)$. This violates property 1 since: $C_2 \subseteq P_1 \subset P_2 : C_2 \cap (P_2 - P_1) = (C_2 \cap P_2) - (C_2 \cap P_1) = C_2 - C_2 = \{\}$. □

283

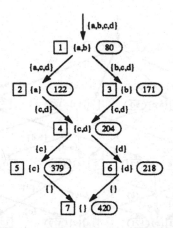

Fig. 4. The Index Benefit Graph for the Brute-Force Graph in Figure 3

Example for Property 2 (and Property 1) Consider $P_1 = \{a, b, c, d\} \to C_1 = \{b, c\}$. Then according to property 2 this implies:

1. $(P_2 = \{b, c\}) \to \{b, c\}$
2. $(P_2' = \{a, b, c\}) \to \{b, c\}$
3. $(P_2'' = \{b, c, d\}) \to \{b, c\}$

Property 3 (Also derived from Property 1) *"For a given query, if the optimizer chooses from a superset of some presented-with set then it cannot choose a subset of the set it chose for this presented-with set before."*

$$\forall P_1, C_1, P_2 \supset P_1, C_2 : (P_1 \to C_1 \land P_2 \to C_2) \Rightarrow C_2 \not\subseteq C_1$$

Proof of (1) $\Rightarrow$ (3) Properties 1 and 3 have the same left hand side. The right hand side of 1 gives: $(C_2 = C_1) \lor (C_2 \cap (P_2 - P_1) \neq \{\})$. If $C_2 = C_1$ then $C_2 \not\subseteq C_1$ follows trivially, else: $C_2 \cap (P_2 - P_1) \neq \{\} \Leftrightarrow \exists x : x \in C_2 \land x \in P_2 \land x \notin P_1 \Rightarrow \exists x : x \in C_2 \land x \notin P_1 \Rightarrow C_2 \not\subseteq P_1 \Rightarrow C_2 \not\subseteq C_1 (\subseteq P_1)$. $\qquad \square$

Example for Property 3 (and Property 1) Consider $P_1 = \{a\}$, $C_1 = \{a\}$ and $P_2 = \{a, b\}$. What are optimizer choices for C_2 adhering to this property?

1. $C_2 = \{a, b\}$ is legal – using both indices may reduce execution time.
2. $C_2 = \{a\}$ is legal – index b is of no use for this query.
3. $C_2 = \{b\}$ is legal – b outperforms a for this query.
4. $C_2 = \{\}$ is illegal – if a is useful when presented with $\{a\}$ then a should still be useful if the optimizer can choose from the superset $\{a, b\}$. If the index set the optimizer can chose from is augmented this should not make subsets useless that were chosen before.

Assume the optimizer violates the property and makes the choice under item 4 above. Then no savings would be recorded for any index because the optimizer did not use any. We missed that the optimizer would have chosen $\{a\}$ if presented with just $\{a\}$ instead of $\{a, b\}$. Property 3 ensures that such cases cannot occur.

Theorem 1 Auxiliary for Cover. *A graph starting with the presented-with superset $X \supset Y$ contains all chosen sets that a graph starting with the subset Y contains if $|X| = |Y| + 1$.*

Proof (by Induction)
Basis: The theorem trivially holds for $|Y| = 0$ $(Y = \{\})$.
Hypothesis: The theorem holds for $|Y| = k - 1$ $(k \geq 1)$.
Step: Let $|Y| = k$, $e \in X - Y$ and let C be the set chosen from X.

1. $e \in C$. Then a graph starting with $X - \{e\} = Y$ is spawned and this graph will trivially contain all the *chosen* sets for a graph starting with Y because it is identical.
2. $e \notin C$. Then due to Property 1 the same set will be chosen for $X = Y \cup \{e\}$ as was chosen for Y. Thus the same sets as before are spawned, but each augmented by e. Figure 5 illustrates this. The problem is reduced to proving that the subgraphs starting with $X_i = (Y \cup \{e\}) - C^i = (Y - C^i) \cup e$ (since $e \notin C$) cover the graphs starting with $Y_i = Y - C^i$ for $1 \leq i \leq |C|$. This is the case due to the hypothesis since $|Y_i| = |Y - C^i| = k - 1$. □

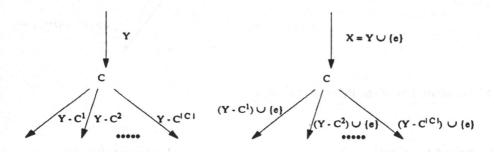

Fig. 5. Illustration of the Proof of Theorem 1

Theorem 2 Cover. *A graph starting with the presented-with superset $X \supset Y$ contains all chosen sets that a graph starting with the subset Y contains.*

Proof Let
$$A_i = \begin{cases} Y & \text{if } i = 0 \\ A_{i-1} \cup (X - Y)^i & \text{if } 1 \leq i \leq |X - Y|, \end{cases}$$

which implies $Y = A_0 \subset A_1 \subset \ldots \subset A_{|X-Y|} = X$ where $|A_i| + 1 = |A_{i+1}|$ for $0 \leq i \leq |X - Y| - 1$. Theorem 2 holds for each pair (A_i, A_{i+1}) due to Theorem 1, so that Theorem 2 holds for (X, Y) by transitivity. □

285

Theorem 3 Auxiliary for Lossless. *The subgraphs not spawned from any node in the graph contain no chosen sets which are not covered by the spawned subgraphs of this node.*

Proof Let P be the *presented-with* set of this node and let C be the set chosen from P. Then $m = |C|$ subgraphs of the form $P_i = P - C^i$ are spawned $(1 \leq i \leq m)$ and $n = |P-C|$ subgraphs of the form $P_j = P-(P-C)^j$ are *not* spawned $(m+1 \leq j \leq m+n)$. Pick an arbitrary non-spawned subgraph P_j. Since $C \subset P_j = P-(P-C)^j \subset P$ the same set C will be chosen for P_j as was chosen for P due to Property 2 (and thus Property 1). The m subgraphs spawned from node j are $P_{j,i} = P-(P-C)^j-C^i$ $(1 \leq i \leq m)$. Figure 6 illustrates this. For all $i \in \{1,\ldots,m\}$ it holds that $P_{j,i} = P-(P-C)^j-C^i \subset P-C^i = P_i$, so that each subgraph starting with $P_{j,i}$ is covered by the subgraph starting with P_i due to Theorem 2. Thus the subgraphs of the node not spawned contain no information that is not already covered by subgraphs which were spawned. □

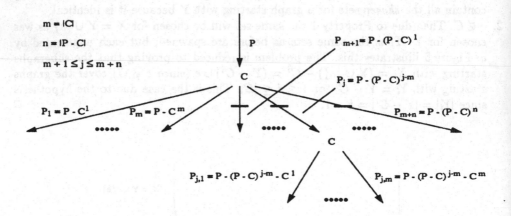

Fig. 6. Illustration of the Proof of Theorem 3

Lemma 4 Lossless. *An Index Benefit Graph contains all index sets the optimizer would choose to process the query if the Sanity Property is assumed.*

Proof Since Theorem 3 holds for all nodes of the graph including the root node the pruning of the graph in this way is lossless and the Index Benefit Graph contains all chosen index sets that the corresponding Brute-Force Graph contains, where no subgraphs are pruned. □

4 Our Tool

An IBG contains all index sets the optimizer would choose for a given query. Retaining all these sets for each query would allow to find the optimal index configuration for a set of queries at the expense of substantial storage cost for these statistics and of an evaluation run exponential in the number of indices. This is a viable methodology for a tool tailoring the index configuration to a small number of given queries like DBDSGN. It is not viable for a run-time tool operating on a continuous query stream due to the large number of queries processed.

Therefore our tool condenses the information contained in an IBG. Condensing the information is necessarily heuristic so that the proposed index configurations are no longer guaranteed to be truly optimal. However the performance of the methodology proved to be excellent in our simulations.

The information we extract is which indices bring which cost savings for a query as compared to processing the query without using any indices. In the simple case of an optimizer choosing at most one index to process a query the savings of an index i in the graph is computed as $c_{seq} - c_i$. Consider the simple IBG of figure 2. For example the savings of index a is computed as $80 - 51 = 29$ cost units. Table 1 contains all savings for the simple IBG in figure 2. No heuristics are involved so far.

An index on column:	a	b	c	d
would bring savings of:	29	57	29	53

Table 1. The Savings for the Simple IBG

In the general case index *sets* will bring savings. This leads to the *savings attribution problem*. Namely, which individual indices of the chosen set should be credited with which savings? If index set $\{a, b, c\}$ provides a savings of 30 then which part of the savings are due to index a? We deal with the *savings attribution problem* in a heuristic way.

Heuristic 1 If the savings of index set $\{i_1, \ldots, i_n\}$ is s then we equally credit the savings for each individual index with $\frac{s}{n}$.

Therefore we loose the information which indices were used *together*, which is relevant information. Consider a hypothetic optimizer which only uses TID (tuple identifier) intersection. In this case using two indices together might be useful but using just one of them is not. However our simulations indicate that such situations are rare.

Heuristic 2 The maximum of all savings an index has been credited with in the graph is retained and this constitutes the savings of this index for the current query.

This means that we take an optimistic view and retain the maximum savings the index *could* bring for the query. For example the savings of index a in the IBG of figure 4 is computed as follows. Due to heuristic 1 its savings in node 1 is $\frac{420-80}{2} = 170$. Its savings in node 2 is $\frac{420-122}{1} = 298$. Due to heuristic 2 the maximum of 170 and 298 is retained so that the savings of index a for the query of this IBG is defined as 298. Table 2 lists all savings for the IBG in figure 4.

All statistics that our tool maintains are the accumulated savings for each possible index. These savings are reset to zero at some time, then for every query the savings

a	b	c	d
298	249	108	202

Table 2. The Savings for the Complex IBG

of each index involved are added to the corresponding overall savings. At a later time (e.g. after one week) the overall savings are transformed into an index configuration proposal. In the simplest case all indices with positive overall savings are taken into the proposed configuration. Several ways to limit the amount of storage consumed by indices are discussed in the *Extensions* section.

5 Simulation of the Tool's Performance

We implemented a prototype of our tool using ORACLE Version 6 on a Sequent Symmetry. The prototype consists of shell scripts and PRO*C[5] programs. Since existing optimizers cannot choose from a virtual set, we actually constructed the indices the optimizer was presented with and dropped the others for every query to simulate an optimizer capable of choosing from a virtual index set. Since we were changing the *actual* (not virtual) index configuration for every query in our prototype these experiments could measure the quality of the proposed index sets but not the runtime overhead of the tool.

We executed each query while enabling ORACLE's trace facility and extracted information about which indices were used from the execution plan and extracted our cost measure from the execution statistics for the query. Therefore the prototype measures the actual execution cost while our tool relies on optimizer cost estimations. We experimented with three cost measures:

1. The *CPU time* used for the query. This measure turned out to yield near optimal index configurations. Its disadvantage is that it is influenced by the machine workload.
2. The *number of logical block accesses* for the query. The term "logical" refers to a block access in the main memory buffer which may or may not require a physical block access on disk. The advantage of this measure is that it does not vary with the machine workload. However it is not proportional to the time required to process the query. Consider a table which fits into the main memory buffer in its entirety. Then a query simply selecting the whole table will use e.g. r_1 logical reads – one per block of the table. Now consider a query joining this table with itself, this will result in $r_2 \gg r_1$ logical reads, but since the table fits into the buffer no more I/O is required than for the query above. Thus the execution time for the second query is not significantly higher than for the first but the number of logical block reads is. In our experiments, measuring the logical block accesses worked fine only if no join queries were involved.

---

[5] ORACLE's version of SQL embedded in C.

3. The number of *physical block accesses*. The reasoning behind this measure is that the processing cost for a query tends to be dominated by the amount of physical I/O needed. Its disadvantage is that it is dependent on the current contents of the main memory buffer. However it still outperformed measuring the logical block accesses in our experiments.

Our tool is capable of using any cost measure for query execution as long as this measure is a simple numeric value. For example it would be possible to combine the measures discussed above.

5.1 Performance Results

Tables 3 and 4 contain the condensed results of our simulation runs. The "Batch" column indicates for which SQL batch the results to the right were obtained. Each such batch consisted of 10 − 20 queries, where a wide range of query types were used. The batches contained Select, Update, Insert, Delete, Create Table and Drop Table statements. Batch 6 contained especially complex queries . We used two tables with four columns each for our benchmarks. All columns were numeric to facilitate automatic tuple generation. The selectivities were close to 0% (single tuple), 25%, 50% and 100% for the columns of both tables, The first table contained 500 tuples, the second contained 5000.

To judge the performance of the index sets our tool proposed, we ran a brute-force script for each batch that simply measured the execution time of a batch for all possible relevant index sets. This brute-force method necessarily finds the best and worst index configuration. The "Best" and "Worst" columns in table 3 contain the best and worst execution times found for every batch. We then ran our tool for the three cost measures "CPU time", "logical block accesses" and "physical block accesses" as described above. The columns CPU, LOGICAL and PHYSICAL in table 3 indicate the execution time when using the index set proposed by our tool for this batch. Table 4 contains the relative ranking of the index sets found by our tool. For example, measuring the logical block accesses with our tool for query batch 4 found the second best out of 16 possible index sets. The tool's performance on query batches with a substantial gap between the best

Batch	Best	Worst	CPU	LOGICAL	PHYSICAL
1	57.6	1:13.3	57.6	1:00.5	57.6
2	3:14.7	4:07.7	3:15.6	3:31.3	3:25.1
3	2:41.6	2:56.2	2:41.6	2:50.8	2:41.6
4	2:55.8	23:44.1	2:55.8	3:36.2	2:55.8
5	1:05.5	1:20.3	1:06.2	1:11.3	1:11.1
6	56.2	1:17.6	1:00.4	1:00.4	56.8

Table 3. Condensed Results - Execution Times

and worst execution times was excellent (see batch 4). The tool performed slightly worse for batches where the best and worst execution time were close to each other (see batch

5). This is reasonable behavior since the index configuration is not of great importance in the latter case anyway. We hypothesize that the performance of the tool decreases with increasing complexity of the IBGs because the effects of our heuristics are more drastic for large IBGs than for moderate ones. The results for a batch of complex queries (batch 6) support this.

Batch	Best	Worst	CPU	LOGICAL	PHYSICAL
1	1	64	1	24	1
2	1	256	3	84	41
3	1	16	1	4	1
4	1	16	1	2	1
5	1	256	11	81	71
6	1	16	5	5	2

Table 4. Condensed Results - Ranking

5.2 Estimation of the Run-Time Overhead

The run-time overhead of our tool is proportional to the number of nodes in the IBG for the query. Therefore the average complexity of the IBGs is critical.

It turned out that for nearly all cases the graphs had a modest number of nodes, even for highly complex queries. For example the optimizer did not use any indices for the quite complex query "select autogen1.col1 from autogen1 where not exists (select * from autogen2 where autogen1.col1 = 10000 and exists (select col1 from autogen1 where exists (select * from autogen2 where autogen1.col1 = autogen2.col1)));". The largest IBG for queries of our test batches contained eight nodes. The exception were queries of the type "select * from X where $X.c_1 = const_1$ and $X.c_2 = const_2$ and ...;" processed by TID intersection, where the particular optimizer we experimented with chose all subsets of the indices on the attributes connected by *and*. The number of nodes in the IBG for this kind of query was exponential in the number of attributes.

6 Limitations

Our approach cannot handle combined indices. It is hypothesized that no efficient statistics gathering and evaluating tool can be built that investigates all possible combined indices because the performance degradation induced by the combinatorial explosion involved in doing this would outweigh the benefits of the tool. To our knowledge no tool was ever presented that is capable of detecting beneficial combined indices.[6]

---

[6] DBDSGN [FST88] has the option of specifying particular combined indices to be evaluated but it cannot detect such desirable combined indices itself.

Our tool was tailored to secondary indices because changing the secondary index configuration is much easier than physically rearranging the data to reassign the clustering property. However, the extension to include primary (clustered) indices is straightforward. The methodology then is to initially present the optimizer with a virtual index set containing a primary and secondary index for every column in the database – a truly virtual configuration since there may be at most one clustered index per table in reality. The optimizer responds with index sets containing at most one primary index per table. Index selection at a reorganization point consists of choosing the clustered index with the highest savings for each relation (or none if the savings for all primary indices on this table are negative), and of adding secondary indices with positive savings to the configuration as before, where the existence of a primary index precludes choosing a secondary index for the same column.

7 Possible Extensions

Let the tool use an additional machine. The idea is to avoid the overhead our tool imposes at query execution time by doing the actual query executions and our tool's evaluations in parallel on different machines. Let A be the machine that executes the queries (e.g. a mainframe) and let B the machine dedicated to our tool (e.g. a workstation). Then A would call the optimizer once for the current index set and execute the plan returned by the optimizer. B would call the optimizer multiple times for different virtual index sets but not actually execute any plan. Figure 7 illustrates this. The requirements are that the optimizer can be called from both machines and that both machines can access the data dictionary consulted by the optimizer to evaluate indices.

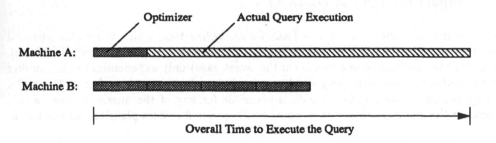

Fig. 7. Using an Additional Machine for our Tool

Allow to combine the results of several recording periods. So far all savings are reset to zero at time t_1 and used to improve the index configuration at $t_2 > t_1$ when they are reset again for the new recording period. It may be desirable to combine the results of the last several recording periods. A standard solution – also used in [HC76] – is to use exponential smoothing to combine the results of the last recording periods.

Take index storage cost into account. So far our tool strictly optimizes the average query execution time without considering the tradeoff between execution time and index storage requirements. The simplest solution is to introduce heuristic restrictions like (1) the total space used by indices should not surpass 20% of the space for the real data, (2) use at most three indices per table, (3) use at most n indices overall. A less heuristic approach is to let the designer specify a factor λ which formalizes the tradeoff between response time r and storage requirements s. λ informs the tool as to which improvement in r will justify what increase in s. For example, an average response time improvement of 0.1 seconds might be worth spending 2 megabytes of disk space, $\lambda = 5 \times 10^{-8} sec/byte$. So an index with the characteristics ($r = 0.2$ sec, $s = 5$ MB) will be disqualified since $r/s < \lambda$. *Allow the specification of exceptions.* The tool assumes that the performance goal is to *always* minimize the average query execution time. This is not necessarily the case. Consider an unconventional database where critical data is rarely accessed but if it is it should be available in minimum time. Then it will be desirable to index this data despite its low reference frequency. Therefore the tool should allow the designer to specify a column set that will be indexed independent of the tool's standard considerations. Implementing exceptions is straightforward.

Take index creation cost into account. If the proposed index configuration yields only slightly better performance than the current one, then the index reorganization cost might be higher than the total savings of the better index configuration. This issue has a low priority for us. First many conventional databases are taken offline at night or at weekends for maintenance – there is no performance penalty for queries if reorganization is done during this time. Second even if indices are constructed and dropped while the system is online it may still be done at times of low database usage where the performance penalty will hardly be noticeable; and the response time during the critical usage peaks will be improved.

8 Comparison against DBDSGN

Our research can also be used as a basis for an *offline* tool, which tailors the physical database design to a batch of queries provided to the tool as does DBDSGN [FST88]. However the run time of our tool is (in the worst case) only exponential in the number of *relevant* indices for each query and linear in the number of queries, whereas DBDSGN is exponential in the number of indices plausible for any of the queries in the batch[7]. Consider the query batch shown in figure 8. There are 9 indices plausible for the batch.

select * from R_1, R_2, R_3 where $R_1.a = R_2.a$ and $R_2.a = R_3.a$;
select * from R_1, R_2, R_3 where $R_1.b = R_2.b$ and $R_2.b = R_3.b$;
select * from R_1, R_2, R_3 where $R_1.c = R_2.c$ and $R_2.c = R_3.c$;

Fig. 8. A Sample Batch

DBDSGN would execute the query batch $2^9 = 512$ times whereas our tool would – in the

---

[7] The effects of various optional heuristics in DBDSGN are not considered here.

worst case – execute each query for $2^3 = 8$ configurations. So DBDSGN would execute $3 \times 512 = 1536$ queries while our tool would execute $3 \times 8 = 24$. However, running DBDSGN in this way would guarantee to find the optimum configuration while our tool yields only near-optimal configurations. DBDSGN is inherently designed to work on query batches (of moderate size) – its methodology cannot be extended to work on continuous query streams.

9 Conclusions and Future Research

This research presents, to our knowledge, the first viable methodology for a run-time facility collecting statistics to optimize the physical design of a database. It has important characteristics which are prerequisites for such a tool: (1) the storage space consumed by the statistics is constant in the number of queries traced (2) the evaluation of the statistics is fast and straightforward.

We demonstrated that the proposed tool will tailor the physical design of the database to the past usage profile if the optimizer can estimate execution costs for virtual index sets, and that the resulting index configuration is reasonably close to the optimum index configuration.

The performance of the index sets proposed by our tool have been verified by simulation, but the actual run-time overhead of the statistics-collection part of our tool could not be measured but only estimated since it would involve modifying an optimizer. The natural extension of this research is to experiment with an actual optimizer.

References

[CB74] D. D. Chamberlin and R. F. Boyce. A Structured English Query Language. In *Proceedings of the ACM SIGMOD Workshop on Data Description, Access and Control*, May 1974.

[FST88] S. Finkelstein, M. Schkolnick, and P. Tiberio. Physical Database Design for Relational Databases. *ACM-TODS*, 13(1), March 1988.

[HC76] M. Hammer and A. Chan. Index Selection in a Self-Adaptive Data Base Management System. In *Proceedings of the ACM-SIGMOD Conference in Washington D.C.*, June 1976.

[Kin74] W. F. King. On the Selection of Indices for a File. *IBM Research, RJ 1341, San Jose*, January 1974.

[Pal70] F. Palermo. A Quantitative Approach to the Selection of Secondary Indexes. *IBM Research, RJ 730, San Jose*, July 1970.

[Sch75] M. Schkolnick. The Optimal Selection of Secondary Indices for Files. *Information Systems*, 1, 1975.

[Sto74] M. Stonebraker. The Choice of Partial Inversions and Combined Indices. *International Journal of Computer and Information Sciences*, 3(2), June 1974.

[WWS81] K.Y. Whang, G. Wiederhold, and D. Sagalowicz. Separability - an Approach to Physical Database Design. In *Proceedings of the Very Large Data Base Conference in Cannes*, September 1981.

Performance of On-Line Index Construction Algorithms

V. Srinivasan and Michael J. Carey

Department of Computer Sciences
University of Wisconsin
Madison, WI 53706, USA

Abstract

In this paper, we study the performance of several on-line index construction algorithms that have recently been proposed. These algorithms each permit an index to be built while the corresponding data is concurrently accessed and updated. We use a detailed simulation model of a centralized DBMS to quantify the performance impact of various factors, including the amount of update activity, resource contention, background load, and the size of a record compared to the size of an index entry. The performance comparison makes use of two new metrics, one of which is a "loss" metric that reflects the amount of on-line work lost due to interference with the index construction activity. In our analysis, we find that there is an important trade-off between the time required to build the index and the throughput achieved by update transactions during the index construction period. An important conclusion of our study is that certain on-line algorithms perform very well in all but extremely resource-bound situations.

1 Introduction

Future databases are expected to be several orders of magnitude larger than the largest databases in operation today. In particular, databases on the order of terabytes (10^{12} bytes) are soon expected to be in active use [Silb90]. In such databases, the utilities for index construction, database reorganization, and checkpointing will take enormous amounts of time to run due to the time it takes to scan the data itself (since scanning a 1-terabyte table may take days). Thus, there is a need for these utilities to operate in an on-line fashion [Dewi90]. In terms of related work, algorithms for on-line checkpointing of a global database state have been discussed [Pu85] and their performance has been studied [Pu88]. Also, the problem of on-line index reorganization has been discussed briefly in [Ston88]. Only recently, however, have algorithms been proposed to tackle the problem of on-line index construction [Srin91b, Moha91]. Since B-trees[1] are the most common dynamic index structure in database systems, the existing work has concentrated on algorithms for on-line construction of B-tree indices.

On-line index construction algorithms typically work as follows: A build process scans the data, copying out information for index entries, concurrently with updaters that modify the same data. The system keeps track of the updates that take place during the scan; the builder then combines these updates with the index entries created during the scan before registering the index in the system catalogs. The proposed on-line index construction algorithms differ in the data structures used for recording the concurrent updates, their strategies for combining these updates with the newly created entries, and finally, in the degree of concurrency supported following the scan phase.

In this paper, we evaluate the relative performance of a number of candidate on-line index construction algorithms. Using a detailed simulation model of a centralized DBMS,

---

[1] By B-tree we mean the variant in which all keys are stored at the leaves, often called B[+]-trees [Come79].

we compare the performance of these on-line index construction algorithms with that of a good off-line algorithm as well as amongst themselves. By running experiments over a wide range of system, workload, and storage conditions, we investigate the performance trade-offs for the proposed algorithms. In particular, to assist in our analysis, we define a new performance metric, "loss," that captures the lost work in terms of update transactions that are unable to execute due to contention caused by conflicts with the index construction process. We also compare algorithms using other relevant metrics, including the "off-line fraction," which characterizes the fraction of time (relative to the response time of an off-line algorithm) during which updaters are unable to proceed.

The rest of the paper is organized as follows. In Section 2, we summarize the proposed on-line index construction algorithms. Section 3 discusses the performance trade-offs involved in choosing one on-line algorithm over another. The simulation model used in our study is described in Section 4. Section 5 describes the performance experiments that we conducted and presents their results. In Section 6 we predict the performance of other proposed algorithms based on our performance results. Finally, in Section 7, we present our conclusions and plans for future work.

2 Index Construction Algorithms

Constructing a B-tree index from a relation usually involves three basic steps. The first step involves scanning the relation and collecting the (key, rid) entries that are needed to build the index. In the second step, the entries collected in the first step are sorted to produce a linked-list of leaf pages for the index. The third and final step involves creating the non-leaf pages of the index in a bottom-up fashion from the leaf page list created in the previous step.

2.1 Off-Line Algorithm

The simplest way to construct a new index on a relation would be to lock the relation in Share mode, build the index using the three basic steps outlined above, and then release the lock. Updaters are assumed to hold an Intention-exclusive lock on the relation while modifying a page of the relation (à la the hierarchical locking scheme of [Gray79]) and would therefore be unable to execute concurrently with the index building process. On the other hand, readers only acquire an Intention-share lock on the relation, and can access the relation's pages concurrently with the building process. Due to the absence of concurrent updaters, this *off-line* strategy is the fastest way to build the index. While the unavailability of the relation for updaters makes the off-line algorithm unacceptable for building indices on large relations, we will use its performance as a baseline for understanding the behavior of alternative on-line algorithms. One way to improve on the off-line approach is to allow updaters to proceed during index construction, somehow communicating their updates to the building process. It is possible that the duration of index construction will be increased due to the presence of concurrent updates, but permitting updates during the index construction phase makes such on-line strategies attractive. Before we describe the on-line algorithms, however, we must first describe the behavior of update transactions.

2.2 Concurrent Updates

Any update to a record in a relation that changes the value of an indexed attribute results in updates to the corresponding index. Update transactions are assumed to obey the following two rules: (i) they hold a short-term Exclusive lock on a relation page while they are making changes to it, and (ii) they do not try to insert the same index entry (key/rid pair) twice successively without deleting it in-between (and vice versa). To ensure correct behavior of our on-line algorithms in a serializability sense, we also require that update transactions hold long-term Exclusive locks on updated record ids until they terminate (commit or abort). Update transactions that encounter an active index construction process will record the necessary index updates in a manner that depends on the type of on-line algorithm being used. We assume for simplicity that this will occur immediately after the corresponding relation update, i.e., the new index entry will be recorded while the updater still holds its Exclusive lock on the modified relation page. (A way to relax this restriction is described in [Srin91b].) It should be mentioned that this approach to transaction execution handles situations like transaction aborts in a straightforward manner (see [Srin91b] for details).

Given that concurrent update transactions behave as described above, we now describe the on-line index construction algorithms of interest here. We will subdivide the on-line algorithms into two classes, list-based algorithms and index-based algorithms, depending on whether they use a list or an index for storing concurrent updates. More details about the on-line algorithms discussed here can be found in an earlier paper [Srin91b].

2.3 List-Based Algorithms

The list-based algorithms for on-line index construction use a list, called the *update-list*, to record concurrent updates. The individual list-based algorithms differ from each other in their method of combining the update-list with the list of index entries obtained by scanning the relation; they also differ in the amount of concurrency provided after the initial scan phase. The various possible list-based algorithms are given in Table 1.

A simple way of combining the scanned entries with the update-list is to first build an intermediate index using the scanned entries alone, and then sequentially apply the update-list entries to this index like ordinary index inserts and deletes. We will call this the *basic* strategy for building the index. Note that the basic strategy may result in several I/Os for any given leaf node of the intermediate index, especially if the number of entries in the update-list is large. A second method of combining the scanned entries with the update-list is to build an intermediate index using the scanned entries, as above, but to sort the update-list before applying its entries to the intermediate index. This method, called the *sort* strategy, ensures that a maximum of one disk I/O is incurred for each leaf page of the intermediate index (since leaf nodes are accessed in sorted order of the keys that they contain). A third method of combining the concurrent updates with the scanned entries is to first sort both the scanned entries and the update-list entries, producing two sorted lists; the index is then built in a bottom-up manner by merging these two sorted lists together, thus producing the leaf pages of the final index in one pass (see [Srin91b] for details). In situations where the update-list is large, this *merge* strategy has some advantages over the sort strategy, as we shall see later.

As mentioned earlier and indicated in Table 1, the list-based algorithms also vary in the amount of concurrency allowed after the scan phase. The simplest strategy involves locking out updaters after the scan phase and applying the concurrent updates using one of the three methods described above. List-based algorithms that use this strategy are called the List-X-* algorithms because they use a list for storing concurrent updates and the build process acquires an X lock on the update-list at the end of the scan phase to lock-out updaters.

The List-X-* Algorithms: Based on the three possible methods for combining concurrent updates with the scanned index entries, there are three possible List-X algorithms, List-X-Basic, List-X-Sort, and List-X-Merge. The execution of the build process and update transactions in the various List-X-* algorithms is illustrated in Figure 1. The exclusive phase in which the update-list entries and the scanned entries are combined is called the *build* phase.

In the List-X-* algorithms, an updater that finds an index building process in the scan phase will append an index update corresponding to its relation update to the update-list (Figure 1). Updater appends are synchronized via short-term exclusive locking of the update-list. During the build phase, however, updaters cannot execute concurrently in the build phase. If the duration of the build phase is significant compared to the duration of the scan phase, there could be a noticeable loss of updater concurrency. To avoid such a loss, we can design list-based algorithms in which updaters can execute concurrently throughout the index construction period; these are called the List-C-* algorithms.

Table 1. List-Based Algorithms.

Name	How Updates Are Applied	Concurrency After Scan Phase
List-X-Basic	Sequentially apply from unsorted list	X lock list, no concurrent updaters
List-X-Sort	Sequentially apply from *sorted* list	X lock list, no concurrent updaters
List-X-Merge	*Merge* sorted list and scanned entries	X lock list, no concurrent updaters
List-C-Basic	Sequentially apply from unsorted list	Concurrent updaters allowed
List-C-Sort	Sequentially apply from *sorted* list	Concurrent updaters allowed
List-C-Merge	*Merge* sorted list and scanned entries	Concurrent updaters allowed

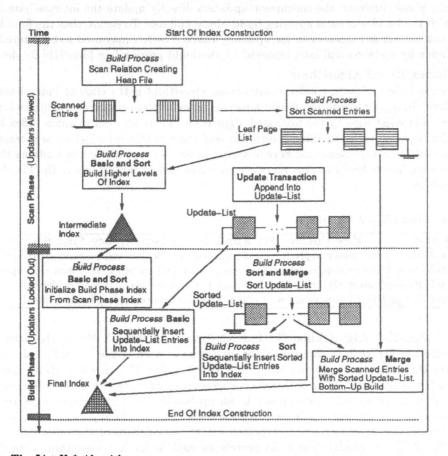

Fig. 1. The List-X-* Algorithms

The List-C-* Algorithms: As for the List-X-* algorithms, there are three possible List-C-* algorithms: List-C-Basic, List-C-Sort, and List-C-Merge. The List-C-* algorithms are illustrated in Figure 2. Notice that the behavior of the build process in the scan and build phases of a particular List-C-* algorithm is the same as that of the corresponding List-X-* algorithm. Since the List-C-* algorithms have a build phase in which updaters can execute concurrently, however, they need an appropriate strategy for merging in a second set of concurrent updates at the end. This is done in a third phase called the *catchup* phase. Each of the three List-C-* algorithms uses the same strategy in the catchup phase to combine the build phase updates with the intermediate index that exists at the end of the build phase. In particular, the intermediate index is made public to updaters (even though it is not yet available for normal use) at the start of the catchup phase. The build process then sorts the list of build phase updates and applies them to the intermediate index concurrently with other updaters. A normal B-tree concurrency control algorithm is used to resolve conflicting accesses to the index by the build process and update transactions during the catchup phase [Srin91b]. When the build process is done processing all of the build phase updates, it makes the index available for normal use.

Updaters in the List-C-* algorithms behave like updaters in the List-X-* algorithms in the scan and build phases; i.e., they append their updates to the update-list. (The update-list is initialized to empty at the start of both the scan and the build phases.) During the catchup phase, however, the concurrent updaters directly update the intermediate index to which the build process is applying build phase updates. To ensure that the final index does not contain any inconsistencies, specially marked entries may need to be entered into this index by updaters and later removed by the build process (see [Srin91b] for details).

2.4 Index-Based Algorithms

The second class of on-line index construction algorithms is the class of index-based algorithms. In these algorithms, updaters use an index to store concurrent updates instead of the update-list used by the list-based algorithms. There are four possible index-based algorithms, as indicated in Table 2; since the leaf pages of this index (which are created by concurrent updates) contain the keys in sorted order, the sort method of building the index is inapplicable here and thus there are no index-based counterparts to the List-*-Sort algorithms.

Table 2. Index-Based Algorithms.

Name	How Updates Are Applied	Concurrency After Scan Phase
Index-X-Basic	Sequentially apply from leaf-page list	X lock index, no concurrent updaters
Index-X-Merge	*Merge* leaf-page list with scanned entries	X lock index, no concurrent updaters
Index-C-Basic	Sequentially apply from leaf-page list	Concurrent updaters allowed
Index-C-Merge	*Merge* leaf-page list with scanned entries	Concurrent updaters allowed

The Index-X-* Algorithms: The Index-X-Basic and Index-X-Merge algorithms are illustrated in Figure 3. In the scan phase, updaters in both of the Index-X-* algorithms register their updates in a temporary public B-tree index. Concurrent updater access to this index is regulated using a B-tree concurrency control algorithm. A difference that arises from using an index, as opposed to an update-list, is that updaters need to leave behind special index entries in certain situations; this avoids any inconsistencies that might otherwise be caused due to repeated inserts and deletes of the same index entry (see [Srin91b] for details). The build process in each Index-X-* algorithm is similar to

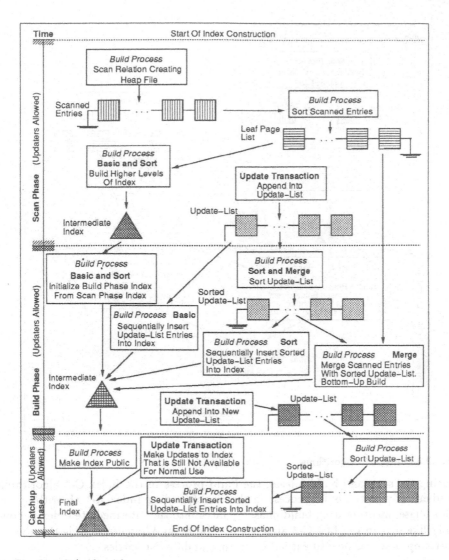

Fig. 2. The List-C-* Algorithms

that of the corresponding List-X-* algorithm; the key difference is that the (sorted) list of concurrent updates is obtained at the end of the scan phase from the leaf pages of the temporary public index rather than from an update-list.

The Index-C-* Algorithms: In the scan and build phases, updaters in the Index-C-* algorithms (Index-C-Basic and Index-C-Merge) register their updates to a temporary public index. This index, just like the update-list in the earlier List-C-* algorithms, is initialized to empty at the start of the scan and build phases. Updaters in the Index-C-* algorithms behave slightly differently (in terms of leaving marked entries in the public index) during the build phase than they do in the scan phase [Srin91b]. In the catchup phase, where updaters share an index with the build process, updaters in the Index-C-* algorithms behave just like updaters in the catchup phase of the List-C-* algorithms. We omit the figure for the Index-C-* algorithms due to lack of space.

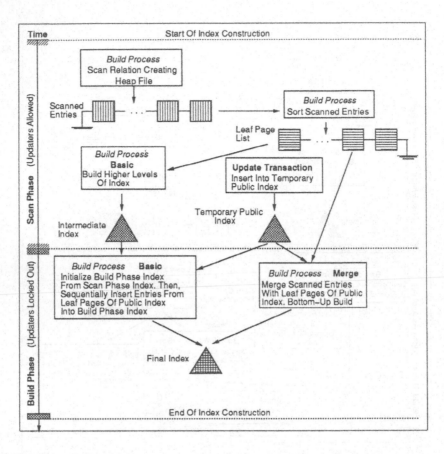

Fig. 3. The Index-X-* Algorithms

During the scan and build phases, the build process in the Index-C-* algorithms behaves identically to the build process in the corresponding Index-X-* algorithms. In the catchup phase, incorporating build phase updates into the intermediate index is done essentially like it is in the List-C-* algorithms. The main difference here is the absence of the sort step that was needed earlier for sorting update-list entries.

3 Performance Trade-Offs

As we mentioned earlier, the off-line algorithm provides the fastest way of building an index at the cost of providing no updater throughput. On the other hand, the on-line algorithms allow concurrent updaters during index construction, with the price being an increase in the time required to build the index. For the on-line algorithms then, the following question arises: How much of an increase in updater throughput is needed to compensate for a corresponding increase in the build response time? We shall try to answer this question by quantifying the *loss* to the database system caused by the index construction activity.

Suppose that the best updater throughput possible in the system *without* the new index is T_{best}. Suppose also that a particular index construction algorithm A has a build response time of R_A seconds and that during its building time it provides an updater throughput of T_A transactions per second. In an on-line algorithm, update transactions face interference from the index construction process in terms of data and resource contention, so T_A will be less than T_{best}. Using R_A, T_A, and T_{best}, we can estimate the loss to the system in terms of the number of potential update transactions that could not execute due to contention caused by index construction activity:

$$loss = (T_{best} - T_A) \times R_A \qquad (1)$$

Interestingly, the formula for loss can also be applied to the off-line algorithm directly. The loss for the off-line algorithm (with response time $R_{offline} = R_{best}$) is simply $T_{best} \times R_{best}$ since the updater throughput ($T_{offline}$) for the off-line algorithm is zero. The loss metric thus gives us a way of comparing the performance of an on-line algorithm both with that of other on-line algorithms and with that of the off-line algorithm. From the loss formula, it can be seen that the loss will be high if index construction takes a long time (if R_A is large) or if the updater throughput is very low (if T_A is small). The loss metric thus offers a simple way to answer the question posed in the previous paragraph regarding the amount of additional updater throughput needed to offset an increase in the build response time. In terms of this metric, an algorithm with a lower loss is better than one with a higher loss. Between two algorithms with the same loss, the one with the smaller response time is better since the index is available earlier in that case. Finally, the *normalized loss* for an algorithm can be defined as the loss for that algorithm divided by the loss for the off-line algorithm.

Though the loss metric provides a clean way to combine the build response time and the updater throughput into one measure, it alone is not sufficient to characterize the performance of an on-line algorithm completely. In particular, recall that some on-line algorithms (e.g., the List-X-* and Index-X-* algorithms) have exclusive phases during their execution. Since high performance transaction processing systems may have severe maximum updater response time requirements, the durations of such exclusive phases may be critical to the performance of such systems. Thus, when evaluating an index construction algorithm, we will also consider the *off-line fraction* of the algorithm, which is defined as the ratio of the duration of its exclusive phase (if any) to that of the off-line algorithm (which has a single exclusive phase equal to its entire build response time).

In our discussion of performance trade-offs thus far, we have ignored certain hidden "lost-opportunity" costs involved in building a new index. These costs arise because the performance of the database system with the new index may be much different from its performance without the index. Not surprisingly, these hidden costs are closely related to the reason for building the new index. The decision to build a new index may be made for either of the following reasons, each of which relates to a performance-improving opportunity:

1. The new index would significantly speed up a class of queries that are currently running inefficiently (i.e., using sub-optimal access plans) in the system.
2. The new index would enable a new class of queries to be executed that cannot be executed at all (reasonably) given the current system configuration. For example, a credit card company might want to provide a new service that involves accessing its customer records using a currently unindexed attribute. A naive way of executing such queries without building a new index on the relevant attribute might involve a relation scan, which could be prohibitively expensive for large relations (e.g., it could take days for a terabyte relation).

Accounting for either of these considerations above is difficult, as the interests of queries that will not be speeded up by the new index conflict with those of the queries that will indeed benefit from the new index (cases 1 and 2 above). In particular, for the queries that will benefit from the new index, the best way to build the index is to build it as soon as possible. On the other hand, for existing queries that will not benefit from the new index, the best way to build the new index is the one that creates the least interference for them during index construction. The question of which class of queries is more important and thus needs to be given priority in the system is application-specific and depends on factors like the economic benefit of preferring one class of queries over another. Such factors are hard to quantify and will vary from system to system. In our discussion of the performance of on-line index construction algorithms, therefore, we assume that the decision to build the index is made off-line, we ignore the hidden performance tradeoffs involved in index construction, and we only consider the impact of index construction on concurrent transactions that use other access paths to efficiently access and/or update the relation on which the index is being built.

4 Simulation Model

Our simulation model is a closed queueing model with a fixed multi-programming level (MPL), and was implemented using the DeNet simulation language [Livn90]. The model of the system hardware assumes a computer system with one or more CPUs and disks. Requests for the CPUs are scheduled using an FCFS (first-come, first-served) discipline with no preemption. Each of the disks has its own disk queue, and each queue is managed using an elevator disk scheduling algorithm. Apart from the CPUs and disks, the physical resource model also includes a buffer pool for holding disk pages in main memory. The buffer pool is managed in a global LRU fashion for all pages except relation pages. Since relation page accesses are either sequential (due to the build process) or random (due to concurrent update or search activity), relation pages are added to the tail end of the LRU list upon being released, effectively giving them lesser priority than index pages. The buffer manager performs demand-driven writes when dirty pages are chosen for replacement. The system model also includes a lock manager for setting and releasing locks on pages and records.

The components of the database storage model include the relation on which an index is being built, an already existing B-tree index on this relation, and auxiliary data structures like the temporary lists and indices needed by the various on-line index construction algorithms. Important parameters of the database storage model include the size of the initial relation in tuples, the maximum number of tuples per relation page, and the maximum fanout of a B-tree index page. In our experiments, the physical size of a page is always the same (4K bytes), so a variation in the maximum capacity of a relation page should be viewed as being due to different tuple sizes. For modeling simplicity, all tuples are assumed to be of the same size, all index entries are assumed to be of the same size, and no duplicate keys are allowed in the index. (These simplifications should not impact our qualitative performance results.) The distribution of values for an indexed attribute of the relation are drawn from a random permutation over an integer key space of 1..400,000.

The workload model consists of the index build process and a fixed set of user terminals, each of which submits one of three types of relation operations (search, insert, or delete). Insert operations find a non-full page in the relation using a bit map and then insert a tuple into that page. After their relation insert, they immediately perform an insert into the relation's existing index. Following this, they take the appropriate action, if any, required by the on-line index building algorithm. Deletes, on the other hand, access a single relation page at random, delete a randomly chosen tuple from that page, and then immediately perform the corresponding delete to the already available index. Like inserts, they then take the action called for by the relevant on-line index building algorithm. Finally, searches andomly access a relation tuple using the available index. Each terminal submits its operations one at a time. As soon as a terminal submits an operation, it becomes active and executes in the system; when the operation completes, it returns to the terminal. In the current study, we use a terminal think time of zero, so the terminal immediately generates another operation of the same type when its current operation completes.

Table 3. Simulation parameters.

num-cpus	Number of CPUs (1)
num-disks	Number of disks (1, 8)
seek-time	Min: 0 msec; Max: 27 msec
cpu-speed	20 MIPS
cc-cpu	Cost for lock/unlock (100 inst.)
buf-cpu	Cost for buffer call (1000 inst.)
search-cpu	Cost for page search (50 inst.)
modify-cpu	Cost for key insert/delete (500 inst.)
copy-cpu	Cost for page copy (1000 inst.)
compare-cpu	Cost for comparing keys (2 inst.)
init-rel-keys	Tuples in initial relation (100,000)
max-fanout	Index-entries/page (200/page)
page-capacity	Tuples/page (2, 20, or 200 /page)
page-size	Size of a disk page (4KB)
alg	On-line algorithm (List-X-Basic, Index-C-basic, etc.)
num-bufs	Size of the buffer pool (250)
search-term	Terminals submitting searches (0 or 50)
MPL	Terminals submitting inserts and deletes (0,2,10,20,40)
insert-frac	Proportion of inserts among updates (50%)

The simulation parameters for our experiments are listed in Table 3. In all of the experiments discussed in this paper, there is exactly one CPU in the system. Apart from the single CPU, a system configuration consists of a fixed number of disks and a fixed capacity for relation pages. In each system configuration, we varied the MPL for updaters from 0 (where only the build process executes) to a maximum of 40, conducting one experiment for each on-line index construction algorithm as well as for the off-line algorithm. At the start of each experiment, the buffer pool is initialized with randomly chosen pages from the initial relation; the build process is then started along with a number of updaters equal to the MPL. The terminal types (search, insert, and delete) are initialized according to the workload parameters. The experiment is stopped when the build process terminates. A special additional experiment is run to calculate the best updater throughput in the system without the new index (for calculating the loss using equation 1). Batch probes in the DeNet simulation language are used with the operation response time metric to generate confidence intervals. For all of the data presented here, the 90% confidence interval for relation operation response times was within 2.5% (i.e., ±2.5%) of the mean.

5 Performance Results

An important factor likely to affect the performance of an on-line index construction algorithm is the relative proportions of time spent in the various phases of index construction. These relative proportions depend on the size of the index relative to the size of the relation itself. We modeled different relative sizes by keeping the size of an index entry constant (20 bytes) and considering three different tuple sizes, small (20 bytes), medium

(200 bytes), and large (2000 bytes). We subdivide the performance experiments into three categories based on the tuple size and present the results for each of these categories.

5.1 Experiment Set 1: Small Tuple Size (20 Bytes)

In this set of experiments, the size of the index is comparable to the size of the relation since an index entry and a tuple are of the same size. The system workload consists of the build process and a set of concurrent updaters. The multiprogramming level (MPL) gives the total number of updaters in the system; half are inserts while the other half are deletes. We will subdivide the small tuple experiments into those involving a system with a single disk and those involving a system with eight disks.

Single Disk Results: The build response times for the various algorithms in the single disk case are given in Figure 4, and the updater throughput curves are given in Figure 5. As expected, the build response time for all of the on-line algorithms increases with the MPL due to an increase in resource contention at higher updater MPLs. We also see from Figure 4 that the List-C-Basic algorithm's build response time increases much faster than those of all the other algorithms. The reason for this is that the build process in List-C-Basic sequentially inserts unsorted entries from the update-list into the intermediate index during the build phase (Figure 2). These sequential inserts cause random leaf page I/Os possibly resulting in multiple I/Os for the same page. Sorting the list before insertion into the intermediate index (as in List-C-Sort) alleviates this problem, so the response time is much lower for List-C-Sort than for List-C-Basic. In contrast to List-C-Basic, List-X-Basic does not suffer as much because its build phase length increases much more slowly due to the absence of buffer and resource contention during this phase.

In Figure 4, the build response time ordering of the on-line algorithms other than List-X-Basic and List-C-Basic reflects the increasing amount of work that they have to do for index construction. Among these eight algorithms, each of the concurrent (*-C-*) algorithms has a higher response time than all of the exclusive (*-X-*) algorithms. This is expected since the *-C-* algorithms allow concurrency throughout the index construction period, resulting in increased contention as well as extra work for catching up. Among the four algorithms within each class, the algorithms that use merging are better than those that perform sequential inserts.

While the various on-line algorithms differ widely in their build response times, all except List-X-Basic attain the same updater throughput (Figure 5). In particular, this means that all of the *-X-* algorithms except List-X-Basic attain the same throughput as the *-C-* algorithms. This is surprising since we would expect the *-X-* algorithms to attain less throughput than the *-C-* algorithms due to their exclusive build phase. The reason is that this effect is swamped by an extremely high level of resource contention in this experiment. In all of the *-X-* algorithms except List-X-Basic, a bottleneck at the lone disk increases the scan phase duration tremendously at high MPLs, while the (exclusive) build phase duration remains about the same due to lack of contention; the build phase therefore forms a negligible part of the build response time, causing a negligible effect on the throughput. In List-X-Basic, however, the extra I/Os during the build phase cause this phase to become a significant fraction of the build response time at higher MPLs, resulting in a significant drop in maximum throughput.

Having looked at the updater throughput and response times separately, we now look at the normalized loss in Figure 6 in order to combine both measures. Note from Figure 6 that the loss for the List-X-Basic and the List-C-Basic algorithms is very high compared to that for the other algorithms (so much so that their values for high MPLs are omitted from

304

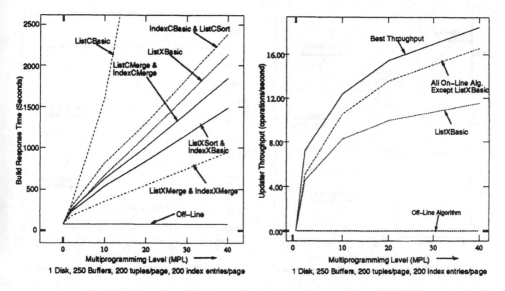

Fig. 4. Build Response Time: 1 Disk.   **Fig. 5.** Updater Throughput: 1 Disk.

he figure). The large loss in List-C-Basic is due to its very high response time (Figure 4), while the loss in List-X-Basic is due to its low updater throughput (Figure 5). The loss curves also show that, at high MPLs, only two merge-based algorithms (List-X-Merge and Index-X-Merge) manage to achieve better loss than the off-line algorithm.

The off-line fractions for this experiment are given in Figure 7. We see that the duration of the exclusive build phase for the List-X-* and the Index-X-* algorithms is a sizable fraction (25% to 50% for all algorithms except List-X-Basic) of the total response time of ' he off-line algorithm. Thus, if it is unacceptable for updaters to wait in the case of the off-line algorithm, it is likely to be unacceptable for them to wait in the *-X-* algorithms as well (since the waiting times are of the same order of magnitude). Using the best among the *-C-* algorithms (List-C-Merge or Index-C-Merge) thus seems to be a better choice here even though they have a higher loss than most of the *-X-* algorithms.

In the single disk experiments, the builder in the on-line algorithms faces very high resource contention. In order to create a less resource-bound situation, the next set of experiments assumes a system with eight disks. Due to the extremely poor performance of the List-X-Basic and the List-C-Basic algorithms, we will omit these two algorithms from all future graphs.

Eight Disk Results: In this experiment, we found that the the ordering of build response times among the various on-line algorithms was the same as in the one disk case. (We omit the curves due to space limitations.) The key difference here was that the best on-line algorithm now had a maximum response time of only a few times the response time of the off-line algorithm, while in the one disk case the best on-line algorithm was more than ten times slower than the off-line algorithm at an MPL of 40 (Figure 4). Adding disks reduced the level of resource contention considerably for the builder, resulting in a faster index building time for all of the on-line algorithms. From the updater throughput curves (again omitted due to lack of space), we found that the List-X-* algorithms and the Index-X-* algorithms had a slightly lower throughput than the corresponding *-C-* algorithms. In the *-X-* algorithms, the (exclusive) build phase now formed a significant proportion of the index construction time, thus leading to a noticeable loss in throughput.

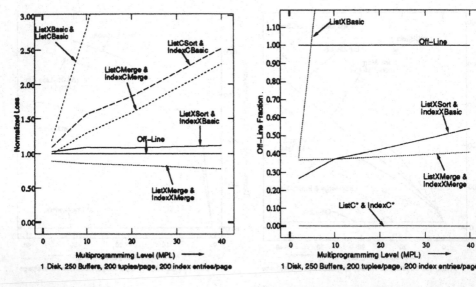

Fig. 6. Loss: 1 Disk.   **Fig. 7.** Off-Line Fraction: 1 Disk.

In Figure 8, we present the normalized loss for the various algorithms in the eight disks case. In contrast to the results of the one disk experiments, where the loss for the *-C-* algorithms was larger than that for the other algorithms, the *-C-* algorithms (which have no exclusive phases) perform better than the other algorithms in terms of the loss metric here. The off-line fractions of the various algorithms for this experiment were the same as in the earlier high contention case (Figure 7), so we omit those curves here; this is to be expected since the duration of the periods during which updaters are locked out should be the same as in the one disk case (since the build process is the only active process in the system during that time). Since the off-line fraction for the *-C-* algorithms is almost zero, and they also have the least loss, they are unequivocally better than the *-X-* algorithms in this situation. Among the *-C-* algorithms, List-C-Merge and Index-C-Merge are the best since they involve the least overhead.

This set of experiments (both the single and eight disk results) examined the case where an index entry is the same size as a tuple. We also ran experiments in cases where the tuple size is ten and then a hundred times the size of an index entry, respectively. Due to space limitations, we will present only the results for the large tuple experiments. Since we found above (and in all our other experiments as well) that the merge method of building the index is better overall than the basic and sort strategies, we will show only the four merge-based algorithms and the off-line algorithm in the remaining graphs.

5.2 Experiment Set 2: Large Tuple Size (2000 Bytes)

In this set of experiments, a tuple is a hundred times larger than an index entry, unlike in the earlier set of experiments where they were the same size. This causes an increase in the relation size (200MB here as compared to 2MB in Experiment Set 1) while the size of the index remains the same as before ($\sim$ 2MB). This increase, in turn, causes the scan phase to dominate the process of index construction (accounting for more than 95% of the build response time). Since a bottleneck at the disk can be expected to swamp the performance differences between the various on-line algorithms in the one disk case, as we saw earlier in the small tuple experiments, we only conducted experiments on a system with eight disks here.

306

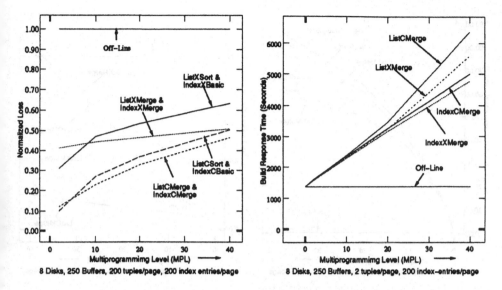

Fig. 8. Normalized Loss, 8 Disks. **Fig. 9.** Response Times, Large Tuples.

Eight Disk Results: The build response time curves for the large tuple experiments on a system with eight disks are given in Figure 9. Compared to the response time differences seen in the corresponding small tuple experiments, the relative response time differences between the various on-line algorithms are smaller here. This is because the scan phase (during which all on-line algorithms perform similarly) is dominant, and the other phases (which are primarily responsible for build response time differences) form only a small portion of the overall index construction time. Another thing to note is that all of the list-based algorithms perform slightly worse at high MPLs here than all of the index-based algorithms. The reason is that the update-list becomes large, due to the large scan phase, and the sorting that takes place during the build phase of the list-based algorithms thus contributes a significant overhead which is absent in the index-based algorithms. Also, between the two list-based algorithms, List-X-Merge is better than List-C-Merge; this is due to the additional catchup phase in List-C-Merge. Similar behavior is seen between the index-based algorithms; the difference is smaller there due to the absence in Index-C-Merge of the sort step that is needed in the catchup phase of List-C-Merge.

The updater throughput curves for this experiment are given in Figure 10. As indicated, the throughput for the index-based algorithms is significantly less (by about 25%) than that of the list-based algorithms at high MPLs. This is because the public index (into which concurrent updaters insert their updates) in the index-based algorithms becomes large enough at high MPLs in this experiment for every index access to have a high probability of performing a disk I/O for a leaf page. This extra disk access causes a significant increase in the overhead of concurrent updaters in the index-based algorithms, while there is no such overhead in the list-based algorithms (since the append to the list almost certainly does not involve a disk access).

The loss curves for this experiment (Figure 11) indicate that the index-based algorithms suffer quite a bit due to their reduction in throughput. In fact, at an MPL of 40, Index-X-Merge and Index-C-Merge are even a bit worse than the off-line algorithm. In contrast, List-X-Merge and List-C-Merge perform much better than the off-line algorithm throughout the entire MPL range, with a maximum normalized loss of 35% for List-X-

307

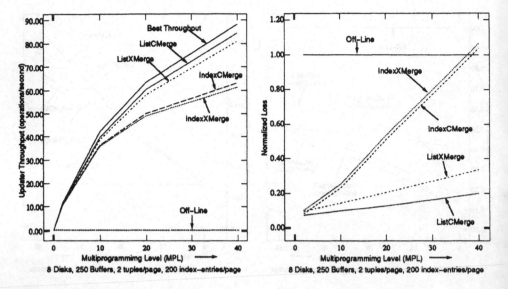

Fig. 10. Throughput, Large Tuples.   **Fig. 11.** Normalized Loss, Large Tuples.

Merge and only 20% for List-C-Merge. Finally, we found that the off-line fractions for the
*-X-Merge algorithms were smaller here than in the small tuple experiments, but they
were still not negligible.

5.3 Other Experiments
Apart from the large (2000 bytes) and small (20 bytes) tuple experiments, we also performed experiments in which the tuple size was intermediate (200 bytes) as mentioned
earlier. The results of the medium tuple experiments were essentially a hybrid of the results of the small and large tuple experiments. We also conducted a series of experiments
where there was a constant background search query load on the relation along with the
concurrent updaters. In these experiments, the relative performance of the various algorithms was essentially the same as in the case with no searches, except that due to the
resource contention generated by the concurrent searches, all algorithms took much longer
to build the index and the on-line algorithms each attained a lower maximum updater
throughput.

6 Discussion
The performance results of the previous section can be summarized as follows:
- Except in extremely resource bound situations, most of the on-line index construction
  algorithms clearly outperformed the off-line algorithm. In other words, the throughput
  that the on-line algorithms achieved for updaters during index construction more than
  compensated for their increase in build response time.
- Among the on-line algorithms, the best among the algorithms with no exclusive phase
  (List-C-Merge) outperformed the best among the algorithms with an exclusive phase
  (List-X-Merge) except in heavily resource bound situations.
- Even in heavily resource bound situations, the best fully concurrent algorithm (List-
  C-Merge) had a loss of only a few times that of the best partially exclusive algorithm
  (List-X-Merge). Furthermore, List-X-Merge was found to have an exclusive phase
  whose length is a non-negligible fraction of the response time of the off-line algorithm
  likely making it unacceptable for use in high performance transaction processing sys-
  tems.

- As should be expected, the relative performance of the various algorithms depended on the proportion of time spent in the initial relation scan phase of index construction. The list-based algorithms performed better than the index-based algorithms when the scan phase was a large proportion (> 95%) of the index building time. When the scan phase was around 50% of the index building time, the fully concurrent (*-C-*) algorithms were found to be superior to the partially exclusive (*-X-*) algorithms.

- The merge strategy for building the index was clearly superior in performance to the basic and sort strategies.

- As a result of the points above, the List-C-Merge algorithm achieved the lowest loss among all of the on-line algorithms over a wide range of tuple sizes, except in heavily resource bound situations.

Even though our simulation results were obtained for relatively small relation sizes (2MB to 200MB), the basic relative performance results should hold for very large database sizes as well. This is because the relative performance of the various algorithms is affected by the ratio of the size of the index to the size of the relation, which in turn determines the time spent by the on-line algorithms in their different phases of index construction. This ratio depends only on the size of an index entry relative to the size of a tuple, and not on the absolute size of the relation itself. Finally, using the above results, we can now make informed projections about the performance of other on-line algorithms that have been proposed in the literature.

Other Candidate Algorithms: Mohan and Narang have proposed two algorithms for on-line index construction [Moha91]. Their first algorithm is index-based and allows updaters and the build process to share the same index throughout. Their second algorithm is list-based and uses an update-list, like the List-C-Basic strategy. While we have not explicitly simulated the two [Moha91] algorithms in our experiments, we believe that their performance can be inferred from that of the Index-C-Basic and the List-C-Basic algorithms (see [Srin91c] for details).

7 Conclusions

In this paper, we have studied the performance of a collection of candidate algorithms for on-line index construction. To aid in our study, we defined a new performance metric that measures the loss to the system due to interference between concurrent updaters and the index building process. An important conclusion of this study is that in most cases, the fully on-line algorithms (which have no exclusive phase) perform very well and do better than the partially on-line algorithms (which have a concurrent relation scan phase but an exclusive build phase) or the off-line algorithm. In fact, even in a highly resource-bound situation, which is the worst case for a fully on-line algorithm, some fully on-line algorithms were only a factor of 2 to 3 worse in terms of loss than the best partially on-line or off-line algorithm. The list-based fully on-line algorithms were found to perform better than the index-based alternatives overall due to the smaller overhead that they impose on concurrent updaters. The fully on-line list-based algorithm that uses the merge strategy (i.e., List-C-Merge) appears to be a very good candidate for use in a real system.

In terms of further work, this study has only examined concurrency issues that affect the performance of on-line index construction algorithms. As mentioned earlier, index construction for a terabyte relation may take days, which means that the index building process must be able to to complete without having to restart from scratch after every crash. Appropriate recovery strategies thus have to be designed for this purpose. (Recovery strategies are described for the algorithms in [Moha91] and could be adapted for the algorithms studied in this paper.) Also, since a terabyte relation is likely to be declustered across several disks, it is necessary to parallelize the various on-line algorithms for use in parallel database systems. Still another interesting issue is to extend our on-line index construction strategies to work for indices other than B-tree indices; a further generalization would be to extend the ideas employed here for use in computing aggregate functions on a relation with minimal interference. These issues are all promising candidates for future work.

Acknowledgements

This research was partially supported by the National Science Foundation under grant IRI-8657323 and by a University of Wisconsin Vilas Fellowship.

References

[Baye72] Bayer, R. and McCreight, E.M. "Organization and Maintainance of Large Ordered Indices", *Acta Informatica*, 1(3), 173–189 (1972).

[Come79] Comer, D. "The Ubiquitous B-Tree", *ACM Computing Surveys*, 11(4), (1979).

[Dewi90] DeWitt, D. J. and Gray, J. "Parallel Database Systems: The Future of Database Processing or a Passing Fad?", *SIGMOD Record*, 19(4), December 1990.

[Gray79] Gray, J. "Notes On Database Operating Systems", *Operating Systems: An Advanced Course*, Springer-Verlag, 1979.

[Lehm81] Lehman, P., and Yao, S. "Efficient Locking for Concurrent Operations on B-trees", *ACM Transactions on Database Systems*, 6(4), December 1981.

[Livn90] Livny, M. "DeNet User's Guide", *version*, 1.5, (1990).

[Moha91] Mohan, C. and Narang, I. "Algorithms for Creating Indexes for Very Large Tables Without Quiescing Updates", *IBM Research Report*, **RJ 8016**, March 1991.

[Pu85] Pu, C. "On-the-Fly, Incremental, Consistent Reading of Entire Databases", *Proceedings of the International Conference on Very Large Data Bases*, 369–375 (1985).

[Pu88] Pu, C., Hong, C. H. and Wha, J.M. "Performance Evaluation of Global Reading of Entire Databases", *Proceedings of the International Symposium on Databases in Parallel and Distributed Systems*, 167–176 (1988).

[Silb90] Silberschatz, A., Stonebraker, M. and Ullman, J. D. "Database Systems: Achievements and Opportunities", *SIGMOD Record*, 19(4), December 1990.

[Srin91a] Srinivasan, V. and Carey, M. J. "Performance of B-tree Concurrency Control Algorithms", *Proceedings of the ACM SIGMOD Conference*, May 1991.

[Srin91b] Srinivasan, V. and Carey, M. J. "On-Line Index Construction Algorithms", *Proceedings of the High Performance Transaction Systems Workshop*, Pacific Grove, CA, September 1991.

[Srin91c] Srinivasan, V. and Carey, M. J. "Performance of On-Line Index Construction Algorithms", *Technical Report, Computer Sciences Department, University of Wisconsin-Madison*, **TR 1047**, September 1991.

[Ston88] Stonebraker, M., Katz, R., Patterson, D. and Ousterhout, J. "The Design of XPRS", *Proceedings of the 14th VLDB Conference*, Los Angeles, CA, August 1988.

[Yao78] Yao, A. C. " On Random 2-3 Trees", *Acta Informatica*, 9, 159–170 (1978).

Hybrid Index Organizations for Text Databases

Christos Faloutsos[†]

University of Maryland
College Park, MD

H. V. Jagadish

AT&T Bell Laboratories
Murray Hill, NJ

ABSTRACT

Due to the skewed nature of the frequency distribution of term occurrence (e.g., Zipf's law) it is unlikely that any single technique for indexing text can do well in all situations. In this paper we propose a hybrid approach to indexing text, and show how it can outperform the traditional inverted B-tree index both in storage overhead, in time to perform a retrieval, and, for dynamic databases, in time for an insertion, both for single term and for multiple term queries. We demonstrate the benefits of our technique on a database of stories from the Associated Press news wire, and we provide formulae and guidelines on how to make optimal choices of the design parameters in real applications.

1. INTRODUCTION

Unformatted databases are rapidly gaining popularity, particularly for the dissemination of text and other "free-format" information. This information is divided into pieces, which we shall refer to as **documents** in this paper, though each piece could well be a page from a book, a "hypercard", an image, a bar of music, or whatever.

Each document has several **terms** that may be used as keys to retrieve the document. For a text document, these terms could simply be all the words in the text. Alternatively, they could be more complex entities, such as, word pairs or triples. There is usually a "stop-list" of common words that cannot be used as key terms. Sometimes a list of "keywords" is explicitly specified and only these may be used as terms that can be used as keys for retrieval. For non-text documents, there is an even greater variety of techniques by which a set of key terms can be obtained for any given document: whether through automated analysis of the document or through human input.

The question we address in this paper is how to create an index over a large number of terms for a large set of documents. Clearly, there are two objective functions: one is to minimize the storage overhead required for the index. The other is to minimize the amount of time taken for a retrieval. If the database is dynamic (e.g., archival, such as a library collection of books), the effort to update the index is also in issue. We address all these issues.

There are several indexing techniques that have been proposed [5] for problems of the sort we are interested in. The most popular commercial approach is the "inverted index" [2]. For each index term, a (variable length) "postings list" is created of the documents that it occurs in. The index terms themselves are usually organized in a B-tree [4], so that given a particular term, one tree traversal is required to get to the appropriate leaf where the required list of documents may be found. The major drawback of this technique is that there is a substantial space overhead – from 50% up to 300% in some cases [8]. In addition, long lists of documents may have to be manipulated when queries involve multiple terms, a task that may be onerous. Also, when a new document is added to the database, an update of the inverted index is required for each term in the document.

---

† This research was sponsored in part by the University of Maryland Institute for Advanced Computer Studies, by the National Science Foundation under grants DCR-86-16833, IRI-8719458 and IRI-8958546 and by the Air Force Office of Scientific Research under Grant AFOSR-89-0303.

The simplest possible indexing technique is to keep a bit matrix, one bit per term per document [10]. If the particular term occurs in the particular document, the bit is on, else it is off (see Figure 1). This technique by itself is rarely used, since the bit matrix is likely to be very sparse, wasting a lot of storage. However, variants of this technique are used, with one or more bits assigned to each term, and superimposing the bit assignments so that each bit may be turned on if any one of several terms occurs in a given document. These techniques as a group are called "signature file" techniques. See, for example, [7]. These techniques can generally be implemented with a smaller storage overhead (10%-20%), and a considerably lower insertion cost, than inverted indices. However, the search time grows linearly as the number of documents in the collection grows, since the signature (a bit or a bit pattern) associated with each individual document has to be examined in response to each query.

	$term_1$	$\cdots$	$term_t$
doc_1	1	$\cdots$	0
$\cdots$			
doc_N	0	$\cdots$	0

Figure 1. Example of a bit matrix (or bitmap or "signature file")

A central motivation for our work is Zipf's law [16], which, informally, states that a few instances occur most of the time and that most instances occur rarely. Variations of Zipf's law are often quoted as the 80-20 rule, or sometimes the 90-10 rule. On account of Zipf's law, it is not reasonable to assume that each index term occurs roughly equally often in the documents to be indexed. In fact, there is likely to be a tremendous imbalance.

In view of this imbalance, it is unlikely that any single technique for indexing text can do well in all situations. In this paper we propose a hybrid approach that merges the good points of both families of techniques discussed above. Hybrid approaches to indexing, in related but different contexts, have previously been proposed in [13] and in [15].

We begin in Section 2 with a review of Zipf's law, and an experimental study of the occurrence frequencies of terms in a database with Associate Press news wire stories. In Section 3, we introduce the main idea behind the proposed hybrid technique. In Sections 4 and 5, we develop the technique for a static (e.g., CD-ROM) database, and for a dynamic (archival) database respectively. In each case, we evaluate our technique analytically, both for single terms and for multi-term queries, and compare the expected performance with respect to the standard inverted index method widely used today. As performance measures, we use storage overhead due to the index, time to perform a query, and, in the dynamic case, time to update the index when a new document is inserted in the database. In Section 6, we recapitulate the results presented earlier in the form of guidelines for a practitioner. We close with some final remarks in Section 7.

2. TERM DISTRIBUTION

We obtained a database of 10,075 documents representing Associated Press newswire stories from 40 random days in 1989. The total database size was a little over 30 Megabytes. Every story from a particular day was selected with some care to eliminate stories that were duplicates or near duplicates. Each story was 300 to 600 words long, and was treated as a separate document. Each alphabetic string in each story was treated as a word, with case being ignored. (All words were converted to lower case for uniformity).

Figure 2 shows a log-log plot of the rank of a word, on the X-axis, versus its frequency, measured as the number of times it occurred in all the documents combined, on the Y-axis. In addition to the full database just described, we also ran experiments on a 10% fraction of the database, of size about 3Mb. Results for this smaller database are plotted in Figure 2, as crosses ("+"). The curves for the two databases are almost identical in shape, indicating that our results are largely insensitive to database size.

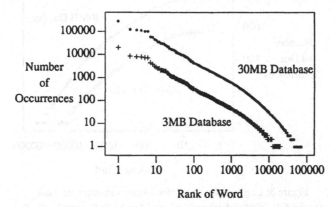

Figure 2: Log-log plot of the frequency vs. rank distribution
for the full (30Mb) database (with "•") and for the sample (3Mb) (with "+").

Zipf [16] observed that not all words occur as often in any given piece of text. In fact, a few words occur very often, and most words occur only infrequently. If words are ranked by their frequency of occurrence, then the following distribution is observed:

$$f_i = F(i) = \frac{K}{i} \tag{2.1}$$

where f_i is the frequency of the word with rank i. K is a constant, usually $K = V$, where V is the vocabulary of the body of the text. Plotted on a log-log graph, the above distribution is a straight line with slope -1.

The curves in Figure 2 are almost straight lines, as predicted by Zipf, but not exactly so. They certainly represent a highly skewed distribution. In other words, even though we have a database that is not a single cohesive document created by a single author, the distribution of the occurrence frequencies of words in the database is highly skewed.

We are interested in not the total frequency of occurrence of a particular word in a document (or set of documents), but rather the **document frequency** of each word, that is, the number of documents that the word appears in (one or more times). That is to say, we discard the second and subsequent occurrences of a word in any document, to obtain a distribution of the number of documents in which each word occurs. Intuitively, we would expect the document frequency distribution to be skewed, too, but not as skewed as the original distribution. The reason is that frequent words will appear many times in the same document, and thus will suffer most from the elimination of duplicate words in a document. We performed measurements. Fig. 3 plots the results in a log-log graph. The X-axis is the rank of the word as before. The Y-axis is the document frequency of the word.

Not every word is worth indexing on. For example, prepositions and common pronouns occur frequently and have little semantic content for purposes of retrieval. In addition, in our particular database, there were a few words that appeared on all stories, such as "est" or "edt" (for the time the story was filed). Words of this nature are called **noise words**, and can be collected into a **stop list**. The rest of the words are called **terms**. In our particular database, we found 128 noise words. These included all of the most common 50 words, and were all within the first 200 ranked words. Without losing much accuracy, we can assume that the first r_n most common words are noise words, with $r_n = 128$ in our case. This causes the flat part of the curves of Figure 3 to be deleted, resulting in a curve that is closer to a Zipf distribution.

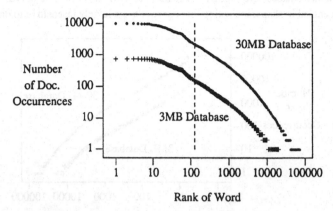

Figure 3: Log-log plot of the document frequency vs. rank
for the full (30Mb) database ("•") and for the 3Mb sample ("+").

When we say **vocabulary** in the following, we mean the total number of different terms in the document, database, or other entity being referred to.

3. PROPOSED APPROACH

Since the inverted index is by far the most common retrieval structure used, let us begin with a description of that as the basic structure. We then address areas for potential improvement.

3.1. The Inverted Index Structure

The traditional inverted index consists of two files: the sorted list of terms, usually organized as a B-tree (although hash implementations have been reported [11] and studied [6]), and the postings file. For the rest of the paper, the first file will be referred to as the "B-tree". Each leaf page contains records of the form,

<term, delimiter, pointer_to_head_of_postings_list>.

Each term is associated with a postings list, that is, a list of pointers to the documents that contain the term. The postings lists are stored in the postings file; depending on the environment, they can be stored contiguously (static environment), or in linked-lists of fixed-length records (dynamic environment), or in some other fashion. Figure 4 illustrates the file structure.

As we shall soon see, most of the storage overhead is due to the postings lists. So minimizing the size of the postings list is very important. Due to the highly skewed distribution, a large fraction of the size of the postings list is contributed by a few commonly occurring terms. Let us see how we can reduce this.

One immediate solution is to maintain a "negative" list, that is, a list of documents in which a term does not occur rather than the ones in which a document does occur. If a term occurs in more than 50% of the documents, this negative list will be shorter than the usual (positive) list. Experimental analysis, for the news story database, showed that while there are a few words that occur in more than 50% of the documents, they are all noise words, such as 'a', 'the', 'to', etc., which are not likely to be useful as index terms, and were all included in the stop list. As such, negative lists are not a useful idea.

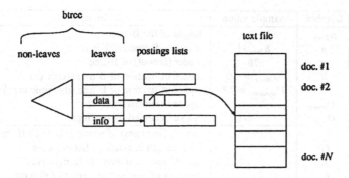

Figure 4: Traditional, inverted-index file structure.

3.2. A Hybrid Strategy

The heart of our proposal is to take advantage of the skew of the frequency distribution, by treating the "frequent" terms in a different way. We still keep the B-tree file, which holds *all* the terms; the "rare" terms are treated the traditional way (variable length postings lists); for each frequent term, we propose storing its postings list as a bit vector. Grouping the bit vectors together, we have a bitmap (see Figure 1 and Figure 5). Notice that we need only one bit, to flag a term as frequent or rare. This bit could be incorporated within another field, e.g., negative number for a postings head can signify a frequent term.

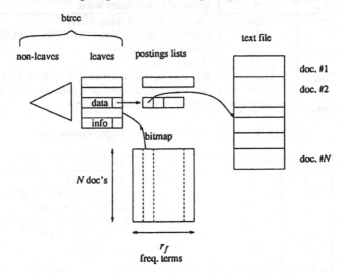

Figure 5: File structure for the proposed hybrid method - static case.

According to the specific environment, we propose different organizations of the bitmap. Moreover, the cut-off for the "frequent terms" is computed based on the parameters of the specific database. Terms 1 through r_f, for some analytically computed cut-off rank r_f, are considered frequent. Terms r_f+1 through V are rare. (Noise words are not considered terms, and are assumed to have been eliminated before ranks are determined for the terms).

Symbol	sample value	Definition
h_{btree}	3	height of the B-tree
h	$h_{btree}-1$	levels of B-tree NOT in core
m	78	order (fanout) of B-tree
U	$U_{static} = 1.0$	space utilization of B-tree (static case)
	$U_{dynamic} = 0.8$	space utilization of B-tree (dynamic case)
O_{tree}		space occupied by B-tree
O_{post}		space occupied by postings
LP_i		length (in pages) of postings list of i-th term
$\overline{LP}$		avg. length of postings list in pages
f_i		no. of docs in which i-th term occurs
C_i		number of postings records of i-th term
$\overline{C}$		avg number of postings records
s	6	pointers per postings record

Table T1: Symbols and Definitions (Data Structure Parameters)

Symbol	sample value	Definition
N	10075	number of documents
S	30Mb	total size of the collection
V_i		vocabulary of the i-th document
V_d	178	avg. vocabulary of a document
V	71,814	vocabulary of collection
l_v	8	length of a vocabulary word
P	1024	page size in bytes (Mag. Disk)
	16K	page size (Optical Disk – CD-ROM or WORM)
p	4	pointer size, in bytes
b	8	bits per byte
T_{rand}	30 msec	avg. time for random disk access (Mag. Disk)
	200 msec	avg. time for random disk access (Optical Disk)
T_{seq}	3 msec	time for sequential disk access

Table T2. Symbols and Definitions (Input Parameters)

Symbol	sample value	Definition
r_f		rank of last "frequent" term
q_i		prob. that the i-th term appears in a query
q	0.33	prob. that a query term is frequent
c		number of terms in a multiple term query
t_1		search time for single term query
t_c		search time for c-term query
t_{IN}		insertion time

Table T3: Symbols and Definitions (Query & Insertion Parameters)

None of the analysis in this and in the following sections assumes any specific distribution of terms, database size, vocabulary, and so forth. Sample values of parameters of interest to us are listed in Tables T1, T2, and T3. These parameter values are obtained from the experiments described in the previous section, are "standard" values that are generally considered reasonable for a practical implementation, or are values computed analytically from other values determined by one of the methods above.

While we have properly determined parameters to evaluate the performance of an indexing technique for any one particular query, we have not said anything about what the queries are like: what sort of distribution do they have over the terms. Unfortunately, this distribution can only be determined by logging the queries posed to a system by users; even worse, it may change over time, as the users' interests shift from one topic to another. However, as we show next, we can choose the cut-off rank r_f in such a way that, for a query on any given term, our hybrid methods will **never do worse** than the traditional method. Under such a design, our methods will always have non-zero speed-up, regardless of the distribution of the queries. The distribution of queries will just determine the magnitude of the savings.

The easiest assumption to make is that each term is equally likely to be specified in a query. Notice that Eq. (3.1) and (3.2) reduce to the uniform case, for $q = r_f/V$. In fact, our analysis would be simplified if we could make such an assumption. Unfortunately, such is not likely to be the case. As it has been pointed out [14], the rarest terms are unusual words that are unlikely ever to be the basis of a query; many of them are often typographic errors or misspellings [1]. In particular, they are unlikely to be the basis of a multi-term query because the typical reason to have a multi-term query is that no single term in it is specific enough.

In order to obtain some arithmetic examples for the speed-up, we have explicitly introduced the parameter "q", which denotes the probability that a term specified in a query is a frequent term. Thus, if q_i is the probability that the i-th term will appear in a query, then we assume that

$$q_1 = q_2 = \cdots = q_{r_f} = q/r_f \qquad (3.1)$$

and

$$q_{r_f+1} = \cdots = q_V = (1-q)/(V-r_f) \qquad (3.2)$$

We have used a value of 0.33 for q, the probability that a term specified in a query is a frequent term.

4. STATIC CASE

Proposed Hybrid Structure

Whereas each document posting recorded in an inverted index for a term requires p bytes of storage, a simple matrix organization would require only 1 bit. We use a hybrid storage structure, recording the usual inverted index, but for "frequent" terms, rather than storing a postings list, we store a reference to an appropriate position in a bit matrix, such as the one shown in Fig. 1. From now on, such a matrix will be referred to as the **bitmap or bit matrix or signature file**; one row of it will be called **document signature**; one column of it will be called **bit slice** or **bit vector**. For the static case, it is most efficient to store the bit matrix in a bit-sliced form (column-wise), since only the columns corresponding to the specified terms need be retrieved in response to a query.

When a retrieval request is supplied, the B-tree is traversed as usual. If the term specified in the query is "rare", then a postings list is obtained at the leaf as usual. However, if the term specified is "frequent", then the appropriate bit vector in the bit matrix is examined.

Space for the traditional method

The traditional inverted index consists of a B-tree with all the terms in the vocabulary, plus a file with postings (pointers to the qualifying documents). Thus the space overhead O_{inv} for the inverted index is

$$O_{inv} = O_{tree} + O_{post} \tag{4.1}$$

For the B-tree, the non-leaf nodes will account for $\approx 1/m$ of the space of the B-tree, where m is the fanout (or "order") of the tree. Typically, $m \gg 1$. Thus the bulk of the B-tree overhead is due to the leaves:

$$O_{tree} \approx (l_v + 1 + p) * V/U \tag{4.2}$$

where V is the total vocabulary of the database and U is the utilization of the leaves. If we pack the tree carefully, we can assume

$$U = U_{static} \approx 1.00 \tag{4.3}$$

Let V_i be the vocabulary of the ith document, and $\overline{V_d}$ be the average vocabulary over all the documents in the database.

$$\overline{V_d} = 1/N \sum_{i=1}^{N} V_i = 1/N \sum_{i=1}^{V} f_i \tag{4.5}$$

We shall find it convenient to divide $\overline{V_d}$ into two parts: $\overline{V_{freq}}$ and $\overline{V_{rare}}$. $\overline{V_{freq}}$ is the average number of frequent terms per document, $\overline{V_{rare}}$ is the average number of rare terms per document, and $\overline{V_{rare}} + \overline{V_{freq}} = \overline{V_d}$.

$$\overline{V_{freq}} = 1/N \sum_{i=1}^{r_f} f_i \tag{4.6}$$

$$\overline{V_{rare}} = 1/N \sum_{i=r_f+1}^{V} f_i \tag{4.7}$$

Then the space required for the postings list can also be divided into two parts corresponding to the rare and frequent terms.

$$O_{post,freq} = N * \overline{V_{freq}} * p \tag{4.8}$$

$$O_{post,rare} = N * \overline{V_{rare}} * p \tag{4.9}$$

$$O_{post} = O_{post,freq} + O_{post,rare} = N * \overline{V_d} * p \tag{4.10}$$

Space for hybrid method

The space overhead for storing the index in the proposed hybrid method is given as:

$$O_{hyb} = O_{tree} + O_{post,rare} + O_{bitmat,freq} = O_{tree} + O_{post} - O_{post,freq} + O_{bitmat,freq}$$
$$= O_{inv} - O_{post,freq} + O_{bitmat,freq} \tag{4.11}$$

Thus the only space difference between the hybrid method and the inverted index is for the frequent terms, which are stored as bit-vectors rather than in postings lists. The space required for the bit-vectors can be computed as

$$O_{bitmat,freq} = N * r_f/b \quad \text{bytes} \tag{4.12}$$

where b is the number of bits in a byte. The savings in storage with respect to the inverted index method is:

$$O_{post,freq} - O_{bitmat,freq} = \sum_{i=1}^{r_f} (p * f_i - N/b) \tag{4.13}$$

We wish to choose r_f such as to maximize this summation. The (finite) differential with respect to r_f is $p * f_{r_f} - N/b$. Since f_i is monotonically non-decreasing in i (by definition of rank), this differential is also monotonically non-decreasing in i. We must choose r_f to be the highest rank, such that this differential is still positive. That is,

$$f_{r_f} \approx N/(b * p) \tag{4.14}$$

Search time for inverted index

For all the analyses that involve page reads and writes, we assume that each page request results in a page fault, except for the root of the B-Tree, which we assume is pinned in memory. We believe that such an assumption is realistic in a typical environment with a large database and users who have a variety of interests. In an inverted index, the time required for a single term query on the i-th term is:

$$t_{1,i} = h*T_{rand} + (T_{rand} - T_{seq} + T_{seq}*LP_i) \tag{4.15}$$

This equation represents h random disk accesses to traverse the B-tree, and one random access followed by $LP_i - 1$ sequential accesses to read the postings list. If h_{btree} is the height of the B-tree, and if the top one or two levels of the B-tree are cached in memory, then h denotes the rest of the levels. Usually, $h = h_{btree} - 1$. The symbols T_{rand} and T_{seq} are the times for a random and sequential disk access, respectively. LP_i is the length of the postings list of the i-th term, in pages:

$$LP_i \approx \left\lceil \frac{f_i*p}{P} \right\rceil \tag{4.17}$$

The above equation is an exact equality if each postings list that spans across pages is guaranteed to be aligned to start at the beginning of a page.

If we know the distribution of queries ($q_i, i = 1 \cdots V$), we can use eq. (4.15) to calculate the average response time. Here, we provide the formulae according to eq. (3.1-2). Let us calculate the response time separately for frequent and for rare terms, so that $\overline{LP_{freq}}$ and $\overline{LP_{rare}}$ denote the average length of a postings list in pages, for frequent and rare terms, respectively. We can then develop equations for the expected time to execute a query against a single frequent term and a single rare term, respectively, as follows:

$$t_{1,rare} = h*T_{rand} + (T_{rand} - T_{seq} + T_{seq}*\overline{LP_{rare}}) \tag{4.18}$$
$$t_{1,freq} = h*T_{rand} + (T_{rand} - T_{seq} + T_{seq}*\overline{LP_{freq}}) \tag{4.19}$$

with

$$\overline{LP_{freq}} = 1/r_f \sum_{i=1}^{r_f} LP_i \tag{4.20}$$

$$\overline{LP_{rare}} = 1/(V - r_f) \sum_{i=r_f+1}^{V} LP_i \tag{4.21}$$

The search time t_1 for a single term query is the average of the search times for rare and frequent terms, weighted by the probability of a rare (respectively, frequent) term being specified. This probability is captured in the parameter q, the probability that the query term is frequent, so that we can write:

$$t_1 = q*t_{1,freq} + (1-q)*t_{1,rare} \tag{4.22}$$

The search time for a multiple-term query with c terms is simply the time to perform c single term queries (plus some additional time to manipulate the postings lists, which we can ignore assuming that this manipulation is entirely in memory).

$$t_c = c*t_1 \tag{4.23}$$

Search time for hybrid method.

In the hybrid structure we propose, the time to perform a retrieval remains exactly the same as before when a single rare term is specified. When a single frequent term is specified, the time to traverse the B-tree is still the same, but now instead of retrieving a postings list, one has to retrieve a bit-slice from the bit-matrix. The time required is:

$$t_{1,freq} = h*T_{rand} + (T_{rand} - T_{seq} + T_{seq} * \lceil N/(b*P) \rceil) \tag{4.24}$$

By our choice of cut-off for frequent words, we know that $N/(b*p) \leq f_i$ for all $i < r_f$. We then have $\lceil N/(b*P) \rceil \leq \left\lceil \dfrac{f_i * p}{P} \right\rceil = LP_i$. Therefore, the time required to perform the retrieval for any term is no worse with our proposed hybrid method than for the standard inverted index, and could be better if the specified term is very frequent. In consequence, the expected time is also less for our technique than for standard inverted index.

Note also, that if we selected r_f to minimize the expected time to perform a single-term retrieval, we would get exactly the same answer as we obtained when we selected r_f to minimize the storage. In other words, the optimum cut-off point is the same for both objectives!

The expected time for a single term query can be computed from $t_{1,freq}$ and $t_{1,rare}$ as before, as well as the time for a multi-term query (eq. (4.22-23)).

$$t_1 = q*t_{1,freq} + (1-q)*t_{1,rare} \tag{4.22}$$
$$t_c = c*t_1 \tag{4.23}$$

Arithmetic example

To estimate the benefit due to the hybrid method quantitatively we use parameter values from our sample 30MB database, as shown in tables T1, T2 and T3: $V = 71,814$ distinct terms and $N=10,075$ documents. From measurements on the database we have that the cut-off rank from eq. (4.14) is

$$r_f = 1214 \quad \text{and that } \sum_{i=1}^{r_f} f_i = 875,951 \,; \, \sum_{i=1}^{r_f} V = 1,792,079$$

Plugging in these values into the formulae above, we get the results shown in Table T4. We see that the hybrid indexing method achieves significant space savings, compared to the standard inverted index method. In addition, it achieves some smaller savings on the search time.

	traditional	hybrid	savings (%)
Space [Mb]	8.10	6.13	32
$t_{1,freq}$ [msec] (magn.disk)	96.99	90.6	7
$t_{1,freq}$ [msec] (CD-ROM)	400	400	0

Table T4: Summary of arithmetic example for the static case.

5. DYNAMIC CASE

Thus far we have not considered any updating of the database. In this section, we include this consideration as well. We assume that the environment is archival, that is, there are insertions of new documents, but deletions and updates are very rare. This is a realistic assumption; most of the text retrieval applications have archival nature, such as library automation [14], patent and law office [9], electronic office filing [3], newspaper articles, *etc.*)

Stability of Frequency Distribution

In order to apply our hybrid method beneficially, the set of frequent terms has to be stable despite the growth of the database. We believe that most archival databases do not radically alter their nature all of a sudden. Therefore, it is reasonable to assume that terms that are frequent will remain frequent as more documents are added to the database, and terms that are rare will remain rare. After a large number of insertions, divergence may begin to appear. In that case we will be forced to re-adjust the indices. This should happen only rarely, and should therefore be acceptable. Moreover, clever incremental reorganization schemes may require rewriting of only a small portion of the index.

To verify our claim above, we performed a small experiment. We considered the most frequent 300 terms in a small sample (representing 5%) of the database we had on hand. We found that over 80% of these terms were in the 300 most frequent terms in the entire database, and almost all of them were within the 600 most frequent. In other words, even as a database grew by a factor of 20, the most frequent terms determined from a small sample remained more or less the most frequent terms in the full database.

We also considered a less extreme situation in which instead of growing the database by such a large factor, we simply doubled the size of the database. Now, the 300 most frequent terms in one half of the database were more than 95% within the 300 most frequent in the full database, and all were within the first 350.

We repeated the above experiments, considering the first 1000, and the first 2000 most frequent terms from a sample (rather than the first 300). The results remained substantially similar. Most frequent terms from the sample remained frequent, provided that the number of terms considered frequent was significantly less than the total vocabulary of the sample (say, less than 10% of it).

Assumptions Regarding Data Organization

In order to allow growth of the database, the postings lists are organized in chains of fixed-length postings records. Each postings record consists of s postings pointers, plus an extra pointer that points to the next postings record (or is null). This organization will add to the space overhead, because of the link pointer and because the last postings record of a chain will be approximately half empty. The choice of the best value for s is an open problem; from the experiments on the 30Mb database, we found that the value of $s = 6$ minimizes the space overhead.

An alternative method of organizing the postings lists is to let the size of the postings records to be adaptive – with a larger postings record obtained on each overflow. Determining the size of each overflow postings record is a non-trivial task, which we are currently studying. Since we do not have a concrete design for the method yet, we cannot study it further.

The retrieval of each postings record requires one random access, *i.e.*, the system does NOT try to cluster the postings records of a chain, because such an attempt would make insertions even more expensive. Moreover, the B-tree cannot be packed, as opposed to the situation in the static environment. Therefore, the utilization factor is lower. Assuming a deferred splitting algorithm (as in a B^*-tree), we have

$$U = U_{dynamic} \approx 0.8 \qquad (5.0)$$

The space overhead and retrieval time criteria remain the same as before, even in a dynamic situation. However, some parameter values change, as discussed above.

Modification to the Hybrid Structure

In most text indexing situations, the primary update activity performed is the insertion of a new document into the database. As such, we shall focus on the effort to insert a new document as the primary cost of update. Consider the hybrid structure that we have been using thus far. In this structure, every time a new document is added to the database, a new row has to be added to the bit matrix corresponding to the frequent terms, and for every other term in the document appropriate entries have to be made in the postings lists, and the B-tree updated if required.

One can readily see that adding a bit to the end of every column bit-vector is a slow procedure. For this reason, in a dynamic environment we propose that the bit matrix be stored row-wise (as a set of document signatures), so that when a new document is added, a new row-vector can be written in one swoop. Of course the rare terms have still to be inserted into the postings lists in the usual way. When a query is specified, instead of reading just a single bit-slice, now all the document signatures will be read, if the specified query term is frequent. (See [12]. for a "group-slice" technique that is a compromise between row-wise and column-wise storage).

Space

The space required for the standard inverted index structure, is computed once more as:
$$O_{inv} = O_{tree} + O_{post} \tag{4.1}$$
with the space for the tree being dominated by the leaves and being obtained as:
$$O_{tree} \approx (l_v + 1 + p) * V/U \quad \text{bytes} \tag{4.2}$$
The space for the postings file has increased, due to the dynamic linking of small groups of postings:
$$O_{post} = (s+1) * p * V * \overline{C} \quad \text{bytes} \tag{5.1}$$
s is the number of postings per postings record, and the additional 1 is for the pointer to the next record. (We have assumed these pointers to be the same size as pointers in the postings list. If not, the formula above can easily be modified accordingly). $\overline{C}$ is the average length of a postings chain (in number of postings records):
$$\overline{C} = \frac{1}{V} \sum_{i=1}^{V} \left\lceil \frac{f_i}{s} \right\rceil \tag{5.2}$$
The quantity inside the summation, the number of postings records for the i-th term, is written as C_i:
$$C_i = \left\lceil \frac{f_i}{s} \right\rceil \tag{5.3}$$
Then, the average number $\overline{C_{freq}}$ of postings records for the frequent terms is
$$\overline{C_{freq}} = \frac{1}{r_f} \sum_{i=1}^{r_f} C_i \tag{5.4}$$
and the respective formula for the rare terms $\overline{C_{rare}}$ is
$$\overline{C_{rare}} = \frac{1}{V - r_f} \sum_{i=r_f+1}^{V} C_i \tag{5.5}$$
Once more, the space required by the postings list in the inverted index method can be expressed in two parts as in eqn. (4.8)
$$O_{post.freq} = (s+1) * p * r_f * \overline{C_{freq}} \tag{5.6}$$

$$O_{post,rare} = (s+1)*p*(V-r_f)*\overline{C_{rare}} \tag{5.7}$$

As in the static case, the space difference between the hybrid method and the inverted method is expressed by

$$O_{hyb} = O_{inv} + O_{bitmat,freq} - O_{post,freq} \tag{4.11}$$

where $O_{bitmat,freq}$ is the same as for the static case, and $O_{post,freq}$ is the overhead of the postings of the frequent terms, as shown above.

Once more, the cut-off rank r_f that minimizes the space overhead can be computed by setting the differential improvement to zero, and works out as follows:

$$C_{r_f} = N/(b*p*(s+1)) \tag{5.8}$$

The cut-off that satisfies the above equation will be called $r_{f,2}$ for the rest of this paper. The $r_{f,2}$ cut-off obtained here is close to, but larger than the cut-off in the static case.

Search Time

Compared to the static case, in the standard inverted index the search time for a single term will be longer, because we have one random disk access for every postings record†. Thus, for a query on the i-th term, we have

$$t_{1,i} = h*T_{rand} + T_{rand}*C_i$$

As in the static case, if the query frequencies q_i are known, t_1 can be calculated as the average of the $t_{1,i}$'s $i=1\cdots V$. If the query frequencies are unknown, then we can use the assumptions implied in eqs. (3.1-2). Then, we have

$$t_{1,freq} = h*T_{rand} + T_{rand}*\overline{C_{freq}} \tag{5.9}$$
$$t_{1,rare} = h*T_{rand} + T_{rand}*\overline{C_{rare}} \tag{5.10}$$

and

$$t_1 = q*t_{1,freq} + (1-q)*t_{1,rare} \tag{4.22}$$

A multi-term query is given by eq. (4.23)

$$t_c = c*t_1$$

For the hybrid structure, $t_{1,rare}$ remains unaltered, and $t_{1,freq}$ can be computed as:

$$t_{1,freq} = h*T_{rand} + t_{bitmap} \tag{5.11}$$

where t_{bitmap} is the time to scan the bit-map sequentially

$$t_{bitmap} = (T_{rand} - T_{seq} + T_{seq}*N*r_f/(b*P))$$

To optimize the search time for single-term queries, the cut-off rank r_f should obey the equation:

$$t_{bitmap} < T_{rand}*C_{r_f} \tag{5.12}$$

or, equivalently,

$$T_{rand} - T_{seq} + T_{seq}*N*r_f/(b*P) < T_{rand}*C_{r_f} \tag{5.13}$$

Let $r_{f,1}$ be the largest value that satisfies eq. (5.13). Eq. (5.13) expresses the requirement that, for the last frequent term, following the chain of postings records will be slower than scanning the bit matrix. Choosing $r_{f,1}$ as the cut-off rank guarantees that the hybrid method will give a better response time for any frequent term, as compared to the traditional method. Of course, for the rare terms, the response

† There is a slight probability that two successive postings records of interest are on the same page. This probability is typically low enough that we have chosen to ignore it (assumed zero) in the formulae derived here.

times are the same for both methods.

In the static case, by having a bit-slice structure for the bit matrix, we were able to guarantee that the time to read the bit-slice would be less than the time to read a corresponding postings record. In fact, the choice of r_f that minimized space was exactly the same as the choice of r_f that minimized expected retrieval time. Unfortunately, we do not have the same situation here. There are several additional factors, such as the respective times for random and sequential access to disk, the number of documents in the database, etc. Since we are forced to scan the entire bit-matrix for every query involving a frequent term, purely in terms of retrieval time, $r_{f,1}$ usually has a lower value. For our example database, this optimum value $r_{f,1}$ is around 690 rather than around 1200. Notice, however, that the hybrid method still improves the space overhead, even with a lower cut-off. Guidelines on how to choose between the two cut-offs are discussed in section 6.

Regardless of the final choice of the cut-off rank, the response time is given by eq. (4.22), assuming that eqs. (3.1-2) hold:

$$t_1 = q * t_{1,freq} + (1-q) * t_{1,rare} \tag{4.22}$$

The calculation of the response time for multi-term queries is the most complicated derivation in this paper. The complication, as well as the savings of the hybrid method, stem exactly from the fact that, if x terms in the query are frequent, the bit matrix has to be scanned only once, instead of x times. Formally:

The response time for a c-term query, under the assumptions of eqs. (3.1-2) is given by

$$t_c = h * c * T_{rand} + (1 - (1-q)^c) * t_{bitmap} + (1-q) * c * \overline{C_{rare}} * T_{rand} \tag{5.14}$$

We see that for multi-term queries, there is an even greater benefit to using the hybrid method relative to a standard inverted index, than in the case of single term queries.

Insertion Cost

For the standard inverted index structure, the time for insertion is

$$t_{IN} = h * \overline{V_d} * T_{rand} + \overline{V_{freq}} * (\overline{C_{freq}} + 1) * T_{rand} + \overline{V_{rare}} * (\overline{C_{rare}} + 1) * T_{rand} + t_{new} \tag{5.15}$$

because we need to traverse the B-tree $\overline{V_d}$ times; for each frequent term ($\overline{V_{freq}}$ of them per document) we need $\overline{C_{freq}}$ reads to traverse a chain of frequent postings plus one disk access to write back the results; and symmetrically for the rare terms. ($\overline{V_{freq}}$ is the average number of frequent terms per doc; $\overline{V_{rare}}$ is the average number of rare terms per doc; $\overline{V_{rare}} + \overline{V_{freq}} = \overline{V_d}$, the average number of terms per doc.). The term t_{new} reflects the cost of introducing a new term, including potential splits of the B-tree this might cause, weighted by the probability of a new term being introduced. This term is common to both this and the hybrid structure, and we do not evaluate it any further.

The above insertion time is extremely long, exactly because we have to scan sequentially all the postings records of a term, to locate and updated the last record. It can easily be shortened, if, e.g., for each term, we store a pointer to its last postings record, in addition to its first postings record. An alternative design would be to link the postings records in the reverse order. Regardless of the low-level details, with negligible or even zero additional space overhead, we can reach the last postings record of each term in one random disk access. Thus, the insertion time becomes

$$t_{IN} = h * \overline{V_d} * T_{rand} + \overline{V_{freq}} * (1+1) * T_{rand} + \overline{V_{rare}} * (1+1) * T_{rand} + t_{new} = (h+2) * \overline{V_d} * T_{rand} + t_{new} \tag{5.16}$$

because we need to descend h levels of the B-tree; one disk access to read the last postings record, and one more to write it back.

For the hybrid structure, the insertion cost is:

$$
\begin{aligned}
t_{IN} = h * \overline{V_d} * T_{rand} + t_{new} && btree && (5.17)\\
+ T_{rand} - T_{seq} + \left\lceil r_f/(b*P) \right\rceil * T_{seq} && bitmap \\
+ (\overline{C_{rare}} + 1) * \overline{V_{rare}} * T_{rand} && postings
\end{aligned}
$$

because we need to descend the B-tree $\overline{V_d}$ times, we need to append the new row at the end of the bitmap and to update the postings lists for $\overline{V_{rare}}$ rare terms. If the last postings record of each term is accessible in one disk access, then, using the same justification as with eq. (5.16), the last term of eq. (5.17) changes, to become

$$
\begin{aligned}
t_{IN} = h * \overline{V_d} * T_{rand} + t_{new} && btree && (5.18)\\
+ T_{rand} - T_{seq} + \left\lceil r_f/(b*P) \right\rceil * T_{seq} && bitmap \\
+ (1+1) * \overline{V_{rare}} * T_{rand} && postings
\end{aligned}
$$

Comparing equations (5.16) and (5.18), we find the saving in insertion cost due to the hybrid method to be

$$
2 * \overline{V_{freq}} * T_{rand} - T_{rand} - \left\lceil r_f/(b*P) \right\rceil * T_{seq} + T_{seq} \qquad (5.19)
$$

If a particular term occurs f_i times in N documents, then the probability that it will occur in a new document is roughly f_i/N. Using this, and ignoring the ceiling function, we can write the differential savings due to including the i-th term in the frequent set as being roughly

$$
2 * f_i * T_{rand}/N - T_{seq}/(b*P) \qquad (5.20)
$$

Let r_f be the largest rank that satisfies (5.22). Once more, since f_i is monotonically non-increasing in i, this function is monotonically non-increasing in i, indicating that the largest benefits are likely to be obtained by marking the most frequent terms as frequent, with diminishing benefits as we include more and more terms. For large enough N, there may be an $r_{f,3}$ cutoff beyond which the quantity in eqn. (5.20) becomes negative indicating a worsening instead of a saving. For smaller databases, due to the large page size and large differential between random and sequential disk access time, no such cutoff maybe found, and it may actually be preferred to treat every term as frequent. This is exactly the case in our 30Mb database: eq. (5.22) gives that every term that occurs in more than $f_i = 0.06$ documents, should be treated as frequent. This is not a very surprising result. Indeed insertion cost is the one criterion on which signature files win handsomely over inverted indices. What our analysis here indicates is that if the insertion cost is to be minimized in our hybrid approach, then the optimum cutoff is very large, making the hybrid technique "closer" to a signature file than an inverted index. A cut-off as large as $r_{f,3}$ will optimize insertion time, imposing heavy penalties on the storage and search time. Thus, we shall not consider the minimization of insertion cost further in this paper. Suffice to say that it can be done, if necessary, as shown above.

Arithmetic Example

Once more, we use data from our example 30MB database, with all parameters values as shown in Tables T1, T2, and T3. As discussed earlier, there is no single optimum value of r_f. The cut-off $r_{f,2}$ that minimizes the space is $r_{f,2} = 1420$; the cut-off $r_{f,1}$ that minimizes the search time for a single term query is $r_{f,1} = 690$ (assuming a magnetic disk as the medium). The cut-off assumes intermediate values when we wish to minimize multi-term retrieval queries.

We have chosen $r_f = 800$ as a representative value for our computations. The size of the postings record is

s=6 pointers. Assume q=0.33. Finally, from statistics on the database, we have:

$$\sum_{i=1}^{V} f_i = 1,792,079 \text{ postings pointers for all terms} \qquad \sum_{i=1}^{r_f} f_i = 721,531 \text{ postings pointers for frequent terms}$$

$$\sum_{i=1}^{V} C_i = 343,320 \text{ postings records for all terms} \qquad \sum_{i=1}^{r_f} C_i = 120,603 \text{ postings records for frequent terms}$$

Table T5 summarizes the results of the comparison using the values discussed above. The main observation is that the proposed method improves every performance measure.

	traditional	hybrid	savings (%)
Space [Mb]	10.7	8.4	27
$t_{1,freq}$ [sec]	4.58	3.0	52
t_1 [sec]	1.61	1.09	47
t_4 [sec]	6.44	3.04	112
t_{IN} [sec]	21.36	17.07	25

Table T5: Summary of arithmetic example for the dynamic case.

6. IMPLEMENTATION CONSIDERATIONS

In this paper we have proposed a hybrid technique for indexing large text databases. A central requirement for the proposed method is that the index terms be divided into two groups: frequent and rare. Here we briefly discuss how a practitioner could do this in a real application.

The classification of terms into two groups hinges on the determination of the occurrence frequencies of the terms. In a static database, these frequencies could be determined by direct measurements on the database. However, in the light of the experimental results presented in Sec. 5, one could get by even with a small sample (5-10%) of the database. The cut-off between frequent and rare terms is then determined analytically as shown in Sec. 4, eq. (4.14).

In an archival situation, the database designer can never have access to the entire database. As documents are added to the database, term frequencies will undoubtedly change. But in view of the experiments described in Sec. 5, we expect that by and large frequent terms will remain frequent and rare terms will remain rare, as the database grows. Thus, by using a snapshot of the database (or even a sample of a snapshot), occurrence frequencies can be determined.

In an archival situation there is the additional complication that the cut-off rank $r_{f,2}$ that minimizes the space (eq. (5.8)) is different (usually, larger) than the cut-off rank $r_{f,1}$ that optimizes the search time (eq. (5.13)). The safe, conservative solution is to choose $r_{f,1}$, the smallest cut-off, which optimizes the response time; this choice achieves sub-optimal, but, nevertheless, positive savings for the space and the insertion time, too. Such a choice guarantees that the response time for any single-term query will be at least as good as in the traditional method.

A larger value for the cut-off rank will improve the space overhead, the insertion time and the search time for multi-term queries, at the expense of a slower performance for single-term queries on the least frequent of the frequent terms. It is up to the designer of the database to decide which value between the two extremes $r_{f,1}$ and $r_{f,2}$ to use as a cut-off; the formulae in section 5 will help to predict the impact of each decision on the performance measures.

Another design decision in the archival case is the choice of the size s of the postings records. Our measurements in the 30Mb database showed that the space overhead is relatively insensitive to s in the vicinity of $s=6$. We also performed the same measurements in two other text databases, that were available on-line: the first was the book, *Wuthering Heights*, and the second was a collection of Grimm stories. The sizes were 659Kb and 1.4Mb, respectively, and the optimal values for s were 4 and 7, respectively. For both databases, the increase on the space overhead was small, for small deviations from the optimal values of s. Thus, we recommend the value of $s=6$ as a good (if not optimal) choice, for databases with English text. It is interesting to examine whether $s=6$ is still a good choice for non-English text databases.

Our experience is summarized in the following pseudo-algorithm, which is intended as a practitioner's guide:

Design Guidelines

1   Obtain a reasonably large sample of the database (10% or more)

2   Sort the words on decreasing occurrence frequencies

3   Decide the list of "noise" words ("I", "the", *etc.*, as well as words specific to the application, like "est" in our Associated Press database)

4   Decide the cut-off rank r_f for the frequent terms:

    4.1   For a static database, use eq. (4.14).

    4.2   For a dynamic database, choose a value of s ($s \approx 6$) to minimize the space of the traditional method; then, use eq. (5.13) and (5.8) to calculate the two cut-off ranks $r_{f,1}$ and $r_{f,2}$, the search-time optimal cut-off and the space-wise optimal cut-off, respectively. Then, try values of r_f in this range, estimate the performance measures (space, search time, insertion effort) and pick the value that gives the best results for the specific application. If in doubt, choose r_f to be the smallest cut-off $r_{f,1}$ (eq. (5.13)); such a choice will give sub-optimal, but positive savings for all the performance measures.

7. CONCLUSIONS

The thrust of this paper is to capitalize on the highly skewed distribution of term occurrence to design better text retrieval methods. We suggest a hybrid approach, that uses a B-tree inverted index for the rare terms, and a signature-like method for the frequent ones. Based on this concept, we fine-tune our designs for two environments: one static and the other archival. We show that, with a careful choice of the frequent terms, the proposed methods *improve all* the performance measures of interest (space, search time and insertion time), when compared to the standard inverted index method. Additional contributions of the paper include:

* the conclusion that even a small sample of the database can be used to determine the frequent terms with good accuracy. This conclusion was drawn after experimenting on a real, text database. The result is essential, because it gives us confidence to propose the hybrid method even in a dynamic

environment.

- the development of analytical models for the space overhead and the response time of the traditional and the hybrid methods for both environments, as well as the study of the insertion time for the dynamic environment. The response time analysis includes multi-term queries, in addition to single-term ones.

- the presentation of statistical data from a real database (30MB) that supports our assertion of a highly skewed term distribution. Based on the above data, the paper presents arithmetic examples that illustrate the superiority of our designs over a plain inverted index.

- Finally, the paper provides guidelines to a practitioner on how to choose the parameters for the hybrid method.

References

1. Bourne, C.P, "Frequency and Impact of Spelling Errors in Bibliographic Databases," *Information Processing and Management* 13(1), pp. 1-12 (1977).

2. Cardenas, A.F., "Analysis and Performance of Inverted Data Base Structures," *CACM* 18(5), pp. 253-263 (May 1975).

3. Christodoulakis, S., M. Theodoridou, F. Ho, M. Papa, and A. Pathria, "Multimedia Document Presentation, Information Extraction and Document Formation in MINOS: A Model and a System," *ACM TOOIS* 4(4) (Oct. 1986).

4. Comer, D., "The Ubiquitous B-Tree," *Computing Surveys* 11(2), pp. 121-137 (June 1979).

5. Faloutsos, C., "Access Methods for Text," *ACM Computing Surveys* 17(1), pp. 49-74 (March 1985).

6. Faloutsos, C. and R. Chan, "Fast Text Access Methods for Optical and Large Magnetic Disks: Designs and Performance Comparison," *Proc. 14th International Conf. on VLDB* , Long Beach, California, pp. 280-293 (Aug. 1988).

7. Faloutsos, C., "Signature-Based Text Retrieval Methods: A Survey," *IEEE Data Engineering* 13(1), pp. 25-32 (March 1990).

8. Haskin, R.L., "Special-Purpose Processors for Text Retrieval," *Database Engineering* 4(1), pp. 16-29 (Sept. 1981).

9. Hollaar, L.A., K.F. Smith, W.H. Chow, P.A. Emrath, and R.L. Haskin, "Architecture and Operation of a Large, Full-Text Information-Retrieval System," pp. 256-299 in *Advanced Database Machine Architecture*, ed. D.K. Hsiao, Prentice-Hall, Englewood Cliffs, New Jersey (1983).

10. King, D. R., "The Binary Vector as the Basis of an Inverted Index File," *J. Lib. Autom.* 7(4), p. 307 (1974).

11. Lesk, M.E., "Some Applications of Inverted Indexes on the UNIX System," UNIX Programmer's Manual, Bell Laboratories, Murray Hill, New Jersey (1978).

12. Lin, Z. and C. Faloutsos, "Frame Sliced Signature Files," CS-TR-2146 and UMIACS-TR-88-88, Dept. of Computer Science, Univ. of Maryland (Dec. 1988).

13. Rothnie, J.B. and T. Lozano, "Attribute Based File Organization in a Paged Memory Environment," *CACM* 17(2), pp. 63-69 (Feb. 1974).

14. Salton, G. and M.J. McGill, *Introduction to Modern Information Retrieval*, McGraw-Hill (1983).

15. Schuegraf, E.J., "Compression of Large Inverted Files with Hyperbolic Term Distribution," *Information Processing and Management* 12, pp. 377-384 (1976).

16. Zipf, G.K., *Human Behavior and Principle of Least Effort: An Introduction to Human Ecology*, Addison Wesley, Cambridge, Massachusetts (1949).

Sampling Issues in Parallel Database Systems

S. Seshadri [†] *and Jeffrey F. Naughton* [*]

Department of Computer Sciences
University of Wisconsin
Madison, WI 53706, USA

Abstract

Sampling has proven useful in database systems in applications including query size estimation, and most recently, probabilistic parallel query evaluation algorithms. In order to apply the full power of modern multiprocessor database systems, sampling techniques must (1) distribute the sampling workload evenly among the processors in the system, and (2) make use of all the data on the pages brought into main memory during the course of the sampling. In this paper we show how to achieve these two goals by proving that for query size estimation, (1) *stratified random sampling* guarantees perfect load balancing without reducing the accuracy of the estimate, and that (2) for a given number of I/O operations, *page level sampling* always produces a more accurate estimate than *tuple level sampling*. For probabilistic parallel query evaluation algorithms, high performance requires tight bounds on the expected skew in the allocation of work to processors as a function of the number of samples. Toward this end we prove a new bound on this skew, and show that our new bound is better than previously known bounds.

1 Introduction

Sampling has proven useful in database applications including query size estimation [HOT88, LNS90], time-constrained evaluation of aggregate queries [HOT89], randomized query evaluation algorithms [DNS91a, DNS91b], and obtaining random samples of answers to queries [OR86]. At the same time, parallel database systems have become more than a research curiosity and in fact have become a commercial success [DG90]. In this paper we consider three issues basic to the efficient implementation of sampling in multiprocessor database systems: load balancing, efficient utilization of disk IOs, and percentile estimation.

Good load balancing is crucial to the performance of any parallel algorithm. In sampling, load imbalances arise at a fundamental level. The most basic definition of what it means to take a "random sample" of n tuples from a database is that the tuples must be selected in such a way that every possible n-element subset of the relation is equally likely. In statistical terms, this is known as a "simple random sample," and it is used by the great majority of statistical tests. Furthermore, simple random sampling is the technique used virtually everywhere in the database literature related to sampling. However, if we use simple random sampling in a parallel database system, poor load balancing results. We study this problem in more detail in Section 3; here we just give one informal example. Suppose we take a simple random sample of size 1000 in a 100 processor system. Then it

---

[†] Work supported by NSF grant IRI-8909795 and by a gift of the IBM Corporation.

[*] Work supported by NSF Presidential Young Investigator Award and by a gift of the IBM Corporation.

is highly likely that some processor will have to take 19 samples, while another processor will take only three samples. Load imbalances such as these can severely degrade speedup as the sampling algorithm is run on more and more processors.

Our proposed solution to this problem is to give up on obtaining a simple random sample. In particular, instead of a simple random sample of size ks on a k processor system, we form a sample consisting of k simple random samples of size s, one from each processor. In the statistical literature, this technique is known as "stratified random sampling." Clearly, with stratified random sampling, perfect load balancing is achieved; the question is whether we have sacrificed the reliability of the estimate in the process. In general, a stratified random sample of a given size may produce less reliable estimates than does a simple random sample of the same size. However, as we show in Section 4, when estimating aggregate queries (which include count, and therefore query size estimation), under the set of parameters commonly encountered in parallel database systems, the difference in reliability between stratified and simple random sampling is so small as to be negligible.

The second issue we consider is how to make the best use of the I/Os performed throughout the course of sampling. (This issue is relevant to uniprocessor as well as multiprocessor systems.) A fundamental disadvantage sampling encounters when compared to most query evaluation algorithms is that naive implementations of sampling require one random disk I/O for each tuple examined, while query evaluation algorithms strive to make use of all tuples on each page as it is read. In [HOT88], Hou et al. propose that this difficulty be removed by using all tuples on a page whenever the page is chosen by the sampling procedure. Of course, a sample chosen in this manner is no longer a simple random sample of tuples from the database, or even a stratified random sample. Hou et al. acknowledge this fact. However, they leave open the basic question of how one can easily decide whether looking at all tuples on the page will improve the estimate. In Section 5 we prove that for aggregate estimation, the answer is extremely simple: using all tuples on the page will always improve the quality of the estimate obtained from a given number of I/Os, independent of the correlation between tuples.

Sections 4 and 5 suggest that page level stratified sampling is the method of choice in parallel database systems. In order to compare this strategy with the other strategies, namely tuple level simple random sampling, page level simple random sampling and tuple level stratified sampling, we conducted experiments on synthetically generated relations. We report the results of these experiments in Section 6.

The final issue we consider is how to estimate percentiles. Estimating percentiles is useful in parallel database systems for the following reason: estimates of percentiles can be used to partition the work in query evaluation. This partitioning can in turn be used to extract parallelism. A fundamental question that arises is how many samples need to be taken to guarantee a given bound on the skew in the estimated percentiles; the tighter this bound on the number of samples, the more efficient the parallel algorithm, since the overhead of sampling can then be reduced to the lowest possible level. In Section 7 we derive a new bound on the number of samples required to guarantee a given skew. This new bound is better than the bounds previously given in [BLM+91, DNS91a].

2 Framework for Sampling

To begin with, we present a framework for sampling. The framework identifies the major components of sampling algorithms, which helps to clarify where and how the issues of page level sampling and stratified sampling fit into a general sampling algorithm.

```
Partition the population into sampling units s₁, s₂, ..., sₙ
L = empty list
While SC(L,p,e)
      Choose a sampling unit sᵢ according to some rule
      Append sᵢ to L
Output g(L) as the desired estimate
```

Fig. 1. A general framework for sampling

Figure 1 gives a general framework for sampling. In the figure, SC is a stopping condition function that decides when to stop sampling, based on L, the list of sampling units seen so far, p, the desired confidence level of the estimate, and e, the maximum error you are willing to tolerate in your estimate. g is the function that estimates some property of the population based on the sampling units seen. The framework is at a very high level and virtually any sampling scheme can be cast into this framework by defining the appropriate functions and parameters.

The important point to note is that there are four major components to the framework:
(C1) the sampling units
(C2) the rule for choosing the sampling units
(C3) the stopping condition function (SC) and
(C4) the estimating function (g)

In most cases, the definitions of the four components are inter-related. Most of the applications of sampling in a database involves estimating the sum or the average of certain quantities. Query size estimation, one of the primary applications of sampling, is one such instance. There have been two approaches proposed for query size estimation based on sampling [LNS90, HOT88]. One of the main differences between these approaches is in their definition of stopping condition detection. In [LNS90], the stopping condition is adaptive, that is depends on the value of the samples seen. In [HOT88, HOD91] the stopping condition is fixed, either before the sampling begins or after an initial "pilot" sampling run to estimate the variance of the samples.

In a parallel database system, there is likely to be very little overhead in detecting a fixed stopping condition. On the other hand, adaptive stopping condition creates the problem of coordinating the processors so that the stopping condition is detected as early as possible by all the sites. For this reason, in this paper we will consider only fixed stopping conditions.

The estimating function g depends on what we are estimating. For example, suppose that their are n sampling units in the database, and that we take m samples, with values $s_1, s_2, \ldots, s_m$. Then we can define

$$g(L) = \frac{n}{m} \sum_{s_i \in L} s_i$$

This is known as the "blowup estimate" in the statistical literature. We will not further discuss components C3 and C4 in this paper. In the remainder of this paper we focus on C1 and C2.

3 Skew in Simple Random Sampling

As mentioned in the introduction, simple random sampling is probably the most natural and common method for obtaining a random sample from a population. (Usually, when a person with no statistical background is asked what a "random sample" is, they will come up with simple random sampling.) If we desire a simple random sample of size n, then we repeatedly choose a sampling unit from the population until we obtain a set of size n. The sampling units are chosen with uniform probability from among all possible sampling units. If we replace the sampling unit after choosing it, it is called sampling with replacement and if we do not, it is called sampling without replacement. We will focus on sampling with replacement for most of the paper. We will now investigate the amount of skew introduced by simple random sampling in a parallel environment.

Suppose we want n sampling units chosen by the simple random sampling rule. Assume that each site has N sampling units and that there are k sites. (For our purposes, a "site" is a processor-disk pair in a shared-nothing [Sto86] parallel database system.) The probability of a particular sampling unit coming from a given site is clearly $1/k$. Therefore, the number of sampling units chosen from a given site is a random number that has a binomial distribution with parameters n and $1/k$, and the number of sampling units chosen will vary from site to site. This leads to a skew in the number of sampling units chosen at each site, which in turn gives rise to load imbalance (or skew) in the system.

We can state a formula for the probability that the maximum of the number of sampling units chosen at each site will be below some specified level as follows. (The lemma can be derived from the results in [KSC78].)

Lemma 1. Let $X_1, X_2, \ldots, X_k$ be the number of sampling units chosen at sites $1, 2, \ldots, k$ respectively. Let $Y_1, Y_2, \ldots, Y_k$ be independent Poisson random variables that have parameter α, where $\alpha = n/k$. Finally, let $Z_1^r, Z_2^r, \ldots Z_k^r$ be random variables such that $P[Z_i^r = m] = P[Y_i = m | Y_i \leq r]$. Then the probability that $X_i \leq r$ for $i = 1, \ldots, k$ is equal to the following probability:

$$\frac{n!}{(k\alpha)^n} \sum_{i=0}^{r} \frac{\alpha^i}{i!} P[Z_1^r + Z_2^r + \ldots + Z_k^r = n]$$

The above lemma gives us a formula for computing the probability that the maximum of X_i is smaller than or equal to some constant r. Unfortunately, the formula does not have a closed form solution that can be easily computed. We can compute the above formula by explicitly computing $P[Z_1^r + Z_2^r + \ldots + Z_k^r = n]$ by a convolution, since we know how the individual Z_i^r's behave. Alternatively, for large k, we can use the central limit approximation for the sum of Z_i^r's and hence compute the formula. However, the resulting formulas are still too complex to be intuitive and are not immediately useful for our purposes.

We can get more useful information by exploring the behavior of the skew as n and k grow. A special case is when n grows in proportion to k, that is, $n/k = O(1)$. In this case we can adapt a result due to Gonnet [Gon81] to yield the following lemma:

Lemma 2. Consider a simple random sample of size n taken over k sites, where $n/k = O(1)$. Then asymptotically, some site will take

$$\frac{\ln k}{\ln \ln k}$$

samples.

Gonnet derived this result in the context of finding the maximum number of keys that will hash to the same location in a hash table.

As n and k grow, this maximum grows fast compared to the average of n/k sampling units you would expect to choose from a site. As another indication of the skew produced by simple random sampling, under the same assumption that $n/k = O(1)$, it can be shown that it is highly likely that there is a site from which no sampling unit is chosen. This follows from the fact that if we are sampling with replacement from a population of n distinct balls, we would need to draw $O(n \log n)$ samples before every ball is drawn at least once.

Table 1 shows the expected maximum and minimum number of samples that would be chosen by the sites for various values of n and k. The table also shows that for a fixed value of n/k, the distribution of the number of sampling units chosen at each site gets more skewed as k grows.

	10 sites	100 sites	1000 sites
10 samples	(3,0)		
100 samples	(15,5)	(4,0)	
1000 samples	(120,80)	(19,3)	(6,0)
10000 samples	(1113,863)	(132,69)	(22,1)

Table 1. Skew in the number of samples

It is clear from the table that even when we choose a lot of sampling units (10000 is a large number of samples for most sampling applications), there is still quite a disparity between the maximum and the minimum number of samples that we would expect to take across all the sites. In the next section, we demonstrate that for a wide class of sampling applications this skew can be eliminated without reducing the quality of the estimate by using a technique known as "stratified sampling."

4 Stratified Sampling for Estimating Averages

As we mentioned in Section 2, estimating averages is one of the primary uses of sampling in database systems. Query size estimation is a typical application of estimating averages, since most query size estimation methods convert the problem of estimating the size of the answer to a query to one of estimating the average or the sum of a set of numbers. In this section we consider the effectiveness of Stratified Sampling for estimating averages.

Like simple random sampling, stratified random sampling is a conceptually simple procedure. First, the domain being sampled is partitioned into disjoint subsets, called *strata*; next, a random sample is taken in such a way that a specified number of samples is taken from each stratum. For example, in our application, the strata can be chosen to be the sites in the database system; if we have k sites, and wish to take a total of n samples, then we take n/k samples at each site. Note again that this is not a simple random sample; in particular, in simple random sampling, there is a non-zero probability that *all* samples will come from a given site, whereas this can never happen with stratified sampling. This raises the question of the relative quality of the estimates obtained from simple random vs. stratified sampling.

In common statistical usage, stratified sampling is used to improve the quality of an estimate when something is known about the properties of the strata involved. Specifically, if the strata can be defined in such a way that the variance between strata is greater than the variance within the strata, stratified sampling can produce estimates that are far more accurate than those obtained by simple random sampling. In other words, if we can divide a heterogeneous population into homogeneous strata, then stratified sampling may produce significant gains in precision.

Our motivation for using stratified sampling is different: we typically know nothing about the relative variances between strata (sites). In this case, it is possible that stratified sampling will perform worse than simple random sampling. However, our goal is efficiency, since stratified sampling produces guaranteed perfect load balancing. In the following theorem, we show that if the system stores the same number of tuples per site, and this number is not "too small," then the reduction in the quality of the estimate due to using stratified random sampling is small enough to be safely ignored.

Theorem 3. *Let there be N tuples stored at each of k sites in a multiprocessor database system, and let V_{strat} be the variance of the estimate produced by taking s samples at each site. Furthermore, let V_{simp} be the variance of the estimate produced by taking a simple random sample of size ks. Then if terms of size $1/N$ are ignored relative to unity, $V_{strat} \leq V_{simp}$.*

5 Page-Level Sampling for Estimating Averages

In this section, we address another basic problem in sampling in database systems. (The material in this section is applicable to uniprocessor as well as multiprocessor systems.) As noted in the introduction, the most obvious way of implementing sampling in a database system is to let the tuples in the relation be the unit of sampling. That is, each individual sample is taken by somehow locating a randomly chosen tuple, then reading in the page on which that tuple is stored. This can cause a severe performance penalty, since it entails a random disk I/O for each sample taken. The alternative is to let the pages themselves be the units of sampling; however, in this case it is less clear how to guarantee the quality of the resulting estimate, since the tuples obtained via page-level sampling may not be independent. (E.g., if we are sampling on the attribute on which the relation is clustered.)

Consider the problem of estimating the size of the result of a select on a relation. This can be easily mapped to the problem of estimating the sum of N integers (estimating a sum is equivalent to estimating an average, when N is known), where N is the number of tuples in the relation, as follows: Associate the integer 1 with every tuple of the relation that satisfies the selection and associate the integer 0 with the other tuples. We could as before define each tuple (number) to be a sampling unit. However, as noted above, it is likely that inspecting n random tuples is likely to cause n disk I/O's. We could alternatively define the set of numbers on a page of the relation to be a sampling unit. Thus, the cost of inspecting n sampling units is again n disk I/O's, but now the total number of integers in the sample is increased by the blocking factor. Theorem 4 shows that the latter definition indeed always produces more accurate estimates.

We need some definitions before we can proceed with the theorem. Let the population consist of NM elements $y_1, y_2, \ldots, y_{NM}$, which is partitioned into N clusters of size M

$(M \geq 1)$ each. (In our application, N is the number of pages, while M is the number of tuples per page.) Let the goal be to estimate the average $\overline{Y}$ of the NM elements. If we take a simple random sample of n elements (tuples), then the sample mean is an unbiased estimate of the population mean. If we take a simple random sample of n clusters (pages), then the mean of the nM elements thus chosen is also an unbiased estimate of the population mean. Then we have the following result relating the variances of the two methods.

Theorem 4. *Let V_{page} be the variance of the estimate obtained from a simple random sample of n pages, and let V_{tuple} be the variance of the estimate obtained from a simple random sample of n tuples. Then $V_{page} \leq V_{tuple}$.*

The above theorem suggests that rather than choosing a simple random sample of n tuples, it makes sense to choose a simple random sample of n pages, since assuming I/O costs dominate the sampling, we would incur approximately the same cost anyway. The theorem assures us that we do not lose any accuracy due to the correlation between the tuples in the pages by choosing the pages as sampling units.

Theorem 4 assumes that the random sample is obtained using simple random sampling. The following theorem extends Theorem 4 to the case when we take a stratified sample of the tuples and the pages. Let the population consist of N elements (tuples) $y_1, y_2, \ldots, y_N$, which is partitioned into k strata (sites), where stratum i is of size N_i (number of tuples at site i). Within each stratum, let the population at that stratum be divided into clusters of size M (number of tuples in a page), where $M \geq 1$. Let the goal be to estimate the average $\overline{Y}$ of the N elements. Let us take a stratified sample of totally n tuples, with n_i tuples chosen from stratum i. Let the n_i tuples be chosen independently in each stratum i by simple random sampling. Then the sample mean $\overline{y_i^{tuple}}$ in stratum i is an unbiased estimate of the stratum mean. It can be shown that

$$\overline{y_{st}^{tuple}} = \sum_{i=1}^{k} \frac{N_i}{N} \overline{y_i^{tuple}}$$

is an unbiased estimate of the population mean. If now instead of choosing n_i tuples at each site, we choose n_i pages by simple random sampling independently at each site, then once again the sample mean $\overline{y_i^{page}}$ in stratum i is an unbiased estimate of the stratum mean. Once again

$$\overline{y_{st}^{page}} = \sum_{i=1}^{k} \frac{N_i}{N} \overline{y_i^{page}}$$

is an unbiased estimate of the population mean.

Theorem 5. *Let V_{st}^{tuple} denote the variance of the estimator $\overline{y_{st}^{tuple}}$, and let V_{st}^{page} denote the variance of the estimator $\overline{y_{st}^{page}}$. Then $V_{st}^{page} \leq V_{st}^{tuple}$*

We should point out that Theorem 4 does not imply that if we were to pick a simple random sample of n pages and a simple random sample of n tuples, the former will always have a greater accuracy. The theorem just states that over a large set of trials the average error of page level sampling will be smaller. A similar comment holds good for Theorems 3 and 5.

Theorem 5 together with Theorem 3 implies that for estimating averages in a parallel database system, the technique of choice is stratified sampling at the page level.

6 Experiments

It is clear now from the previous sections that we can obtain four sampling schemes for estimating aggregates. They are

1. tuple level simple random sample (TLSRS)
2. page level simple random sampling (PLSRS)
3. tuple level stratified sampling (TLStr)
4. page level stratified sampling (PLStr)

In order to compare these strategies, we built synthetic relations and estimated the size of a select query on the relation using each of the above four strategies. Notice that since we are estimating the size of selects, as far as the estimating algorithm is concerned, the relation consists of 1's and 0's according to whether the tuple satisfies the select or not. We shall therefore treat the relation as if it consisted of 0's and 1's only (in the strict sense of the word, this can no longer be called a relation).

All our experiments were run simulating a million tuple relation that was declustered across 100 sites. We assumed that each page of the relation contained 40 tuples. In the following, when we say we chose n samples per site, it means that stratified sampling chose n samples (pages/tuple) per site, and simple random sampling chose $100n$ samples. All our results are the average over 100 runs.

We ran four types of experiments, each one corresponding to a different synthetic relation. Figure 2 graphs the average absolute error of each of the four schemes against the number of samples per site. The figure contains one graph for each of the four synthetic relations. The four synthetic relations we considered were:

- **R1:** In this relation, 10% of the relation was 1's and the rest were 0's. The 1's and 0's were randomly distributed in the relation. It is clear that the page level schemes outperform the tuple level schemes by a huge margin. The reason is that the random distribution aids the page level schemes. Since there is no correlation between the tuples in a page, it is as if we were choosing 40 times more samples for the page level schemes. There is very little difference between simple random sampling schemes and stratified sampling schemes because both the inter-site variance and the intra-site variance are approximately the same.

- **R2:** In this relation, the pages of the relation were either all 1's or all 0's. 10% of the pages were all 1's and the rest were 0's. The pages themselves were randomly distributed across the system. This is a case of high correlation among the tuples of a page. It can be seen that page level schemes are close to tuple level schemes. This is one of the worst scenarios for page level schemes and yet it can be seen that their accuracy is comparable to the tuple level accuracy. Once again, the stratified schemes do not differ much from the simple random sampling schemes because of the random distribution of the pages.

- **R3:** 50% of this relation at each site were 1's while the rest were 0's. Therefore, the inter-site variance is zero in this case while the intra-site variance is 0.25. It can be seen that the stratified schemes are very close to the simple random schemes. This is despite the fact that the distribution favors simple random sampling. This shows the applicability of Theorem 3.

- **R4:** In this relation 50% of the sites have 95% 1's and the rest 0's while the other 50% of the sites have 5% 1's and the rest 0's. This gives rise to a high inter-site variance

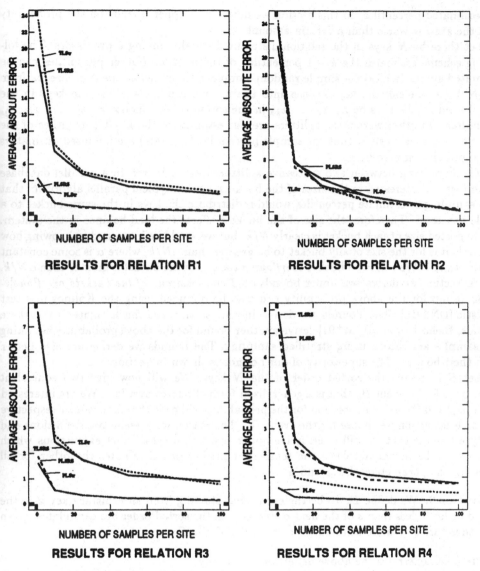

Fig. 2. Experimental Results

while keeping the intra-site variance reasonably low. It can be seen that stratified sampling is more accurate than simple random sampling as would be expected.

7 Estimating Percentiles

Estimating percentiles is a problem that has received much attention in recent literature. It has found applications in Parallel Sorting [BLM+91, DNS91b] and Non Equijoin Computation [DNS91a]. In each case, the efficiency of the resulting algorithm depends how few samples can be taken while still guaranteeing an upper bound on the resulting skew in the estimated percentiles. In this section we derive new upper bounds on the probability that the skew is worse than a certain amount.

Let there be N keys in the relation distributed equally among k processors. The following scheme estimates the $k - 1$ percentiles of the relation. (Other percentiles can be estimated similarly.) Take a simple random sample without replacement of size ks from the N keys and call the keys chosen into the sample *candidates*. Sort the keys in the sample and let the keys be $x_1, x_2, \ldots, x_{ks}$ in the sorted order. Choose $x_s, x_{2s}, \ldots, x_{(k-1)s}$ as *splitters*. In other words, the splitters are our estimate of the $k - 1$ percentiles of the N keys. It is easy to show that the sample percentiles (splitters) are unbiased estimators of the population percentiles.

The keys lying between two successive splitters form a *bucket*. In a parallel database system we are interested in the sizes of the buckets, since a typical parallel algorithm that uses sampling to estimate percentiles would redistribute the keys in the same bucket to a single processor. Therefore, the size of the buckets affects the load balance in the system. The expected size of each bucket is clearly N/k, but we would be interested in knowing how probable it is for the size of any bucket to be greater than $\alpha N/k$, where α is some constant greater than 1. We will say a bucket *overflows* if the size of the bucket is greater than $\alpha N/k$. In this section we derive two upper bounds on $Pr[at\ least\ one\ of\ the\ buckets\ overflows]$.

A bound for the above probability can also be obtained using the Kolmogorov test statistic [DNS91a]. The bounds we derive in this section are much tighter than these bounds. Blelloch et al. [BLM+91] derive another bound for the above probability assuming the samples are chosen using stratified sampling. The bounds we derive are also better than their bounds. The superiority of our bounds is shown in Section 7.

Let S represent the sorted order of the N keys. We will now give two equivalent definitions for an event B_x that is a generalized form of bucket overflow. We are interested in $Pr[B_x]$ and the exact expression for the probability will have the same value irrespective of which definition we choose for the event B_x. The reason we present two definitions and analyze them is that we will later derive upper bounds on these exact expressions which turn out to be incomparable in the sense that neither one dominates the other for all values of the parameters N, k, s and α.

Definition 6. We define B_x to be the event that starting from an arbitrary key x in the sorted order S, less than s of the next $\alpha N/k$ keys in the sorted order are candidates, given that there are s or more candidates to the right of x in S.

Figure 3 demonstrates the above definition pictorially.

The same event can alternatively be described by the following definition.

Definition 7. B_x is the event that the sth candidate starting from x is after the next $\alpha N/k$ keys in S.

Figure 4 demonstrates the above definition pictorially.

We now present an overview of the technique we use for proving those two bounds. We will denote by y_i the key just after x_{is} in S. y_0 will be the first key in S. It is easy to see that the probability that the $i + 1$st bucket overflows is $Pr[B_{y_i}]$ for $0 \le i \le k - 2$. The event that the last bucket overflows is not the same as the event $B_{y_{k-1}}$, but the probability of both the events are the same since we can envisage the reverse of the sorted order S and then the event of the last bucket overflowing is same as B_{y_0}. We will demonstrate in Lemma 12 that the probability of occurrence of B_{y_0} is the same as $B_{y_{k-1}}$. Therefore, the

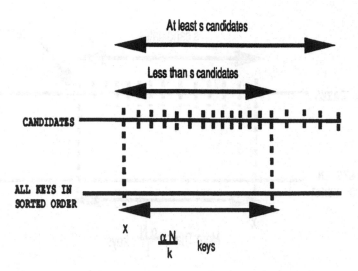

Fig. 3. Definition for the event B_x

probability that at least one of the buckets overflows is less than $\sum_{i=0}^{p-1} Pr[B_{y_i}]$. Our final goal is then to derive an upper bound on this sum so that we have an upper bound on the probability that any of the buckets overflow.

We will use Definition 6 for the event B_x in the following sequence of lemmas leading up to Theorem 13, which gives an upper bound on the probability that one or more of the buckets overflow. We will then use Definition 7 for B_x and derive yet another upper bound on the probability that one or more of the buckets overflow.

We will in the following lemma derive an exact expression for $Pr[B_x]$ using Definition 6 for the event B_x, where x is an arbitrary key. Since the exact expression is difficult to compute, we will then in the subsequent lemma derive an upper bound for this exact expression. The final lemma in this sequence will show that $Pr[B_{y_i}]$ is the same as $Pr[B_x]$, where x is an arbitrary key. In other words, the information that we have chosen exactly is samples up to y_i does not affect $Pr[B_{y_i}]$. Once we have the above lemmas, we can derive an upper bound on the desired probability. This bound is stated in the Theorem 13 after these three lemmas.

We will need the following definitions before we can proceed with the lemmas.

Definition 8. We will need the following standard definition of the falling factorial: $n^{\underline{m}} = n(n-1)\ldots(n-m+1)$, where m is a positive integer.

Lemma 9. *Let x be an arbitrary key. Then*

$$Pr[B_x] = \sum_{j=0}^{s-1} \binom{ks}{j} \frac{(\alpha N/k)^{\underline{j}}(N - \alpha N/k)^{\underline{ks-j}}}{N^{\underline{ks}}}$$

The preceding lemma gave an exact expression for $Pr[B_x]$. We now derive an upper bound for the expression. We will need a lemma from [Hoe63] before we can prove our upper bound.

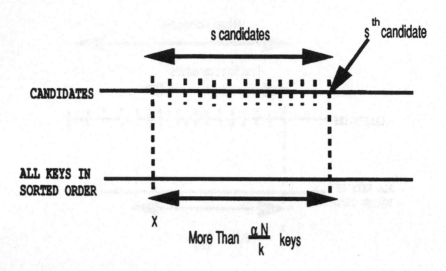

Fig. 4. Definition for the event B_x

Lemma 10. *[Hoe63] Let $X_1, X_2, \ldots X_n$ be n independent random variables such that $0 \leq X_i \leq 1$ for $i = 1, \ldots, n$. Let $S = X_1 + X_2 \ldots + X_n$, let $\overline{X} = S/n$ and let $\mu = E\overline{X} = ES/n$. Then for $0 < t < \mu$,*

$$Pr[\mu - \overline{X} \geq t] \leq \left\{ \left(\frac{1-\mu}{1-\mu+t} \right)^{1-\mu+t} \left(\frac{\mu}{\mu-t} \right)^{\mu-t} \right\}^n$$

Lemma 11. *Let x be an arbitrary key. Then $Pr[B_x] \leq \alpha^s (\frac{k-\alpha}{k-1})^{ks-s}$*

We will now show that $Pr[B_{y_i}]$ is the same as $Pr[B_x]$, where x is an arbitrary key. Recall that when we derived the expression for $Pr[B_x]$ we assumed nothing about how the samples have been chosen since x was an arbitrary key. On the other hand while considering the event B_{y_i} we already know that exactly is samples are chosen from among the keys up to y_i in S. This lemma shows that this information does not cause $Pr[B_{y_i}]$ to be different from $Pr[B_x]$, where x is an arbitrary key.

Lemma 12. $Pr[B_{y_i}] = Pr[B_x]$.

We are now ready to state a theorem which gives an upper bound on the probability that at least one of the buckets overflow.

Theorem 13. *$Pr[\text{at least one of the buckets overflows}] \leq k\alpha^s \left(\frac{k-\alpha}{k-1} \right)^{ks-s}$*

Proof: Recall that the probability that at least one of the buckets overflows is less than $\sum_{i=0}^{p-1} Pr[B_{y_i}]$. By Lemma 12 $\sum_{i=0}^{p-1} Pr[B_{y_i}] = k Pr[B_x]$ where x is an arbitrary key. Therefore the probability that at least one of the buckets overflow is less than or equal to $k\alpha^s \frac{k-\alpha}{k-1}^{ks-s}$ by Lemma 11. $\square$

Recall that the preceding theorem was derived using Definition 6 for the event B_x. We now derive a similar theorem using Definition 7 for the event B_x. As in the preceding case, we will first derive an exact expression for $Pr[B_x]$ using Definition 7 for the event B_x, where x is an arbitrary key. We will then in the subsequent lemma derive an upper bound for the exact expression. Finally we derive an upper bound on the probability that one or more of the buckets overflow. This bound is stated in Theorem 17 after these two lemmas.

We will need the following definition before we can proceed with the lemmas.

Definition 14. Let us denote the expression

$$\binom{ks}{s-1} \frac{m^{s-1}(N-m)^{ks-(s-1)}}{N^{ks}} \frac{ks-(s-1)}{N-m}$$

by $A(m)$.

The following lemmas gives an exact expression for the probability of the event B_x (using Definition 7).

Lemma 15. *Let x be an arbitrary key. Then*

$$Pr[B_x] = \sum_{m=\alpha N/k}^{n-1} A(m)$$

The following lemma gives an upper bound on the expression in the preceding lemma.

Lemma 16. *Let x be an arbitrary key. Then*

$$Pr[B_x] \le A(\alpha N/k)(1 - r^{N-\alpha N/k})/(1-r)$$

where

$$r = \frac{(\alpha N/k + 1)(N - \alpha N/k - 1 - (ks - s))}{(\alpha N/k + 1 - (s-1))(N - \alpha N/k - 1)}$$

Theorem 17. *Let $p = kA(\alpha N/k)(1 - r^{N-\alpha N/k})/(1-r)$ where*

$$r = \frac{(\alpha N/k + 1)(N - \alpha N/k - 1 - (ps - s))}{(\alpha N/k + 1 - (s-1))(N - \alpha N/k - 1)}$$

Then $Pr[$at least one of the buckets overflows$] \le p$

Proof: Notice that Lemma 12 holds irrespective of which definition we use for the event B_x. Recall that the probability that at least one of the buckets overflows is less than $\sum_{i=0}^{p-1} Pr[B_{y_i}]$. By Lemma 12 $\sum_{i=0}^{p-1} Pr[B_{y_i}] = kPr[B_x]$ where x is an arbitrary key. Therefore the probability that at least one of the buckets overflow is less than or equal to p by Lemma 16. □

As we stated before, the bounds of Theorems 13 and 17 are incomparable in the sense that neither one dominates the other for all values of n, s, k and α. Therefore, we have the following theorem.

Theorem 18. *Let $p_1 = k\alpha^s \frac{k-\alpha}{k-1}^{ks-s}$ and let $p_2 = kA(\alpha N/k)(1 - r^{N-\alpha N/k})/(1-r)$ where*

$$r = \frac{(\alpha N/k + 1)(N - \alpha N/k - 1 - (ps - s))}{(\alpha N/k + 1 - (s-1))(N - \alpha N/k - 1)}$$

Then $Pr[$at least one of the buckets overflows$] \le min\{p_1, p_2\}$

Comparison with other Bounds

There have been quite a few bounds suggested in literature for the probability that at least one of the buckets overflows. Blelloch et al. [BLM+91] choose the candidates as follows: First, each of the k sites partitions its N/k keys into s groups of size N/ks and then selects one key from each group at random. They proved that for $\alpha > 1$, the probability that any bucket is of size greater than $\alpha N/k$ is at most $Nexp(-(1-1/\alpha)^2\alpha s/2)$. It is easy to show that $exp(-(1-1/\alpha)^2\alpha s/2)$ is greater than $\alpha^s((k-\alpha)/(k-1))^{ks-s}$, for all $\alpha > 1$ and all $k > \alpha$. Therefore, the upper bound of Theorem 18 is smaller than $Nexp(-(1-1/\alpha)^2\alpha s/2)$. In fact, the bounds differ significantly when N, the number of keys in the relation is much bigger than k, the number of sites, which usually is the case.

There is yet another bound that has been used while estimating percentiles. This bound is derived from Kolmogorov test statistic and is used for estimating percentiles in [DNS91a]. The way they choose the buckets is exactly the same as the way the buckets are chosen by our simple random sampling method. The Kolmogorov statistic says that the estimated percentile will differ from the actual percentile by at most $x_p/\sqrt{ks}$, where ks is the number of keys chosen in the simple random sample and x_p is a constant that depends on the confidence level of the estimate. For example, x_p is 1.63, if confidence level desired is 99%, while it is 1.36, if confidence level desired is 0.95. Therefore, if we take a simple random sample of size 256, then the median of the sample is at most $1.63/\sqrt{256} = 0.1$ (approximately) away from the actual median with probability 0.99. This means that there are at most $0.1N$ keys between the sample median and the actual median with 99% certainty. This means that the maximum size of any bucket is $N/k+2Nx_p/\sqrt{ks}$, since N/k is the number of keys between two consecutive $k-1$ percentiles (we are talking about the elements that divide the population into k equal parts) and Nx_p/ks the maximum number of keys between one of the estimated percentiles and actual percentiles. We want $N/k + 2Nx_p/\sqrt{ks}$ to be less than or equal to $\alpha N/k$. Simplifying, we obtain $ks \geq 4x_p^2k^2/(\alpha-1)^2$.

We compare the bounds of Theorem 18 with the bounds of Blelloch et al. and the bounds derived from the Kolmogorov statistic in Tables 2, 3 and 4. In each of the tables B is the number of samples required according to the bound of Blelloch et al., K, the number of samples required according to the bound derived from Kolmogorov's statistic and New, the number of samples required by the bound of Theorem 18. In all cases the number of samples shown is per site, therefore, the total number of samples is the number of samples times the number of sites. p is kept constant at 0.95 in all cases.

k	B	K	New
10	201	295	29
20	201	591	37
30	201	887	42
40	201	1183	44
50	201	1479	47
60	201	1775	48
70	201	2071	49
80	201	2367	51
90	201	2663	51
100	201	2959	52

Table 2. Samples per site for $\alpha = 1.5$, $N = 10^6$, k varying

α	B	K	New
1.1	3698	36992	1441
1.2	1008	9248	180
1.3	485	4110	108
1.4	294	2312	68
1.5	201	1479	47
1.6	149	1027	34
1.7	116	754	26
1.8	94	578	20
1.9	78	456	17
2.0	67	369	14

Table 3. Samples per site for $k = 50$, $N = 10^6$, α varying

N	B	K	New
25000	157	1479	29
50000	165	1479	35
100000	174	1479	39
200000	182	1479	43
400000	190	1479	45
800000	199	1479	46
1600000	207	1479	47
3200000	215	1479	47
6400000	224	1479	48
12800000	232	1479	48

Table 4. Samples per site for $k = 50$, $\alpha = 1.5$, N varying

8 Conclusion

We presented a framework for sampling that gives a high-level view of sampling. The framework helped identify areas of interest to database research. We showed that simple random sampling leads to skew in the number of samples to be chosen at each site in a parallel database system. On the other hand, stratified sampling produces exact load balancing without significantly reducing the quality of the estimates. We also showed that page level sampling is preferable to tuple level sampling, if we are estimating averages. Our experiments verified our theoretical analysis that for estimating averages (and, hence, for query size estimation) in parallel database systems, stratified sampling at the page level is the method of choice.

In another direction, we derived a new bound for estimating percentiles. This bound is better than the previous bounds for percentile estimation, which in turn leads directly to more efficient algorithms for parallel external sorting and non-equijoin computations.

We are currently investigating the relationship between the accuracy of the percentile estimates produced by simple random sampling and stratified sampling. We are also investigating whether page level sampling always helps while estimating percentiles as is the case for estimating averages. Finally, we have designed algorithms for estimating the sizes of answers to queries in a parallel database system and are currently evaluating their performance.

343

References

[BLM+91] G. E. Blelloch, C. E. Leiserson, B. M. Maggs, C. G. Plaxton, S.J. Smith, and M. Zagha. A comparison of sorting algorithms for the connection machine CM-2 In *3rd Annual ACM Symposium on Parallel Algorithms and Architectures*, Hilton Head, South Carolina, July 1991.

[Coc77] William G. Cochran. *Sampling Techniques*. John Wiley and Sons, Inc., New York New York, 3 edition, 1977.

[DG90] David J. Dewitt and Jim Gray. Parallel database systems: The future of database processing or a passing fad? *SIGMOD Record*, 19(4):104–112, December 1990.

[DNS91a] David J. DeWitt, Jeffrey F. Naughton, and Donovan A. Schneider. A comparison of non-equijoin algorithms. In *Proceedings of the Eighteenth International Conference on Very Large Databases*, Barcelona, Spain, August 1991.

[DNS91b] David J. DeWitt, Jeffrey F. Naughton, and Donovan A. Schneider. Parallel external sorting using probabilistic splitting. In *Proceedings of the Parallel and Distributed Information Symposium*, Miami Beach, Florida, Dec 1991. To appear.

[Gon81] Gaston H. Gonnet. Expected length of the longest probe sequence in hash code searching. *JACM*, 28(2):289–304, April 1981.

[HOD91] W. C. Hou, G. Ozsoyoglu, and E. Dogdu. Error constrained count query evaluation in relational databases. In *Proceedings of the SIGMOD International Conference on Management of Data*, pages 278–287, Denver, Colorado, May 1991.

[Hoe63] Wassily Hoeffding. Probability inequalities for sums of bounded random variables. *American Statistical Association Journal*, pages 13–30, March 1963.

[HOT88] Wen-Chi Hou, Gultekin Ozsoyoglu, and Baldeo K. Taneja. Statistical estimators for relational algebra expressions. In *Proceedings of the Seventh ACM Symposium on Principles of Database Systems*, pages 276–287, Austin, Texas, March 1988.

[HOT89] Wen-Chi Hou, Gultekin Ozsoyoglu, and Baldeao K. Taneja. Processing aggregate relational queries with hard time constraints. In *Proceedings of the ACM-SIGMOD Conference on the Management of Data*, pages 68–77, Portland, Oregon, June 1989.

[KSC78] V. F. Kolchin, B. A. Sevastyanov, and V. P. Chistyakov. *Random Allocations*. V. H. Winston and Sons, Washington, D.C., 1978.

[LNS90] Richard J. Lipton, Jeffrey F. Naughton, and Donovan A. Schneider. Practical selectivity estimation through adaptive sampling. In *Proceedings of the ACM SIGMOD International Conference on Management of Data*, Atlantic City, New Jersey, May 1990.

[OR86] Frank Olken and Doron Rotem. Simple random sampling for relational databases. In *Proceedings of the Twelfth International Conference on Very Large Databases*, pages 160–169, Kyoto, Japan, August 1986.

[Sto86] M. Stonebraker. The case for shared nothing. *Database Engineering*, 9(1), 1986.

Parallelism For High Performance Query Processing

Vincent G. Winters

Department of Computer Science, University of Cincinnati Cincinnati, Ohio USA

Abstract

We present a new method for a type of processing required in data base management systems. The method efficiently determin s t! relevance of a given query value to each of many (target) sets of data. By using a new type of data structure, the method allows complete parallelism both for operations on different target sets and for those within each target set. The method never generates a false drop (*i.e.* indicates that an irrelevant target set is relevant to the query) and always identifies all relevant target sets. This eliminates the the overhead of reading each selected target set to ensure that the selection was not a false drop. A good deterministic bound on the system's performance is established.

With $O(\ln N_V + \ln \ln M)$ processors, the relevance of any target set can be completely determined in $O(1)$ time against a query consisting of a subset of N_V vocabulary items. The space complexity is $O(N_i(\ln N_V + \ln \ln N_V))$ bits , where N_i is the number of items relevant to target set i. As a concrete example, for a database using 64 byte keys, having a 100,000 word vocabulary (potentially valid keys) and in which a target set can have up to 64 distinct relevant elements, the relevance of a target set can be determined in 2 parallel operations using 6 processors. In other words, with 64K processors a database of one million target sets can be processed in 184 parallel operations. No probability distribution assumptions are necessary.

Keywords: Signatures, Searching, Retrieval, Parallel Algorithms, Complexity.

Key words: Signatures, Searching, Retrieval, Parallel Algorithms, Complexity.

1 Introduction

Data filtering is an important function necessary in a wide variety of database applications. The goal of data filtering is the rapid and efficient determination, from a large number of sets of data, of all and only those sets that are relevant to a given input query. One popular type of filtering is that using "signatures". In this method, a data structure (the signature) is associated with each "block" (we refer to each set of data whose relevance is to be determined as a block). The filtering then involves some type of matching a derivative of the input value to each signature. Some examples of signature based filtering are superimposed coding [6] and word signatures [10]. Filtering with signature files has been used in searching unformatted documents (to locate those that are relevant to a subject area of interest), in spelling checkers [2], in accessing change files for database systems [5], in partial match retrieval against databases [7] and in event counting systems [8]. A good review of filtering for text retrieval can be found in [3]. In this article we propose a new method for filtering with signatures. The new method has a number of desirable features not present in earlier systems.

A common characteristic of previous filtering systems has been a probabilistic foundation. In such systems, there exists a non-zero probability of generating "false drops". A false drop occurs when the system indicates that a block is relevant to the input set but, in fact, it is not. False drops are costly since their possibility requires that every block that the system indicates is relevant must be processed to ensure that the indication is not a false drop. Much research in this area has had as its subject the prediction of and/or reduction in the rate of false drops for various signature systems. In addition, it is often the case that results concerning the performance of such systems require the assumption of a particular probability distribution. Assumptions are made about the probability distributions of values in the target sets and/or of the values that can be entered as query values.

In the new system it is guaranteed that no false drops will occur regardless of the probability distributions of values in the query or target sets. The system also exhibits other features that make it an attractive filtering mechanism. First, the system allows almost complete inter-block and intra-block parallelism. It can make use of as much parallelism as is available up to the point of being able to filter an entire database, of any size, with 2 parallel operations. Also, a great majority of the processing requires single bit operations. Thus, processing in parallel can be accomplished with relatively inexpensive hardware. A second benefit is a low space requirement (relative to the underlying data base) for the system's data structures. The parallel processing of a target set does not require exclusive access to common storage. Rather it consists of parallel AND and OR operations along with parallel read operations on data in distributed storage.

The remainder of this work is organized as follows. In Sect. 2, terminology is defined and some environments in which the system is applicable are identified. Sect. 3 motivates the method and presents its algorithms. In Sect. 4, the complexity of the system is formally derived. Sect. 5 contains a small example and discusses some tradeoffs available to implementors of the method. Sect. 6 concludes and discusses future research.

2 Background and Terminology

The system is applicable in any situation requiring the processing of queries against a large body of data that is divided into subsets (called blocks). We assume that the data is static or slowly changing. An example of the former situation is a database contained on a CD-ROM. An example of the latter would be a very large database. The system services queries, each of which consists of one or more data values. Each block will either be relevant (for example, contains the data values) or be irrelevant for a given query. The task is to efficiently identify exactly the set of relevant blocks. An example frequently cited in the literature [3],[1], is that of a large text database in which those blocks containing user supplied keywords must be identified. Other examples include partial match retrieval [7] and determination of the currency of replicated data [5].

For each problem of this type, there will be a "vocabulary". The vocabulary consists of those data values for which at least one block (now or potentially in the future) is (could be) relevant. That is, the vocabulary is the set of query data values for which the system could return a nonempty set of block identifiers. In many situations the contents of the vocabulary will be delineated naturally. For example, in a database of text it could be the words contained in all the text or all words of the native language or terms that are key to a specific subject area. In database records it could be the legal values for attributes. We use N_V to denote the cardinality of the vocabulary and M to denote the number of possible values that can occur in the encoded reperesentation of data values (in or out of the vocabulary). That is, M is the largest binary integer containable in the field that holds an encoded term (at least $\lceil \log N_V \rceil$ [1]). Using the concept of a vocabulary does not cause any loss of generality since one can always choose as the vocabulary the set of all possible values containable in the encoded data field.

The number of blocks (target sets) in the database is represented by N_B. For the ith block, we denote the jth distinct vocabulary item that is relevant to it by $V_{i,j}$. The cardinality of $\{V_{i,j}\}$ is N_i.

3 Motivation and Algorithms

In order to exemplify the utility of the system we will sometimes refer to its performance in two "example" environments. The first environment is a database in which key values are 8 bytes in length, the vocabulary consists of 10,000 words, each block holds 8192 bytes of data and contains at most 64 distinct relevant words. In the second environment keys are 64 bytes long, the vocabulary size is 100,000 and each block is 131,072 bytes long. In this environment there can be as many as 512 distinct relevant words associated with a block.

We now motivate our algorithms via a discussion of the functions performed by the various parts. [2] To start we outline the method used to create the signature for an arbitrary block - block i. It begins by reducing the magnitude of vocabulary items relevant to the block such that none is greater than $(N_V^2 \ln M)$, where N_V is the number of items in the vocabulary and M is the magnitude of the largest value that can be contained in a key field. The jth reduced value, $W_{i,j}$, is obtained via $W_{i,j} = (V_{i,j} \bmod R_V)$ where R_V is an integer determined from the vocabulary. It is known [4] that for any set of N integers bounded above by M, there must be an integer $R \le N^2 \ln M$ such the N integers are incongruent modulo R. By making use of this fact we obtain unique representations of the vocabulary items satisfying the above bound. With respect to the example one situation, any of the reduced values can be contained in 32 bits. The example two situation results in values that can be contained in 42 bits.

Letting M_R represent the maximum of all reduced values generated by the vocabulary, the system determines the smallest prime number, P_C, such that $\prod_{1 \le j \le C} P_j \ge M_R$. It is

---

[1] We use $'\ln'$ for natural logarithms and $'\log'$ for base 2 logarithms

[2] All discussion of vocabulary items and input query items refers to encoded representations considered as non-negative binary integers.

shown in Sect. 5 that C, the number of primes necessary to satisfy the above inequality, is $O(\ln M_R)$. Again considering our two example situations we find that the value of P_C is 29 (the tenth prime) for example one and 37 (the twelfth prime) for example 2.

The signature for a block is made via the concatenation of C components that are bit vectors. The kth component is generated using the kth prime number. The kth component is itself composed of a concatenation of P_k sub-component bit vectors. The length of each subcomponent bit vector is N_i (the number of distinct vocabulary items relevant to this block). Initially, all signature bits are set to 0. To generate component k of our signature, each $W_{i,j}$ (reduced value of an item relevant to this block) is taken mod P_k, giving an index $I_{k,W_{i,j}}$. Each $I_{k,W_{i,j}}$ is used as a zero origin index to a subcomponent vector of component k. The jth bit (corresponding to the jth relevant vocabulary item) in this subcomponent vector is set to one. As is demonstrated later, the space complexity of a signature (in *bits* not words) is $O(N_i \ln^2(N_V \ln M))$. The upper bounds on the number of bits in any signature for our examples are 8,256 and 100,884 respectively. Thus, the worst possible overhead for signature storage in our examples are 12.6% and 9.6% respectively. Further, since the total number of one bits in any signature cannot exceed the product $N_i \times C$ (640 in example one and 6144 in example two), employing data compression algorithms could significantly reduce storage overhead.

We now turn to the processing of query requests using the previously created signatures for blocks. We consider the steps required to determine whether or not an arbitrary block (given its associated signature) is relevant to an arbitrary single item query. To start, the input value (treated as a binary integer) is reduced mod R_V as was done in signature creation. The final output of this operation we denote by Q_R. Then a single parallel operation is performed in which the value of Q_R (the reduced query value) is taken mod P_j for $j = 1 \ldots C$. This gives index values $I_1, \ldots I_C$. Note that these values will also be used in determining the relevance of other blocks. Thus, for any given prime, the modulo operation need be done only once per search of the entire database. This is especially important since the other operations involved in relevance determination can be accomplished with inexpensive processors having an instruction set of only basic boolean operators. Each index value is used to select one subcomponent vector from each of the C components of the signature. All selected subcomponent vectors are $ANDed$ in parallel (e.g. via common bussing) with the result being stored into a vector of N_i bits. For any query value that is contained in the vocabulary, the block with this signature is relevant if and only if the result vector is non-zero.

Let us now consider the system's performance for our two examples. We assume an architecture employing 64 bit words with the capability for 12 processors to simultaneously AND one word from each of 12 local storage areas into a common word. The reduction of a query value takes one step involving only one processor. Obtaining the subcomponent indices takes one parallel step involving no more than 10 processors for example one and 12 processors for example two. (We reiterate that the operation of obtaining the indices is done only once for processing the entire database and *not* for each block.) The final step is $ANDing$ all indexed subcomponents of the signature into a common area and comparing the result to zero. In example one, subcomponent vector size can be no greater than 64 and the number of components is 10. Therefore, this step requires only one parallel operation. In example two, since N_i can be as large as 512 and a signature has 12 components, up to 8 iterations of this step (each operating on 64 bits) may be required. Naturally, if there were 8 processor groups with 12 processors in each group example two would also require only one parallel operation.

In the next section we discuss several ways in which the flexibility of such a system can be enhanced and present a small illustrative example.

4 Implementation Considerations and Example

It is often desirable for a retrieval system to accomodate dynamic changes in its data base. For example, allowing incremental extension and contraction of the database by adding and deleting blocks. In our system these functions can be implemented simply and performed efficiently. For the addition of a new block a signature is created as previously described. Deletion of a block requires only removal of its signature.

Another type of dynamic change is the addition of a new vocabulary item to the set of items that are relevant to a block. Adding the item is accomplished by simply adding one more bit to each subcomponent and setting to one the new bit in those subcomponents indexed by the new item. Making a previously relevant item irrelevant to this block is done by simply setting off the signature bits that correspond to that item.

A small pedagogical example is now presented. This is intended to clarify the manner in which the method functions. Fig. 1 lists a 442 word vocabulary (derived from several articles on space program topics). Contained in Fig. 2 is a 106 word subset of the vocabulary. This subset consists of all vocabulary words that occur in one of the original articles. Also in Fig. 2 are the unique values generated by the vocabulary reduction. For this vocabulary the reduction consists of taking the binary encoding of each word mod 12882. Fig. 3 gives the reduced values and the subcomponent indices for each of these 106 relevant words. There are five components corresponding to the primes 3, 5, 7, 11 and 13.

Consider, for example, the relevant word "aerospace". When the binary representation of "aerospace" is taken modulo 12882 the value 8735 is obtained. Any bijective mapping of relevant words to subcomponent bit positions may be chosen at the time signatures are created. In this example the relevant words are mapped in alphabetical order. Thus, "aerospace" corresponds to the first bit in every subcomponent of the signature. Now 8735 taken modulo 3,5,7,11 and 13 gives the values 2, 0, 6, 1 and 12 respectively. Thus, the creation of this signature includes setting to one the first bits of subcomponent 2 in the component corresponding to 3, subcomponent 0 in the component corresponding to 5, subcomponent 6 in the component corresponding to 7, subcomponent 1 in the component corresponding to 11 and subcomponent 12 in the component corresponding to 13. The relevance of "aerospace" to this block would be detected via the fact that the first bit is a one in the all of the indexed subcomponents - subcomponent 2 (of the component for 3), subcomponent 1 (of the component for 5), subcomponent 0 (of the component for 7), subcomponent 1 (of the component for 11) and subcomponent 2 (of the component for 13). The result of *ANDing* these subcomponents would be non-zero since bit position one would be on. The (uncompressed) size of this block's signature is 65 storage words (at 64 bits per word). The complete determination of an input's relevance to the block can be made in 2 parallel operations using 10 processors. This assumes that the reduction and modulo operations have been done once for processing of the entire database.

The total size of the block for which this signature was created is 3874 bytes giving an overhead of 13.4%. Since more than 87% of the bits in this signature are zeros, the potential for reducing overhead via compression is great.

5 Analysis

In this section some properties of the method are formally derived. Theorem 5.1 establishes the effectiveness of the method. Theorems 5.2-5.3 bound the complexities of the system. In the first theorem, it is shown that the system will select all and only those blocks relevant to a single valued query. The extension to queries in the form of boolean functions of multiple values is straightforward. To accomplish this, boolean operations are incorporated into signature checking. A binary OR can be accomplished by taking the modulos of primes on both operands and checking if either set of selected subcomponents gives a non-zero resultant vector. Binary AND can be obtained similarly except that a block is selected only if both results are non-zero vectors. To implement NOT, a block is selected if the result is the zero vector.

Theorem 5.1 *Assume that vector signatures have been created using bit vectors as described in Sect. 3 - that is, by setting on bits in subcomponents that are indexed via the reduced relevant vocabulary values modulo a set of k primes. Further assume that the set of primes has the property that $\prod_{1 \leq j \leq k} p_j \geq M_R$. Then for any Q_R (reduced query input value) generated by a vocabulary item and any block B_i,*
$$RELEVANT(Q_R, B_i) \Leftrightarrow \forall p_j, \bigwedge S_i[j, (Q_R \bmod p_j)] \neq 0.$$
That is, a block is relevant if and only if the AND of all selected subcomponent vectors results in a non-zero vector.

PROOF:
In creating the signatures, a relevant data value caused every subcomponent vector that it indexed to have the same bit position set to one. Thus, ANDing the subcomponents indexed by a relevant data value must have a one in that bit position of the resultant vector. Therefore,
$$RELEVANT(Q_R, B_i) \Rightarrow \forall p_j, \bigwedge S_i[j, (Q_R \bmod p_j)] \neq 0.$$

Now, assume $\exists Q_e$ such that $\neg RELEVANT(Q_e, B_i)$ and $\bigwedge S_i[j, (Q_e \bmod p_j)] \neq 0$. Any resultant vector bit position containing a one can have been set in each indexed subcomponent by only one value, I_s, from the set of relevant vocabulary. Therefore, $\forall p_j, I_s \equiv Q_e \bmod p_j$ and so $p_j \mid (I_s - Q_e)$. Since p_j is prime, we have the contradiction that $(\prod p_j) \mid (I_s - Q_e) \leq M_R$.
Thus, $(\forall p_j, \bigwedge S_i[j, (Q_e \bmod p_j)] \neq 0) \Rightarrow RELEVANT(Q_e, B_i)$.

Having established the effectiveness of the procedure, we now consider its efficiency. This is done by bounding the space and time complexities of the system. Theorem 5.2 derives a limit on the number of primes that will be needed. Theorem 5.3 establishes the space and time complexities (in bits and bit operations) of a block's signature and its processing. We note that, for parallel processing, each component of a signature need reside only in a storage area local to its processor(s). This alleviates problems associated with interprocessor communication and memory interference.

Theorem 5.2 $O(\ln M_R)$ *primes are sufficient to ensure that* $\left(\prod_{1 \leq j \leq k} p_j \right) \geq M_R$.

PROOF:

Let k represent the number of primes that are needed to obtain a product $\geq M_R$ and assume that k is not $O(\ln M_R)$ - that is, $\not\exists C$, such that $\forall M_R$ ($\prod_{1 \leq j \leq P_{C \ln(M_R)}} p_j) \geq M_R$.

Let P_k represent the kth prime number. It is known [9] that $\exists A$ (a constant) such that
$P_k \geq (A \, k \, \ln k)$. Thus, $\exists A$ such that $P_{C \ln(M_R)} \geq (A \, C \ln(M_R) \ln(C \ln(M_R)))$, where C is a constant to be chosen.

Let Θ_X represent $\sum_{p_i < X} \ln p_i$. It is known [9] that

$\exists$ constant B such that $\forall X$, $\Theta_X \geq B \, X$.
Since Θ_X is an increasing function, we have that
$\Theta_{P_{C \ln(M_R)}} \geq \Theta_{A \, C \ln(M_R) \ln(C \ln(M_R))} \geq B \, A \, C \, \ln(M_R) \, \ln(C \, \ln(M_R))$.
Now, if we choose $C > 1$ such that $(B \, A \, C) > 1$, we have that, for $M_R \geq 16$,
$\Theta_{P_{C \ln(M_R)}} \geq \ln(M_R)$. But since $\left(\prod_{p \leq x} p \right) = \exp^{\Theta_x}$, we have the contradiction

$\left(\prod_{1 \leq j \leq P_{C \ln(M_R)}} p_j \right) \geq M_R$.

Theorem 5.3 *The space complexity (in bits) of the signature of a block, B_i, is*
$O(N_i \ln^2(N_V \ln M))$ *and the sequential bit operation time complexity of determining relevance is* $O(N_i \ln(N_V \ln M))$.

PROOF:

For each prime, p_j, used there are p_j subcomponents. Each subcomponent has N_i bits. The total number of subcomponents for B_i is $\sum_{p_j \text{ is used}} p_j$ and the magnitude
of p_j is $O(j \ln(j))$. Since the maximum number of items that could be relevant to a block is N_V and the maximum magnitude of a relevant item item is $O(N_V \ln M)$, the number of primes used is $O(\ln(N_V \ln M))$, the total number of subcomponents
for B_i is $O\left(\sum_{j=1}^{\ln(N_V \ln M)} j * \ln(j) \right)$.

Because $\sum_{k=1}^{M} k \ln(k)$ is $O(M^2)$, we have that the total number of bits required for the
signature of B_i is $O(N_i \ln^2(N_V \ln M))$.
To determine the relevance of a query to a block, the system must choose and process $O(\ln(N_V \ln M))$ subcomponents (one from each component in the block's signature). Since each subcomponent has at most N_i bits that need to be examined, the time complexity is $O(N_i \ln(N_V \ln M))$.

Also of concern is the time complexity of creating the structures necessary for the algorithms. Generating a signature for block B_i requires $O(N_i \ln(N_V \ln M))$ operations. Since it has been shown [4] that the construction time required for determining the reducer is $O(N_V^3 \ln M)$, we have that the algorithms' overall complexity is $O(MAX[N_V^3 \ln M, N_i N_B \ln(N_V \ln M)])$, where N_B is the number of blocks in the system.

This concludes the formal analysis of the method.

6 Conclusion

We have described a new system for rapidly determining the relevance of given inputs to existing sets of data. The method uses signatures and provides some significant new benefits. Specifically, it never generates false drops even though it does not explicitly store the vocabulary, it has provably good performance bounds, and it allows complete parallelism for intra-block as well as inter-block operations. Implementing a system based on the method is not difficult.

There are a number of areas in which further research could prove beneficial. An effective and efficient compression scheme could significantly reduce the storage requirements of the system. Also, the method seems, intuitively, likely to lend itself to a hierarchichal structuring - that is, using signatures of signatures to enhance performance even further. Such a structuring would eliminate the need for examining every signature to determine the set of relevant blocks.

acir acreages acres across adapt adapted advanced advances aerial aerospace agdisp agreement agricultural agriculture aid aim aircraft airplane airplanes analysis analyzed analyzer analyzes analyzing annual annually antenna application applicators appraisal appraise appraiser appraisers areas assessing atmospheric atx-100 auger aurora automatically aviation batteries bearings bi-monthly blasques block boring borings briefs building built cameras cause causes center change changes characteristic characteristics characters charlotte chemical chemicals citrus classification cloud coatings code color commercially company compiled complete composed compositions computer concentration concentrations connected conservation consideration contract cooperation costs counties county crop crystal damage data decline denver depth depths design designed designers detect detecting determine developed developing development differences different dig dispersal document double-check downward dozen dr drift dual dusting dynamics economical education electric electromagnetic elements eliminate eliminating emissions emit employing enabling energies energy engineers entirely environmental equipment estimate examine exist expensive experience failures faster fatiguing feasible features feet field findings flight flights florida flow fluorescence focused following forest four-wheel-drive funded funds gear gears geologists government graphic graphs ground grove growers growth hardware haul height heightening helicopters help holes hour identify image images immersed important inc including incorporate incorporated increase industry information infrared innovations input instrument instruments interfaces interpretation interpreted interpreting inventories inventory investigating investigations invited involved involves irradiation irrigation jersey jointly june kennedy laboratory lake lander landers langley large layers learned licensing lindsay line liquid loads locations long losses low-friction lowe lubricants lubrication maintenance major man-made manufactured manufacturers manufacturing mapping marietta marketed mars marshall martian martin material materials matter measurements measures metal method midwest mineral minimizing models modifications monitors motion motions motor mounted multichannel nasa nasa-developed nebraska necessary network normally north nozzle nozzles objects–of occurred offers office oliver operated operates operator originated oscilloscope output paired park patterns penetrate penetrating personal photographic photographing photographs photointerpret photos pipes pivot planet plant plants plus pounds power predictions predicts princeton principle printer printout probable problem problems process processes produce produces program properties property protective protects prototype provide provides publication pulses radar radio radioisotopes readout recorder redesigned redesigning reducing reference reflected relays released report require required requires research responsible resulting revenue revolution rock rocks rotates routinely salt sample samples scientists scs seconds selecting self-contained series serve service seven several sewage since single sites siting slow software soil solve source space spacecraft spectrometer spectrum spray spraying state stemming step straight stress strike studies subsurface successful such supported surface surfaces survey surveying surveys swa-h swath system target tech technology three-ton total towers traditional transect transmits tree trees turbulent two types typical uniform university updated utah utilization valuations vehicle verified version video viking visual wake wasteful water watering waves wear wearing weighs wheel wheeled wheels whole wide width with x-ray x-rays year years zimmatic

Fig. 1. Vocabulary Words

8735 aerospace	8137 agreement	3323 analysis
945 analyzed	2317 analyzer	2137 analyzing
9447 atx-100	4467 aurora	3281 automatically
8252 batteries	11092 built	7979 causes
2253 center	1679 characteristic	11169 characteristics
8987 characters	10121 commercially	9007 complete
11653 compositions	7893 contract	11257 crystal
9908 denver	10454 detecting	9268 developed
1010 different	6804 document	8826 dozen
5545 elements	7521 emissions	1247 emit
1939 energies	11915 energy	2994 field
2592 fluorescence	9888 following	11611 geologists
11122 haul	6189 incorporated	3125 instrument
4479 instruments	173 investigating	4795 irradiation
1630 laboratory	7286 lake	4928 lander
10350 landers	506 langley	1834 licensing
8200 liquid	2890 loads	2355 manufactured
10315 marietta	12515 marketed	8087 mars
3963 marshall	2177 martian	10505 martin
7035 measures	9201 metal	7509 mineral
2459 multichannel	7114 nasa	4590 nasa-developed
5732 network	3980 north	9999 offers
781 operated	2251 operates	8553 oscilloscope
9194 photographing	8832 planet	9632 pounds
12574 power	110 principle	408 radioisotopes
1782 readout	874 redesigned	10430 research
4030 rock	4484 rocks	10231 salt
12139 sample	4679 samples	7237 seconds
387 self-contained	9255 several	9547 soil
12807 spacecraft	4613 spectrometer	10227 spectrum
5999 subsurface	11425 surface	9813 surfaces
10851 system	10594 tech	11610 technology
4728 two	11265 updated	5511 utah
9138 version	9124 viking	11757 weighs
6233 with	12342 x-ray	6044 x-rays
3673 years		

Fig. 2. 106 vocabulary words relevant to block.

8735-	2 0 6 1 12	8137-	1 2 3 8 12	3323-	2 3 5 1 8
945-	0 0 0 10 9	2317-	1 2 0 7 3	2137-	1 2 2 3 5
9447-	0 2 4 9 9	4467-	0 2 1 1 8	3281-	2 1 5 3 5
8252-	2 2 6 2 10	11092-	1 2 4 4 3	7979-	2 4 6 4 10
2235-	0 0 2 2 12	1679-	2 4 6 7 2	11169-	0 4 4 4 2
8987-	2 2 6 0 4	10121-	2 1 6 1 7	9007-	1 2 5 9 11
11653-	1 3 5 4 5	7893-	0 3 4 6 2	11257-	1 2 1 4 12
9808-	1 3 1 7 6	10454-	2 4 3 4 2	9268-	1 3 0 6 12
1010-	2 0 2 9 9	6804-	0 4 0 6 5	8826-	0 1 6 4 12
5545-	1 0 1 1 7	7521-	0 1 3 8 7	1247-	2 2 1 4 12
1939-	1 4 0 3 2	11915-	2 0 1 2 7	2994-	0 4 5 2 4
2592-	0 2 2 7 5	9888-	0 3 4 10 8	11611-	1 1 5 6 2
11122-	1 2 6 1 7	6189-	0 1 4 7 1	3125-	2 0 3 1 5
4479-	0 4 6 2 7	173-	2 3 5 8 4	4795-	1 0 0 10 11
1630-	1 0 6 2 5	7286-	2 1 6 4 6	4928-	2 3 0 0 1
10350-	0 0 4 10 2	506-	2 1 2 0 12	1834-	1 4 0 8 1
8200-	1 0 3 5 10	2890-	1 6 4 8 4	2355-	0 0 3 1 2
10315-	1 0 4 8 6	12515-	2 0 6 8 9	8087-	2 2 2 2 1
3963-	0 3 1 3 11	2177-	2 2 0 10 6	10505-	2 0 5 0 1
7035-	0 0 0 6 2	9201-	0 1 3 5 10	7509-	0 4 5 7 8
2459-	2 4 2 6 2	7114-	1 4 2 8 3	4590-	0 0 5 3 1
5732-	2 2 6 1 12	3980-	2 0 4 9 2	9999-	0 4 3 0 2
781-	1 1 4 0 1	2251-	1 1 4 7 2	8553-	0 3 6 6 12
9194-	2 4 3 9 3	8832-	0 2 5 10 5	9632-	2 2 0 7 12
12574-	1 4 2 1 3	110-	2 0 5 0 6	408-	0 3 2 1 5
1782-	0 2 4 0 1	874-	1 4 6 5 3	10430-	2 0 0 2 4
4030-	1 0 5 4 0	4484-	2 4 4 7 12	10231-	1 1 4 1 0
12139-	1 4 1 6 10	4679-	2 4 3 4 12	7237-	1 2 6 10 9
387-	0 2 2 2 10	9255-	0 0 1 4 12	9547-	1 2 6 10 5
12807-	0 2 4 3 2	4613-	2 3 0 4 11	10227-	0 2 0 8 9
5999-	2 4 0 4 6	11425-	1 0 1 7 11	9813-	0 3 6 1 11
10851-	0 1 1 5 9	10594-	1 4 3 1 12	11610-	0 0 4 5 1
4728-	0 3 3 9 9	11265-	0 0 2 1 7	5511-	0 1 2 0 12
9138-	0 3 3 8 12	9124-	1 4 3 5 11	11757-	0 2 4 9 5
6233-	2 3 3 7 6	12342-	0 2 1 0 5	6044-	2 4 3 5 12
3673-	1 3 5 10 7				

Fig. 3. Reduced values and subcomponent indices for block's signature.

5191 3837 6735 61 9089 11521 11883 471 1527 8735 4135 8137 4589 5979 3041 8795 4885 11681
11457 3323 945 2317 2415 2137 8831 241 4491 5639 9979 617 11749 11863 8955 12231 9307 10191
9447 8823 4467 3281 4757 8252 10016 1888 8300 12772 8622 1162 5066 2860 11092 3079 1395
7979 2253 287 5709 1679 11169 8987 2695 1491 1267 673 5037 1987 6069 10319 12309 10121
2505 10495 9007 8007 11653 3411 7277 10471 10455 5295 2499 7893 11777 11211 8563 5657 7589
11257 10988 10606 10364 9908 8568 2270 3938 6066 7214 7134 10454 7876 9268 7260 6954 5444
1010 668 9156 6804 3802 9448 8826 1810 630 8048 7076 5860 8139 3227 6699 7135 5545 10509
195 7521 1247 7623 2811 1939 11915 2149 11405 7047 329 7413 3179 6063 12087 4199 1302 6372
5722 990 4414 11980 2994 2480 4628 10050 5364 1408 2592 6528 9888 6852 3208 3656 10532
3201 3655 11611 5967 10317 509 4043 485 5003 7469 3506 11122 3734 1036 3578 8306 148 10112
8781 2911 9495 11767 5045 187 3617 10627 6189 5635 4911 1447 7155 9079 11191 3125 4479
3933 9275 5549 7105 2447 11233 173 5167 1593 4091 5561 4795 7065 1472 3326 7468 1229 1630
7286 4928 10350 506 9384 11484 4392 1834 5138 5934 8200 2890 8400 1474 2776 6668 12456
2078 5988 7923 3523 841 2355 6215 8293 4475 10315 12515 8087 3963 2177 10505 3295 3071
9881 1159 7035 9201 2689 1509 7509 8647 2105 3431 8167 11449 3989 1689 10917 2459 7114
4590 4032 4572 5732 9538 3980 7548 88 2843 6067 9999 3499 6187 781 2251 5985 3159 8553
12323 11410 3238 11778 6872 9440 9324 1572 9194 2482 12222 1544 514 8608 8832 2474 9058
7122 9632 12574 12162 3360 10 110 8138 7562 3236 4354 2742 10638 7430 12560 10948 12474
2090 2058 3194 8078 10292 4948 3336 8794 4798 6230 10062 408 1782 6674 874 1490 10980
10882 12166 5076 1470 10746 3848 766 2236 10430 6946 6848 2212 12740 4030 4484 8504 10586
10231 12139 4679 7265 3293 7237 8217 387 11259 9339 8919 6435 9255 7889 6863 1545 1643
1993 1421 11635 9547 2489 7895 879 12807 4613 10227 8031 5239 8481 2069 11487 10149 2631
11393 1065 5999 7515 12641 12233 11425 9813 8569 11889 1109 2249 9885 10851 7968 10594
11610 508 10488 6280 6394 11170 5862 1340 1794 5474 4728 2566 1012 10997 3865 11265 5511
3585 11556 11064 3636 9138 8664 9124 12840 7297 743 283 10373 7627 3217 11649 11757 11019
569 4721 12479 9571 5721 6233 12342 6044 3219 3673 11500

Fig. 4. Vocabulary reduced values.

References

1. S. R. Ahuja and C. S. Roberts, "An Associative/Parallel Processor for Partial Match Retrieval Using Superimposed Codes," in *Annual Symposium on Computer Architecture*, 1980, pp. 218-227.
2. J. Bentley, "A Spelling Checker," *Communications of the ACM,"* vol. 28, no. 5, pp. 456-462, 1985.
3. C. Faloutsos, "Access Methods for Text," *Computing Surveys*, vol. 17, no. 1, pp. 49-74, 1985.
4. M. Fredman, J. Komlos and E. Szemeredi, "Storing a Sparse Table with O(1) Worst Case Access Time," *Journal of the ACM*, vol. 31, no. 3, pp. 538-544, 1984.
5. L. L. Gremillion, "Designing a Bloom Filter for Differential Access," *Communications of the ACM*, vol. 25, no. 7, pp. 600-604, 1980.
6. D. E. Knuth, 1973. *The Art of Computer Programming, vol. 3: Sorting and Searching*. Reading, Mass.: Addison-Wesley, 1973.
7. J. W. Lloyd, "Optimal Partial Match Retrieval," *BIT*, vol. 20, pp. 406-413, 1980.
8. P. E. McKenney, "High Speed Event Counting and Classification Using a Dictionary Hash Technique," in *Proceedings of the International Conference on Parallel Processing*, pp. 218-227, 1989.
9. H. N. Shapiro, *Introduction to the Theory of Numbers*. New York: John Wiley and Sons, 1983.
10. D. Tsichritzis D. and S. Christodoulakis, "Message Files," *ACM Trans. Office Inf. Systems*, vol. 1, no. 1, pp. 88-98, 1983.

This article was processed using the LaTeX macro package with LMAMULT style

Dynamic and Load-balanced Task-Oriented Database Query Processing in Parallel Systems

Hongjun Lu   *Kian-Lee Tan*

Department of Information Systems and Computer Science
National University of Singapore

ABSTRACT

Most parallel database query processing methods proposed so far adopt the task-oriented approach: decomposing a query into tasks, allocating tasks to processors, and executing the tasks in parallel. However, this strategy may not be effective when some processors are overloaded with time-consuming tasks caused by some unpredictable factors such as data skew. In this paper, we propose a dynamic and load-balanced task-oriented database query processing approach that minimizes the completion time of user queries. It consists of three phases: task generation, task acquisition and execution and task stealing. Using this approach, a database query is decomposed into a set of tasks. At run-time, these tasks are allocated dynamically to available processors. When a processor completes its assigned tasks and no more new tasks are available, it steals subtasks from other overloaded processors to share their load. A performance study was conducted to demonstrate the feasibility and effectiveness of this approach using join query as an example. The techniques that can be used to select task donors from overloaded processors and to determine the amount of work to be transferred are discussed. The factors that may affect the effectiveness, such as the number of tasks to be decomposed to, is also investigated.

1. Introduction

Today's DBMS will have to deal with complex queries that take a long time to complete. The conventional von-Neumann architecture will soon reach its speed limit, and parallelism represents the most feasible alternative to achieve any significant breakthrough in performance. With the advances in hardware technology and computer architecture, a large number of parallel computers are already being employed to solve database applications [DeWi90, Engl89, Ozka86, Su88, Tera88].

To explore parallelism and to fully utilize the system resources, most proposed parallel database query processing methods use a *task-oriented* approach. In general, the approach consists of three phases: *task generation, task allocation* and *task execution*. In the task generation phase, a query is decomposed into a set of tasks that are allocated to all available processors in the second phase, the task allocation phase. Tasks are assigned to processors according to some criteria such as the tuple sizes of data associated to tasks [Hua91, Kits90] or the estimated execution time of tasks [Wolf90, Wolf91]. Finally, in the third phase, *task execution phase*, all the processors concurrently execute the tasks allocated to them according to some predetermined order. This task-oriented approach is most effective when the load of tasks to be executed concurrently at each processor is approximately the same. In this case, the completion time of the query is near-optimal if not optimal. However, in real situation, the processing load across the processors will not be the same for the following reasons:

1. Some tasks are more time-consuming or expensive, for example join in relational database systems is often recognized as the most costly operation.

2. The criteria on which the tasks are assigned to processors fail to allocate the tasks evenly across the system.

3. Even when all tasks seem evenly distributed across the processors, some unpredictable factors such as the skew in the data may cause a load-imbalance across the processors during execution [Laks90, Walt91].

In such cases, the minimum completion time for the query depends on the task(s) that finishes last. Moreover, under-loaded processors will soon become idle. All these indicate the need to develop new algorithms to evenly distribute the processing load across the processors.

The problem has been addressed by researchers from different directions — intra-operation [Hua91, Kits90, Omie91, Wolf90, Wolf91] and inter-operation [Deen90, Lu91, Murp91]. Wolf, Dias and Yu propose a parallel sort-merge join algorithm [Wolf90] and a parallel hash-based join algorithm [Wolf91] to handle data skew. Both algorithms introduce a *scheduling phase* that employs two optimization algorithms iteratively to minimize the overall completion time of the join based on the estimated execution time of the tasks. Instead, in [Hua91, Kits90] the skew problem is alleviated by allocating the tasks to the processors such that the bucket sizes are balanced. Omiecinski's approach to handle skew, in a shared-everything environment, is to allocate more processors for large buckets [Omie91]. In [Deen90], the processors are distributed evenly across the number of joins. Lu, Shan and Tan allocate more processors to more expensive joins such that the completion time for the joins is minimized [Lu91]. In [Murp91], the *execution plan balancing* strategy prioritizes the operations and allocates resources (memory and processors) to the most critical operation first.

In this paper, we propose a dynamic task-oriented query processing method with load-balancing capabilities. The proposed approach is robust to data skew and is able to achieve a minimum completion time for a query. It is different from the conventional method in the following ways. First, our approach is a *dynamic* approach and task allocation is *demand-driven*. For most of the previous work, the allocation of tasks to processors is *static*, that is, all the tasks are allocated to the processors before the execution of any tasks. Thus each processor knows exactly which (and how many) tasks are allocated to it. In our approach, a processor *acquires* a task to be processed at run-time. Each processor has, at any time, at most one task to process and it does not know which is the next task to process until the current task finishes. Once the current task is completed, the processor will acquire another task until there is no more tasks. Second, a *task transfer* strategy is employed to handle load-imbalances across the processors when there is no more tasks in the system. Most of the existing work does not transfer any task or sub-tasks once it is allocated to a processor. Once a task is allocated to a processor, it will only be executed by the processor. In our approach, an idle processor can *steal* some load — pages of data that have not been processed — from an overloaded processor.

In the next section, we discuss the general dynamic and load-balanced task-oriented query processing approach. Section 3 describes the detailed implementation of the approach when apply to single join queries. A performance study and its results are also presented. We summarize this research and briefly discuss some future work in section 4.

2. The General Approach

In this paper, we assume the system to be a multiprocessor system with *shared disks (SD)*. In SD systems, each processor has its own private memory but each processor can directly access any disk. The processors cooperate by message passing through an interconnection network connecting processors. Each relation is horizontally partitioned across the disks in the system. However, we assume that the system has a certain amount of global memory and the global memory is used to keep up-to-date information of the tasks. We also assume a locking mechanism is used to regulate access to the global memory.

The proposed approach, a *dynamic and load-balanced task-oriented query processing method* provides a solution to the problem of minimizing the completion time of a query by using the system resources to the fullest. The approach comprises three phases — *task generation, dynamic task acquisition and execution* and *task stealing (load-balancing)*.

2.1. Task generation

The first phase of our approach is the task generation phase where a query is decomposed into a set of tasks as in conventional methods. In the database query processing environment, task decomposition can be *operation oriented*, that is, a *task* represents a single operation on the associated data. However, task decomposition can also be *data oriented*. That is, data to be operated on by certain operations can be partitioned into subsets and a task becomes the application of the same operation(s) on a subset of the data. By applying these two decomposition techniques alternatively and recursively, a database query can be decomposed into a set of tasks that can be ordered and allocated to processors in the task allocation phase.

First issue in task generation is that the decomposition should guarantee the correctness of the operation. That is, the results from subtasks should be easily assembled into the same final result as that from the operation without decomposition. This is especially important to data oriented decomposition. With different operations, the way in which the data is partitioned to form tasks will be different to guarantee the correctness. For example, for the hash-based joins, both participating relations, say R and S, can be partitioned into corresponding buckets. A task will then be the join operation on a set of two buckets from two relations. However, if a nested-loops join method is used, a task could be a join on whole relation R and any subset of S.

Second issue in task generation is the optimal number of tasks to be generated. The number of tasks to be generated is limited by the decomposibility of the tasks. It is also limited by the amount of memory at each processor. The optimal number of tasks to be generated is closely associated with the size of the data that an operation works on. A large number of tasks may be generated such that an operation is applied on only few tuples of data. This may result in poor performance because of the overhead incurred in splitting the data and duplicating the operation. Fragmentation may also cause additional I/Os. On the other hand, a small number of tasks will limit the flexibility of allocating tasks to the processors and result in uneven load among the processors.

Our task generation, or query decomposition follows the same strategy as that in conventional methods. However, the portions of data across the disks that correspond to a task are *not transferred* until the task is to be executed during the execution phase. Instead, these data form a logical system pool of tasks with the following information for each task stored in the global memory: 1) what is the operation, 2) the number of tasks associated with the operation, and 3) the addresses of the data that is associated with this task. The global memory also stores the information of the processing at each processor. Such information includes 1) the size of data left (in pages) and 2) the size of the resultant relations generated so far.

2.2. Dynamic task acquisition and execution

In the second phase, processors acquire tasks from the system task pool and execute them if the acquisition is successful. Initially, the size of the task left is the number of pages of data associated with the task and the size of the result generated is zero. Whenever a page of data is processed, the global information is updated accordingly. Whenever a processor finishes the processing of the acquired task, it checks whether there are more tasks in the system. If there are tasks available in the system, the processor will be assigned the next task for execution. This process of *dynamic acquisition and execution* of tasks is repeated until all the tasks have been allocated.

2.3. Task stealing

In the third phase, a load-balancing strategy is employed when there is no more tasks to be assigned. When all the tasks have been assigned, idle processors may help to bear the burden of overloaded processors to minimize the completion time. This may require the *stealing* of some load from overloaded processors. Based on the global information, the idle processor determines the *donor* (the overloaded processor) and the amount of load to be transferred. This process of stealing is repeated until some criterion, which indicates that the minimum completion time has been achieved, is satisfied. In this case, no further transfer is necessary and each processor may finish up its processing for the entire query to complete. In this way, the load is balanced across all the processors and the completion time is minimized.

3. DLPJ: A Dynamic and Load-balanced Parallel Join Processing Algorithm

In this section, we present a detailed implementation of the above dynamic and load-balanced query processing method for join queries. The join algorithm obtained is *dynamic* as there is no prior allocation of tasks to any processor before execution begins. Tasks are assigned at run-time. As such, some processors in the system may perform more "light" tasks while others may perform few tasks with "heavy" load. The task generation is *hash-based* as in conventional hash-based join methods. We will describe the three phases of the join algorithm that corresponds to the three phases of the proposed approach followed by a discussion of the experiments conducted and their results.

3.1. Phase 1: Task Generation — Partitioning Phase

The task generation phase of the join algorithm is essentially a partitioning phase since the number of buckets determines (equals) the number of tasks. As in all previous parallel hash-based algorithms, this phase scans the relations R and S and creates partitions for the joining phase. Each processor i ($1 \leq i \leq p$) allocates one output buffer for each of the B partitions where B is the number of partitions desired (the number of partitions is limited by the amount of memory that is available). Each processor reads a subset R_i of relation R and hashes the tuples to the corresponding output buffers based on the hash results. When the buffer is full, it is written out to the disk. The same hash function is used to create partitions for relation S. We call the portions of R_i (S_i) that hash into the jth output buffer the sub-buckets of R_i (S_i) and denote them as R_{ij} (S_{ij}), where $1 \leq j \leq B$.

During the partitioning of data, each sub-bucket on each disk has associated with it a *directory*. The directory for a sub-bucket stores the *disk identifier* and *page identifier* for pages belonging to a partition. With this directory, a processor assigned a partition will have direct access to the pages. Moreover, such a structure facilitates the balancing of load in the joining phase, which we will describe in Section 3.3. It should be noted that the sizes of the directories are not large. Assuming the disk identifier requires 1 byte and the page identifier requires 2 bytes, a 4 Kbytes page can house the addresses for more than 1300 pages of data.

For hash-based join algorithms, the number of partitions may have an impact on the performance of the algorithm [Naka88, Kits89]. When the number of buckets is small, more tuples will be hashed to a bucket and the probability of the size of a bucket exceeding the main memory size increases. Such overflow buckets will degrade the performance of the algorithm. On the other hand, too many buckets may also lead to poor performance as the number of fragmented pages increases resulting in more I/Os. A compromise is to generate a large number of buckets first. The small buckets are then merged into larger ones that can still be staged in memory [Kits83]. The maximum number of partitions is constrained by the memory size since each page corresponds to a partition. We do not consider the case when a partition is recursively split to generate more partitions since this will incur additional I/Os. Once the partitioning is performed, each processor will store the information of the sub-buckets in the global memory. Such information includes 1) the task number, 2) the size of the sub-buckets of the source and target relations and 3) the addresses to the directories of the sub-buckets. A processor (with smallest index) will then build a single *task table* containing the task number with its associated information for a partition of R and S. This task table is used in subsequent phases. Figure 3.1 illustrates this process. The size of each partition is the sum of the corresponding sub-buckets. The addresses of the directories are stored as it is.

3.2. Phase 2: Task Acquisition and Execution — Joining Phase

This phase is the joining phase of the algorithm. During the joining phase, a free processor reads the global information and acquires a task to process. Once a task is available, the directories associated with the sub-buckets of R and S that correspond to this task are collected at the processor. The directories from all disk are then linked as shown in Figure 3.2(a). In this way, each processor has the addresses to all pages that correspond to the task. The task is then executed, that is the join is performed, as in a uniprocessor environment. Any uniprocessor join algorithm may be employed. In our study, we use the *hash-based nested-loops join* (HNL) algorithm for simplicity. The result can be easily generalized. This algorithm is shown to be superior over the other algorithms when we handle medium-sized source relations, that is the size of the source relation is no more than 5 times the size of the memory [Naka88]. The algorithm comprises two phases: 1) Several pages of the source relation, which is determined by the available memory, is read and the hash table is built; 2) The whole of target relation is read a page at a time and each tuple is probed for joinability with the partially staged hash table. These two phases are repeated until all the pages of the source relation are read. We denote the time for the entire join to be $T_{HNL}(|R|, |S|, |Res|)$ where

Information on disk 1				
j	$|R_{1j}|$	$|S_{1j}|$	$AddrR_{1j}$	$AddrS_{1j}$
1	100	100	(1, 2)	(1, 7)
...	...	...	...	...
.	.	.	.	.
.	.	.	.	.
B	...	...	...	...

Information on disk n				
j	$|R_{nj}|$	$|R_{nj}|$	$AddrR_{nj}$	$AddrS_{nj}$
1	100	100	(n, 5)	(n, 9)
...	...	...	...	...
.	.	.	.	.
.	.	.	.	.
B	...	...	...	...

(a) Initial set of tables.

Task# j	$|R_j|$	$|S_j|$	$AddrR_{1j}$	.....	$AddrR_{nj}$	$AddrS_{1j}$	.....	$AddrS_{nj}$
1	1000	1000	(1, 2)	.....	(n,5)	(1, 7)	.....	(n,9)
...	...	...	...	...	...	...	...	...
.	.	.	.	..	.	.	.	
.	.	.	.	..	.	.	.	
B	...	...	...	...	...	...	...	...

(b) Task table.

Figure 3.1. Build information in global memory

$|R|$, $|S|$ and $|Res|$ represent the size (in pages) of the source, target and result relations respectively. We also denote the time to perform phase 2 when r pages are of R are staged in memory and s pages of S are used to probe for a match to generate result res as $T_{join}(r, s, |res|)$.

As each page is read, the processor will update the global information — number of pages of each relation left and the number of pages of the result relation generated thus far. Whenever a processor finishes the processing of the allocated task, it acquires a new task. This process of *acquisition and execution* of tasks is repeated until all the B tasks have been allocated. When there is no more tasks, the processor will enter into the *task stealing (load-balancing) phase*.

3.3. Phase 3: Task Stealing — Load-balancing Phase

Once all the tasks have been acquired, that is there is no more tasks from the system task pool for the idle processor to process, the processor will try to *steal* some load from a processor that has not completed the execution of its acquired task. The load at a processor is the amount of unfinished work to be performed and is measured as the estimated time needed to finish up the task. We will discuss how to determine the appropriate candidate processor(s) that is overloaded and the amount of load to steal in the subsequent sub-sections. The stealing process is realized by transferring bucket directories among two processors. Let p_a be the candidate over loaded processor and p_a is the idle one. After the amount of work to steal has been determined, the work load of p_a, represented by a chain of directories are divided into two portions. That is, each directory in the chain is split into two. The upper portion remains in

Directories that are associated with a
bucket are linked

Load at overloaded
processor

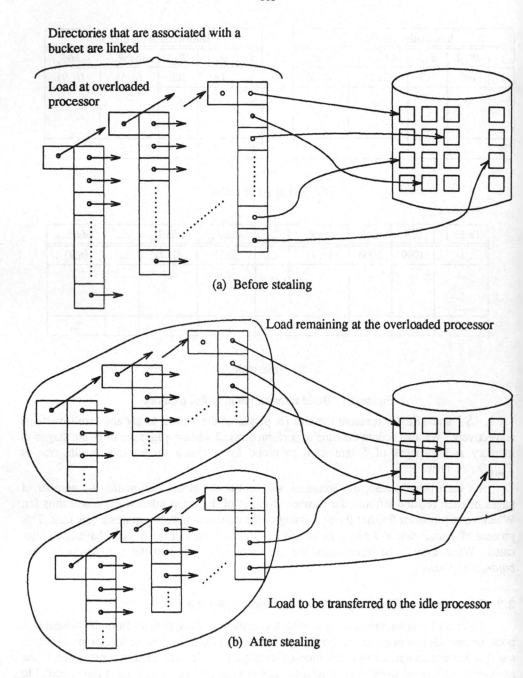

(a) Before stealing

Load remaining at the overloaded processor

Load to be transferred to the idle processor

(b) After stealing

Figure 3.2. Stealing of load.

p_a, that is to be processed by p_a. The lower portion is chained up and sent to p_b. Thus the load is shared between p_a and p_b without physical movement of data — only the directories are shipped. Figure 3.2 illustrates the process. This process of *stealing* is repeated until the criterion, which indicates that the minimum completion time has been achieved, is satisfied. In this case, one just need to wait for all the processors to finish up its processing for the entire join operation to complete.

3.3.1. Determination of donor

Any processor that is executing its acquired task when an idle processor tries to steal some load from other processors can be a donor. Naturally, we hope that the donor is the most heavily loaded processor since it will be the last processor to finish up the entire processing. However, it is impossible to provide an exact measure of the load of a processor. We propose to use the *estimated finish time (EFT)* as the measure of the load of a processor. When task stealing happens, the EFTs of those processors with tasks are computed and the processor with the maximum EFT will be chosen as the donor, that is, processor i is the donor (ties are arbitrary broken) when

$$EFT_i = \max_{j=1}^{p}(EFT_j)$$

Note that the estimated finish time is both data and operation dependent since a task is defined as an operation on certain amount of data. In our example, where each task is a hash-based nested loops join on two buckets T_1 and T_2, the finish time will depend on the relative size of the outer bucket, say T_1, on which a hash table is built.

1. If $|T_1| \times F \leq |M|$ (we assume a hash table for R occupies $|R| \times F$ pages), the hash table for T_1 is staged in memory, and the joining process is to scan T_2 once and probe for a match for each tuple of T_2 scanned. The load of the processor at any time after building the hash table is determined by the unprocessed pages of T_2.

2. If T_1 is too large for the available memory, that is $|T_1| \times F > |M|$, T_2 needs to be scanned several times, each with a portion of T_1 that can be staged in memory. The load therefore is dependent on both the unprocessed pages of T_1 and T_2.

With this in mind, we can proceed to estimate the EFT for a processor.

Case 1: $|T_1| \times F \leq |M|$.

The time to perform the join of T_1 and T_2 with result *Result* is estimated by

$$T_{HNL}(|T_1|, |T_2|, |Result|) = T_{HNL}(|T_1|, n_2, |Res|) + EFT$$

where n_2 denotes the number of pages of T_2 that have been processed, inclusive of the page that is processed at the time of the task request and $|Res|$ is the size of the resultant relation generated so far, using n_2 pages of T_2, inclusive of the page that is being generated. The size of *Result* may be estimated by [1]

$$\frac{|Result|}{|Res|} = \frac{|T_2|}{n_2}$$

Therefore,

---

[1] In the case when $|Res| = 0$, that is when no tuple has been generated yet, *Result* can be estimated using the number of distinct join attribute values in T_1 and T_2 respectively.

$$EFT = T_{HNL}(|T_1|, |T_2|, |Result|) - T_{HNL}(|T_1|, n_2, |Res|) \qquad (1)$$

Case 2: $|T_1| \times F > |M|$.

The number of loops required to scan T_2 is Loop $= |T_1| \times F/|M|$. Let n_1 denotes the number of pages of T_1 processed. If $n_1 = |T_1|$, then all the pages of T_1 have already been read and the current loop is the last loop. In this case, EFT is derived in the same way as the case when $|T_1| \times F \le |M|$ using Equation (1) (It should be noted the value of $|T_1|$ in Equation (1) should be replaced by $|T_1| - (Loop - 1) \times |M|/F$). Otherwise, the following computation is done. Let n_2 denotes the number of pages of T_2 processed in the current loop. Then the number of loops processed, inclusive of the loop that is currently being processed, is LoopProcessed $= n_1/T_1 \times$ Loop. The estimated time to perform the join is

$$T_{HNL}(|T_1|, |T_2|, |Result|) = T_{HNL}((LoopProcessed - 1) \times \frac{|M|}{F}, |T_2|, |Res\,1|) +$$

$$T_{HNL}(\frac{|M|}{F}, n_2, |Res\,2|) + EFT$$

where $|Res1|$ and $|Res2|$ are estimated using the following two expressions:

$$\frac{|Res\,1|/(LoopProcessed - 1)}{|Res\,2|} = \frac{|T_2|}{n_2} \quad \text{and} \quad |Res\,1| + |Res\,2| = |Res|$$

where $|Res|$ is the size of results generated thus far. Therefore,

$$EFT = T_{HNL}(|T_1|, |T_2|, |Result|) -$$

$$T_{HNL}((LoopProcessed - 1) \times \frac{|M|}{F}, |T_2|, |Res\,1|) -$$

$$T_{HNL}(\frac{|M|}{F}, n_2, |Res\,2|)$$

3.3.2. Determination of the amount of data to be transferred

The amount of data to be transferred is determined in such a way that two processors sharing the load are expected to complete their tasks at the same time.

Case 1: $|T_1| \times F \le |M|$.

If $|T_1| \times F \le |M|$, then the idle processor needs the entire relation T_1 and portion of the unprocessed T_2. Let k be the number of pages of T_2 to be stolen. k should satisfy the following expression: [2]

$$EFT - T_{join}(|T_1|, k, Res_k) \ge \begin{cases} T_{HNL}(|T_1|, k, Res_k) & \text{if } k \ge |T_1| \\ T_{HNL}(k, |T_1|, Res_k) & \text{otherwise} \end{cases}$$

where Res_k, the result size of the k pages, is estimated as follows:

$$\frac{|Res_k|}{|Res|} = \frac{k}{n_2}$$

---

[2] We have ignored the transmission of directories since their sizes are expected to be small (in number of pages).

We can determine the optimal number of pages to be transferred by solving the following equation:

$$EFT - T_{join}(|T_1|, k, Res_k) = \begin{cases} T_{HNL}(|T_1|, k, Res_k) & \text{if } k \geq |T_1| \\ T_{HNL}(k, |T_1|, Res_k) & \text{otherwise} \end{cases}$$

Case 2: $|T_1| \times F > |M|$.

On the other hand, if $|T_1| \times F > |M|$, then we should transfer portion of the unprocessed T_1 and the entire T_2. We would like to transfer enough pages of T_1 such that a hash table can be built in memory for these pages. If all pages of T_1 have already been read, the number of pages to be transferred is determined in the same way as case (1) using the number of pages processed in the last loop instead of T_1. Otherwise, the k pages of T_1 to be transferred should satisfy the following expression:

$$T_{HNL}(k, |T_2|, Res_k) \leq EFT - T_{HNL}(k, |T_2|, Res_k)$$

where $|Res_k|$ may be estimated using

$$\frac{|Res_k|}{|Res\,1|/(LoopProcessed - 1)} = \frac{k}{|M|/F}$$

where $|Res|$ is the size of results generated thus far. We can determine the number of pages to be transmitted that will optimize the load-balancing, that is

$$T_{HNL}(k, |T_2|, Res_k) = \frac{EFT}{2}$$

However, if k pages turn out to be too large to be staged in memory, we will only transmit sufficient amount that can be staged in memory. This, we believe, will minimize thrashing, that is too much load may be transferred to an idle processor which forces it to become over-loaded leading to its load being stolen.

3.4. Performance Study of DLPJ

We conducted a simulation study for join algorithm DLPJ described above. We vary the skewness of the join attribute (which follows the Zipf-distribution) and the number of processors involved. We also study different memory sizes, different relation sizes and obtained similar results reported here.

To evaluate the performance of the proposed algorithm, we assume that the values of the join column follow a *Zipf-like distribution* [Knut73]. For a relation R with a domain of D distinct values, the ith distinct join column value, for $1 \leq i \leq D$, has such number of tuples as given by the following expression:

$$\|D_i\| = \frac{\|R\|}{i^\theta \cdot \sum_{j=1}^{D} \frac{1}{j^\theta}} \tag{2}$$

where θ is the skew factor. When $\theta = 0$, the distribution becomes *uniform*. With $\theta = 1$, it corresponds to the highly skewed *pure* Zipf distribution [Zipf49]. Though the join column is skewed, we assume that the relations to be joined are, initially, evenly distributed among the processors to facilitate full concurrent access to the relation.

We also study the effect of different correlations between the skew values in the two relations. Two types of correlation are modeled: *Ordered correlation* and *random correlation*. For ordered correlation, the values in both the attributes have the same ranking sequences. For example, the highest ranked value in attribute R_A of relation R is also the highest ranked value in the corresponding attribute S_A in relation S. On the other hand, random correlation randomly correlates the attribute in R and S.

We compare the performance of DLPJ with 3 other algorithms. The first, *join algorithm 1* (JA1) is similar to DeWitt's approach where the number of partitions generated is the same as the number of processors available [DeWi85]. Using this approach, given p processors, the relations are partitioned into p partitions generating p tasks. Each task is allocated to a processor and the p tasks are simultaneously executed. The second algorithm, *join algorithm 2* (JA2) is similar to Kitsuregawa's method where a large number of tasks will be generated first. These partitions are then merged into p partitions so that each partition of the source relation will have approximately equal size [Kits83]. The last algorithm, *no load balancing* (NLB) is essentially equal to the DLPJ but no load-balancing is performed.

As in [Wolf90, Wolf91], we substitute the *actual* distribution of data into the cost formulas for the join algorithm HNL to compute the elapsed time. That is, the actual number of pages (and tuples) of the source, target and result relations of each partition are used in the computation. The distribution of data for the source and target relations is generated using Equation (2). A hashing function is then used to partition the relations into B partitions. Two hashing functions are used — *range-based* where partition i contains tuple in the range

$$\left[1 + (i - 1) \times \frac{D}{B} \ , \ i \times \frac{D}{B} \right],$$ for $1 \le i \le B$, and *modulo-based* where tuple with value tu

belongs to partition $[tu \ \text{MOD} \ B + 1]$. Both hashing functions show similar results. To compute the result size, we introduce a selectivity factor of the join operation, Sel. Sel gives the number of distinct tuples in the source relation that has a matching value in the target relation. For example, $Sel = 0.5$ means that for each tuple in the source relation, there is a probability of 0.5 that it will find a match in the target relation. Sel is modeled using a uniform distribution UD(0,1). When the ordered correlation is used, for each distinct value of the source relation examined, if the value of UD(0,1) is in the range $0 - Sel$, the corresponding distinct value in the target relation is a match and the join result size equal to the product of the number of tuples with this value in the source and target relations. Otherwise, the result size is 0. For random correlation, for each distinct value of the source relation examined, a random tuple is picked from the target relation and the result size is computed in the same manner as that of ordered correlation.

For purpose of illustrating the performance study here, the following test values are used: The system has 16 disks. The number of processors is varied from 2 — 32 and each processor has 512K of memory. The CPU processing rate is 10 MIPS and the I/O bandwidth 10 Mbytes/s. It takes 50 instructions to compare two keys/attributes. The computation of hash function of a key costs 100 instructions. The time to move a tuple in memory is 500 instructions. We also vary the number of tuples in relation R (S) from 100K — 1M. Each page of relation R(S) and the resultant relation contains 50 tuples. The number of distinct tuples in relations R and S is 10K. Three skew factors, 0.1, 0.5 and 1.0, are used to represent low, medium and high skew respectively. The selectivity factor (Sel) is 0.5.

3.4.1. Experiment 1: Vary the number of processors

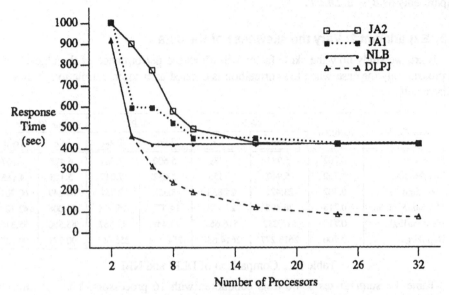

Graph 3.1. Response time as the number of processors varies.

In this experiment, we study the performance of the algorithms as the number of processors varies. We present here only the results when both relations are highly skewed. With the other parameter settings, similar behaviors are obtained. Graph 3.1 shows the result of the experiment. While the response time for all the algorithms decreases as the number of processors increases, the 3 algorithms, *JA* 1, *JA* 2 and *NLB* , perform poorly as compared to the DLPJ algorithm. This is so because of data skew which results in some tasks dominating in the join outputs. As the number of processors increases, the response time becomes dominated by a few partitions. Since there is no load-balancing in all these 3 algorithms, the most time-consuming task will determine the completion time of the algorithms. The NLB algorithm performs slightly better than the other 2 approaches since it generates a larger number of tasks (partitions). This implies that lesser number of tuples per partition and this may avoid some overflow partitions that the other 2 approaches may generate.

It is obvious that DLPJ outperforms other algorithms as it is able to balance the load across the processors. Idle processors for the JA1, JA2 and NLB algorithms remain idle once every task is allocated and the processor finishes the tasks that are allocated to it. On the other hand, for DLPJ, idle processors steal some load from some overloaded processors. However, DLPJ may not be able to achieve 100% speedup. In particular, the gain in performance is significant with each additional processor when the number of processors is small (between 2 to 10). Once the number of processors reaches a certain value, the gain is not significant (from 16 processors onwards). This is so for the following reasons. First, less than half the load from the candidate processor is transferred each time. Second, especially for high data skew, when a single processor is active (no transfer is possible because the page is currently being executed or because the estimation criterion is inaccurate), the currently executing page and any remaining pages may be the most time-consuming pages that generate a huge number of output.

Since *JA*1 and *JA*2 perform poorly, we will not present their results subsequently but will compare only *NLB* with *DLPJ*.

3.4.2. Experiment 2: Vary the skewness of the data

Next, we study how the skew factor will affect the performance of the algorithms. We will present only the case when the correlation is ordered as random correlation of data shows similar results.

Skew/Skew	Partition	NLB		DLPJ		Gain (%) w.r.t.	
		Join	Total	Join	Total	Join	Total
Low/Low	0.702	5.985	7.389	5.600	7.004	6.428	5.207
Low/Medium	0.702	5.940	7.355	5.632	7.047	5.183	4.185
Low/High	0.702	23.426	24.833	8.352	9.759	64.349	60.701
Medium/Medium	0.713	26.498	27.925	14.572	15.998	45.008	42.709
Medium/High	0.713	515.232	516.651	74.448	75.867	85.550	85.316
High/High	0.706	2613.277	2614.688	254.249	255.661	90.271	90.222

Table 3.1. Comparison of DLPJ and NBL.

Table 3.1 summarizes some tests conducted with 16 processors. The column labeled "Skew/Skew" represents the skews for the source and target relations respectively and the values for Low, Medium and High correspond to the skew factor of 0.1, 0.5 and 1 respectively. From the table, we see that DLPJ is superior over the other approaches. The performance gain ranges from 5% to 90%. When the skew is low, the performance gain is not significant. The reason is that, with low skew, most of the tasks have approximately the same processing times. As such, there is little or even no load being transferred between processors. However, as the skew increases, some tasks are more time-consuming than others. Without balancing the load, some processors will remain lightly loaded while the heavily loaded ones will determine the completion time of the join. By balancing the load, the completion time may be, as discussed above, drastically reduced.

3.4.3. Experiment 3: Vary the number of partitions

For hash-based join algorithms, the number of partitions may have an impact on the performance of the algorithm [Naka88, Kits89]. When the number of partition is small, more tuples will be hashed to a partition and the probability of the size of a partition exceeding the main memory size increases. Such overflow partitions will degrade the performance of the algorithm. On the other hand, too many partitions may also lead to poor performance as the number of fragmented pages increases resulting in more I/Os.

In this experiment, we perform two tests on DLPJ. The first varies the number of partitions statically, that is the number of tasks to be generated. The second is more complicated. After the relations are partitioned, the number of partitions is further fined-tuned as in [Kits83] by merging partitions of smaller size to form larger-sized partitions that can still be staged in memory. The joining phase will then work with the new number of tasks.

The results of the experiment are shown in Graph 3.2. [3] First, it is observed that, for test

---

[3] The curve for test 2 is drawn according to the initial number of partitions and not the final number of

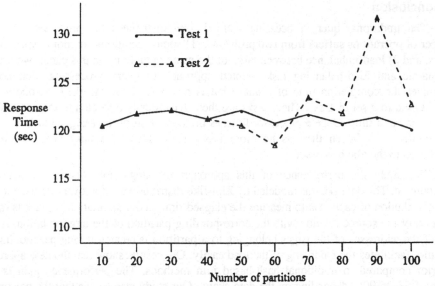

Graph 3.2. Response time as the number of partitions varies.

1, the number of partitions does not seem to affect the performance significantly. This is because the tasks are CPU-bound and so the algorithm is able to balance the load across all the processors. [4] The performance difference between the best and worst case is less than 5% of the response time. Second, both tests 1 and 2 have the same performance when the number of partitions is small. For test 2, when the initial number of partitions is small, the partition size is large and the opportunity for merging decreases. However, when the initial number of partitions is larger, the opportunity for merging increases. While this has the benefit of reducing I/Os for fragmented pages, it also has the overhead cost during the balancing stage of the joining phase. During the balancing phase, if the partition whose load is to be transferred is a merged partition (that is it has been merged from several smaller partitions), additional cost would be incurred for building a larger hash table by the idle processor than it would if no merging has been performed. In Graph 3.2, when the number of partitions is large (> 70), each partition contains lesser tuples. Therefore, there are more opportunity for merging smaller partitions to form a larger one. Thus during the balancing stage, the overhead incurred exceeds the benefit gained. As the result, the performance is poorer than the case when no fine-tuning is performed. On the other hand, as shown in Graph 3.2, when the number of partitions is moderate, fewer partitions need to be integrated and therefore the gain is greater than the overhead. Thus, we propose that the number of partitions be chosen to be as large as possible to avoid overflow partitions. Moreover, partition-size tuning is not necessary for CPU-bound tasks.

---

partitions after partition-size tuning.

[4] We assume a quite high I/O bandwidth. With a low I/O bandwidth, the I/O will always be the bottleneck and the performance will not be improved much by increasing the number of processors. With new technology, such as optical erasable disks and parallel I/Os, the high bandwidth is also realizable.

371

4. Conclusion

The traditional query processing method that distributes the processors across the number of operations suffers from two problems: 1) some operations are more expensive than others, and 2) load imbalance between tasks of the same operation. In this paper, we proposed a dynamic and load-balancing task-oriented approach to query processing that not only minimizes the completion time of a query but is also robust to data skew. A query is first decomposed to a set of tasks. These tasks are then dynamically allocated to the available processors one at a time. Once a processor finishes the execution of the assigned task, it requests for another one. When there is no more tasks, some load of a busy processor may be transferred to the idle processor.

We study the performance of this approach for single join queries in shared-disk environment. The data skew is modeled by Zipf-like distribution. Moreover, we use the actual data distribution of each task to measure the elapsed time in our simulation. A task is to join a partition of the source relation with the corresponding partition of the target relation. A directory of the addresses of the pages belonging to a partition is created during partitioning. This structure facilitates the balancing of the load easily. Our results show that the new approach is superior compared to traditional hash-based join methods. The performance gain is in the range of 5% to 90% depending on the data skew. Our study also shows that the performance of the approach is not sensitive to the number of partitions. This is an important feature since it can simplify the algorithm design and implementation.

We plan to extend this work in the following area. First, we are planing to extend our study to more general queries. We have applied the same approach to multi-join queries. The preliminary results are very promising. With more general query plans, some other issues, such as task ordering, pipelined processing versus task stealing, etc. make the problem more complicated. Second, we can enhance the load-balancing strategy for the join algorithm when the source relations can be staged in memory. Instead of reading the source relations and built the hash table by the idle processor, we may transfer the content from memory to memory, that is from the candidate processor to the idle processor. Since the cost of communication is expected to be cheaper than that of disk I/Os, this enhancement may provide a slightly better performance. Finally, we have considered only hash-based nested loop join algorithm in which the load to be transferred can be determined easily. It would be interesting to explore how the load for other algorithms, such as sort-merge join, may be determined and transferred.

References

[Deen90]   Deen, S. M., Kannangara, D. N. P. and Taylor, M. C., "Multi-join on Parallel Processors," *Proc. 2nd Intl. Symp. Databases in Parallel and Distributed Systems*, Dublin, Ireland, Jul. 1990, pp. 92-102.

[DeWi85]   DeWitt, D. J., and Gerber, R., "Multiprocessor Hashed-Based Join Algorithms," *Proc. VLDB 85*, Stockholm, Aug. 1985, pp. 151-164.

[DeWi90]   DeWitt, D. J., et al., "The GAMMA Database Machine Project," *IEEE Trans. Knowledge and Data Engineering*, Vol. 2, No. 1, Mar. 1990, pp.44-62.

[Engl89]   Englert, S., et al., "A Benchmark of Nonstop SQL Release 2 Demonstrating Near-linear Speedup and Scaleup on Large Databases," Tandem Tech. Rep. 89.4, May 1989.

[Hua91]   Hua, K. A. and Lee, C., "Handling Data Skew in Multicomputer Database Systems Using Partition Tuning," to appear in *Proc. VLDB 91*, Barcelona, Spain, Sept. 1991.

[Kits83]   Kitsuregawa, M., Tanaka, H. and Motoka, T., "Application of Hash to Database Machines and its Architecture," *New Generation Computing*, Vol. 1, No. 1, 1983, pp. 63-74.

[Kits89]   Kitsuregawa, M., Nakayama, M. and Takagi, M., "The Effect of Bucket Size Tuning in the Dynamic Hybrid GRACE Hash Join Method," *Proc. VLDB 89*, Amsterdam, Netherlands, Aug. 1989, pp. 257-266.

[Kits90]   Kitsuregawa, M. and Ogawa, Y., "Bucket Spreading Parallel Hash: A New, Robust, Parallel Hash Join Method for Data Skew in the Super Database Computer (SDC)," *Proc. VLDB 90*, Brisbane, Australia, Aug. 1990, pp. 210-221.

[Knut73]   Knuth, D. E., The Art of Programming, Vol. 3: Sorting and Searching, Addison-Wesley, 1973.

[Laks90]   Lakshmi, M. S., and Yu, P. S., "Effectiveness of Parallel Joins," *IEEE Trans. Knowledge and Data Engineering*, Vol. 2, No. 4, Sept. 1990, pp.410-424.

[Lu91]   Lu, H., Shan, M. C., and Tan, K. L., "Optimization of Multi-Way Join Queries for Parallel Execution," to appear in *Proc. VLDB 91*, Barcelona, Spain, Sept. 1991.

[Murp91]   Murphy, M. C., and Shan, M. C., "Execution Plan Balancing: A Practical Technique for Multiprocessor Query Optimization," *Proc. 7th Intl. Conf. on Data Engineering*, Kobe, Japan, Apr. 1991, pp. 698-706.

[Naka88]   Nakayama, M. and Kitsuregawa, M., "Hash-partitioned Join Method Using Dynamic Destaging Strategy," *Proc. VLDB 88*, Los Angeles, CA., Aug. 1988, pp. 468-478.

[Omie91]   Omiecinski, E., "Performance Analysis of a Load Balancing Relational Hash-Join Algorithm for a Shared Memory Multiprocessor," to appear in *Proc. VLDB 91*, Barcelona, Spain, Sept. 1991.

[Ozka86]   Ozkarahan, E., Database Machines and Database Management, Prentice Hall, 1986.

[Su88]   Su, S. Y. W., Database Computers, McGraw-Hill, 1988.

[Tera88]   Teradata Corporation, DBC/1012 Data Base Computer Concepts and Facilities, Teradata Document C02-0001-05, Los Angeles, CA, 1988.

[Walt91]   Walton, C. B., Dale, A. G., and Jenevein, R. M., "A Taxonomy and Performance Model of Data Skew Effects in Parallel Joins," to appear in *Proc. VLDB 91*, Barcelona, Spain, Sept. 1991.

[Wolf90]   Wolf, J. L., Dias, D. M. and Yu, P. S., "An Effective Algorithm for Parallelizing Sort Merge Joins in the Presence of Data Skew," *Proc. 2nd Intl. Symp. Databases in Parallel and Distributed Systems*, Dublin, Ireland, Jul. 1990, pp. 103-115.

[Wolf91]   Wolf, J. L., Dias, D. M. and Yu, P. S., "An Effective Algorithm for Parallelizing Hash Joins in the Presence of Data Skew," *Proc. 7th Intl. Conf. on Data Engineering*, Kobe, Japan, Apr. 1991, pp. 200-209.

[Zipf49]   Zipf, G. K., Human Behavior and the Principle of Least Effort, Addison Wesley, 1949.

The Demarcation Protocol: A Technique for Maintaining Linear Arithmetic Constraints in Distributed Database Systems

Daniel Barbará
Matsushita Information Technology Laboratory
182 Nassau St; 3rd Floor
Princeton, New Jersey 08542   USA

Hector Garcia-Molina
Department of Computer Science
Stanford University
Stanford, California 94305   USA

Abstract

Traditional protocols for distributed database management have high message overhead, lock or restrain access to resources during protocol execution, and may become impractical for some scenarios like real-time systems and very large distributed databases. In this paper we present the demarcation protocol; it overcomes these problems through the use of explicit linear arithmetic consistency constraints as the correctness criteria. The method establishes safe limits as "lines drawn in the sand" for updates and gives a way of changing these limits dynamically, enforcing the constraints at all times.

1. Introduction

Traditional protocols used to manage distributed data, such as two-phase commit, require one or more rounds of messages, lock or restrain access to resources during the protocol execution, and have a high overhead. Moreover, these protocols could render data unavailable during failure periods, decreasing system availability. This may be impractical for some scenarios, like those involving very large distributed data bases or real-time systems. In this paper we propose an alternative protocol that overcomes these problems through the use of explicit consistency constraints as the correctness criteria. The method gives the nodes involved substantial autonomy for performing changes to individual data items.

To illustrate, consider an application where "items" are stored in two separate locations. Assume there must be sufficient stock of these items among the two locations. This could, for instance, correspond to a military application where planes are stationed at two different bases, with the requirement that at all times the total number of stationed planes cannot be below some specified limit. (Perhaps out of fear of being short of planes in case of an attack.) Or it could also correspond to a retail business application where the "parts" stock at two warehouses must be maintained above a certain limit all the time. Transactions will run trying to withdraw or add to the stock, and the system should verify that the constraint is obeyed at all times. In the military application, planes can be put out for maintenance, or sent off to missions, but the minimum number of planes should be kept stationed at all times.

In this example, we have two nodes, each storing the value of the stock kept at the location. Let A and B be the data items at locations a and b respectively. Let the constraint be $A + B \geq 100$. Consider a typical transaction that attempts to withdraw Δ units from A:

$$\text{If } A - \Delta + B < 100 \text{ then abort}$$
$$\text{else } A = A - \Delta$$

In a conventional transaction processing system, such a transaction would have to lock data item B at location b, and A at a, verify whether the updated value satisfies the constraint and in that case, update A and follow a two-phase commit protocol to ensure that the transaction commits. Notice that this would require two rounds of

374

messages, and will lock and limit access by other transactions to A and B during protocol execution, resulting in a high overhead. The protocol could also render the data unavailable if one node or the network fails during execution, thus decreasing the availability of the system. This can occur because the two-phase commit protocol can block, i.e., after a failure the nodes may not be able to determine the outcome (commit or abort) of the transaction. Therefore, the nodes cannot release the locks and other transactions cannot run.

Alternatively, we could have a variable A_l at node a that acts as a limit, and state that transactions can continue withdrawing units of A as long as the final value of A remains above A_l ($A \geq A_l$). Similarly, a variable B_l will be stored in node b, serving as a limit for the updates made to B ($B \geq B_l$). (Think of A_l and B_l as "lines drawn in the sand.") The transactions will produce correct results as long as we ensure that $A_l + B_l \geq 100$. Notice that now, A (or B) can be modified by a transaction without involving the other node, as long as the updated value remains larger than the limit A_l (B_l). In these cases, what used to be a global transaction has become a local one, so there is no need for global concurrency control nor a two phase commit protocol. This increases data availability since transactions of this type may run even if the other node (or the network) is unavailable. One would expect that in many applications there is often slack in the constraints, so that in a very large number of cases transactions will be able to run locally as illustrated. In the aircraft example, say each base has 80 aircraft and that a total of 100 aircraft must be kept between the two bases. If we set $A_l = B_l = 50$, we satisfy the global constraint, leaving each base with a slack of 30 aircraft. Thus, each base could dispose of 30 aircraft without consulting the other.

The limits do not have to be static, but can change over time as needed. However, the changes have to be made in such a way that the constraint $A_l + B_l \geq 100$ is obeyed at all times. This is the goal of the *demarcation protocol* presented in this paper. The protocol is designed for high autonomy. Clearly, some changes in limits must be delayed because they are not "safe;" however, these delays do not block safe changes nor transactions that operate within the current limits. Besides a protocol for changing limits, we also need a *policy* for selecting the values of the desired new limits. (In our aircraft example, do we set $A_l = B_l = 50$ or should we pick $A_l = 30, B_l = 70$?) Policies will also be discussed in this paper.

Our approach does *not* guarantee global serializable schedules. Local executions are serializable, though, since each node uses conventional techniques (e.g., two phase locking) to run local transactions. Our approach does guarantee that inter-node constraints, which we assume are given, are satisfied. A conventional global concurrency control mechanism, on the other hand, would guarantee globally serializable schedules and the satisfaction of all constraints without the need to explicitly give them to the system.

One could argue that having to explicitly list the global consistency constraints is a disadvantage of our method. We can counter this argument, first by noting that with conventional approaches programmers still have to know and understand consistency constraints in order to write transactions. (A transaction must preserve all constraints.) Second, by knowing the constraints, the system can exploit their semantics, yielding better availability and performance.

Third, we are only talking of specifying constraints that span more than one node (local control ensures local constraints are satisfied). If we look at inter-node consistency constraints in practice, we see that they tend to be very simple. It is very unlikely for instance that we encounter an application with employee records in New York and an index to those records in Los Angeles. Data that is closely interrelated tends to be placed on a single node. (In a parallel database machine or in a local cluster, there may be complex inter-computer constraints. But in this case, the autonomy of each computer and network delays are not the critical issues. We are focusing on geographically distributed systems.) If we look at the types of constraints that are found in databases [DAT83], we claim that the following ones are the most likely to involve data stored in different nodes of a distributed system:

(1) Linear arithmetic inequalities. For example, the available funds for a customer at an ATM machine should be less than or equal to the actual balance of his or her account.

(2) Linear arithmetic equalities. For instance, the hourly wage rate at one plant must equal the rate at another plant.

(3) Referential integrity constrains. Example: if an abbreviated customer record exists on one node, then the full customer record must exist at headquarters.

(4) Object copies. The employee benefits brochure must be a copy of the brochure at the personnel office.

Our main focus in this paper will be on linear arithmetic inequalities. If an arithmetic equality is tight, e.g., $A = B + \delta$, then maintaining it will be expensive. Every change involves two phase commit or the equivalent, since each time A changes, B must immediately change. However, in many applications a tight equality can be treated as an inequality, e.g., $|A - B - \delta| \le \epsilon$. This is simply the two constraints $A - B - \delta \le \epsilon$ and $-A + B + \delta \le \epsilon$, which can be handled via our demarcation protocol. In Section 6 we show that the same principles that are used for arithmetic constraints can be applied to existential and copy constraints.

This paper is organized as follows. We start by listing related research in Section 2. In Section 3 we offer additional examples and an informal description of our approach. The protocol and a policy under a particular arithmetic inequality are presented in Section 4. (The generalization to arbitrary linear arithmetic constraints is in Appendix I for reference.) In Section 5 we discuss the performance of the demarcation protocol while in Section 6 we cover other types of constraints.

2. Related Research

There has been a lot of recent interest in trying to reduce the delays associated with conventional transaction processing and on exploiting semantics. In this section we briefly summarize research that is related to the demarcation protocol.

The idea of setting limits for updates has been suggested informally many times, e.g., [HS80, DAV82]. These ideas were formalized by Carvalho and Roucairol [CR82] in the context of enforcing assertions in distributed systems. Their limit changing protocol is more general than ours, but it is substantially more complex. For example, to maintain a constraint distributed among n nodes (each holding one variable) requires n^2 limit variables, while our protocol only uses n limits, one at each node. Their protocol requires many more update messages when limits are changed, and also forces changes to be done serially. Furthermore, [CR82] does not discuss policies for changing limits.

The demarcation protocol is related in a way to O'Neil's escrow mechanism [ONE86]. This technique was devised to support high-speed transaction updates without locking items, by enforcing integrity constraints. However, the mechanism was designed to be used only in a single database management system. (The application to the management of replicated data was proposed in the paper as a research topic.) Also, Kumar and Stonebraker [KuS88] have proposed a strategy for the management of replicated data based on exploiting application semantics. They present an algorithm to implement the constraints $B > B_{min}$ and $B < B_{max}$. However, their technique relies heavily in the commutativity of the transactions involved and does not generalize to arbitrary arithmetic constraints. Soparkar and Silbershatz [SS90] have developed a protocol to partition a set of objects across nodes. A node may "borrow" elements from neighbors. This approach does not deal with arbitrary constraints but does guarantee serializable global schedules.

The notion of quasi-copies is defined in [ABG90] as a way of managing copies that may diverge in a controlled fashion. The goals of this work are the same as for the demarcation protocol. However, quasi-copies are not useful for arithmetic constraints. For managing copies, the notion of quasi-copies is more flexible in some ways. For instance, one may specify that a copy must be equal to some value that the primary had within the last 24 hours. This type of constraint is not handled by the demarcation protocol. On the other hand, with quasi-copies updates may only occur at a primary location. The demarcation protocol allows updates at any site containing an arithmetic value.

Finally, there are other papers that deal with weaker notions of serializability and use of application semantics [FGL82], [LBS86], [GAR83], [KS88], [DE89], [FZ89].

3. Examples

In this section we present two examples that illustrate how the demarcation protocol works and the kinds of
problems that are to be dealt with. First we return to the example presented in Section 1. The proposed method of
operation imposes some restrictions. As pointed out, a transaction that attempts to lower A (or B) under the limit A_l
(B_l) would be aborted. The only way to run such a transaction would be first to get the site to lower its limit. Since
this is not a "safe" operation (lowering A_l may violate the constraint $A_l + B_l \geq 100$), it can only be achieved by
asking the other node to raise its limit first. The only safe operation in this example is to raise the limit above the
current value.

To see how limits can be changed, assume that $A = 61$ while $B = 69$, and the limits are chosen initially to
be $A_l = 45$ and $B_l = 55$. Figure 3.1 shows the setting of the base scenario for this example. Notice that transactions at node a can update A without further intervention from b, as long as the final value remains greater than or
equal to 45. The same is true for b and B, as long as $B \geq 55$.

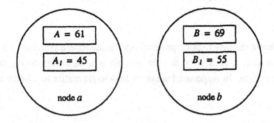

Figure 3.1 The base scenario for the sufficient supply problem

Assume now that for some reason, node a wants to raise its limit A_l to 50. Since this is a safe operation, a can go
ahead and do it. Node a will send a message to b informing it of the increment to A_l by 5 units. Upon receipt of
this, b may lower B_l by 5 to 50 (an originally unsafe operation). No reply to a is necessary. If instead of raising
A_l, a wants to lower it, the situation is not as easy. Lowering the limit is an unsafe operation in this case, so node
a would have to send a request to b asking it to raise B_l by the necessary amount. Node b is free to reject this
request. However, if it does honor it by raising B_l, it will send a a message informing it, and only then a could
lower A_l. If the nodes follow this protocol, it can be assured that at all times $A_l + B_l \geq 100$.

This is essentially the way the demarcation protocol operates. Whenever a node wishes to perform an unsafe
operation, it requests that the other node perform a corresponding safe operation and waits for notification. Notice
that the demarcation protocol is not two-phase commit. (The decision to give another node slack by increasing a
limit is made by one node only.) The nodes are still autonomous and there is no need for locking remote resources.
While limits are being changed, transactions that modify A or B can still run (as long as $A \geq A_l$, and $B \geq B_l$.)

There are still two issues to be discussed. The first is the establishment of a policy for when to invoke the protocol. The policy is orthogonal to the protocol, and the changes can be triggered at any time. For instance, the
changes could be triggered whenever A (B) gets too close to A_l (B_l). The second issue is the selection of the new
limits. Each node needs a formula for computing the new limits when a change is to be made. For instance, in this
example it may be desirable to split the "slack" evenly, i.e., to make the distance between A_l and A equal to the
one between B_l and B.

As an example, using the initial values of Figure 3.1, consider a transaction that updates B to 57. Say that
$B - B_l = 2$ is considered "close," so the change mechanism is triggered. However, node b does not know how
to split the slack since it does not know the value of A, plus it cannot lower B_l safely anyway. Therefore, b sends

a message to a requesting that A_l be raised, and including the current value of B. Upon receipt of this message, a knows that $B = 57$ and $A = 61$. The slack is $A + B - 100 = 18$. Subtracting half of this from each value we get $A_l = A - 9 = 52$, and $B_l = B - 9 = 48$. These are the new limits that split the slack evenly. Finally, a can safely increase A_l from 45 to 52 (increment of 7), sending a message to b, allowing it to decrement B_l by 7 to 48.

So far we have only discussed one type of constraint, i.e., $A + B \geq \delta$. Do the ideas generalize to other types of arithmetic inequalities? Fortunately, they do. For any constraint, some operations are safe while others are not. To illustrate, consider the following example: ensuring that project expenses E do not exceed budget B. Assume that we store B at a node b and E at another node e. Node b could be located at company headquarters, while e is at the project location. We require that at all times $E \leq B$. Both the expenses and the budget get to be updated over time. For the demarcation protocol we shall keep two limits E_l and B_l such that $E \leq E_l, B_l \leq B$, and $E_l \leq B_l$. In the supply example, it was safe to increase the limits of both variables. In this budget problem, the limit E_l can be *decreased* safely by e, while B_l can be *increased* safely by b. On the other hand, the operations of incrementing E_l at e, or decrementing B_l at b are unsafe. Notice again that once one node performs a safe operation, it leaves room for the other to perform what was originally an unsafe change. Consider that initially $E = 0, B = 20$ and that limits E_l and B_l have been set to 10. As long as E stays under 10, node e is free to modify E without consulting b. Similarly, node b can lower B to 10.

4. A Protocol and a Policy

In this section we present the demarcation protocol and its associated policies. To simplify the explanation, we assume a particular constraint, $A \leq B + \delta$. We also show a particular policy choice for splitting slack, although many others are possible. In Appendix I we show how to generalize to a linear arbitrary inequality and to more than two variables.

4.1 The Demarcation Protocol

The protocol consists of two operations, one for changing a limit and one for accepting the change performed by the other node. Recall that the constraint we are dealing with is $A \leq B + \delta$. Let the predicate SAFE(X, σ), where X is either A or B, and σ is a desired change in value, be defined as follows:

$$\text{SAFE } (X, \sigma) = if\,(X = A \text{ and } \sigma \leq 0) \text{ or } (X = B \text{ and } \sigma \geq 0)$$
$$then \text{ TRUE } otherwise \text{ FALSE}$$

Essentially, SAFE is TRUE when we decrement the limit of A or increment the limit of B. The other two operations are unsafe. We also define the following predicate to signal when the change in a limit exceeds its data value:

$$\text{LIMIT\_BEYOND } (X, \sigma) = if\,(X = A \text{ and } A_l + \sigma < A) \text{ or } (X = B \text{ and } B_l + \sigma > B)$$
$$then \text{ TRUE } otherwise \text{ FALSE}$$

When we refer to one of the values as X, we will use Y to refer to the complementary variable in the constraint $A \leq B + \delta$, i.e., $Y = A$ if $X = B$ and viceversa. We use the notation $N(X)$ for the node holding X. The demarcation protocol is composed by two procedures: *change_limit()* and *accept_change()*:

P1: *The Demarcation Protocol*

```
change_limit(X,σ)
  if SAFE(X,σ) is FALSE then
    Send message to N(Y) requesting it to perform change_limit(Y,σ)
  else if LIMIT_BEYOND(X,σ) is TRUE then
    abort the change
  else
    { Xₗ ← Xₗ + σ;
    send message to N(Y) requesting it to perform accept_change(Y,σ) }.

accept_change(Y,σ)
```

$$Y_l \leftarrow Y_l + \sigma.$$

Conventional database techniques should be used at each node to make changes in the limits and variables atomic and persistent. For instance, the values of the limits should not be lost due to a node failure. Loss of messages is undesirable but does not cause the constraint to be violated. For example, say $N(A)$ decreases its limit by 5 and sends an *accept_change* message to $N(B)$. If this message is never delivered, B_l will be 5 units higher that it need be. This is safe, but means that $N(B)$ will be unable to "use" these 5 units. Thus, for proving our protocol correct (Theorem 4.1) we make no assumptions about message delivery. However, in practice it is desirable to use persistent message delivery (messages are delivered eventually, without specifying how long this might be). Also note that since messages from different calls to *change_limit* only include decrements/increments, they need not be delivered in order at the other node.

For simplicity, in the protocol we have assumed that nodes are always willing to cooperate with their partners. In reality, nodes need not comply with *change_limit* or *accept_change* requests. When node a gets a request from b to decrease A_l by 10 units, a is free to ignore the request, decrease A_l by 10, or to decrease A_l by whatever amount it wishes. Similarly, when a receives *accept_change*$(A, 10)$, it may increase A by any amount up to 10. Of course, in most cases it is advantageous for a to perform the full increment, as indicated by the code. This is what we assume here.

Theorem 4.1: The demarcation protocol ensures that at all times $A_l \leq B_l + \delta$, assuming that the system starts with limits A_l^0 and B_l^0, where $A_l^0 \leq B_l^0 + \delta$.

Proof: All the increments or decrements to limits are done by adding a value v_i or subtracting a value u_i to the old limits, where i is simply an ascending index. For data value A, v_i^A represents a change performed via the *accept_change* call, while u_i^A represents a change made via *change_limit*. For B, v_i^B represents a change made using *change_limit*, and u_i^B one made using *accept_change*. At any time, we have

$$A_l = A_l^0 + \sum_{i \leq k_1} v_i^A - \sum_{i \leq k_2} u_i^A \quad \text{and} \quad B_l = B_l^0 + \sum_{i \leq k_3} v_i^B - \sum_{i \leq k_4} u_i^B,$$

where k_1 and k_3 are the indexes of the last increments seen by nodes $N(A)$ and $N(B)$ respectively, and k_2 and k_4 are the indexes of the last decrements seen by nodes $N(A)$ and $N(B)$ respectively.

Every increment v_i^B performed by *change_limit* produces an equivalent increment v_j^A done by *accept_change*. The increments for A may not be done in the same order as for B. However, the increment v_i^B is always done before the increment of the same magnitude v_j^A is done. Thus,

$$\sum_{i \leq k_1} v_i^A \leq \sum_{i \leq k_3} v_i^B$$

By a similar argument,

$$\sum_{i \leq k_4} u_i^B \leq \sum_{i \leq k_2} u_i^A$$

We can combine these two inequalities with $A_l^0 \leq B_l^0 + \delta$ by adding all left hand sides and all right hand sides, obtaining that at all times $A_l \leq B_l + \delta$ •

Note incidentally that δ plays a limited role in the protocol (and proof). As long as A_l and B_l are initially δ units apart, the protocol ensures they continue to be that far apart.

Corollary 4.1 Using the demarcation protocol, we ensure that at all times $A \leq B + \delta$.

Proof: The line in *change_limit* that checks LIMIT_BEYOND(X, σ) ensures that $B \geq B_l$ and $A \leq A_l$. Then, by Theorem 4.1, the result follows. •

Corollary 4.2 Suppose that $A_l^0 = B_l^0 + \delta$, that all update activity stops and that all messages have been delivered. Then $A_l = B_l + \delta$ (note equality).

Proof. Same as the proof for Theorem 4.1, except that after all messages are delivered,

$$\sum_{i \le k_1} v_i^A = \sum_{i \le k_3} v_i^B \quad \text{and} \quad \sum_{i \le k_4} u_i^B = \sum_{i \le k_2} u_i^A \bullet$$

4.2 Policies

The policies associated with the demarcation protocol specify when to initiate limit changes, how to compute new limits, and what to do in case a transaction tries to change the data value beyond its limit. We describe here the framework for such policies, and present some choices for them. However, the reader should bear in mind that other policies exist.

We begin by explaining how a transactions will actually perform changes on the data items. In order to change a value, a transaction will use a system call *change_value*(X, θ), where X is the data item and θ is the amount (positive or negative) to change. Within this call, we will have invocations of three policies. The first will be triggered whenever the change would exceed the limit. The second will be fired up when the final value gets "too close" to the limit. The last one will be triggered if the final value gets "too far" from the limit. These policies are implemented by procedures associated with the constraint that we are enforcing. Since a data value may be involved with more than one constraint (and thus, have more than one limit), we will have to test the limits on a per constraint basis. We will denote the constraints by the symbol Φ_j, where $1 \le j \le m$ and m is the number of constraints. Up to this point we have only discussed the constraint $A \le B + \delta$, but we are now generalizing to emphasize that the policies are constraint dependent.

Before presenting the *change_value* procedure, we introduce the following predicate, for the case Φ_j is the constraint $A \le B + \delta$. (A generalization is presented in Appendix I.)

VALUE_BEYOND $(X, \theta) = if(X = A \text{ and } A + \theta > A_l)$ or $(X = B \text{ and } B + \theta < B_l)$
    then TRUE *otherwise* FALSE

This predicate is analogous to LIMIT_BEYOND, in this case checking whether a change would violate the limit constraint.

The system call for changing a data value is as follows. Again, X refers to the variable being changed (A or B is our sample constraint). The limit for X under constraint Φ_j is X_{l_j}. Parameter T_{code} is a pointer to the code that runs the calling transaction and is explained below. (Note that the procedure below is valid for any constraint, not just our sample one.)

change_value(X, θ, T_{code})
  for each constraint Φ_j $(1 \le j \le m)$ in which X is involved *do*
    { *if* Φ_j.VALUE_BEYOND(X, θ) is TRUE *then*
      { Fire up process Φ_j.*policy*$1(X, \theta, T_{code})$ at $N(X)$
      abort calling transaction; }
    if $|X + \theta - X_{l_j}| < \Phi_j.\varepsilon$ *then*
      Fire up process Φ_j.*policy*$2(X, \theta, T_{code})$ at $N(X)$;
    if $|X + \theta - X_{l_j}| > \Phi_j.\beta$ *then*
      Fire up process Φ_j.*policy*$3(X, \theta, T_{code})$ at $N(X)$ }
  $X \leftarrow X + \theta$.

The procedures Φ_j.*policy*1, Φ_j.*policy*2 and Φ_j.*policy*3 are associated with the constraint Φ_j. The first policy is invoked when a change exceed one of the limits. In some cases *policy*1 may be null, but in other it may be important to initiate some action, like for example trying to increase the limit. The code pointer parameter T_{code} is useful for restarting the transaction once the limit has been changed. (An alternative would be to move the "abort transaction" command in *change_value* into *policy*1. This way, *policy*1 could chose between aborting the transaction or simply delaying it until the limit has been successfully changed.) The second procedure deals with the case where the value is getting close to the limit. What close means is defined by the constraint specific constant $\Phi_j.\varepsilon$. It may be desirable at this point to initiate a change in limits. For instance, if a base is running low on planes, it may be a good idea to renegotiate its limits with the other base. The third procedure handles the case in which the value is getting too far away from the limit, as defined by constant $\Phi_j.\beta$. In our example, if a base has too many planes, it may wish to notify the other base to arrange new limits.

A fourth policy is needed to cover the case where procedure *change_limit* encounters a change that exceeds the data value. In Section 4.1, we opted for aborting the change, but in general we can have a policy that decides what action is to be taken. This $\Phi_j.policy4$ can be invoked when the LIMIT_BEYOND check in *change_limit* detects a violation. Due to space limitation we will not present the modified *change_limit* procedure here; a more general version is presented in Appendix I.

The policies must also implement some form of load control. For example, say the system has reached a point where $A = A_l$ and $B = B_l$. Transactions that attempt to increase A will repeatedly try to increase A_l by sending a message to $N(B)$ to increase B_l. Since B_l cannot be raised, all these attempts will fail. Instead of wasting $N(B)$'s time, $N(A)$ may remember how many times it has attempted to change the limits and based on that, decide to wait for a given period of time before trying again.

Finally, there is the issue of how to compute the limits. A formula should be agreed upon to compute the new values when needed. We illustrate one possible formula for splitting the available slack, for the constraint $A \le B + \delta$. (A generalization is presented later.)

$$A_l = A + (B - A + \delta)k \tag{4.1}$$

$$B_l = A_l - \delta$$

Equation (4.1) is derived by computing the slack between A and B, and giving a fraction k of it to variable A as the "room to move up". The remaining $1 - k$ of the slack is given to variable B. By setting up k, one can tune the system in order to favor or constraint more one of the two variables. By setting $k = 0.5$ one divides the interval evenly.

Notice, however, that computing the new limits by using (4.1) requires information about both variables A and B, and neither one of the nodes know it. However, we can design *policy2* and *policy3* to overcome this problem as follows.

$\Phi_j.policy2(X,\theta,T_{code})$
 send message to $N(Y)$ requesting it to perform $\Phi_j.split\_slack(X)$

$\Phi_j.policy3(X,\theta,T_{code})$
 send message to $N(Y)$ node requesting it to perform $\Phi_j.split\_slack(X)$

$\Phi_j.split\_slack(X)$;
 *** local variable is Y; value of remote variable is parameter X; ***
 compute new limits, $Y_{l_j}{}^{new}$ and $X_{l_j}{}^{new}$, using Eq. (4.1) and X, Y values.
 let $\sigma = Y_{l_j}{}^{new} - Y_{l_j}$;
 if SAFE(Y,σ) *then* invoke $\Phi_j.change\_limit(Y,\sigma)$
 else send message to $N(X)$ requesting it to perform $\Phi_j.split\_slack(Y)$

Notice that we prefixed the function *split_slack* with the constraint identification Φ_j. In general, the way the slack is split will depend on the specific constraint. (The generalization of Eq. (4.1) is given in Appendix I.) It may be desirable to include a timestamp in a *split_slack* message, so that the receiving node may discard messages that took "too long" in transit and represent stale data. Also note we have ignored load control issues in these policies.

To illustrate how limit changing and slack splitting work, consider the following example. Assume that we are using the single constraint $A \le B + \delta$ so that all our constants and policies refer to it. Initially $A = 0$, $B = 20$, with $\delta = 10$, $\beta = 20$ and $\varepsilon = 2$. The limits have been set to $A_l = 15$ and $B_l = 5$, assuming that we are using $k = 1/2$. Figure 4.1 shows the initial scenario.

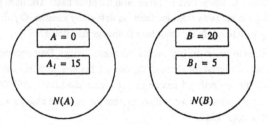

Figure 4.1 Initial scenario.

Now assume that a transaction calls *change_value* at $N(B)$ to update B to 30. (Notice that this update is allowed since $B \geq B_l$.) Since $B - B_l > \beta$, the request to change limits is initiated by $N(B)$, by triggering *policy3*. A message is sent to $N(A)$ requesting it to perform *split_slack*$(B = 30)$. Using Equation 4.1, node $N(A)$ computes the new limits obtaining a value of 20 for A_l. (The slack is 30 - 0 + 10 = 40; half of this is added to A to give the desired new limit.) To obtain $A_l = 20$, $N(A)$ must add 5 to the current limit; since this is an unsafe increment it does not perform the change. Instead, it sends a message to $N(B)$ requesting it to perform *split_slack*$(A = 0)$. Node $N(B)$ will compute the same limits, and this time the change in B_l will be performed there, updating it to 10. Node $N(B)$ will send a message to $N(A)$ requesting *accept_change*$(A, 5)$. Finally, $N(A)$ will raise A_l to 20. This example illustrates the case where *split_slack* is called twice. In other cases, *split_slack* is only called once (e.g., from initial scenario, A is updated to 15).

Now consider a scenario with concurrent updates. Starting with the values of Figure 4.1, assume both $N(A)$ and $N(B)$ complete transactions. The transaction at $N(A)$ updates A to 13, while the one in $N(B)$ updates B to 5. Both nodes send their new values to the other node, since both want to change their limits. Upon receipt at $N(A)$ of the new value of $B = 5$, the limit A_l is computed to be 14 and therefore the change is made, and a message to $N(B)$ is sent requesting it to perform *accept_change*$(B, -1)$. In the meantime, $N(B)$ processes the first message from $N(A)$, computing a desired new limit B_l^{new} of 4. Since this change is not safe, a message is sent to $N(A)$ requesting that the change is made there first. Next, each node receives the second message generated by its partner. When the *accept_change*$(B, -1)$ arrives at $N(B)$, B is updated to 4. When the second *split_slack*$(B = 5)$ message arrives at $N(A)$, it is ignored. ($A = 13$, $B = 5$ in Eq. (4.1) implies that A_l should be 14, but that is already the value of the limit, so nothing is done.) The final values are thus $A_l = 14$, $B_l = 4$, which evenly split the slack. Notice how the limits converge to the correct values, without any tight coordination. Each node still makes decisions autonomously.

In general it is difficult to prove formal properties for the policies, first because they can be arbitrary programs, and second because on purpose we do not wish to guarantee any properties that may hurt autonomy. For instance, for slack splitting, one may be tempted to prove that the selected limits are indeed the ones that split the current slack. However, there is no such thing as the "current slack" as the nodes may autonomously change A and B at any time (within limits). To enforce such a property, we would have to restrict updates in one way or another, which is clearly undesirable.

In the sample slack splitting policies, we simply assume that the value received in a *split_slack* message is current, and act accordingly. If indeed it is current, then the slack is split properly; if not, the selected limits will be out of date. But remember that no matter what the policies do, the underlying constraints are always guaranteed by the demarcation protocol.

5. A Simple Performance Evaluation

As discussed in the introduction, the main advantage of the demarcation protocol is the added autonomy and fault tolerance that it provides. However, a second advantage of the demarcation protocol may be improved performance during normal operation, because for some transactions (hopefully the majority), no communication between nodes is needed for commit. In this section we present a comparative performance analysis of the demarcation protocol versus the standard two phase commit protocol.

Analyzing the performance of a transaction processing system, under either the demarcation or the two phase commit protocol, is very hard. It is difficult to predict performance because it depends on many unknown parameters and issues: How many conflicts will there be among transactions? How expensive is getting a lock? Checking a limit? How often will limits have to be changed? Given the complexity of these issues we pick two simple, but in our opinion key scenarios: one where there are no conflicts and we can evaluate the maximum system throughput, and one where there is a single remote conflict. We believe these two scenarios will be by far the most common, so it is instructive to study performance in those cases.

The analysis assumes a system with two nodes, each one holding a portion of the database. In the first scenario no conflicts arise. That is, in the demarcation protocol, all transactions are able to run to completion, without triggering any change of limits, while in the two phase commit protocol, no transaction blocks due to lock contention. This extreme case maximizes throughput for both protocols; therefore we use that metric for comparison. In the second scenario every transaction encounters a conflict when it is run for the first time. In the two phase commit protocol, the transaction waits for a remote lock before it can proceed. In the demarcation protocol, the predicate VALUE_BEYOND is TRUE when the transaction is submitted for the first time. The transaction is aborted, and a change of limits is triggered. After the limits are changed, the transaction is rescheduled and run to completion. In this case, we compute the response time for a transaction under both protocols.

Table 5.1 presents the parameters used in the analysis. The second column explains the meaning of each symbol. In order to illustrate the performance gains of the demarcation protocol, we consider two "representative" parameter settings, given in Columns 3 and 4. There are obviously a great many possible settings, and by only selecting two of them we are leaving many out. However, to visualize the performance gains we think it is useful to at least have two concrete settings to study, at opposite ends of the transaction cost spectrum. The first setting represents with a system with lightweight transactions and low cost for sending a message. The second setting represents a system with larger transactions and high message costs (a more conventional transaction processing system). The only parameters that change in the two cases are the running time and the time to send/receive a message. All the values are in microseconds.

Parameter	Meaning	Case 1	Case 2
t_s	context switch	100	100
t_l	request locks	100	100
t_{cl}	check limits	300	300
t_T	running time	1,000	100,000
t_r	release locks	50	50
t_m	send/receive a message	1000	10,000
t_d	message delay	100,000	100,000
t_{ch}	change limits	300	300
t_x	scheduling delay	10,000	10,000

Table 5.1 Parameters (times in microseconds)

In the first scenario (no conflicts), a transaction running under the demarcation protocol arrives to the node and it is scheduled for processing. Before the transaction starts, a request message is received (t_m), a context switch takes place (t_s), then the transaction requests local locks (t_l), runs (t_T), and the system check the limits

(t_{cl}). Since there are no conflicts, limits do not have to change, so the locks are released (t_r) and the transaction commits, sending the answer back to the user (t_m). Therefore, the total CPU resources consumed by a transaction in this case are:

$$t_{dc}^1 = 2t_m + t_s + t_l + t_T + t_{cl} + t_r$$

For the same transaction running under two phase commit, the timing is as follows. First a message is received (t_m), a context switch is done (t_s), the locks are requested (t_l), then a message is sent to the other node (t_m) to request remote locks. At this point, this node switches to run another transaction while waiting for the answer to the lock request. (We assume an infinite supply of transactions to maximize throughput.) At the other node, the transaction produces a context switch (t_s), requests the remote locks (t_l), and a message is sent back acknowledging the locks (t_m). When this message arrives, the first node can switch back to the original transaction (t_s), run it (t_T), release the locks (t_r), and commit sending a message to the other node (t_m) which in turn releases the locks (t_r). Finally, a message to the user is sent (t_m). The CPU resources consumed *at both nodes* by the transaction are:

$$t_{2pc}^1 = 3t_s + 2t_l + 5t_m + t_T + 2t_r$$

In analyzing the throughput, we must notice that since we have two nodes, in one second we have two units of CPU resources available. Then, the respective throughputs are:

$$T_{dc}^1 = \frac{2}{t_{dc}^1} \quad \text{and} \quad T_{2pc}^1 = \frac{2}{t_{2pc}^1}$$

From the equations above, one can immediately establish that $T_{dc}^1 > T_{2pc}^1$ if the following equation holds:

$$t_{cl} < t_l + 3t_m + t_r + 2t_s$$

That is, the demarcation protocol throughput will be greater than the one for two phase commit if the cost of checking limits is less than the sum of the costs on the right hand side. We believe that, in general, this will be true, since checking limits is a simple operation whose cost should be comparable to that of locking an item. To see the gains for our two parameter settings, we substituted the values in the respective equations. For the values shown in Table 5.1, the throughput values are shown in Table 5.2 As can be seen, the performance of the demarcation protocol is significantly better: 83% higher throughput in Case 1, 25% in Case 2. In Case 2 gains are smaller because the transaction processing cost, t_T (equal for both protocols) is much higher.

Protocol	Case 1	Case 2
T_{dc}^1	563 Trans./sec.	16.6 Trans./sec.
T_{2pc}^1	308 Trans./sec.	13.3 Trans./sec.

Table 5.2 Throughput values for Scenario 1.

Let us turn our attention to the second scenario. Recall that in this scenario every transaction encounters a conflict when it is run for the first time. Under the demarcation protocol a request message is received (t_m), a context switch takes place (t_s), locks are requested (t_l), the transaction is run (t_T), and the limits checked (t_{cl}). Since the value goes beyond the limit, the transaction is aborted, the locks released (t_r), and a message is sent to the other node requesting a change of limits (t_m). This message takes t_d time to arrive. When it arrives, there is a scheduling delay t_x until the processor can service the request. Then a context switch takes place (t_s), the limits are changed (t_{ch}), and a message acknowledging the changes is sent back (t_m). This message arrives at the first node t_d units later, and there is a scheduling delay (t_x). Finally, after a context switch (t_s), the limits are changed (t_{ch}) and the transaction can be resubmitted. Resubmitting the transaction takes again $t_s + t_l + t_T + t_{cl} + t_r$. Finally, a message is sent to the user with the answer t_m. Thus, the total response time for the transaction is:

$$t_{dc}^2 = 4t_m + 4t_s + 2t_l + 2t_T + 2t_{cl} + 2t_r + 2t_d + 2t_x + 2t_{ch}$$

384

For two phase commit, we can use part of the analysis of Case 1. To the value t^1_{2pc} we should add $2t_d$, i.e., two message delays, and $2t_x$, i.e., the scheduling delay at both nodes when the messages arrive (we did not take this into account before because we were computing throughput, not response time). This yields t_n, the response time with no conflicts. But, since we are assuming the remote locks will be taken, the transaction will wait until the locks are released. We assume that the transaction will wait on the average half of the total running time of the transaction holding the locks, i.e., half of t_n. Therefore, the total response time for the transaction is:

$$t^2_{2pc} = \frac{3}{2}(t^1_{2pc} + 2t_d + 2t_x)$$

Table 5.3 compares the response times for the two protocols and the two cases (values in milliseconds).

Protocol	Case 1	Case 2
t^2_{dc}	228	462
t^2_{2pc}	340	556

Table 5.3 Response times for the second Scenario (times in milliseconds)

Even in this conflict scenario, the demarcation protocol outperforms two phase commit. In Case 1, the response time for the demarcation protocol is 33% better than the one for two phase commit. The difference is less marked for setting 2, again since the dominating factor is the transaction length. Even in this case we get non-trivial improvement (17%).

6. Other Constraints

In the introduction we argued that inter-node constraints tend to be simple. So far we have studied one class of such simple constraints, arithmetic inequalities. In this section we illustrate how the demarcation protocol and its policies can be used to manage other types of simple constraints. The key idea is to convert these other constraints into arithmetic inequalities.

To illustrate, consider a referential constraint of the form

$$Exist(A, a) \Rightarrow Exist(B, b) \qquad (6.1)$$

where A, B are data objects, a, b are nodes, and $Exist(A, a)$ is a predicate that is TRUE if object A is stored in node a and $Exist(B, b)$ is TRUE if B is at node b.

We can define the following function

$$f(X,x) = \text{if } Exist(X, x) = \text{TRUE } then \ 1 \ otherwise \ 0 \qquad (6.2)$$

where X stands for either A or B, and x corresponds to either node a or b. With this equation, the referential constraint becomes:

$$f(A,a) \leq f(B,b) \qquad (6.3)$$

This constraint can now be enforced via the demarcation protocol, as long as we interpret arithmetic an operation on $f(X,x)$ to be the appropriate create or delete operation. That is, changing $f(A,a)$ from 1 to 0 means that A is deleted at a; changing it from 0 to 1 means that A is created. We must also define policies that implement the correct semantics for this case. One possibility is to define the following policies. (Policies 2 and 3 are not necessary in this case.)

Φ_j.policy1($f(X,x)$, δ , T_{code})
*** An invalid change to $f(X,x)$ has been attempted;
    first change limit and then try transaction later ***
Φ_j.change_limit($f(X,x)$, δ);
resubmit later T_{code}.

Φ_j.policy4($f(X,x)$, δ)
*** An unsafe limit change has been attempted ***
Φ_j.change_value($f(X,x)$, δ , *null*)
resubmit Φ_j.change_limit($f(X,x)$, δ).

To illustrate, assume that A and B are stored in nodes a and b respectively. Thus, $f(A,a) = 1$, and $f(B,b) = 1$. Equation 6.3 must be enforced at all times. Therefore, the system establishes two limits $f(A,a)_l$ and $f(B,b)_l$, such that at all times $f(A,a) \leq f(A,a)_l$, $f(B,b) \geq f(B,b)_l$, and $f(A,a)_l \leq f(B,b)_l$. In this initial scenario, these limits can be $f(A,a)_l = f(B,b)_l = 1$. The safe operations are for a to decrease $f(A,a)_l$ and for b to increase $f(B,b)_l$.

Assume now that there is a transaction T that wants to delete B at b. The transaction will try to change $f(B,b)$ by -1 to 0. However, since the limit $f(B,b)_l = 1$, the transaction will be aborted and *policy1* fired. This policy will force the change of -1 on limit $f(B,b)_l$, invoking *change_limit*($f(B,b)$, -1). However, this is not a safe operation for b, so a message to a will be sent requesting it to change $f(A,a)$ by -1 to 0. In turn, a will invoke *change_limit*($f(A,a)$, -1). Since the desired new limit $f(A,a)_l = 0$ violates the constraint $1 = f(A,a) \leq f(A,a)_l$, *policy4* will be triggered (and the limit change aborted). This policy will force the change in $f(A,a)$ by -1 to 0, deleting A from a. The policy also resubmits the change in the limit $f(A,a)_l$ to 0. This time, the change will be successful. As a consequence of the change, a message will be sent to b allowing it to change $f(B,b)_l$ by -1. This makes $f(B,b)_l = 0$. When T is resubmitted and attempts the deletion of B again, it will find that the new limit allows it, and will proceed to delete B. Thus, the existential constraint is obeyed at all times. Note that if T is resubmitted early, before $f(B,b)_l$ has had a chance to change, unnecessary (but unharmful) messages will be triggered. One way to avoid this is to have the change in the limit $f(B,b)_l$ trigger the re-submission of the pending transaction.

While this may not be the most efficient way to enforce existential constraints, we believe it is very useful to have a uniform strategy for handling a significant fraction of all distributed constraints. The demarcation protocol provides such a strategy.

As stated in Section 1, approximate equality constraints of the form $| A - B - \delta | \leq \varepsilon$ can be implemented via the two constraints $A - B - \delta \leq \varepsilon$ and $-A + B + \delta \leq \varepsilon$. Each constraint can then be enforced by the demarcation protocol. We do not have space to describe the associated policies in detail but the key idea is as follows. Node a, holding A, will have an upper and a lower bound for A. Changes to A that leave it in this range can be done autonomously. If A gets "too close" to its upper limit, and thus "too far" from its lower one, two messages are sent to b: one stating that A's lower limit has been moved up (a safe operation for a), the second requesting that b up its lower limit (so that A upper limit can be moved accordingly). After these operations finish, A range will have moved up, so that A is no longer too close to its limit. To avoid unnecessary messages, the first message sent by a needs to be processed by b before the second one. What we have described here can be accomplished by writing the appropriate policies for the two constraints we have.

Finally, note that the demarcation protocol may also handle object copy constraints (see Section 1). The basic idea is to associate with each object a version number or counter that is incremented each time period. Constraints such as "the copy of O at a site must be within two version of the master copy" can be translated into arithmetic inequalities that can be managed via the demarcation protocol.

7. Conclusions

We have presented a strategy for enforcing linear arithmetic inequalities in distributed databases. Limits are defined for each of the participating variables; a node is free to update a variable as long as it stays within its bounds. The demarcation protocol is used to change the limits in a dynamic fashion. We also showed how this strategy can be used for other types of constraints, such a referential constraints and approximate equalities.

Intuitively, we may view a system that uses the demarcation protocol as a "spring." When a constraint has a lot of slack, limits will not be tight, and many transactions will be able to perform their updates locally. This corresponds to a loose spring. This corresponds to the first scenario considered in Section 5. As the slack is reduced, the spring is compressed, and more and more transactions will hit against the limit. The transactions will be more expensive to run, as they will require negotiations with the other node to change limits. When there is no slack e.g., $A = A_l$ and $B = B_l$, the spring is compressed the most. Even at this point, the system may be more efficient than a conventional one (which requires two phase commit for every transaction) because transactions that move a variable away from its limit may be done locally.

The demarcation protocol is limited because it only applies to linear arithmetic constraints. However, we have argued that a very large number of distributed constraints fall in this simple category. As a matter of fact, we have difficulty envisioning more complex constraints that would arise in a practical distributed system.

There are two ways to implement the demarcation protocol in a database system. One is to use an existing system, and provide the user with a library of procedures (e.g., *change_value*), sample policies (e.g., for splitting slack), and definitions (e.g., for limit variables). The user's code could then call these procedures to update values or change limits. The disadvantage of this approach is that a user could circumvent the rules, e.g., by updating a constraint variable directly and not through *change_value*. The other option is to incorporate the procedures into the system itself. The database administrator (or possibly an authorized user) would define the constraints and policies and give them to the system. The variables involved would be tagged. When a transaction updated one of these variables, it would trigger the necessary procedures. With either one of these approaches, there are clearly many issues that still need to be resolved, such as language used for defining the constraints, load control strategies, dealing with contradictory constraints, and so on.

Acknowledgments

We would like to thank Luis Cova and Ken Salem for helpful discussions, and Naftaly Minsky and Patrick O'Neil for pointing out some useful references.

8. References

[ABG90]   R. Alonso, D. Barbará, and H. Garcia-Molina, "Data Caching Issues in an Information Retrieval System," *ACM Transactions on Database Systems*, Vol. 15, No. 3, September 1990.

[CR82]   O.S.F. Carvalho and G. Roucariol, "On the Distribution of an Assertion," *Proceedings of the ACM-SIGOPS Symposium on Principles of Distributed Computing*. Ottawa, 1982.

[DAT83]   C.J. Date, "An Introduction to Database Systems," Volume 2, Addison-Wesley.

[DAV82]   S. B. Davidson, "An Optimistic Protocol for Partitioned Distributed Database Systems," Ph.D. Dissertation, Princeton University. October 1982.

[DE89]   W. Du, and A. Elmagarmid, "Quasi-Serializability: A Correctness Criterion for Global Concurrency Control in InterBase," *Proceedings of the 15th Conference on Very Large Data Bases*, Amsterdam, Aug. 1989.

[FGL82]   J.M. Fischer, N.D. Griffeth, and N.A. Lynch, "Global States of a Distributed System," *IEEE Transactions on Software Engineering*, SE-8, 3. May 1982.

[FZ89]   M. F. Fernández and S. B. Zdonik, "Transaction Groups: A Model for Controlling Cooperative Work," *Proceedings of the Third International Workshop on Persistent Object Systems*. Queensland, Australia, January 1989.

[GAR83]   H. Garcia-Molina, "Using Semantic Knowledge for Transaction Processing in a Distributed Database," *ACM Transactions on Database Systems*, Vol.8, No. 2, June 1983.

[HS80]   M.M. Hammer and D. W. Shipman, "The Reliability Mechanisms of SDD-1: A system for Distributed Databases," Computer Corporation of America Technical Report CCA-80-04, January 1980.

[KS88]   H. F. Korth, and G.D. Speegle, "Formal Model of Correctness Without Serializability," *Proceedings of the ACM SIGMOD International Conference on Management of Data*, Chicago, June 1988.

[KuS88]   A. Kumar, and M. Stonebraker, "Semantics Based Transaction Management Techniques for Replicated Data," *Proceedings of the ACM SIGMOD 1988 International Conference on Management of Data*, Chicago, 1988.

[LBS86]   N.A. Lynch, B. Blaustein, and M. Siegel, "Correctness Conditions for Highly Available Replicated Data," *Proceedings of the Fifth Annual ACM Symposium on Principles of Distributed Systems*, Calgary, August 1986.

[ONE86]   P. O'Neil, "The Escrow Transactional Method," *ACM Transactions on Database Systems*, Vol. 11, No. 4, December 1986.

[SS90]   N. Soparkar, A. Silberschatz, "Data-Value Partitioning and Virtual Messages," *Proceedings of the Conference on Principles of Database Systems*, 1990.

Appendix I: Generalizing the Protocol

In this appendix we generalize the demarcation protocol to operate on an arbitrary constraint of the form $c_1 A + c_2 B \leq \delta$, where $c_1, c_2 \neq 0$. We also discuss how to extend it to more than two data items.

We start by generalizing the predicates SAFE, LIMIT_BEYOND and VALUE_BEYOND for the constraint Φ_j: $c_1 A + c_2 B \leq \delta$. As before, we use X to refer to either A or B, and X_{l_j} for its limit. We use the notation c_{X_j} to refer to the corresponding constant in the constraint (either c_1 or c_2).

$$\Phi_j . \text{SAFE}(X, \sigma) = if \ c_{X_j} \sigma \leq 0 \ then \ \text{TRUE} \ otherwise \ \text{FALSE}.$$

(For instance, for the constraint $A \leq B + \delta$, if we wish to increase the limit B_l by $\sigma > 0$, the predicate SAFE would be TRUE.)

$$\Phi_j . \text{LIMIT\_BEYOND}(X, \sigma) = if \ (X_{l_j} + \sigma - X) c_{X_j} < 0 \ then \ \text{TRUE} \ otherwise \ \text{FALSE}.$$

(For instance, for the constraint $A \leq B + \delta$, the predicate is true if $A_l + \sigma < A$.)

$$\Phi_j . \text{VALUE\_BEYOND}(X, \theta) = if \ (X + \theta - X_{l_j}) c_{X_j} > 0 \ then \ \text{TRUE} \ otherwise \ \text{FALSE}.$$

(For the constraint $A \leq B + \delta$, the predicate is true if $A + \theta > A_l$.)

Procedure *change_value* (Section 4.2) is unchanged, except that it uses the new definition of VALUE_BEYOND given here. Procedure *accept_change* (Section 4.1) is simply generalized for an arbitrary constraint Φ_j, i.e., Y_l is replaced by Y_{l_j}. Procedure *change_limit* must be modified as follows. In the original procedure (Section 4.1), when one node changed its limit by σ, the second one would perform a change of the same value later. For the general constraint, however, the sign of the second change depends on the constants c_1 and c_2. For example, for the constraint $A + B \leq \delta$, a positive change in A's limit must be followed by a negative change in B's limit. In the procedure below, we also incorporate *policy4* discussed in Section 4.2.

Φ_j.change_limit(X, σ)
  if Φ_j.SAFE(X, σ) is FALSE *then*
    Send message to $N(Y)$ requesting it to perform
      Φ_j.change_limit$(Y, -sign(c_{1_j})\,sign(c_{2_j})\sigma\ )$
  else if Φ_j.LIMIT_BEYOND(X, σ) is TRUE *then*
    { fire up Φ_j.policy4(X, σ);
    abort this change }
  else
    { $X_{l_j} \leftarrow X_{l_j} + \sigma$;
    send message to $N(Y)$ requesting it to perform
      Φ_j.accept_change$(Y, -sign(c_{1_j})\,sign(c_{2_j})\sigma\ )$ }.

For splitting the slack in the constraint $c_1 A + c_2 B \leq \delta$, $c_1.c_2 \neq 0$, we generalize Equation 4.1 as follows:

$$A_l = A + (\delta - c_1 A - c_2 B)\frac{k}{c_1} \qquad B_l = \frac{B - (\delta - c_1 A - c_2 B)k}{c_2} \qquad (A.1)$$

Equation A.1 can be easily derived from $c_1 A + c_2 B \leq \delta$, noticing that the slack is equal to $\delta - c_1 A - c_2 B$.

To conclude this appendix, let us consider constraints of more than two variables. First, observe that if only two nodes are involved, nothing is different. For example, if we have the constraint $A + B + C \leq \delta$, and the items A, B are stored in one node, while C is stored at another, A and B can be treated as a single variable as far as the demarcation protocol is concerned. That is, it would be enough to have two limits: AB_l and C_l and follow the protocol.

If there are three or more nodes involved, then whatever node performs a safe operation must indicate what other node gets the amount. For unsafe operations, a node must select a particular node for its request to change limits. For instance, consider the inequality $A + B \leq C + \delta$. Say $N(A)$ wants to raise its limit, an unsafe operation. $N(A)$ has a choice: it may ask $N(B)$ to lower its limit, or $N(C)$ to increase its. Suppose that $N(C)$ is selected. If $N(C)$ does raise C_l, a message to perform *accept_change* is sent only to $N(A)$, so only it consumes the available slack. Now suppose that both $N(A)$ and $N(B)$ want to raise their limits concurrently, and send requests to $N(C)$. $N(C)$ should indicate to each the amount of their change. For example, if $N(C)$ raises C_l by 10, it may indicate to $N(A)$ that A_l can be raised by 6 and to $N(B)$ that B_l can be raised by 4. The generalizations we have illustrated here are straightforward and will not be discussed further.

Fragmentation of Recursive Relations in Distributed Databases

Sakti Pramanik

Computer Science Department
Michigan State University
East Lansing, MI 48824

&
David T. Kao

Computer Science Department
Michigan State University
East Lansing, MI 48824

&
David Vineyard

Computer Science Department
University of Michigan - Flint
Flint, MI 48502

ABSTRACT

In a distributed database system, it is advantageous to fragment a relation and store the fragments at various sites. In this paper, the fragmentation problem of recursive relations is studied. A distributed database model is established for studying the general fragmentation issues. Based on the concept of partial order sets, we have proposed two approaches for fragmenting recursive relations. The first approach uses the union of lattices to represent a fragment. The second approach defines a fragment by using a maximal node and the recursive part of the relation.

1. Recursive Relations

Recursive relations include two attributes with the same domain whose values are related by some recursive rule. Recursive queries are defined over recursive relations. One example of recursive relation is the part/subpart relation as defined by the following rule.

subpart(X,Z) :- subpart(X,Y), subpart(Y,Z)

Here, subpart (X,Y) represents the relation that Y is a subpart of X. Thus, the above rule is read as "Z is a subpart of X if Z is a subpart of Y and Y is a subpart of X." Recursive relations are useful in knowledge-base systems in which rules are defined recursively.

The properties of partial order sets and lattices will be used for modeling recursive relations, since if the recursive join attributes are considered to be related by an inclusion (the recursive relation), then the original relation is a poset. Transitive closure will be the model for recursive join as in [Val86]. A recursive relation is a relation in which two sets of attribute values are related by some transitive relation. We extend the transitive relation to include reflexivity, if it is not already present, in order to use the properties of posets. This will not change the transitive relation between any two different attribute values in the original relation thus the result of a recursive query will be unchanged. In the subpart example, this is equivalent to adding the rule subpart(X,X).

The user of the database may view the recursive relation as all tuples of the form $(attribute_1, attribute_2, \cdots attribute_n)$ where $attribute_1$ and $attribute_2$ have the same domain and are related by an inclusion relation, and $attribute_3$ through $attribute_n$ describe $attribute_1$. For example, the part/subpart relation may have tuples

part	subpart	color	quantity	weight	dimensions	cost
engine	cylinder head	black	1	800	3 by 2 by 2	1000
engine	fan belt	black	1	800	3 by 2 by 2	1000

For efficient implementation, the view is decomposed into two smaller relations, namely parts(part,color,quantity,weight,dimensions,cost) and part_subpart(part,subpart). The parts relation contains the part attribute and the attributes which describe the part. Every part is represented once in this relation. The recursion can be represented by the relation part_subpart containing attributes part and subpart, where a (part,subpart) tuple indicates that part is a cover of subpart.

The recursive relation may now be represented as a digraph whose nodes represent the values of the recursive join attributes (part in the example) and whose arcs represent covers, i.e., (x, y) is an arc in the digraph if x covers y in the poset. Inclusion is then represented as a path in this digraph, $x \geq y$ if there is a path of 0 or more arcs from x to y.

2. Fragmentation in Distributed Databases

It is advantageous to fragment a relation and store the fragments at various sites in a distributed database system. A relation whose tuples are stored at different sites is *horizontally fragmented*, or simply *fragmented*. The tuples at a site are called a *fragment*. This fragmentation is *disjoint* if each tuple is in a unique fragment. The fragmentation is *non-disjoint* if some tuple occurs in more than one fragment. If each fragment is the entire relation, this is called *replication*. If every site stores the entire relation, this is called *total replication*; if a subset of the sites store the entire relation, this is called *partial replication*. Consider the example of a bank with branches, each branch having local customers. Each branch requires the tuples corresponding to the accounts of the local customers for that branch. Ceri, et.al., have considered the problem of how to fragment a relation horizontally [Cer82]. Mukkamala, et.al., have investigated the problem of determining the minimal number of sites to access in order to answer a query when the data are partially replicated [Muk88]. Yu, et.al., have shown that choosing the optimal set of sites to access in order to answer a query is NP-hard if each relation is partially replicated at various sites [Yu82]. Yu, et.al., have considered the selection problem where a relation may be completely replicated or fragmented across sites and the fragmentation is disjoint, but no relation is both fragmented and replicated, in order to reduce transmission costs [Yu].

In performing a distributed query, the *relevant* fragments are those fragments which contain tuples needed to answer the query. A relevant fragment is said to be *essential* if there is some tuple in it which is needed by the query and that tuple does not occur in any other fragment. Two problems of interest in this scheme are how the relation is fragmented, and how a fragment is identified and described. These two issues are actually closely related.

In a traditional (nonrecursive) databases, fragmentation is accomplished through use of logical rules which the tuples of the various fragments must satisfy [Cer82]. A *predicate* is a boolean function defined on a relation. Thus it is a logical function composed of conjoining, disjoining, and negating statements defined on the attribute values of the relation tuples. The *fragmentation criteria*, or simply *criteria*, for a fragment F is a predicate which is applied to a relation R to determine which tuples of R belong to F. To determine whether the fragment is relevant, the fragmentation criteria is compared with the predicate used for selection by the query.

Fragmentation of recursive relations should preserve recursive properties in each of its fragment. Recursive relations are more well-structured in a way that two sets of attributes are related by some transitive relation. Most fragmentations are based on the transitive relation. If we represent a recursive relation as a digraph, a fragment is a subgraph of the original digraph. In reasonable fragmentations, the subgraph is unlikely to be a set of random unrelated nodes. Most likely, it is either a connected component or a collection of several connected components.

Our model for fragmentation of recursive relations is as follows. Again, we use the part/subpart relation in Section 1 as an example. At first, the view of the recursive relation part/subpart is decomposed into two smaller relations, namely parts and part_subpart. It is the parts relation that get fragmented and distributed over various sites. The part_subpart relation is actually a collection of ordered pairs that represent the recursion in the original recursive relation. Storage can be saved by replacing each attribute value of those ordered pairs by a smaller system-defined identifier, called a *surrogate* [Val86]. This relation of surrogate pairs is called a *join index* [Val86] since the user's original view can be recovered by performing self joins on the index, and then joining the result with the relation. Each site has a copy of the join index. In this regard, each site has a global view of the recursion part of the whole recursive relation.

To keep the fragmentation information, each site also has a copy of the *fragments table* of the recursive relation. A fragments table is actually a binary relation of the form (f,d) where f is the fragment identifier and d is its corresponding description. To find the fragments containing the tuples needed by a query issued at any given site, its local copy of join index and fragments table are all it has and all it takes to find those fragments.

When a recursive relation is updated, its corresponding join index as well as fragments table at each site also has to be updated. In the case of refragmentation, only fragments tables have to be modified. It is important to keep the integrity of those join indexes and fragments tables all the time.

In the above model, a fragmentation approach is defined as the way to interpret and utilize the fragment description part of the fragments table. A naive approach is as follows. We define d in the fragments table as the set of key attributes of the tuples in that fragment. For instance, in the example of part/subpart relation, the key attribute is the part attribute. Given a tuple t and a fragment description d, to determine whether t is in that fragment, we only have to look through the elements in d, one by one, and compare it with the key attribute of t.

This naive approach is quite flexible in a sense that any fragment can be represented and described by grouping the key attributes of its elements. However, it suffers from two serious drawbacks. First, the fragment description grows linearly as the size of fragment grows. Second, in order to find the fragments containing the tuples needed by a query, a search of all fragment descriptions is needed. This can be very costly, especially when the original relation is large and fragments are not disjoint.

Thus, better approaches are required for practical purposes. As it might have been noticed, that in determining the membership of a given fragment in the above naive approach, only fragments table is needed while the join index is left unused. With proper exploitation of the join index, a fragment can be defined and described in a more efficient way.

In the following two sections, we suggests two concise and flexible fragmentation approaches based on the model we just established. It is interesting to see how the join index, or in other word, transitive relation can be utilized in two different ways to put a boundary on a fragment.

3. Fragmentation by Sets of Lattices

A fragment is defined as a subset of the tuples of the original relation. The original relation is a poset. Each subset of a poset is itself a poset, thus each fragment of the relation is also a poset. The properties of posets can therefore be used to define and identify fragments.

3.1. Upper Bounds and Lower Bounds

A fragment can be viewed as a subgraph of the digraph of the original relation. Given a digraph G, a node $x \in G$ is *maximal* if there does not exist a node $y \in G$ such that y is x's ancestor. Similarly, a node $x \in G$ is *minimal* if there does not exist a node $y \in G$ such that y is x's descendant. One way to exploit the join index is to define the fragment by two sets of nodes, U and L, where U is the set of maximal nodes of the subgraph and L is the set of minimal nodes. Let F be a fragment. Then

$$F = <U,L>$$

and a node z is in F if and only if there exist $a \in U$ and $b \in L$ such that $a \geq z \geq b$.

In other words, a fragment is described by its upper bounds (maximal nodes) and lower bounds (minimal nodes), and a node is in the fragment if it falls between these upper and lower bounds. However, a careful examination of this approach reveals one limitation. Consider the relation in Figure 3.1. Given a fragment consisting of the six nodes {1,2,3,7,8,9}, finding its maximal and minimal nodes, we have the description as <{1,7},{3,9}>. According to the interpretation of this definition, this fragment must also contain node 6 which is not desired. It is easy to see that there is no proper description to describe this fragment in this approach. All we can do is to break down the fragment into two smaller ones which might not be desired or practical. Nonetheless, this approach provides us with some insights about the utilization of join index information. With some modification, the above limitation can be removed. In the next section, we will present a lattice method for representing this type of fragments.

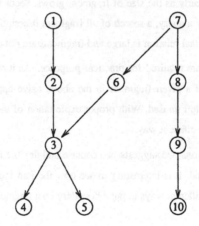

Figure 3.1: Example of the Upper and Lower Bounds Approach

3.2. Lattice Approach

As we have mentioned that the original relation is a poset. In this approach, each fragment is represented by a union of lattices defined on the poset. For each lattice describing the fragment's tuples, require that for x_L, the lattice lub, and for y_L, the lattice glb, for any z in the poset representing the original relation, if $x_L \geq z \geq y_L$ then z is in the lattice and thus in the fragment. Each fragment, represented by a set of lattices, is thus represented by a set of lub, glb pairs. Let F_i be a fragment. Then

$$F_i = \bigcup_j L_{i,j}$$

where lattice $L_{i,j}$ is represented by $(lub_{i,j}, glb_{i,j})$ and z is in F_i if $lub_{i,j} \geq z \geq glb_{i,j}$ for some lattice $L_{i,j}$ in F_i. In order to distinguish a pair of nodes and the corresponding lattice it determines, in subsequent context, we will use <x,y> to represent the lattice determined by node pair (x,y).

In this way, we have a powerful approach to describe general fragments no matter how the membership of those fragments are determined. Given a fragment, for each connected component of the fragment, we can decompose the component into a set of lattices, such that each node in that component falls into one or more lattices. Then, the set of lattices is called a *lattice cover* for the component. A connected component may have many different lattice covers. Since a fragment may consist of more than one connected component, the union of the lattice covers of those components forms a lattice cover of the fragment.

Comparing this approach to the one of upper and lower bounds, it is easy to see that this approach is just a variation of the former approach. First, we restrict U and L to consist of one node only. Second, we allow a fragment description to be a collection of those pairs of U and L. These two modifications provides us with a lot more flexibility in representing fragments.

Figure 3.2 shows a digraph for a recursive relation. Figures 3.3 shows three fragments for this relation. Figure 3.4 shows a lattice cover for the Fragment 2.

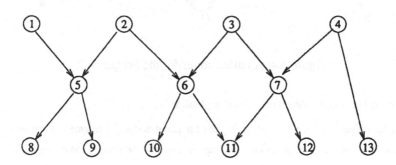

Figure 3.2: A digraph for a recursive relation

3.3. Finding Lattice Covers

As we have mentioned earlier, given a fragment, there might be lots of different lattice covers. Thus, before we try to derive a lattice cover from a fragment, it is important to define the criteria for good lattice covers. There are two desirable characteristics for a good lattice cover. First, there should not be too much redundancy. That is, the overlaps between lattices should be small. To evaluate this property, the sum of the sizes of all the lattices in a lattice cover can be used as an index, called *cover size*. Second, the number

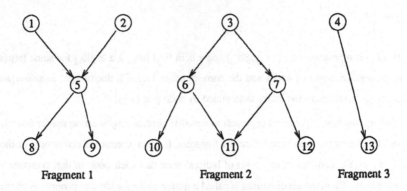

Fragment 1   Fragment 2   Fragment 3

Figure 3.3: Three fragments

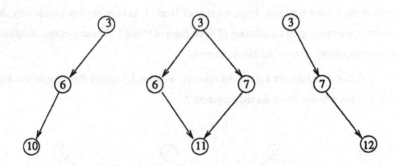

Figure 3.4: A lattice cover for the Fragment 2

of lattices in the lattice cover should be as small as possible.

Consider the extreme case in which each pair of adjacent nodes in a fragment is regarded as a lattice of two nodes. The result is a trivial lattice cover, and it is easy to remove the redundant lattices in this lattice cover in order to reduce cover size as well as the number of lattices in the cover. Given a digraph of n nodes, this trivial approach will provide us with a lattice cover with worst case cover size of 2n−2; this happens when the given digraph is a star. A star of 9 nodes is shown in Figure 3.5a. Figure 3.5b shows the same digraph as a tree. In general, a lattice cover generated by this approach will have an average cover size of n+c where c is independent of n. As far as only the first criterion is concerned, this trivial lattice cover is quite good. However, the number of lattices in this cover will range anywhere from $\frac{n}{2}$ to n−1 which is certainly too large.

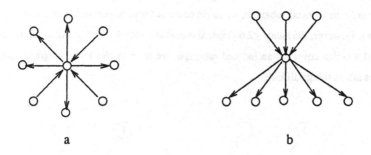

Figure 3.5: A star of 9 nodes

In fact, the two criteria are somehow related. Thus, a good lattice cover should achieve a balance between these two factors. However, with two criteria, in general, it is not possible to define an absolute index for evaluating different lattice covers. Nonetheless, we have the idea of what we are looking for. The following two propositions will establish the relationship between the number of lattices required in a lattice cover and the number of maximal and minimal nodes in the digraph.

Proposition 3.1: Given a digraph G with M maximal nodes and N minimal nodes. Any lattice cover of G must have at least max(M,N) lattices.

Proof: Assume that M≥N. Since two maximal nodes can not belong to the same lattice, to cover all those maximal nodes, we need as least M lattices. Similarly, if N≥M, we need at least N lattices to cover those minimal nodes. □

Proposition 3.2: Given a digraph G with M maximal nodes and N minimal nodes. There must be a lattice cover of G which has less than or equal to M×N lattices.

Proof: Let C={<m,n>: m, n are maximal and minimal nodes respectively} be a set of M×N lattices. For arbitrary node x∈G, there are maximal node m′ and minimal node n′ such that m′≥x≥n′. Then, x∈ <m′,n′>∈C, and C is a lattice cover of G. □

In the general case, to derive a good lattice cover for a fragment which is specified by a random subset of the nodes in the original digraph is a hard problem. The reason is that looking at just the subgraph induced by the nodes of a fragment alone is not enough to derive a lattice cover. To illustrate this problem, take the digraph in Figure 3.6a as an example. It is a digraph consists of six nodes. Given a fragment specified by node set {1,2,3,5,6}, we have the induced subgraph for this fragment in Figure 3.6b. By investigating only the induced subgraph, we might come out several possible lattice covers. One of them is {<1,5>,<2,6>}. However, the lattice <2,6> must also contain node 4 which is not in the fragment. In other words, to find a lattice cover for an induced subgraph, we have to check the subgraph against the whole digraph. This makes things difficult.

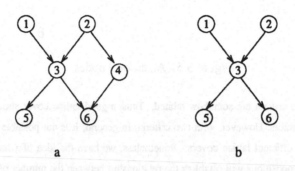

a   b

Figure 3.6: A digraph and its induced subgraph

Although an efficient algorithm for solving the general case is still not available, we do have an algorithm which works in limited situations. Algorithm 3.1 can be applied to one of the following cases to get a correct lattice cover.

(1)   any stand-alone (non-induced) digraph

(2)   any induced subgraph in which no internal nodes (nodes which are neither maximal nor minimal in the subgraph) are adjacent to any node which is not in the subgraph

In Algorithm 3.1, we tend to follow the second criterion more closely than the first one. Assume that the input is in the digraph format which is stored as adjacency lists, and M, N denote respectively the sets of maximal and minimal nodes in the digraph. The following algorithm generates a lattice cover for that input digraph.

Algorithm 3.1: Find a Lattice Cover for a Digraph

Stage 1.

1.   For each node v in the digraph, create a corresponding ancestor set A(v). For each edge (i,j), create a corresponding edge label set $E_{i,j}$. Originally, all these ancestor sets as well as the edge label sets are empty, and all nodes are unmarked.

2.   For each maximal node m, let A(m)={m}. For every v which is a descendant of m, let also A(v)=A(v)∪{m}. Therefore, given a node v, its ancestor set A(v) contains all the maximal nodes

which are ancestors of v. These ancestor sets will not be changed thereafter, but the edge label sets will be updated in Stage 2 of the algorithm.

Stage 2.

For each minimal node n, and each m∈ A(n), node pair (m,n) suggests a lattice <m,n>. There are $\sum_{n\in N}$ |A(n)| such pairs, where N is the set of minimal nodes in the digraph.

3. Repeat choosing one minimal node and one maximal node in its ancestor set, carrying out Step 4 through Step 7 to construct the corresponding lattice, until all nodes in the digraph are marked — in other words, the lattices already constructed form a lattice cover for the input digraph.

4. Suppose the node pair picked in Step 3 is (m,n). Let S={n}, S'=ø, L={n}, T=ø, where S, S' and L are sets of nodes, T is a set of edges. If the node n has not been marked, let SUCCESS=true, else let SUCCESS=false, where SUCCESS is a Boolean variable.

5. Choose arbitrary x∈ S such that x is not a maximal node;

> If such x exists then goto Step 6.
> else
>> if SUCCESS=true, then
>>> if S'=ø, then goto Step 7.
>>> else let S=S∪S' and S'=ø, goto Step 5.
>> else abort, the lattice <m,n> is not established.
>> Goto Step 3.

6. Find x's parents whose ancestor sets contain m. Assume that there are k such parents. Let those parents be v_i, i=1,...k and m∈ A(v_i) ∀i. If m∈ $E_{v_i,x}$ i=1,...k and SUCCESS=false, let S=S−{x} and S'=S'∪{x}; goto Step 5. If ∃i such that the node v_i has not been marked, set SUCCESS=true. Let S=S∪{v_i: i=1,...k}−{x}, L=L∪{v_i: i=1,...k}, T=T∪{(v_i,x): i=1,...k}. Goto Step 5.

7. The lattice determined by (m,n) is created successfully. All the elements in L are the nodes defined by the lattice <m,n>. Mark all the nodes in L. For each element (i,j)∈ T, let $E_{i,j}=E_{i,j}\cup\{m\}$. Goto Step 3.

To demonstrate the algorithm, the digraph in Figure 3.7 is taken as an example. In order to show how the algorithm will work under different situations, we deliberately construct lattices in the order of <1,12>, <3,15>, <2,14>, <3,13>, and <1,13>. Only the construction process of the second lattice <3,15> and the fifth lattice <1,13> will be shown. Figure 3.7 shows the ancestors set for each node and the edge label sets after the construction of first lattice <1,12>. In Figure 3.7 and 3.8, the nodes which have been included in one or more constructed lattices are marked by an asterisk. There are 6 variables used in the algorithm. The execution of the algorithm can be easily traced by showing the changes in these variable values.

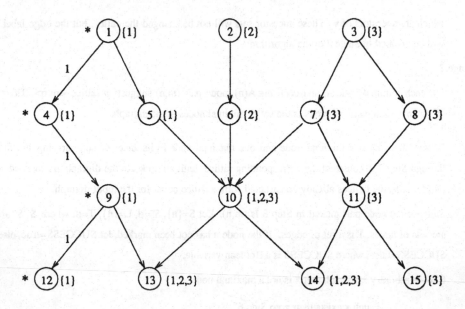

Figure 3.7: Digraph after the constructing of first lattice <1,12>

(1)   <m,n>=<3,15> (construction of the second lattice)

x	S	S'	L	T	SUCCESS
-	{15}	∅	{15}	∅	true
15	{11}	∅	{15,11}	{(11,15)}	true
11	{7,8}	∅	{15,11,7,8}	{(11,15),(7,11),(8,11)}	true
7	{8,3}	∅	{15,11,7,8,3}	{(11,15),(7,11),(8,11),(3,7)}	true
8	{3}	∅	{15,11,7,8,3}	{(11,15),(7,11),(8,11),(3,7),(3,8)}	true
-	{3}	∅	{15,11,7,8,3}	{(11,15),(7,11),(8,11),(3,7),(3,8)}	true

Since there is no node in S which is not maximal, SUCCESS=true, and S´=∅, according to Step 3 and 7, lattice <3,15>={15,11,7,8,3} is created successfully. Mark nodes 15, 11, 7, 8 and 3. Edge label sets $E_{11,15}$, $E_{7,11}$, $E_{8,11}$, $E_{3,7}$ and $E_{3,8}$ have to be updated by adding node 3.

We omit the construction process for lattices <2,14> and <3,13>. The updated edge labels information after these constructions is shown in Figure 3.8.

(2)   <m,n>=<1,13> (construction of the fifth lattice)

x	S	S'	L	T	SUCCESS
-	{13}	ø	{13}	ø	false
13	{9,10}	ø	{13,9,10}	{(9,13),(10,13)}	false
9	{10}	{9}	{13,9,10}	{(9,13),(10,13)}	false
10	{5}	{9}	{13,9,10,5}	{(9,13),(10,13),(5,10)}	true
5	{1}	{9}	{13,9,10,5,1}	{(9,13),(10,13),(5,10),(1,5)}	true
-	{1,9}	ø	{13,9,10,5,1}	{(9,13),(10,13),(5,10),(1,5)}	true
9	{1,4}	ø	{13,9,10,5,1,4}	{(9,13),(10,13),(5,10),(1,5),(4,9)}	true
4	{1}	ø	{13,9,10,5,1,4}	{(9,13),(10,13),(5,10),(1,5),(4,9),(1,4)}	true
-	{1}	ø	{13,9,10,5,1,4}	{(9,13),(10,13),(5,10),(1,5),(4,9),(1,4)}	true

The table above needs a little more explanations than the one we saw in the construction of lattice <3,15>.

1. After the second row in the table, S={9,10}. Choosing arbitrarily node 9 from S, we find its only parent is node 4. Since $1 \in E_{4,9}$ and SUCCESS is still false, the node 9 is moved from S to S'.

2. After the fifth row in the table, S={1}. Since no non-maximal node can be chosen from S, SUCCESS=true, and $S' \neq \emptyset$, let $S = S \cup S'$ and $S' = \emptyset$.

At the end of the table, since there is no node in S which is not maximal, SUCCESS=true, and $S'=\emptyset$, according to Step 3 and 7, lattice <1,13>={13,9,10,5,1,4} is created successfully. Mark nodes 5 only, because all the other nodes in <1,13> have already been marked. Edge label sets $E_{9,13}$, $E_{10,13}$, $E_{5,10}$ and $E_{1,5}$ have to be updated by adding node 1.

The lattice cover generated by the algorithm is not optimal in a sense that the number of lattices and the overlaps between lattices are not minimal. In fact, the quality of the results depends on the order of of lattices we tried to construct. There are $(\sum_{n \in N} |A(n)|)!$ possible permutations, and some of them will lead us to good results while some others will not. Here is where heuristics can help.

For this purpose, at first, we define a new digraph G^b based on the original digraph G. G^b consists of only the maximal and minimal nodes of G and two nodes are connected by an arc in G^b if and only if there is a directed path from one node to the other in G. Obviously, G^b is *bipartite*. A bipartite graph is one whose node set can be partitioned into two subsets, say X and Y, so that each edge has one end in X and one end in Y. In the case of G^b, X=M and Y=N. To get G^b, all we have to do is to transform the ancestor sets of the minimal nodes into adjacency lists of G^b. Then we can find a *maximum matching* of G^b. A *matching* is a subset of all edges in which no two edges are incident with the same node. A maximum matching is a matching containing the largest number of edges. In performing the algorithm, try those edges, i.e. node pairs, in the maximum matching first. Only after all lattices suggested by the pairs in the matching have been tried, and there are still some nodes have not been covered by a lattice yet, we will try

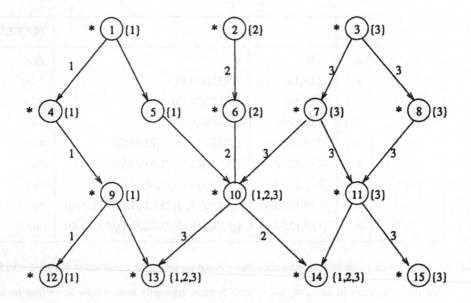

Figure 3.8: Digraph after the constructing of the fourth lattice <3,13>

other possibilities.

The above algorithm is a greedy algorithm. From Step 3., it is easy to see that each edge is traced at most $\sum_{n \in N} |A(n)|$ times. Since $|A(n)| \leq |M|$, the time complexity is $O(|M| |N| |E|)$, where M, N, E are the sets of maximal nodes, minimal nodes, and edges in the input digraph respectively. However, this is the worst case situation. Although, the real time required by this algorithm is affected by $|M|$, $|N|$ and the connection of the digraph, on the average, the time complexity is $O(|E|)$.

3.4. Finding Relevant Fragments

A query on this fragmented database will specify which tuples must be accessed. The join index and the lattice lub's and glb's can be used to determine which fragments those tuples are in. Algorithm 3.2 finds all the relevant fragments of the query. In the algorithm, the sets S_i and P_i are the successor and predecessor sets as defined by Schnorr [Sch78] in his algorithm, the set A is the set of tuples needed by the query, the set B is the set of lub's for determining the fragments, and the set C is the set of glb's.

Algorithm 3.2: Find the Relevant Fragments in a Recursive Relation

1.   For all i in A find S_i, P_i.

2.   For all j in C find P_j.

3.   For each (i,j) from A crossproduct C determine if $i \geq j$.

4.   For all (k,j) where $k \in B$ and j is the corresponding glb in C, if $i \geq j$ is false for all i in A, remove this (k,j) pair. Recalculate B and C.

5.   For all k in B, find S_k.

6.   If $k \geq i \geq j$ for some $i \in A$ and some (k,j) where (k,j) is a (lub,glb) pair, then mark the fragment with lattice <k,j> as containing i.

4. Recursive Fragments in Recursive Relations

A fragment is *recursive* if for any element x in the fragment, all descendants of x are in the fragment. This is a much cleaner definition for a fragment than in the last section, however, it is not as general. The motivations for defining this type of fragmentation derive from the applications for this type of relation. The most common type of query is a recursive query in which descendants will be the result of the query.

A "recursively fragmented" relation is a relation in which all fragments are recursive. This is not always practical. Consider the case in which there is a single maximal node. The fragment which contains this node contains the entire relation, therefore, queries are assured of accessing tuples by accessing this one fragment. However, if there are many maximal nodes, it makes sense to have a recursively fragmented relation. Assume the case where there are many maximal nodes and that the relation is recursively fragmented. Each fragment is uniquely determined by a set of maximal nodes, that is, nodes which have no ancestors in the fragment.

Proposition 4.1: A nontrivial fragmentation of a recursive relation with a single maximal element must have at least one non-recursive fragment.

Proof: If all fragments are recursive, then the fragment containing the maximal tuple of the relation contains the entire relation, hence the fragmentation is trivial. □

Proposition 4.2: If a recursive relation is recursively fragmented, and if the fragmentation is non-trivial, then there does not exist one fragment which contains all the maximal tuples.

Proof: Assume that some recursive fragment contains all the maximal tuples. Let x be a tuple. Then a maximal ancestor of x lies in the given fragment. But the fragment is recursive, therefore x lies in the same fragment. We chose x arbitrarily, therefore this fragment contains the entire relation and the fragmentation is trivial. □

It is very quick to find relevant fragments in recursively fragmented relations. Traverse the join graph backwards looking for ancestors. Each ancestor which is a maximal node for a fragment determines a fragment a given tuple is in. If all such ancestors are in the same fragment, then the fragment is essential. Given the query "find all descendants of node x", once a fragment containing x is found, all nodes for the query can be accessed from that fragment.

A common query for a recursive relation is "find all descendants of a set of nodes". A naive way to approach this query is to find all descendants of each node in the set, then use intersection to find the common descendants. However, recursive fragments have a helpful property, intersections of recursive fragments are recursive.

Proposition 4.3: The intersection of two recursive fragments is recursive.

Proof: Let F_1 and F_2 be recursive fragments and let F_3 be the intersection. F_3 is recursive if all descendants of any tuple in F_3 are in F_3. If F_3 is empty, then Proposition 4.3 is trivially true. Let $x \in F_3$. Then we have that $x \in F_1$ and hence all descendants of x are in F_1. Similarly, all descendants of x are in F_2. Therefore all descendants of x are in F_3. $\square$

Proposition 4.4: The union of two recursive fragments is recursive.

Proof: The descendants of a tuple t in the union must be in one of the fragments containing t, therefore these descendants are in the union. $\square$

5. Conclusion

In this paper, we have established a distributed database model for studying the general fragmentation issues of recursive relations. Based on the concept of partial order sets, we have examined two different approaches to fragment recursive relations. The lattice approach gives us great flexibility in defining and handling fragments, while requiring sophisticated operations to create and maintain the fragments. On the other hand, recursive fragments approach provides a simple definition of fragments at the price of flexibility. Besides, it has a clear edge over the lattice approach in performing queries like "find all the descendants."

There are special problems with updating fragmented recursive relations which do not occur with updating fragmented non-recursive relations. Issues related to fragmented recursive relations have been addressed in [Pra91]. [Pra91] also describes an efficient method to find common descendants as well as common ancestors by using tag sets information. The applications of this method go beyond the distributed databases. The same algorithm can be applied to compute transitive closure of any poset.

6. References

[Ccr82] Ceri, S., Negri, M., Pelagatti, G., "Horizontal partitioning in database design", *in Proc. ACM SIGMOD Intl. Conf. on Management of Data*, 1982.

[Muk88] Mukkamala, R., Bruell, S.C., Shultz, R.K., "A heuristic algorithm for determining a near-optimal set of nodes to access in a partially replicated distributed database system", *in Proc. 4th Intl Conf. on Data Engineering*, February 1988.

[Pra91] Pramanik, S., Kao, D. T., Vineyard D., "Fragmentation of recursive relations in distributed databases", Technical Report, Department of Computer Science, Michigan State University, August 1991.

[Sch78] Schnorr, C., "An Algorithm for transitive closure with linear expected time", *SIAM J. Compute.*, vol 7, no. 2, May 1978.

[Val86] Valduriez, P., Boral, H., "Evaluation of recursive queries using join indices", in *Proc. 1st Intl. Conf. on Expert Database Systems*, pp. 197-208, 1986.

[Vin89] Vineyard, D. R., "Query optimization in distributed databases by predicate analysis and semi-join techniques", *Ph.D. Dissertation*, Department of Computer Science, Michigan State University, East Lansing, Michigan, 1989.

[Yu] Yu, C.T., Chang, C.C., Templeton, M., Brill, D., Lund, E., "FREDS - a query processing algorithm for fragmented relational distributed systems", technical report, Dept. of Electrical Engineering and Computer Science, University of Illinois at Chicago, Chicago, Illinois 60680.

[Yu82] Yu, C.T., Lam, K. Chang, C.C., Chang, S.K., "Promising approach to distributed query processing", *in Proc. of 6th Berkeley Workshop on Distributed Data Management and Computer Networks*, February 1982.

A Geometric Approach to Indexing Large Rule Bases*

Timos Sellis[†] and Chih-Chen Lin[‡]
Department of Computer Science
University of Maryland
College Park, MD 20742

Abstract

The efficiency of finding qualifying rules against updates in large production systems has always been an important research issue. In database implementations of rule systems, this problem is even more critical. *Predicate Indexing* is a reduced version of the above problem when only selection conditions are considered. In this paper we draw a similarity between predicate indexing and indexing of geometric data, and discuss index design issues. Results from experiments using special data structures are also presented.

1 Introduction

Efficiency of execution has always been a major issue for production systems and forward-chaining rule systems. In particular, finding all qualifying rules, commonly called the *Match phase*, is the most time consuming step in the *recognize-select-act* cycle of a typical production system like OPS5 [FORG81]. It has been reported that the match phase constitutes around 90% of the execution time of a production system [GUPT86]. Several algorithms have been proposed to enhance the speed of the match phase, such as the Rete algorithm [FORG82] used in OPS5. When the knowledge base of a production system is too large to fit in main memory, the use of database management systems (DBMS) for the implementation of production systems is a natural solution [SELL89a], and has been extensively studied by many researchers [STON87, STON88]. The efficiency of the match phase becomes even more critical in DBMS rule systems because of the size of data involved. In this work we are interested in production (or forward-chaining) rules only.

A rule base consists of a collection of (production) rules of the form

IF *[CONDITION]* **THEN** *[ACTION]*

which operate on data stored in the database, also called *working memory* (WM) in production systems. The conditions in the *IF* part of a rule can be roughly classified into

---

*This research was sponsored partially by the National Science Foundation under Grants IRI-8719458 and IRI-9057573 (PYI Award), by DEC and Bellcore, and by the Air Force Office for Scientific Research under Grant AFOSR-89-0303.

†Also with University of Maryland Institute for Advanced Computer Studies (UMIACS).

‡Current Address: AT&T Bell Labs, Rm. 4A217, 200 Laurel Avenue, Middletown, NJ 07748.

selection conditions and *join* conditions, using database terms. This paper concentrates on the efficient testing of selection conditions, which is also referred to as *predicate indexing* [STON87]. We draw a similarity between predicate indexing and spatial data indexing, and show how spatial access methods, such as R-trees [GUTT84], can be used for indexing selection conditions. However, the design of such indexes has to be done carefully, in order to maintain good performance. In particular, we are interested in the problem of deciding what kind and how many spatial indexes have to be built, given a set of rules; this problem is similar to the index-selection problem in relational database management systems [FINK88].

The rest of the paper is organized as follows: in the next section we introduce the problem and discuss our approach of viewing predicate indexing as a geometric problem. The problem of designing efficient predicate indexing schemes is then discussed in Section 3. Experimental results using R-trees are then presented in Section 4. Section 5 is a summary.

2 Predicate Indexing and Geometric Interpretation

Suppose we are given a set of rules with selection-only condition clauses (hereafter also called *predicates*). For example, the following two selections

Predicate-1: salary > 60K
Predicate-2: 20 < age < 35 and 10K < salary < 30K

may be used to monitor incoming employee tuples so that, whenever a qualifying tuple is inserted, the DBMS can take some action (e.g. send a message to the personnel department). The predicate indexing problem accounts to finding which of the rules' conditions are satisfied, given a value substitution for attributes involved in the selection clauses.

One can think of selection clauses as areas in a multi-dimensional space defined by the various attributes of a relation. As an example, the above two predicates can be mapped to a region and a rectangle respectively in the 2-dimensional space defined by the two attributes **age** and **salary** of a relation **Emp**, as shown in Figure 1. Similarly, a tuple being inserted into (or deleted from) **Emp** can be mapped to a point in the same space. Finding all predicates satisfied by a tuple, i.e. the match problem, is therefore the same as finding all rectangles which contain the corresponding point in the multi-dimensional space.

Although matching can be clearly performed by sequentially checking all selections defined in conditions of rules, this process can be very inefficient when large numbers of rules are defined. However, if we view matching from the geometric perspective outlined above, spatial indexing techniques, such as multi-attribute index trees, can be used to efficiently identify satisfied conditions. Multi-attribute indexing methods are discussed in detail in [SAME90]; they include the R-tree [GUTT84], the R^+-tree [SELL87], the k-D-B-tree [ROBI81], and others. The ideal candidate for predicate indexing should be able to accommodate point as well as regional data, and should allow dynamic insertion and deletion of data. The most promising method suggested up to this point has been Guttman's R-trees and its variants. In the following sections we use R-trees to design predicate indexes and discuss their performance. An example of a 2-dimensional R-tree and the corresponding rectangles are shown in Figure 2.

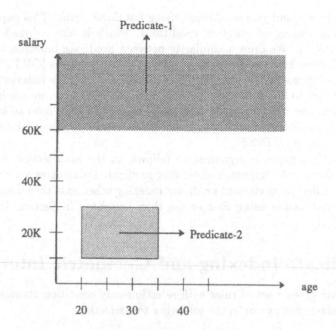

Figure 1: Mapping predicates to geometric areas

Another significant advantage of using indices lies in the capability they offer in processing queries on the rule base itself. For example, questions of the form

Give me all the rules that apply on employees older than 55

can be easily answered using an index (an overlap query). Supporting rule base queries is very important in the design of expert database systems; they can provide information on the effect of various rules, even if data that satisfy the conditions of the rules *has not* already been inserted into the database. Notice that this is not possible in systems, such as POSTGRES, where rule information is stored together with the actual data [STON88].

3 Predicate Indexing Algorithms

The problem we are addressing in this work is the design of predicate indexing schemes for a given set of rules. An indexing scheme includes the partitioning of the attributes used in rule conditions to sets, and the creation of a multi-dimensional indexing structure for each of these sets. A closely related problem is the index-selection problem in physical database design for relational database systems [FINK88]. Given a set of tables and a set of statements, together with their expected frequencies of use, the *index-selection problem* involves selecting for each table

- the ordering rule for the stored records (which determines the clustered index, if any), and

- a set of nonclustered indices,

so as to minimize the total processing cost, subject to a limit on total index space. It has been proven that the index-selection problem is in the class of NP-hard problems

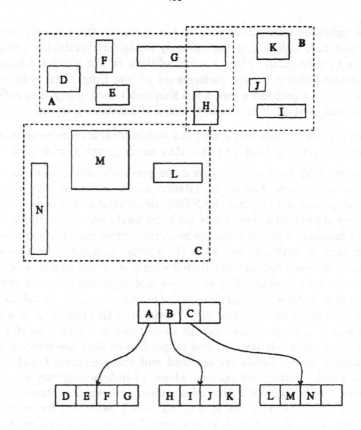

Figure 2: Some rectangles and their corresponding 2-dimensional R-tree

[COME78]. Therefore, there appears to be no fast algorithm that will find the optimal solution. However, by an appropriate use of some heuristics, combined with more exact techniques, it is possible to find a set of *reasonable solutions* quickly as suggested in [COME78].

Although the problem of designing predicate indexes is similar to the index-selection problem, they differ in the following respects:

- Predicates are static since they correspond to rules, not data. As a result, the cost of creating and updating indices for predicates is less important in the predicate indexing problem. The most important issue is search performance.

- Multi-attribute indexing is of major concern in predicate indexing while it is normally ignored in the index-selection problem.

- Queries to traditional database systems are dynamically created. A particular set of indices selected may be good for some queries, but may be terrible for some other queries. That is why frequencies of use of typical queries are so important in the index-selection problems. On the contrary, there is only one major query to a predicate indexing system, namely finding all qualifying predicates for any update to a relation. Thus, a good solution to the predicate indexing problem can almost guarantee good performance all the time. This is in contrast to the index-selection problem where a less frequently used query may suffer badly with a bad configuration of indices in traditional database systems.

- Range queries are normally considered non-indexable in index-selection, but are so common in predicate indexing that they are of primary consideration.

Alternatives that have been proposed for predicate indexing in database systems include sequential search, hashing on relation name combined with sequential search, physical locking, and the IBS-tree [HANS90]. Sequential search is an obvious choice for small numbers of predicates, but clearly performs badly when the number of predicates is large. When hashing on relation name is used, the system maintains one list of predicates for each relation. It performs well when the average number of predicates per relation is small, and the predicates are distributed evenly over the relations. Physical locking depends heavily on the availability of indices and degenerates into a sequential search when there are no indices, or a large number of predicate clauses are defined on attributes which do not have an index [STON88]. Finally, the IBS-tree is an augmented binary search tree which allows indexing intervals as well as point data. One IBS-tree is needed for each attribute in a relation. To find all predicates that are satisfied by a tuple, all IBS-trees defined on a relation are searched and the predicates found to satisfy all of them are isolated. This is one extreme where all indices only use one attribute. The other extreme is to build a multi-dimensional index tree which contains all attributes in a relation. This is the approach analyzed in [STON87]. Searching for matching predicates is easier because only one tree needs to be searched and no merging is necessary. However, the performance of the index tree can be poor due to the overhead of building indices of high dimensionality. This issue is further discussed in Section 4.

A better solution is to build a set of multi-dimensional index trees which can give optimal performance given a set of predicates, thus avoiding the disadvantages of the above two extreme methods. Each multi-dimensional index is defined on a set of attributes involved in rule conditions. Hereafter, we call these sets *partitions*. It is clear that the predicate indexing problem is also an NP-Complete problem; this can be proven by showing that it is a special case of the "Minimum Sum of Squares" problem [GARE79]. Therefore, it is not practical to try to solve the problem by exhaustive search. In [SELL91], we demonstrate how the problem can be mapped to a space search problem and how an A^* search algorithm over that space can be used to solve the problem. The output of the algorithm is a pair $(\mathcal{P}, \mathcal{N})$ where

$\mathcal{P}$ is a set of partitions created, and
$\mathcal{N}$ is a set of attributes which will not be indexed.

All attributes found in selection predicates are either in $\mathcal{P}$ or in $\mathcal{N}$. Each partition in $\mathcal{P}$ is a set of attributes which are to be used to build a multi-dimensional index tree. For example, if a partition contains the set $\{A_1, A_2, A_3\}$, a 3-dimensional index tree T will be created using A_1, A_2 and A_3. If an attribute A is in set $\mathcal{N}$, that means that A will not be considered in any index tree; every predicate which contains A has to check the selection condition on A separately, if the rest of the conditions of the predicate are satisfied by the rest of the attributes.

In [SELL91] we give the details of the index-selection algorithm and discuss several heuristics to reduce its execution cost. These details are outside the scope of this paper. Instead, we concentrate in the next section on evaluating the performance of alternative indexing schemes.

4 Using the R-tree for Predicate Indexing

We have conducted an experimental study to demonstrate the importance of the predicate indexing problem and the advantages of using an adaptive system, instead of one of the two extremes mentioned in Section 3. Depending on the cost model used, many criteria can be used to compare the performance of different algorithms. We chose to use the CPU time used as the basis for performance comparison. In the case where predicate indexing is assumed to be done in main memory, this can be very valuable. If secondary storage is required to store predicates, the number of disk accesses may be a better performance indicator; we record this number also in our experiments.

In all the experiments, a series of N predicates were created, where N is between 1,000 and 10,000. A fraction a of predicates were simple ones of the form $attribute = constant$ (i.e. zero length intervals), and the remaining fraction $1-a$ were non-zero length intervals. The points and interval boundaries were drawn randomly from a uniform distribution of integers between 1 and 10,000. The length of the intervals was drawn randomly from a uniform distribution of integers between 1 and 1,000. The values of a tested are 0, 0.5 and 1. After all predicates had been inserted, 100 points were randomly generated and the time to search the corresponding indices was measured. For range queries, the interval boundaries of a search region were generated the same way as with predicates. In each of the figures shown in the following, the y-axis shows the search time in seconds for 100 point or range queries, and the x-axis is the number of predicates indexed. Equivalently, the y-axis is the average search time in 0.01 seconds for each search. The selectivity, i.e. the fraction of predicates matching a single attribute, is roughly 0.05, 0.02 and 0.001 for a equal to 0, 0.5 and 1, respectively. The cost of merging results of searches (i.e. intersecting results in the case of multiple index searches) depends on the algorithm used for intersection and the number of rules that qualified, which in turn depends on the selectivity. For simplicity, the merge cost is ignored for a equal to 1 since the corresponding selectivity is very small. The merge cost is set to 0.5 milliseconds and 0.2 milliseconds per 1000 predicates indexed for a equal to 0 and 0.5, respectively, based on the experiments run. All tests were performed on a DECstation 2100 workstation.

The following sub-sections present the results of our experiments.

4.1 Overhead of Dummy Ranges

As illustrated in Figure 1, and for Predicate-1, if an attribute is not used by a predicate in the R-tree, the range $[-\infty, \infty]$ is used as the interval for the corresponding dimension, in order to satisfy any query on that attribute (in the example the attribute age). In the rest of this paper, the $[-\infty, \infty]$ range is called the "dummy" range. Also, R-trees with one dimensional data are denoted as 1-d R-trees, and similarly R-trees with k dimensional data are referred to as k-d R-trees.

In our first experiment, a 1-d R-tree storing single attribute conditions was generated as described above. To test the overhead of the R-trees with dummy ranges, k-d R-trees

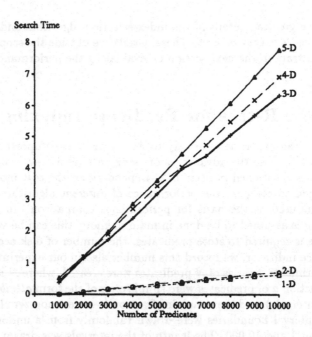

Figure 3: Overhead of dummy ranges (range predicates) – Point Queries

were generated by augmenting the 1-d R-tree with a range $[-\infty, \infty]$ for each additional dimension, where $2 \leq k \leq 5$.

Figure 3 shows the performance of R-trees in various dimensions. The value of a is set to 0 in Figure 3, which means all predicates are non-zero length intervals. Similarly, Figure 4 shows the same comparison with a equal to 1 where all predicates are point intervals. Search time in Figure 4 is clearly smaller than that in Figure 3 which is expected since the selectivity for a equal to 1 is much lower than that for a equal to 0. The search time is lower because the number of tree nodes that need to be searched is smaller for lower selectivity. Another experiment was to test the performance of R-trees for range queries. Figure 5 shows the result of this comparison using the same parameters as in Figure 3 except that the search data used are range queries which are randomly generated. It is clear that range queries are slightly more expensive than point queries, but the relative performance of the R-trees in different dimensions is similar to that for point queries.

In summary, an R-tree with dimension greater than 2 does not perform well and the search time needed grows almost in proportion to the number of predicates indexed. A similar result can be obtained when comparing the number of disk pages accessed. We can thus conclude that the R-tree has a very large overhead when dummy ranges are used in higher dimensions. Therefore, when most predicates use few attributes in a relation, building an R-tree using all attributes in the relation, i.e. the second extreme case [STON87], is definitely a bad idea.

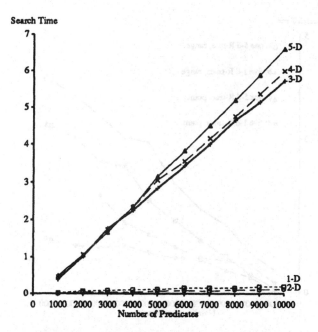

Figure 4: Overhead of dummy ranges (point predicates) – Point Queries

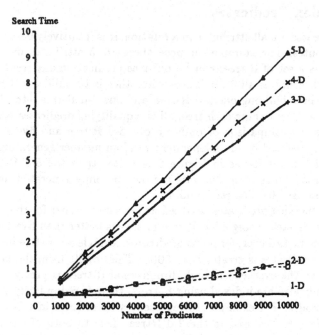

Figure 5: Overhead of dummy ranges (range predicates) – Range Queries

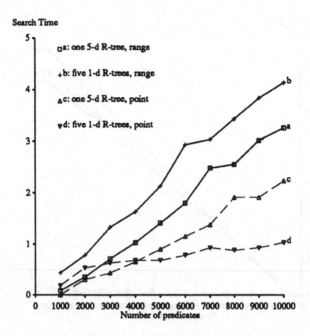

Search Time

□a: one 5-d R-tree, range

+b: five 1-d R-trees, range

▲c: one 5-d R-tree, point

▼d: five 1-d R-trees, point

Number of predicates

Figure 6: 5-d R-tree vs. 5 1-d R-trees – Point Queries

4.2 Complex Predicates

When all predicates use all attributes in a relation, it is intuitively best to build an R-tree using all attributes. For example, suppose there are 5 attributes in a relation. There are several ways a set of R-trees can be built as predicate index trees. One is to build an R-tree which contains all 5 attributes, the other is to build five 1-d R-trees. Other possibilities include building one 2-d R-tree and one 3-d R-tree, etc. If more than one R-tree is built, after searching each tree, all the qualifying predicates need to be merged. Figure 6 shows the comparison of building one 5-d R-tree and five 1-d R-trees. Each dimension was generated by an independent random number generator. Notice that the performance of the 5-d R-tree in Figure 6 is better than the 5-d R-tree in Figures 3 and 4, as expected, since each attribute is now randomly generated, unlike the infinite (dummy) ranges used for Figures 3 and 4.

The cost of merging predicates is added as described earlier for the 1-d case in Figure 6. For range predicates, a single 5-d R-tree is always better than five 1-d R-trees, as can be seen in Figure 6. However, for point predicates, a single 5-d R-tree is not as good when the number of predicates is greater than 5000. This results from the fact that when the selectivity is low, the overhead of high dimensional R-trees is pretty high. In addition, when point predicates are indexed using R-trees, there is redundancy in the information stored in tree nodes. For example, to represent a point (x,y) in a 2-dimensional space, the rectangle (x,y,x,y) is used in the 2-d Rtree. Due to both of the above reasons, it is not always true that a single n-d R-tree is better than n 1-d R-trees, even when all

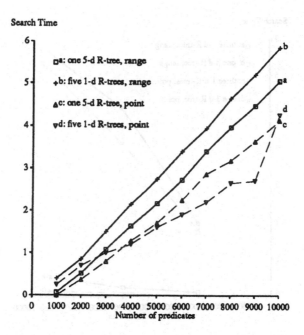

Figure 7: 5-d R-tree vs. 5 1-d R-trees – Range Queries

predicates use all attributes. A similar result for range queries is shown in Figure 7.

4.3 Simple Predicates

When every predicate uses **only one** attribute in a relation, intuitively the best way is to build one index tree per attribute. Clearly no merging is needed in this case. Figure 8 compares the performance of 1-d and 3-d R-trees under this condition, with the assumption that the number of predicates using each attribute is the same. The x-axis shows the total number of predicates indexed, in other words, it is three times the number of predicates indexed in each 1-d R-tree. For example, suppose 9000 predicates are to be indexed. Three 1-d R-trees are constructed, each with 3000 predicates. Another 3-d R-tree is created which contains all 9000 predicates. The first 3000 predicates use the first attribute, the other two attributes are padded by $[-\infty, \infty]$. Similarly, the second and third 3000 predicates use the second and third attribute respectively with the other attributes padded with dummy ranges. It is clear from Figure 8 that a single 3-d R-tree is always worse than three 1-d R-trees, which agrees with our intuition. Figure 9 compares the performance of two 1-d R-trees and one 2-d R-tree. Again, 1-d R-trees are better in this case. The performance of the 2-d R-tree in Figure 9 is much worse than that of Figures 3 and 4. This is because the first attribute is always checked first in R-trees and since there are many predicates with dummy ranges as their first attributes in this experiment, the overlapping is too high.

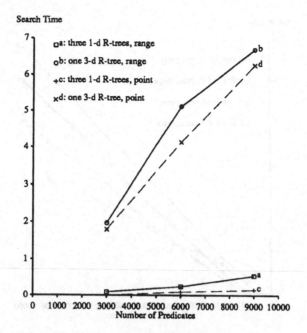

Figure 8: One attribute per predicate: 1-d vs. 3-d

4.4 A Mixed Case

A more complex and practical example follows: suppose there are 5 attributes in a relation, and there are 2000 predicates which contain one attribute each. Another 2000 predicates contain 3 attributes each, and another 2000 predicates contain all 5 attributes. There are several ways we can build a set of R-trees as predicate index trees for these 6000 predicates. Among others:

1. Build five 1-d R-trees for the first 2000 predicates, each containing 400 predicates, ten (i.e. the number of ways to select 3 attributes out of 5) 3-d R-trees for the second 2000 predicates, each containing 200 predicates, and one 5-d R-tree for the last 2000 predicates.

2. Build one 5-d R-tree for all 6000 predicates.

3. Build one 1-d R-tree on each attribute. Each R-tree will have 6000 predicates.

4. Build five 1-d R-trees for the first 2000 predicates, each containing 400 predicates, and one 5-d R-tree for the remaining 4000 predicates.

5. Build five 1-d R-trees for the first 2000 predicates, each containing 400 predicates, one 5-d R-tree for the second 2000 predicates, and another 5-d R-tree for the last 2000 predicates.

6. Build three 5-d R-trees for the first, second, and third 2000 predicates.

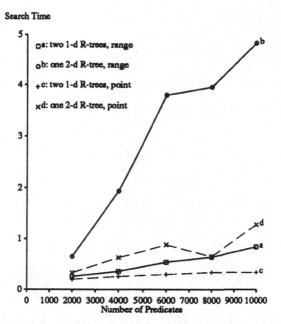

Figure 9: One attribute per predicate: 1-d vs. 2-d

Except for the third method which needs merging of predicates after searching the R-trees, all other methods are set up in a way such that a predicate will only appear in one R-tree, so no merging is necessary. Figure 10 shows the search time in seconds for 100 point queries using each method. Method 3, which uses five 1-d R-trees for all predicates, is the worst, even before adding the merge cost in Figure 10. The best method is Method 5 in which a 5-d R-tree is built for the second 2000 predicates separately. Method 4 is about the same as Method 1. It is clear that the best way to index the second 2000 predicates is to build a 5-d R-tree. A single 5-d R-tree (Method 2) is not good because of the overhead of dummy ranges. For the first 2000 predicates, the best method is to build one 1-d R-tree for each attribute. Method 6 is also not that good because a 5-d R-tree is used, with a large overhead of dummy ranges for the first 2000 predicates. The number of total disk accesses is shown in Figure 11. The y-axis is the total number of disk accesses in 10K for 100 point queries. The pattern is very similar to Figure 10 except that Method 1 is slightly better than Method 4 in Figure 11.

This experiment shows that if predicates can be partitioned into groups according to their characteristics, such as sharing of attributes, it is easier to choose the best indexing method for each group separately. For example, there are three groups in the example above and the best method is to build independent R-trees for each group, as in Method 5.

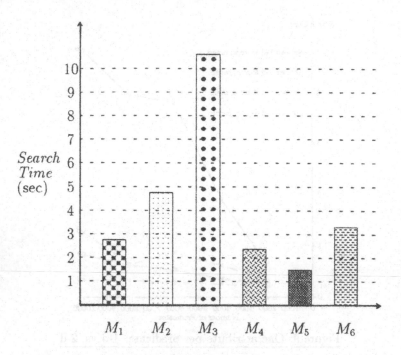

Figure 10: <u>Mixed case: Search time</u>

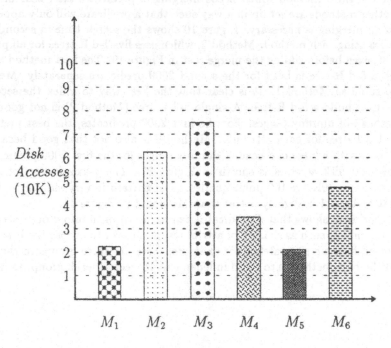

Figure 11: <u>Mixed case: Disk accesses</u>

4.5 Summary of the Experiments

We have conducted several experiments using R-trees to index selection predicates. Based on the results we obtained in these experiments, we conclude the following:

- The R-tree is designed to be a height-balanced tree, similar to the B-tree, which is suitable for spatial data objects in multi-dimensional spaces. However, for large amounts of data and dimensions higher than 2, the performance is not good enough for predicate indexing as observed in our experiments.

- Analysis of the R-tree and its variants is a very hard problem and the only work we have seen so far on this topic is in [FALO87]. Most papers only provide empirical results, as we have done in this paper. However, experiments have been previously reported only for 2-dimensional data. Our experiments show that the performance of the R-tree deteriorates in higher dimensions which has never been studied before. Improvements to the R-tree, such as the R^+-tree [SELL87], claim to perform better than R-tree by eliminating overlapping rectangles in intermediate nodes of the tree (R^+-tree) or using special optimization techniques to minimize the area, margin and overlap of each enclosing rectangle in the directory (R*-tree). However, experimental results in higher dimensions for these improvements are not available.

- If a predicate does not use all attributes in an R-tree, dummy ranges $[-\infty, \infty]$ need to be used for missing attributes. Our experiments show that the overhead associated with dummy ranges is very high. When a dummy range is used for the first attribute, the overhead is even higher. Whether R^+-trees or R*-trees can do better under this condition is interesting and should be examined.

- Because of the poor search performance of the R-tree in high dimensions, sometimes the intuition of index selection is not always correct, e.g. a single n-d R-tree is not always better than n 1-d R-trees even when all predicates use all attributes, as shown in Figure 6 and 7.

- Partitioning the predicates is also very important, as can be seen in Figures 10 and 11. Therefore, good algorithms need to be developed to decide on these partitions; the algorithm of [SELL91] is a first step in this direction.

5 Conclusions

In this paper we studied the problem of predicate indexing in database rule systems. First, we showed how this problem can be mapped to a geometric problem and suggested the use of multi-attribute indexing techniques to support efficient condition monitoring. We then presented empirical results using the R-tree as a predicate indexing structure. One of the advantages of using R-trees, or its variants, is that the structures support dynamic insertion and deletion, which therefore makes the addition of new or deletion of old rules very easy to handle. The results of our study can be used in developing algorithms for multi-attribute index design to support predicate indexing.

Currently, we are looking into the performance of the R^+-tree, the R*-tree and other spatial indexing techniques to see if they could substitute the R-tree for more efficient predicate indexing. We are also investigating the problem of integrating predicate indexing with a prototype rule-system implemented on top of a relational DBMS [SELL89b].

References

[COME78] D. Comer. The Difficulty of Optimum Index Selection. *ACM Transactions on Database Systems*, 3(4):440–445, December 1978.

[FALO87] C. Faloutsos, T. Sellis, and N. Roussopoulos. Analysis of Object Oriented Spatial Access Methods. In *Proceedings of the ACM-SIGMOD International Conference on the Management of Data*, pages 426–439, 1987.

[FINK88] S. Finkelstein, M. Schkolnick, and P. Tiberio. Physical Database Design for Relational Databases. *ACM Transactions on Database Systems*, 13(1):91–128, March 1988.

[FORG81] C. L. Forgy. OPS5 User's Manual. Technical Report CMU-CS-81-135, Dept. of Computer Science, Carnegie-Mellon University, Pittsburgh, PA, July 1981.

[FORG82] C. L. Forgy. Rete: A Fast Algorithm for the Many Pattern/Many Object Pattern Match Problem. *Artificial Intelligence*, 19:17–37, 1982.

[GARE79] M. R. Garey and D. S. Johnson. *Computers and Intractability: A Guide to the Theory of NP-Completeness*. W. H. Freemand and Company, New York, 1979.

[GUPT86] A. Gupta. *Parallelism in Production Systems*. PhD thesis, Department of Computer Science, Carnegie-Mellon University, March 1986.

[GUTT84] A. Guttman. R-Trees: A Dynamic Index Structure for Spatial Searching. In *Proceedings of the ACM-SIGMOD International Conference on the Management of Data*, pages 47–57, 1984.

[HANS90] E. N. Hanson, M. Chaabouni, C.-H. Kim, and Y.-W. Wang. A Predicate Matching Algorithm for Database Rule Systems. In *Proceedings of the ACM-SIGMOD International Conference on the Management of Data*, pages 271–280, Atlantic City, NJ, May 1990.

[LIU68] C. L. Liu. *Introduction to Combinatorial Mathematics*. McGraw-Hill Book Company, New York, 1968.

[ROBI81] J. T. Robinson. The K-D-B Tree: A Search Structure for Large Multidimensional Dynamic Indexes. In *Proceedings of the ACM-SIGMOD International Conference on the Management of Data*, 1981.

[SAME90] H. Samet. *The Design and Analysis of Spatial Data Structure*. Addison-Wesley Publishing Company, Inc., 1990.

[SELL87] T. Sellis, N. Roussopoulos, and C. Faloutsos. The R$^+$-tree: A Dynamic Index for Multi-Dimensional Objects. In *Proceedings of the 13th International Conference on Very Large Data Bases*, Brighton, England, 1987.

[SELL89a] T. Sellis. *Special Issue on* Rule Management and Processing in Expert Database Systems. *SIGMOD Record*, 18(3), September 1989.

[SELL89b] T. Sellis, L. Raschid, and C.-C. Lin. Data Intensive Production Systems: The DIPS Approach. In [SELL89a].

[SELL91] T. Sellis and C.-C. Lin. A Study of Predicate Indexing for DBMS Implementations of Production Systems. Technical Report, Dept. of Computer Science, University of Maryland, College Park, MD, February 1991.

[STON87] M. Stonebraker, T. Sellis, and E. Hanson. An Analysis of Rule Indexing Implementations in Database Systems. In *Expert Database Systems: Proceedings From the First International Conference*, pages 465–476. Benjamin/Cummings Publishing Company, Inc., Menlo Park, CA, 1987.

[STON88] M. Stonebraker, E. N. Hanson, and S. Potamianos. The POSTGRES Rule Manager. *IEEE Transactions on Software Engineering*, 14(7):897–907, July 1988.

Database Support
for
Problematic Knowledge

W. Kießling[1] ,   H. Thöne[2] ,   U. Güntzer[2]

[1] Institut für Informatik,   [2] Wilhelm-Schickard-Institut,
Technische Universität München,   Universität Tübingen,
Orleansstr. 34, 8000 München 80, FRG   Sand 13, 7400 Tübingen 1, FRG
wk@informatik.tu-muenchen.de   {thoene|guentzer}@informatik.uni-tuebingen.de

Abstract

Recently substantial research efforts have been spent on extending database technology in various ways towards a better support of applications of the nineties. In contrast, the tough problems of adding the right uncertainty reasoning capabilities have received relatively modest attention despite evident importance. Among the many faces of uncertainty we focus on what we call problematic knowledge, which is - e.g. - inherent in what-if decision scenarios. Based on a rule calculus with probability intervals introduced lately [GKT 91] we show how to do rule chaining under independence and how to add comparative probability. Also a method for reasoning with uncertain facts, founded on the notions of maximal context and detachment, is given. Full database support can be given to the calculus. We discuss some aspects of the optimization problem and how to deliver uncertainty reasoning to the user's application by interoperability in a heterogeneous database environment.

1. Introduction

Database systems have been successful over the years for applications requiring deductive capabilities on completely specified knowledge domains. Founded on the principles of classical logic, SQL or extended declarative DB-languages like DATALOG could be seen to be appropriate. However, when it comes to deal with not so well-behaved knowledge, like uncertain or imprecise knowledge, DB-technology currently lacks to offer almost any support. Many researchers, trying out to extrapolate future demands on advanced DB-functionality, have identified this deficiency (see e.g. [Lag 90], [LKM 90]). If we look across the rim of databases towards the AI shore, we see a quite substantial number of approaches to this very complex and complicated subject. At the moment a variety of proposals exist, such as fuzzy sets, Dempster-Shafer theory, modal logics, Bayesian networks or probabilistic logics, only to name a few ([KSH 91]). Within the DB-community there are currently only a few exceptions, e. g. [BMP 90] and [SSGKAB 89]. In our opinion this will have to improve, if DB-technology still should be considered as an attractive delivery vehicle for many forthcoming challenging applications. Important social or commercial application areas like medical information systems, environmental planning, technical and financial risk assessment (e. g. credit approval or portfolio management in banking) or biological applications could benefit a lot, provided future DB-systems offer the right functionality and performance. Among the many faces of uncertainty and vagueness, we want to focus on uncertainty reasoning for -what we call- problematic knowledge. Hereby, we are typically confronted with uncertain, but at the same time incomplete and often highly subjective information. Expert systems in such fields are often used to give decision support based on what-if scenarios.

The rest of this paper is organized as follows. Section 2 confronts the DB-folks with surprising phenomena from the world of uncertainty and discusses a new probabilistic rule calculus to cope with this kind of problems. Section 3 then is concerned with the problem how to include factual knowledge into the probabilistic reasoning process. We introduce an inference rule called detachment within a maximal context and demonstrate its usefulness. Thereafter, in section 4 various implementation and optimization issues are explored, including direct utilization of deductive DB-technology and cooperative solutions in an interoperable DB-environment. Finally, section 5 summarizes our results and outlines areas for future work.

2. Probabilistic Reasoning with Rules

2.1 Reasoning Phenomena under Uncertainty

At first glance, familiar reasoning paradigms from certain knowledge domains seem to carry over to uncertainty. Conclusions look quite convincing in many cases. However, this is sometimes more coincidentally than due to the soundness of the reasoning process. To give a brief idea to the unfamiliar reader, we shall pick out a few characteristic examples subsequently. (Moreover we encourage the reader to try out his/her favorite uncertainty reasoning methods against these examples.)

The problem of correct rule chaining:

Example (Barking cats)
For illustrative purpose, assume that 70% of all domestic animals are dogs and 90% of all dogs can bark:

$$domestic\_animals \xrightarrow{0.7} dogs$$
$$dogs \xrightarrow{0.9} bark$$

Putting these assumptions together by multiplying certainties, as many expert systems do, we may come to the conclusion that 63% of all domestic animals can bark. This seems to be true. But now consider the following situation:

$$cats \xrightarrow{1.0} domestic\_animals$$
$$domestic\_animals \xrightarrow{0.63} bark$$

With the same naive chaining method we come to the conclusion that 63% of all cats can bark, what is obviously strange.

Aspects of non-monotonicity:

Example (Drunk or Injury) (cf. [Pea 88])
Consider the following story:

> When I saw that Jack cannot walk straight (A),
> I thought he was drunk (B).
> However, upon noticing his blood stained shirt (C),
> I realized it was a different matter (D).   ("explaining away")

The **causal diagram** in figure 1 reflects this situation of non-monotonicity by "explaining away" (arrows indicate causal relationships).

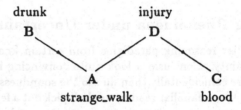

Figure 1: Non-monotonic reasoning (explaining away)

A general inference mechanism must be able to cope with these phenomena. Doing so, no implicit assumptions by the system should be allowed for whatever reasons. This issue is very critical, if the knowledge is not only **uncertain**, but likewise **incomplete** and even coming from **subjective** sources. We call this class of knowledge **problematic** and will focus on it throughout. Many commercially and socially important applications are of this type, medical diagnosis being a prominent representative.

2.2   The New Probabilistic Calculus

The early expert system shells employing ad hoc reasoning mechanisms for uncertainty turned out to be dead-end lanes after some initial successes. Consequently approaches relying on well-established theories like probability theory began to gain more interest. Besides, newer investigations revealed that "probabilistic inference is epistemologically

adequate to perform important kinds of reasoning humans are capable of " ([Hen 86]).
An orthogonal point of view concerns fundamental design decisions made by most expert
system shells. There, the inference mechanisms rely on various implicit assumptions like
independence of events or complete information. Obviously, this is a problematic way to
go in particular for applications with problematic knowledge. The incomplete nature of
this kind of knowledge is very sensitive to any kind of unwarranted information and thus
might produce completely unjustified or wrong results. (Just think about risk assessment
in nuclear power plants.) This means that to construct a general reliable system, one has
to pursue a **cautious** approach: only knowledge explicitly entered must be used during
the uncertain inference process [1]. Below we give a brief review of our cautious approach
to problematic knowledge as presented first in [GKT 91].

Definition 2.1 (Conditional probability)

*Let A, B be sets of events and let AB denote the intersection of A and B. The conditional
probability of B given A is defined as*

$$P(B|A) = \frac{P(AB)}{P(A)}, \quad if \quad P(A) > 0.$$

The equivalent rule-based interpretation is: $A \xrightarrow{P(B|A)} B$
That is $P(B|A)$ among the events in A are also events in B. If we have both $A \xrightarrow{x} B$
and $B \xrightarrow{y} A$, we also write $A \underset{y}{\overset{x}{\longleftrightarrow}} B$.
Since precise conditional probabilities are often hard to get or not available, working with
intervals makes much more sense in practice:

Definition 2.2 (Uncertain rule)

*Let $C_1, C_2, \ldots, C_k$ be the set of events. C_l and its complement $\overline{C_l}$, $1 \leq l \leq k$, are called basic
events. We consider conjunctive events $A = A_1 \cdots A_n$, $B = B_1 \cdots B_m$, where $n, m \geq 1$
and A_i, B_j are basic events, and $P(A) > 0$. An uncertain rule consists of an upper and
a lower bound for a conditional probability:*

$$A \xrightarrow{x_1, x_2} B \quad iff \quad 0 \leq x_1 \leq P(B|A) \leq x_2 \leq 1.$$

If lower and upper bound coincide we simply write $A \xrightarrow{x} B$.

The **axioms** of the calculus are given by a collection $\mathcal{R}$ of uncertain rules, respecting
the Kolmogorov axioms of probability theory. The advantage of this purely axiomatic
approach is that both main interpretations of probability are supported [KSH 91]: **Objective** probability is interpreted as relative frequency in the long run. In the context
of building expert systems **subjective** probabilities as personal degree of confirmation is
often more relevant. Our approach supports even both interpretations occurring within
a single application, e.g. think about stock market decisions.

---

[1]These design principles were applied first in the INFERNO system [Qui 83].

Given a knowledge base for an application involving uncertainty in form of such axioms $\mathcal{R}$ among a set of events $C_1, \ldots, C_k$, we want to draw other uncertain conclusions, not explicitly listed in $\mathcal{R}$. This is accomplished by a collection of **inference rules**, which achieve to combine few pieces of influence into new evidence.

Definition 2.3 (Inference mechanism)
Let $\mathcal{R}$ be a set of uncertain rules, A and B be conjunctive events.

$$\mathcal{R} \vdash A \xrightarrow{x_1, x_2} B \quad \text{iff} \quad A \xrightarrow{x_1, x_2} B \text{ can be generated, given } \mathcal{R}, \text{ by the}$$
following inference rules in a finite number of steps.

Inference Rules [2]

(A, B, C and D denote conjunctive events, F denotes a basic event.)

(I1) **Chaining (C):**

(a) $\{A \xrightarrow{x_1, x_2} FC, A \xrightarrow{y_1, y_2} \overline{F}C\} \vdash A \xrightarrow{z_1, z_2} C, \; z_1 = x_1 + y_1, \; z_2 = \min(1, x_2 + y_2)$

(b) $\{A \xrightarrow{x_1, x_2} BC\} \vdash A \xrightarrow{x_1, 1} C$

(c) $\{A \xrightarrow{x_1, x_2} BC, C \xrightarrow{y} B\} \vdash A \xrightarrow{z_1, z_2} C,$

$$z_1 = \begin{cases} 0 & \text{if } y = 0 \\ x_1 & \text{if } y = 1 \end{cases} \qquad z_2 = \begin{cases} 0 & \text{if } y = 0 \\ x_2 & \text{if } y = 1 \end{cases}$$

(d) $\{A \xrightarrow{x_1, x_2} BC, A \xrightarrow{y} B\} \vdash A \xrightarrow{z_1, z_2} C,$

$$z_1 = \begin{cases} 0 & \text{if } y = 0 \\ x_1 & \text{if } y = 1 \end{cases} \qquad z_2 = \begin{cases} 0 & \text{if } y = 0 \\ x_2 & \text{if } y = 1 \end{cases}$$

(I2) **Sharpening (S):**

$\{A \xrightarrow{x_1, x_2} B, A \xrightarrow{y_1, y_2} B\} \vdash A \xrightarrow{z_1, z_2} B, \; z_1 = \max(x_1, y_1), \; z_2 = \min(x_2, y_2)$

(I3) **Conjunction left (CL):**

$\{A \xrightarrow{x_1, x_2} B, x_1 > 0, A \xrightarrow{y_1, y_2} BC\} \vdash AB \xrightarrow{z_1, z_2} C, \; z_1 = \frac{y_1}{x_2}, \; z_2 = \min(1, \frac{y_2}{x_1})$

(I4) **Conjunction right (CR):**

$\{A \xrightarrow{x_1, x_2} B, AB \xrightarrow{y_1, y_2} C\} \vdash A \xrightarrow{z_1, z_2} BC, \; z_1 = x_1 \cdot y_1, \; z_2 = x_2 \cdot y_2$

(I5) **Weak conjunction left (WCL):**

$\{A \xleftarrow{x_1, x_2} B, x_1 > 0, B \xrightarrow{y_1, y_2} C\} \vdash AB \xrightarrow{z_1, z_2} C,$

$$z_1 = \max(0, \frac{x_1 + y_1 - 1}{x_1}), \; z_2 = \min(1, \frac{y_2}{x_1})$$

(I6) **Weak conjunction right (WCR):**

(a) $\{A \xrightarrow{x_1, x_2} B, A \neq C\} \vdash A \xrightarrow{0, x_2} BC$

---

[2](C) and (WCR) are generalizations and (CRN) is added compared to [GKT 91].

(b) $\{A \xrightarrow{x_1, x_2} B, B \xrightarrow{y} C, A \neq C\} \vdash A \xrightarrow{z_1, z_2} BC,$

$$z_1 = \begin{cases} 0 & \text{if } y = 0 \\ x_1 & \text{if } y = 1 \end{cases} \qquad z_2 = \begin{cases} 0 & \text{if } y = 0 \\ x_2 & \text{if } y = 1 \end{cases}$$

(I7) Negation (N):

$$\{A \xrightarrow{x_1, x_2} F\} \vdash A \xrightarrow{z_1, z_2} \overline{F}, \; z_1 = 1 - x_2, \; z_2 = 1 - x_1$$

(I8) Conjunction right with negation (CRN):

$$\{A \xrightarrow{x_1, x_2} C, A \xrightarrow{y_1, y_2} FC\} \vdash A \xrightarrow{z_1, z_2} \overline{F}C,$$
$$z_1 = \max(0, x_1 - y_2), \; z_2 = \max(0, x_2 - y_1)$$

(I9) Weak conjunction right with negation (WCRN):

$$\{A \xleftarrow[v_1, v_2]{u_1, u_2} F, \; v_1 > 0, \; F \xleftarrow[y_1, y_2]{x_1, x_2} C, \; y_1 > 0, \; A \neq C\} \vdash A \xrightarrow{z_1, z_2} \overline{F}C,$$
$$z_1 = 0, \; z_2 = \min\left(1, (1 - y_1) \cdot \frac{u_2 \cdot x_2}{v_1 \cdot y_1}\right)$$

(I10) Annulment (A):

$$\{A \xleftarrow{}_{0} B, A \xrightarrow{x_1, x_2} B\} \vdash A \xrightarrow{0} B$$

We denote all uncertain rules that can be generated out of a set of axioms $\mathcal{R}$ by applying these inference rules as **deduced rules**. Already deduced rules can be used as premises for deducing further rules. As shown in [GKT 91], deduced rules are sound within the laws of probability.

Example (Drunk or Injury) (continued)
Suppose we know the following uncertain rules:

$$\mathcal{R} = \{A \xleftarrow[0.8]{0.9} B, A \xleftarrow[0.3]{0.1} D, C \xleftarrow[0.9]{0.95} D\}$$

(1) Event A is observed first: As $A \xrightarrow{0.9} B$ and $A \xrightarrow{0.1} D$, B (Jack is drunk) obviously is a more probable explanation than D.

(2) Now events A and C are observed together: By deduction within the calculus we get [3]:

$$\mathcal{R} \vdash AC \xrightarrow{0.76, 1.0} D$$
$$\mathcal{R} \vdash AC \xrightarrow{0.0, 1.0} B$$

Thus, D (Jack is injured) is a more probable explanation now, explaining B away. If we knew additionally $C \xrightarrow{0.1} B$, then with $\mathcal{R} \cup \{C \xrightarrow{0.1} B\} \vdash AC \xrightarrow{0.0, 0.47} B$ explanation D would gain even more credit relatively to B.

---

[3] For the interested reader the deduction steps are given in [KTG 91].

2.3 Conditional Independence

One of the critical knowledge engineering tasks in developing uncertainty applications is concerned with the acquisition of numerical data; in our case the interval estimates for base rules. For domains with objective probabilities classical statistics can be applied (sampling). In case of subjective probabilities or when sampling is not feasible, expert opinions have to be acquired. So far we have neglected one rich source of statistical information, namely independence information.

Definition 2.4 (Conditional independence)
A is independent of C under condition B, denoted $I(A, B, C)$, iff $P(A|BC) = P(A|B)$.

As the calculus does not make any implicit independence assumptions, we have to enter such information explicitly in the form of triples $I(A, B, C)$. Conditional independence information is included into the inference process by adding the following two sound rules to the basic calculus:

(I11) Invariance (I):

$$\text{(a)} \quad \{ B \xrightarrow{x_1, x_2} C, \, I(A, B, C) \} \;\vdash\; AB \xrightarrow{x_1, x_2} C$$

$$\text{(b)} \quad \{ AB \xrightarrow{x_1, x_2} C, \, I(A, B, C) \} \;\vdash\; B \xrightarrow{x_1, x_2} C$$

A third sound inference rule is gained as follows: If $B \xrightarrow{1} A$, then $B \subseteq A$ and hence $AB = B$. Therefore $P(C|AB) = P(C|B)$ for some C, implying $I(C, B, A)$.

(I12) Independence (IND): $\{ A \xleftarrow{\quad} {}_1 B, \, B \xrightarrow{x} C \} \;\vdash\; I(A, B, C)$

In [GKT 91] we have stated a general rule chaining theorem, which has to be used if no other correlation information is available. If conditional independences are known, rule chaining can be specialized and produces tighter intervals.

Lemma 2.5 (Rule chaining under independence)
Let A and C be conjunctive events, B be a basic event,

$$\mathcal{R} = \{ A \xrightarrow{u} B, \, B \xrightarrow{x} C, \, \overline{B} \xrightarrow{y} C, \, I(A, B, C), \, I(A, \overline{B}, C) \}.$$

Then

$(RCI1) \quad \mathcal{R} \;\vdash\; A \xrightarrow{w} C, \, w = u \cdot x + (1 - u) \cdot y$

$(RCI2) \quad \mathcal{R} \cup \{ w > 0 \} \;\vdash\; AC \xrightarrow{z} B, \, z = \dfrac{u \cdot x}{w}$

Proof: (By deduction in the calculus)

$(1) \quad \{ A \xrightarrow{u} B \} \;\vdash_{\scriptscriptstyle N}\; A \xrightarrow{a_1} \overline{B}, \, a_1 = 1 - u$

$(2) \quad \{ B \xrightarrow{x} C, \, I(A, B, C) \} \;\vdash_{\scriptscriptstyle I}\; AB \xrightarrow{x} C$

$(3) \quad \{ \overline{B} \xrightarrow{y} C, \, I(A, \overline{B}, C) \} \;\vdash_{\scriptscriptstyle I}\; A\overline{B} \xrightarrow{y} C$

(4) $\{A \xrightarrow{u} B, AB \xrightarrow{x} C\} \overset{|}{\underset{CR}{\vdash}} A \xrightarrow{a_2} BC, a_2 = u \cdot x$

(5) $\{A \xrightarrow{a_1} \overline{B}, AB \xrightarrow{y} C\} \overset{|}{\underset{CR}{\vdash}} A \xrightarrow{a_3} \overline{B}C, a_3 = a_1 \cdot y$

(6) $\{A \xrightarrow{a_2} BC, A \xrightarrow{a_3} \overline{B}C\} \overset{|}{\underset{C}{\vdash}} A \xrightarrow{w} C, w = a_2 + a_3$

(7) $\{A \xrightarrow{w} C, w > 0, A \xrightarrow{a_2} BC\} \overset{|}{\underset{CL}{\vdash}} AC \xrightarrow{z} B, z = \frac{a_2}{w}$

The last two derived uncertain rules make up $(RCI1)$ and $(RCI2)$. ∎

Example (Metastatic cancer) (cf. [Spie 86])
Metastatic cancer is a possible cause of a brain tumor and is also an explanation for increased total serum calcium. In turn, either of these could explain a patient falling into a coma. Severe headache is also possibly associated with a brain tumor. Figure 2 shows the diagram representing these causal influences among others.

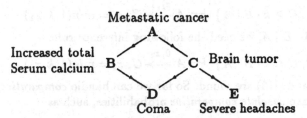

Figure 2: Causal diagram for metastatic cancer

These influences are expressed in terms of conditional probabilities and additional independences:

$$\mathcal{R} = \{A \xrightarrow{0.8} B, A \xrightarrow{0.2} C, BC \xrightarrow{0.8} D, \overline{B}C \xrightarrow{0.8} D, B\overline{C} \xrightarrow{0.8} D, \overline{B}\,\overline{C} \xrightarrow{0.05} D,$$
$$C \xrightarrow{0.8} E, \overline{C} \xrightarrow{0.6} E, I(A, BC, D), I(A, \overline{B}C, D), I(A, B\overline{C}, D), I(A, \overline{B}\,\overline{C}, D),$$
$$I(A, C, E), I(A, \overline{C}, E), I(B, A, C), I(\overline{B}, A, C)\}$$

With the rule chaining lemma 2.5 we can directly deduce:

$$\{A \xrightarrow{0.2} C, C \xrightarrow{0.8} E, \overline{C} \xrightarrow{0.6} E, I(A, C, E), I(A, \overline{C}, E)\} \overset{|}{\underset{RCII}{\vdash}} A \xrightarrow{0.64} E$$

For the more complicated conclusion $A \xrightarrow{?} D$, applying inference rules I, N, CR, C properly we get the sharp result $A \xrightarrow{0.68} D$. (See [KTG 91] for detailed inferences.)

2.4 Further Extensions of the Calculus

Absolute probabilities:

Let Ω be the so-called **frame of discernment**, which contains all events of interest for a particular application. Hence Ω has the properties $P(\Omega) = 1$ and $A \cup \overline{A} = \Omega$ for all events $A \subseteq \Omega$. Since $P(A|\Omega) = \frac{P(A\Omega)}{P(\Omega)} = P(A)$, we can model absolute probabilities by conditional probabilities.

We extend the calculus by admitting absolute probabilities $\xrightarrow{x_1, x_2} A$ with the interpretation $x_1 \leq P(A) \leq x_2$. The following inference rule does the proper transformation to the familiar uncertain rules.

(I13) Absolute probabilities: $\xrightarrow{x_1, x_2} A \vdash \Omega \xleftarrow[1]{x_1, x_2} A$

Comparative probabilities:

Sometimes no numerical values for uncertain events are at hand, but only comparative information like "under condition A, event C is at least twice as likely as event B" is known (see also [Rim 90]). We extend the calculus by admitting statements of the form $P(C|A) \geq k \cdot P(B|A)$, which will be denoted by

$$C \geq k \cdot B \mid A \quad , \quad \text{for some parameter } k \epsilon I\!\!R^+.$$

The appropriate inference rule is:

(I14) $\{A \xrightarrow{x_1, x_2} B, C \geq k \cdot B \mid A\} \vdash A \xrightarrow{z_1, 1} C,\ z_1 = min(1, k \cdot x_1)$

If we state $C \leq k \cdot B \mid A$, we need the following inference rule:

(I15) $\{A \xrightarrow{x_1, x_2} B, C \leq k \cdot B \mid A\} \vdash A \xrightarrow{0, z_2} C,\ z_2 = min(1, k \cdot x_2)$

Obviously (I14) and (I15) are sound. So far we can handle *comparative conditional* probabilities. If we have *absolute comparative* probabilities, such as

$$C \geq k \cdot B, \text{ with the interpretation "C is at least k times as likely as B",}$$

we can employ the same trick as before, rewriting this into $C \geq k \cdot B \mid \Omega$.

Due to space limitations we cannot compare our approach here to other proposals coming from AI, most of which have serious problems when dealing with problematic knowledge. So we have to refer the interested reader to [KTG 91].

3. Probabilistic Reasoning with Facts

We have developed a calculus for managing uncertain rules so far. This section extends it by introducing a mechanism to combine uncertain *rules* and individual *facts* stored in a database. To draw our attention to the main issues, let us start with a well-known example from default logic (see e. g. [Rei 80]).

Example (Penguin triangle)
Suppose we have the predicates *penguin*, *bird* and *fly* with the following uncertain rules and (certain) facts:

Uncertain rules: $penguin \xrightarrow{1.0} bird$ Facts: $bird(Ted)$,

$bird \xrightarrow{0.9} fly$ $bird(Tweety), penguin(Tweety)$,

$bird \xrightarrow{0.01} penguin$ $bird(Sam), \overline{penguin(Sam)}$

$penguin \xrightarrow{0.0} fly$

We might ask whether individual Ted, Tweety or Sam can fly?

The fact $bird(Ted)$ refers to an individual bird, namely Ted, while we talk about a set of birds in the given uncertain rules. It may be that Ted is an ostrich and cannot fly, or that Ted is an eagle with good flying abilities, but we don't know that for sure. Because of the non-monotonic nature of probabilistic reasoning we can not jump to any conclusions about Ted or another individual unless we know the maximal context for that individual.

Definition 3.6 (Maximal context)
Let t be an individual. The maximal context $C[t]$ of t is defined as

$$C[t] \;=\; \bigwedge_{\substack{A \text{ is predicate} \\ \text{with } A(t) \,\epsilon\, DB}} A.$$

Informally, the maximal context of an individual t can be defined to accumulate everything known in the database concerning t. For instance, $C[Ted] = bird$, $C[Tweety] = bird \wedge penguin$ and $C[Sam] = bird \wedge \overline{penguin}$. If this knowledge is fragmentary, i.e. incomplete, then of course the maximal context must be incomplete, too. However, if we learn somehow additional information about an individual we are due to include it to the maximal context.

Although rules can be applied to facts to deduce new facts by modus ponens in classical logic, probability theory does not posses an equivalent inference mechanism to combine particular facts and uncertain rules. The straightforward generalization $\{A(t), A \xrightarrow{x_1,x_2} B\}$ $\vdash \xrightarrow{x_1,x_2} B(t)$ is not sound. A counter-example is: $\{\, bird(Tweety), bird \xrightarrow{0.9} fly \,\} \vdash \xrightarrow{0.9} fly(Tweety)$. Therefore we define a new inference rule to assign probabilities to conclusions about individuals within their maximal context.

Definition 3.7 (Detachment)
Let $C[t]$ be the maximal context of an individual t, B be a conjunctive event. The detachment rule is an inference rule defined by:

$$\{\, C[t] \xrightarrow{x_1,x_2} B \,\} \;\underset{D}{\vdash}\; \xrightarrow{x_1,x_2} B(t)$$

The interpretation of $\xrightarrow{x_1,x_2} B(t)$ is that the fact $B(t)$ for individual t is concluded to hold with a probability between x_1 and x_2. Thus, the detachment rule plays the role of the classical modus ponens. For a given individual the premise can be detached from an uncertain rule, provided the premise is equal to the maximal context.

$$\{\, C[Ted] \xrightarrow{0.9} fly \,\} \qquad \underset{D}{\vdash} \quad \xrightarrow{0.9} fly(Ted)$$
$$\{\, C[Tweety] \xrightarrow{0.0} fly \,\} \qquad \underset{D}{\vdash} \quad \xrightarrow{0.0} fly(Tweety)$$
$$\{\, C[Sam] \xrightarrow{0.91} fly \,\} \qquad \underset{D}{\vdash} \quad \xrightarrow{0.91} fly(Sam)$$

The boundaries in the uncertain rules are computed as described previously. Expectedly we conclude that Ted can fly with a probability of 90%. The property "penguin" reduces our belief in Tweety's flying to 0, while we are due to believe that Sam is a little bit more likely to fly than Ted, i.e. we get a probability of 91% for his flying ability, because we know that he is not a penguin being unable to fly.

The detachment rule provides features that extend the usual framework known from reasoning with defaults [GePe 90] and for Bayesian networks [Pea 88]. On the one hand large fact and rule bases can be utilized and on the other hand conclusions can be quantified numerically.

Although the maximal context depends on given facts, it doesn't depend on facts that are deducible from the rules in a logical sense. Suppose we have a fact $A(t)$ and a rule $A \xrightarrow{1} B$, it is sufficient to show that for an uncertain rule $A \xrightarrow{z_1, z_2} C$ we get:

$$A \xrightarrow{z_1, z_2} C \quad \text{iff} \quad AB \xrightarrow{z_1, z_2} C$$

Thus the deducible certain fact $B(t)$ is not relevant for the detachment process. The proof of the equivalence is listed in [KTG 91].

Example (Blood test) (cf. [Hen 86])

Assume that James is engaged to be married, and takes the routine pre-married blood test. To his horror, the test comes back positive for Aids. His physician explains to him that the test is very reliable having a false positive rate of 1%.

Fortunately, James' fiancee, Alice, is not only understanding, but finds out from the physician that the prevalence of Aids among men from James' intercourse is about 1 in 10000. Based on this, she decides to go ahead with the wedding.

Alice's decision can be justified within the given context. It is assumed that a positive test result is independent from being not in a risk group given that Aids isn't supposed. With the abbreviations NR for "no risk" and TP for "test positive" we have:

$$\text{Uncertain rules:} \quad \overline{Aids} \xrightarrow{0.01} TP \qquad \text{Facts:} \quad TP(James),$$
$$NR \xrightarrow{0.0001} Aids \qquad \qquad NR(James)$$
$$\text{Independences:} \quad I(NR, \overline{Aids}, TP)$$

Deduction within the calculus yields:

(1) $\{ NR \xrightarrow{0.0001} Aids \} \vdash_{N} NR \xrightarrow{0.9999} \overline{Aids}$

(2) $\{ \overline{Aids} \xrightarrow{0.01} TP, I(NR, \overline{Aids}, TP) \} \vdash_{I} NR\,\overline{Aids} \xrightarrow{0.01} TP$

(3) $\{ NR \xrightarrow{0.9999} \overline{Aids}, NR\,\overline{Aids} \xrightarrow{0.01} TP \} \vdash_{CR} NR \xrightarrow{0.009999} \overline{Aids}\,TP$

(4) $\{ NR \xrightarrow{0.0001} Aids \} \vdash_{WCR} NR \xrightarrow{0.0, 0.0001} Aids\,TP$

(5) $\{ NR \xrightarrow{0.0, 0.0001} Aids\,TP, NR \xrightarrow{0.009999} \overline{Aids}\,TP \} \vdash_{C} NR \xrightarrow{0.009999, 0.010099} TP$

(6) $\{ TP \xleftarrow{0.009999, 0.010099} NR, NR \xrightarrow{0.0001} Aids \} \vdash_{WCL} TP\,NR \xrightarrow{0.0, 0.01} Aids$

(7) $\{ C[James] = TP\,NR, TP\,NR \xrightarrow{0.0, 0.01} Aids \} \vdash_{D} \xrightarrow{0.0, 0.01} Aids(James)$

Surprisingly, considering the maximal context correctly James' risk can be assessed to drop from 99% to below 1% for having Aids.

Summarizing, detachment within a maximal context is a reliable and extremely useful way to infer uncertain facts about individuals in problematic domains.

4. Implementation Issues

4.1 The DUCK approach

The calculus has been designed with the intention to directly exploit deductive database technology for the complicated inference processes.

The result of the knowledge acquisition process is a set of axioms $\mathcal{R}$ as described previously. $\mathcal{R}$ plus the set of sound inference rules can be mapped straightforwardly into a $DATALOG^{fun+set}$ rule program ([CGT 89], [Ull 89]). For this purpose we define five base relations as follows:

$$br(A, B, X1, X2) \quad :\Longleftrightarrow \quad A \xrightarrow{X1, X2} B \in \mathcal{R}$$

$$br2(A, X1, X2) \quad :\Longleftrightarrow \quad \xrightarrow{X1, X2} A \in \mathcal{R}$$

$$ir(A, B, C) \quad :\Longleftrightarrow \quad I(A, B, C) \in \mathcal{R}$$

$$con(C, \theta, k, B, A) \quad :\Longleftrightarrow \quad C \, \theta \, k \cdot B | A \in \mathcal{R} \text{ where } \theta \in \{\leq, \geq\}$$

$$bar(C, Cbar) \quad :\Longleftrightarrow \quad Cbar = \overline{C}, C \text{ is a basic event.}$$

Deduced uncertain rules and facts are implemented by virtual relations:

$$dr(A, B, X1, X2) \quad :\Longleftrightarrow \quad \mathcal{R} \vdash A \xrightarrow{X1, X2} B$$

$$df(B, t, X1, X2) \quad :\Longleftrightarrow \quad \{C[t] \xrightarrow{X1, X2} B\} \vdash_{D} \xrightarrow{X1, X2} B(t)$$

Then dr can be defined by a (nonlinearly) recursive $DATALOG^{fun+set}$ program as given in [GKT 91]. For the calculus extensions, the mapping is achieved as follows:

(I13) $dr(\Omega, A, X1, X2) \quad \leftarrow \quad br2(A, X1, X2).$
         $dr(A, \Omega, 1, 1) \quad \leftarrow \quad br2(A, X1, X2).$
(I14) $dr(A, C, Z1, 1) \quad \leftarrow \quad dr(A, B, X1, X2), con(C, \theta, K, B, A),$
                              $\theta = '\geq', Z1 = \min(1.0, K \cdot X1).$

The remaining inference rules can be treated similarly.

The gross system architecture, named DUCK (Deduction with UnCertain Knowledge) was given in [GKT 91], where we have already pointed out some optimizations applicable to this complex rule program. Here we will elaborate the chances that the possibly huge deduction space can be pruned intelligently by goal-directed deduction. Let us study an example for goal-directed deduction.

Example (Sunburn) (cf. [Mor 89])
Suppose it is Saturday and you work in a windowless office. You look forward to going to a baseball game later. If it rains, there is a 95% chance that the game will be cancelled

and otherwise it is certain that the game will be played. You assume that it is cloudy 10% of the time. Clouds cause rain 60% of the time and rain cannot occur if clouds are absent. *Question 1*: Will the game be rained out?

Now suppose a somewhat unreliable rain alarm sounds in your office and you wish to determine a revised probability of rain. Experience with the alarm tells you that the probability of the alarm sounding when there is rain is 0.8, but 4% of the time the alarm will sound falsely. *Question 2*: How are the chances for the game now?

Later that afternoon your son calls you on the telephone. He is reluctant to discuss the weather, but insists on spending the night with his nearby aunt. After consenting, you muse over the conversation, remembering that he tends to visit her only when he has something to hide. You know that he is at the local beach. If it is sunny, it is 70% probable he will have a sunburn, but if it is cloudy, there is only a 10% chance that he will have a sunburn. You estimate that he would certainly visit his aunt if he is sunburned, while the probability that he would visit her otherwise is only 2%. *Question 3*: How does this new evidence affect the ball game?

The full scenario is depicted in the causal diagram of figure 3.

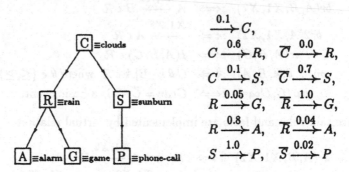

Figure 3: Causal influences and uncertain rules

Question 1:

$$\{ \xrightarrow{0.1} C, C \xrightarrow{0.6} R, \overline{C} \xrightarrow{0.0} R \} \qquad \underset{RC11}{\vdash} \xrightarrow{0.06} R$$

$$\{ \xrightarrow{0.06} R, R \xrightarrow{0.05} G, \overline{R} \xrightarrow{1.0} G \} \qquad \underset{RC11}{\vdash} \xrightarrow{0.94} G \blacksquare$$

Question 2:

$$\{ \xrightarrow{0.06} R, R \xrightarrow{0.8} A, \overline{R} \xrightarrow{0.04} A \} \qquad \underset{RC12}{\vdash} A \xrightarrow{0.56} R$$

$$\{ A \xrightarrow{0.56} R, R \xrightarrow{0.05} G, \overline{R} \xrightarrow{1.0} G, I(A,R,G), I(A,\overline{R},G) \} \quad \underset{RC11}{\vdash} A \xrightarrow{0.47} G \blacksquare$$

Question 3:

$$\{ C \xrightarrow{0.1} S, S \xrightarrow{1.0} P, \overline{S} \xrightarrow{0.02} P, I(C,S,P), I(C,\overline{S},P) \} \quad \underset{RC11}{\vdash} C \xrightarrow{0.12} P$$

$$\{ \overline{C} \xrightarrow{0.7} S, S \xrightarrow{1.0} P, \overline{S} \xrightarrow{0.02} P, I(\overline{C},S,P), I(\overline{C},\overline{S},P) \} \quad \underset{RC11}{\vdash} \overline{C} \xrightarrow{0.71} P$$

$$\{ \xrightarrow{0.1} C, C \xrightarrow{0.12} P, \overline{C} \xrightarrow{0.71} P \} \qquad \underset{RC12}{\vdash} P \xrightarrow{0.02} C$$

$$\{ P \xrightarrow{0.02} C, C \xrightarrow{0.6} R, \overline{C} \xrightarrow{0.0} R, I(P,C,R), I(P,\overline{C},R) \} \quad \underset{RC11}{\vdash} P \xrightarrow{0.01} R$$

$$\{P \xrightarrow{0.01} R, \; R \xrightarrow{0.8} A, \; \overline{R} \xrightarrow{0.04} A, \; I(P,R,A), \; I(P,\overline{R},A)\} \;\; \underset{\text{RCI2}}{\vdash} \;\; AP \xrightarrow{0.18} R$$

$$\{AP \xrightarrow{0.18} R, \; R \xrightarrow{0.05} G, \; \overline{R} \xrightarrow{1.0} G, \; I(AP,R,G), \; I(AP,\overline{R},G)\} \;\; \underset{\text{RCI1}}{\vdash} \;\; AP \xrightarrow{0.83} G \; \blacksquare$$

The same numbers as in [Mor 89] are deduced, where a Bayesian network was used to solve the problem [4].

It is conspicuous that a low amount of inferences needs to be executed only and that only two simple corollaries are required to do the job. It is an open research problem currently, how to detect such situations, where the deduction space can be narrowed down by proper selection of inference rules. Provided that proper pruning heuristics can be discovered, the DBA*-algorithm ([SKGB 89]) is conjectured to be efficient in a DB environment.

4.2 Interoperability

Facts about individuals are stored in databases or other data repositories, often in a heterogeneous environment. Therefore, to determine the maximal context of an individual requires to issue a query against heterogeneous databases in general. This intern suggests to construct a system based on *interoperability* ([IMS 91], [KLK 91]) between cooperative, but mostly autonomous sites. Figure 4 shows how one might envision a future development environment for applications with problematic knowledge, including components for knowledge acquisition.

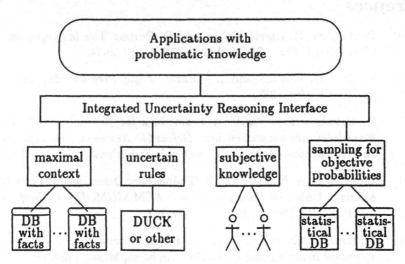

Figure 4: Uncertainty reasoning and interoperability

---

[4]Therefore many independence assumptions had to be enforced implicitly by the Bayesian network; some of them show up in our inferences as needed.

5. Summary and Outlook

We have presented a sound uncertainty calculus particularly suited for reasoning in problematic domains. Founded on a cautious approach to uncertain inference, only knowledge entered explicitly into the system is used. The expressiveness of the user interface comprises conditional probability rules allowing intervals, conditional independence, comparative and absolute probabilities, conjunctive and negated events. Though we are able to give a direct implementation of the full calculus with deductive DB-technology, the overall performance problem is largely unsolved right now. Though not discussed here related approaches from expert systems, experimenting with operations-research methods, exhibit only initial successes either. But we are guardedly optimistic that one eventually can come up with viable optimizations for practical demands, the thrust being on discovering proper heuristics to prune the deduction space through sloppy-delta iteration ([SKGB 87]). Furthermore, we demonstrated how to incorporate factual knowledge by detachment. As an appropriate architecture for complex uncertainty applications we favor interoperability in a heterogeneous DB-environment (instead of building one monolithic super-DB). The design of an integrated user interface for conventional and uncertain reasoning with a familiar look and feel to the average DB-programmer is a further next step to accomplish.

References

[BMP 90] D. Barbara, H. Garcia-Molina and D. Porter: The Management of Probabilistic Data. *Proc. EDBT*, Venice, 1990, pp. 60-74.

[CGT 89] S. Ceri, G. Gottlob and L. Tanca: *Logic Programming and Databases.* Springer-Verlag, 1989.

[GePe 90] H. Geffner and J. Pearl: A Framework for Reasoning with Defaults. In *Knowledge Representation and Defeasible Reasoning*, H. Kyburg, R. Loui and G. Carlson (eds.), Kluer Academic Publishers, 1990, pp. 69-87.

[GKT 91] U. Güntzer, W. Kießling and H. Thöne: New Directions for Uncertainty Reasoning in Deductive Databases. *Proc. ACM SIGMOD Int. Conf. on Management of Data*, Denver, 1991, pp. 178-187.

[Hen 86] M. Henrion: Should we use probability in uncertain inference systems. *Proc. Cognitive Science Society Meeting*, Amherst, Mass., 1986, pp. 320-330.

[IMS 91] 1st International Workshop on Interoperability in Multidatabase Systems, Kyoto, April 7-9, 1991.

[KLK 91] R. Krishnamurthy, W. Litwin, W. Kent: Language Features for Interoperability of Databases with Schematic Discrepancies. *Proc. ACM SIGMOD Int. Conf. on Management of Data*, Denver, 1991, pp. 40-49.

[KSH 91] R. Kruse, E. Schwecke and J. Heinsohn: *Uncertainty and Vagueness in Knowledge Based Systems.* Springer-Verlag, 1991.

[KTG 91]   W. Kießling, H. Thöne and U. Güntzer: Database Support for Problematic
            Knowledge. *Technical Report TUM-I9109*, Institut für Informatik, Techni-
            sche Universität München, June 1991.

[Lag 90]   Lagunita Beach Report: Database Systems: Achievements and Opportu-
            nities. Report of the *NFS Invitational Workshop on Future Directions in
            DBMS Research*, Palo Alto, Febr. 1990.

[LKM 90]   P.C. Lockemann, A. Kemper and G. Moerkotte: Future Database Technol-
            ogy: Driving Forces and Directions. *Lecture and Notes in Computer Science
            No. 466, Database Systems of the 90s*, A. Blaser (ed.), Springer-Verlag, 1990,
            pp. 15-33.

[Mor 89]   P. Morawski: Understanding Bayesian Networks. *AI Expert*, 1989, pp. 44-48.

[Pea 88]   J. Pearl: *Probabilistic Reasoning in Intelligent Systems*. Morgan Kaufmann,
            San Mateo, 1988.

[Qui 83]   J.R. Quinlan: INFERNO: A cautious approach to uncertain inference. *The
            Computer Journal 26*. 1983, pp. 255-269.

[Rei 80]   R. Reiter: A logic for default reasoning. *Artificial Intelligence 13*, 1980, pp.
            81-132.

[Rim 90]   M. v. Rimscha: The Determination of Comparative and Lower Probability.
            "Uncertainty in Knowledge-Based Systems". Workshop at the FAW in Ulm
            1990, FAW-B-90025, Vol.2, pp. 344-376.

[SKGB 89]   H. Schmidt, W. Kießling, U. Güntzer and R. Bayer: DBA*: Solving Combi-
            natorial Problems with Deductive Databases. *Proceedings GI/SI-conference
            on "Datenbanksysteme in Büro, Technik und Wissenschaft"*, Zürich, 1989.

[SKGB 87]   H. Schmidt, W. Kießling, U. Güntzer and R. Bayer: Compiling Exploratory
            and Goal-Directed Deduction into Sloppy Delta-Iteration. *4th IEEE Symp.
            on Logic Programming*, San Francisco, 1987, pp. 234-243.

[SSGKAB 89] H. Schmidt, N. Steger, U. Güntzer, W. Kießling, R. Azone and R. Bayer:
            Combining Deduction by Certainty with the Power of Magic. *Proceedings
            First Int. Conf. on Deductive and Object-Oriented Databases*, Kyoto, 1989,
            pp. 205-224.

[Spie 86]   D.J. Spiegelhalter: Probabilistic Reasoning in Predictive Expert Systems.
            In *Uncertainty in Artificial Intelligence*, L.N. Kanal and J.F. Lemmer (ed.),
            Elsevier Science Publishers B.V., North Holland, 1986, pp. 47-68.

[Ull 89]   J. Ullman: *Principles of Database and Knowledge-Base Systems*. Vols. 1,2,
            Computer Science Press, New York, 1989.

A Knowledge-Based Approach to Statistical Query Processing[1]

Carla BASILI°, Roberto BASILI^, Leonardo MEO-EVOLI°

°) Istituto di Studi sulla Ricerca e Documentazione Scientifica (ISRDS)
   Consiglio Nazionale delle Ricerche (CNR) / Via C. de Lollis 12 / 00185-ROMA (Italy)
^) Dipartimento di Ingegneria Elettronica
   Università di Roma II 'Tor Vergata' / Via O. Raimondo / 00173-ROMA (Italy)

Key-words: Statistical Data Modelling, Query Processing, Statistical Data Manipulation, Knowledge Bases

Abstract

Representation of statistical data is achieved by means of complex data structures. Such a complexity transfers directly to statistical data manipulations. Furthermore, the most meaningful statistical indicator resides in complex data structures. Our work is focused on simplifying manipulations of statistical data structures by means of StEM (Statistical database Expert Manager), a knowledge-based kernel. StEM acts as a deductive query processor between a high level query language and the set of low level DBMS primitives required for query resolution. StEM contains a Prolog knowledge base that provides transparency of complex data manipulations, allowing a real conceptual interaction with a statistical database.

1. Introduction

A computational aspect of the decision-making process is statistical data analysis, which requires a set of elementary activities, such as: collection of relevant data, production of indicators representing trends in phenomena, transformation of indicators into forms which can be more easily and significantly used, comparison of real trends with estimated and projected trends and, lastly, evaluation aimed at producing a range of alternative choices and cost-benefit analysis.

---

1 This work has been partially supported by CNR under project MULTIDATA

background notions. Section 4 describes some fundamental concepts which constitute the foundation of our query processing mechanism. Section 6 shows a Prolog query processor prototype. The last section provides an example of a user session.

2. Guide-lines for our proposal

In order to simplify manipulations of statistical data structures we developed StEM (Statistical database Expert Manager), a knowledge-based module acting as a deductive query processor between a high level query language Staquel* [Me] and a set of DBMS primitive. The focal points of our StEM design are described in the following.

KNOWLEDGE-BASED QUERY PROCESSING

The final goal of our work is to achieve the *transparency* of aggregate data manipulations. Transparency refers to the capability of freeing the user from the burden of algorithmic details, thus allowing high level manipulation. Henceforth, we will call query the user formulation of an aggregate data manipulation. In fact, the resolution of a single manipulation of aggregate data involves several elementary operations and data.
Transparency is achieved by means of a query processing mechanism with the following steps:
1. *query validation* according to the applicability criteria of the manipulation with respect to the data; query validation is a syntactic and semantic analysis of the arguments explicitly expressed in the query;
2. query *feasibility verification* consisting of deduction and search for the availability in the database of data required for the query solution; the feasibility verification qualifies StEM as a problem solving system (see section 5.) guided by a specific control strategy; the result of this step is a *resolution plan* of DBMS primitives, i.e. a sequence of DBMS operations suitable combined to ensure the query solution;
3. *activation* of the resolution plan of DBMS primitives over the located data;
4. *result acquisition* of the manipulation as a new datum properly inserted within existing data definitions.
Step 4 enhances the descriptive information on statistical data; we call this step "result acquisition" since the term "learning" implies a generalisation process currently not supported by StEM.
The query validation, feasibility verification and result acquisition steps lead us to the choice of a knowledge-based mechanism for achieving transparency. Query validation and feasibility verification are not deterministic processes because they appear to be highly dependent on the current content of the statistical database when the query is activated. Therefore, a purely algorithmic approach cannot be used. More specifically:
- query validation needs knowledge of applicability criteria of manipulations and aggregate data descriptions;

Since our interest is focused on the representation and manipulation of statistical data in order to perform the above-mentioned activities, let us examine some problems in statistical data manipulation.

Statistical data exists in two forms: as elementary data recording in detail a measure of a real-world phenomenon; as aggregate data, representing indicators, i.e. synthetic information of a real-world phenomenon; aggregate data are produced by aggregation from elementary data; a typical user form of aggregate data is a statistical table, like the one shown in fig.1.a. From the point of view of statistical analysis aggregate data are the most meaningful and at the same time the most difficult structures to manipulate.

Many researchers in the area of statistical databases [Kl], [Oz], [Su], [Wo], [Jo], [Ch], [Ik], [Ta], [Gh], obtain aggregate data directly from elementary data and perform manipulations of aggregate data only when they have additive (i.e. count or sum) values. It should be noted that the user usually operates on aggregate data produced by national or international statistical bureaus and has no access to elementary data. Therefore, the need arises to manipulating aggregate data without accessing to elementary data and without limitations on the kind of data (additive or not).

Let us assume statistical data, both elementary and aggregate, are stored in a database, henceforth called "statistical database".

As an example of aggregate data let us examine the statistical table "average age of employees by economic branch and by sex" in fig. 1.a.

Average age of employees by economic branch and sex in 1985			Number of employees by economic branch and sex in 1985		
sex			sex		
economic branch	M	F	economic branch	M	F
agriculture	46,5	44	agriculture	1485	812
industry	38,5	33,9	industry	5270	1626
other activities	40,1	37,2	other activities	7232	4318
Figure 1.a			Figure 1.b		

Source: Istat,"Rilevazione delle forze di lavoro - Media 1985", Supplemento al bollettino mensile di statistica, anno 1985, n.26

Let us take the case of a user interested in knowing the distribution of "average age of employees by economic branch". The user must suppress the details determined by "sex". To solve this conceptually simple manipulation, data that are different from those shown in fig. 1.a are needed. The query solution needs, at least, the weights corresponding to each numeric entry of fig. 1.a that can be represented by another aggregate data "Number of employees by economic branch and sex in 1985" in fig. 1.b or the elementary data used for the generation of the aggregate data in fig. 1.a.

The above example shows that a single manipulation can be processed in different ways, each with its own computational cost. Furthermore, the computational details may distract the user's attention from the statistical analysis objectives.

Section 2 of this paper introduces the guide-lines of our proposal in order to achieve transparency of high level aggregate data manipulations. Section 3 illustrates the

- feasibility verification needs knowledge of the current status of the statistical database, i.e. of the context, in terms of: aggregate data descriptions, elementary data descriptions and semantic and operative relationships between data.

THE GLOBAL ARCHITECTURE OF THE SYSTEM

StEM is a query processor within the Aggregate Data Management System ADAMS [Feb]. The result of StEM activation is a plan of DBMS primitives to be executed by the DBMS in order to achieve the query resolution.

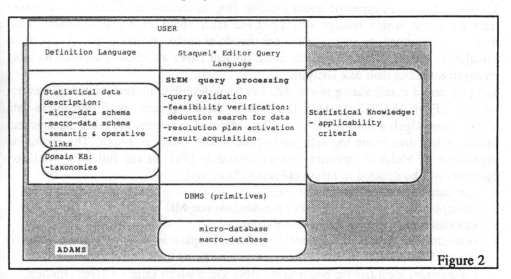

Figure 2

Our architecture splits the knowledge base into three areas: description of statistical data, representation of the application domain by means of taxonomies and reasoning through applicability criteria. Ours may be defined as a loosely coupling approach [Ce].
The concepts in figure 2 not yet defined will be discussed later on in this paper.

3.   Background

MICRO-DATA AND MACRO-DATA [WO]

A *micro-datum* (mD) is a data structure suitable for recording elementary observations. It is a linear structure consisting of an ordered set of measured properties denoted by Ai; then   mD(A1,A2,...,An) is a micro-datum scheme. All data models of DB technology are suitable for representing micro-data. For the sake of convenience, henceforth micro-data will be represented by means of Codd's Relational Model [Co]. According to this hypothesis a micro-datum is a *relation*, a micro-datum scheme is a *relation scheme,* a property is an *attribute*, each attribute varies over a *domain*.
A *macro-datum* (MD) is a data structure built up from a mD by means of an aggregate function [Oz], [Kl]. A macro-datum is a complex data structure [Ra] given by the

following constructs: a *summary attribute*, a set of *variables* (Vi), a *data type*. Each construct is related to a domain of its possible values: the summary attribute is related to a set of *summary values*; a variable is related to a set of *modalities*, a data type varies over the set {SUM, COUNT, %, ...}; the data type denotes the aggregate function generating the MD from the mD. The full cartesian product of the set of modalities of the variables is the *table space* (TS).

MACRO-DATA MANIPULATION ALGEBRA

There are two main types of transformation [Fa] of macro-data:*Table Management* transformations which enlarge or restrict the table space of a macro-datum; *Data Analysis* transformations are manipulations that do not affect the table space but perform calculations on the summary values. In the present paper attention is focused on table management rather than data analysis.

The problem of manipulating macro-data has been described in the literature by several authors ([Fab], [Kl], [Su], [Oz], [Fo], [Ra]). In the present work the micro-data manipulation algebra used is Mefisto* [Ra]. Mefisto* operators are table management operators and thus retain the data type of the macro-datum *operand*. The resolution algorithms of Mefisto* operators are expressed in [Fa]. In the following Mefisto* operators will be denoted as macro-operators. They are:

- *summarization*: eliminates a variable;
- *enlargement*: "merges" two MD's operands into one MD result;
- *extension*: adds a variable to a macro-datum;
- *restriction*: decreases the cardinality of the table space in order to focus attention on a part of the table;
- *comparison*: identifies the points in the table space which satisfy a given criterion.
- *reclassification*: replaces one variable with another.

4.   Basic concepts

This section introduces the concepts used in StEM knowledge base. The Prolog definition of the concepts introduced here is provided in section 6.

4.1.   Macro-data as a view on micro-data

A statistical database containing both elementary data and aggregate data is based on two data levels: micro-data and macro-data. A generic macro-datum can be thought of as a view on micro-data [Ba]. The macro-datum thus becomes a way of extracting information from the elementary data. In our case, however, the macro-datum schema not only defines the structure of the stored statistical data, but also lays down the micro-datum from where the macro-data is aggregated, the kind of classification of the micro-datum tuples and the aggregate function selected to generate the macro-datum itself.

For the statistical data description we choose to model:

- micro-data;
- macro-data described in terms of view on micro-data;

The result acquisition step of StEM query processing will create a new macro-datum schema together with the representation of the processed manipulation. The representation of a manipulation will be discussed in the next section.

4.2. Semantic, taxonomic and operative links

Between micro-data and macro-data structures described two main types of link are perceived [Bab]: *static* and *dynamic*. Static links support a semantic network between data; dynamic links hold between an operand and the result of a manipulation. Static links include *semantic* and *taxonomic* links; dynamic links are the *operative M-M* links.
A *semantic* link is defined between data, both micro-data and macro-data, related to the same real-world *topic*. Such links are useful in view of a semantic *navigation* through the statistical database to understand the kind of information available.
A *taxonomic* link is set up between variables which defines the intrinsic properties of the *application domain* independently of the existing statistical data (e.g. link between 'Los Angeles' city and state of 'California'). Taxonomic links actually implemented are *set-of* relationships.
An *M-M operative* link represents the manipulation which generated the MD and therefore an M-M operative link exists between two macro-data: the operand and the result of a manipulation. Such a link is represented in terms of the macro-operator expressed in the query.

4.3. Reducibility among macro-data

We decided to model links in StEM in order to define a fundamental concept: the *reducibility* of one macro-datum to another [Bab]. When the feasibility of a query is not verified with respect to a certain macro-datum operand, reducibility enables StEM to infer all usable alternative macro-data. A macro-datum MDcan is said to be reducible to a macro-datum MD if MDcan can be transformed into MD by a Mefisto* operator. More rigorously it is possible to state the following definition:

Def 1.: a macro-datum MDcan with table space TScan is said to be *reducible* to a macro-datum MD with table space TS under the following conditions:
1) MDcan and MD are generated from the same micro-datum mD
2') TScan $\supseteq$ TS   *(simple reducibility)*
     or
2") $\exists$ taxonomic links between the variables Vi of MD and Vican of MDcan such that
      Vi *set-of* Vican.   *(semantic reducibility)*
Reducibility is fundamental in our approach since most Mefisto* operators require a macro-datum of the additive data type (i.e. count or sum data type). Reducibility is used (see the query feasibility verification of section 5) when the macro-datum operand is not

additive (e.g. it has data type=%); in this case StEM will search for an additive MDcan reducible to MD.

5.   StEM Query Processing

QUERY VALIDATION

For each Mefisto* operator we found a set of applicability criteria establishing constraints in the data structure of the operand. These applicability criteria are explicitly represented in 6.

QUERY FEASIBILITY VERIFICATION

StEM can be classified as a heuristic problem solving system using a problem reduction method. The StEM reasoning is set out below.

Def 2. a *macro-data manipulation* is a mapping:

$$\Omega: \quad MD_{op} \quad \rightarrow \quad MD_{res}$$

where Ω is a macro-operator, MD_{op} is the schema of the operand macro-datum and MD_{res} is the schema of the result macro-datum.

Def 3. a *resolution plan* of a MD manipulation is an ordered set of transformations

$$C(\Omega) = \quad \{f: x \rightarrow \quad y \quad / x = mD \text{ or } x = MD \text{ and } y = MD\}$$

where each f is a DBMS primitive generating a macro-datum from the statistical database.

It should be noted that for a single statistical manipulation different sets $C(\Omega)$ may exist.

In view of the above definitions StEM query feasibility verification consists in solving the following

Problem: given a macro-datum scheme MD_{res} find the most economical sequence of primitive components to obtain it, with the following problem constraints:

-    Ω applicability criteria;
-    MD_{op} as starting schema.

The StEM reasoning process proceeds from the initial problem (the schema of the result macro-datum) until it is decomposed into sub-problems (the set of f). There may be many alternative decompositions of the problem into sub-problems.

The choice of the most economical $C(\Omega)$ is guided by the control strategy described in the next section.

CONTROL STRATEGY

Suppose $\Omega(MD) = MD_{res}$ a statistical query where:

-    Ω is a macro-operator;
-    MD is the operand schema of a macro-datum aggregated from micro-datum mD;
-    MD_{res} is the result schema.

StEM will infer the resolution plan $C(\Omega)$ as:

1. <u>direct computation of Ω on MD</u>; this happens when MD has additive data type; in this case $C(\Omega) = \{\Omega(MD)\}$;
2. <u>indirect computation of the result using aggregate data different from MD</u>; this happens when MD has not additive data type; is this case:
   2.1. StEM searches a macro-datum MDcan aggregated from the same mD and with the same table space as MD, but with additive data type; in this case $C(\Omega) = \{A_\Omega(MDcan)\}$;
   2.2. StEM searches a macro-datum MDcan aggregated from the same mD, with additive data type and reducible to MD. Two kinds of reducibility can occur:
      2.2.1. simple reducibility: in this case $C(\Omega) = \{T=restriction(MDcan), A_\Omega(T)\}$;
      2.2.2. semantic reducibility: in this case $C(\Omega) = \{T=reclassification(MDcan), A_\Omega(T)\}$;
3. <u>generation of the result accessing micro-data</u>; StEM searches the micro-datum mD; if mD exists $C(\Omega) = \{aggregate(MDres)\}$

Where:
- A_Ω are algorithms defined in [Fa] transforming the MDcan data type into MD data type and performing at the same time the macro-operator Ω; these algorithms are dependent from the macro-operator and the MD data type;
- T are intermediate results.

It should be noted that previous points are ordered steps of a single query processing control strategy, converting the feasibility of Ω into a resolution plan <u>performed by the DBMS on available data</u>.

The above query processing control strategy attempts to perform less expensive actions before those requiring more computational effort. Step 2 implies the use of the previously introduced links, both static and dynamic. These links reduce the search space of the suitable data in the database; in fact they constitute the heuristic information used by the StEM problem-solving procedure to find a solution with the minimum search effort. Following (see figure 2) the semantic and operative links in the statistical data description together with the taxonomic links in the domain knowledge, StEM limits the number of data explored in the database for the purpose of reducibility (see 4.3).

RESULT ACQUISITION

Macro-operator feasibility verification enables the system to activate the DBMS with the inferred resolution plan. At the conclusion of the query resolution the statistical database will consequently have been modified and new macro-data will have been generated. Any subsequent access to the statistical database will reap the benefit of the new situation. Maintaining an updated representation of the mD and MD thus appears to be an essential activity of StEM. The StEM result acquisition nevertheless allows the system to check the final state of the database after the macro-operators have been applied. For the representation of a manipulation the system will be able to create the result schema and the M-M operative link.

6. The representation in Prolog

In order to capture in the StEM knowledge base the taxonomies, as well as the static and dynamic aspects governing the definition and production of micro-data, it was also necessary to represent the concepts of variable, modality, primitive domains and taxonomic relations in StEM.

MICRO-DATA, MACRO-DATA AND LINKS
According to the previous definition a micro-datum may be defined as a *<Micro,Attributes>* pair where *Attributes* is the list of micro-datum attributes. Each attribute is characterized by its own primitive Domain. A micro-datum mD is thus represented by predicates of the type

(6.1.1) micro(Micro, Attributes_List)
in which each *[Attr,Domain]* element of the *Attributes_List* will be further characterized by a predicate *domain (Domain,Elements,Unit)*, describing the allowed values (*Elements*) for *Attr* and the unit of measurement (*Unit*).

Macro-data are obtained from micro-data by applying aggregate functions. An aggregate function Fa is characterized by:
- a list of attributes (*Attr*) of the micro-datum on which it acts.
- the data type (*Dt*) that it produces.

A macro-datum will thus be represented by:

(6.1.2) macro(Macro, Micro, [Attrs,Dt], Table_Space).
where: *Micro* refers to the original micro-data, *Attrs* are the attribute of mD on which Fa acts, *Dt* is the Fa data type and *Table_Space* is the list of variables pairs and their modalities *[V, Modalities]*. Each variable is related to a predicate *domain(Domain,Elements,Unit)* equivalent to that used for mD attributes.

By way of example reference may be made to a classical sample about employees of an enterprise, represented by 'People' mD and expressed by predicate

(6.1.3) micro('People', [[name, surnames], [activity, activities],
[salary, income], [sex, sexes],
[birth_day, dates]]).
where, correspondingly,

(6.1.4) domain(surnames, ['Rossi', 'Dupont', ...], _).[2]
(6.1.5) domain(activities, [lands_irrigation, ...], _).
(6.1.6) domain(income, range(50, 10000, 1), '$').
(6.1.7) domain(sexes, [m,f], _).
(6.1.8) domain(dates], range(0, ∞[3]*, 1), yy_mm_dd).*

---

2 In the formalism used, upper case terms express variables. '\==' refers to inequality and '_' (underscore) to a mute variable. Lower case terms address the elements of the language, or atoms. Square parentheses are used to represent lists of atoms, and the 'l' operator separates the first element from the remaining list. '!' avoids for alternative solutions search when satisfied [Ko].
3 ∞ is considered as the upper limit of the date.

Having to aggregate, from the mD in 6.1.3, the employees by sex and activity, and by high income and sex it is possible to represent the result macro-data

(6.1.9)   macro('employed by sex and activity', 'People',, [[], #[4]], [
[sex, sexes], [activity, activities]]).
and

(6.1.10) macro('employed by income and sex, 'People',, [[], #], [
[sex, sexes], [income, high_salary]]).
in which *sexes*, *activities*, have been defined in (6.1.6), (6.1.7), and

(6.1.11) domain(high_salary, range(5000,10000,1), '$').
defines modalities of *income* variable. For a percentage aggregation of young employees by activities and high income, we shall have a new macro-datum:

(6.1.12) macro('Young employees by activity and high salary', 'People',
[[birth_day], %], [[income, high_salary],
[activity, activities]]).
(6.1.12) represent the macro-data schema.
Semantic links are useful in the conceptual navigation through data. They are centred on the definition of topics grouping micro-data and macro-data. Semantic links can easily be declared by means of logic predicates over attributes, summary attributes, variables and domains. Taxonomic links, indeed, are able to imply reclassification. By way of example it is easy to obtain a reclassification of a MD 'average life expectancy by region' through a mapping between the 'district' variable and the 'region' one; this operation is allowed by the taxonomic link set-of existing between the involved variables, i.e. region set-of district.

QUERY VALIDATION
Macro-operators will be represented by a predicate of the arity of the operator itself:

(6.2.1)   Op(Macro1, .., MacroN, Attr1, .., AttrM)
For instance:

(6.2.2)   summarization(Macro, V)
expresses the summarization of a given macro-datum *Macro* with respect to its variable *V*. Just as

(6.2.3)   comparison(Macro1, Macro2, Op)
expresses the comparison between the instances of two operands MD (*Macro1* and *Macro2*) and the comparison criterion (*Op*).
It is possible to express an applicability criterion of a macro-operator by a rule of the type

---

4 #, +, % will represent respectively count, sum and percentage data types; it is clear that only the first two
  are additive data types.

(6.2.4) cn(*Macrooperator, Output_Parameters*) :- *{ set of necessary conditions}*
where the *Output_Parameters* are optional and depend from the Macrooperator itself.

SUMMARIZATION: summarization(Macro, V)

(6.2.5) cn(*summ(Macro, V), Macro*) :-
  macro(Macro, _, [_,Dt], Table_space),
  member([V _], Table_space),
  is_additive(Dt).
  cn(*summ(Macro, V), Macro1*) :-
  macro(Macro, _, _, Table_space),
  member([V, _], Table_space),
  to_add(Macro, Macro1).

EXTENSION: extension(Macro, V, Mod, Unit)

(6.2.6) cn(*extension(Macro, V, Mod, Unit)*) :-
  macro(Macro, Micro, _, Table_space),
  micro(Micro, Attributes),
  not(member([V_], Table_space)),
  member([V Domain], Attributes),
  in(Mod, Unit, Domain).
where *in* establishes the membership of a single modality (*Mod*) to a certain domain
description (*Domain*).

ENLARGEMENT: enlargement(Macro1, Macro2)

(6.2.7) cn(*enlargement(Macro1, Macro2*)) :-
  macro(Macro1, Micro, [_,Dt], _),
  macro(Macro2, Micro, [_,Dt], _).

RESTRICTION: restriction(Macro, V, Mod)

(6.2.8) cn(*restriction(Macro, V, Mod*)) :-
  macro(Macro, _, [_,Dt], Table_space),
  member([V, Mods], Table_space),
  in(Mod, _, Mods),
  is_additive(Dt).

COMPARISON comparison(Macro1, Macro2, Op)

(6.2.9) cn(*comparison(Macro1, Macro2, Op)*) :-
  is_boolean(Op).

RECLASSIFICATION: reclassification(Macro, V1, V2)

(6.2.10) cn(*ricl(Macro, V1, V2*)):-
  macro(Macro, _, _, Table_space),

```
member([V1,_], Table_space),
tax_rel( V2, V1, _, _ ).
```

where *tax_rel* is as in (4.2): it establishes the existence of a taxonomic link between *V1* and *V2*.

REDUCIBILITY AMONG MACRO-DATA

It is important to relate back to the definition of two fundamental concepts, i.e. simple reducibility and semantic reducibility among different macro-data.

The following definition of reducibility among macro-data may be given:

(6.3.1)
```
reduce_to( Macro1, Macro2 ) :-
        find_candidate( Macro1, Macro2),
        macro( Macro1, Micro, _, Tab_space1),
        macro( Macro2, Micro, _, Tab_space2),
        included( Tab_space1, Tab_space2).
```

where *included* is defined by:

(6.3.2)
```
included([],_).
included([[V,Modalities1]|Rest_tab_sp],Tab_space) :-
        member( [V, Modalities2], Tab_space),
        s_included( V, Modalities1, Modalities2),
        included( Rest_tab_sp, Tab_space).
included([[V,Modalities1]|Rest_tab_sp],Tab_space) :-
        member( [V2, Modalities2], Tab_space),
        tax_rel( V, V2, Modalities1, New_mods1),
        s_included( V2, New_mods1, Modalities2),
        included( Rest_tab_sp, Tab_space).
```

tax_rel detects the existence of a taxonomic link between *V* and *V2*, and consequently transforms the modalities expressing *V* (*Modalities1*) into the new (*New_mods1*),
s_included establishes the inclusion of the second argument (a set of modalities of the *V* at first argument) into the third one, *find_candidate* support the selection of likely useful (reducible) macro-data for the definitive check, avoiding useless processing.

In view of the conditions of reducibility of a macro-datum to an additive data type given in section 4.3, the definition

(6.3.3)
```
to_add( Macro, Macro1) :-
        reduce_to( Macro, Macro1),
        macro( Macro1, _, [_, Dt], _),
        is_additive( Dt).
to_add( Macro, none) :-
        macro( Macro, Micro, _,_),
        micro( Micro,_).
        % availability of microdata
```

can be accordingly given.

RESULT ACQUISITION

An M-M operative link is set up by the system between the result macro-datum and the set of operands of an operator. This link is expressed declaratively at the end of each successful resolution plan activation, by the following predicate:

(6.4.1)   op_linked(Source_Macro,Result_Macro, Macro_operator).

These links augment the representation of the micro and macro-data of new semantic contents. Subsequent queries can benefit from the inference of reducibility. Obviously this new form of knowledge is not present in the content of the statistical database but is acquired by the system from scratch. One example of inference is given by:

(6.4.2)   assert_new_macrodata(summ(Macro, V), none) :-
                new_macro(summ, Macro, V, none, Macro0),
                macro(Macro, Micro, [Attr,_], Table_space),
                member([V, Modalities], Table_space),
                retract_el([V, Modalities], Table_space, New_table_space),
                assert(macro(Macro0, Micro, [Attr,#], New_table_space)).
          assert_new_macrodata(summ(Macro, V), Macro) :-
                new_macro(summ, Macro, V, Macro, Macro0),
                macro(Macro, Micro, [Attr,Dt], Table_space),
                member([V, Modalities], Table_space),
                retract_el([V, Modalities], Table_space, New_table_space),
                assert(macro(Macro0, Micro, [Attr,Dt], New_table_space)),
                assert(op_linked(Macro, Macro0, summ(V)).
          assert_new_macrodata(summ(Macro, V), Macro1) :-
                Macro \== Macro1,
                macro(Macro1, Micro, [Attr, Dt], Table_space),
                new_macro(summ, Macro, V, Macro1, Macro0),
                member([V,Modalities], Table_space),
                retract_el([V, Modalities], Table_space, New_table_space),
                assert(macro(Macro0, Micro, [Attr,Dt], New_table_space)),
                assert(op_linked(Macro1, Macro0, summ)(V)).

where retract_el eliminates the first argument from the list appearing in the second argument, and new_macro generates the name of the result macro-data. In short, the process of analysing a manipulation is thus represented in StEM by the following rule:

(6.4.3)   process(Macro_operator) :- exists(Macro_operator), !,
          process(Macro_operator) :- cn(Macro_operator, Res), !,
                assert_new_macrodata(Macro_operator, Res).
          process(Macro_operator) :- send_error(Macro_operator).

where exists(Macro_operator) tests if the result macro-data from the application of Macro_operator has already been obtained in previous sessions.

7. User session

In the following a user session is described in order to show StEM query processing. At first the user may select the macro-data of interest and the required macro-operator (See fig. 3.a, 3.b and 3.c). This way he can control the current content of the statistical DB. Once the query validation has been verified and a name to apply to the result macro-data asked for, the system displays the data of the resolution plan inferred by the control strategy implemented by the feasibility verification. At the same time it shows the induced new links that will augment its knowledge of the statistical DB (see fig. 4). Further attempts to submit the same queries will impact on such acquired information (see Fig.5).

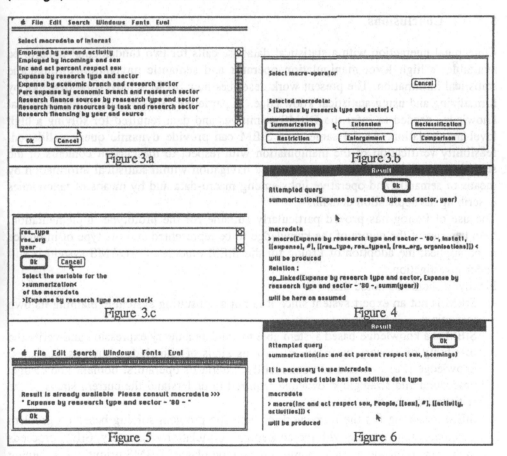

Figure 3.a

Figure 3.b

Figure 3.c

Figure 4

Figure 5

Figure 6

In fig. 7 an attempt to summarize a table is reduced to the summarization of a different table with an equivalent table space.

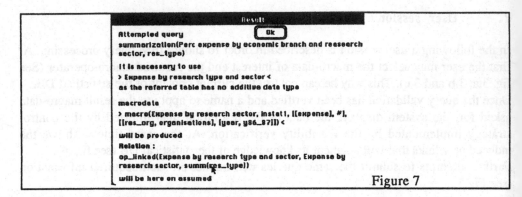

Figure 7

8. Conclusions

Conceptual interaction with a statistical database calls for two fundamental tools to be available: a high level manipulation operator and semantic navigation through the statistical information. The present work describes how StEM achieves the first tool by formalizing and using statistical knowledge. In particular, StEM contains the statistical knowledge needed to infer the DBMS primitives and data required for solving a high level manipulation. At the same time StEM can provide dynamic query validation, feasibility verification of the manipulation with respect to the current contents of the statistical database. StEM enables semantic navigation within statistical information by means of semantic and operative links among macro-data and by means of taxonomies describing the application domain.

The use of Prolog has proved particularly suitable for the prototype implementation, both because of the nature of the knowledge to be represented and the type of inference to be applied; the adoption of Prolog for the StEM module of ADAMS system is still under investigation.

Finally, it should be noted that:

- StEM is not an expert system since it is not a consulting system explaining its own reasoning;
- StEM is a knowledge-based system able to validate a query expression and verify the feasibility of a query by means of various kinds of knowledge, such as: statistical knowledge [Fa] in terms of applicability criteria of operators, domain knowledge, procedural and strategic knowledge required to understand the current status of the statistical database;
- StEM reasoning fits the framework of heuristic problem-solving based on problem decomposition: starting with the conceptual formulation of a query, StEM proceeds in the search for the most economical resolution plan of DBMS primitives, assuming as constraints the schema of the result and the current status of the database;
- StEM can be defined as a query processor inside a Statistical Database Management System, ADAMS [Feb], actually operating on computer Macintosh.

References

[Ba],   Basili, C., L. Meo-Evoli, *A statistical Knowledge Model for Aggregated Data Manipulation*, Proceedings "Eighth International Symposium Applied Informatics", Innsbruck, Austria, Feb 1990.

[Bab], Basili, C., R. Basili, L. Meo-Evoli, *A Logic-Based Knowledge Base for Statistical Table Management*, Proceedings "Ninth International Symposium Applied Informatics", Innsbruck, Austria, Feb 1991

[Ce],   Ceri, S., G. Gottlob and L.Tanca, *Logic Programming and databases*, Springer Verlag, Berlin Heidelberg, 1990

[Ch],   Chan, P., A. Shoshani, *SUBJECT: a directory driven system for organizing and accessing large statistical databases*, Proc. Very Large Data Bases Conference 1980

[Cl],   Clocksin, W.F., and C.S. Mellish, *Programming in Prolog*, Springer Verlag, 1981

[Co],   Codd, E.F., *A relational model of data for large shared data bank*, Com. ACM, Vol.13, N.6, June 1970

[Fa],   Falcitelli, G., L. Meo-Evoli, E. Nardelli, F.L. Ricci, *The Mefisto* model: an object oriented representation for statistical data management*, in Data Analysis, Learning Symbolic and Numeric Knowledge, ed. E. Diday, Nova Science Publishers, 1989

[Fab], Fortunato, E., M.Rafanelli, F.L.Ricci, *The statistical functional model for the logical representation of a statistical table*, Technical Report n. RT11/87, CNR-ISRDS, 1987

[Fe],   *The handbook of artificial intelligence, Vol. 1*, Eds. Feigenbaum, E.A. and A. Barr, William Kaufmann, 1981

[Feb], Ferri, F., P. Grifoni, L. Meo-Evoli, F.L. Ricci: *ADAMS: An Aggregate Data Management System with Multiple Interaction Techniques* Proceedings of the 2nd International Conference on Database and Expert Systems Application DEXA '91,Springer-Verlag, August 1991

[Fo],   Fortunato, E., M.Rafanelli, F.L.Ricci, A.Sebastio, *An algebra for statistical data*, Proceedings of the III° International Workshop on Statistical and Scientific Database Management, 1986

[Gh],   Ghosh, S.P., *Statistical relational table for statistical database management*, IBM Research Laboratory, San Jose, Tech. Rep. RJ 4394, 1984

[Ik],   Ikeda, H., Y. Kobayashi, *Additional facilities of a conventional DBMS to support interactive statistical analysis*, Proceeding 1st Lawrence Berkeley Laboratory Workshop Statistical Database Management, Menlo Park, Dec. 1981

[Jo],   Johnson, R., *Modelling summary data*, Proc. of "ACM SIGMOD Conference" 1981

[Kl],   Klug, A., *Equivalence of relational algebra and relational calculus query language having aggregate functions*, Journal of the ACM, Vol.29, N.3, July 1982

[Ko],   Kowalski, R., *Logic for problem solving*, Elsevier Science, 1979

[Me],   Meo-Evoli, L., *Interaction model for Man-Table Base System*, Proceedings of "Eighth International Symposium Applied Informatics", Innsbruck, Austria, feb 1990

[Oz],   Ozsoyoglu, G., Z.M. Ozsoyoglu, V. Matos, *Extending relational algebra and relational calculus with set-valued attributes and aggregate functions*, ACM Transactions on Database Systems, 12, 4, 1987

[Ra],   Rafanelli, M., F.L. Ricci, *A functional model for statistical entities*, Proceedings of "Database and Expert Systems Applications: DEXA '90", Springer Verlag, 1990

[Su],   Su, S.Y.W., *SAM*: a semantic association model for corporate and scientific-statistical databases*, Information Sciences, Vol.29, N.2 and 3, May and June 1983

[Ta],   *Table Producing Language Systems, version 5*, Bureau of Labor Statistics, Washington, Jul. 1980

[Wo],   Wong, H.K.T. *Micro and macro statistical/scientific database management*, I° IEEE International Conference on Data Engineering, 1984

Efficient Locking and Caching of Data in the Multisystem Shared Disks Transaction Environment

C. Mohan
Inderpal Narang

Data Base Technology Institute, IBM Almaden Research Center, San Jose, CA 95120, USA

{*mohan, narang*}@*almaden.ibm.com*

Abstract This paper describes a technique for use when multiple instances of a data base management system (DBMS), each with its own cache (buffer pool), can directly read and modify any data stored on a set of shared disks. Global locking and coherency control protocols are necessary in this context for assuring transaction consistency and for maintaining coherency of the data cached in the multiple caches. The coordination amongst the systems is performed by a set of local lock managers (LLMs) and a global lock manager (GLM). This typically involves sending messages. We describe a technique, called **LP locking**, which saves locking calls when the granularity of locking by transactions is the *same* as the granularity of caching by the cache manager. The savings are gained by making the LLMs hide from the GLM the distinction between a transaction lock, called the L lock, and a cache-ownership lock, called the P lock, for the *same* object. The L and P locks for an object, though distinct at an LLM, are known as a single lock at the GLM. An LLM can grant an L or P lock request on an object *locally* if the combined lock mode of the L and P locks already held on that object by that LLM is equal to or higher than the requested mode. Such optimizations save messages between the LLMs and the GLM. Our ideas apply also to the client-server environment which has become very popular in the OODBMS area and to the distributed shared memory environment.

1. Introduction

This paper describes a technique which saves messages for transaction locking and cache coherency when multiple instances of a data base management system (DBMS) are accessing the same data via shared disks. Such a multisystem *shared disks (SD)* architecture is also called *data sharing* [DIRY89, Haer88, MoNa91a, MoNa91b, MoNP90, MoNS91, Rahm86, Rahm91, Reut86, Shoe86]. With SD, all the disks containing the data base are shared among the different systems. Any instance of the DBMS may access and modify any portion of the data base on the shared disks. As a result, a given transaction makes all its data base accesses through only one DBMS instance. The SD approach is used in IBM's IMS Data Sharing product [StUW82], TPF product [Scru87] and the Amoeba research project [MoNa91a, MoNa91b, MoNP90, MoNS91, SNOP85], and in DEC's VAX DBMS[1] and VAX Rdb/VMS[1] [Josh91, KrLS86, ReSW89]. More recently, for the VAXcluster[1] environment, third-party DBMSs like ORACLE[1] and INGRES have been modified to support SD. Hitachi and Fujitsu also have products which support the SD environment. SD has also, of late, become popular in the area of distributed virtual memory [NiLo91].

---

[1] DB2 and IBM are trademarks of the International Business Machines Corp. DEC, VAX DBMS, VAX, VAXcluster and Rdb/VMS are trademarks of the Digital Equipment Corp. Oracle is a registered trademark of the Oracle Corp.

Global locking is required to preserve transaction semantics in a multisystem environment. Locks acquired by transactions are called the **L locks**. The global locking function requires coordination among multiple instances of the DBMS. This is typically done by sending messages between the systems. Without any loss of generality, we assume the following configuration for lock management: there is a **global lock manager (GLM)** which coordinates locks among the **local lock managers (LLMs)** of the sharing systems.[2] The GLM and the LLMs communicate efficiently via messages by batching messages. Unfortunately, messages have processing overhead, and batching increases latency. These, in turn, impact transactions' lock hold times and response times. Therefore, optimizations to save lock and unlock calls to the GLM are important performance considerations.

In a multisystem environment, each DBMS instance has its own local **cache** (also called **buffer pool** [TeGu84]) for retaining copies of recently accessed pages. It is required that coherency of the data in the different caches be preserved so that a DBMS instance always uses the current copy of data. To accomplish this, the cache manager (also called buffer manager) follows certain coherency control protocols which are based on locking. To cache a page in the system, a page-cache lock, called the **P lock**, may be acquired. The actual protocols depend on whether the DBMS follows the no-force-at-commit policy or the force-at-commit policy in the multisystem environment. **Force-at-commit** [HaRe83] requires that, by the time a transaction is allowed to commit, all the data base pages updated by it should have already been written to disk. With **no-force-at-commit**, updated pages can be written to disk in a leisurely fashion, even long after the updating transaction has committed.[3] As a result, no-force-at-commit improves transactions' response times and reduces lock hold times, thereby leading to more concurrency. Since the modern industrial-strength DBMSs (e.g., DB2 [HaJa84]) implement the no-force-at-commit policy, we assume that the DBMS follows the no-force-at-commit policy.

One of the primary goals of a DBMS which operates in a multisystem environment with shared disks is to reduce messages involved in acquiring and releasing locks for assuring transaction consistency and cache coherency. In this paper, we describe a novel technique, called **LP locking**, which saves messages for locking when the unit of locking of an object by a transaction is the *same* as the unit of caching of that object by the cache manager. This would be the case when page locking is being used (our algorithms for finer-granularity (e.g., record) locking are covered in [MoNa91a, MoNS91]). The savings result from the following observation: an LLM can hide the distinction between the L lock and the P lock for the same object from the GLM. The L and P locks for an object, though distinct at an LLM, are known as a single **(LP)** lock at the GLM. The GLM knows about this lock with the following owner and lock mode attributes: the owner is an LLM; the lock mode is the combined lock modes of the L and P locks held at that owning LLM. Hence, the name LP lock.

When LP locking is being used, an LLM already owning an LP lock at the GLM can grant a new L or P lock request for the corresponding object *locally* (i.e., without communicating with the GLM) in many cases. Also, an LLM can suppress the transmission of an unlock call of an L (respectively, P) lock to the GLM in many cases if the P (L) lock is still held. These optimizations avoid some of the lock and unlock calls from an LLM to the GLM and the replies

---

2 Algorithms for recovering from failures of the LLMs and the GLM are presented in [MoNa91a].

3 We do support the *steal* policy of cache management [HaRe83]. This means that updated pages are allowed to be written to disk even before the updates are committed. The approach of [Rahm91] does not support it.

from the GLM to the LLM for those calls, thereby saving some message exchanges between them and hence improving response times. The key point is that the LLM can grant a lock locally or suppress an unlock call to the GLM based on the ownership of another related lock.

In addition to the shared disks architecture, the ideas presented here can also be applied to the client-server environment which has become very popular in the context of the object oriented data base (OODB) area [CFLS91, DeRo91, DMFV90, KSDVM90, MoNa91b, RoDe91, WaRo91, WiNe90] and to the distributed shared memory environment [NiLo91].

The rest of the paper is organized as follows. In section 2, we describe in detail the transaction lock, the L lock, and the page-cache lock, the P lock. Then, in section 3, we describe how P locking supports cache coherency in conjunction with the no-force-at-commit policy. We count the number of lock and unlock calls when the L and P locks are treated as separate locks at GLM. We describe the LP locking technique in section 4 and show the savings of the lock and unlock calls to the GLM. In section 5, we discuss related work. We summarize our work in section 6.

2. L and P Locks

A DBMS which operates in a multisystem environment, with each system running an instance of the DBMS each with its own cache, requires (1) global logical locking to ensure isolation and serializability of transactions across multiple systems, and (2) coherency control protocols to ensure that if the same data is cached in different systems, then the copies are kept coherent so that the correct version is used by the transactions [DIRY89, MoNa91a, Rahm91, ReSW89]. The logical locking and coherency control protocols use a distributed lock manager which consists of an LLM in every system and a GLM. The LLMs and the GLM use messages

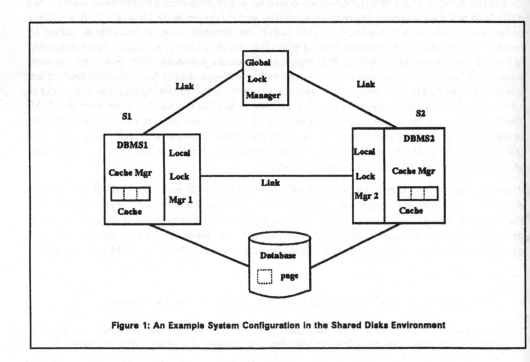

Figure 1: An Example System Configuration in the Shared Disks Environment

for communicating locking primitives such as lock and unlock, and responses to those requests. Communication links exist between all the sharing systems. The connectivity between systems is required for many reasons such as (1) command processing in the multisystem environment and (2) for transferring changed pages between systems for assuring coherency, as described in [MoNa91a] and in the section "3.1. Coherency Control via P Locks". Figure 1 depicts an example system configuration in the shared disks environment.

The coherency protocols described in this paper support the no-force-at-commit policy. That is, a changed page does not have to be written to disk before the modifying transaction commits. However, when a transaction in another system accesses the changed page, the coherency control protocols ensure that the most recent version of the page is accessed. This is explained in more detail in the section "3.1. Coherency Control via P Locks" and in [MoNa91a].

2.1. Logical or Transaction Locking

A *transaction* obtains ownership of a piece of data via a *logical* (*L*) *lock*. For the purpose of discussions in this paper, we assume that the object being locked is a *page* in the data base (fine-granularity (e.g., record) locking is discussed in [MoNa91a, MoNS91]). The transaction provides, on a lock call to LLM, the following parameters which are of relevance to the discussions in this paper:

- *Lock name*: name of the page being locked

- *Type of lock*: "L"

  The reason for specifying the type of lock would become clear when we discuss the page-cache lock.

- *Mode of the requested lock*: Share (S) or Exclusive (X)

- *Owner of the lock*: ID of transaction which is requesting the lock

A transaction has to acquire an L lock in S mode to read a page and in X mode to update the page. The compatibility matrix of the two lock modes is shown in Figure 2. The resultant modes of the two lock modes is shown in Figure 3. The resultant mode of X is considered to be greater than S. A transaction's lock call is processed by the LLM as follows: if the LLM does not have the page name in its lock table, then it sends the request to the GLM with the owner being specified as the requesting LLM (**not** the requesting transaction). Below, we explain why the ownership of locks is tracked in the name of the LLM at the GLM.

Requested	Held	
	S	X
S	grant	wait
X	wait	wait

Figure 2: Lock Compatibility Matrix

Lock Mode Held (Tx1)	Lock Mode Held (Tx2)	Resultant Lock Mode
S	Null	S
S	S	S
X	Null	X

If transactions Tx1 and Tx2 in a system hold locks in the modes shown, then the resultant lock mode is as shown. If the lock is not held, then it is shown as being held in the Null mode.

Figure 3: Resultant Lock Mode of L Locks

If a transaction in a system were to request a lock on a resource which is already locked by one or more transactions in the requesting system and the requested mode is less than or equal to the *preexisting* resultant lock mode at that system's LLM, then it is possible for the LLM to avoid sending the lock call to the GLM by granting the lock locally. This is because (1) the GLM already knows about the lock and no change needs to be made to the lock mode, and (2) the GLM does not track transaction level lock ownership information. However, if the lock cannot be granted locally, then the lock call is sent to the GLM. The lock call flow to the GLM is shown in Figure 4. For simplicity, the possibility of batching of multiple lock and unlock calls is not shown in the figure. The GLM sends the lock grant reply to the requesting LLM when the requested lock is compatible with locks, if any, that are already held on that page by the other LLMs. In the figure, we also show the interactions between the LLM and the GLM for the unlock call. Once the DBMS issues an unlock call, it need not wait for the processing of that call to be completed. That is, the unlock call can be handled asynchronously.

2.2. Physical or Page-Cache Locking

The *cache (buffer) manager* in a system which wants to cache a page obtains *permission* to cache that page by acquiring a **physical (P) lock** on that page. A P lock is different from an L lock

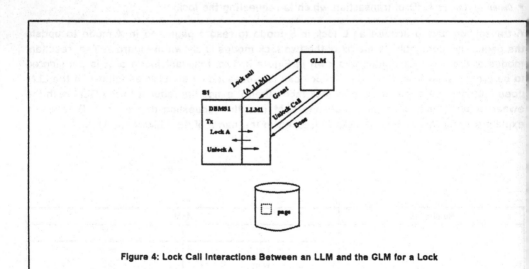

Figure 4: Lock Call Interactions Between an LLM and the GLM for a Lock

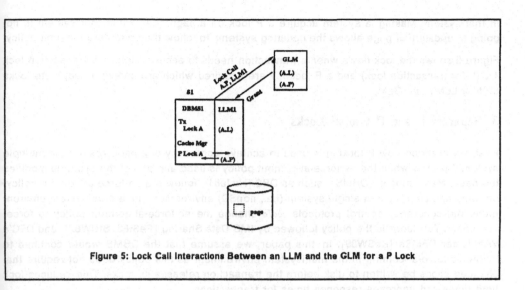

Figure 5: Lock Call Interactions Between an LLM and the GLM for a P Lock

in that the purpose behind acquiring it is different from that behind acquiring an L lock. A P lock is acquired to ensure cache coherency *between* systems, whereas an L lock is acquired for assuring intra- and inter-system isolation and serialization of usage of the corresponding page by different *transactions*. As a result, a P lock requested in the X mode in a system should not conflict with the L locks held by transactions on the same system.

For the purposes of the discussions in this section and the next one, we assume that the distinction between these two locks is made by having different lock names for the L and P locks on the same page. (In the LP locking technique which we describe in the section "4. LP Locking Technique", the distinction between the L and P locks is kept only at the LLM level and GLM is unaware of this distinction.) The cache manager provides, on a lock call to LLM, the following parameters which are of relevance to the discussions in this paper:

- *Lock name*: name of the page being locked

- *Type of lock*: "P"

  The type information is required so that the LLM can invoke the cache manager's routines as explained in the section "3.1. Coherency Control via P Locks".

- *Mode of the requested lock*: Share (S) or Exclusive (X)

- *Owner of the lock*: ID of cache manager (distinct from the IDs of the transactions) requesting the lock.

The cache manager acquires the P lock in the S mode to read the page and in the X mode to update the page. The compatibility rules for the P lock are the same as those shown in Figure 2. But they apply only between different systems since, for a given page, there is only one P lock which is owned by the cache manager in a system. The latter implies that when multiple transactions use the page which is already cached in a system, only one of them pays the overhead of acquiring the P lock. The P lock is held as long as the page is cached in that system. Making a system acquire a P lock on a page even when that system is not going to update that page allows the updating systems to follow the no-force-at-commit policy.

Figure 5 shows the lock flows when a transaction needs to access page A. A transaction lock $A.L$ (L for transaction lock) and a P lock $A.P$ are acquired which are known as separate locks both at LLM1 and GLM.

3. Separate L and P Global Locks

First, we describe how P locking is used to achieve coherency of a page residing in multiple systems' caches when the no-force-at-commit policy is used and one of the systems modifies the page. Many modern DBMSs, such as DB2 [HaJa84], follow the no-force-at-commit policy, but they operate only in a single system (i.e., nonSD) environment. In a multisystem environment, the coherency control protocols *could* change the no-force-at-commit policy to force-at-commit. The latter is the policy followed by IMS Data Sharing [PeSt83, StUW82], and DEC's VAXcluster DBMSs [ReSW89]. In this paper, we assume that the DBMS would continue to follow no-force-at-commit in the multisystem environment as this policy does not require that changed pages be written to disk before the transaction releases its locks. This reduces lock hold times and improves response times for transactions.

The other aspect of a coherency control protocol is whether the so-called *notification messages* are going to be sent for a changed page to the other sharing systems as part of termination processing for the transaction which updated the page. These messages let the other systems which have cached older versions of the modified page invalidate those versions. They require an acknowledgement from the other systems to ensure that those systems have invalidated their cached pages before the relevant locks are released by the terminating transaction. With no-force-at-commit, these messages are not sent. This approach can considerably reduce lock hold time and response time of a transaction.[4]

In this section, we assume that L and P locks on a page are treated as separate locks at GLM. That is, an LLM has *no* knowledge of the relationship between the L and the P locks on a page. Therefore, the LLM sends the lock and unlock calls for both the L and the P locks to the GLM. We will compare the number of lock and unlock calls when this approach is used versus when the LP locking technique is used.

3.1. Coherency Control via P Locks

In this subsection, we explain how P locking supports the maintenance of coherency of a page cached in multiple systems when the no-force-at-commit policy is used. Since the cache manager always acquires a P lock when it caches a page in its system and this lock call is communicated to the GLM, the GLM knows from its lock table which system(s) holds the lock and hence has cached that page. If the P lock is held in the S mode, then the page could be cached in multiple systems; if the P lock is held in the X mode, then the page can be cached only in one system. GLM's lock table entry has the ID(s) of the LLM(s) which hold the P lock.

Example: Assume that DBMS S1 has a changed copy of page A cached. In this case, the GLM's lock table entry for A would show that the LLM of S1 holds the P lock in the X mode.

---

4 In IMS Data Sharing, notification messages are used; in DEC's VAXcluster [KrLS86], notification messages are not used, rather the *check-on-access* scheme is used. That is, when a cached page is about to be used, its currency is checked with the assistance of the lock manager. Check-on-access is also described in [Rahm86] and in [MoNa91a].

Assume that the transaction which updated A has committed. Note that A was not written to disk as the DBMS is following the no-force-at-commit policy. Now, let a transaction in S2 attempt a read of A. Then, S2 would request the L lock on A in the S mode. LLM in S2 would send the lock call A.L to GLM. The lock would be granted by GLM since there is no other transaction which is holding the lock in a conflicting mode (remember that A.L is a different lock from A.P). Then, S2's cache manager would request the P lock on A in the S mode which would be sent as A.P to GLM by S2's LLM. GLM would detect the lock conflict for A.P and send a message to the LLM in S1 informing it of the lock conflict for page A due to S2's request. The LLM in S1 would do the following processing in response:

It would invoke cache manager's lock conflict routine [Josh91, MoNa91a, ReSw89] with the following parameters: (1) lock name for which the conflict occurred (A), (2) the requested lock mode (S), and (3) the requesting system (S2). The cache manager would do the following processing which would ultimately resolve the P lock conflict:

- If the page is still *dirty* (i.e., more up to date than the disk version), then it would write the page to disk.[5]

- In parallel with the disk I/O, it would send A via the communication link to S2.[6]

- After the disk I/O is complete, it would request the LLM to change the P lock mode from X to S. By downgrading the P lock to the S mode, rather than releasing it, A can continue to be cached in S1.

The LLM in S1 would pass the new P lock mode for A to the GLM. The GLM would update its lock table entry for A to note that S1 holds the P lock in the S mode and grant the P lock in S mode to S2. Note that S1's sending of the page by communication link is overlapped with the lock conflict and the lock grant processing. Therefore, it is expected that in almost all cases A would be cached in S2 by the time the P lock request is granted.[7] Thus, the current changed copy of A in S1 is propagated to S2. This is how coherency control is achieved via P locking when a DBMS follows the no-force-at-commit policy.

To summarize, (1) a cache manager would hold a P lock on a cached page whether it is changed or unchanged, (2) the lock mode for a changed page would be different from that for an unchanged page, (3) a lock conflict at the GLM would trigger the GLM to inform the LLM where the P lock on the changed page is held, and (4) the LLM would invoke the cache

---

5 It is possible to avoid this disk I/O by using one of the fast page transfer techniques described in [MoNa91a]. The fast page transfer techniques would send the page via the communication link to the system needing it without writing it to disk. However, the techniques require a merged log in a multisystem environment even for restart recovery.

6 Discussions relating to the handling of failure to receive the page or the late arrival of the page via the communication link are beyond the scope of this paper. The possibility of late arrival of the page must be handled carefully to ensure that an outdated version of the page does not get used by any transactions. These problems and associated solutions are described in [MoNa91a].

7 We have not described here the details of the manner in which S2 receives the page (see [MoNa91a]). It is possible to send the page via GLM to forward it to the requesting system, but we choose to send the page directly to the requesting system. This is because the latter approach would save the memory and processing overheads required by the other approach to store and forward the page using the GLM. Also, it would reduce the link utilization between the processors and the GLM.

manager routine which would take the necessary actions to provide the current copy of the page to the requesting system and to resolve the P lock conflict. This way, the system which updates the page can continue to cache the changed page beyond transaction usage without writing the page to disk and informing other systems of the change within the transaction commit scope. The changed page could be written to disk under the normal write policy of the cache manager [TeGu84]. The system in which the changed page is cached would react only when some other system develops interest on that page.

3.2. Global Locking Overhead

A DBMS incurs the following processing and response time overheads in a multisystem environment for each page when it follows the no-force-at-commit policy.

- There will be the overheads relating to the lock/unlock *calls* from the LLM to the GLM and replies for them. However, these are *not* counted as *separate messages*. The number of actual messages sent will depend on the batching or bundling of the calls and the replies traffic between the LLMs and the GLM. It should be noted that such a batching has its costs since it increases the processing overheads, and the transaction's lock hold time and response time.

- The lock calls for the L lock and the P lock from the LLM to the GLM are in the transaction response time. That is, the transaction does not proceed until the GLM sends the grant reply to the LLM. In contrast, we assume that the unlock calls and the "Done" reply are handled asynchronously to the transaction's processing and hence do not affect the transaction's response time.

Now, we count the locking calls to read a page. The reason for choosing the read operation is that typically it is much more frequent than the update operation. We choose the no-contention case because that way we can make our point on the advantages of LP locking without getting into the details of the contention case(s). For the contention case, the savings would be even more with the LP locking method.

- Lock call from the LLM to the GLM for the L lock.
- "Grant" reply from the GLM to the LLM for the L lock.
- Lock call from the LLM to the GLM for the P lock.
- "Grant" reply from the GLM to the LLM for the P lock.
- Unlock call from the LLM to the GLM for the L lock.
- "Done" reply from the GLM to the LLM for the unlocking of the L lock.
- Unlock call from the LLM to the GLM for the P lock.

  The P lock would continue to be held as long as the page is cached. That is, the cache manager would write the page to disk if it was changed, and then, as part of stealing the cache slot occupied by the page, it would release the P lock. We do *not* count the release of this lock as it would be common in our comparison with the LP locking technique.

Therefore, if a transaction were to access N pages, then there would be 2N lock calls and N unlock calls, giving a total of 3N calls for the GLM to process. There would be 3N replies for the LLM to process. The 2N lock calls to the GLM would be synchronous, thereby causing an increase in the transaction response time.

L Lock	P Lock	Resultant Mode of L and P Locks
Null	Null	Null
Null	S	S
Null	X	X
S	Null	S
S	S	S
S	X	X
X	Null	X
X	S	X
X	X	X

$$X > S > Null$$

Figure 6: Resultant Mode of L and P Locks

4. LP Locking Technique

We now describe an alternative technique, called LP locking, which is based on the following observation: the cache manager acquires the P lock for the *same* resource and perhaps in the same mode for which the L lock is already held by the transaction. Even though the owners of the L lock and the P lock are different (i.e., transactions versus the cache manager), that distinction is important only for the LLMs since the GLM tracks lock ownership with LLMs as the holders. As shown in Figure 7, the L and P locks for page A, though distinct at an LLM (A.L and A.P, respectively) are known as a single lock (A) at the GLM. The GLM knows about this lock with the owner being an LLM and in the mode which is the resultant mode of the L and P locks. The resultant mode of the L and the P locks is determined by the lock modes

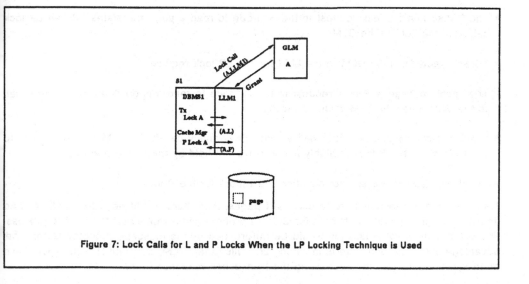

Figure 7: Lock Calls for L and P Locks When the LP Locking Technique Is Used

in which they are held by the transactions of that system and the cache manager of that system. Figure 6 shows the resultant mode of L and P locks held on a page.

An LLM can grant an *L* lock request for a page *locally* if the resultant mode of any already held L locks and P lock at that LLM for that page is greater than or equal to the requested mode, where the X mode is considered to be greater than the S mode and the S mode is considered to be greater than the Null mode. When the *P* lock is requested, if the resultant mode of all held, if any, L locks is equal to or greater than the requested mode, then the P lock can be granted locally. In all cases, if the resultant mode is *less than* the requested mode, a GLM interaction is needed to upgrade the lock. For unlock requests, an LLM would suppress passing on to the GLM the unlock call of an L (respectively, P) lock if the P (L) lock, and possibly other L locks, are still held with the resultant mode which is the same or greater than the mode of the lock being released. Thus, some lock and unlock calls from an LLM to the GLM can be avoided.

A few points need to be made about the parameters on the lock call which were discussed in the sections "2.1. Logical or Transaction Locking" and "2.2. Physical or Page-Cache Locking". The fact that the LLM could recognize that a P lock could be granted without sending the lock call to the GLM because the L lock on the corresponding page is held, led us to name these special type of locks, L and P, as having the attribute called **LP**. Hence, the name LP locks. In fact, when a transaction makes a lock call to the LLM, it specifies that it is an L type lock with the LP attribute; when the cache manager makes a lock call to the LLM, it specifies that it is a P type lock with the LP attribute. Based on this attribute information, the LLM optimizes its interactions with the GLM as described before.

As before, we will next count the number of locking related calls to read a page when the LP locking technique is used.

4.1. Global Locking Overhead

We compare the number of lock and unlock calls for the no-contention case for a read operation. For the contention case, the savings would be even more with LP locking.

- The transaction's L lock request in the S mode to read a page translates into an LP lock call from the LLM to the GLM.

- "Grant" reply from the GLM to the LLM for the LP lock request.

- The cache manager's P lock request in the S mode to read a page does not cause a call to the GLM since the LLM grants it locally.

- The transaction's unlock L lock call would not normally cause the LLM to issue a call to the GLM since the P lock is highly likely to be still held by the cache manager.

As explained earlier, we are not counting the unlock for the P lock.

Therefore, if a transaction were to access N pages, then there would be N lock calls and no unlock calls, giving a total of N calls for GLM to process and N replies for the LLM to process. The actual number of messages would be determined by the message batching factor. The advantage of the LP technique is in saving 2N calls to the GLM, of which N calls would have been synchronous, thereby decreasing the transaction response time.

4.2. Coherency with LP Locking

In the section "3.1. Coherency Control via P Locks", we described how P locks achieve coherency of a page which is cached in many systems and is updated in one of them. Below, we describe a few differences which come about as a result of treating the L and P locks on a page as a single lock at the GLM.

- Without LP locking, the GLM detects the lock conflict for L and P locks separately, when a corresponding incompatible lock request is made from another system. With LP locking, the GLM would detect a lock conflict on a page when an incompatible LP request is made by another LLM due to either an L or a P lock request made to that LLM in its system. The GLM would send a lock conflict message to the LLM which owns the lock.

- Without LP locking, an LLM invokes the cache manager's lock conflict routine when it receives a lock conflict message for the *P* lock request from the GLM. In that case, because the L and P locks are treated as separate locks at the GLM, the LLM does not have to be aware of a tie-in with the L lock as is needed for LP locking. With LP locking, the owning LLM would invoke the cache manager's lock conflict routine only *after* the locally held L lock, if any, becomes compatible with the mode in which the request has been made by the other system.

Example: A transaction in system S1 holds the L lock in the X mode to update a page, and the cache manager in S1 holds the P lock also in the X mode because it is a changed page; a transaction in another system S2 requests an L lock on the same page. In this scenario, the LLM in S1 would invoke the cache manager's lock conflict routine after the transaction in S1 releases the L lock (i.e., when the transaction terminates). This ensures that the cache manager's lock conflict routine would transfer only that version of the page which has the final version of the updated data. Transferring a version of the page which has intermediate updates is wasteful.

An example of a situation in which an LLM would invoke the cache manager's lock conflict routine immediately is as follows: (1) in system S2, a transaction (respectively, the cache manager) requests the L (P) lock on a page in the S mode, (2) in S1, the P lock is held in the X mode and the L lock is held in the S mode or is not held at all. In this scenario, the cache manager in S1 has the changed page cached but no transaction is updating the page. The changes to the page are already committed. Therefore, the page can be transferred to another system without waiting for any transaction to release any locks. However, if a transaction in system S2 were to request the lock in X mode to update the page, then the LLM in S1 would have to wait for any transactions which held the L lock in the S mode to release their locks before invoking the cache manager's routine. Note that an L lock which is held in the S mode may be released before the transaction terminates if the transaction is using the cursor stability option (degree 2 consistency of System R [GLPT76]).

5. Related Work

The method described in [ShTr90] assumes hierarchical locking between the cache lock (P lock) and the record lock (L lock). Hierarchical locking requires that locks be obtained in the order dictated by the hierarchy. In our work, the L and P locks cannot be treated as hierarchical locks since those locks may have to be acquired in different orders at different times. For example, when a cache manager fetches pages prior to transaction usage of those pages to improve I/O performance for sequential and skip-sequential scans of data (see [CHHIM91, MHWC90, TeGu84]), the P locks on those pages would be acquired *before* the L locks are acquired; for a typical random access of data by a transaction, the L lock on a page would be acquired before the P lock is acquired assuming that the page is not already cached.

In comparing our work with related work, we found that there is very little mention of the combination of (1) no-force-at-commit policy, (2) page level granularity of transaction locking, and (3) combining the L and P locks into one lock at the GLM.

The IMS data sharing product [PeSt83, StUW82] which supports the SD environment uses the force-at-commit policy. The DEC VAXcluster DBMSs [KrLS86, ReSW89] follow the force-at-commit policy. They do not distinguish between the transaction locks and the cache manager's locks, and adopt the idea of combining them.

The work reported in [DIRY89] assumes the force-at-commit policy. Also, the L and P locks are treated as separate locks at the GLM. Further, in that work, the GLM tracks *transactions*, rather than *LLMs*, as the owners of locks. This means that the number of locks acquired, and the message and processing overhead will be higher if multiple transactions within a system access the same page. Further, *separate* page level (global) locks are used for coherency control and these locks are acquired by the cache manager. The message overhead is reduced for these extra locks by piggybacking them on transaction lock requests.

[CFLS91] describes various schemes for caching data in the client-server environment. We compare the scheme *Caching Two-Phase Locking* (C2PL) with LP locking. In C2PL, even though an updated page may be cached at the client site between transactions, a subsequent access to the page by a transaction requires obtaining a lock from the server. The validity of the cached page is checked by sending the page's log sequence number (LSN) with the lock request (this is the check-on-access scheme of [KrLS86, Rahm86]). This lock request causes a round-trip message flow. In LP locking, as long as the page is cached in a system, the P lock is held on the page and that allows the L lock to be granted locally without sending messages to the GLM. For update, LP locking could have more messages depending on the number of systems where the page is cached, whereas with C2PL those messages are not needed. Since we assume that in typical workloads read access is much more predominant than update, the LP scheme would have fewer messages overall.

[WaRo91] discusses retaining locks on cached objects beyond transaction usage but does not mention anything about a separate cache lock (*a la* our P lock). It is not clear how, in that work, the following issues are handled without much complexity: when the last transaction releases the lock on an object, who owns the lock and how is it transferred to this unknown owner. The LP locking scheme handles it in a simpler way by using the cache lock as a separate lock. Caching is independent from transaction locking of the object. That is, the cache manager can purge the object if no transaction is currently actively using it even though the transaction may hold a lock on it. The purging of the object from the cache may become necessary because of cache storage constraints.

6. Summary

We have described a technique which saves messages for transaction locking and controlling cache coherency when multiple instances of a DBMS can access for read and modification *any* data stored on a set of shared disks. In such a multisystem environment, the locking function requires coordination among the multiple instances of the DBMS. This is typically done via messages sent between the systems. Messages have processing overhead and increase latency. They impact transaction lock hold times and response times. Therefore, saving any lock and unlock calls is an important performance consideration.

The cache manager follows the no-force-at-commit policy in the multisystem environment. It maintains coherency among multiple instances of the caches via physical (*P*) locks. We described a technique, called **LP locking**, which saves messages for locking when the unit of ownership of an object by a transaction is the *same* as the unit of caching of that object by the cache manager. The savings result from the observation that a local lock manager (LLM) can hide the distinction between the transaction lock, called the L lock, and the page-cache lock, called the P lock, for the same object from the global lock manager (GLM). The L and P locks for an object, though distinct at the LLMs, are known as a single lock at the GLM. An LLM can grant a lock locally (i.e., without communicating with the GLM) based on the already-held ownership by the same LLM of another related lock or the LLM can suppress an unlock call since the information kept at the GLM does not change.

The performance benefits of the LP locking technique in the no-contention case are estimated as follows (the benefits for the contention case would be even better). If a transaction were to access N distinct pages, the LP locking technique can save 2N calls and their replies involving the GLM out of a total of 3N calls and their replies which would be required were the LP locking technique not used. In the savings of 2N calls, N calls are of the synchronous kind which increase the transaction response time. The extent of savings of messages would depend on the amount of batching of these calls.

The LP locking idea presented here can also be used in the distributed shared memory environment [NiLo91] and in the client-server environment. The latter has become very popular in the context of the object-oriented data base area. Our algorithms for fine-granularity (e.g., record) locking are presented in [MoNa91a, MoNS91]. Most of the recovery related discussions in those papers are applicable to the current context also.

7. References

CFLS91 Carey, M., Franklin, M., Livny, M., Shekita, E. *Data Caching Tradeoffs in Client-Server DBMS Architectures*, **Proc. ACM SIGMOD International Conference on Management of Data**, Denver, May 1991.

CHHIM91 Cheng, J., Haderle, D., Hedges, R., Iyer, B., Messinger, T., Mohan, C., Wang, Y. *An Efficient Hybrid Join Algorithm: a DB2 Prototype*, **Proc. 7th International Conference on Data Engineering**, Kobe, April 1991. Also available as IBM Research Report RJ7884, IBM Almaden Research Center, December 1990.

DeRo91 Delis, A., Roussopoulos, N. *Performance Comparison of Three Modern DBMS Architectures*, **Technical Report CS-TR-2679**, University of Maryland, May 1991.

DIRY89 Dias, D., Iyer, B., Robinson, J., Yu, P. *Integrated Concurrency-Coherency Controls for Multisystem Data Sharing*, **IEEE Transactions on Software Engineering**, Vol. 15, No. 4, April 1989.

DMFV90 DeWitt, D., Maier, D., Futtersack, P., Velez, F. *A Study of Three Alternative Workstation-Server Architectures for Object Oriented Database Systems*, **Proc. 16th International Conference on Very Large Data Bases**, Brisbane, August 1990.

GLPT76 Gray, J., Lorie, R., Putzolu, F., Traiger, I. *Granularity of Locks and Degrees of Consistency in a Shared Data Base*, **Proc. IFIP Working Conference on Modelling of Database Management Systems**, Freudenstadt, January 1976. Also Available as IBM Research Report RJ1654, IBM San Jose Research Laboratory.

Haer88   Haerder, T. *Handling Hot Spot Data in DB-Sharing Systems*, **Information Systems**, Vol. 13, No. 2, p155-166, 1988.

HaJa84   Haderle, D., Jackson, R. *IBM Database 2 Overview*, **IBM Systems Journal**, Vol. 23, No. 2, 1984.

HaRe83   Haerder, T., Reuter, A. *Principles of Transaction Oriented Database Recovery - A Taxonomy*, **Computing Surveys**, Vol. 15, No. 4, December 1983.

Josh91   Joshi, A. *Adaptive Locking Strategies in a Multi-Node Shared Data Model Environment*, **Proc. 17th International Conference on Very Large Data Bases**, Barcelona, September 1991.

KrLS86   Kronenberg, N., Levy, H., Strecker, W. *VAXclusters: A Closely-Coupled Distributed System*, **ACM Transactions on Computer Systems**,Vol. 4, No. 2, May 1986.

KSDVM90   Koch, B., Schunke, T., Dearle, A., Vaughan, F., Marlin, C., Fazakerley, R., Barter, C. *Cache Coherency and Storage Management in a Persistent Object System*, **Proc. 4th International Workshop on Persistent Object Systems**, Martha's Vineyard, September 1990, Morgan Kaufmann Publishers, Inc.

MHWC90   Mohan, C., Haderle, D., Wang, Y., Cheng, J. *Single Table Access Using Multiple Indexes: Optimization, Execution and Concurrency Control Techniques*, **Proc. International Conference on Extending Data Base Technology**, Venice, March 1990. An expanded version of this paper is available as **IBM Research Report RJ7341**, IBM Almaden Research Center, March 1990.

MoNa91a   Mohan, C., Narang, I. *Recovery and Coherency Control Protocols for Fast Intersystem Page Transfer and Fine-Granularity Locking in Shared Disks Transaction Environment*, **Proc. 17th International Conference on Very Large Data Bases**, Barcelona, September 1991. A longer version of this paper is available as **IBM Research Report RJ8017**, IBM Almaden Research Center, March, 1991.

MoNa91b   Mohan, C., Narang, I. *Data Base Recovery in Shared Disks and Client-Server Architectures*, **IBM Research Report**, IBM Almaden Research Center, November 1991.

MoNP90   Mohan, C., Narang, I., Palmer, J. *A Case Study of Problems in Migrating to Distributed Computing: Page Recovery Using Multiple Logs in the Shared Disks Environment*, **IBM Research Report RJ7343**, IBM Almaden Research Center, March 1990.

MoNS91   Mohan, C., Narang, I., Silen, S. *Solutions to Hot Spot Problems in a Shared Disks Transaction Environment*, **Proc. 4th International Workshop on High Performance Transaction Systems**, Asilomar, September 1991. Also available as **IBM Research Report RJ8281**, IBM Almaden Research Center, August 1991.

NiLo91   Nitzberg, B., Lo, V. *Distributed Shared Memory: A Survey of Issues and Algorithms*, **Computer**, August 1991.

PeSt83   Peterson, R.J., Strickland, J.P. *Log Write-Ahead Protocols and IMS/VS Logging*, **Proc. 2nd ACM SIGACT-SIGMOD Symposium on Principles of Database Systems**, Atlanta, March 1983.

Rahm86   Rahm, E. *Primary Copy Synchronization for DB-Sharing*, **Information Systems**, Vol. 11, No. 4, 1986.

Rahm91   Rahm, E. *Recovery Concepts for Data Sharing Systems*, **Proc. 21st International Symposium on Fault-Tolerant Computing**, Montreal, June 1991.

ReSW89   Rengarajan, T.K., Spiro, P., Wright, W. *High Availability Mechanisms of VAX DBMS Software*, **Digital Technical Journal**, No. 8, February 1989.

Reut86   Reuter, A. *Load Control and Load Balancing in a Shared Database Management System*, **Proc. International Conference on Data Engineering**, February 1986.

RoDe91   Roussopoulos, N., Delis, A. *Modern Client-Server DBMS Architectures*, **Technical Report CS-TR-2719**, University of Maryland, June 1991.

Scru87   Scrutchin, T. *TPF: Performance, Capacity, Availability*, **Proc. IEEE Compcon Spring '87**, San Francisco, February 1987.

Shoe86   Shoens, K. *Data Sharing vs. Partitioning for Capacity and Availability*, **Database Engineering**, Vol. 9, No. 1, March 1986.

ShTr90   Shoens, K., Treiber, K. *Method for Lock Management, Page Coherency, and Asynchronous Writing of Changed Pages to Shared External Store in a Distributed Computing System*, **U.S. Patent 4,965,719**, IBM, October 1990.

SNOP85   Shoens, K., Narang, I., Obermarck, R., Palmer, J., Silen, S., Traiger, I., Treiber, K. *Amoeba Project*, **Proc. IEEE Compcon Spring '85**, San Francisco, February 1985.

StUW82   Strickland, J., Uhrowczik, P., Watts, V. *IMS/VS: An Evolving System*, **IBM Systems Journal**, Vol. 21, No. 4, 1982.

TeGu84   Teng, J., Gumaer, R. *Managing IBM Database 2 Buffers to Maximize Performance*, **IBM Systems Journal**, Vol. 23, No. 2, 1984.

WaRo91   Wang, Y., Rowe, L., *Cache Consistency and Concurrency Control in a Client/Server DBMS Architecture*, **Proc. ACM-SIGMOD International Conference on Management of Data**, Denver, May 1991.

WINe90   Wilkinson, K., Neimat, M.-A. *Maintaining Consistency of Client-Cached Data*, **Proc. 16th International Conference on Very Large Data Bases**, Brisbane, August 1990.

A Non-Restrictive Concurrency Control for Object Oriented Databases*

D. Agrawal and A. El Abbadi

Department of Computer Science, University of California,
Santa Barbara, CA 93106, USA

Abstract

We propose an algorithm for executing transactions in object oriented databases. The object oriented database model generalizes the classical model of database concurrency control by permitting accesses to *class* and *instance* objects, by permitting *arbitrary operations* on objects as opposed to traditional read and write operations, and by allowing for the *nested* execution of transactions on objects. In this paper, we first develop a uniform methodology for treating both classes and instances. We then develop a two phase locking protocol with a new relationship between locks called *ordered sharing* for an object oriented database. Ordered sharing does not restrict the execution of conflicting operations. Finally, we extend the protocol to allow for nesting. The resulting protocol permits more concurrency that other known locking-based protocols.

1 Introduction

In this paper, we present a concurrency control protocol to deal with the problem of shared access to objects in object oriented databases. Traditionally, database systems are modeled as a collection of objects that can only be read or written by transactions [BHG87]. More recently, many researchers have shown that greater concurrency can be achieved in object oriented databases by using the type specific properties of objects [Kor83, SS84, BR87, Wei89a, Wei89b]. An object oriented database differs from classical databases since information is maintained in terms of *classes* and *instances* of these classes. Both classes and instances are referred to as *objects*. Classes define both attributes and the procedures through which instances can be manipulated. The procedures associated with a class are referred to as *methods*, and a method may invoke other methods on other objects in the database. This model of execution generalizes the classical model of database concurrency control by permitting *nested transactions* as opposed to flat transactions and by permitting *arbitrary operations* on objects as opposed to traditional read and write operations. Nested transactions increase performance and reliability, because synchronization of transactions becomes more flexible, and also because they provide

---

* This research is supported by the NSF under grant numbers IRI-9004998 and IRI-9117904.

finer control over failures than the flat transactions. Another aspect of object oriented databases is related to the notion of *extensibility* or *schema evolution*. That is, object oriented databases allow the classes to be modified concurrently with the accesses to the objects defined by these classes.

In this paper, we present protocols for executing atomic transactions on objects. We begin by introducing the notion of atomic operations to modify the methods and attributes of a class. This approach is novel since it provides a methodology for uniform treatment of both classes and objects from a concurrency control point-of-view. We then propose a new relationship between locks called *ordered sharing* [AE90] for synchronizing the execution of concurrent transactions in object oriented databases. We first describe an extension of two phase locking with ordered sharing for executing flat transactions, which are sequences of arbitrary atomic operations on classes and instances. The new lock relationship does not block the execution of conflicting operations, and hence increases concurrency and improves performance [AEL91]. The protocol permits more concurrency than the original two phase locking protocol for abstract data types [Wei89b]. Also, unlike previous protocols for object oriented databases [GK88, CF90], our protocol performs schema evolution at a fine granularity and uses the semantics of these update operations on classes.

We then extend the model of the database to include nested executions of transactions on objects. We present a two phase locking protocol with ordered sharing for synchronizing the execution of nested transactions. We show that the proposed protocol permits more concurrency than the nested two phase locking protocol (N2PL) [Mos85]. Also, given an execution with an acyclic serialization graph [HH91], the proposed protocol can accept this execution without reordering the order of atomic operations. The commit order, however, may be altered. To the best of our knowledge, this is the first attempt to integrate two distinguishing aspects of object oriented databases, i.e., schema evolution and nested execution of transactions.

The paper is organized as follows. In the next section, we develop a model for operations on classes and objects and present a synchronization mechanism for method executions on objects. In Section 3, we extend this protocol to nested execution of atomic transactions on objects. The paper concludes with a summary of our results.

2 Atomic Transactions in Object Oriented Databases

In this section, we present the model of an object oriented database [BKKK87, BBB+88, LRV88, RGN90] and present the correctness criterion used in such databases. Next, we present a concurrency control protocol to synchronize the execution of concurrent transactions in object oriented databases. The section concludes with a brief discussion about the implementation of the protocol.

2.1 Model

An *object oriented database* is a collection of *classes* and *instances* of these classes. A class defines a set of attributes for its instances and atomic methods or atomic procedures that are used to manipulate these instances. We allow inheritance of properties (attributes and methods) between classes, i.e., the class is structured as a hierarchy[2]. All subclasses of a class inherit all properties defined for the class and can have additional properties local to the subclass. We assume that each class definition is physically represented as a *class object* and each instance is represented as an *instance object*. Thus, we use the generic term *object* to refer to both classes and instances of these classes. This provides a uniform approach for dealing with all types of objects in object oriented databases.

Users access the instance objects by executing methods. An object inherits the methods from all its ancestors in the class hierarchy. In addition to accessing the instances, users may also update the class definitions dynamically in the system thus permitting *extensibility* or *schema evolution*. This is the main distinction between object oriented databases and standard database systems. For example, a class can be modified by replacing an old method implementation by a new and perhaps more efficient method implementation. Also, methods may be added or deleted from a class object. Similarly, attributes may be added or deleted from a class object. For example, the ORION database allows about twenty types of dynamic changes to the database schema [BKKK87]. We assume that the execution of methods as well as modifications to classes are executed as atomic operations.

Often users of an object oriented database may need to access several classes and instances in an atomic manner. The traditional transaction model for database systems can be used to ensure atomicity of user interactions. Users access the database by executing transactions, where a *transaction* is a partially ordered set of operations on the class and instance objects. We assume that two operations *conflict* with each other if they do not *commute*. The notion of commutativity depends upon the implementation and representation of the objects and will be discussed later. Formally, a *transaction* T_i is a partial order $\langle t_i, <_{T_i} \rangle$ such that:

1. t_i is a set of operations.
2. The relation $<_{T_i}$ orders at least all conflicting atomic operations in t_i.

Consider a set of transactions $T = \{T_1, T_2, \ldots, T_n\}$. The execution of the transactions in T is modeled by a structure called a *history*. A *history* is a partial order $\langle \Sigma, < \rangle$ such that:

1. Σ is the set of all operations executed by transactions in T.
2. Relation $<$ is a partial order on the operations of H and must satisfy the following conditions:
   (a) For every $T_i = \langle t_i, <_{T_i} \rangle \in \Sigma$, $< \supset <_{T_i}$.
   (b) For every pair of conflicting atomic operations o and o', either $o < o'$ or $o' < o$.

A *serial* history is a totally ordered history where for any two transactions all the operations of one precede the other or vice-versa. A history H is *serializable* if there is a history H_s over the same set of transactions such that $o <_H o'$ in H if and only if $o <_{H_s} o'$ in H_s. The correctness of a history H can be determined by checking the acyclicity the serialization graph of H denoted as $SG(H)$ [Pap79, BSW79]. $SG(H)$ is a directed graph

---

[2] In this paper, we do not deal with the problem of multiple inheritance of properties among classes which results in a class lattice structure instead of class hierarchy [GK88, CF90].

whose nodes correspond to the transactions in H and which has an edge $T \rightarrow T'$ iff T and T' execute conflicting operations o and o' such that $o < o'$.

Concurrency control and recovery protocols are used to ensure serializability and failure atomicity of transactions. In this paper, we have opted to use the update-in-place (UIP) approach [Ver78, HR83] for recovery due to its simplicity and better performance [AD85]. In the standard read/write model two operations conflict if they are executed on the same object and one of them is a write operation. We now use the model developed by Weihl [Wei89a] to extend this notion to objects that support arbitrary operations and where results of the operation executions may also be taken into consideration. We assume that operations are executed by invoking the corresponding methods atomically at each object. At any time, the current state of an object consists of a committed state, and a set of operations belonging to active transactions (i.e., transactions that have neither committed nor aborted). When an operation op is submitted to an object, it is executed returning a result res. Conflict relations among operations on an object are determined from the commutativity properties of the operations. Since we are using the UIP approach for recovery, conflict relations can be derived from the notion of *right backward commutativity* of operations [Wei89b]. An operation o *right backward commutes with* o' on an object if for every state in which o' can be executed after o, executing o' followed by o results in the same state as executing o followed by o'. Also, the results of o and o' are the same in both executions.

The notion of right backward commutativity is illustrated with the following example of an instance object that is derived from a bank account class. The state of a bank account object is the amount of money in the account. At any time, the amount of money cannot be negative. Three types of operations, namely, *deposit*, *withdraw* and *balance* can be invoked by transactions. The response to a *deposit* operation is always *ok*. The response to a *withdraw* operation may be *ok* or *no* whereas the response to a *balance* operation is the amount of money in the account. The right backward commutative relation for the operations of a bank account is depicted in Table 1. A "yes" entry indicates that the operation for the given row right commutes backward with the operation for the column and a "no" entry indicates that the row operation does not right commute backward with the column operation. Note that right backward commutativity is an asymmetric relation. In [Wei89b], it is shown that any concurrency control protocol must use a conflict table that is at least as restrictive as the complement of the right backward commutativity relation. In the rest of the paper, we will be using the term commute to refer to right backward commutativity.

Table 1. Right Backward Commutativity Table for a Bank Object

BA:[deposit(i),ok]	BA:[withdraw(i),ok]	BA:[withdraw(i),no]	BA:[balance,i]	
yes	yes	no	no	BA:[deposit(j),ok]
no	yes	yes	no	BA:[withdraw(j),ok]
yes	no	yes	yes	BA:[withdraw(j),no]
no	no	yes	yes	BA:[balance,j]

Note that depending upon the response to operation op, $\langle op, res \rangle$ may have differ-

Table 2. Right Backward Commutativity Table for Method Operations in Class C

[use(m),ok]	[use(m),no]	[add(m),ok]	[del(m),ok]	[del(m),no]	[rep(m),ok]	[rep(m),no]	
yes	⊥	no	⊥	⊥	yes	⊥	[use(m),ok]
⊥	yes	⊥	no	yes	⊥	yes	[use(m), no]
⊥	no	⊥	no	no	⊥	no	[add(m),ok]
no	⊥	no	⊥	⊥	no	⊥	[del(m),ok]
⊥	yes	⊥	no	yes	⊥	yes	[del(m),no]
yes	⊥	no	⊥	⊥	no	⊥	[rep(m),ok]
⊥	yes	⊥	no	yes	⊥	yes	[rep(m),no]

Table 3. Right Backward Commutativity Table for Attribute Operations in Class C

[use(a),ok]	[use(a),no]	[add(a),ok]	[add(a),no]	[del(a),ok]	[del(a),no]	
yes	⊥	no	yes	⊥	⊥	[use(a),ok]
⊥	yes	⊥	⊥	no	yes	[use(a), no]
⊥	no	⊥	⊥	no	no	[add(a),ok]
yes	⊥	no	yes	⊥	⊥	[add(a),no]
no	⊥	no	no	⊥	⊥	[del(a),ok]
⊥	yes	⊥	⊥	no	yes	[del(a),no]

ent conflict relations with respect to another operation. For example, if $withdraw(j)$ yields an ok response then $\langle withdraw(j), ok \rangle$ conflicts with any prior $\langle balance, i \rangle$ pair since the former does not right commute backward with the latter. On the other hand, $\langle withdraw(j), no \rangle$ does not conflict with previous $\langle balance, i \rangle$ pairs because $\langle withdraw(j),$ right commutes backward with all previous $\langle balance, i \rangle$ pairs. If the response to the operations is not considered then a withdraw operation would always conflict with prior balance operation.

Next we model the conflict relation for method executions and operations that modify the methods of a class. We consider only three types of update accesses to the methods of a class and a single access operation. For a class object C, operation $add(m)$ adds a method m to C, $del(m)$ deletes a method m from C, and $rep(m)$ replaces the implementation of method m by a new implementation. Note that all these operations may result in a response ok if the operation is successful otherwise the response is no; we assume that $add(m)$ is always successful. In addition, if a method m of class C is being executed by a transaction then the transaction executes an operation $use(m)$ on that method. Table 2, summarizes the right backward commutativity relations among the operations on methods in a class.

In Table 2, an entry "⊥" indicates that such an execution of the operations with the indicated response is not possible or is undefined. For example, if a delete of a method m was successful then $use(m)$ cannot return with a response ok. A "yes" indicates that the operation in the row right backward commutes with the corresponding column operation. For example, if a transaction used a method m and later another transaction changed the representation, the order between the two operations is irrelevant. However, if a successful addition of method m is followed by a replacement of m's representation, the order is important since the final states and the returned values would have been different if the operations were executed in the reverse order. The case when order is important is indicated by a "no" entry.

Finally, we develop the conflict relationship among the operations that modify the attributes of a class object C. We will restrict ourselves to operations that add or delete an attribute to or from a definition of a class. Furthermore, we assume that if a transaction accesses an attribute a in class C through a method execution, it issues an operation $use(a)$. Thus, we assume that the definition of a method lists all the relevant attributes that may be used as a result of its execution. Consider a transaction T that executes a method m on instance o and let m be defined in class C. Before m is executed, T issues operation $use(m)$ on the class object C. Furthermore, for all attributes a in the class hierarchy of o that may be accessed as a result of the method execution m, T issues operations $use(a)$. The right backward commutativity relation for the operations for accessing the attributes of a class is illustrated in Table 3.

Note that by defining operations on classes, we are providing methods for manipulating class objects. Classes provide methods for manipulating instance objects. We therefore have a uniform treatment of all types of objects in the system. Furthermore, we use the same notion of right backward commutativity to determine conflict relation between operations on classes as well as instances.

2.2 Protocol

In the traditional read/write model, locks have two relationships: shared and non-shared. A transaction acquires a read lock for executing a read operation and a write lock for a write operation. A read lock has a shared relationship with other read locks and non-shared relationship with write locks. Write locks, on the other hand, have non-shared relationships with both read and write locks. This allows several active transactions to concurrently execute read operations on an object, while ensuring a single active write operation. Weihl extended this approach to abstract data types by using the notion of right backward commutativity [Wei89b]. An operation o is first executed, and if any active transactions are executing conflicting operations o', i.e., o does not right backward commute with o', o is delayed for later execution; otherwise o is added to the set of currently active operations and is assigned a shared lock.

We now introduce a protocol, which uses a recently introduced relationship between locks, called *ordered sharing* [AE90]. When ordered sharing is used, an operation is never delayed: once it is executed it either acquires a shared or an ordered shared relation with respect to other active operations. Informally, once the results of an operation o are known, the set of operations executed by active transactions are partitioned into two sets: the set of operations that commute with o and the set of operations that do not commute with o. If o commutes with some operation o' or if the commute relation between o and o' is undefined, then o does not conflict with o'. In this case, o has a shared relation with respect to o' and the execution order between the two operations is not important, i.e., in an equivalent serial execution the order between o and o' can be reversed. On the other hand, if o does not commute with o', then o conflicts with o' and o has an *ordered shared* relation with o'. In this case, the order of execution between o and o' is important, and any other conflicting operations executed by the corresponding transactions must be executed in the same order.

We now describe more formally the protocol, and describe how the restrictions on execution are maintained. An operation and its results $\langle p, res \rangle$ partition the set of concurrent operations into two categories:

1. $\langle p, res \rangle$ has a shared relation with all operations $\langle q, res' \rangle$ that do not conflict with $\langle p, res \rangle$.
2. $\langle p, res \rangle$ has an ordered-shared relation with all operations $\langle q, res' \rangle$ that conflict with $\langle p, res \rangle$.

In order to enforce the above relations among operations we associate locks with each operation and response pair. In particular, $\langle p, res \rangle$ is given a lock which has a shared relationship with respect to all operations in the first category and has an ordered shared relationship with respect to all operations in the second category. We employ a strict two phase locking policy, i.e., all locks are released when a transaction commits or aborts. In the case of the bank account, for example, an operation has shared relations with all column operations with "yes" entries and has ordered shared relations with all column operations with "no" entries.

Transactions that employ locks with shared and ordered shared relationships must observe the following rules:

1. A lock $l(t)$ is associated with each atomic operation t. The lock $l(t)$ has a shared relationship with respect to locks of all operations with which t has a shared relation and has an ordered shared relationship with respect to locks of all operations with which t has an ordered shared relation.
2. All locks of a transaction are released when the transaction commits or aborts, i.e., transactions observe the strict two phase locking rule.
3. *Ordered Commitment Rule.* A transaction T_i is said to be *waiting for* T_j if T_i was granted a lock with an ordered shared relationship with respect to a lock held by T_j on an object. In this case, T_i cannot commit its operations on any object as long as any transaction T_j, for which T_i is waiting for, has not committed or aborted.

Recall as discussed in the model, a transaction must execute all appropriate *use* operations before executing each method. In particular, the method being executed and all attributes involved in the method must be locked as the result of these operations.

We are using the strict version of two phase locking in which all locks are released at transaction commit/abort for several reasons. First, often it is difficult for the application to determine when locks can be released. At the time of transaction commitment, it is always certain that the transaction has completed and hence would not need any more locks. Second, the recovery mechanism is considerably simplified if locks are released at termination. Finally, in a distributed system, strict two phase locking is used to implement the two phase rule easily and efficiently. Otherwise, whenever a transaction issues an operation on an object, the object must communicate with every other database objects to ensure that this transaction has not released locks elsewhere [BHG87]. The strict policy eliminates the need for this communication, which would be prohibitively expensive in a distributed environment.

In order to implement the protocol, we have to ensure that operation execution is carried out correctly and the ordered commitment rule is enforced. The execution of operations is completely local to the objects where they are being executed and, hence, can be implemented in a straightforward manner. However, the ordered commitment rule requires that a transaction may not commit at any object as long as it is waiting for some other transactions on some other objects. This rule can be enforced by requiring a committing transaction to send commit requests to all objects accessed by the transaction. An object responds only if the transaction is not waiting for any other transactions at that object. After receiving the responses from all objects, the transaction can commit by sending a commit message to all the objects. The above implementation can be easily incorporated into the standard two phase commit protocol [Gra78] which is generally necessary for ensuring atomicity.

The correctness of the protocol can be informally argued as follows. Let H be a history produced by the protocol and let $SG(H)$ be the corresponding serialization graph induced by H. If $T_1 \rightarrow T_2 \in SG(H)$, then T_1 and T_2 executed conflicting operation o_1 and o_2 such that $o_1 < o_2$. Since o_1 and o_2 conflict, either T_1 committed before T_2 executed o_2 or o_2 has an ordered shared relation with respect to o_1. Hence from the restriction on transaction commitment, if $T_1 \rightarrow T_2$ in $SG(H)$ then $c_1 < c_2$. By induction, if $T_1 \rightarrow \cdots \rightarrow T_n$ in $SG(H)$ then $c_1 < c_n$. Hence, a cycle in $SG(H)$ would imply $c_i < c_i$ for some transaction T_i, a contradiction. Thus, H is serializable.

We now summarize the results in this section. Previous concurrency control protocols for object oriented databases [GK88, CF90] only consider read and write operations. By exploiting the rich structure that is already available in an object oriented database and by using the semantics of both methods on instances as well as the semantics of operations on classes, we are able to achieve higher concurrency. Our approach differs from earlier approaches with respect to the granularity of schema updates. In particular, we allow for schema updates at the level of attribute and methods whereas previous work required the locking of an entire class [GK88, CF90]. Finally, an advantage of uniform treatment of both classes and instances allow users to atomically update both types of objects through a single atomic transaction. This is particularly beneficial from the point-of-view of extensibility and experimentation that are needed for continuously evolving object oriented database applications.

3 Nested Transactions in Object Oriented Databases

As mentioned in the introduction, the notion of nesting is natural in object oriented databases. In this section, we first extend the model of objects to include methods that are not necessarily atomic and these methods may invoke other methods [HH91, RGN90]. This results in transaction executions with a nested structure. We then present a concurrency control protocol to synchronize the execution of nested transactions in object oriented databases. We conclude this section by analyzing the proposed protocol.

3.1 Model

We now extend the object model to include nested transactions. In this model, a method execution is a transaction which may invoke atomic operations or invoke other methods on other objects. This results in the method execution or transaction having a *nested* structure.

We now extend our definition of objects and transactions to allow for nesting [HH91]. A *transaction* T_i is a partial order $\langle t_i, <_{T_i} \rangle$ such that:

1. t_i is a set of operations, where an operation may be another transaction $T_j = \langle t_j, <_{T_j} \rangle$ or an atomic operation.
2. The relation $<_{T_i}$ orders at least all conflicting atomic operations in t_i.

From the above definition, T_i imposes a tree structure such that the operations in t_i appear to be atomic to T_i. Standard tree terminology is used to refer to the relationship among the nodes. The members of t_i are *children* of T_i. T_j is a *descendent* of T_i if $T_j = T_i$ or T_j is a child of a descendant of T_i. T_j is a *proper descendant* of T_i if it is a descendant other than T_i itself. *Ancestor* relationship is defined analogously. T_i is a *top-level* transaction if it has no proper ancestors. The *least common ancestor* of a set of transactions t is a transaction T such that T is an ancestor of every transaction $T_i \in t$ but no proper descendent of T has this property. We denote the least common ancestor of transactions T_1 and T_2 as $lca(T_1, T_2)$.

Consider a set of transactions $T = \{T_1, T_2, \ldots, T_n\}$. The execution of the transactions in T is modeled by a structure called a *history*. Formally, a history H over T is a tuple $(\Sigma, <)$ such that:

1. Σ is the set of all operations executed by transactions in T.
2. Relation $<$ is a partial order on the operations of H and must satisfy the following conditions:
   (a) For every $T_i = \langle t_i, <_{T_i} \rangle \in \Sigma$, $<\supset<_{T_i}$.
   (b) For every pair of conflicting atomic operations o and o', either $o < o'$ or $o' < o$.
   (c) If $T_i < T_j$ then $desc(T_i) < desc(T_j)$.

T and T' are *incomparable* if neither is a descendent of the other.

The correctness of a history H can be determined by constructing the serialization graph of H denoted as $SG(H)$. $SG(H)$ is a directed graph whose nodes correspond to the transactions in H and which has an edge $T \to T'$ iff T and T' are incomparable and either

1. there exists descendents $desc(T)$ and $desc(T')$ such that some operation of $desc(T)$ precedes and conflicts with an operation of $desc(T')$; or
2. if $T_i = lca(T, T')$ and there exist ancestors such that $ancest(T) <_{T_i} ancest(T')$.

Hadzilacos and Hadzilacos [HH91] show that if $SG(H)$ is acyclic then H is serializable. Note that this is a sufficient condition for correctness because the correctness of nested transaction execution is based on view serializability.

3.2 The Protocol

In this section, we present a protocol that ensures that the execution of nested transactions is serializable. The protocol is an extension of the two phase locking protocol with ordered sharing presented in the previous section. A transaction execution must observe the following rules:

1. A lock $l(t)$ is associated with each atomic operation t. The lock $l(t)$ has a shared relationship with respect to locks of all operations with which t has a shared relation and has an ordered shared relationship with respect to locks of all operations with which t has an ordered shared relation.

2. A transaction maintains all its locks until it commits or aborts, i.e., transactions observe the strict two phase locking rule.

3. Transaction T_i cannot commit or abort until all its children have terminated, i.e., committed or aborted.

4. *Ordered Commitment Rule.* T_i is said to be *waiting for* T_j if T_i was granted a lock with an ordered shared relationship with respect to a lock held by T_j on an object and T_j is a proper descendant of $parent(T_i)$. In this case, T_i cannot commit its operations on any object as long as any transaction T_j, for which T_i is waiting for, has not committed or aborted.

5. When a transaction aborts, all its locks are discarded.

6. *Lock Inheritance Rule.* When T_i commits its locks are inherited by $parent(T_i)$. Thus, $parent(T_i)$ inherits all locks $l(t)$ for all atomic operations t executed by its committed descendants. When T_0 inherits the locks, they are discarded.

We will refer to the above protocol as N2PL with ordered sharing. In order to implement the above protocol, we associate with each transaction T a unique transaction identifier $tid(T)$. A transaction identifier $tid(T)$ encodes all the information about the ancestors of T. The ordered commitment rule is enforced as follows. If T_i is a top-level transaction, i.e., $parent(T_i) = T_0$, then we use the two-phase commit protocol as outlined in the previous section to enforce the ordered commitment rule. On the other hand, if T_i is not a top-level transaction then T_i requests its commitment to $parent(T_i)$. The request includes the set of transactions for which T_i is waiting for. Note that all such transactions are proper descendants of $parent(T_i)$ and, therefore, $parent(T_i)$ will eventually know when they terminate. Thus, $parent(T_i)$ can commit T_i when all transactions for which T_i is waiting for have committed. The lock inheritance rule is implemented by using the tids. When a top-level transaction commits, it explicitly informs each accessed object of its commitment and, hence, the object can discard its locks. On the other hand, if a transaction that is not a top-level transaction commits, its commitment is passed to its parent but no information is sent to the objects it accessed. This results in the parent implicitly inheriting the locks on all such objects.

The correctness of the protocol can be argued by using the notion of serialization graphs for nested transactions [HH91]. Let H be a history resulting from the execution of a set of nested transactions using the protocol. We now argue that $SG(H)$ is acyclic. It can be shown that if $T_1 \rightarrow T_2$ then $\text{lca}(T_1, T_2)$ has two children, C_1, which is an ancestor of T_1, and C_2, which is an ancestor of T_2, such that C_1 commits before C_2 commits. By induction, this can be extended to a path in the serialization graph. That is, if there is a path in $SG(H)$: $T_1 \rightarrow T_2 \rightarrow \cdots \rightarrow T_{n-1} \rightarrow T_n$, then $\text{lca}(T_1, T_n)$ has two children, C_1, which is an ancestor of T_1, and C_n, which is an ancestor of T_n, such that C_1 commits before C_n commits. A cycle in the serialization graph implies that there is a transaction T_i that has an ancestor C_i that commits before C_i itself. Hence, $SG(H)$ must be acyclic and hence H is serializable.

479

3.3 Relationship with Other Protocols

We now compare N2PL with ordered sharing with the original N2PL protocol for nested transactions proposed by Moss [Mos85]. In particular, we show that any history accepted by N2PL is accepted by our protocol. Next, we show that the class of histories with acyclic serialization graphs as defined by Hadzilacos and Hadzilacos [HH91] is accepted by our protocol without reordering atomic operations. We conclude with a brief discussion on optimistic protocols for concurrency control and their relationship with N2PL with ordered sharing.

Theorem 1. The class of histories accepted by N2PL [Mos85] is a strict subset of the class of histories accepted by N2PL with ordered sharing.

Proof: Let H be a history accepted by N2PL [Mos85]. The only restriction that is imposed by N2PL with ordered sharing is that a transaction T's commit must follow the commitment of all transactions that are proper descendants of $parent(T)$ and with which T has an ordered shared relation. Let T' be such a transaction. Then in H, T' executed an operation o' and T executed an operation o such that o' and o conflict and $o' < o$ in H. However, in that case, N2PL requires that $o' < c' < o$ in H, where c' is the commit action of T'. Since, the definition of a transaction require that $o < c$ in H, the commitment of T' precedes T in H. Thus, the restriction imposed by N2PL with ordered sharing would not result in H being rejected. Thus, N2PL with ordered sharing accepts all histories that are accepted by N2PL.

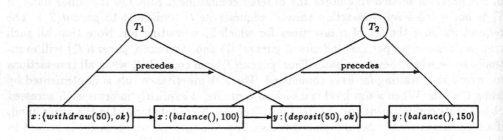

Fig. 1. A history accepted by N2PL with ordered sharing

In order to show strict containment, consider the history shown in Figure 1. This history would be accepted by N2PL with ordered sharing but would be rejected by N2PL. Hence, N2PL with ordered sharing permits more concurrency than N2PL [Mos85]. □

Theorem 2. N2PL accepts all histories with acyclic serialization graph without reordering non-commit atomic operations.

Proof: Let H be a history such that $SG(H)$ as defined in [HH91] is acyclic. Since we are using ordered shared relationships between locks, an operation will never be delayed or blocked in N2PL with ordered sharing. The only restriction is imposed on the order of commitment of transactions or method executions.

Consider a transaction T in the history. We argue that all atomic operations of T can be executed in the original order, however, the commits of some method executions of T may be delayed. Since $SG(H)$ is acyclic, there exists a serialization order of method executions of T. Without loss of generality, let that order be $T_1, T_2, \ldots, T_n$. We now argue that all T_i's can be committed in this serialization order. A transaction T_i may be waiting for T_j only if T_j executed an operation before another conflicting operation executed by T_i. This implies that T_j must appear before T_i in the equivalent serial order. Otherwise, $SG(H)$ would contain a cycle. Since the transactions are committed according to the serial order of transactions, T_i cannot be waiting for any transaction when it commits. Thus, all atomic operations of T are executed in the order in which they appear in H.

The above argument can be applied recursively to $parent(T)$ and so on. Thus, N2PL with ordered sharing preserves the order of execution of non-commit operations in a history H which has an acyclic serialization graph. $\qquad\square$

Theorem 2 is significant from the perspective of concurrency in the system. In particular, transactions do not block other transactions for concurrency control purposes. However, the commit points of transactions may be delayed to ensure serializability. Note that if the same histories were submitted to N2PL, it would have delayed the execution of conflicting operations. Hence at the earliest, N2PL would commit the transactions at the same points as our protocol.

N2PL with ordered sharing as well as two phase locking with ordered sharing have an optimistic flavor in terms of executing conflicting operations. Both allow conflicting operations to be executed and ensure serializability using the ordered commitment rule when transactions commit. This is similar to optimsitic protocols in which transactions execute operations and are later subject to validation [KR81]. However, optimistic protocols generally use deferred update strategy for performing updates while we use update-in-place which has superior performance [AD85]. Furthermore, it can be easily shown that the class of histories accepted by the optimistic concurrency control protocol [KR81] is a strict subset of histories accepted by the standard two phase locking protocol [EGLT76]. Our protocol, on the other hand, is a superset of two phase locking. From Theorem 3, it is clear that similar advantages are carried over for N2PL with ordered sharing.

4 Conclusion

Object oriented databases generalize the traditional database model in several ways. First, objects in the database can be of two types: classes and instances of classes. Second, instead of simple read and write operations on database objects, object oriented databases permit arbitrary operations, viz. methods, on objects. Third, unlike traditional database systems where the database schema is static, object oriented databases support dynamic evolution of schema through operations on classes. Finally, nested executions of methods on objects are possible since a method may invoke another method on some other object. In this paper, we proposed concurrency control protocols for providing transactional access to object oriented databases. We provided a uniform treatment for dealing with both class and instance objects and extended the two phase locking protocol with ordered sharing [AE90] to objects with arbitrary operations. The novel aspect of this protocol is that conflicting operations may share locks on the same objects, provided that the order between the operations is preserved. We then present a protocol for synchronizing nested executions of transactions on objects. Allowing updates to both classes and instances of these classes makes the proposed protocol beneficial for extensibility and experimentation, which are needed for continuously evolving object oriented database applications.

References

[AD85]   R. Agrawal and D. J. Dewitt. Integrated concurrency control and recovery mechanisms: Design and performance evaluation. *ACM Transactions on Database Systems*, 10(4):529–564, December 1985.

[AE90]   D. Agrawal and A. El Abbadi. Locks with Constrained Sharing. In *Proceedings of the Ninth ACM Symposium on Principles of Database Systems*, pages 85–93, April 1990. An expanded version of this paper appears as technical report TRCS 90-14, Department of Computer Science, University of California, Santa Barbara.

[AEL91]   D. Agrawal, A. El Abbadi, and A. E. Lang. Performance Characteristics of Protocols with Ordered Shared Locks. In *Proceedings of the Seventh IEEE International Conference on Data Engineering*, April 1991.

[BBB+88] F. Bacilhon, G. Barbedette, V. Benzaken, C. Delobel, S. Gamerman, C. Lécluse, P. Pfeffer, P. Richard, and F. Velez. The Design and Implementation of O2 an Object-Oriented Database System. In *Advances in Object-Oriented Database Systems, Springer-Verlag*, September 1988.

[BHG87]   P. A. Bernstein, V. Hadzilacos, and N. Goodman. *Concurrency Control and Recovery in Database Systems*. Addison Wesley, Reading, Massachusetts, 1987.

[BKKK87] J. Banerjee, W. Kim, H. J. Kim, and H. F. Korth. Semantics and Implementation of Schema Evolution in Object-Oriented Databases. In *Proceedings of the International Conference on Management of Data*, May 87.

[BR87]   B. Badrinath and K. Ramamritham. Semantics Based Concurrency Control: Beyond Commutativity. In *Proceedings of the International Conference on Data Engineering*, pages 304–311, February 1987. To appear in the ACM Transactions on Database Systems.

[BSW79]   P. A. Bernstein, D. W. Shipman, and W. S. Wong. Formal aspects of serializability in database concurrency control. *IEEE Transactions on Software Engineering*, 5(5):203–216, May 1979.

[CF90]   M. Cart and J. Ferrié. Integrating Concurrency Control into an Object-Oriented Database System. In *Proceedings of the International Conference on Extending Data Base Technology, Springer-Verlag, LNCS 416*, pages 363–376, 1990.

[EGLT76] K. P. Eswaran, J. N. Gray, R. A. Lorie, and I. L. Traiger. The Notion of Consistency and Predicate Locks in Database System. *Communications of the ACM*, 19(11):624–633, November 1976.

[GK88]   J. F. Garza and W. Kim. Transaction Management in an Object-oriented Data Model. In *Proceedings of the International Conference on Management of Data*, pages 37–55, June 88.

[Gra78]   J. N. Gray. Notes on database systems. In R. Bayer, R. M. Graham, and G. Seegmuller, editors, *Operating Systems: An Advanced Course*, volume 60 of *Lecture Notes in Computer Science*, pages 393–481. Springer-Verlag, 1978.

[HH91]   T. Hadzilacos and V. Hadzilacos. Transaction Synchronization in Object Bases. *Journal of Computer and System Sciences*, 43(1):2–24, August 1991. Special issue on the 7th Annual ACM SIGACT-SIGMOD Symposium on the Principles of Database Systems, March 21-23, 1988.

[HR83]   T. Härder and A. Reuter. Principles of Transaction-Oriented Database Recovery. *ACM Computing Surveys*, 15(4):287–317, December 1983.

[Kor83]   H. F. Korth. Locking primitives in a database system. *Journal of the ACM*, 30(1):55–79, January 1983.

[KR81]   H. T. Kung and J. T. Robinson. On Optimistic Methods for Concurrency Control. *ACM Transactions on Database Systems*, 6(2):213–226, June 1981.

[LRV88]   C. Lécluse, P. Richard, and F. Velez. O₂, an Object-Oriented Data Model. In *Proceedings of the International Conference on Management of Data*, pages 424–433, June 88.

[Mos85]   J. E. B. Moss. *Nested Transactions: An Approach to Reliable Distributed Computing*. MIT Press, Cambridge, Massachusetts, 1985.

[Pap79]   C. H. Papadimitriou. The Serializability of Concurrent Database Updates. *Journal of the ACM*, 26(4):631–653, October 1979.

[RGN90]   T. C. Rakow, J. Gu, and E. J. Neuhold. Serializability in Object-Oriented Database Systems. In *Proceedings of the Sixth International Conference on Data Engineering*, pages 112–120, April 1990.

[SS84]   P. M. Schwarz and A. Z. Spector. Synchronizing shared abstract types. *ACM Transactions on Computer Systems*, 2(3):223–250, August 1984.

[Ver78]   J. S. M. Verhofstad. Recovery Techniques for Database Systems. *ACM Computing Surveys*, 10(2):167–196, 1978.

[Wei89a]   W. E. Weihl. Local Atomicity Properties: Modular Concurrency Control for Abstract Data Types. *ACM Transactions on Programming Languages and Systems*, 11(2):249–283, April 1989.

[Wei89b]   W. E. Weihl. The Impact of Recovery on Concurrency Control. In *Proceedings of the Eighth ACM Symposium on Principles of Database Systems*, pages 259–269, March 1989.

This article was processed using the LaTeX macro package with LMAMULT style

An Execution Model for Distributed Database Transactions and Its Implementation in VPL*

Eva Kühn and Franz Puntigam

University of Technology Vienna
Institute of Computer Languages
Argentinierstr. 8, A-1040 Vienna
Austria, Europe
{eva,franz}@mips.complang.tuwien.ac.at

Ahmed K. Elmagarmid

Indiana Center for Database Systems
Department of Computer Sciences
Purdue University
West Lafayette, IN 47907, USA
ake@cs.purdue.edu

Abstract

We present an execution model for distributed transactions that can be employed for multidatabase systems. We use the Flex Transaction model that has been proposed as a highly general and flexible tool for the specification of distributed transactions and extend it by allowing nested and possibly recursive transaction specifications. We show how a given transaction specification and its execution model can be mapped into a representation in a new concurrent Prolog language, the VPL (Vienna Parallel Logic) language. The representation in VPL can be considered as an executable specification. We show some optimizations concerning this mapping and define a significant subclass of Flex Transactions with a declarative representation in VPL that can be modeled by AND/OR structures. We argue that it is more advantageous to use VPL directly for the transaction specification because it provides more flexibility and more control aspects than the Flex Transaction model.

1 Introduction

A transaction model, called *Flex Transactions* [2, 8], has been proposed for the specification of the control of multidatabase transactions. In particular, this model extends commonly used transaction models by allowing the transaction programmer to release the atomicity and isolation requirements [1]. Function replication is provided in that the goal of a local subtransaction can also be achieved by other subtransactions. This model distinguishes between subtransactions that can be compensated and subtransactions that cannot be compensated after they have committed. Compensatable transactions, also called *sagas* [3], may commit before the global transaction completes and may therefore reduce the lock time in local databases. As compensatable and non-compensatable

---

*The work is supported by the Austrian FWF (Fonds zur Förderung der Wissenschaftlichen Forschung), project "Interoperability of Autonomous Databases", contract number P7773-PHY.

transactions are supported by the Flex Transaction model, we speak of *mixed transactions*. Flex Transactions specify the control plan, i.e., parallel or sequential execution of transactions due to given dependencies. However, Flex Transactions are not runnable transactions. For the transaction processing in a heterogeneous environment, we need
(a)   a specification model for the transaction control (we use Flex Transactions), and
(b)   an execution model for transactions.

In Section 2, we extend the Flex Transaction model by allowing nested and recursively defined Flex Transactions. A subtransaction may either be a transaction on a local database or again a Flex Transaction. We present an execution model for this extended definition and prove its correctness in Section 3. This model allows a maximum of parallelism: as soon as all pre-conditions for a subtransaction are fulfilled, this subtransaction may be scheduled for execution. The locking time in local databases is kept as short as possible by immediately committing compensatable transactions after they have succeeded. This feature contributes to the autonomy of local database systems [7]. We assume that the corresponding local database systems provide the two phase commit protocol for non-compensatable transactions.

In [5, 6] we have proposed a new concurrent logic programming language, the VPL (Vienna Parallel Logic) language. This language has been influenced by the family of concurrent Prolog languages [9] and provides explicit language constructs to control the parallelism. VPL differs from existing concurrent Prolog languages in many aspects: VPL is transaction oriented, supports the compensation of committed code, and allows full backtracking. Synchronization and communication in VPL is done by *communication variables*. Section 4 gives a brief survey of VPL.

In Section 5 we show how a Flex Transaction specification can be mapped into a VPL program. This program can be considered as a runnable specification. We prove that the execution of this program is equivalent to the previously defined execution model concerning the produced output and the execution time. Next we prove that VPL's control mechanisms are at least as powerful as the Flex Transaction model. In particular, VPL provides even more mechanisms for the control of distributed transactions. We argue to use VPL directly as the specification language because there exists a significant subclass of Flex Transactions with a highly declarative representation in VPL: they can be modeled by AND/OR structures (Section 6). Thus, VPL can serve for the specification and execution of flexible multidatabase transactions.

2   Flex Transactions and Definitions

We give a definition of nested Flex Transactions and some definitions that we use to prove the correctness of the execution model in Section 3. Our definition of Flex Transactions differs from that in [2] and [8] in that also nested Flex Transactions are considered and only relevant internal dependencies are tested.

Definition 2.1 (*Flex Transaction*). A *Flex Transaction* T is a 5-tuple $(D, \prec_S, \prec_F, \Pi, C)$ where
(a) $D = \{t_1, \ldots, t_n\}$ is a finite set of *typed subtransactions* called the *domain* of T;
(b)   the ordering relation $\prec_S$ specifies the *success order* of T (a partial order on D);

(c)   the ordering relation $\prec_F$ specifies the *failure order* of T (a partial order on D);

(d) $\Pi = \{\pi_1, \ldots, \pi_n\}$ is a set of predicates on D called the *external dependencies* of T. Each $\pi_i \in \Pi$ is a predicate on $t_i \in D$;

(e) $C = \{C_1, \ldots, C_m\}$ where $C_i \subseteq D$ is called a *commit-set* of T ($i = 1, \ldots, m$).

$\prec_S$ and $\prec_F$ must be chosen so that the *order* of T, with ordering relation $\prec$, is a partial order of D where $t_i \prec t_j$ iff $t_i \prec_S t_j$ or $t_i \prec_F t_j$ (for all $t_i, t_j \in D$).

In the following, we use the notions of transaction and subtransaction interchangeably to denote typed subtransactions. Transactions are either local transactions that are executed at a database system or Flex Transactions. Informally, a Flex Transaction succeeds if all subtransactions in one of its commit-sets are a success. $\prec_S$ and $\prec_F$ specify an execution order on the subtransactions (*internal dependencies*). $t_i \prec_S t_j$ ($t_i \prec_F t_j$) is called a *success dependency* (*failure dependency*) between t_i and t_j. The external dependencies specify extra constraints, e.g., time constraints.

Definition 2.2 (*transaction type, compensate-action*). For a Flex Transaction T with the domain D, the function $type : D \rightarrow \{C, NC\}$ determines the *type* of each subtransaction $t_i \in D$. If $type(t_i) = C$, then t_i is *compensatable;* otherwise t_i is *non-compensatable*. A transaction c_i, called *compensate-action*, is associated with each compensatable transaction t_i; c_i *compensates* the effects of t_i.

Compensate-actions are Flex Transactions. They have to be specified so that they cannot fail. This can be achieved by function replication. A compensatable subtransaction t_i may be committed before it is known that t_i is needed. If t_i is committed but not needed, the execution of the compensate-action c_i (Definition 2.2) compensates all effects of t_i. A non-compensatable subtransaction t_j must not be committed before it is known that t_j is really needed.

Definition 2.3 (*execution state, local execution state*). Let T be a Flex Transaction with the domain $\{t_1, \ldots, t_n\}$. The *execution state* x^τ of T at time τ is an n-tuple $(x_1^\tau, \ldots, x_n^\tau)$ where (for $i = 1, \ldots, n$) the *local execution state* of subtransaction t_i at time τ

$$x_i^\tau = \begin{cases} N & \text{if } t_i \text{ has not yet been submitted for execution at time } \tau; \\ S & \text{if } t_i \text{ has succeeded and is committed at time } \tau; \\ P & \text{if } t_i \text{ has succeeded and is in a prepared state at time } \tau; \\ F & \text{if } t_i \text{ has failed (has been aborted) at time } \tau' \le \tau; \\ E & \text{otherwise } (t_i \text{ is executing at time } \tau). \end{cases}$$

We use the following transition network to describe all possible local execution states of a subtransaction: Initially, each subtransaction t_i is in the state N. After t_i has been submitted to the database system for execution (i.e., t_i has been started), t_i is in the state E. When the execution has terminated, the state of t_i changes to S (successfully terminated and committed) or to F (failed) if t_i is compensatable; the state of t_i changes to P (successfully terminated and not yet committed) or to F if t_i is non-compensatable. S and F are final states that will never change. P is the prepared state of the two phase commit (2PC) protocol. We assume that each database system where non-compensatable subtransactions are executed supports 2PC. When it is known whether t_i is needed or not, the state of t_i changes from P to S (commit) or to F (abort).

Definition 2.4 (*initial execution state, history*). Let T be a Flex Transaction with the domain $\{t_1, \ldots, t_n\}$. The execution state $x^{\tau_0} = (x_1^{\tau_0}, \ldots, x_n^{\tau_0})$ with $x_i^{\tau_0} = \text{N}$ ($i = 1, \ldots, n$) is called the *initial* execution state of T. A *history* H^k of T is a set of execution states $\{x^{\tau_0}, x^{\tau_1}, \ldots, x^{\tau_k}\}$ where τ_j ($j = 1, \ldots, k$) is chosen as follows: $x^{\tau_j} \neq x^{\tau_{j-1}}$ and there does not be a time τ' with $\tau_{j-1} < \tau' < \tau_j$ and $x^{\tau'} \neq x^{\tau_{j-1}}$.

Definition 2.5 (*prefix*). Let $H^k = \{x^{\tau_0}, \ldots, x^{\tau_k}\}$ and $H'^{k'} = \{x'^{\tau_0'}, \ldots, x'^{\tau_{k'}'}\}$ be two histories. $H'^{k'}$ is a prefix of H^k, denoted by $H^{k'}$, iff $k' < k$, $\tau_i = \tau_i'$, and $x'^{\tau_i'} = x^{\tau_i}$ for all $i = 0, \ldots, k'$.

A history reflects all transitions of the execution state of a Flex Transaction. Let H^k be a history of the Flex Transaction T with n subtransactions and let $(x_1^{\tau_j}, \ldots, x_n^{\tau_j}) = x^{\tau_j} \in H^k$ ($j = 1, \ldots, k$) denote the execution states in H^k. From the possible local execution state transitions of subtransactions it is clear that for $i = 1, \ldots, n$

(a) if $x_i^{\tau_j} = \text{N}$, then $x_i^{\tau_v} = \text{N}$ for $0 \leq v \leq j$;

(b) if $x_i^{\tau_j} = \text{E}$, then there is an $x_i^{\tau_w} = \text{N}$ with $x_i^{\tau_v} = \text{E}$ for $w < v \leq j$;

(c) if $x_i^{\tau_j} = \text{P}$, then $type(t_i) = \text{NC}$ and there is an $x_i^{\tau_w} = \text{E}$ with $x_i^{\tau_v} = \text{P}$ for $w < v \leq j$;

(d) if $x_i^{\tau_j} = \text{S}$ and $type(t_i) = \text{C}$, then there is an $x_i^{\tau_w} = \text{E}$ with $w < j$ and $x_i^{\tau_v} = \text{S}$ for $w < v \leq k$;

(e) if $x_i^{\tau_j} = \text{S}$ and $type(t_i) = \text{NC}$, then there is an $x_i^{\tau_w} = \text{P}$ with $w < j$ and $x_i^{\tau_v} = \text{S}$ for $w < v \leq k$;

(f) if $x_i^{\tau_j} = \text{F}$, then there is either an $x_i^{\tau_w} = \text{E}$ or an $x_i^{\tau_w} = \text{P}$ with $w < j$ and $x_i^{\tau_v} = \text{F}$ for $w < v \leq k$.

All possible histories of a Flex Transaction T do not be correct (because of the success and failure order of T). There need not exist a history that is correct for all commit-sets of T. We must define the correctness of a history with respect to a specific commit-set (Definition 2.8).

Definition 2.6 (*acceptable state*). Let T be a Flex Transaction with domain $\{t_1, \ldots, t_n\}$. Let C_i be a commit-set of T. The *acceptable state* A_i of T with respect to C_i is a tuple $(a_{i,1}, \ldots, a_{i,n})$ where for $j = 1, \ldots, n$

$$a_{i,j} = \begin{cases} \text{S} & \text{if } t_j \in C_i \text{ and } type(t_j) = \text{C}; \\ \text{P} & \text{if } t_j \in C_i \text{ and } type(t_j) = \text{NC}; \\ \text{F} & \text{if there is a } t_v \in C_i \text{ with } t_j \prec_F t_v \text{ and } t_j \notin C_i \ (j \neq v); \\ \text{Y} & \text{otherwise.} \end{cases}$$

S, P, and F are used with the same meaning as the local execution states defined above. Y stands for any local execution state. Note that a local execution state $a_{i,j}$ must be F if there is a failure dependency so that a subtransaction in the commit-set must wait for the failure of t_j and t_j is not in the commit-set. A failure dependency between t_j and t_v is not important if both t_j and t_v are in the same commit-set. Otherwise this definition would cause a contradiction.

Definition 2.7 (*executable subtransaction*). Let $T = (D, \prec_S, \prec_F, \Pi, C)$ be a Flex Transaction with $D = \{t_1, \ldots, t_n\}$ and the execution state $x^\tau = (x_1^\tau, \ldots, x_n^\tau)$ at time τ. Let $A_i = (a_{i,1}, \ldots, a_{i,n})$ be the acceptable state of T with respect to $C_i \in C$. The subtransaction $t_j \in D$ is *executable* at time τ with respect to C_i if the following conditions hold (for $v = 1, \ldots, n; v \neq j; z_v, z_j \in \{\text{P}, \text{S}\}$):

(a) $\pi_j \in \Pi$ is true for t_j at time τ;

(b)   if $t_v \prec_S t_j$, $a_{i,v} = z_v$, and $a_{i,j} = z_j$, then $x_v^\tau = z_v$;

(c)   if $t_v \prec_F t_j$ and $a_{i,v} = $ F, then $x_v^\tau = $ F.

Definition 2.8 (*correct history*). Let T be a Flex Transaction with domain $\{t_1,\ldots,t_n\}$ and history H^k. Let C_i be a commit-set of T. Let $(x_1^{\tau_v},\ldots,x_n^{\tau_v}) = x^{\tau_v} \in H^k$ ($v = 0,\ldots,k$). H^k is a *correct* history of T with respect to C_i if $k = 0$ or if the following conditions hold:

(a) H^{k-1} is a correct history of T with respect to C_i;

(b)   if $t_j \in C_i$ and $x_j^{\tau_k} \neq $ N, then t_j is executable at time τ_k with respect to C_i ($j = 1,\ldots,n$).

By Definitions 2.6 through 2.8, a success dependency between t_v and t_j is important for a history H^k with respect to a commit-set C_i only if both t_v and t_j are in C_i. As stated above, a failure dependency between t_v and t_j is important only if t_j is in C_i but t_v is not. Dependencies that do not be important for H^k with respect to C_i may be important for H^k with respect to C_w where $C_w \neq C_i$ is a commit-set.

Definition 2.9 (*comply*). Let T be a Flex Transaction with the domain $\{t_1,\ldots,t_n\}$, let C_i be a commit-set of T, let $x^\tau = (x_1^\tau,\ldots,x_n^\tau)$ be the execution state of T at the time τ, and let $A_i = (a_{i,1},\ldots,a_{i,n})$ denote the acceptable state of T with respect to C_i. If $a_{i,j} = x_j^\tau$ or $a_{i,j} = $ Y for all $j = 1,\ldots,n$, then x^τ *complies* with C_i.

Definition 2.10 (*succeed, fail, selected commit-set, execution time*). Let T be a Flex Transaction with the set of commit-sets C and the history H^k. Let $x^{\tau_j} \in H^k$ denote an execution state in the history ($j = 0,\ldots,k$). T *succeeds* with the *selected* commit-set $C_s \in C$ and the *execution time* $\tau_e = \tau_k - \tau_1$ if the following conditions hold:

(a) H^k is a correct history of T with respect to C_s;

(b) x^{τ_k} complies with C_s;

(c) $x^{\tau_{k-1}}$ does not comply with C_s.

T *fails* with execution time $\tau_e = \tau_k - \tau_1$ if the following conditions hold:

(a)   there does not exist a history $H^{k'}$ with $k < k'$ and T succeeds with the execution time $\tau_{k''} - \tau_1$ where $1 < k'' \leq k'$;

(b) T has not failed with execution time $\tau_{k-1} - \tau_1$.

When a Flex Transaction T succeeds, a commit-set C_s is selected. On commitment of T, all subtransactions in C_s that are in a prepared state must be committed, all subtransactions that are not in C_s either have not yet been started or must be aborted or compensated. If T is aborted, then all subtransactions that have already been started must be aborted or compensated (i.e., the same actions must occur as if $C_s = \emptyset$ has been selected):

Definition 2.11 (*completed transaction*). Let T be a Flex Transaction with the domain $\{t_1,\ldots,t_n\}$. Let $x^\tau = (x_1^\tau,\ldots,x_n^\tau)$ be the execution state of T at the time τ. T has *completed* at time τ if one of the following conditions holds:

(a) T has succeeded with a selected commit-set C_s;

(b) T has failed ($C_s = \emptyset$);

and the following conditions hold for $i = 1, \ldots, n$ where $C_s' = C_s$ if T has succeeded and is committed, and $C_s' = \emptyset$ otherwise:

(a) $x_i^\tau = \text{F}$ or $x_i^\tau = \text{S}$ or $x_i^\tau = \text{N}$;

(b) if $t_i \in C_s'$, then $x_i^\tau = \text{S}$;

(c) if $t_i \notin C_s'$ and $type(t_i) = \text{NC}$, then $x_i^\tau \neq \text{S}$;

(d) if $t_i \notin C_s'$ and $x_i^\tau = \text{S}$, then the compensate-action c_i which is associated with t_i has completed at time τ;

(e) there is not a time $\tau' > \tau$ with $x_i^\tau \neq x_i^{\tau'}$.

The definition of Flex Transactions in this section is not an execution model. The main problem is the interdependency between the selection of a commit-set and the correctness of a history. It is not useful to select a commit-set before a Flex Transaction starts execution because this would imply the loss of function replication. On the other side, starting the subtransactions so that the resulting history is correct with respect to all commit-sets is impossible in general. In the next section we describe an execution model for Flex Transactions that keeps a correct history for all commit-sets that eventually may be selected.

3 An Execution Model for Flex Transactions

Before we can give an algorithm for the execution of Flex Transactions, we need additional definitions and a proposition:

Definition 3.1 (*commit-set state*). Let $T = (D, \prec_S, \prec_F, \Pi, C)$ be a Flex Transaction with $D = \{t_1, \ldots, t_n\}$ and $C = \{C_1, \ldots, C_m\}$. Let $x^\tau = (x_1^\tau, \ldots, x_n^\tau)$ be the execution state of T at the time τ. Let $A_i = (a_{i,1}, \ldots, a_{i,n})$ denote the acceptable state of T with respect to C_i (i=1,...,m). The *commit-set state* r^τ of T at time τ is an m-tuple $(r_1^\tau, \ldots, r_m^\tau)$ where

$$
r_i^\tau = \begin{cases}
\mathcal{F} & \text{if there is an } a_{i,v} = \text{F with } x_v^\tau = z \\
& \text{or there is an } a_{i,v} = z \text{ with } x_v^\tau = \text{F } (z \in \{\text{P}, \text{S}\}); \\
\mathcal{S} & \text{if } x^\tau \text{ complies with } C_j; \\
\mathcal{E} & \text{otherwise.}
\end{cases}
$$

Proposition 3.2 (*final commit-set state*). Let $T = (D, \prec_S, \prec_F, \Pi, C)$ be a Flex Transaction with $D = \{t_1, \ldots, t_n\}$ and $C = \{C_1, \ldots, C_m\}$. Let H^k be a history of T, let $(x_1^{\tau_j}, \ldots, x_n^{\tau_j}) = x^{\tau_j} \in H^k$ denote an execution state in H^k, and let $r^{\tau_j} = (r_1^{\tau_j}, \ldots, r_m^{\tau_j})$ denote the commit-set state of T at time τ_j $(j = 1, \ldots, k)$. Let there not be an j' $(j < j' \leq k)$ with $x_u^{\tau_j} = \text{P}$ and $x_u^{\tau_{j'}} \neq \text{P}$ $(u = 1, \ldots, n)$. If $r_i^{\tau_v} = \mathcal{S}$ $(r_i^{\tau_v} = \mathcal{F})$, then $r_i^{\tau_w} = \mathcal{S}$ $(r_i^{\tau_w} = \mathcal{F})$ for $i = 1, \ldots, m$; $v = 0, \ldots, k$; $v \leq w \leq k$.

Proof. Since H^k does not contain a transition of a local execution state from P to S or to F, there does not be a transition of a local execution state that is in a P, S, or F state into another state. ∎

Definition 3.3 (*startable subtransaction*). Let T be a Flex Transaction with the domain $D = \{t_1, \ldots, t_n\}$ and the set of commit-sets $C = \{C_1, \ldots, C_m\}$. Let $r^\tau = \{r_1^\tau, \ldots, r_m^\tau\}$ be the commit-set state of T at time τ. A subtransaction t_i $(i = 1, \ldots, n)$ is *startable* at time τ if $r_j^\tau = \mathcal{F}$ or t_i is executable at time τ with respect to C_j for all $j = 1, \ldots, m$.

Algorithm 3.4 (*execute a Flex Transaction specification*).

Input: A Flex Transaction T with the domain $\{t_1, \ldots, t_n\}$ and the set of commit-sets $\{C_1, \ldots, C_m\}$, $type(T)$, and a Boolean variable in that specifies whether or not to commit T.

Output: The selected commit-set C_s.

Global Variables: The current execution state $x = (x_1, \ldots, x_n)$ of T, the commit-set C_s, a set of indices f, and a Boolean variable b.

1. Set $x = (N, \ldots, N)$; set $f = \emptyset$; set $b = $ false.

2. Execute Steps (a) through (e) in parallel and break execution when $b = $ true during wait operations:

   (a) Execute Steps (i) and (ii) for $i = 1, \ldots, n$ in parallel:

       (i) Wait until t_i is startable; then start t_i and set $x_i = $ E.

       (ii) Wait until t_i has succeeded or failed; if t_i has succeeded and $type(t_i) = $ C, then set $x_i = $ S; if t_i has succeeded and $type(t_i) = $ NC, then set $x_i = $ P; otherwise (t_i has failed) set $x_i = $ F.

   (b) Execute this step if $type(T) = $ C: Wait until there is an $r_j = \mathcal{S}$ in the current commit-set state $r = (r_1, \ldots, r_m)$; then set $C_s = C_j$ and set $b = $ true.

   (c) Execute this step if $type(T) = $ NC: Execute Steps (i) and (ii) in sequence:

       (i) Wait until there is an $r_j = \mathcal{S}$ with $j \notin f$ in the current commit-set state $r = (r_1, \ldots, r_m)$; then set $C_s = C_j$.

       (ii) Wait for an input in; if $in = $ true, then set $b = $ true; otherwise set $f = f \cup \{j\}$ and continue with Step (i).

   (d) Wait until $r_j \neq \mathcal{E}$ for all $j = 1, \ldots, m$ in the current commit-set state $r = (r_1, \ldots, r_m)$ and $j \in f$ if $r_j = \mathcal{S}$; then set $C_s = \emptyset$ and set $b = $ true.

   (e) Wait until T is caused to abort during its execution; then set $C_s = \emptyset$ and set $b = $ true.

3. Execute Steps (a) through (d) for $i = 1, \ldots, n$ in parallel:

   (a) If $t_i \in C_s$ and $x_i = $ P, then cause t_i to commit.

   (b) If $x_i = $ E or $x_i = $ P and $t_i \notin C_s$, then cause t_i to abort.

   (c) If $t_i \notin C_s$ and $x_i = $ S, then execute the compensate-action c_i of t_i, wait until the execution of c_i returns a result, cause c_i to commit, and wait until c_i has completed.

   (d) If $x_i \neq $ N, then wait until t_i has completed.

We assume a sufficiently fine grained clock so that all execution state transitions can be observed. Further we assume that just those steps in Algorithm 3.4 need time that explicitly wait for an event to occur. Algorithm 3.4 produces an output whenever the output variable C_s is set.

The following theorems show the correspondence between the output of Algorithm 3.4 and the success or failure of a Flex Transaction T (Definition 2.10), and between the termination of Algorithm 3.4 and the completion of T. We will give sufficient conditions for the production of an output and the termination of the algorithm.

Theorem 3.5 (*output, succeed, fail*). If Algorithm 3.4 with input T produces an output C_s with $C_s \neq \emptyset$ after run time τ_r, then T succeeds with the selected commit-set C_s and the execution time $\tau_e \leq \tau_r$. If C_s with $C_s \neq \emptyset$ is the first output, then $\tau_e = \tau_r$. If C_s is the first output, $C_s = \emptyset$, and T is not caused to abort, then T fails with the execution time $\tau_e = \tau_r$.

Proof. Let $H^k = \{x^{\tau_0}, \ldots, x^{\tau_k}\}$ be the history corresponding to the execution of T. Step 1 of Algorithm 3.4 initializes x to the initial execution state. τ_0 is the time when T was created (not the start time of T). Step 2(a)(i) immediately starts some subtransactions and changes some components of x from N to E. Since we assume that internal calculations do not need time, these transitions occur at the same time τ_1 when the transaction is started and are reflected in x^{τ_1}. Each subsequent transition of a component of x in Step 2(a) may cause a new element $x = x^{\tau_{k+1}}$ to be inserted into H^k whereby x denotes the execution state immediately after the transition at time τ_{k+1}.

Let $r^\tau = (r_1^\tau, \ldots, r_m^\tau)$ denote the commit-set state of T at time τ. During execution of Step 2, the history does not contain a state transition from P to S or to F. If $r_i^\tau = \mathcal{S}$ ($r_i^\tau = \mathcal{F}$), then $r_i^{\tau'} = \mathcal{S}$ ($r_i^{\tau'} = \mathcal{F}$) for all $\tau \leq \tau' \leq \tau_k$. An $r_i^\tau = \mathcal{F}$ can never be selected, thus the history H^k need not be correct with respect to C_i if $r_i^{\tau_k} = \mathcal{F}$.

We have to show that T succeeds with the selected commit-set C_s whenever $C_s \neq \emptyset$ is set. H^0 trivially is a correct history with respect to all commit-sets $C_i \in C$. Let H^{k-1} be correct with respect to $C_i \in C$ for all $i = 1, \ldots, m$ with $r_i^{\tau_{k-1}} \neq \mathcal{F}$ and let there be such $r_i^{\tau_{k-1}} \neq \mathcal{F}$. H^k is correct with respect to $C_j \in C$ for all $j = 1, \ldots, m$ with $r_j^{\tau_k} \neq \mathcal{F}$ by Definitions 2.8 and 3.3 since a subtransaction $t_v \in D$ is not started before t_v is startable. If there is an $r_j^{\tau_k} = \mathcal{S}$, then Step 2 sets the selected commit-set $C_s = C_j$. Since $r_j^{\tau_k} \neq \mathcal{F}$, H^k is correct with respect to $C_s = C_j$. Because of Definition 3.1, x^{τ_k} complies with C_s.

Step 2 of Algorithm 3.4 sets the first result as soon as x^{τ_k} complies with C_s, so $x^{\tau_{k-1}}$ cannot comply with C_s. Thus, T succeeds with the selected commit-set C_s and the execution time $\tau_r = \tau_e = \tau_k - \tau_1$. For all subsequent results $C'_{j'}$, let $\tau_{k'}$ denote the time when $r_{j'}^{\tau_{k'}}$ becomes $\mathcal{S}$. T succeeds with the selected commit-set $C'_{j'}$ and the execution time $\tau'_e = \tau_{k'} - \tau_1$ since $x^{\tau_{k'-1}}$ cannot comply with $C'_{j'}$. The run time τ'_r may be longer than the execution time τ'_e because the output may be delayed by waiting for the input *in* to eject the previously produced output.

It remains to show that T fails with execution time τ_r if the first output of Algorithm 3.4 is $\emptyset$ and T has not been caused to abort. The commit-set state $r^{\tau_k} = (\mathcal{F}, \ldots, \mathcal{F})$. There cannot be a τ' with $\tau' > \tau^k$ and $r^{\tau'} \neq r^{\tau_k}$. There is not a correct history $H^{k'}$ ($k' \geq k$) with respect to any $C_i \in C$. But there is a correct history $H'^{k'}$ ($k' \geq k$) with respect to $C_i \in C$ with prefix H^{k-1} because there must be an $r_j^{\tau_{k-1}} = \mathcal{E}$. Thus, T fails with the execution time $\tau_r = \tau_e = \tau_k - \tau_1$. ∎

Theorem 3.6 (*termination and completed transaction*). If Algorithm 3.4 with input T stops at time τ, then T is completed at time τ.

Proof. The theorem directly follows from Step 3 of Algorithm 3.4 (Definition 2.11). ∎

Theorem 3.7 (*sufficient conditions for output*). Algorithm 3.4 with input $T = (D, \prec_S, \prec_F, \Pi, C)$ produces an output if following conditions hold:

a) t_i eventually stops for all $t_i \in D$;

b) π eventually is true for all $\pi \in \Pi$.

Proof. Let $H^k = \{x^{\tau_0}, \ldots, x^{\tau_k}\}$ be a history corresponding to the execution of T, let $r^{\tau_j} = (r_1^{\tau_j}, \ldots, r_m^{\tau_j})$ denote the commit-set state of T at time τ_j $(j = 0, \ldots, k)$ and let $D = \{t_1, \ldots, t_n\}$. k is finite since n is finite and T has at most 3^n execution state transitions. There is a time $\tau_{k'}$ with $r_i^{\tau_{k'}} = S$ or $r_i^{\tau_{k'}} = \mathcal{F}$ for all $i = 1, \ldots, m$, where H^k is a prefix of $H^{k'}$. Thus Step 2 of Algorithm 3.4 stops if all time intervals between execution state transitions are finite.

Step 2(a)(ii) does not wait forever if t_i eventually stops for $i = 1, \ldots, n$. We assume that this condition is satisfied.

In Step 2(a)(i) each $t_i \in D$ waits until t_i is startable. By Definition 3.3, t_i is startable if (for each $C_v \in C$) t_i is executable or C_v is no longer a candidate for the selected commit-set. t_i is executable if the external and internal dependencies on which t_i depends are satisfied. We assume that all external dependencies eventually become true. If Step 2(a)(ii) stops and there are no cyclic internal dependencies, then the internal dependencies on which t_i depends eventually are satisfied or some $C_v \in C$ are no longer candidates for the selected commit-set so that t_i does not longer depend on these internal dependencies. There are no cyclic internal dependencies because the order of T is a partial order. Thus Step 2(a)(i) eventually terminates. ∎

Theorem 3.8 (*sufficient conditions for termination*). Algorithm 3.4 with input $T = (D, \prec_S, \prec_F, \Pi, C)$ eventually stops if following conditions hold:

(a) Step 2 of Algorithm 3.4 with input T produces an output;
(b) if $type(T) = \text{NC}$, the input whether or not to commit T eventually is made for each output of Algorithm 3.4.
(c) if $type(t_i) = \text{C}$, the compensate-action c_i that is associated with t_i stops when being executed by Algorithm 3.4 (for all $t_i \in D$);
(d) t_i is not aborted by the local database system if t_i is in a prepared state for all $t_i \in D$ (2PC for all non-compensatable subtransactions).

Proof. The conditions of the theorem guarantee that Steps 2(b) and 3 of Algorithm 3.4 do not wait forever. ∎

4 The VPL (Vienna Parallel Logic) Language

Parlog, Concurrent Prolog and Guarded Horn Clauses [9] are parallel logic languages with explicit language constructs to express communication and synchronization. Our proposal for a parallel logic language (VPL) differs in the following aspects. It is a real superset of sequential Prolog. VPL supports parallelism *and* the possibility to try several search paths: backtracking is extended by the property to undo non-committed and to compensate committed side-effects. VPL is transaction oriented and allows a dynamic granularity of committed code. Communication and synchronization are supported by *communication variables*.

A VPL program is a finite set of procedures consisting of several clauses.

$Head :- Body_1.$
$Head :- Body_2.$

The above two clauses represent a procedure with sequential clause search. To prove a call (viz. query) to *Head*, clause 1 is taken first. If it fails, clause 2 is tried. Clauses form a procedure with parallel clause search if "::–" is used instead of ":–". In order to prove *Head*, all clauses are started in OR-parallel. *Body*$_i$ consists of goals (viz. subqueries) connected by "&" (sequential AND operator) or "&&" (parallel AND operator). If *Body*$_i$ is defined by $(G_1 \; \&\& \; G_2) \; \& \; G_3$, the VPL system starts G_1 and G_2 in parallel. If both succeed, G_3 is started. If G_1 (G_2) fails, then G_2 (G_1) is aborted and G_3 is not started.

Communication variables are created by the primitive "#" and have a single assignment property. The "=" unification primitive serves for synchronization when used with communication variables. If X is a communication variable created by $\#X$ and Y is a normal variable, then $X = Y$ waits until X has received a non-variable value and then reads the value. Goal-Head unification is the same as $Goal = Head$ and thus also waits until all communication variables are bound. If we want to bind a communication variable, we use the primitive "=#=". $X =\#= Z$ requests the writing of Z to X (if Z is a non-variable term) and replaces all free normal variables in Z by new communication variables. But this primitive does not immediately write to X. X is written only on commitment.

VPL includes the "!" (cut, known from Prolog) that disables backtracking over the solutions found so far within the clause executing the cut. In parallel procedures, the semantics of the cut operator is the same as the semantics of the "commit" operator in committed choice parallel logic languages (e.g., Parlog), i.e., OR-parallel running clauses are aborted when executing the "!". The commit operator "|" of VPL is an extended version of the cut. It commits all bindings of communication variables as requested by the execution of "=#=" in goals to the left of the commit operator. On backtracking, committed procedures are compensated instead of undone. The programmer must specify a compensate-action. Backtracking over a committed procedure without a compensate-action raises an error.

In this paper, we introduce the special, immediately committing, access primitive "⇐" for communication variables: $X \Leftarrow Y$ writes Y to the communication variable X and immediately commits the written value. "⇐" may be defined in VPL as follows:

$$X \Leftarrow Y \; :\!- \; X =\#= Y \; | \; .$$
$$\text{compensate}(X \Leftarrow Y) \; :\!- \; \text{true}.$$

The compensation of "⇐" is an empty action because communication variables can be written only once.

The primitive process(*Goal*, *PID*) creates a new parallel process that executes *Goal*. *PID* is an identifier of the process. A difference between this primitive and the parallel AND operator is that a call to process immediately succeeds without waiting for the result. The primitive unbound(X) tests whether X is an unbound communication variable. For a more detailed language description see [5].

5 Mapping Flex Transactions into VPL

Program 5.1 is constructed from some Flex Transaction specifications. The execution of a procedure in this VPL program, constructed from the Flex Transaction T^w, corresponds to the application of Algorithm 3.4 to T.

Program 5.1 (*implementation of Flex Transactions in VPL*). VPL program for the execution of Flex Transactions according to Algorithm 3.4. Let $T^1 = (D^1, \prec_S^1, \prec_F^1, \Pi^1, C^1), \ldots, T^k = (D^k, \prec_S^k, \prec_F^k, \Pi^k, C^k)$ be Flex Transactions. If $t_j^w \in D^w$ is a Flex Transaction, there is a $T^{w'} = t_j^w$ ($w, w' = 1, \ldots, k$). The VPL program consists of the following procedures:[1]

(a) The procedure t^w executes the Flex Transaction T^w:

$$t^w :- \#X_1 \ \& \ \cdots \ \& \ \#X_n \ \& \ \text{process}(p_1^w(X_1, \ldots, X_n), P_1) \ \& \ \cdots$$
$$\cdots \ \& \ \text{process}(p_n^w(X_1, \ldots, X_n), P_n) \ \& \ p_0^w(X_1, \ldots, X_n).$$

(b) The procedure p_0^w tests whether T^w has succeeded or failed. Let $A_i^w = (a_{i,1}^w, \ldots, a_{i,n}^w)$ be the acceptable state of T^w with respect to $C_i^w \in C^w$. For $i = 1, \ldots, m$, there is a clause

$$p_0^w(X_1, \ldots, X_n) ::- h_{i,1}^w \ \& \ \cdots \ \& \ h_{i,n}^w.$$

The subgoal $h_{i,j}^w$ is defined as follows (for $j = 1, \ldots, n$):

$$h_{i,j}^w = \begin{cases} X_j = \text{result}(Y_j) \ \& \ Y_j =\#= \text{success} & \text{if } a_{i,j}^w = \text{S or } a_{i,j}^w = \text{P}; \\ X_j = \text{result(failure)} & \text{if } a_{i,j}^w = \text{F}; \\ X_j =\#= \text{result(failure)} & \text{otherwise (i.e. } a_{i,j}^w = \text{Y).} \end{cases}$$

(c) The procedure p_j^w controls the execution of the subtransaction $t_j^w \in D^w$ (for $i = j, \ldots, n$) and it is defined as follows ($\pi_j^w \in \Pi^w$):

$$p_j^w(X_1, \ldots, X_n) :- e_{1,j}^w(X_1, \ldots, X_n) \ \& \ \cdots \ \& \ e_{m,j}^w(X_1, \ldots, X_n) \ \& \ \pi_j^w \ \&$$
$$t_j^w \ \& \ X_j \Leftarrow \text{result}(Y_j) \ \& \ Y_j = \text{success}.$$
$$p_j^w(X_1, \ldots, X_n) :- X_j \Leftarrow \text{result(failure)}.$$

(d) The procedure $e_{i,j}^w$ tests whether $t_j^w \in D^w$ is executable with respect to $C_i^w \in C^w$ (except the external dependencies) or the commit-set C_i^w is not a candidate for being the selected commit-set. Let $A_i^w = (a_{i,1}^w, \ldots, a_{i,n}^w)$ be the acceptable state of T^w with respect to C_i^w. $e_{i,j}^w$ is defined as follows:

$$e_{i,j}^w(X_1, \ldots, X_n) ::- g_{i,j,1}^w \ \& \ \cdots \ \& \ g_{i,j,n}^w.$$
$$e_{i,j}^w(X_1, \ldots, X_n) ::- f_i^w(X_1, \ldots, X_n).$$

The subgoal $g_{i,j,v}^w$ is defined as follows (for $v = 1, \ldots, n$):

$$g_{i,j,v}^w = \begin{cases} X_v = \text{result}(Y_v) \ \& & \text{if } t_v^w \prec_S^w t_j^w, \ a_{i,v}^w = z_v, \text{ and } a_{i,j}^w = z_j \\ \text{unbound}(Y_v) & \text{where } v \neq j \text{ and } z_v, z_j \in \{\text{S,P}\}; \\ X_v = \text{result(failure)} & \text{if } t_v^w \prec_F^w t_j^w \text{ and } a_{i,v}^w = \text{F where } v \neq j; \\ \text{true} & \text{otherwise.} \end{cases}$$

(e) The procedure f_i^w tests whether the commit-set $C_i^w \in C^w$ is not a candidate for the selected commit-set. Let $A_i^w = (a_{i,1}^w, \ldots, a_{i,n}^w)$ be the acceptable state of T^w with respect to C_i^w. f_i^w contains the following clauses ($j = 1, \ldots, n$):

$$f_i^w(X_1, \ldots, X_n) ::- X_j = \text{result(failure).} \qquad \text{if } a_{i,j}^w = \text{S or } a_{i,j}^w = \text{P};$$
$$f_i^w(X_1, \ldots, X_n) ::- X_j = \text{result}(Y_j) \ \& \ \text{unbound}(Y_j). \quad \text{if } a_{i,j}^w = \text{F}.$$

(f) The procedure t_j^w executes the subtransaction $t_j^w \in D^w$. $t_j^w = t^v$ if t_j^w is a Flex Transaction; otherwise t_j^w is a subtransaction at a local database system. c_j^w denotes the compensate-action associated with t_j^w. t_j^w is defined as follows:

---

[1] Please note the use of the italic style to denote the local subtransaction at a local database system.

$$t_j^w \;:\!-\; t_j^w \;|\;.$$
$$\left.\begin{array}{l} \text{compensate}(t_j^w) \;:\!-\; c_j^w \;|\;. \\ t_j^w \;:\!-\; t_j^w. \end{array}\right\} \quad \begin{array}{l} \text{if } type(t_j^w) = \text{C}; \\[4pt] \text{if } type(t_j^w) = \text{NC}. \end{array}$$

Example 5.2 (*two of three*). The Flex Transaction T reserves a table in a restaurant on two of three days. Each of the transactions t_1, t_2, and t_3 reserves a table at a specific day. For $i = 1, 2, 3$, $type(t_i) = \text{NC}$ and the Flex Transaction is

$$T = (\{t_1, t_2, t_3\}, \emptyset, \emptyset, \{\text{true}, \text{true}, \text{true}\}, \{\{t_1, t_2\}, \{t_1, t_3\}, \{t_2, t_3\}\}).$$

The VPL implementation of T applies some obvious optimizations and uses intuitive symbols. The code for all p_i^w is essentially the same, so there is only one procedure c that is called with different arguments for different i.

```
two_tables :- #X1 & #X2 & #X3 & process(c(day1,X1),_) &
    process(c(day2,X2),_) & process(c(day3,X3),_) & control(X1,X2,X3).

control(X1,X2,X3) ::- X1 = result(Y1) & Y1 =#= success &
    X2 = result(Y2) & Y2 =#= success & X3 =#= result(failure).
control(X1,X2,X3) ::- X1 = result(Y1) & Y1 =#= success &
    X3 = result(Y3) & Y3 =#= success & X2 =#= result(failure).
control(X1,X2,X3) ::- X2 = result(Y2) & Y2 =#= success &
    X3 = result(Y3) & Y3 =#= success & X1 =#= result(failure).

c(D,X) :- reserve_table(D) & X <= result(Y) & Y = success.
```

Theorem 5.3 (*correspondence to Algorithm 3.4*). The execution of the procedure t^w of program P corresponds to the application of Algorithm 3.4 to the Flex Transaction T^w.

Proof. After declaring $X_1, \ldots, X_n$ to be communication variables, t^w starts the processes to execute p_0^w, $p_1^w, \ldots, p_n^w$ in parallel. The procedure p_j^w ($j = 1, \ldots, n$) waits until t_j^w is startable, then it calls the procedure t_j^w that executes t_j^w; if t_j^w succeeds (the local execution state is either S or P), then p_j^w writes result(Y_j) to the communication variable X_j to report the execution state. If t_j^w fails, then p_j^w writes result(failure) to the communication variable X_j. This corresponds to Step 2(a) of Algorithm 3.4. It is not necessary to distinguish between the states S and P.

Steps 2(b) through 2(d) of Algorithm 3.4 are executed by the call to p_0^w. Each clause of p_0^w waits until the execution state of T^w, reflected in the variables $X_1, \ldots, X_n$, complies with the commit-set, represented by this clause, by testing $X_j = \text{result}(Y_j)$ and $X_j = \text{result(failure)}$ accordingly to the definition of the acceptable state. Furthermore, p_0^w reports that a subtransaction t_j^w is in the selected commit-set by executing $Y_j =\#=$ success (which also ensures that $Y_j \neq$ failure) or that t_j^w is not in the selected commit-set by executing or $X_j =\#=$ result(failure). As soon as a clause of p_0^w succeeds, t^w succeeds and waits until the found solution (selected commit-set) is committed or rejected. If $type(T^w) = \text{C}$, the first solution is committed immediately by the procedure $t_{j'''}^w$ that calls t^w. Otherwise the commitment or abortion is delayed until one of the calling procedures (Flex Transactions) commits a solution. This corresponds to the waiting for the input *in* in Algorithm 3.4.

If a commit-set C_i^w (i.e., the clause of p_0^w representing C_i^w) is committed by the caller of t^w, the bindings of all communication variables $X_1, \ldots, X_n$ and $Y_1, \ldots, Y_n$ become visible as requested by the corresponding clause of p_0^w. The first clause of p_j^w $(j = 1, \ldots, n)$ will succeed if Y_j is bound to success and will fail otherwise. If it fails, t_j^w also fails and causes t_j^w to abort (if $type(t_j^w) = \mathrm{NC}$) or compensate (if $type(t_j^w) = \mathrm{C}$) by calling compensate(t_j^w). This corresponds to step 3 of Algorithm 3.4 if $C_s \neq \emptyset$.

If p_0^w does not contain a succeeding clause or all selected commit-sets have been rejected or t^w is caused to abort, then p_0^w fails and causes t^w to fail. By this, the parallel processes executing $p_1^w, \ldots, p_n^w$ are aborted and cause $t_1^w, \ldots, t_n^w$ to abort. This corresponds to step 3 of Algorithm 3.4 if $C_s = \emptyset$.

It remains to show that $e_{1,j}^w(X_1, \ldots, X_n)$ & $\cdots$ & $e_{m,j}^w(X_1, \ldots, X_n)$ & π_j^w succeeds iff t_j^w is startable. The first clause of $e_{i,j}^w$ $(i = 1, \ldots, n)$ together with π_j^w tests whether t_j^w is executable with respect to C_i and the second clause of $e_{i,j}^w$ tests whether for the i-th component of the commit-set state $r^{w,\tau}$ of T^w at the current time τ the condition $r_i^{w,\tau} = \mathcal{F}$ holds (i.e., whether C_i^w is not a candidate for a selected commit-set). Each subgoal $g_{i,j,v}^w$ in the first clause of $e_{i,j}^w$ ensures that the conditions (b) and (c) of Definition 2.7 are satisfied. Condition (a) of Definition 2.7 is satisfied by the call to π_j^w. Thus t_j^w is not called before the conditions of Definition 3.3 are satisfied and t_j^w will be started as soon as these conditions are satisfied. ∎

6 A Declarative Subclass of Flex Transactions

We give four theorems that allow the specification of all useful Flex Transactions with two subtransactions as declarative VPL procedures. Two further theorems describe, for an important subclass of Flex Transactions, the transformation of a Flex Transaction T into an equivalent Flex Transaction T' with two subtransactions. T' can be specified as a declarative VPL procedure. Complex Flex Transactions can be specified as declarative VPL procedures by repeatedly applying these theorems in any sequence.

Two VPL procedures are *equivalent* if they produce the same output after the same execution time and the conditions under which they produce an output and terminate are the same. Analogously, two Flex Transactions T and T' are equivalent if Algorithm 3.4 applied to T produces the same output after the same execution time and produces output and terminates under the same conditions as Algorithm 3.4 applied to T'.

Theorem 6.1 (*parallel AND*). If $T^w = (\{t_1^w, t_2^w\}, \emptyset, \prec_F^w, \{\pi_1^w, \pi_2^w\}, \{\{t_1^w, t_2^w\}\})$ is a Flex Transaction, the VPL procedure t'^w is equivalent to the VPL procedure t^w in Program 5.1:

$$t'^w :- (\pi_1^w \ \& \ t_1^w) \ \&\& \ (\pi_2^w \ \& \ t_2^w).$$

Proof. The procedures $e_{1,1}^w$ and $e_{1,2}^w$ in Program 5.1 immediately succeed since there are no success dependencies and can be omitted. t_1^w and t_2^w are startable as soon as π_1^w and π_2^w are true. This is expressed in the body of t'^w. t'^w succeeds when both subtransactions have succeeded. If the found result is rejected or one of the subtransactions fails, t'^w fails and aborts or compensates the subtransactions. This behavior is the same as that of t^w in Program 5.1. ∎

Theorem 6.2 (*sequential AND*). If $T^w = (\{t_1^w, t_2^w\}, \{t_1^w \prec_S^w t_2^w\}, \prec_F^w, \{\pi_1^w, \pi_2^w\}, \{\{t_1^w, t_2^w\}\})$ is a Flex Transaction, the VPL procedure t'^w is equivalent to the VPL procedure t^w in Program 5.1:

$$t'^w :- \pi_1^w \;\&\; t_1^w \;\&\; \pi_2^w \;\&\; t_2^w.$$

Proof. The proof is analogous to that of Theorem 6.1, but the success dependency is expressed by the sequential AND-operator instead of the parallel one. t_2^w will not be executed before t_1^w has succeeded. ∎

Theorem 6.3 (*parallel OR*). If $T^w = (\{t_1^w, t_2^w\}, \prec_S^w, \emptyset, \{\pi_1^w, \pi_2^w\}, \{\{t_1^w\}, \{t_2^w\}\})$ is a Flex Transaction, the VPL procedure t'^w is equivalent to the VPL procedure t^w in Program 5.1:

$$t'^w ::- \pi_1^w \;\&\; t_1^w.$$
$$t'^w ::- \pi_2^w \;\&\; t_2^w.$$

Proof. The proof is analogous to that of Theorem 6.1, but there are two disjunct commitsets. The procedure t'^w succeeds as soon as one of the two subtransactions has succeeded. The other one is aborted on commitment of t'^w (as in Program 5.1). ∎

Theorem 6.4 (*sequential OR*). If $T^w = (\{t_1^w, t_2^w\}, \prec_S^w, \{t_1^w \prec_F^w t_2^w\}, \{\pi_1^w, \pi_2^w\}, \{\{t_1^w\}, \{t_2^w\}\})$ is a Flex Transaction, the VPL procedure t'^w is equivalent to the VPL procedure t^w in Program 5.1:

$$t'^w :- \pi_1^w \;\&\; t_1^w \;!.$$
$$t'^w :- \pi_2^w \;\&\; t_2^w.$$

Proof. The proof is analogous to that of Theorem 6.3, but there is a failure dependency. If the first clause succeeds, the second clause will not be started (as in Program 5.1). ∎

Theorem 6.5 (*OR partition*). Let $T = (D, \prec_S, \prec_F, \Pi, C)$ be a Flex Transaction with $D = \{t_1, \ldots, t_n\}$ and $C = \{C_1, \ldots, C_m\}$. Let there be a v with

(a) $D_1 = \bigcup_{i=1}^{v} C_i$ and $D_2 = \bigcup_{i=v+1}^{m} C_i$;

(b) $D_1 \cap D_2 = \emptyset$;

(c) if $t_j \prec_F t_{j'}$, then $t_j, t_{j'} \in D_1$ or $t_j, t_{j'} \in D_2$.

The Flex Transaction $T' = (\{T_1', T_2'\}, \emptyset, \emptyset, \{\text{true}, \text{true}\}, \{\{T_1'\}, \{T_2'\}\})$ with

(a) $T_1' = (D_1, \prec_S^1, \prec_F^1, \Pi_1, \{C_1, \ldots, C_v\})$ where
   (i) $t_j \prec_S^1 t_{j'}$ iff $t_j \prec_S t_{j'}$ and $t_j, t_{j'} \in D_1$;
   (ii) $t_j \prec_F^1 t_{j'}$ iff $t_j \prec_F t_{j'}$ and $t_j, t_{j'} \in D_1$;
   (iii) $\Pi_1 = \{\pi_j | \pi_j \in \Pi \text{ and } t_j \in D_1\}$;

(b) $T_2' = (D_2, \prec_S^2, \prec_F^2, \Pi_2, \{C_{v+1}, \ldots, C_m\})$ where
   (i) $t_j \prec_S^2 t_{j'}$ iff $t_j \prec_S t_{j'}$ and $t_j, t_{j'} \in D_2$;
   (ii) $t_j \prec_F^2 t_{j'}$ iff $t_j \prec_F t_{j'}$ and $t_j, t_{j'} \in D_2$;
   (iii) $\Pi_2 = \{\pi_j | \pi_j \in \Pi \text{ and } t_j \in D_2\}$.

equals T if $\{T_1'\}$ represents the selected commit-set $C_\bullet \subseteq D_1$ and $\{T_2'\}$ represents $C_\bullet \subseteq D_2$.

Proof. There are two groups of subtransactions D_1 and D_2 in D so that no commitset contains subtransactions of both groups. Thus T succeeds with a selected commit-set containing subtransactions from either D_1 or D_2. T' succeeds with the selected commit-set

$\{T_1'\}$ ($\{T_2'\}$) as soon as T_1' (T_2') succeeds with the selected commit-set $C_{\bullet} \subseteq D_1$ ($C_{\bullet} \subseteq D_2$). If $\{T_1'\}$ represents $C_{\bullet} \subseteq D_1$ ($\{T_2'\}$ represents $C_{\bullet} \subseteq D_2$) and the same dependencies that are tested in T are also tested in T', T' is equivalent to T.

A success dependency between a subtransaction in D_1 and one in D_2 is not important since a commit-set contains only subtransactions of one group of subtransactions (Definition 2.6). All internal and external dependencies that are tested in T are also tested in T' and vice versa. ∎

Theorem 6.6 (*AND partition*). Let $T = (D, \prec_S, \prec_F, \Pi, C)$ be a Flex Transaction with $D = \{t_1, \ldots, t_n\}$ and $C = \{C_1, \ldots, C_m\}$. Let there be a v with

(a) $B^1 = \{B_1^1, \ldots, B_{m_1}^1\}$ and $B^2 = \{B_1^2, \ldots, B_{m_2}^2\}$ where $B_{i'}^1 = \{t_j | t_j \in C_i$ and $1 \le j \le v\}$ and $B_{i''}^2 = \{t_j | t_j \in C_i$ and $v < j \le n\}$ for $i = 1, \ldots, m; i' = 1, \ldots, m_1; i'' = 1, \ldots, m_2$;

(b) $C = \{B_1^1 \cup B_1^2, \ldots, B_1^1 \cup B_{m_2}^2, \ldots, B_{m_1}^1 \cup B_1^2, \ldots, B_{m_1}^1 \cup B_{m_2}^2\}$, i.e. $m_1 \cdot m_2 = m$;

(c) if $t_j \prec_S t_{j'}$, then $1 \le j, j' \le v$ or $v < j, j' \le n$ or for all $1 \le j \le v$ and all $v < j' \le n$ the success dependency $t_j \prec_S t_{j'}$ holds;

(d) if $t_j \prec_F t_{j'}$, then $1 \le j, j' \le v$ or $v < j, j' \le n$.

The Flex Transaction $T' = (\{T_1', T_2'\}, \prec_S', \emptyset, \{\text{true}, \text{true}\}, \{\{T_1', T_2'\}\})$ with

(a) $T_1' = (\{t_1, \ldots, t_v\}, \prec_S^1, \prec_F^1, \Pi_1, B^1)$ where

    (i) $t_j \prec_S^1 t_{j'}$ iff $t_j \prec_S t_{j'}$ and $1 \le j, j' \le v$;

    (ii) $t_j \prec_F^1 t_{j'}$ iff $t_j \prec_F t_{j'}$ and $1 \le j, j' \le v$;

    (iii) $\Pi_1 = \{\pi_j | \pi_j \in \Pi$ and $1 \le j \le v\}$;

(b) $T_2' = (\{t_{v+1}, \ldots, t_n\}, \prec_S^2, \prec_F^2, \Pi_2, B^2)$ where

    (i) $t_j \prec_S^2 t_{j'}$ iff $t_j \prec_S t_{j'}$ and $v < j, j' \le n$;

    (ii) $t_j \prec_F^2 t_{j'}$ iff $t_j \prec_F t_{j'}$ and $v < j, j' \le n$;

    (iii) $\Pi_2 = \{\pi_j | \pi_j \in \Pi$ and $v < j \le n\}$;

(c) $T_1' \prec_S' T_2'$ iff there is a $t_j < t_{j'}$ with $1 \le j \le v$ and $v < j' \le n$.

is equivalent to T if $\{T_1', T_2'\}$ represents the selected commit-set $C_{\bullet}^1 \cup C_{\bullet}^2$ of T where $C_{\bullet}^1 \in B^1$ and $C_{\bullet}^2 \in B^2$.

Proof. Each commit-set $C_i \in C$ is divided into two subsets $B_{i'}^1$ and $B_{i''}^2$. For all $i' = 1, \ldots, m_1$ and $i'' = 1, \ldots, m_2$ there is an $i = 1, \ldots, m$ with $B_{i'}^1 \cup B_{i''}^2 = C_i \in C$. Thus there is a $C_{\bullet}$ with $C_{\bullet}^1 \cup C_{\bullet}^2 = C_{\bullet}$ for all $C_{\bullet}^1 \in B^1$ and $C_{\bullet}^2 \in B^2$. For all $C_{\bullet}$, there are $C_{\bullet}^1 \in B^1$ and $C_{\bullet}^2 \in B^2$ with $C_{\bullet}^1 \cup C_{\bullet}^2 = C_{\bullet}$. Thus T and T' are equivalent if $\{T_1', T_2'\}$ represents the selected commit-set $C_{\bullet}^1 \cup C_{\bullet}^2$ of T and the same dependencies that are tested in T are also tested in T'.

The success dependencies between t_j and $t_{j'}$ with $1 \le j \le v$ and $v < j' \le n$ are ensured by $T_1' \prec_S' T_2'$ since there are success dependencies of this form for all $1 \le j \le v$ and all $v < j' \le n$ and all unions of an element in B^1 with an element in B^2 are elements in C. All other internal and external dependencies are tested by T_1' and T_2'. There do not be dependencies that are tested in T' but not in T. ∎

Example 6.7 (*recursion*). Let us assume a log-in procedure as the Flex Transaction T. The subtransactions test whether a log-in can be granted (t_1) for a request π_1, recursively call T if t_1 fails ($t_2 = T$), and, after the next successful login, write a message to the terminal for each try of a log-in (t_3):

$$T = (\{t_1, t_2, t_3\}, \{t_1 \prec_S t_3, t_2 \prec_S t_3\}, \{t_1 \prec_F t_2\}, \{\pi_1, \text{true}, \text{true}\}, \{\{t_1, t_3\}, \{t_2, t_3\}\}).$$

The types of all transactions are C. T has a declarative representation. We use the predicates read/3 for π_1, test/2 for t_1, login/0 for t_2 and T, and message/2 for t_3.

```
login :- do_login(Name,Time) & message(Name,Time) |.
compensate(login) :- logout.

do_login(Name,Time) :- read(Name,PWD,Time) & test(Name,PWD).
do_login(_,_) :- login.
```

The procedures read/3, test/2, message/2, logout/0, and the compensate-actions of test/2 and message/2 must be specified properly.

Conclusions

We have shown an execution model for nested Flex Transactions and conditions under which this model is deadlock free. With nested and recursive Flex Transaction specifications, it is possible to model long-lived and ever-lasting transactions with endless repetition and variable-sized commit-sets. We have given a mapping of all nested Flex Transactions into programs in the parallel Prolog language VPL. We have identified an important subclass of Flex Transactions with a declarative representation in VPL. For this class, a specification in VPL provides not only more convenience but is also an implementation of the execution model for the Flex Transaction.

Acknowledgements: We thank Manfred Brockhaus for encouraging our work.

References

[1] Ph. Bernstein, V. Hadzilacos, and N. Goodman, *Concurrency Control and Recovery in Database Systems*, Addison-Wesley, 1987.

[2] A. K. Elmagarmid, Y. Leu, W. Litwin, and M. Rusinkiewicz, "A Multidatabase Transaction Model for InterBase", *Proceedings of the 16th International Conference on Very Large Data Bases*, Australia, 1990.

[3] H. Garcia-Molina and K. Salem, "Sagas", *Proceedings of the ACM SIGMOD Annual Conference*, San Francisco, May 1987.

[4] J. Gray, "The Transaction Concepts: Virtues and Limitations", *Proceedings of the International Conference on Very Large Data Bases*, 1981.

[5] e. Kühn and F. Puntigam, "Programmed Backtracking and Concurrency in Logic Programming", technical report TR-1851-91-4, University of Technology Vienna, Dep. of Computer Languages, 1991.

[6] e. Kühn, F. Puntigam, and A. K. Elmagarmid, "Transaction Specification in Multidatabase Systems based on Parallel Logic Programming", *First International Workshop on Interoperability in Multidatabase Systems*, Kyoto, April 1991.

[7] Witold Litwin, Leo Mark, and Nick Roussopoulos, "Interoperability of Multiple Autonomous Databases", *ACM Computing Surveys*, Vol. 22, No. 3, 1990.

[8] Y. Leu, "Composing Multidatabase Applications using Flex Transactions", *IEEE DE Bulletin*, 1991.

[9] E. Shapiro, "The Family of Concurrent Logic Programming Languages", *ACM Computing Surveys*, Vol. 21, No. 3, September 1989.

Approximate Query Processing with Summary Tables in Statistical Databases

*Soraya Abad-Mota**

Rutgers University, Department of Computer Science
New Brunswick NJ 08903, USA

Abstract

Statistical Databases usually allow only statistical queries. In order to answer a query some kind of summarization must be performed on the raw data. If the size of the original data is too large, e.g. as in Census data and the Current Population Survey, obtaining accurate answers is extremely time consuming. Thus, if the application allows for some precision loss in the answer, the mechanism for query answering could take advantage of previously computed summaries to answer other summary queries. In this paper we describe the necessary notions to *maintain a database of previously computed summary information to allow fast query answering of new summary queries with a qualified accuracy and without having to go back to the original data.* We use the concept of *summary tables*, study the potential of sets of summary tables for answering queries, and organize these sets in a lattice structure.

1 Introduction

As public and large statistical databanks like the Census and the Current Population Survey become available on CD-ROM over a network, the number of "casual users" will grow tremendously. By casual users we mean the general public, with varying degrees of computer expertise and diverse needs of economic, demographic and planning information.

Statistical Databases usually allow only statistical queries, and questions requiring information about the individuals cannot be answered. Therefore, in order to answer a query some kind of summarization must be performed on the raw data. If the size of the original data is too large, accessing it to obtain accurate answers is extremely time consuming and requires human intervention (even with CD-ROM's). This is specially cumbersome for "casual users" who need to access the data in an exploratory manner to find trends, correlations, and the like. These users would be happy to first check candidate conjectures that can later be verified with the raw data. Therefore, if the application allows for some precision loss in the answer, the mechanism for query answering could take advantage of previously computed summaries to answer other queries. The answers

* Partially supported by a scholarship from FUNDAYACUCHO, Caracas, Venezuela.

provided in this fashion could be qualified in terms of the level of imprecision they carry, and of the additional conditions under which such answers will be good approximations of the "real values" (the ones obtained from the raw data).

An idea that could be used to satisfy the informational needs of the community described here, is to *cache previously requested summary information to allow fast query answering of new summary queries with a qualified accuracy and without having to go back to the original data.*

In this paper we use *summary tables* (Section 2) obtained from the raw data, and some additional information to process queries. We define two operators S and C to produce summary tables from the raw data or from other summaries. There are cases in which an expression gives an exact answer (Section 2.1), but there are other cases in which it does not. For the latter we provide some approximate computations (Sections 2.3, 2.4, and 2.5). Instead of providing the "exact answer" or a single approximate answer, we establish *bounds* on the answer, and qualify those bounds with specific assumptions. We study the potential of sets of summary tables for answering queries, and organize them in a lattice structure (Section 3). We have paid special attention to grouping data into "quanta" and to how to answer queries about different groupings of the same data.

2 Summary Tables

A *table* in our domain is a two-dimensional (rows vs columns) arrangement of data. The columns of the table have names called the *attributes*. An attribute is defined over a *domain*, from which the column gets its values.

There are two main differences between the *tables* used here, and the relations as defined in the Relational Model. First, the information contained in our tables usually comes in three different flavors, i.e. we can separate three types of attributes, category attributes, measurement attributes and aggregate attributes[2]. Second, the manipulations allowed on tables will be different from the operations defined in relational algebra; for example, some rearrangements of the elements of the tables are allowed, new columns can result from the application of an aggregate function, tables can be combined with or without having common attributes.

Category attributes define classes in which the individuals are classified. Usually they have discrete values known in advance. Examples of this type of attributes are: sex or gender, year, race, country. Category attributes can be simple or compound. Gender alone is a simple attribute with values in D(gender) = {female, male}, race is a simple attribute with values in D(race) = {white, black, indian}. The combination gender-race is a compound attribute, and its domain is formed by taking the cartesian product of the domains for gender and race, i.e. D(gender-race) = {female-white, male-white, female-black, male-black, female-indian, male-indian}.

Measurement attributes refer to numeric data items whose values are "measured" in some experiment or survey. Any aggregate function can be applied to their value. These attributes can be obtained from the answer to a question in a questionnaire, like annual

---

[2] In the Statistical Database Management literature measurement and aggregate attributes are considered one type and are often called *summary attributes* (Shoshani 1982).

income, or they could also come from the output of some measuring equipment, for example as in the case of the blood pressure, or the weight.

Aggregate attributes, have values obtained by applying an aggregate function to another attribute. Examples of aggregate functions are: count, sum, maximum, minimum, median and weighted average. In this paper we use count only. Count has a special meaning: given a raw table, we can generate a count attribute by literally counting the number of individuals for each combination of values of a set of attributes, e.g. the column named # in Table 3.[3] In fact, we will use the symbol # to name all the count columns in our tables.

Measurements can be treated as either aggregate or category attributes. For example, the GPA is a measurement, it measures the student's performance and it is obtained by applying the average function to individual grades. But one can also use GPA to classify the students according to its value, in this case GPA is used as a category attribute.

We distinguish two types of tables. *Base Tables* have the raw data which includes information about some individuals. Sometimes we will refer to them as the original or raw tables. A sample of a portion of a base table is shown in Table 1. *Summary Tables* can be defined by their structure and by the way they are computed. Structurally, they have three sets of attributes: category, measurement and aggregate. A summary table should have at least two attributes, one of them should be a category or a measurement, and the other one should be a count aggregate attribute. Functionally, a summary table is obtained from a base table or from another summary table.

Table 1. Base Table

student id	IQ	GRE	GPA
140829	140	800	4
516729	140	700	3.7
655784	150	770	3.6
953722	170	820	3.8
.	.	.	.
.	.	.	.

2.1 The Summary Operator.

We define the operator S to produce summary tables. For simplicity reasons, let us assume that any base table has an additional column containing a count of the number of tuples for each combination of values of its attributes. For Table 1 we would add an attribute named # containing a column of ones, as we show in Table 2.

The operator S takes three arguments, $S[A \mid p](T)$:

- an attribute name, A;
- a partition p of the domain D of the attribute A, i.e. p is a set of mutually exclusive subsets of $D(A)$, which covers the whole domain $D(A)$, and

---

[3] GRE stands for graduate record examination grade, GPA is the grade point average.

502

Table 2. Base Table with the count column

student id	IQ	GRE	GPA	#
140829	140	800	4	1
516729	140	700	3.7	1
655784	150	770	3.6	1
953722	170	820	3.8	1
.	.	.	.	.
.	.	.	.	.

Table 3. Count Summary Table

IQ	GRE	GPA	#
140	[500,700)	[2,2.5)	121
140	[500,700)	[2.5,3)	63
140	[500,700)	[3,3.5)	70
140	[500,700)	[3.5,4)	60
140	[700,900)	[2,2.5)	67
140	[700,900)	[2.5,3)	50
140	[700,900)	[3,3.5)	67
140	[700,900)	[3.5,4)	31
150	[500,700)	[2,2.5)	212
150	[500,700)	[2.5,3)	116
150	[500,700)	[3,3.5)	103
150	[500,700)	[3.5,4)	101

IQ	GRE	GPA	#
150	[700,900)	[2,2.5)	132
150	[700,900)	[2.5,3)	83
150	[700,900)	[3,3.5)	69
150	[700,900)	[3.5,4)	66
170	[500,700)	[2,2.5)	14
170	[500,700)	[2.5,3)	9
170	[500,700)	[3,3.5)	8
170	[500,700)	[3.5,4)	5
170	[700,900)	[2,2.5)	8
170	[700,900)	[2.5,3)	4
170	[700,900)	[3,3.5)	9
170	[700,900)	[3.5,4)	6

— a summary table T.

Assume for a moment that Table 2 above, had only the 4 rows shown. If we applied the expression: $S[\text{student id} \mid \emptyset](S[\text{GRE} \mid \{[700,900]\}])(S[\text{GPA} \mid \{[3.5,4)\}])(T2)$, we would obtain the following summary table:

IQ	GRE	GPA	#
140	[700,900)	[3.5,4)	2
150	[700,900)	[3.5,4)	1
170	[700,900)	[3.5,4)	1

There is a special notation for describing the partition of the domain of an attribute in an S expression:

- The partition is described as: $\{p_1, p_2, ...\}$, where each p_i is a subset of D(A).
- If D(A) is the set of reals or the set of integers, one specifies intervals as: [x,y), including x and excluding y; [x,y], including x and y, and with the special case of [x,*) meaning from x to infinity.
- There is a special value called OTH, which stands for all the other values not specified in any subset within p. Therefore one could specify some ranges of an attribute and leave the values not considered within these ranges, in the unspecified category of OTHERS. For example, if we have ages ranging from 1 to 85 years, and one would like to consider some ranges including ages from 1 to 65 only, this could be expressed with the following partition: { [1,4], [5,17], [18,44], [45,64], [65,*), [OTH] }.

The effect of using $S[A \mid p](T)$ is described in two steps below.

1. In every row the value of A is replaced by the appropriate class within the partition p of D; the value of A must fall in one of the subsets in p. The domain of A in the resulting summary table is redefined to be $\mathcal{P}(D(A))$. There is a special case worth mentioning. If $p = \emptyset$, then A is eliminated from the output, and all the rows with the same value in all the other attributes are collapsed into one row, by adding its entries in the count column. In this case step 2 below, does not apply.

2. All the rows with the same value in A are collapsed into one row, by summing up its entries in the count column and leaving the result of the sum in the new count column.

The following rules hold for S expressions.

- $S[A \mid p](S[B \mid q](T)) = S[B \mid q](S[A \mid p](T))$ if A and B are different attributes in T.
- $S[A \mid p](S[A \mid q](T)) = S[A \mid p](T)$ if q is a refinement of the partition p i.e., each set in p is the union of sets in q.

When using S for different attributes in the same table, we use the abbreviation $S[A \mid p, B \mid q](T)$ for $S[A \mid p](S[B \mid q](T))$. For example, if we denote Table 2 by T2, Table 3 is the result of evaluating the following expression:
$S[\text{student id} \mid \emptyset, \text{GRE} \mid \{[500,700),[700,900)\}, \text{GPA} \mid \{[2,2.5),[2.5,3),[3,3.5),[3.5,4)\}](T2)$.

When computing S expressions we can distinguish two situations. The first situation arises when the operations have an *exact computation*, this is the case of collapsing existing quanta and when selecting some attributes from an existing table. For example, to find the number of students with GPA between 2.5 and 3.5 from Table 3, we can collapse the two quanta 2.5-3 and 3-3.5, and the following expression will do the job: $S[\text{GPA} \mid \{[2,2.5),[2.5,3.5),[3.5,4)\}](T3)$. Another example: to compute the table with only IQ and the count from Table 3 we can use the following expression: $S[\text{GRE} \mid \emptyset, \text{GPA} \mid \emptyset](T3)$. The result is shown in Table 4.

However, if in Table 3 we want to now divide GPA into the following quanta: 2.5-2.9, 2.9-3.2, 3.2-3.5, 3.5-3.7, and 3.7-4, several special cases arise, as we show below, and the partition could not be done with the operator S with the semantics described here. The range 2.5-2.9 is a "subset of a single existing quanta"; 2.9-3.2 is a "subset of more than one existing quanta", and 3.7-4.1 "contains a subset which does not exist in the original data", i.e., there is no data available for 4-4.1.

Similarly, if we have to answer the query: *How many students are there with IQ = 140 and GPA between 3.5 and 4?*, from the summary tables 8, 9, and 10 in Section 3 we do not have any single table containing both, the IQ and the GPA attributes.

For these last two examples which could not be answered precisely, it is desirable to have some way of giving an *approximate answer*. In the following sections we describe two mechanisms for coping with these uncertain situations; the case of the unknown joint table will be covered in Section 2.3, and the overlapping quanta will be discussed in Section 2.5. But first let us establish some standards by defining a canonical form for summary tables.

2.2 Summary Tables in Canonical Form

The summary table in Table 3 could have been shown in various different formats, all conveying the same information; Table 5 shows one of these possible formats. These

Table 4. Marginal Table for IQ

IQ	#
140	529
150	882
170	63

formats can be seen as three-dimensional versions of the information in Table 3. For instance, in Table 5 the attribute *IQ* is one dimension (y), the compound attribute *GRE-GPA* is another dimension (x), and the aggregate attribute count (#) is the third dimension (z), which does not appear as a column any more. Similarly, if we put GRE in the y dimension, and the compound IQ-GPA in the x dimension, we obtain another possible three-dimensional format. In order to have a uniform way of referring to the information conveyed in all the possible formats, a *canonical or standard form* of the table is defined. The canonical form of a table is always two-dimensional, with one column per category, one column per measurement and one column per aggregate. Categories go first, followed by the measurements and finally the aggregates. Table 3 is in canonical form.

Although the canonical form is useful for homogeneity reasons, users should be allowed to view the data in any format they want. The *transposition operation* is defined to produce data in a specified format. It can be applied to a table in canonical form to produce any three-dimensional format of the same information. Transposition can also be applied to three-dimensional tables to modify their format.

In summary, we have two complementary operations: one to build the canonical form, and transposition to build the table in any three-dimensional format.

In many situations in the following discussions it will be necessary to *"interpret some attributes as random variables"*. For instance, the values for the number of students (column #) in Table 9 in Section 3 can be transformed into a relative frequency distribution by dividing each number by the total number of students, yielding Table 6.

In this case the *GRE* is seen as a random variable with two possible values: [500,700) and [700,900), and a relative frequency distribution given by f(GRE). The value [500,700) (or 600 which is the midpoint) is observed with relative frequency of 60% and the value [700,900) (or 800 which is the midpoint) is observed with relative frequency of 40%. By following the procedure described in this example we can interpret any numeric attribute in our tables as a random variable. Hereafter when we refer to an attribute as a variable we mean the interpretation just described.

In fact any summary table with a count attribute has a probabilistic interpretation. Let T be a summary table with more than one attribute and one count attribute. Table T represents the *joint frequency distribution* of all the attributes. If we interpret all the attributes in T as random variables and divide each value of the count by the total number of individuals, the transformed Table T shows the *joint relative frequency distribution* of all the attributes. For example, Table 7 is the probabilistic interpretation of Table 3, and it contains the joint distribution for the variables, GRE, GPA and IQ (f(IGG)). Moreover, Table 7 is the canonical form of the joint distribution.

Among the aggregate functions which can be applied to the tables, the most important

Table 5. Transposed Table

	GRE-GPA							
	[500,700)				[700,900)			
IQ	[2,2.5)	[2.5,3)	[3,3.5)	[3.5,4)	[2,2.5)	[2.5,3)	[3,3.5)	[3.5,4)
140	121	63	70	60	67	50	67	31
150	212	116	103	101	132	83	69	66
170	14	9	8	5	8	4	9	6

Table 6. Relative Frequency Distribution of GRE grades

GRE	f(GRE)
500-700	0.60
700-900	0.40

is the *count* function. It allows a probabilistic interpretation of the tables and makes possible the use of the methods for combining tables described in Sections 2.3 and 2.5.

2.3 Combining Summary Tables

Assume a situation where a query has to be answered and the necessary information for it is not contained in a single summary table. The answer could be obtained from the raw data, but given the size of the original table, such task will often require too much time. The goal is to get a quick approximate answer using the summary tables, which should be significantly smaller than the raw data.

For instance, suppose we have available the Summary Tables 8, 9 and 10 in Section 3, and our query is: *How many students are there with IQ = 140 and GPA between 3.5 and 4?*. What we need in order to answer this query is the joint frequency distribution of IQ and GPA, and to select from it the appropriate entry. If we cannot afford to use the raw data, the problem of answering this query can be reduced to the problem of *"guessing" the entries of the joint frequency distribution, given the individual frequencies of each variable separately*. In other words, we have to complete the entries of the joint table given some constraints.

The problem of *"completing"* two-dimensional tables given constraints on the sum by columns and the sum by rows has been studied in many domains. In particular, in Statistics and in Linear Algebra (Seneta 1980). We consider here, two procedures from the statistical domain that have been applied to completing or "guessing" joint distributions. To illustrate these procedures we use an example of two variables, A and B, each with three possible values, 1, 2, and 3, and with marginal constraints given by the following two tables:

A	1	2	3
	7	11	18

B	1	2	3
	5	16	15

— *Mutual Independence Approach*[4]. According to this approach, the joint table is computed assuming independence between the variables. This means that we multiply

---

[4] or Maximum Entropy Approach, or Idiot Bayes Approach.

Table 7. Count Summary Table with relative frequency distribution

IQ	GRE	GPA	f(IGG)
140	[500,700)	[2,2.5)	0.082
140	[500,700)	[2.5,3)	0.043
140	[500,700)	[3,3.5)	0.047
140	[500,700)	[3.5,4)	0.041
140	[700,900)	[2,2.5)	0.045
140	[700,900)	[2.5,3)	0.034
140	[700,900)	[3,3.5)	0.045
140	[700,900)	[3.5,4)	0.021
150	[500,700)	[2,2.5)	0.144
150	[500,700)	[2.5,3)	0.079
150	[500,700)	[3,3.5)	0.070
150	[500,700)	[3.5,4)	0.069

IQ	GRE	GPA	f(IGG)
150	[700,900)	[2,2.5)	0.090
150	[700,900)	[2.5,3)	0.056
150	[700,900)	[3,3.5)	0.047
150	[700,900)	[3.5,4)	0.045
170	[500,700)	[2,2.5)	0.009
170	[500,700)	[2.5,3)	0.006
170	[500,700)	[3,3.5)	0.005
170	[500,700)	[3.5,4)	0.003
170	[700,900)	[2,2.5)	0.005
170	[700,900)	[2.5,3)	0.003
170	[700,900)	[3,3.5)	0.006
170	[700,900)	[3.5,4)	0.004

their individual frequencies to obtain the joint frequency. If we want the result in absolute frequencies, we multiply the absolute frequencies, divide by the total number of individuals, and round off the result. If we want the joint relative frequencies we multiply the individual relative frequencies. In the example above this method would yield the following table of absolute frequencies.

	1	2	3	
1	1	2	2	(5)
2	3	5	8	(16)
3	3	4	8	(15)
	(7)	(11)	(18)	TOTAL=36

– *Fréchet's method.* (Maximum or Minimum Correlation Approach.) Fréchet (1960) describes a method for filling the entries of a two-dimensional table given the marginal constraints for each row and column. Each dimension in the table corresponds to a random variable. The values are ordered in increasing order in both dimensions. There are two variations of the method, one gives the joint table with the maximum correlation possible between the variables, the other gives a table with minimum correlation. The method is described here with the same example used above. The table is filled by columns, assigning numbers according to the horizontal and vertical constraints. The table to be filled and the constraints are shown below.

	1	2	3	
1				(5)
2				(16)
3				(15)
	(7)	(11)	(18)	TOTAL=36

For maximum correlation, we put the largest possible number in each entry. When a column is completed the numbers assigned are subtracted from the horizontal constraints.

	1	2	3	
1	5			(0)
2	2			(14)
3	0			(15)
	(7)	(11)	(18)	TOTAL=36

The method is applied succesively to the remaining columns according to the modified constraints.

	1	2	3	
1	5	0		(0)
2	2	11		(3)
3	0	0		(15)
	(7)	(11)	(18)	TOTAL=36

The final table with maximum correlation between A and B is shown below. In fact this final table gives a correlation factor of 0.76 (computed with *relative* frequencies), the maximum that can be obtained with the given constraints.

	1	2	3	
1	5	0	0	(0)
2	2	11	3	(0)
3	0	0	15	(0)
	(7)	(11)	(18)	TOTAL=36

For a minimum correlation, the same procedure applies, except that the smallest possible number is assigned to each entry at each step.

A possible extension to Fréchet's method is to define it for more than two variables. A way to do this is to first construct the joint table of two attributes, then consider the two attributes a compound attribute, and build a joint table with the third attribute, and in this manner "add" one attribute at a time. At the end we will have a joint table with all the attributes.

If we have more than two variables the extended Fréchet algorithm gives the same results independently of the order in which the variables are included in the joint table. Since the concept of correlation is not suitable for more than two variables, the interpretation of the final table using the extended algorithm is that it yields values which correspond to the maximum *pairwise correlation* of the variables. In other words, if from the final table one selects the summary subtable containing only two variables, then one obtains a table with maximum correlation between the two chosen variables.

The three methods described in this section provide us with the desired bounds. The notion of correlation gave us the key to the bounds. A correlation factor can take values between −1 and 1. The negative extreme corresponds to a negative correlation, meaning that when one variable increases the correlated one decreases; the positive extreme corresponds to a positive correlation, meaning that when one variable increases the other also increases. The midpoint of the interval, the zero, corresponds to no correlation. Independence between the variables gives us a zero correlation. Therefore these three values of a joint distribution seem to be a natural bound to offer in our case. In the worst case we will be conservative, but the exact answer must be within those bounds.

2.4 The Combine Operator C

The special computations for combining tables to produce a joint frequency distribution described in Section 2.3 can be specified with the use of a special operator denoted by C.

The operator C takes four arguments, $C[A:f](T1;T2)$:

1. an attribute name A, which is a common attribute to the tables to be combined;
2. a frequency distribution function f, describing the distribution of attribute A when interpreted as a random variable, three arguments are specified for f:
   (a) the type of distribution, e.g. normal, chi-square;
   (b) the mean of the distribution;
   (c) the standard deviation of the distribution;
3. the names of the two summary tables to be combined.

The attribute and its distribution function are optional arguments because we can combine two tables without a common attribute by using, for example, the mutual independence method and assuming mutual independence between all the variables. However, if we specify a common attribute, it is mandatory to include the distribution function data if the quanta splitting operation must be performed. Actually, the attribute's distribution function is only necessary in the case of unmatched quanta.

The C operator can take various different forms depending on which method of computation will be used to combine the tables. When combining tables with a common attribute with identical values in both tables, the method could be the mutual independence method or Fréchet's maximum or minimum correlation method. In each case we can put a superscript to the operator to indicate the method to be used: C^I indicates mutual independence method, C^{Fmax} indicates Fréchet's method with maximum correlation, and C^{Fmin} indicates Fréchet's method with minimum correlation. When the common attribute does not have the same partition in both tables one should first make the two partitions agree. To make the partitions agree, one writes an S expression with the agreed partition for one of the tables. This might be an uncertain expression if it involves quanta splitting, and if this is the case, we use the method described in the next section to compute the expression.

2.5 Splitting Quanta

As we mentioned in Section 2.1 there are some partitions of an attribute's domain that cannot be computed exactly with S operations. Such is the case of partitioning GPA into the following quanta: $\{[2.5,2.9), [2.9,3.2), [3.2,3.5), [3.5,3.7), [3.7-4)\}$ in Table 3.

There are two situations where the need to split quanta arises. First is the case when a user asks a query about an attribute partitioned in a way that does not exist in any computed summary table. In this case, we have a single summary table with the desired attribute, but in different quanta than what we need. We assume that we do know the distribution type, mean and standard deviation for that attribute. The mean and the standard deviation can always be computed from the frequency distribution of the attribute. If the distribution type is not known, one can use a statistical procedure to estimate it.

To adjust the table to the new quanta follow these steps:

1. Transpose the table in such a way that the attribute to be partitioned appears alone in the y dimension.
2. Use the frequency distribution of the attribute to compute an approximation to the number of individuals in each new range of the attribute.
3. Apply a procedure similar to Fréchet's to compute the entries in the new summary table. When computing the entries by columns, notice that now we have three constraints: the new marginal (horizontal constraints), the marginal for the other attributes (vertical constraints), and the old marginal for the given attribute. Notice also that the new range must be either part of a previous range, or of various previous ranges.

The other case where the need for splitting quanta arises is when we want to combine the information from two summary tables which have a common attribute but are partitioned in different quanta. In this case, we first force the partitions for the attribute in the two tables to be the same by modifying the partition in one table to be exactly the same as the partition in the other table. Later we can combine the two tables with the assumption of independence, or finding the maximum correlation, or the minimum correlation.

3 The Query Answering Lattice

Assume that we have computed several summary tables by applying the following S operations: $S[\text{GPA}\,|\,\emptyset, \text{IQ}\,|\,\emptyset](\text{T3})$, $S[\text{GRE}\,|\,\emptyset, \text{IQ}\,|\,\emptyset](\text{T3})$, $S[\text{GPA}\,|\,\emptyset](\text{T3})$, $S[\text{GRE}\,|\,\emptyset](\text{T3})$. In fact, after executing the above operations we have the tables 9 and 10, and the joint tables for GRE-IQ and GPA-IQ, respectively. Name T^{GRE-IQ} the joint table GRE-IQ and name T^{GPA-IQ} the joint table GPA-IQ. Now suppose a user asks the query: *How many students with a GPA between 2 and 2.5 obtained a grade greater than 700 in the GRE?* If we assume mutual independence between the variables GRE, IQ and GPA, we have two alternative ways of computing this query, depending on which summary tables are available, namely:

- $C^I(S[\text{GPA}\,|\,\{[2,2.5),\text{OTH}\}](\text{T10}); S[\text{GRE}\,|\,\{[700),\text{OTH}\}](\text{T9}))$, or
- $C^I(S[\text{GPA}\,|\,\{[2,2.5),\text{OTH}\}](T^{GPA-IQ}); S[\text{GRE}\,|\,\{[700),\text{OTH}\}](T^{GRE-IQ}))$.

Therefore it is desirable to have a way of deciding among alternative computations. In the following sections we define a lattice of sets of summary tables to help us decide among alternative strategies for query answering.

3.1 A Hierarchy of Sumary Tables

All the summary tables which can be computed from a given base table can be organized in a hierarchy defined according to the number of attributes contained in the summary tables.

At the top of the hierarchy we find the *global summary tables* which contain all the category or measurement attributes, and a column containing a count attribute summarizing the individual information in the base table. The bottom of the hierarchy has tables with only one category or measurement attribute and one count attribute.

For example, if we consider as the only aggregate attribute a frequency count of the number of individuals, each summary table in this level corresponds to one *"histogram table"* for some attribute. All the histogram tables obtained from Table 3 are shown in tables 8, 9, and 10. Intermediate points in the hierarchy correspond to summary tables whose attributes are proper subsets of the original set of attributes. In Figure 1 we show an example of a hierarchy of summary tables which can be obtained from Table 1. The notation T(GRE,GPA,#) stands for the table of the number of students for each value of GRE and GPA. As we go down in the hierarchy we lose information and we need less space to store the tables. Since the tables get smaller, it is faster to operate on them.

In this section we study the properties of sets of summary tables with respect to their ability to answer queries. We compare the sets of tables according to such ability, and define a partial order on them.

Table 8. Students per IQ

IQ	140	150	170
	529	882	63

Table 9. Students per GRE grades

GRE	500-700	700-900
	882	592

Table 10. Students per GPA

GPA	2-2.5	2.5-3	3-3.5	3.5-4
	554	325	326	269

3.2 The Lattice of Sets of Summary Tables

Consider all the summary tables that can be obtained from a base table by applying S operations to it. Call these tables the *Count Summary Tables*. Let $\mathcal{P}(A)$ be the power set of the attributes, and let N be the total number of attributes in the base table, excluding the count. We define a *Non-Redundant Set of Count Summary Tables* as the summary tables formed using as attributes the elements of $\mathcal{P}(A)$, and for which the following conditions hold:

1. Exhaustive condition. All the attributes in the base table are covered by the union of the attributes in the non-redundant set.

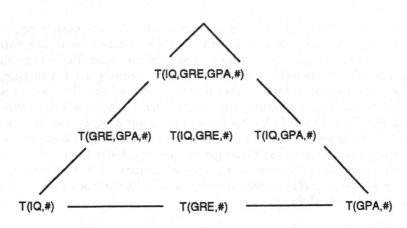

Fig. 1. Example of a Hierarchy of Summary Tables

2. Minimality condition. If we eliminate any summary table in the set, its information cannot be reconstructed "exactly" from the remaining summary tables.

Examples of non-redundant sets of count summary tables are: {T(GRE,GPA,#), T(IQ,#)} and {T(IQ,GRE,#), T(IQ,GPA,#)}. An example of a redundant set is: {T(IQ,GRE,#), T(IQ,GPA,#), T(GPA,#)}.

The Query Answering Lattice of *sets* of count summary tables is organized by defining the relationship *less-informed-than* using the criteria: *best answers queries about N − 1 or less attributes.*

Given two sets of count summary tables, S1 and S2, S1 is less-informed-than S2, if S1 can answer all the queries that S2 can answer provided the following independence assumptions hold:

1. If two tables T_1^1 and T_2^1 in S1 have schemas (A,C,#) and (B,C,#), respectively, where A, B and C can be single or compound attributes, and if S2 contains a table with schema T^2(A,B,#), then variables A and B are independent given C, when A,B,C are interpreted as random variables.
2. For every pair of tables $T_1^1(Z)$ and $T_2^1(Y)$ in S1, with no common attributes, and such that S2 contains a table with schema $T^2(Z,Y)$, all the single attributes contained in Z and Y are mutually independent random variables.

Regarding assumption 1 above, and queries involving the joint distribution of A and B, S1 is less-informed-than S2 unless A and B are independent given C, i.e. when we combine T_1^1 and T_2^1 to produce the joint table T(A,B,#), this gives exactly T^2(A,B,#). In other words, if the independence assumptions do not hold, the answer to some queries computed using the tables in S1, will not be as accurate as would be the answer using the tables in S2, therefore S1 has less information than S2.

In Figure 2 we show the lattice for the students example. The solid lines mean that the relationship "less-informed-than" holds for the two connected sets. The dotted lines define pairs of sets that are not comparable using the relationship "less-informed-than" and the mentioned criteria. For example, the sets S1={T(GRE,GPA,#), T(IQ,#)} and S2={T(IQ,GRE,#), T(IQ,GPA,#)} are not comparable because S1 can answer queries

about the joint distribution of GRE and GPA, but S2 cannot, and S2 can answer queries
about the joint distributions of IQ-GRE and IQ-GPA, but S1 cannot.

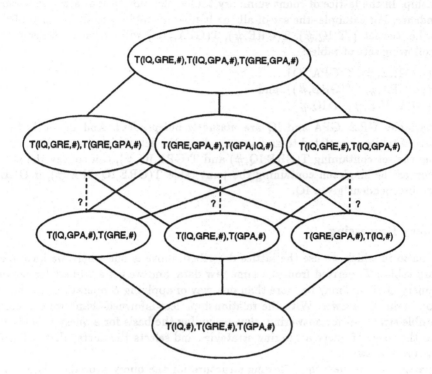

Fig. 2. Example of the lattice for IQ, GRE, and GPA

The relationship less-informed-than provides a partial order on the sets of count
summary tables, because it is not possible to compare all the pairs of sets according to
the criteria defined above.

The lower bound of the lattice is the set of all summary tables with a single attribute
and a count with the number of individuals in each value of the attribute. The upper
bound of the lattice is the non-redundant set of summary tables each with N-1 attributes.

If we modify slightly the criteria for building the lattice to: *best answers queries about
ALL the attributes*, the same lattice would still be valid, but with an additional element
at the top. The additional element is the new upper bound, and consists of the global
summary table containing all the attributes. In the example of Figure 2, the singleton
{T(IQ,GRE,GPA,#)}, i.e. the joint summary table with all the attributes, is the new
top element.

When we consider four attributes or more (excluding the count) things get very
complicated quickly. To count the number of summary tables in the intermediate levels
of the lattice is a non-trivial combinatorial problem.

At each level of the lattice, the different sets of summary tables can be "annotated" to
describe its potential for answering queries. This potential refers to the ability of a set of

tables, to produce a valid approximation of the "more-informed-tables" contained in a set above the annotated level, and related to this one according to the "less-informed-than" relationship. In the lattice of count summary tables, the annotations are *assumptions of independence*. For example, the set of all the histogram tables are shown in tables 8, 9, and 10, i.e. the set { T(IQ,#), T(GRE,#), T(GPA,#) } will be "as-informed-as" each of the following sets of tables:

- {T(IQ,GRE,#), T(GPA,#)},
- {T(IQ,GPA,#), T(GRE,#)}, and
- {T(GPA,GRE,#), T(IQ,#)},

if the variables GRE, GPA and IQ are *mutually independent*. And in the lattice, the three sets of tables are related to and appear above the set of histogram tables. Another example: the set containing T(GRE,IQ,#) and T(GPA,IQ,#), can convey the same information as the singleton containing the joint table T(GRE,IQ,GPA,#), if GRE and GPA are independent given IQ.

3.3 Query Processing

The scenario in which we use the lattice described above is one where we have a set of summary tables, T, derived from the same raw data, and we get a request for answering a new query Q. There may be more than one way of applying S operations to the tables in T to obtain the answer. With the relationship "less-informed-than" we can compare the possible strategies for answering, thus providing the basis for a query processor that searches the space of query answering strategies and selects the one(s) that will provide more accurate answers.

In particular, we view the following structure for the query processor: Given T and a new query Q, if there is an expression using S operations, that provides an exact computation of the answer to Q, use it and give the resulting answer. Otherwise, follow the next steps:

1. Select all the non-redundant sets of summary tables among the existing ones, from which the answer could be computed.
2. Choose the non-redundant set that is higher in the lattice.
3. Compute the following three joint tables using the chosen set of summary tables:
   - A table showing independence among the variables.
   - A table with maximum pairwise correlation.
   - A table with minimum pairwise correlation.

Rather than offering a single approximate value, these three tables give bounds for the answer. The answer computed directly from the raw data *should* be within these bounds.

4 Conclusions

For large statistical databases, used by the general public as a "fishing pond" for obtaining trends and correlations, it is sometimes unaffordable to obtain precise answers due to the size of the raw data. If we only use summaries to compute answers, in general we lose some precision, although there may be cases where we can obtain exact answers; for the other cases there are methods that allow the computation of approximate answers from the summaries. If we had a mechanism for keeping track of already computed summaries, then we could use these summaries to quickly answer a new request for summary information.

In this paper we have described such a mechanism. We have presented a fundamental operator, the S operator, to build summary tables. With it we can compute some answers exactly. For the cases where there is no exact answer obtainable from the available summaries we defined the operator C which combines summary tables in an approximate manner to provide bounds for the answer.

Since sometimes we have a choice of answering strategies, we defined the structure of a lattice to help us decide which strategy to use when facing a new query and a set of summary tables previously computed. The mechanism described here can be used as the basis for building a data exploration facility and a query optimization technique within the environment defined above.

When we include non-numeric attributes the probabilistic interpretation described in Section 2.2 is no longer valid, because random variables must take real values. A possible solution is to assign numeric values to the non-numeric attributes, although this imposes a structure and an order in the attributes which might not be appropriate. In particular in Fréchet's method, since the order imposed in the non-numeric attributes is arbitrary, one could have different possible sets of constraints by using different permutations of the "non-numeric values" when assigning numbers to them. One alternative is to generate all the possible answers with the different permutations and compare them or average them. In any event, the existence of non-numeric data in statistical databases requires new notions of correlation and independence.

The idea of taking advantage of previously computed summary tables to answer new queries was inspired by the work of Finkelstein (1982) on query optimization. Rather than starting a new computation with every new query, Finklestein's query optimization philosophy is to use what was computed before to help answer the new query.

Regarding related work, Rowe (1982) uses precomputed summary values to improve access speed to large amounts of data requiring statistical calculations. There are two main differences between our work and Rowe's work: first, he uses a set of inference rules to estimate some statistics in terms of precomputed ones, and second, his system builds the database abstract, whereas in our case we just *keep* some of the summaries previously computed by the users, and we do not need inference rules.

Malvestuto (1987) gives a method for building a joint distribution table from two summary tables with a common attribute. He uses the assumption of conditional independence of the variables to do this, which leads to a joint distribution with maximum entropy. Although we do not use Malvestuto's method here, we do use the notion of conditional independence to build some of our joint summary tables.

Sato (1981) and Malvestuto (1987) deal with tables on which the common attribute has different categorizations. They both provide specific methods to "match" the different categorizations of the same attribute, but do not compute approximate values when there is not a clear cut correspondence, as we try to do in Section 2.5.

Oszoyoglu (1986) and Su (1989) also use a lattice model, but for security in statistical databases rather than for query answering. The way the lattice is defined is very different from the one proposed here.

Ozsoyoglu et al. (1987), have proposed algebraic operators for summary tables which are based on a nested-attribute model of data. In contrast, we propose here a two level approach: a simple base level where there are only traditional tuples, and a surface level, which would allow all sorts of inversions and transpositions of base relations as a way of displaying the data in a fashion more traditional in statistical data. The exact relationship between the expressiveness of the resulting languages is subject to further research.

Acknowledgement

The author wishes to express her heartfelt thanks to Prof. Alex Borgida for enlightening discussions and suggestions, and for reading previous versions of this manuscript, and to Prof. José Luis Palacios for many useful comments.

References

S. Finkelstein: *Common expression analysis in database applications.* Proceedings of the ACM SIGMOD Conference, 1982, Orlando, Florida, pp 235-245.

M. Fréchet: Sur Les Tableaux dont les marges et des bornes sont données. Review of the International Institute of Statistics 28:1/2 (1960), pp 10-32.

M. Fréchet: Les Tableaux dont les marges sont données. Trabajos de Estadística, 1960, pp 3-18.

F. M. Malvestuto: *Answering Queries in Categorical Data Bases.* Proceedings of the Sixth ACM-SIGMOD Symposium, San Diego 1987, pp 87-96.

F. M. Malvestuto: *The derivation problem for summary data.* Proceedings of the ACM-SIGMOD Symposium, 1988, pp 82-89.

A. Shoshani: *Statistical Databases: Characteristics, Problems and some Solutions.* Proceedings of the 8th VLDB, Mexico City, Mexico 1982, pp 208-222.

G. Ozsoyoglu and J. Chung: *Information Loss in the Lattice Model of Summary Tables due to Cell suppression.* Second IEEE Data Engineering Conference, Los Angeles, California, Feb. 1986, pp. 75-85.

G. Ozsoyoglu, Z. M. Ozsoyoglu and V. Matos: *Extending Relational Algebra and Relational Calculus with Set-Valued Attributes and Aggregate Functions.* ACM Transactions on Database Systems, Vol 12, No 4, Dec. 1987, pp 566-592.

N. C. Rowe: *Rule-based statistical calculations on a "Database Abstract".* Proceedings of the First LBL Workshop on Statistical Database Management, March 1982, pp 163-175.

H. Sato: *Handling Summary Information in a Database: Derivability.* Proceedings of SIGMOD, 1981, pp 98-107.

E. Seneta: *Non-negative matrices and Markov Chains.* Springer-Verlag, New York 1980.

T-A. Su, J. Chung and G. Ozsoyoglu: *On the Cell Suppression by Merging Technique in the Lattice Model of Summary Tables.* IEEE Symposium on Computer Security and Privacy, April 1989, pp 126-137.

Pipelined Query Processing in the DBGraph Storage Model [1]

Philippe Pucheral, Jean-Marc Thévenin

INRIA - Rocquencourt BP. 105, 78153 Le Chesnay, France

Abstract

The DBGraph storage model, designed for main memory DBMS, ensures both data storage compactness and efficient processing for all database operations. By representing the entire database in a unique graph-based structure, called DBGraph, it fully exploits the direct-access capability of main memory systems. Complex database queries can be processed in either set-oriented or pipelined mode depending on the way the DBGraph is traversed. In this paper we concentrate on the pipelined mode. Its advantages are the ability to produce result tuples as early as possible (during query processing) and the low cost of memory utilization in managing temporary results. We analyze different strategies for translating a query into a pipelined program and compare their performance with the set-oriented mode. Based on these results, we propose a compiler/optimizer algorithm translating relational queries into an optimal pipelined program.

1. INTRODUCTION

In a previous paper [Puch90], we proposed the DBGraph model as a main memory storage and access model which achieves both compactness and efficiency. Compared to previous work in the area of main memory DBMS, this model integrates the advantages of compact data structures [Amma85, Lehm86a, Lehm86b] with the direct (pointer-based) data access capability of main memory [DeWi84, Vald87, Agra89, Shek90]. A DBGraph is a bipartite graph composed of a set of tuple-vertices and a set of value-vertices connected together by edges. Compactness is obtained by storing each attribute value only once [Miss83] and by using the same edges to precompile all database operations. A DBGraph naturally supports vertical partitionning making possible the loading of a subpart of the DBGraph in main memory and the clustering on disk. By representing the entire database in a unique graph-based data structure, this model provides efficient support for all database operations, unlike disk-based storage models [Miss83, Cope85, Vald86] which optimize some operations at the expense of others. Selection, join and transitive closure operations over base or temporary relations can be performed by a DBGraph traversal without any tuple comparison or move. Compared to other methods, DBGraph demonstrates good storage occupancy and excellent performance for both set-oriented retrieval and update operations involving integrity constraints checking.

An attractive property of the DBGraph is that complex database queries can be processed by either set-oriented or pipelined mode depending on the way the graph is traversed. The set-oriented execution of a query, considered in [Puch90], induces a *breadth-first search* traversal of the DBGraph. Each operation produces a temporary result which must be materialized and consumed by the next operation. A pipelined execution of a query can be obtained by a *depth-first search* traversal of the DBGraph. A pipelined execution has two major advantages. First temporary results need not be generated. Thus, minimizing the space occupancy for temporary data [Bitt86, Lehm86b] is no more required to save main memory space for the permanent active data. Second, tuples already produced can be displayed while the query processing is still in progress. This drastically reduces the elapsed time for a query.

---

[1] This work has been partially funded by the Esprit project Stretch n° 2443.

517

In this paper, we propose a compiler/optimizer algorithm translating relational selection queries into optimal pipelined programs exploiting the DBGraph. This algorithm first parses the query into a sequence of relational operations represented as a relation-connection-graph [Ullm82], then rearranges this graph for optimization purpose and finally generates a pipelined program involving DBGraph traversal primitives. Different strategies are proposed for translating a subquery into a pipelined sequence of code. We introduce an analytical model to compare these strategies one to another in terms of performance. These strategies are then compared to the set-oriented mode on a DBGraph which has excellent performance compared with other well known main memory set-oriented strategies [Puch90].

The paper is organized as follows. Section 2 recalls from [Puch90] the definition of the DBGraph model including its graph structure and primitive operations as well as the select and join algorithms involved in a set-oriented query processing. In Section 3, we study several strategies to translate a subquery into a pipelined sequence of code and propose a code generator algorithm for complete queries relying upon these strategies. In Section 4, we analyze the performance of the different translation strategies and compare them to the set-oriented strategy. In light of these results, Section 5 proposes an optimizer algorithm producing an optimal query execution plan. Section 6 concludes.

2. DBGRAPH STORAGE MODEL

First of all, we introduce a few notations used in the sequel of the paper. We consider a database DB composed of a set of relations. In most of our examples we will use only two relations named R and S. These relations are defined over a number of domains, each domain j being denoted by Dj. A relation schema is an aggregation of attributes, each from a given domain of values. We denote by R.k the kth attribute of relation R and $t_{R.k}$ the value of attribute k for tuple t. Finally, we denote by T the set of all the tuples of a database DB and V the set of all the domain values of DB.

2.1. DBGraph Definition and Primitive Traversal Operations

A DBGraph is a bipartite graph composed of a set of *tuple-vertices* holding all the tuples of T, a set of *value-vertices* holding all the domain values of V, and *valued-edges* connecting these two sets (see example Figure 1). Each edge, denoted by (t, v, R.k), is bi-directional and connects a tuple-vertex t with a value-vertex v. The valuation R.k indicates that t belongs to relation R and that v is the value of its kth attribute. A tuple-vertex is linked by one edge to each of its attribute values and a value-vertex is linked by an edge to each tuple that references it for one of its attributes. Tuple vertices (resp. value vertices) may be grouped on a relation basis (resp. domain basis). The DBGraph concept can be more formally defined as follows:

Definition: *The DBGraph of a database DB is a valued bipartite graph G(X,A) where X=(T,V) is the set of vertices of G, A is the set of edges of G and the edge (t, v, R.k)∈A iff t∈T, v∈V and $t_{R.k} = v$.*

Complex database operations can be expressed in a simple and uniform fashion by composition of two traversal operations, regardless of the physical DBGraph implementation. This provides a high-level description of all algorithms which should result in higher modularity. Update operations have also been defined in [Puch90].

- the *succ_val* operation is an application from V to T that delivers the subset ΔR of tuple vertices corresponding to all the tuples of relation R whose k^{th} attribute value is equal to a given value v.
  $ΔR = succ\_val(v, R.k)$ *where* $ΔR = \{t \in T / v \in V, (t, v, R.k) \in A\}$

- the *succ_tup* operation is an application from T to V that determines the V vertex connected to a given T vertex by an edge valued by R.k.
  $v = succ\_tup(t, R.k)$ *where* $v \in V$ *and* $(t, v, R.k) \in A$

2.2. Set oriented processing

The DBGraph model is able to support set-oriented database languages based on different data models. In this section, we show how relational operators can be composed easily using the DBGraph primitive operations. For the sake of conciseness, only the select and join operators are recalled below. Other retrieval and update relational operators (including transitive closure) are detailed in [Puch90].

The select operator, denoted by σ_Q, applied to relation R, determines the subset R_σ of T vertices corresponding to all the tuples of relation R which satisfy the qualification Q. For simplicity, we assume that Q is a simple predicate (R.k θ c) where c is a constant and θ is a comparator. The corresponding algorithm is given below. Function $Select_Q(V)$ builts the set $\Delta V = \{v \in V / (v \theta c)$ is true}. It can be optimized using indices on V (see details in Section 4). The generalization of Q to handle conjunctions (resp. disjunctions) of predicates requires unions (resp. intersections) of the R_σ sets corresponding to each predicate.

> Function $\sigma_Q (R) : R_\sigma$
> $\quad R_\sigma := \emptyset;$
> $\quad \Delta V := Select_Q(V);$
> $\quad$ for each $v \in \Delta V$ do
> $\quad\quad \Delta R := succ\_val(v, R.k);$
> $\quad\quad R_\sigma := R_\sigma \cup \Delta R$

The join operator, denoted by $\otimes_M$, applied to R and S determines the set $RS_\otimes$ of couples of T vertices corresponding to the matching tuples. We consider a join predicate M of the form (R.k = S.l) where R.k and S.l take values on the same domain Dj. The DBGraph definition insists that the matching tuples are connected by a path of length two. A first join algorithm, named Join1, consists of scanning Dj and reaching for each value the matching tuples of R and S. As domains are shared among relations, Card(Dj) can be high compared to Card(R) or Card(S) (Card denotes the cardinality of a set). In this case, a better algorithm, named Join2, consists of first scanning the smallest operand relation and retrieving the join attribute value of each tuple through the succ_tup primitive. Then, applying the succ_val primitive gives access to the subset of tuples of the other operand relation having the same value of join attribute. These two algorithms are given below.

> Function $Join1_M(R,S) : RS_\otimes$
> $\quad RS_\otimes := \emptyset;$
> $\quad$ for each $v \in Dj$ do
> $\quad\quad \Delta R := succ\_val(v, R.k);$
> $\quad\quad \Delta S := succ\_val(v, S.l);$
> $\quad\quad RS_\otimes := RS_\otimes \cup (\Delta R \, X \, \Delta S)$

> Function $Join2_M(R,S): RS_\otimes$
> $\quad RS_\otimes := \emptyset;$
> $\quad$ for each $t \in R$ do
> $\quad\quad v := succ\_tup(t, R.k);$
> $\quad\quad \Delta S := succ\_val(v, S.l);$
> $\quad\quad RS_\otimes := RS_\otimes \cup (t \, X \, \Delta S)$

X denotes the cartesian product operation. In the Join2 algorithm, we assume Card(R) ≤ Card(S) ≤ Card(Dj). In both algorithms, the union $RS_\otimes \cup (\Delta R \, X \, \Delta S)$ (resp. $RS_\otimes \cup (t \, X \, \Delta S)$) is in fact a concatenation because the generation of duplicates in $RS_\otimes$ is impossible.

Set-oriented processing requires the management of temporary results. In most data storage models, it is difficult to speed up operations on temporary results using indices [Puch90]. As join operations are frequently preceded by selections, this limitation is severe. In the DBGraph model, temporary results are materialized by temporary vertices connected through temporary links with the tuples of the basic relations from which they are extracted. The degree (number of edges) of a temporary vertex is equal to the number of basic tuples involved in the temporary result. The main advantage is that temporary results preserve the links to basic tuples. Consequently, operations on temporary relations are speeded up by a DBGraph traversal in a way similar to operations on basic relations. For example, consider the query $\otimes_M(\sigma_Q(R),S)$ with Q = (R.2="mouse") and M = (R.2=S.1), illustrated in Figure 1. Scanning the temporary result $\sigma_Q(R)$ determines a set of entry vertices in the DBGraph that can be directly exploited by the join operator, using the Join2 algorithm introduced earlier.

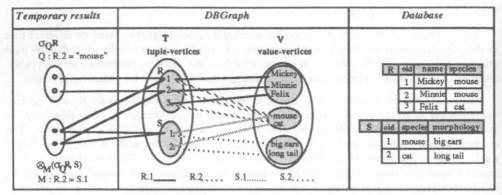

Temporary results	DBGraph	Database

Figure 1: DBGraph extended with temporary results

3. PIPELINED PROCESSING

Let us consider a generic query QR involving relations R1, R2, ... Rn. A naïve algorithm performing the pipelined execution of QR is given in Figure 2. This algorithm is composed of several nested loops, one for each relation involved in the query. Each loop scans the corresponding relation in order to select the tuples matching the query predicate.

> **for each** $t1 \in R_1$ **do**
>   **if** $(t1, *, *, ...)$ *satisfies QR* **then**
>   **for each** $t2 \in R_2$ **do**
>   **if** $(t1, t2, *, *, ...)$ *satisfies QR* **then**
>   ⋮
>   **if** $(t1, t2, t3, ..., tn)$ *satisfies QR* **then** *PROJECT the answer*

Figure 2: Pipelined strategy [Amma85]

Using the DBGraph, this algorithm can be optimized by restricting each loop to the tuples matching with the current tuple of the previous loop. Intuitively, the pipelined strategy performs a *depth-first search* traversal of the DBGraph as follows. The number of joins in QR determines the length of a *pertinent-path* connecting a tuple of R1 to a tuple of Rn where the edges valuations are determined by the join predicates. These paths are explored one after the other and a result tuple is produced each time the extremity of a pertinent-path is reached.

Like with other strategies, the join ordering has a strong influence on the query execution time, since it determines the number of paths to be explored in the DBGraph. The translation of a query into an optimal pipelined program which exploits the DBGraph proceeds in three steps. First, a parser decomposes the query into a sequence of relational operations represented as a relation-connection-graph [Ullm82] (named RCG). Second, an optimizer rearranges the RCG to produce an oriented RCG which indicates the optimal join ordering (see Figure 3). Third, the oriented RCG is translated by a code generator into a pipelined program composed of nested loops calling the succ_val and succ_tup primitives in order to traverse the DBGraph.

relation-connection-graph   Oriented relation-connection-graph

• *Each node denotes a relation involved in the query* • *An edge between two nodes stands for a join and a loop stands for a selection* • *Each edge (resp. loop) is valuated by a join (resp. selection) predicate. To simplify the figure, these valuations are not pictured* • *This oriented RCG of root U expresses the following optimal join ordering :* $(\sigma U \otimes R \otimes T) \otimes (\sigma W \otimes S)$

Figure 3: Oriented Relation-Connection-Graph

In the rest of this section, we show how subparts of the oriented RCG can be translated into sequences of code to be combined together. Then, we give a generic algorithm which translates an oriented RCG into a pipelined program. The parser is not detailed since it corresponds to a well known process, the optimizer is presented in Section 5 and the code generator is detailed below.

3.1. Characterization of query execution plans

In the general case, the RCG of a query may contain chains, forks, cycles, meets and loops where loops stand for selections and the other arcs stand for joins (see Figure 4). In the following, we detail the sequence of instructions which should be generated in each case. When several alternatives apply, the query optimizer annotates the RCG to indicate the best translation strategy.

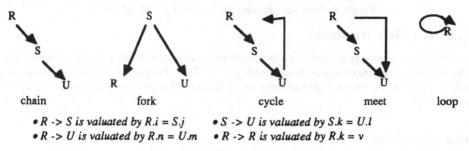

| chain | fork | cycle | meet | loop |

- $R \to S$ is valuated by $R.i = S.j$ • $S \to U$ is valuated by $S.k = U.l$
- $R \to U$ is valuated by $R.n = U.m$ • $R \to R$ is valuated by $R.k = v$

Figure 4 : Oriented RCG structure

Chain translation

Each join which is part of a chain can be translated as a loop on the first relation containing a call to the succ_tup primitive, then a call to the succ_val primitive in a way similar to the Join2 algorithm (see Section 2.2). These loops are nested and the result is produced in a final loop on the last relation, as illustrated in Figure 5a. A second solution is to perform the first join in a way similar to the Join1 algorithm, by replacing the external loop on the first relation by a loop on the domain of the join attribute (see Figure 5b). This solution applies only if the chain root is the root of the RCG.

```
for each t₁ ∈ R do
    v₁ = succ_tup (t₁, R.i)
    ΔS = succ_val (v₁, S.j)
    for each t₂ ∈ ΔS do
        v₂ = succ_tup (t₂, S.k)
        ΔU = succ_val (v₂, U.l)
        for each t₃ ∈ ΔU do
            project (t₁, t₂, t₃)
```

```
for each v∈ Dj do
    ΔR:= succ_val(v, R.i)
    ΔS:= succ_val(v, S.j)
    for each t₁ ∈ ΔR do
        for each t₂ ∈ ΔS do
            v₂ = succ_tup (t₂, S.k)
            ΔU = succ_val (v₂, U.l)
            for each t₃ ∈ ΔU do
                project (t₁, t₂, t₃)
```

5a: Chain1   5b: Chain2

Figure 5: Pipelined program for the chain $R \otimes S \otimes U$

Fork translation

In case of a fork, out-edges are considered left to right, splitting the oriented RCG into subgraphs. The translation of a subgraph is nested into the internal loop of its left neighbor subgraph. Figure 6a illustrates this translation for a fork which is the root of two chains. As we will see in Section 4, it could be more efficient to perform all the joins corresponding to the out-edges of the fork in the external loop of the program instead of nesting them. This optimization is illustrated in Figure 6b.

for each $t_1 \in S$ **do**	**for each** $t_1 \in S$ **do**
$\quad v_1 = succ\_tup\,(t_1, S.j)$	$\quad v_1 = succ\_tup\,(t_1, S.j)$
$\quad \Delta R = succ\_val\,(v_1, R.i)$	$\quad \Delta R = succ\_val\,(v_1, R.i)$
$\quad$ **for each** $t_2 \in \Delta R$ **do**	$\quad v_2 = succ\_tup\,(t_1, S.k)$
$\quad\quad v_2 = succ\_tup\,(t_1, S.k)$	$\quad \Delta U = succ\_val\,(v_2, U.l)$
$\quad\quad \Delta U = succ\_val\,(v_2, U.l)$	$\quad$ **for each** $t_2 \in \Delta R$ **do**
$\quad\quad\quad$ **for each** $t_3 \in \Delta U$ **do**	$\quad\quad$ **for each** $t_3 \in \Delta U$ **do**
$\quad\quad\quad\quad project\,(t_1, t_2, t_3)$	$\quad\quad\quad project\,(t_1, t_2, t_3)$
6a: Fork1	**6b:** Fork2

Figure 6: Pipelined program for the fork $R \otimes S \otimes U$ of root S

Cycle and Meet translation

The last join of a cycle or a meet can be considered as an inter-attribute selection. Indeed, this last join involves two relations that have been already joined. Thus, this join consists in comparing the join attribute values of the current tuples of these two relations. This process is illustrated Figure 7 on a cycle example.

Loop translation

Selections in a pipelined program may be evaluated in two different ways. The first solution, called SelOntheFly, consists of checking the selection qualification each time a tuple of the selected relation is accessed during a path traversal. Such on-the-fly selection does not benefit from indices. The second solution, called SelIndexed, consists of checking the selection qualification before any path traversal and marking the tuples satisfying this qualification. Then, at DBGraph traversal time, all the paths traversing a non-marked tuple are discarded. This second solution can exploit indices to speed up the selection. However, it incurs the overhead of managing a bit array implementing the marking protocol. Note that when applying the second strategy to the relation involved in the external loop, marking is not necessary. Indeed, this selection directly restricts the external loop to the tuples satisfying the selection criteria, as shown in Figure 8.

for each $t_1 \in R$ **do**
$\quad v_1 = succ\_tup\,(t_1, R.i)$
$\quad \Delta S = succ\_val\,(v_1, S.j)$
$\quad$ **for each** $t_2 \in \Delta S$ **do**
$\quad\quad v_2 = succ\_tup\,(t_2, S.k)$
$\quad\quad \Delta U = succ\_val\,(v_2, U.l)$
$\quad\quad$ **for each** $t_3 \in \Delta U$ **do**
$\quad\quad\quad v_3 = succ\_tup\,(t_3, U.m)$
$\quad\quad\quad v_4 = succ\_tup\,(t_1, R.n)$
$\quad\quad\quad$ **if** $v_3 = v_4$ **then**
$\quad\quad\quad\quad project\,(t_1, t_2, t_3)$

Figure 7: Pipelined program for the cycle
$R \otimes S \otimes U \otimes R$

{Eventually build a marking bit array for σS }
$V' = Select_{Q1}(V)$
for each $v \in V'$ **do**
$\quad \Delta R = succ\_val\,(v, R.k)$
$\quad$ **for each** $t_1 \in \Delta R$ **do**
$\quad\quad v_1 = succ\_tup\,(t_1, R.i)$
$\quad\quad \Delta S = succ\_val\,(v_2, S.j)$
$\quad\quad$ **for each** $t_2 \in \Delta S$ **do**
$\quad\quad\quad$ **if** $check\,(t_2, Q2)$ **then**
$\quad\quad\quad\quad project\,(t_1, t_2)$

$check(t_2, Q2)$ verify the qualif. Q2
or the marking for tuple t2

Figure 8: Pipelined program for the query
$\sigma_{Q1} R \rightarrow \sigma_{Q2} S$

3.2. Generating pipelined programs

We now propose an algorithm that generates an optimized pipelined program from the oriented RCG produced by the optimization step. This algorithm traverses the oriented RCG starting from the root and marks the visited nodes in order to detect the cycles and meets, and to avoid going twice through the same path. In case of a fork, the subgraphs are traversed in left to right order. During this traversal, the algorithm produces sequences of code according to the four particular cases introduced above. The code generator algorithm is recursive. It considers one node at a time and performs the following operations on that node (see Figure 9): mark the node, generate a loop on the tuples of the corresponding relation, call the *check* primitive for each of these tuples in case of selection, generate the sequence of succ_tup and succ_val primitives implementing the join corresponding to each out-edge of that node then call itself recursively for each successor of this node (extremity of these out-edges). As shown in the previous section, some edges can be translated in different ways. For the sake of simplicity, the code generator algorithm shown in Figure 9 translates always chains with algorithm Chain1 (see Figure 5a), forks with algorithm Fork2 (see Figure 6.b) and selections with a generic *check* primitive. The complete version of this algorithm should take into account the annotations produced by the optimizer to indicate the best translation strategy.

procedure CodeGenerator (OrientedRCG, Node, i, j)

mark (Node)
generate ("for each t<i> ∈ Δ<Node> do")
if *there is a loop on Node* **then**   /* selection */
    generate ("if check (t<i>, Q(Node)) then ")

for each *outEdge of Node from left to right* **do**
    generate ("v<j> = succ_tup (t<i>, outEdge.valuation.att1)") ;
    if (outEdge.endNode ¬marked)
        then   /* join involved in a chain or a fork */
            generate ("Δ<outEdge.endNode> = succ_val (v<j>, outEdge.valuation.att2)")
        else   /* join involved in a loop or a meet */
            generate ("v<j+1> = succ_tup (t<Indice(outEdge.endNode)>, outEdge.valuation.att2)
                        if v<j> = v<j+1> then ")
            j = j + 1
    end if
    j = j + 1
end for

for each *outEdge of Node from left to right* **do**   /* evaluate the subgraph if not yet visited */
    i = i + 1
    if *(outEdge.endNode ¬marqued)* **then** *CodeGenerator (OrientedRCG, outEdge.endNode, i, j)*
end for

if *Node is the rightmost leaf* **then**   /* the rightmost leaf has been reached */
            generate ("project (t1, t2, ..., tn)")
end procedure

• *In a string "xx <i> xx", <i> stands for the content of variable i* • *Variable Node contains a marking boolean and pointers to potential loop and outEdges* • *Variable outEdge contains a valuation composed of two join attribute names and a pointer to its endNode* • *Q(Node) returns the selection qualification corresponding to the valuation of the loop on Node* • *Indice(Node) returns the indice used for the tuple variable in the "for each" loop generated for Node.*

Figure 9: Code generator algorithm

4. PERFORMANCE EVALUATION

In [Puch90], we compared the DBGraph model with other storage and access models. Storage cost evaluation demonstrated the compactness of the DBGraph model. Compared to a flat file storage model, the DBGraph model is less compact for short attribute values without duplicates but becomes rapidly better in other cases or when indices are considered. Performance evaluation showed the following results: selections on a DBGraph are equivalent to selections using inverted indices; joins on a DBGraph outperforms joins using join indices or inverted indices especially on temporary relations; and transitive closure on a DBGraph outperforms transitive closure by join waves using join indices. Finally, update cost evaluation shown that updates on a DBGraph are equivalent to updates on a flat file model with inverted indices. In addition, the DBGraph has the ability of checking important integrity constraints (unique key, referential) during updates with no significant overhead.

This section analyzes the previous alternatives to translate queries into pipelined programs and compares them with set-oriented processing. The remainder of this section is organized as follows. A DBGraph implementation is first proposed and the evaluation parameters are defined accordingly. Then, the translation alternatives introduced Section 3.1 are evaluated. Each comparison between two alternatives is expressed in a ratio form in order to determine when a strategy is better than the other and by how much. This will give the basis for the optimization strategies developed in Section 5. Finally, pipelined processing and set-oriented processing are compared on a DBGraph.

4.1. DBGraph Implementation

We detail below a particular DBGraph implementation which achieves data compactness and supports vertical partitionning. This DBGraph implementation is shown in Figure 10.

Domain values are stored only once to preserve compactness as in [Miss83]. To achieve vertical partitionning [Hamm79], all the values varying over the same domain are clustered in a separate segment and can thus be loaded independent of the others. Similarly, tuples are clustered in separate segments on a relation basis. Each object stored in a segment has a unique and invariant identifier (OID). Thus, tuples and values are referenced by OID's. Indices may be added on domain values to speed up selections on all attributes varying on the same domain. We choose indices containing only OID's referencing the key values in order to reduce the storage cost for variable length keys [Amma85].

In the formal definition of a DBGraph, edges of A are bi-directional. In the implementation, an edge (t, v, R.k) is split in two arcs (oriented edges) (t—>v) and (v—>t) by means of OID-pointers. We call OID-pointer an OID that can be translated into a direct pointer in main memory. A tuple is implemented as an array of OID-pointers referencing each of its attributes values. The valuation R.k of an arc (t—>v) is implicit since tuple t belongs to the segment containing relation R and the OID-pointer corresponding to this arc is stored in place of the kth attribute of tuple t. An arc (v—>t) is implemented by an OID-pointer stored in an inverted list attached to the value v. The valuation R.k of this arc is represented by the fact that inverted lists are divided in as many sublists as there are attributes sharing this value. Thus, all arc valuations are determined by the relations and domains schema. They remain implicit at the instance level and do not compromise the DBGraph compactness.

Following the vertical partitioning strategy adopted for domain values, all the inverted sublists corresponding to one attribute R.k are grouped in one segment. With each domain value is associated a sublist array containing the OID-pointers referencing all the sublists attached to this value. It contains one entry per attribute R.k varying on that domain and is indexed by R.k. Inverted lists corresponding to key attributes contain only one OID-pointer. In this case, much space is saved by storing the OID-pointer directly in the sublist array.

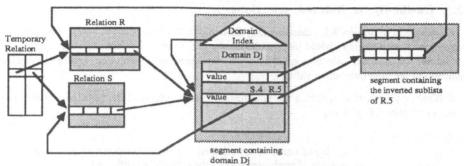

The attribute S.4 is assumed to be a key attribute.

Figure 10: Proposed DBGraph implementation

When processing a query in a set-oriented way, temporary links are always traversed along the same direction. Thus, they can be implemented by arcs instead of bi-directional edges to reduce the cost of building temporary results. The result of a selection on a base relation R can be implemented by either keeping in a list the OID-pointers of all selected tuples or marking these selected tuples via a bit array of length Card(R). A join result between two relations is materialized by an array of couples of OID-pointers where each couple references two tuples matching together. See [Puch90] for further information.

For the sake of uniformity, the proposed implementation is fully inverted. Note that the DBGraph model easily supports a mix of inverted and non inverted attributes. Only the succ_val and succ_tup primitives have to be adapted to handle this mix. Joins and selections involving non inverted attributes are then penalized while projections are improved. The choice of not inverting an attribute is a physical design decision.

4.2. Evaluation parameters

We first introduce the following structural parameters:

$Card(R), Card(S)$ cardinality of relation R (resp. S);

S_R, S_S selectivity factor of one attribute of R (resp. S);
$S_R = Card(\pi_i(R))/Card(R)$, where π_i denotes project on attribute i;

S_{avg} average attribute selectivity factor for the attributes varying over domain Dj;

J_{RS}, J_{SR} semi-join selectivity factor of relation R (resp. S) for a join between R and S;
$J_{RS} = Card(Semi\text{-}join(R,S))/Card(R)$; note that $J_{RS} \neq J_{SR}$;

J_{avg} average semi-join selectivity factor;

L overlaping factor expressing the intersection between the values taken by the n attributes varying over domain Dj $(1/n \leq L \leq 1)$; $L=1/n$ when each domain value is shared by the n attributes and $L=1$ when the n attributes do not share any value.

These parameters help to determine the cardinalities of the select and join results as follows. The average cardinality of the inverted lists attached to an attribute value of relation R is defined by $1/S_R$. The cardinality of the $\sigma_Q R$ result, where Q is an equi-predicate of the form (attribute = value), is thus: $Card(\sigma_Q R) = 1/S_R$. The cardinality of the R⊗S result is given by : $Card(R \otimes S) = J_{RS} Card(R)/S_S$.

In addition, we introduce the following system parameters:

u: time for a memory access, all algorithm execution times will be evaluated in terms of u,

d: time for decoding an OID, assumed to be $3u$, (OID beeing considered as pointers)

o: time for comparing two OID, assumed to be $2u$,

v: time for comparing two values, assumed to be $2ul$ where l is the average size of a domain.

w: time for writing a word in memory, assumed to be u.

4.3. On-the-fly vs indexed selections

As discussed in Section 3.1, selections may be computed in two different ways. The performance comparisons detailed below should help to choose the best strategy for each selected relation. In this evaluation, we consider selection qualifications expressed as conjunction and/or disjunction of predicates of the form (attribute = value).

SelOntheFly consists of checking the qualification for each tuple of the selected relation accessed during a path traversal, yielding :

$time(SelOntheFly)$ =
  $nbtup\_acc$ /* number of tuples of the selected relation accessed at traversal time
    $(nbpred$ /* number of predicates part of the selection qualification
      $((u + d)$ /* access the attribute value on which the predicate applies
      $+ v)$ /* check the predicate
        $= nbtup\_acc\,(nbpred\,(4 + 2l))\,u$

SelIndexed consists of checking the qualification before any path traversal by exploiting domain indices in order to mark the tuples satisfying this qualification via a bit array of the size of the selected relation. At DBGraph traversal time, the bit array is accessed to check whether the corresponding tuple satisfy the qualification or not.

$time(SelIndexed)$ =
  $nbpred$ /* number of predicates part of the selection qualification
    $((Card(R)/32)\,w$ /* initialize a bit array to mark the selected tuples of relation R
              /* 32 is the number of bits in a memory word
    $+ log_2(Card(D))\,(u + d + v)$ /* dichotomizing search in the index of the domain of the selected
              /* attribute domain indices contain only OID that must be decoded to
              /* access the domain values (see Section 4.1) in order to compare them
    $+ o + d$ /* access the inverted sublist of the selected value
    $+ 1/S_R$ /* cardinal of this inverted sublist
      $(u + w)$ /* mark each tuple referenced by the inverted sublist in the bit array
    $+ (nbpred - 1)$ /* conjunction/disjunctions of predicates imply to do ∩ / ∪ of bit arrays
    $((Card(R)/32)\,(2u + w))$ /* merge two bit arrays
  $+ nbtup\_acc\,(o)$ /* check the bit array for each accessed tuple at traversal time
    $= (nbpred\,((Card(R)/8) + (4 + 2l)\,log_2(Card(D)) + 5 + 2/S_R) - 3Card(R)/32) + 2nbtup\_acc)\,u$

Intuitively, SelOntheFly performs better when few tuples of the selected relation are accessed at traversal time, since SelIndexed incurs the constant overhead of building a bit array. Thus, we have to determine the percentage of accessed tuples after which SelIndexed becomes cheaper than SelOntheFly. For this, we evaluate the ratio $time(SelOntheFly)/time(SelIndexed)$. To reduce the number of parameters involved in this ratio, we approximate the cardinality of the domains of the selected attributes (which is not a deciding factor) by: $Card(D) = S_R Card(R)$ which roughly corresponds to a maximum overlaping between all attributes varying on the same domain ($L=1/n$). The ratio is expressed as follows:

$$\frac{time(SelOntheFly)}{time(SelIndexed)} =$$
$$\frac{nbtup\_acc\,(nbpred\,(4 + 2l))}{nbpred\,((Card(R)/8) + (4 + 2l)\,log_2(S_R Card(R)) + 5 + 2/S_R) - 3Card(R)/32) + 2nbtup\_acc}$$

This ratio is plotted in Figure 11 in terms of $nbtup\_acc/Card(R)$ for different values of $Card(R)$, $nbpred$ and l. Parameter S_R has negligible influence on this ratio. These curves show that SelIndexed generally performs better than SelOntheFly, except for very low values of the ratio $nbtup\_acc/Card(R)$ or for very small relations. Indeed, the extra cost of scanning the domain index and of creating the bit array is not profitable in this case. High value of l and $nbpred$ disadvantages SelOntheFly since it increases the qualification checking cost for each accessed tuple.

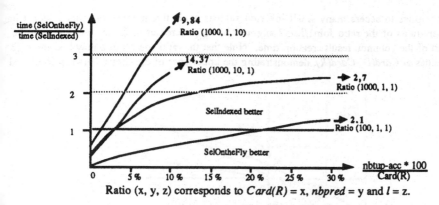

Ratio (x, y, z) corresponds to $Card(R)$ = x, $nbpred$ = y and l = z.

Figure 11: SelOntheFly vs SelIndexed

4.4.   Domain-based vs relation-based joins

As discussed in Section 3.1, the first join involved in a chain can be translated in two different sequences of code similar to the Join1 and Join2 algorithms. In a chain involving a single join, the code produced is exactly the one of Join1 or Join2 that we compare below. In a chain involving many joins, the subpart of these algorithms performing the result construction is postponed to the end of the query.

Join1 scans the domain D of the join attributes and for each value checks whether there is an inverted list associated with the join attribute of each relation to join. If there is one, a Cartesian product between the two inverted lists is performed, yielding:

$$
\begin{aligned}
time(Join1) \ = \ & Card(D) && \textit{/* scan the domain of the join attributes} \\
& (2o) && \textit{/* check the existence of an inverted sublist for each join attribute} \\
& + J_{RS}\, S_R Card(R) && \textit{/* number of R inverted sublists participating to the join} \\
& (\ 2d && \textit{/* access to the inverted sublist for each join attribute} \\
& + 1/S_R(u + (u + 2w)/S_S))) && \textit{/* Cartesian product of these two inverted sublists} \\
& = 4\,Card(D) + J_{RS}\,Card(R)\,(6\,S_R + 1 + 3/S_S)\,u
\end{aligned}
$$

Join2 scans the smallest relation (assumed to be R) and for each tuple checks whether there is an inverted list associated with the join attribute of the second relation (S). If there is one, a Cartesian product between the current tuple of R and the inverted list is performed, yielding :

$$
\begin{aligned}
time(Join2) \ = \ & Card(R) && \textit{/* scan the smallest relation} \\
& ((u + d) && \textit{/* call succ\_tup to get the join attribute value of each tuple} \\
& + o) && \textit{/* check the existence of an inverted sublist for the join attribute of S} \\
& + J_{RS}\,Card(R) && \textit{/* number of R tuples matching with an S tuple} \\
& (d && \textit{/* access to the inverted sublist for the join attribute of S} \\
& + (u + (u + 2w)/S_S)) && \textit{/* Cartesian product of an inverted list and an OID} \\
& = Card(R)\,(6 + J_{RS}\,(4 + 3/S_S))\,u
\end{aligned}
$$

The ratio between these costs is expressed by :

$$
\frac{time(Join1)}{time(Join2)} = \frac{4\,Card(D)/Card(R) + J_{RS}\,(6\,S_R + 1 + 3/S_S)}{6 + J_{RS}\,(4 + 3/S_S)}
$$

This ratio is plotted in Figure 12 in terms of $Card(D)/Card(R)$ for different values of J_{RS}, S_R and S_S. We can show that all curves cut the *equality* axis in the interval $0.9 < Card(D)/Card(R) < 2.25$. Thus, for $Card(D)/Card(R) < 0.9$ (resp. >2.25), Join1 (resp. Join2) is always better independently of the values of J_{RS}, S_R and S_S. This property simplifies the optimization process. High values of S_R disadvantage

Join1 since it implies to access many small inverted sublists while this number remains constant in Join2. The variations of the ratio Join1/Join2 augment as J_{RS} decreases or S_S increases due to the decreasing part of the common result creation time. Note that the ratio Join1/Join2 may become high for extreme values of $Card(D)/Card(R)$, demonstrating the importance of the choice between Join1 and Join2.

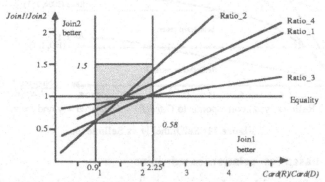

$Ratio\_1$ corresponds to $J_{RS}=1$, $S_R=0.1$ and $S_S=1$. $Ratio\_2$ corresponds to $J_{RS}=0.1$, $S_R=0.1$ and $S_S=1$. $Ratio\_3$ corresponds to $J_{RS}=1$, $S_R=0.1$ and $S_S=0.1$. $Ratio\_4$ corresponds to $J_{RS}=1$, $S_R=0.5$ and $S_S=1$.

Figure 12: Join1 vs Join2

4.5. Chain vs fork joins

A sequence of joins $R \otimes S \otimes U$ can be translated in a chain or a fork. A fork can itself be translated following two different strategies. The query optimizer has in charge to determine the best strategy and orientate the RCG accordingly. The evaluation given below compares the algorithms Chain1, Fork1 and Fork2.

The cost formula of Chain1 is expressed as follows:

```
time(Chain1) =
     Card(R)                        /* scan relation R
       (((u + d)                    /*  call succ_tup to get the join attribute value (R.i)
        + o)                        /* check the existence of an inverted sublist for the join attribute S.j
        + J_RS                      /* ratio of R tuples matching with an S tuple
        (d                          /* access to the inverted sublist for the join attribute S.j
        + 1/S_S                     /* cardinal of this inverted sublist
          (((u + d)                 /* get one S tuple referenced by the inverted sub-list
          (u + d)                   /*  call succ_tup to get the join attribute value (S.k) of this tuple
          + o)                      /* check the existence of an inverted sublist for the join attribute U.l
          + J_SU                    /* ratio of S tuples matching with a U tuple
          (d                        /* access to the inverted sublist for the join attribute U.l
        + (2u + (u + 3w)/S_U))      /* Cartesian product of this inverted list and the two OID
                                    /* corresponding to the current tuples of R and S
     = Card(R) (6 + J_RS (3 + 1/S_S (10 + J_SU (5 + 4/S_U)))) u
```

Chain1 and Fork1 have the same structure. Consequently they have similar cost formulas except that $Card(R)$, J_{RS} and S_S are replaced by $Card(S)$, J_{SR} and S_R since program Fork1 starts from relation S. Moreover program Fork1 does not access tuples of relation R, saving a cost of $(u + d) = 4$. Thus, constant 10 is replaced by constant 6 in the cost formula of Fork1 given below.

$time(Fork1) = Card(S) (6 + J_{SR} (3 + 1/S_R (6 + J_{SU} (5 + 4/S_U)))) u$

The cost formula of Fork2 is expressed as follows:

$$time(Fork2) =$$

$Card(S)$	/* scan relation S
$(((u + d)$	/* call succ_tup to get the join attribute value (S.j)
$+ o)$	/* check the existence of an inverted sublist for the join attribute R.i
$+ J_{SR}$	/* ratio of S tuples matching with an R tuple
$(d$	/* access to the inverted sublist for the join attribute R.i
$+ (u + d)$	/* call succ_tup to get the join attribute value (S.k)
$+ o$	/* check the existence of an inverted sublist for the join attribute U.l
$+ J_{SU}$	/* ratio of S tuples matching with a U tuple
$(d$	/* access to the inverted sublist for the join attribute U.l
$+ u$	/* Cartesian product of the OID corresponding to the current tuple of S
$+ 1/S_R$	/* and the two current inverted sublists of R and U

$$(u + 1/S_U(u + 3w)))))$$
$$= Card(S)\,(6 + J_{SR}\,(9 + J_{SU}\,(4 + 1/S_R(1 + 4\,/S_U))))\,u$$

These cost formulas depend on the cardinality of each relation and the selectivity factors involved in the sequence of joins. Indeed, these parameters determine the number of non pertinent paths traversed. Minimizing the number of non pertinent paths traversed is a global optimization problem which we discuss in Section 5. The goal of this analysis is to compare the behavior of chain and fork strategies for equivalent values of these parameters. Thus, we use average cardinalities and average selectivities to study the ratio $time(Chain)/time(Fork2)$ given below. For the sake of conciseness, we ignore the ratio $time(Fork1)/time(Fork2)$. Indeed, considering average cardinalities and selectivities, Chain and Fork1 algorithms have similar behavior with a small advantage to algorithm Fork1 (see the formulas given earlier).

$$\frac{time(Chain)}{time(Fork2)} = \frac{6 + J_{avg}\,(3 + 1/S_{avg}\,(10 + J_{avg}\,(5 + 4/S_{avg})))}{6 + 12\,J_{avg} + J_{avg}/S_{avg}\,(1 + 4\,J_{avg}/S_{avg})}$$

This ratio is plotted in Figure 13a in terms of S_{avg} for different values of J_{avg}. As expected, algorithm Fork2 is always better than algorithm Chain (and than algorithm Fork1). This superiority increases as S_{avg} decreases, up to an optimum after which the ratios comes down to near 1. Indeed, Fork2 optimizes the inner loop of the program by checking all join predicates in the outer loop and $1/S_{avg}$ determines the size of the inverted lists and consequently the number of iterations in each loop. The ratio $1/S_{avg}$ determines also the cardinal of the result. Thus, after the optimum, the difference between all algorithms decreases to disappear as the common result construction cost increases. Low values of J_{avg} emphasize the effects of the $1/S_{avg}$ parameter.

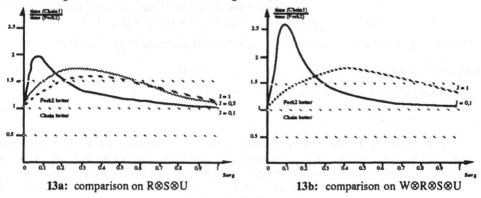

13a: comparison on R⊗S⊗U   13b: comparison on W⊗R⊗S⊗U

Figure 13: Chain vs fork

Chain and Fork strategies are now compared for queries involving more than two joins. Let us consider the sequence W⊗R⊗S⊗U where S is the root of the fork. The loop corresponding to join S⊗U is deeper nested than in the sequence R⊗S⊗U since joins are evaluated left to right. This reinforce the optimization of algorithm Fork2 for this join. The corresponding gain is plotted in Figure 13b.

4.6. Pipelined vs set-oriented processing

In a single processor system, pipelined processing is generally less efficient than set-oriented processing since it involves nested loops on relations. On a DBGraph, pipelined and set-oriented processing are intuitively equivalent since *depth first search* and *breadth first search* strategies have roughly the same temporal complexity [Gibb85] (respectively $O(max(Card(X),Card(A)))$ and $O(Card(A))$, where X is the set of vertices and A is the set of edges of a graph). We demonstrate this intuitive result below.

As discussed in Section 4.3, the best strategy to perform selections in a pipelined mode is in most cases the indexed selection strategy. The corresponding algorithm is almost the same as the one used for set-oriented selections (see Section 2.2). Thus, no main difference exists between selections in the two processing modes. Concerning a single join operation, pipeline and set-oriented strategies are again equivalent since both use the Join1 or Join2 algorithm (see Section 4.4). Thus, pipelined and set-oriented processing will be compared in the following on sequences of joins of the form $R \otimes S \otimes U$.

In set-oriented processing, the sequence of joins $R \otimes S \otimes U$ implies a first join $R \otimes S$ performed by Join1 or Join2, followed by a second join between the temporary result ($R \otimes S$) and U. The second join is performed by the $Join2_{TP}$ algorithm detailed in [Puch90] which performs a join between a temporary relation and a permanent relation. Algorithm $Join2_{TP}$ scans the ($R \otimes S$) result, materialized by an array of couples of OID (see Section 4.1), and decodes the second OID of each couple to access the corresponding tuple of S. The join of this tuple of S with relation U is performed like in Join2, which gives:

$time(Join2_{TP}) =$

$Card(R \otimes S)$	/* scan the temporary relation $R \otimes S$
$((u + d)$	/* read and decode the OID of S of each couple $\in R \otimes S$
$+ (u + d)$	/* apply succ_tup to get the join attribute value of the S tuple
$+ o$	/* check the existence of an inverted sublist for the join attribute of U
$+ J_{SU}$	/* ratio of $R \otimes S$ tuples matching with a U tuple
$(d$	/* access to the inverted sublist for the join attribute of U
$+ (2u + (u + 3w)/S_U))$	/* Cartesian product of an inverted list and a couple of OID
	/* the $R \otimes S \otimes U$ result is materialized by a triplet of OID
$= Card(R \otimes S) (10 + J_{SU} (5 + 4/S_U))$ u	

$time(set\text{-}oriented) = time(Join2) + time(Join2_{TP})$

/* in the formula $time(Join2_{TP})$, $Card(R \otimes S) = J_{RS}Card(R)/S_S$ */

$= Card(R) (6 + J_{RS} (4 + 3/S_S) + J_{RS}/S_S (10 + J_{SU} (5 + 4/S_U)))$ u

The time to perform the same sequence of joins $R \otimes S \otimes U$ in a pipelined way is (see Section 4.5) :

$time(Chain1) = Card(R) (6 + J_{RS} (3 + 1/S_S (10 + J_{SU} (5 + 4/S_U))))$ u

The difference between the two formulas is expressed by:

$time(set\text{-}oriented) - time(chain) = J_{RS} Card(R) (1 + 3/S_S)$

Pipelined is always more efficient than set-oriented since this difference cannot be negative. This difference is mainly due to the cost of constructing the temporary result of the first join, which is avoided by the pipelined processing. Although this difference may become high when S_S increases, the ratio $time(set\text{-}oriented)/time(chain1)$ remains always close to 1. Note however that in the pipelined mode, a fork execution of the same sequence of joins provides optimizations that are not possible in a set-oriented mode (see Section 4.5). Thus, pipelined processing on a DBGraph is as least equivalent to set-oriented processing and more efficient in most cases.

5. OPTIMIZATION STRATEGIES

Query optimization has to be reconsidered for main memory DBMS in order to be simplified. Indeed the relative cost of optimization w.r.t execution is higher because query execution in memory is speeded up by avoiding the I/O bottleneck [Eich89]. Some observations help to lighten the optimization process: the cost formulas do not have to consider I/O nor clustering thus simplifying the choice of the best algorithm for each operation; introducing intermediate projections is not required since temporary results are stored in a compact way by means of OID's [Amma85, Lehm86b]. This section proposes lightweight query optimization strategies for pipelined programs taking advantages of these observations.

The query execution cost depends on the number of paths traversed in the DBGraph and on the way these paths are traversed. Roughly speaking, minimizing the number of paths to traverse is a problem of global optimization which consists of choosing the best join ordering. Optimizing the way these paths are traversed is a problem of local optimization which consists of choosing the best translation strategy for each operation. Consequently, we propose a two step optimizer algorithm performing first global optimization then local optimization. Dividing the optimizer algorithm in two steps greatly reduces its combinatorial complexity. The performance evaluation results presented Section 4 are exploited during local optimization to choose the best selection and join strategies for each operation. The choice between a chain and a fork to translate a sequence of joins is performed during the global optimization step. The remainder of this section is organized as follows. The statistics maintenance required by the optimization process is first discussed. Then, the two steps of the optimizer algorithm are presented.

5.1. Statistics maintenance

The performance evaluation of both set-oriented processing [Puch90] and pipelined processing on a DBGraph depends on a few structural parameters introduced in Section 4.2. The relation and domain cardinalities, the attribute selectivity factors and the semi-join selectivity factors are sufficient to determine the number of paths traversed in the DBGraph and the cost of each operation. In conventional DBMS, maintaining relation and domain cardinalities is obvious while maintaining the other parameters incurs an important overhead. The DBGraph storage model provides an efficient way to maintain all the parameters needed.

The selectivity factor of an attribute R.i is determined using a counter $nblist_{R.i}$ maintaining the number of inverted sublists created for this attribute. Thus, $S_{R.i}$ is computed by: $S_{R.i} = nblist_{R.i}/Card(R)$. The semi-join selectivity factor J_{RS} of relation R for a join R.i$\otimes$S.j is more complex to maintain. A precise estimation of J_{RS} and J_{SR} is obtained by the means of a counter $nblist_{R.i,S.j}$ maintaining the number of domain values for which the two inverted sublists of R.i and S.j exist. Thus, J_{RS} can be computed as follows: $J_{RS} = nblist_{R.i,S.j}/(S_{R.i}Card(R))$ since $1/S_{R.i}$ determines the average cardinality of an inverted sublist of attribute R.i. Note that maintaining semi-join selectivities in this way incurs $n(n-1)/2$ counters for a domain shared by n attributes and that $(n-1)$ counters have to be incremented when an inverted sublist creation occurs. The semi-join selectivities maintenance can be greatly simplified under the assumption that values of a given attribute are equi-distributed among the domain values. In this case, J_{RS} can be approximated by: $J_{RS} = nblist_{S.j}/Card(D)$. Indeed, this ratio corresponds to the percentage of domain values for which the inverted sublist of S.j exists and only the tuples of R referencing these values participate to the semi-join. Finally, the selectivity $\sigma_{R.i}$ of a selection of the form (R.i=constant) (resp. R.i>constant) is computed by $1/(S_{R.i}Card(R))$ (resp. $Card(R)/2$). For selection qualifications involving conjunctions (resp. disjunctions) of predicates, the selectivities of each predicate are multiplied (resp. added).

5.2. Global optimization

The main objective of the global optimization process is to determine the join ordering which will minimize the number of paths to traverse in the DBGraph, considering the attribute selectivities, the semi-join selectivities and the selection selectivities. This process evaluates exhaustively the number of paths to traverse, considering each relation as a possible root of the oriented RCG. It is recursive, since each son of the root is in turn root of a subgraph to be optimized (see Figure 14). This process is still quite inexpensive due to the small number of relations generally involved in a query and to the simplicity of the formulas.

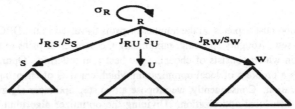

Figure 14: Number of paths issued from a fork

The ordering of the edges issued from a fork has a strong influence on the total number of paths to traverse in the DBGraph. Indeed edges of the RCG are translated by nested loops in the pipelined program traversing the DBGraph. Thus, sequences of code corresponding to each son of the fork and its associated subgraph are nested in the order the edges issued from this fork are considered (see Section 3.1). Let us consider the example presented in Figure 14. The total number of paths to traverse from the root R is determined recursively by the following formula:

totalNbPath(R) = Card(R) nbpath(R)   where

$nbpath(R) = \sigma_R\, J_{RS}\, J_{RU}\, J_{RW}$
$(\ 1/S_S\,(1 + nbpath(S))$ /* $1/S_S$ = number of S tuples matching with one R tuple
$+\ [1/S_S\, nbpath(S)]\ 1/S_U\,(1 + nbpath(U))$
                              /* $[1/S_S nbpath(S)]$ = nb of iterations involving the U subgraph
$+\ [1/S_S\, nbpath(S)]\ [1/S_U\, nbpath(U)]\ 1/S_W\,(1 + nbpath(W))\ )$
                              /* $[1/S_S\, nbpath(S)]\ [1/S_U\, nbpath(U)]$ =
                              /* nb of iterations involving the W subgraph

Minimizing nbpath(R) consists in exploiting the R sons in ascending cost order where the cost is expressed in terms of number of paths to traverse. The factor $J_{RS}\, J_{RU}\, J_{RW}$ corresponds to the Fork2 algorithm optimization which consists in checking the join predicates between the root and all its sons in the outer loop of the fork (see Sections 3.1 and 4.5).

The algorithm performing the global optimization is given in Figure 15. It is recursive in the same way as the *nbpath* formula. Each stage of the recursive process computes the number of paths to traverse (nbpathFromRi) from the current node Ri of the RCG, as follows. The cost of each subgraph issued from the Ri sons is first computed independent of the others. Then, these subgraphs are considered one after the other in ascending cost order. The cost of each subgraph is multiplied by the number of paths to traverse in its predecessors and the result is added to nbpathFromRi. When all subgraphs have been considered, nbpathFromRi is multiplied by the selectivity of the joins between Ri and each of its son. This algorithm deals with chains in the same way as with a single branch fork. Indeed, the ordering of joins in a chain is induced by the choice of the root of the RCG and cannot be changed.

This algorithm is intentionally simplified and the complete version should rearrange the out-edges of each fork in the RCG so that the best join ordering consists for the code generator to consider the out-edges from left to right. Note that the global optimization algorithm may consider as equivalent a join ordering starting by a chain and an other one starting by a fork, on a number of paths to traverse basis. As detailed in Section 4.5, the join ordering starting by a fork will be preferred in this case.

GlobalOptimizer *(RCG)*
        for each *Ri* ∈ *RCG* **do**
                currentCost = Card(Ri) nbpath(Ri)
                minCost = min (minCost, currentCost)

nbpath*(Ri)*
{
        nbpathFromRi = 0
        nbpathPred = 1
        /* sort the subgraphs of root Ri on their respective cost: nbpath(R_j)/S_{Rj} */
        for each *Rj son of Ri* **do**
                insert ((Rj, nbpath(Rj)), SortedList)
        /* treat each subgraph in ascending cost order */
        for each *Rj of SortedList* **in sorted order**
                nbpathFromRj = extract (SortedList)
                nbpathFromRi = nbpathFromRi + nbpathPred/S_{Rj} (1 + nbpathFromRj)
                if *Rj ends a path in RCG*
                        then *nbpathPred = nbpathPred/S_{Rj}*
                        else *nbpathPred = nbpathPred * nbpathFromRj/S_{Rj}*
        end for
        /* take into account an eventual selection on Ri */
        if *loop on Ri* **then** *nbpathFromRi = nbpathFromRi * σ_{Ri}*
        /* take into account the selectivity of the joins between Ri and each of its son */
        for each *son Rj of Ri* **do**
                nbpathFromRi = nbpathFromRi * J_{RiRj}
        return(nbpathFromRi)
}

        Ri, Rj, Rk,... are the relations involved in RCG
        A relation Rj ends a path in RCG if it constitutes a leaf of RCG or if its son has already
        been treated (ie. end of a loop or a meet)

Figure 15: Global optimizer algorithm

5.3. Local optimization

Local optimization may provide substantial gains without incurring an important overhead. The local optimization is activated after the join ordering has been fixed by the global optimization. It consists of choosing the best strategy to translate an operation, in accordance with the performance comparisons detailed in Section 4. The choice between on-the-fly selections and indexed selections depends on the ratio *nbtup_acc/Card(R)* (see Section 4.3). Factor *nbtup_acc* corresponds in fact to the number of paths traversing the selected relation. It can be determined during the global optimization process and be exploited for local optimization purposes. It can also be recomputed at low cost due to the simplicity of the cost formulas. Let us now consider join optimization. If the first join of the join ordering selected by the global optimization process is root of a chain, it can be translated with Join1 or Join2 algorithms. Materials for this choice are provided in Section 4.4. The best strategy depends on the relation and domain cardinalities and on the semi-join and attribute selectivities. The choice is thus obvious since the values of all these parameters are provided to the optimizer (see Section 5.1). Finally, in light of the result of Section 4.5, algorithm Fork2 will always be preferred to perform a fork. The local optimizer annotates the oriented RCG to inform the code generator on the way each operation should be translated.

Note that a two step optimization process may fail in finding the best strategy. For instance, a join ordering starting by a fork may be discarded considering the number of traversed paths even though it could be globally more efficient than the selected chain alternative. On the other hand, this dichotomy between global and local optimization leads to a quite simple and efficient optimizer.

6. CONCLUSION

The DBGraph storage model supports either set-oriented and pipelined execution of database queries depending on the way the graph is traversed. In both cases, queries are performed without any tuple comparison or move, yielding high performance in a main memory context. In this paper we concentrated on the pipelined mode. We studied the translation of a query into an optimal pipelined program and we compared the pipelined mode to the set-oriented mode. A pipelined execution has two major advantages. First temporary results need not be generated, saving main memory space for the permanent active data. Second, tuples already produced can be displayed while the query processing is still in progress, drastically reducing the elapsed time for a query.

We proposed a three steps algorithm to translate a query into an optimal pipelined program. First, a parser decomposes the query into a sequence of relational operations represented as a relation-connection-graph (named RCG). Then, an optimizer rearranges the RCG to produce an oriented RCG which indicates the optimal join ordering for the query. Finally, a code generator translates the oriented RCG into a pipelined program composed of nested loops calling the succ_val and succ_tup primitives in order to traverse the DBGraph.

An analytical model has been introduced to compare different alternatives for translating subparts of the oriented RCG into a pipelined sequence of traversal primitives. This model is exploited to perform first global optimization then local optimization. The global optimization chooses the best join ordering in order to minimize the number of paths to traverse in the DBGraph while the local optimization determines the best algorithm to translate each operation. The fully inverted structure of the DBGraph provides an efficient way to maintain the statistics required by the analytical model. This leads to accurate and inexpensive optimization strategies. It is of main interest in a main memory context where the optimization overhead has to be minimized.

ACKNOWLEDGEMENTS

We wish to thank Dennis Shasha and Patrick Valduriez for their helpful comments on this paper.

REFERENCES

[Agra89]   Agrawal R., Bargia A., and Jagadish H.V., "Efficient Management of Transactions Relationships in Large Data and Knowlage Bases", Proc. of ACM SIGMOD, Portland, June 1989.
[Amma85]   Ammann A., Hanrahan M., and Krishnamurthy R., "Design of a Memory Resident DBMS", IEEE COMPCON, San Fransisco, California, February 1985.
[Bitt86]   Bitton D., Turbyfill C., "Performance Evaluation of Main Memory Database Systems", Cornell University, TR 86-731.
[Cope85]   G. Copeland, S. Khoshafian, "The Decomposition Storage Model", ACM SIGMOD Int. Conf., Austin, May 1985.
[Dewi84]   DeWitt D., Katz R., Olken F., Shapiro L., Stonebraker M., Wodd D., "Implementation Techniques for Main Memory Database Systems", ACM SIGMOD Int. Conf., Boston, June 1984.
[Eich89]   Eich M.H., "Main Memory Database Research Directions", Int. Workshop on Database Machines, Deauville, France, June 1989.
[Gibb85]   Gibbons A., "Algorithmic Graph Theory", Cambridge University Press, 1985.
[Hamm79]   Hammer M., Niamir B., "A heuristic approach to attribute partitioning", Proc. of ACM SIGMOD, 1979.
[Lehm86a]   Lehman T., Carey M., "A Study of Index Structures for Main Memory Database Management Systems", Int. Conf. on VLDB, Kyoto, Japan, August 1986.
[Lehm86b]   Lehman T., Carey M., "Query Processing in Main Memory Database Management Systems", ACM SIGMOD Int. Conf., Washington, D.C., May 1986.
[Miss83]   Missikov M., Scholl M., "Relational Queries in a Domain Based DBMS", ACM SIGMOD Int. Conf., San Jose, May 1983.
[Puch90]   Pucheral P., Thévenin J.M., Valduriez P., "Efficient Main Memory Data Management Using the DBGraph Storage Model", Int. Conf. on VLDB, Brisbane, Australia, August 1990.
[Shek90]   Shekita E., Carey M., "A Performance Evaluation of Pointer-Based Joins", ACM SIGMOD Int. Conf., Atlantic City, New Jersey, May 1990.
[Ullm82]   Ullman J., "Principle of Database Systems", Computer Science Press, 1982.
[Vald86]   Valduriez P., Khoshafian S., Copeland G., "Implementation Techniques of Complex Objects", Int. Conf. on VLDB, Kyoto, August 1986.
[Vald87]   Valduriez P., "Join Indices", ACM TODS, Vol. 12, No 2, June 87.

Optimizing Object-Oriented Database Queries using Cost-Controlled Rewriting

Georges Gardarin[1], *Rosana S.G. Lanzelotte*[2]

[1] MASI CNRS University P-M CURIE 78000 Versailles, France
[2] INRIA Rocquencourt 78153 Le Chesnay, France, on leave from PUC-RIO, Brazil

Abstract

Declarative languages for Object-oriented DBMSs combine navigational accesses, expressed as path traversals, to associative ones. Works on query optimization for OODBs usually focus on optimizing one of the aspects (e.g., path traversals) neglecting others (e.g., associative joins). This work proposes a rule-based approach for optimizing uniformly all features encountered in queries in OODBs. Queries and rules are expressed using an easily readable functional formalism, functional symbols providing a natural way to represent both path traversals and method calls. Cost estimations are assigned to each functional equation. This enables the application of transformation rules on systems of equations under the control of deterministic cost-based search strategies, such as Iterative Improvement or Simulated Annealing.

1 INTRODUCTION

Object-oriented DBMSs aim at offering declarative interfaces to users, where associative accesses are combined with navigation through objects and their components through path traversals (e.g., O1.A1.A2.....An-1.An where O1 is an object, A1 is an attribute of O1, A2 is an attribute of O1.A1, ..., and An is an attribute of O1.A1.A2.....An-1). At first glance, path traversals contrast with the declarative nature of query languages. To preserve the latter, the query optimizer should be able to choose the best way to navigate provided that information concerning the physical storage of objects is available.

Extensibility through a rule-based approach, where the optimizer proceeds by applying rewriting rules to the input query, was first adopted in relational query optimization [Freytag87, Graefe87, Lee88, Finance91]. Recently the approach was applied to OODBs as well [Beeri90, Kemper90a]. The rule-based approach contributes to achieving extensibility, but introduces a control problem. For example, in [Beeri90] no cost model is proposed and a deterministic cost-based search strategy cannot be applied. Although a cost model is mentioned in [Kemper90a], the application of transformation rules is not controlled by a search strategy. Besides, associative operations such as joins are not considered in the same optimization framework together with path traversals. This prevents the investigation of solutions where path traversals are interleaved with associative operations, which may be effective ones (e.g., due to the existence of selective value indexes on an attribute at the middle of a path).

This work proposes a uniform framework for optimizing object-oriented queries using cost-controlled rewriting. The approach consists in translating the input query to a system of functional equations which can be further transformed by rewriting rules. Functions can either express elementary path traversals or method invocations. Thus, the functional formalism provides a natural and easily readable way for representing queries or rewriting rules. Another advantage of our approach is that, as the systems of functional equations are globally optimized, there is no need of rewriting rules for factoring common path expressions as in [Kemper90a]. As we associate cost estimates to any functional form, we are able to apply deterministic cost-based search strategies, thus preventing the control problem faced by rule-based systems. We also illustrate how to achieve extensibility at the search strategy level by applying specialization rules to a basic algorithm that implements the search strategy.

The rest of this work is organized as follows. Section 2 sketches the model over which queries as functional equations are built and briefly describes ESQL, the query language supported by the approach proposed here. Section 3 shows how queries are translated to a system of functional equations. In section 4 we present a significant subset of the transformation rules used for query optimization. Section 5 sketches the cost model that enables the application of deterministic search strategies, which is shown in Section 6. Also in Section 6 we illustrate how to customize the search strategy by specializing a basic algorithm. Section 7 concludes the paper.

2 DATA MODEL OVERVIEW

Our data model is a simplified object-oriented data model, composed of types, classes and methods. Objects are instances of classes with single valued or multiple valued attributes of atomic or complex types. Methods are associated with classes. We present a graphical representation of classes, attributes and methods that provides a uniform view of a conceptual schema.

2.1 Types, Classes and Methods

A type is an arbitrary set of abstract values with associated operations. There exists a pre-defined set of atomic types, including integer, real, string and boolean. A complex type is built by using constructors, also known as generic types. For simplicity and compactness, we consider only the set constructor, denoted { }.

An object is simply an entity of the real world, which is implemented with a system identifier and described via attributes of given names. A class is a collection of objects with identical attributes. Each attribute is either a reference to an object of another class C, denoted obj(C), or a value of a given type t. Ai(O) denotes the projection function on attribute Ai of object O. If Ai is of type t, then Ai(O) is a value of type t; if Ai is a reference such as obj(C), then Ai(O) is an object of class C.

A method is a partial function from a class to a type. For simplicity, we do not consider functions with multiple arguments, which can be introduced by defining intermediate types composed of the multiple arguments as attributes. When invoked in the scope of an object, a method returns an answer and possibly changes the state of that object. The answer is of the target type, which can be a single valued type or a set-valued type; the answer can be undefined, as a method is a partial function. Methods can be scalar or set-valued, like attributes. We do not really distinguish between methods and attributes, the latter being simply methods with a standard implementation (i.e., the projection and assignment functions).

2.2 Schema Example

The schema of a sample database that will be used in the examples is presented in Figure 1. It includes five classes built from atomic types and the Note user type. The attributes are self explanatory. In addition, we assume that a method Age is attached to the Composer class that computes the composer age from his or her birthdate.

```
Class Composer =
[ Name : String, Birth : Obj(Date), Masters : { String }, Works : { Obj(Composition) } ]
Class Composition =
[ Title : String, Movements : { String }, Duration : Float,Use : { Obj(Instrument) } ]
Class Instrument =
[ Name : String, Family : String, Lowernote : Note, Uppernote : Note ]
Class Concert =
[ Program : { Obj(Composition) }, Date : Obj(Date), City : String ]
Class Date =
[ Day : Int, Month : Int, Year : Int ]
```

Fig. 1. Database schema example

Figure 2 is a graphical representation of the database schema defined in Figure 1. The proposed representation is similar to that of DAPLEX [Shipman81], except that classes are introduced. The rounded enclosures indicate types and the square boxes represent classes. A single headed arrow represents a single valued attribute, while a double headed arrow portrays a set-valued attribute. Arrows are labelled by the corresponding attribute names. Note that method signatures may be also portrayed on the diagram, according to their argument types, as, for example, the Age method.

2.3 The Query Language

The query language supported by the approach proposed here is an upward compatible version of SQL2 called ESQL2 [Gardarin92]. The user sees classes as relations and can manipulate them using SQL. However, since classes may be defined over complex domains (tuples or sets), it is also possible to manipulate data inside a complex structure using built-in or user defined methods. In general, any method attached to a given type may be applied to an element of that type. The result of a method applied to a class attribute

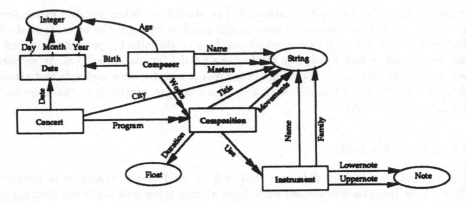

Fig. 2. Graphical representation of the sample database.

has a type derived from the method signature; a new method can in turn be applied to that result. Thus, methods can be applied in cascade to an SQL attribute expression.

Data manipulation using user-defined or generic methods of ESQL is now illustrated. The following query on the Composer class lists "all the names of all fourty years old composer". Note that the Age user defined method is applied in the selection qualification.

SELECT Name
FROM Composer
WHERE Age(Composer) = 40

The project method defined on the tuple type may be used to extract an attribute from a tuple. As mentioned above, we use the attribute name directly as a projection method, i.e., A(t) in place of Project (t,A), where t is a tuple with attribute A. Consequently, the next query gives the year of birth of Bach; it illustrates the use of the projection function Year.

SELECT Year(Birth)
FROM Composer
WHERE Name = "Bach"

The next query retrieves the names of instruments used in all concerts taking place in Rio in 1990; it illustrates functional navigation through the Program and Use references. Note that variables are used for Concert and Instrument, as in SQL.

SELECT Name
FROM Concert c, Composition, Instrument i
WHERE City(c) = "Rio" AND Year(Date(c)) = 1990 AND Program(c) = Composition
AND Use(Composition) = i

In summary, the query language is an extended SQL in which classes are used as relations and functional notations is used for projecting tuples, navigating through references and calling methods. Sets, and more generally collections like bags, lists, arrays, are manipulated through built in functions, such as union, intersection, contains, map, etc. [Gardarin92], which can be invoked within SQL queries.

3 QUERIES AS FUNCTIONAL EQUATIONS

In this section, we extend the definition of the set valued functions initially introduced in [Gardarin87]. Originally they were called magic functions and were induced by relations. In the present context we call them database functions and generalize them to classes. We introduce basic operations as database functions. The composition of database functions may be seen as a set oriented functional representation of path traversals and method calls. This approach provides a natural way to express queries as database functions.

3.1 Database Functions

Let C (A1, A2, ...) be a class, where A1, A2, ... are the attributes of class C. We denote by Obj(C) the set of objects in C, i.e., the extension of class C. Let X be any group of attributes of class C. The extension of class C yields two database functions X and X^{-1}, which are defined as follows :

1. Let o = {o1, o2, ..., oq} be a subset of Obj(C); X : o (i.e., X applied to o) is the subset of dom(X) defined by { xk | There exists oi $\in$ o such that X (oi) = xk }.
2. Let x = {x1, x2, ..., xq} be a subset of dom(X); X^{-1} : x (i.e., the inverse of function X applied to x) is the subset of Obj(C) defined by {op | There exists xk $\in$ x such that X(op) = xk }.

Clearly, Ai : o is obtained by projecting the objects in o on attribute Ai and grouping the results in a set. Ai^{-1} : x is obtained by restricting C to those objects having for Ai's value x1 or x2 or ... xn, keeping only the object identifiers as a set.

3.2 Operations with Database Functions

For convenience and simplicity, we shall use the following standard operations over set valued functions and function results, defined by the given formula:

- Union $(f \cup g) : x = f : x \cup g : x$.
- Composition $(g \circ f) : x = g : (f : x)$.
- Intersection $(f \cap g) : x = f : x \cap g : x$.
- Difference $(f - g) : x = f : x - g : x$.

We further use the tupling operation on two functions having the same source domain. Tupling is defined by : $[f, g] : x = [f : x, g : x]$. A tuple equality is a short notation for specifying the equality of each components, as usual. Thus, [f,g]:x = [a,b] is equivalent to f:x = a and g:x = b. Note that the inverse of a tupling function is defined for a tuple of its component domains; its effect is defined by: $[f, g]^{-1} : [x, y] = f^{-1} : x \cap g^{-1} : y$ which derives from the fact that a tuple equality encodes a conjunction of simple equalities.

One complexity of the use of database functions in the context of an object oriented databases is due to the existence of set-valued attributes. This yields to results of database functions that are set of sets. To simplify queries and query answers, we introduce an automatic collapsing of a set of sets into a single set. Thus, in the following, f:{{a},{b}}=f:{a,b}, which means that we do not consider sets of sets; in other words, sets are one level sets. This restriction does not penalize the generality of the approach: if one wants to keep set of sets, it is always possible to label sets with object identifiers (by introducing an intermediate classes in the schema), and thus keep them. Automatic set collapsing does not change the properties of the set-valued database functions introduced above.

3.3 Queries as Functional Equations

ESQL queries can be translated into systems of functional equations. Equations are built from database functions applied to variables or constants. A variable range either on the powerset of a type (i.e., a value-based variable) or on the powerset of objects in a class (i.e., an object-based variable). Variables are denoted x, y, z, ... as usual and are set valued. The domain of a variable is context defined, i.e., it is defined by the function which is applied to the variable. For simplicity, we assume that all function names are unique in a schema. If not so, a function name is completed with the name of the class it applies to (e.g., Name going from Instrument to String is denoted NameInstr).

Functional equations are built as follows. An atomic functional equation is built using the set comparison predicate = . It is a comparison of a database function expression applied to a variable or a constant, of the form F:x = G:y, where x and y are set variables or constants, and F and G are either set-valued functions (including the identity function) or functional expressions built using composition, union, intersection, Cartesian product and difference of database functions. Note that queries with predicates less than ($<$), greater than ($>$) or not equal to ($\neq$) are translated into set equalities by defining intensional sets. For example, $z < 10$ where z is a real can be translated into $z = \{<10\}$, where $\{<10\}$ is the set of reals less than 10. A functional system is simply a set of functional equations. A conjunctive query generates one functional system which constrains the variables that stand for the query answer. A disjunctive query may generate several functional systems, one for each conjunctive component.

We now sketch the algorithm to translate a conjunctive query into a system of functional equations. The translation process requires first the attachment of object variables to classes of the conceptual schema. Then, an output variable is assigned to each element of the query answer (i.e., the elements of the SELECT list). Next, each attribute expression either in the SELECT or WHERE clauses is translated into its set valued functional expression counterpart. Each constant is replaced by a set containing this constant. A first set of equations is written to specify the query answer in term of the corresponding output variables. Then, each predicate in the WHERE clause is simply rewritten as one equation. Thus, the translation of a conjunctive query yields one system of equations, each equation being a constraint on the output variables.

To illustrate the translation of queries into functional equations, we now give the translation of the queries introduced in section 3 :

1. Name of all fourty years old composers :
   y | {Age : x = {40} ; y = NameComposer : x }
2. Year of birth of Bach :
   y | {NameComposer : x = {"Bach"} ; y = Year : Birth : x }

3. Name of the instruments used in all concert taking place in Rio in 1990 :
   y | { y = NameInstr : i; Use : x = i ; Program : c = x ; Year : Date : c = {1990} ;
   City : c = {"Rio"} }

4 QUERY TRANSFORMATIONS

The goal of the optimizer is to rewrite the input query to get to an "optimal" form, where optimal means the least costly among the investigated options. We showed above that a conjunctive query may be interpreted as a set of functional equations that constrains the query answer. The problem is then to transform the system of equations into a least-costly-to-execute equivalent one. We adopt a rule-based approach to transform equation systems, which makes the optimizer extensible. Rules express possible rewriting for functional equations. Other authors have proposed to rewrite functional terms for query optimization [Freytag87, Finance91, Sciore90, Beeri90]. Our approach is more general in several ways:

- The proposed functional equations capture both algebraic operations (e.g., projection or join), method applications and navigational accesses.
- Functional equations are transformed globally, not one term at a time, which enables the simultaneous optimization of overlapping path expressions.
- A cost model is integrated in the approach to enable evaluating the cost of processing a given system of equations.
- Deterministic cost-based search strategies are modeled.

In this section, we present a set of available transformation rules applicable to the system of equations that constitute the query to be optimized. We distinguish syntactic transformations from semantic transformations. Syntactic transformations are basically rules to solve equations and to eliminate useless intermediate variables. Such rules allow the optimizer to normalize queries, to eliminate redundancy and to select the best navigation in the object base. Semantic transformations use semantic knowledge such as integrity constraints, method properties and operator properties (e.g., transitivity of equality) to further simplify the query.

4.1 Rules for Query Rewriting

Rules express valid transformations of systems of equations into equivalent systems. The general form of a rule is as follows:

$$\{Equations\}[|\ Constraint] \longrightarrow \{Equations\}$$

The meaning of a rule is: when the equations of the left-side match equations of the input query (expressed as a system of equations), they are transformed into the form specified on the right-side of the rule, provided that the (optional) constraint is true. Equations may use generic function letters to represent generic functions or function expressions. They can also refer to precise function names, such as Age or NameInstr or Add. Throughout this section we represent functions and variables using the following conventions:

- F, G, H, ... for denoting any generic functions, including the identity function.
- o, o1, o2, ... for denoting variables ranging over the powerset of objects of a class (i.e., for variables denoting a set of objects).
- v, v1, v2, ... for variables ranging oves the powerset of a type (i.e., for variables denoting a set of values).
- x, y, z, ... for variables ranging independently over a set of objects or values.
- a, b, c, ... for denoting a set of constants.
- α, β, γ, ... for denoting any functional term.

As rules are applied to the whole system of equations that constitute a query, all the occurrences of a functional expression are optimized at the same time. This removes the need of rewriting rules for factoring common path expressions such as done in [Kemper90a].

4.2 Syntactic Transformation Rules

In this section, we give typical examples of syntactic transformation rules. We illustrate them with the following query that "retrieves the name of the instruments used in all concert taking place in Rio in 1990": y | { y = NameInstr : i ; Use : x = i ; Program : c = x ; Year : Date : c = {1990} ; City : c = {"Rio"} }. This query is graphically represented in Figure 3. In graphical representations of queries, as for schemas, we use square nodes to represent domains of objects and rounded nodes to represent value domains. The query bindings are specified by the values or variable names written inside the nodes. By applying rewriting rules given below, the query can be transformed into the following one: y | { y = NameInstr:Use:Program: (Date^{-1}:Year^{-1}:1990 ∩ City^{-1}{"Rio"}) }

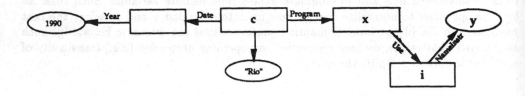

Fig. 3. A Graphical Representation of the Query

Variable Elimination Rule. The simplest approach to query simplification is to eliminate useless variables, which represent in some sense temporary object references or relations not required for query computation. The following transformation enables the elimination of free variables, i.e., variables which are not referred to elsewhere in the query:

$$\{\alpha = F : y, y = \beta\} \mid free(y) \longrightarrow \{\alpha = F : \beta\}$$

For example, a query to retrieve the title of all compositions which have been played in all concerts may be written as x | { x = Title : y ; y = Program : z }. It is transformed to x | { x = Title : Program : z } by the above rule.

Inversion Rules. Let F be a generic function and F^{-1} denotes the function that corresponds to a reverse traversal of the path corresponding to F in the database graph representation. The following transformation computes values from a function that applies to that values :

$$\{F^{-1} : v = \alpha\} \mid (F \ reverse \ of \ F^{-1}) \longrightarrow \{v = F : \alpha\}$$

This rule can be used for transforming queries such as x | { x = Age^{-1}: {40} }, which is replaced by x | { Age : x = {40}}. A similar rule can be specified for functions that apply to objects and not to values, but it has to be constrained by a condition that prevents the consideration of previously (in the same query) constrained objects. The condition must guarantee that all objects in the class are candidates for selection; thus, the object set variable should be free before applying the transformation. Finally, the rule is :

$$\{F : o = \alpha\} \mid (F^{-1} \ reverse \ of \ F) \ and \ free(o) \longrightarrow o = F^{-1} : \alpha$$

where C is the class on which F applies. For example, if C is the class of composer, then Age : x = {40} may be replaced by x = Age^{-1} : {40}, if x range over all the composers.

Intersection Rule. The following rule enables the simultaneous application of conjuntions:

$$\{\alpha = \beta; \ \alpha = \gamma\} \longrightarrow \{\alpha = (\beta \cap \gamma)\}$$

For example, a query which retrieves the titles of compositions where a harpsichord and a flute are used written as : $y \mid \{y = Title : Use^{-1} : NameInstr^{-1} : \{"harpsichord"\}; y = Title : Use^{-1} : NameInstr^{-1} : \{"flute"\}\}$ is rewritten as : $y \mid \{y = (Title : Use^{-1} : NameInstr^{-1} : \{"harpsichord"\} \cap Title : Use^{-1} : NameInstr^{-1} : \{"flute"\})\}$.

Tupling Rule. When the answer of a query consists of the projection of some object in subsets of its attributes, it is useful to apply the following transformation:

$$\{x = F : z, y = G : z\} \mid \longrightarrow \{[x, y] = [F, G] : z\}$$

For example, the query [d, m, y] | { d=Day: date: c ; m=Month: date : c ; y=Year: date: c } is transformed to [d, m, y] | [d, m, y] = [Day, Month, Year] : date : c.

Tupling Intersection Rule. The form of the example given for the intersection rule suggests combining both selections into one single operation. This is done through the following rule, which transforms an intersection of functions (whose counterdomains are the same class) into a tuple functional access:

$$\{(F : x \cap G : y) = \alpha\} \longrightarrow \{[F, G] : [x, y] = [\alpha, \alpha]\}$$

Then, the example that illustrates the Intersection Rule becomes : $y \mid \{[y, y] = [Title : Use^{-1} : NameInstr^{-1}, Title : Use^{-1} : NameInstr^{-1}] : [\{"harpsichord"\}, \{"flute"\}]$ which will be less expensive because both criteria can be verified at the same time.

4.3 Semantic Transformation Rules

Traditionally in query optimizers, decisions are mainly conditioned by syntactic knowledge and data structures. However, this is not sufficient in object oriented DBMSs, where users can define their own structures, their own methods and even their own operators. Thus, it is useful that the query optimizer support the introduction of new query transformation rules. In this section, we briefly demonstrate through examples that semantics rules can be introduced as transformation rules on functional equations.

Abstract Data Type Equations. Let us assume for example that a Min method is defined on sets to compute the minimum value of a set. Then, it is well known that the minimum of the minimums of two sets is the minimum of the union set. Using the rule paradigm, it can be simply written as follows :

$$\{Min : \{Min : x, Min : y\} = F : \alpha\} \longrightarrow Min : (x \cup y) = F : \alpha$$

Then, semantic properties of methods can also be introduced as systems of functional equations.

Integrity Constraints. Choosing appropriate integrity constraints that simplify query processing is a difficult task. In our approach, integrity constraints may be also added to queries as functional equations. For example, to add a constraint specifying that the Age function applied to a Composer gives a result between 0 and 120, we simply add the rule :

$$\{G : Age : x = F : a\} \longrightarrow \{G : Age : x = F : a; Age : x = \{0 < int < 120\}\}$$

If applied, this rule adds the equation "Age : x is included in the set 0 to 120" to queries having a function of the corresponding form, for example x | { Age : x = {40} }. Whether it is useful or not to add integrity constraint equation(s) should be determined by the cost estimation component. Clearly in this example the application of the given rule does not reduce the query cost because it does not further restrict the answer set.

Properties of Operators. In object oriented systems, operators can be overloaded or specific operators can be defined. Thus, it is useful to be able to introduce rules to use the properties of operators in query optimization. An example of such a rule is the transitivity of equality. It can be introduced by the following rule:

$$\{\alpha = \beta, \ \beta = \gamma\} \longrightarrow \{\alpha = \beta, \ \alpha = \gamma\}$$

5 PHYSICAL MODEL AND COST ESTIMATION

Cost estimations depend on the physical model and on the execution model associated to functional equations. This section presents the assumptions for the physical model, a default execution semantics for functional equations and, then, sketches the cost model

5.1 Storage Model for Objects

We assume that all atomic attributes are represented by their values, while non-atomic attributes (which always belongs to a class) are represented by their object identifiers (oid's). Also we assume that oid's are physically implemented, i.e., given an oid it is possible to know the physical page where the corresponding object is. The values of atomic attributes are stored inside the owner object record. Non-atomic attributes are represented by storing their oid's inside the owner instance (e.g., the oid's of the compositions that constitute the Program attribute of a Concert are stored inside the record of Concert). This approach is referred to as the direct storage model [Valduriez86]. These assumptions correspond to those of most OODBs.

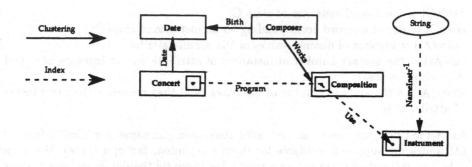

Fig. 4. A Sample Physical Schema for the Conceptual Database

Figure 4 shows a possible physical DB schema for the conceptual schema of Figure 2. The physical model provides for clustering of objects and sub-objects. When clustering is specified, sub-objects are stored close to the owner object record (e.g., in the same or neighbor disk page) usually by depth-first placement. For example, the instances of Composition which are the *works* of a Composer are clustered with it. Clustering contributes to speeding the access of entire objects (i.e., an object together with its component objects). The physical DB schema of Figure 4 specifies that the objects of classes Date and Composition are clustered with the owner object Composer. Also instances of Date are clustered with the owner instances of Concert.

As auxiliary structures, the model provides for value indexes (e.g., NameInstr^{-1} in Figure 4) and path indexes (e.g., Program.Use). Value indexes are similar to the usual selection indexes, whose entries have the form <value,oid>. Path indexes [Maier86] provide fast access through objects and their components and have entries of the form <oidO1, oidO2, ..., oidOn>.

5.2 Execution Model

To establish the cost model we make some assumptions concerning the execution model. We suppose that equations are evaluated left to right, which determines the bindings of variables. For example, when the cost of the query $x = \{NameInstr : Use : x = $

$\{$*"harpsichord"*$\}$; $NameComp : Works^{-1} : x = \{$*"Bach"*$\}\}$ is estimated, variable x is not constrained in the first equation and is bound to a set in the second one. Then, changing the order of the equations may change the cost of the query. A pipelined execution is assumed whenever possible. Any available index that can speed up access is supposed to be used. With these assumptions, a system of equations can be considered as an execution plan. However, to relax these assumptions, annotations for denoting execution options could be appended to functional terms and equations.

5.3 Cost Modeling

The class extensions related parameters used in the cost model are [Kemper90b]:

- card(C) = number of instances of class C;
- size(C) = size of a record corresponding to an instance of class C;
- ndist(Ai) = number of distinct values of the atomic attribute Ai;
- fan(Ai) = the average number of instances of attribute Ai per instance of C (=1 if Ai is single-valued);
- share(Ai) = the average number of instances of C that reference the same instance of attribute Ai.

As method calls are viewed as *computed* attributes, the same statistical information for attributes are supposed available for them (i.e., ndist, fan and share). We assume that the cost estimate for computing a method is given by the database implementor.

The cost formulas measure the number of transfers (either I/O or memory) needed for computing a query. For each functional equation $\alpha = \beta$, we evaluate the cost of α and β separately. Then, the cost of $\alpha = \beta$ is estimated as that of the intersection between the results of α and β supposing a sort-merge algorithm.

A composition of functions $F_n : ... : F_2 : F_1 : v$ is evaluated from the innermost function (i.e., F_1) to the outermost (i.e., F_n). The cost of a composition $F_i : F_{i-1} : x$ is estimated as that of a join between the class extensions corresponding to F_{i-1} and F_i, taking indexes and clustering into account.

We also give estimates for the number of instances (i.e., the cardinality) returned by each functional equation. Cardinalities propagate from left to right through variable bindings, conditioning the estimation of the subsequent functional equations of the query. Cost formulas are established assuming uniform distribution of values among domains and sub-domains. A more detailed description of a cost model analogous to the one used here can be found in [Lanzelotte91b].

6 APPLYING COST-BASED SEARCH STRATEGIES

The search strategy is a key issue in query optimization. One of the great achievements of the relational technology has been to propose cost-based search strategies which guarantee the convergence and termination of the optimization process [Lanzelotte91a]. Rule-based query rewriters are often unable to apply such search strategies because of their inability to directly measure the cost impact of rewriting transformations. Either no search strategy is proposed at all [Beeri90] or the optimizer proceeds by heuristically applying rules from successive groups (i.e., chosen to avoid antagonistic effects) to approach a query form expected to be optimal [Finance91, Kemper90a]. In both cases, an undecidable control problem arises and the convergence of the optimization process cannot be assured. Furthermore, extending the set of available transformation rules becomes non-trivial in the second approach, in which rules interfere among them. This limits the extensibility, which is one of the main goals of rule-based optimizers.

In the approach proposed here, the convergence of the optimization process is guaranteed by the application of cost-based search strategies, as shown in this section. Also we show how to use the rewriting rules for customizing the search strategy: we propose a basic algorithm which can be specialized to produce a given search strategy.

6.1 Transformation-based Search Strategies

Among known search strategies, randomized ones are transformation-based in the sense that they proceed by applying transformations to one or several start solutions. Examples of randomized strategies are Simulated Annealing [Ioannidis87] and Iterative Improvement [Swami89]. As they have several similar features, they can be captured by the same basic algorithm, shown in Figure 5. The adoption of a deterministic cost-based randomized strategy enables the random choice of transformation rules but assures the convergence and termination of the optimization process.

```
begin
setInitState (); set start solution s and parameters
while not stopCond ()
    begin
    nmoves := 0;
    while localStopCond ()
        begin
        s' := transform (s); apply a transformation rule
        if acceptTransform (s,s') conditioned by the costs of s and s'
        then s := s';
        nmoves := nmoves + 1
        end;
    insert(S,s); S is the set of all investigated solutions
    setNextState ();
    end;
return optimal(S);
end
```

Fig. 5. Basic Algorithm for Randomized Strategies

Throughout the randomized algorithm of Figure 5, a query plan (stored in s and s') is a system of functional equations derived from the input query. The basic step in the algorithm is to apply a transform (i.e., a transformation rule) to a current solution s to generate s'. The transformed query plan replaces the original one depending on the acceptTransform method, which checks a strategy-specific condition on the costs of s and s'. The generated solutions are gathered in a set S and the optimal (i.e., the least costly) solution is returned at the end of the algorithm. The methods in bold are specific for each strategy and are discussed in the next sections.

6.2 Iterative Improvement

Iterative Improvement is characterized by the choice of several start solutions, one for each run (the inner loop in the basic algorithm). The method *setInitState* generates s as the first start solution by simply parsing the input query. For each start solution s, neighbor solutions are obtained (i.e., by applying transformation rules) until a local mininum is reached. The transformed solution replaces the original one if the *accept-Transform* method returns true (i.e., if the cost of the transformed solution is less than that of the original one). The method *stopCond* corresponds usually to a time constraint [Swami89]. A local minimum is defined as the least costly solution in the neighborhood of the current one. So, to guarantee that a local minimum was reached, all the neighbors of the current solution should be tested, which would be very expensive. We simplify the criterion, by setting to zero the counter of transformations, nmoves, every time the current solution is replaced by a neighbor conditioned by *acceptTransform*. Then, the method *localStopCond* can be related to the number of neighbors of a solution. This number should be proportional to the size of the problem (i.e., the number of entities of the physical schema referenced by the query). The method *setNextState* must generate different start solutions for the subsequent runs of Iterative Improvement that do not belong to the neighborhood of the previous ones. It can be implemented by randomly permuting equations.

In the approach proposed here, the search strategy is also extensible. A generic optimization algorithm as the previous one can be specialized for iterative improvement (denoted II) by specifying the strategy-specific methods through the specialization rules given in Figure 6.

$$
II = \begin{array}{|ll|}
\hline
setInitState() & \longrightarrow s := parse(inputQuery) \\
stopCond() & \longrightarrow elapsedTime > maxTime \\
localStopCond() & \longrightarrow nmoves > card(Extensions) * k \\
acceptTransform() & \longrightarrow cost(s') < cost(s) \\
setNextState() & \longrightarrow s := randomTraversal(inputQueryGraph) \\
\hline
\end{array}
$$

Fig. 6. Specialization Rules for Iterative Improvement

6.3 Simulated Annealing

Contrary to Iterative Improvement, all the stages in Simulated Annealing (the inner loop in the basic algorithm) are performed over the same start solution, generated by setInit-State by simply parsing the input query. Besides nmoves, the system has a temperature property, temp, that is set by setInitState (e.g., temp := 2 * cost(s)) and reduced by setNextState (e.g., temp := 0.95 * temp). The method stopCond, which is the global stop condition, is related to the temperature and not to the elapsed time (it corresponds to the fact that the system has frozen, e.g., stopCond = (temp < 1 and s unchanged for 4 stages) [Ioannidis90]). The specification of localStopCond is the same as in Iterative Improvement, which depends on the number of neighbors (related to the size of the problem). The criterion for accepting a transformation is different: transformed solutions with higher cost than the original solution are accepted with a low probability. Then, the method acceptTransform uses Prob, which is a boolean function. The specialization rules for simulated annealing (i.e., SA) to replace the generic methods of the basic algorithm are given in Figure 7.

$$
SA = \begin{array}{|l l|}
\hline
setInitState() & \longrightarrow s := parse(inputQuery); temp := 2 * cost(s) \\
stopCond() & \longrightarrow temp < 1\,and\,s\,unchanged\,for\,4\,stages \\
localStopCond() & \longrightarrow nmoves > card(Extensions) * k \\
acceptTransform() & \longrightarrow cost(s') < cost(s)\,or\,Prob(cost(s), cost(s'), temp) \\
setNextState() & \longrightarrow temp := 0.95 * temp \\
\hline
\end{array}
$$

Fig. 7. Specialization Rules for Simulated Annealing

7 CONCLUSION

This paper proposed a cost-controlled rewriting approach for optimizing queries involving objects. With this approach we are able to support new declarative database languages with complex object constructors and methods (e.g., ESQL [Gardarin92]). We first translate the input query to a system of functional equations. A cost model enables the association of a cost estimate to each equation of the system and, therefore, to the whole system. Then, we apply available transformation rules to the system of equations under the control of a cost-based search strategy.

Functional expressions are a good formalism for specifying path traversals through objects. Queries as systems of functional equations can be manipulated by equivalence preserving transformations. Furthermore, the functional formalism proposed here is quite natural and therefore eases the task of a database implementor when extending the set of available transformation rules. We also sketched a cost model which takes into account several options for storing objects. Although cost estimation assumed a by-default execution semantics, the approach can be extended by appending execution annotations to functional constructs to deal with different execution alternatives.

As we are able to associate costs to every query representation, we can apply deterministic cost-based search strategies. Thus, our approach avoids the control problem faced by other rewriting systems [Beeri90, Kemper90a]. We also achieved extensibility at the search strategy level: by applying rewriting rules to a generic algorithm, we generated two transformation-based search strategies. Although we demonstrated this extensibility by modelling Iterative Improvement and Simulated Annealing, we showed elsewhere that the same approach can be used for modelling several different search strategies, as it is currently being done in the EDS optimizer [Lanzelotte91a].

References

[Beeri90] C. BEERI, Y. KORNATZKY: "Algebraic Optimization of Object-Oriented Query Languages", In *Proc. Int. Conf. on Database Theory*, Paris, France, December 1990.

[Finance91] B. FINANCE, G. GARDARIN: "A Rule-Based Query Rewriter in an Extensible DBMS", In *Proc. 7th IEEE Int. Conf. on Data Engineering*, Kyoto, Japan, 1991.

[Freytag87] J.C. FREYTAG: "A Rule-Based View of Query Optimization", In *Proc. ACM SIGMOD Int. Conf. on Management of Data*, 1987.

[Gardarin87] G. GARDARIN: "Magic Functions: A Technique to Optimize Extended Datalog Recursive Programs", In *Proc. 13th Int. Conf. on Very Large Data Bases*, Brighton, England, 1987.

[Gardarin92] G. GARDARIN, P. VALDURIEZ: "ESQL2, an Extended SQL with F-Logic Semantics", In *Proc. 8th IEEE Int. Conf. on Data Engineering*, Salt Lake City, USA, 1992.

[Graefe87] G. GRAEFE, D.J. DEWITT: "The EXODUS Optimizer Generator", In *Proc. ACM SIGMOD Int. Conf. on Management of Data*, 1987.

[Ioannidis87] Y.E.IOANNIDIS, E. WONG: "Query Optimization by Simulated Annealing", In *Proc. ACM SIGMOD Int. Conf. on Management of Data*, San Francisco, USA, 1987.

[Ioannidis90] Y.E.IOANNIDIS, Y. CHA KANG: "Randomized Algorithms for Optimizing large join queries", In *Proc. ACM SIGMOD Int. Conf. on Management of Data*, USA, 1990.

[Kemper90a] A. KEMPER, G. MOERKOTTE: "Access Support in Object Bases", In *Proc. ACM SIGMOD Int. Conf. on Management of Data*, USA, 1990.

[Kemper90b] A. KEMPER, G. MOERKOTTE: "Advanced Query Processing in Object Bases Using Access Support Relations", In *Proc. 16th Int. Conf. on Very Large Data Bases*, Brisbane, Australia, 1990.

[Lanzelotte91a] R.S.G. LANZELOTTE, P. VALDURIEZ: "Extending the Search Strategy in a Query Optimizer", In *Proc. 17th Int. Conf. on Very Large Data Bases*, Barcelona, Spain, 1991.

[Lanzelotte91b] R.S.G. LANZELOTTE, J.-P. CHEINEY: "Adapting Relational Optimization Technology to Deductive and Object-oriented Declarative Database Languages", In *Proc. 3rd Int. Workshop on Database Programming Languages*, Nafplion, Greece, 1991.

[Lee88] K.M. LEE, J.C. FREYTAG, G.M. LOHMAN: "Implementing an Interpreter for Functional Rules in a Query Optimizer", In *Proc. 14th Int. Conf. on Very Large Data Bases*, Los Angeles, 1988.

[Maier86] D. MAIER, J. STEIN: "Indexing in an Object-Oriented DBMS", In *Proc. Int. Workshop on Object-Oriented Database Systems*, Asilomar, California, September 1986.

[Sciore90] E. SCIORE, J. SIEG JR.: "A Modular Query Optimizer Generator", In *Proc. 6th IEEE Int. Conf. on Data Engineering*, Los Angeles, 1990.

[Shipman81] D.W. SHIPMAN: "The Functional Data Model and the Data Language DAPLEX", *ACM Transactions on Database Systems*, Vol. 6, N. 1, March 1981.

[Swami89] A. SWAMI: "Optimization of Large Join Queries: combining Heuristics and Combinatorial Techniques", In *Proc. ACM SIGMOD Int. Conf. on Management of Data*, Portland, USA, 1989.

[Valduriez86] P. VALDURIEZ, S. KHOSHAFIAN, G. COPELAND: "Implementation Techniques of Complex Objects", In *Proc. 12th Int. Conf. on Very Large Data Bases*, Kyoto, August 1986.

This article was processed using the LaTeX macro package with LMAMULT style

Panel
Object-Oriented Models for Multidatabase Interoperability

Witold Litwin

Many organizations including industrial and academic research laboratories and information systems vendors are addressing various aspects of heterogeneous multidatabase interoperability. Research prototypes are being built and information systems vendors are working together to bring solutions which meet the requirements of emerging multidatabase applications.

Some of these requirements are interoperability of databases and of nontraditional data sources such as file systems or multimedia systems, queries and updates in presence of semantic heterogeneity in federated environment, mappings between heterogeneous data models, concurrency control and transaction management, methods for finding relevant information in very many sources, and security of the participating information sources.

Up to now, the relational model was the common basis for the solutions to these problems. Recently, OO models also started to be investigated. While the emergence of OODBMS was responsible for the integration of programming language advances with a DBMS, the use of object-oriented models and languages for heterogeneous multidatabase management appears very promising as well.

The new goal requires enhancements to OO models, languages and systems. The language should allow for nonprocedural multidatabase manipulations despite the semantic heterogeneity of autonomous databases, and for the definition of mappings to popular database models, the relational one especially. It should also allow for mappings to other OO models, for easy use of methods from different OO systems, and for the integration of data from nondatabase applications, e.g. multimedia. The system should be able to uniformly manage OIDs accross databases, to move structured data accros heterogeneous representations, should support interoperative transaction processing, and, last but not least, should be efficient. In particular, existing transaction models should be generalized to better fit the new environment.

The panel will discuss the state-of-the-art and trends in this new area. The panelists are all working on related prototype systems. They will discuss problems they encountered, the solutions choosed, and will conclude on emerging trends, perspectives, and research issues.

Panelists:

Witold Litwin (Panel Chair, Univ. Paris 9, visiting Santa Clara Univ. and HP Laboratories in Palo Alto)
Mohammad Ketabchi (Santa Clara Univ.)
Erich Neuhold (GMD, Darmstadt)
Ming Shan (HP Labs.)
Amit Shet (Bellcore)
Marek Rusinkiewicz (Houston Univ.)

W. Litwin will introduce the topic of the panel. M. Ketabchi will address the interoperability of heterogeneous OO systems, under investigation in Object Technology Lab. he heads at Santa Clara University. E. Neuhold will talk about the current work on VODAK model he proposed as the vehicle for OO multi-database integration. M. Shan will present lessons from the implementation of the 1st version of Pegasus OO heterogeneous multidatabase system he heads at HP Labs, especially related to the access to SQL databases, and multimedia applications. Furthermore, A. Sheth will talk about experiences based on use of two object-oriented data models, CANDIDE and Dual Model, for integration of traditional database schemas. Finally, M. Rusinkiewicz will present the OO Transaction Model he develops at Houston University, where transactions are objects within transactions classes that define semantics of a class of transactions, have OIDs, can inherit methods of a superclass, can support refinements, and can act over multiple autonomous OODBs, provided the interoperability.

Lecture Notes in Computer Science

For information about Vols. 1–491
please contact your bookseller or Springer-Verlag